Police & Society

Police & Society

Fifth Edition

Roy Roberg

Kenneth Novak

Gary Cordner

Brad Smith

New York Oxford

OXFORD UNIVERSITY PRESS

Oxford University Press, Inc., publishes works that further Oxford University's
objective of excellence in research, scholarship, and education.

Oxford University Press, Inc., publishes works that further
Oxford University's objective of excellence
in research, scholarship, and education.

Oxford New York
Auckland   Cape Town   Dar es Salaam   Hong Kong   Karachi
Kuala Lumpur   Madrid   Melbourne   Mexico City   Nairobi
New Delhi   Shanghai   Taipei   Toronto

With offices in
Argentina Austria Brazil Chile Czech Republic France Greece
Guatemala Hungary Italy Japan Poland Portugal Singapore
South Korea Switzerland Thailand Turkey Ukraine Vietnam

Copyright © 2012, 2009, 2005, 1999, 1993 Oxford University Press

For titles covered by Section 112 of the US Higher Education Opportunity Act,
please visit www.oup.com/us/he for the latest information about pricing
and alternate formats.

Published by Oxford University Press, Inc.
198 Madison Avenue, New York, New York 10016
www.oup.com

Oxford is a registered trademark of Oxford University Press

Library of Congress Cataloging-in-Publication Data
Police & society / by Roy Roberg...[et al.].—5th ed.
    p. cm.
Includes index.
ISBN 978-0-19-977256-8 (alk. paper)
1. Police—United States. 2. Police administration—United States.
3. Community policing—United States. I. Roberg, Roy R.
II. Title: Police and society.

HV8141.R6 2011
363.2'30973—dc22   2010046590

5 7 9 8 6 4

Printed in the United States of America
on acid-free paper

Dedicated to Jack Kuykendall (1940–2005), who helped to initially develop this text and worked tirelessly on the first two editions. Always a great friend, colleague, and gentleman. You will forever be in our thoughts.

BRIEF CONTENTS

Preface xiii
Acknowledgments xiv
About the Authors xv

PART 1: Policing Foundations 1
Chapter 1: Police in a Democracy 2
Chapter 2: Police History 29
Chapter 3: Legal Issues 56
Chapter 4: Community Policing 88

PART II: Police Administration 123
Chapter 5: Police Management 124
Chapter 6: Organizational Change 156
Chapter 7: Selection and Development 184
Chapter 8: Field Operations 226

PART III: Police Behavior 269
Chapter 9: Behavior and Misconduct 270
Chapter 10: Force and Coercion 310
Chapter 11: Accountability and Ethics 350

PART IV: Contemporary Issues 385
Chapter 12: Diversity 386
Chapter 13: Stress and Officer Safety 418
Chapter 14: Higher Education 454
Chapter 15: Emerging Issues 484

Glossary 523
Name Index 540
Subject Index 546

CONTENTS

Preface xiii
Acknowledgments xiv
About the Authors xv

CHAPTER 1 Police in a Democracy 2

Policing a Free Society 4
    Police and Government 5
    Police and Rule of Law 6
    Police, Terrorism, and Homeland Security 8
Police Systems 9
The U.S. Police System 11
    Other Types of Law Enforcement Agencies 15
    Similarities and Differences 16
Police Role and Purpose 18
    Law Enforcement or Politics? 20
    Crime Fighting or Social Service? 20
    Proactive or Reactive? 21
    Police Activities and Workload 21
    Police Goals and Strategies 23
Looking Ahead 25
Summary 26

CHAPTER 2 Police History 29

Foundations of Policing 30
    Early Policing 30
    Policing in Nineteenth-Century England 32
The Emergence of Modern Policing in the United States 34
    The First City Police Forces 34
    The County Sheriff 36
Vigilance Committees 36
Modern American Policing 37
    The Political Era 37
    Police Development 37
    Criticism in the Political Era 40
    The Reform Era 40
    Minority Perspective on to the Development of American Police 46

State Police 46
    Texas and Massachusetts 46
    Pennsylvania 47
    Highway Patrol 47
Federal Law Enforcement 50
    The Revenue Cutter Service and the U.S. Marshal Service 50
    Postal Inspectors 50
    The Secret Service 50
    The Federal Bureau of Investigation 50
Summary 53

CHAPTER 3 Legal Issues 56

Criminal Procedure 57
    Searches and Seizures of Persons 58
    Searches and Seizures of Property 64
    Interrogations and Confessions 68
Civil Liability 71
    Costs of Liability in Policing 71
    Avenues of Liability 73
    Civil Liability in State Courts 74
    Civil Liability in Federal Courts 75
    Emerging Liability Issues for the Twenty-First Century 79
    Use of Force 80
    Impact on Officers 81
Summary 84

CHAPTER 4 Community Policing 88

Evolving Strategies of Policing 89
Early Forms of Community Policing 90
    Police–Community Relations 90
    Crime Prevention 91
    Team Policing 94
    Foot Patrol and Broken Windows 95
Community Policing 96
Elements of Community Policing 98
    The Philosophical Dimension 98

The Strategic Dimension 101
The Tactical Dimension 104
Implementing Community Policing 110
Positive Indications 111
Questions and Doubts 113
Evaluating Community Policing 115
Community Policing Today 117
Summary 118

CHAPTER 5 Police Management 124
The Managerial Process 125
The Development of Police Management 127
Classical Police Management 128
Behavioral Police Management 128
Contemporary Police Management 129
Organizational Design 131
Restructuring and Community Policing
Implementation: Fact or Fiction? 132
Criticisms of the Paramilitary Design 133
Increasing Influence of Police Paramilitary
Units 134
Broken Windows and Zero-Tolerance Policing 135
Compstat, Police Legitimacy, and Procedural
Justice 136
Police Goals and Organizational Performance 140
Impact of Supervisory Styles on Officer
Behavior 140
Measuring Police Performance 141
Changing Performance Masures 144
Managing Group Behavior 145
Police Subcultures 145
Employee Organizations 148
Police Unions 148
Media Relations 150
Summary 151

CHAPTER 6 Organization and Change 156
The Change Process 157
Resistance to Change 158
Overcoming Resistance to Change 159
The Madison Experience 161
Laying the Foundation 162
Key Elements to Change 162
Results From Madison 163
The Chicago Experience 165
Laying the Foundation 165
Key Elements to Change 165
Results From Chicago 168
Lessons Learned from Madison and Chicago 170
A Final Lesson: Surviving Leadership Change 171

Job Redesign and Community Policing 171
Changing Officer Performance Measures 173
Innovation 174
Compstat as a Change Process 176
Police Departments as Learning Organizations 178
Organizational Learning 180
Police-Researcher Partnerships 180
Utilize Middle Managers 180
Summary 181

CHAPTER 7 Selection and Development 184
Recruitment 186
Recruitment Methods 186
Targeting Females and Minorities 187
Targeting the Service Oriented 188
Cop Crunch 189
Selection 190
Preemployment Standards 191
General Suitability 193
Preemployment Testing 196
Written Exams and Performance 197
Too Smart for Policing? 198
Development 201
Recruit Training 201
Community Policing Training 205
Terrorism-Related Training 207
Field Training 212
Career Growth 216
Summary 220

CHAPTER 8 Field Operations 226
The Patrol Function 228
Historical Development 228
Patrol Methods 231
Use of Patrol Methods 234
Selected Research on Patrol Operations 238
Random Patrol 238
Response Time 239
Differential Response to Calls 240
Focused Interventions 241
Proactive Arrests and Crackdowns 241
Guns and Gang Violence 242
Policing Disorder: Zero-Tolerance and Quality-of-
Life Policing 245
Problem-Oriented Policing Focused on
Disorder 246
Juvenile Curfews 248
Reactive Arrests and Intimate Partner
Violence 249
Police Pursuits 250

The Investigative Function 252
    Historical Development 253
Selected Research on Investigative
Operations 255
    Investigative Effectiveness 255
    Career Criminal Programs 259
    Bias Crime Programs 260
    Detective–Patrol Relationships 260
    Enticement and Entrapment 261
Summary 262

CHAPTER 9 Behavior and Misconduct 270

Perspectives of Police Behavior 271
    Universalistic Perspectives 271
    Particularistic Perspectives 273
    Socialization Versus Predisposition 273
Classic Studies of Police Behavior 276
    Violence and the Police 276
    Justice Without Trial 277
    Varieties of Police Behavior 277
    City Police 278
    Working the Street: Police Discretion 278
Decision Making and Police Discretion 280
    Organizational Variables 281
    Neighborhood Variables 282
    Situational Variables 283
    Individual (Officer) Variables 288
    Career Orientation 290
Police Deviance 290
    Types of Deviance and Misconduct 291
    The Prevalence of Police Deviance 292
    The Trouble With Gratuities 294
    Deviant Officers 295
    The Persistence of Corruption 297
    Police Sexual Misconduct 299
    The Drug War and Police Deviance 301
Summary 303

CHAPTER 10 Force and Coercion 310

Police-Citizen Interactions 312
    Context of Force 312
    National Estimates on Police
    Use of Force 315
Learning to Use Force 317
    Training 317
    Areas of Training 321
    Police Culture and the Use of Force 323
    Controversy and the Use of Force 324
Inappropriate Force 327

Brutality and Excessive Force 327
Physical and Psychological Force in Police
History 329
Frequency of Excessive Force and Brutality 331
Brutality in the Twenty-First Century 332
Deadly Force 338
    Individual and Situational Factors 340
    Environmental and Departmental Variations 341
    Racial Considerations 342
    Legal and Policy Changes 343
Summary 344

**CHAPTER 11 Accountability
and Ethics 350**

Internal Accountability Mechanisms 352
    Bureaucratic Organization and Management 352
    Internal Investigation 354
    Issues in Internal Investigations 358
    Early Warning/Early Identification
    Systems 360
    Effectiveness of Internal Investigations 362
External Accountability Mechanisms 362
    Civilian Review 362
    Police Auditor Systems 365
    Legal Control 366
The Limits of Oversight Mechanisms 368
Professional Standards 369
    The Police Professionalization Movement 369
Criteria of Police Professionalization 370
Ethical Standards 374
    Ethical Perspectives 375
    Ethical Dilemmas 377
The Limits of Professional and Ethical
Standards 378
Summary 380

CHAPTER 12 Diversity 386

Racial Minorities in Policing 389
    Unequal Treatment 389
    Performance of African American Police 390
Women in Policing 393
    Unequal Treatment 393
    Performance of Women Officers 394
Affirmative Action 396
Equal Employment Opportunity 397
Reverse Discrimination 398
Increasing Diversity in Police Departments 400
    Promotional Opportunities 404
Integration of Minorities and Women

Into Policing 406
    Police Culture 407
    Structural Characteristics 408
    Pregnancy and Maternity 409
    Sexual Harassment 410
Future Prospects 412
Summary 413

CHAPTER 13 **Stress and Officer Safety 418**
The Concept of Stress 419
Occupational Stress 420
Overview of Stressors 421
    Police Stressors 421
    Emerging Sources of Stress 424
Line-of-Duty and Crisis Situations 425
    Posttraumatic Stress Disorder 426
    Shift Work 428
    Social Supports and Police Stress 429
Consequences of Stress 431
    Alcohol Abuse 431
    Drug Abuse 433
    Suicide 433
    Marital and Family Problems 435
    Policies and Programs 436
Officer Safety 438
    Danger and Police Work 440
    Safety and the Mentally Ill 444
    Improving Safety and Reducing Fatalities 445
Summary 447

CHAPTER 14 **Higher Education 454**
The Development of Higher Education Programs
for Police 456
    Federal Programs and Support for Higher
    Education 457
    Quality of Higher Education Programs 458
    Higher Education Requirements for Police 461
    Police Chiefs, Promotion, and Higher
    Education 462
The Impact of Higher Education on
Policing 463
    Higher Education and Attitudes 463
    Higher Education and Performance 465
    Use of Force and Liability 466
    Leadership and Promotion 467
    Other Significant Findings 467
    Summary of Higher Education Findings and
    Directions for Future Research 468

Higher Education and Job Satisfaction 470
Higher Education, Community Policing, and
Terrorism 470
Police Executives' Views on Higher Education 471
Chief's Scholar Program 472
Validating Higher Education for Police 473
    Higher Education as a Bona Fide Occupational
    Qualification 473
    Higher Education and Discrimination 474
Higher Education Incentive Programs 475
    Higher Education Requirements and Policy
Implications 477
Summary 480

CHAPTER 15 **Emerging Issues 484**
Changes in American Society 486
    The Aging Population 486
    Diversity 488
    Economics 489
    Immigration and Migration 491
Modern Problems 494
    Racial Profiling 494
    Immigration Enforcement 495
    Eyewitness Identification 496
    Persons With Mental Illness 497
    Cyber Crime 498
Modern Technology 499
    Suspect Control and Officer Safety 501
    Crime Detention and Crime Solving 501
    Information Technology 502
    Communications and Interoperability 504
    Social Media 504
Long-Term Trends 505
    Collaboration 505
    Privatization 506
    Federalization 507
    Militarization 508
    Globalization 509
Competing Police Strategies 510
    Terrorism and Homeland Security 510
    Compstat and Performance
Management 512
    COP, POP, and ILP 513
Summary 516

Glossary of Key Terms 523
Name Index 540
Subject Index 546

PREFACE

*P*olice and Society offers a comprehensive introduction to policing in the United States. The text is both descriptive and analytical in nature, covering the process of policing, police behavior, organization, operations, and historical perspectives. Contemporary issues and future prospects are also addressed. Throughout the text, an emphasis is placed on describing the relationship between the police and the public and how this relationship has changed through the years. To adequately explain the complex nature of police operations in a democracy, we have integrated the most important theoretical foundations, research findings, and contemporary practices in a comprehensible, yet analytical, manner.

Because of the substantial increase of published research in the field, in the fifth edition we have attempted to include only the most valid and reliable research available, leading to the "best policies and practices" in policing. We emphasize in-depth discussions of critical police issues rather than attempting to cover—in a relatively brief manner—every conceivable topic or piece of research in the field. We believe this approach contributes more substantially to the intellectual and practical development of the field of policing.

While all chapters have been revised, important new topics include the following:

- Dual arrest and primary aggressor laws in domestic violence
- Use of forensic evidence by detectives
- Official complaints on police brutality
- Community policing implementation: fact or fiction?
- Procedural justice
- Organizational learning
- Police–researcher partnerships
- Recruitment strategies for females and minorities
- Problem-based learning training
- Immigration enforcement
- Social media/social networking
- Predictive policing

In addition, numerous topics have been significantly expanded, as follows: criminal procedure, misconduct and deviance, racial and gender diversity, officer stress and safety, focused interventions, intimate partner violence, national estimates on police use of force, brutality/extralegal police aggression, deadly force, limits of accountability systems, impact of higher education on police, use/abuse of the Compstat process, Homeland Security, intelligence-led policing, competing police strategies, and bottom line of policing.

To provide the most realistic and up-to-date view of the police, several types of offsets are provided. *Inside Policing* boxes provide a brief description of real-world police issues and operations as well as biographical sketches that highlight the contributions of important police leaders. *Voices From the Field* boxes highlight nationally recognized experts, who provide their insights into contemporary police practices and problems in a thought-provoking Q&A format. This edition contains perspectives from six new experts.

The fifth edition features an expanded glossary of key terms, and each chapter begins with a listing of key terms. Ancillaries to enhance instruction include an **Interactive Student Study Guide** on CD that is included with each copy of the book and a revised and expanded **Instructor's Manual/Testing Program**.

We thank the many police officers, police executives, and students with whom we have interacted over the years. Their experiences and insights have given us the basis for many of our ideas and have provided us a basis for conceptualizing critical issues in policing. We hope this book increases the understanding and appreciation of policing in society and encourages thought-provoking dialog among students and the police.

ACKNOWLEDGMENTS

We continue to enjoy an outstanding working relationship with Oxford University Press and thank those who contributed significantly to the production of this edition, including Sherith Pankratz, our editor, and her assistants, Richard Beck and Taylor Pilkington. Appreciation is also extended to the graduate students who provided helpful research reviews, including Seth Fallik (University of Missouri–Kansas City), Jay Kennedy (Wayne State University), and Craig Short (University of Missouri–Kansas City). We also thank those who reviewed the book for their thoughtfulness and insight, including Lorenzo M. Boyd, Fayetteville State University; Anthony P. Chiarlitti, Pace University; Kent R. Kerley, University of Alabama at Birmingham; Paul A. Magro, Ball State University; Susan L. Miller, University of Delaware; Daniel Price, Westfield State College; Jerome Randall, University of Central Florida; Thomas D. Stucky, Indiana University Purdue University at Indianapolis; and DeVere Woods, Indiana State University.

We especially thank all of the contributors to the *Voices From the Field* offsets throughout the text. These individuals are experts in policing and academe and have served in policymaking positions in police departments throughout the United States. Their contributions to our discussion on the police are significant, and they have provided a perspective on policing that cannot be found in any other forum.

ABOUT THE AUTHORS

Roy Roberg received his doctorate from the University of Nebraska, Lincoln, where he also taught. Other teaching experiences include Louisiana State University and San Jose State University, where he is currently a Professor of Justice Studies. He has published extensively in the areas of police organizational behavior and change, managerial issues, and higher education in policing. He is the editor of an anthology on policing and co-editor of an anthology on corrections and is the author or co-author of numerous texts, including the third edition of *Police Management.* He served as a police officer in a large county department of public safety in Washington State.

Kenneth Novak is associate professor and chair of the Department of Criminal Justice and Criminology at the University of Missouri–Kansas City. He received his Ph.D. in criminal justice from the University of Cincinnati in 1999. He has published numerous research articles on a variety of topics in policing, including officer decision making, citizens' attitudes toward the police, racially biased policing, and policy analysis. He has conducted research with a number of criminal justice agencies, including the Kansas City Police Department, the Cincinnati Police Department, and the U.S. Attorney for the Western District of Missouri. He co-authored the Third Edition of *Police Management* (2002, Roxbury). Novak previously worked as an undercover law enforcement officer for the Ohio Department of Public Safety.

Gary Cordner is Professor of Criminal Justice at Kutztown University in Pennsylvania. He taught for 21 years at Eastern Kentucky University, also serving as Director of the Kentucky Regional Community Policing Institute and Dean of the College of Justice & Safety. He received his doctorate from Michigan State University and served as a police officer and police chief in Maryland. Cordner has co-authored textbooks on police administration and criminal justice planning and co-edited several anthologies on policing. He edited the *American Journal of Police* from 1987 to 1992 and *Police Quarterly* from 1997 to 2002. Cordner is past president of the Academy of Criminal Justice Sciences and founder and former chair of that organization's Police Section. He currently serves as a Commissioner on the Commission on Accreditation for Law Enforcement Agencies.

Brad Smith received his Ph.D. in criminal justice from the University of Cincinnati. He is Associate Professor in the Department of Criminal Justice at Wayne State University in Detroit. His research focuses on policing, and he has published in a variety of areas, including articles on police discretionary behavior, citizens' attitudes toward the police, the use of deadly force, and police brutality. Recently, he co-authored the book *Race and Police Brutality: Roots of an Urban Dilemma* (2008, State University of New York Press).

Part I

Policing
Foundations

CHAPTER 1

Police in a Democracy

CHAPTER OUTLINE

- Policing a Free Society
    - Police and Government
    - Police and Rule of Law
    - Police, Terrorism, and Homeland Security
- Police Systems
- The U.S. Police System
    - Other Types of Law Enforcement Agencies
    - Similarities and Differences
- Police Role and Purpose
    - Law Enforcement or Politics?
    - Crime Fighting or Social Service?
    - Proactive or Reactive?
    - Police Activities and Workload
    - Police Goals and Strategies
- Looking Ahead
- Summary
- Critical Thinking Questions
- References

- case law
- civil law
- consolidated agencies
- contract law enforcement
- counterterrorism
- criminal justice system
- criminal law
- discretion

- federalism
- homeland security
- jurisdiction
- private police
- proactive
- procedural law
- public police
- public safety agencies

- reactive
- regional police
- rule of law
- separation of powers
- special-jurisdiction police
- substantive law
- task forces
- tribal police

THE POLICE HAVE POWER and authority. Sometimes they use it well and wisely, sometimes not. The actions they take are frequently controversial. Consider a few current events in the United States that illustrate some of the issues and challenges surrounding modern policing as we forge ahead into the twenty-first century:

- Responding to a school shooting in Pennsylvania in October 2006, a state trooper ripped apart a window frame with his bare hands, enabling him to gain entry. Ten young girls had already been shot, five of whom died, but the trooper's quick and courageous action helped end the situation before more innocent lives were taken (Scolforo 2007).

- Police in High Point, North Carolina, developed a unique strategy for reclaiming neighborhoods plagued by open drug markets. The strategy threatens to arrest every single dealer in the neighborhood, but uses the families and friends of offenders, along with wraparound social services, to offer the dealers one last chance at redemption. The strategy worked flawlessly in High Point, has won several awards, and is being replicated in other cities around the country (High Point Police Department 2006; Smalley 2009).

- An off-duty New Jersey state trooper was stopped 10 times within 14 months during 2007–2008 for traffic violations, including 3 times for driving under the influence (DUI). The trooper was not given a ticket or arrested on any of the occasions (Megerian 2010).

- Two police officers in Martinsville, Indiana, were suspended after using a Taser on a 10-year-old boy who was reportedly screaming, kicking, and out of control at Tender Teddies Day Care (Tuohy 2010). Police use of Tasers makes the news on a regular basis.

- After the Los Angeles Police Department used force to control a peaceful immigration-related demonstration in May 2007, public and media outcry led the mayor to launch an investigation and Police Chief William Bratton to reassign several top commanders (Kahn 2007).

- Police in Pittsburgh and Detroit have adopted aggressive tactics aimed at reducing violence and getting guns off the street. In both cities, street officers have achieved impressive results, but questions have also arisen about whether the tactics are fair and legal (Gurman 2010; Hunt 2010).
- The San Francisco Police Department crime lab closed its drug-testing section after an employee was accused of skimming cocaine from evidence, a revelation that led to the dismissal of hundreds of cases (Begin 2010). Problems at crime labs in Baltimore (Harris 2009), Houston (Mendoza and Olson 2009), and other police departments have also been in the news in recent years.

To begin to understand these kinds of situations and controversies, we must start with some basic questions: Why do the police exist? What do they do? What are their problems? How has policing changed over the years? The central theme of this book is to attempt to answer these and related questions about police in the United States.

One quick note about semantics: Throughout this book the terms *police* and *law enforcement* are used interchangeably. With either term, the intent is to refer to all those who provide police services, whether they work for a police department, sheriff's office, state police, or federal agency.

There is a lot of information in this book. To help you digest it, you should notice that the book is organized into four sections:

1. *Policing foundations*, including a discussion of the democratic context of policing and the police role, the history of police, legal issues, and the transition toward community policing.
2. *Police administration*, which includes a discussion of management and organizational behavior, change and innovation, selection and development, police field operations, and selected problems.
3. *Police behavior*, which includes a discussion of behavior and discretion, police authority and the use of coercion, and police professionalism and accountability.
4. *Contemporary issues*, including higher education, cultural diversity, stress and officer safety, and the future of policing.

Each chapter contains special sections called "Voices from the Field" and "Inside Policing." These sections provide brief descriptions of "real-world" police issues, excerpts from research studies, and brief descriptions of the contributions of important historical and contemporary figures in law enforcement.

Policing a Free Society

The police play a two-edge role in a free society. On one hand, they protect our freedom—not just our right to own property, to travel safely from place to place, and to remain free from assault, but also such fundamental rights as freedom of speech, freedom of assembly, and freedom to change the government through elections. However, the police also have the power to limit our freedom through surveillance, questioning, search, and arrest. It is particularly important to understand this anomalous situation when thinking about policing in the United States, because "the police...are invested with a great deal of authority under a system of government in which authority is reluctantly granted and, when granted, sharply curtailed" (Goldstein 1977, 1).

In our democratic system, government is based on consensus of the people, but policing often comes into play when agreement breaks down. In our system, government is expected to serve the people, but police often give out "services" that people do not want—orders, tickets, arrests. In our system, people are largely free to do as they please, but police can force them to stop. In our system, everyone is considered equal, but police have more power than the rest of us. It has been said that "democracy is always hard on the police" (Berkeley 1969, 1). It might also be said that police can be hard on democracy.

These factors indicate why the opposite of a democratic state is often called a police state. Democracy represents consensus, freedom, participation, and equality; the police represent regulation, restriction, and the imposition of government authority upon the individual. That is why the police in a democracy are often confronted with hostility, opposition, and criticism no matter how effectively or fairly they may operate.

Police and Government

The word *police* is derived from the Greek words *politeuein,* which means to be a citizen or to engage in political activity, and *polis,* which means a city or state. This derivation emphasizes that policing is every citizen's responsibility, although it is a responsibility that is often delegated to certain officials who do it on a full-time basis. Also, the derivation emphasizes that policing is political—not in the sense of Republicans versus Democrats, but in the sense that policing entails carrying out decisions made by the people and their representatives, decisions that benefit some members of society but not others.

Today, we would tend to say the same thing in a slightly different way—police enforce the law and carry out the policies of the government. Governments are vested with *police power* to regulate matters of health, welfare, safety, and morality because a society requires structure and order if it is to be effective in meeting the needs of its members. One important expression of police power in a society is a police, or law enforcement, organization.

The activities and behavior of the police are determined, in part, by the type of government of which they are a part. In more totalitarian governments, power is exercised by only one person (e.g., a dictator), a very small number of individuals, or one political party. The established laws and policies that control all aspects of life in a totalitarian state are intended to maintain the interests of those in power; the social order is preserved at the expense of individual freedom. More democratic governments, by contrast, are based on the principle of "participation of the governed." The members of a democratic society either directly participate in deciding the laws or they elect representatives who make such decisions for them.

The United States has a republican form of government known as **federalism**. Some powers are exercised by the national government but many others are decentralized to state and local units of government to allow more people to participate in the political system and to limit the power of those individuals elected to national political office. Among the governmental functions that are largely delegated to state and local governments is policing.

Another important organizational feature of the U.S. government is **separation of powers**, which results in three branches of government: executive, judicial, and legislative. This separation exists to provide a system of "checks and balances" so that one branch of government will not become too powerful. In the United States, the combination of federalism and separation of powers results in a governmental system that is highly fragmented, with power and authority widely dispersed. This system is sometimes criticized for being inefficient and incapable of governing effectively, but of course that is exactly what its designers intended—they wanted a limited form of government (including police) that would not interfere with peoples' freedoms any more than absolutely necessary.

Law enforcement is a responsibility of the executive branch of government in our system. Checks and balances help to constrain policing in two fundamental ways. First, the police do not get to make the laws they enforce—the legislature does this, along with appropriating the money that police agencies need to operate. Second, the police do not get to decide what happens to people who violate the law and get arrested—the judicial branch does that, along with interpreting and reinterpreting the meaning of laws in our changing society.

Government and laws are created through a political process or system. Voters, special-interest groups (e.g., the National Rifle Association, the American Medical Association, or the National Association for the Advancement of Colored People), political parties, and elected officials are active participants in the political process. Theories of political decision making in a democracy take both pluralistic and elitist perspectives. The pluralistic perspective argues that debates, bargains, and compromises determine the allocation of resources and the enactment of laws and policies. Further, although there are many different interests and groups in a society, some more influential than others, no one group dominates. In contrast, the elitist or class perspective argues that only a limited number of persons (e.g., the rich or special-interest groups) have any real influence in the political process. The playing field is not level, so politics results in preferential treatment for the most influential and discrimination against those with little or no influence or power.

These two contrasting perspectives are very important for our understanding of the police. From the pluralist perspective, police can be seen as a benign institution that helps implement laws and policies that result from an honest and fair political contest, as well as one of the interest groups competing in the process to advance its own interests. From the elitist perspective, police are usually characterized as the "iron fist" that helps protect the powerful and repress everyone else. Obviously, policing is a more noble enterprise within the pluralist framework than within the elitist framework. From either perspective, however, the police wield power and thus deserve careful attention.

Police and Rule of Law

Democracies are concerned about the rights and freedoms to be given to individuals and about the limits to be placed on government's use of police power. This concern is usually addressed by creating a constitution. Constitutions may be written or unwritten, but they serve the same basic purpose: to establish the nature and character of government by identifying the basic principles underlying that government. The Constitution of the United States identifies the functions of government and specifies in its first 10 amendments (the Bill of Rights) the most important rights of individuals relative to the government.

The United States has a constitutional democracy in which the exercise of power is based on the **rule of law**. Ideally, laws created through a democratic process are more reasonable and more likely to be accepted by citizens than laws created by only a few influential persons. And although democratic government does not always work in this fashion, ours has evolved so that the rule of law in practice has gradually become less tyrannical and more representative of the concerns of all citizens. One of the reasons that the rule of law is considered necessary is that proponents of democracy assume that individuals in power will be inclined to abuse their power unless they are controlled by a constitution, democratically developed laws, and the structure or organization of government.

Police accountability to the rule of law is an important tradition in democratic societies. According to Reith (1938, 188), the basis for democratic policing "is to be found in rational and humane laws." The significance of the rule of law to democracy and the police is further described in a Royal Commission Report on the British police:

> Liberty does not depend, and never has depended, upon any particular form of police organization. It depends upon the supremacy of…the rule of law. The proper criterion [to determine if a police state exists] is whether the police are answerable to the law and ultimately, to a democratically elected [government]. In the countries to which the term police state is applied…, police power is controlled by a [totalitarian] government [that] acknowledges no accountability to democratically elected (representatives), and the citizens cannot rely on the [law] to protect them. *(1962, 45)*

There are a number of ways to categorize laws; for example, laws may be civil or criminal and substantive or procedural (legal issues are discussed further in Chapter 3). **Civil laws** are concerned with relationships between individuals (e.g., contracts, business transactions, family relations); **criminal laws** are concerned with the relationship between the individual and government. Those behaviors that pose a threat to public safety and order (e.g., failure to get a driver's license, theft, rape, murder) are considered crimes. The prosecution of a crime is brought in the name of the people as represented by government officials (e.g., a prosecuting attorney). While police need to be familiar with both civil and criminal law, their primary concern is with criminal law.

In the realm of criminal law, **substantive laws** are those that identify behavior, either required or prohibited, and the punishments for failure to observe these laws. For example, driving under the influence of alcohol is prohibited, and such behavior may be punished by a fine or imprisonment or both, along with suspension of the privilege to drive a motor vehicle. **Procedural laws** govern how the police go about enforcing substantive laws. Procedural laws specify the level of evidence required to justify an arrest, for example, and whether the police can arrest based on their own authority or, instead, must first obtain a warrant.

Important frames of reference for procedural criminal laws are the Bill of Rights (the first 10 amendments of the U.S. Constitution; see Table 1.1) and **case law** (the written rulings of state and federal appellate courts), which more specifically define when and how each procedure is to be used. When enforcing substantive laws, officers are supposed to follow procedural laws, which exist to restrict the power of government and to reduce the possibility that police will abuse the power they have been given. The law not only provides a framework for police activity and behavior but also is intended to ensure that the police have a good reason (e.g., "reasonable suspicion" or "probable cause") to intrude into the lives of citizens. Procedural laws also balance what would otherwise be an unequal relationship between government and the individual because the government usually has more resources, and often more public support, than a person suspected of committing a crime.

Even when the police have legal authority, however, they do not always enforce the law because of limited resources, public expectations, organizational priorities, and officer preferences. Rather, both the organization and the officer exercise **discretion**; that is, they make a choice concerning what laws will be enforced and how that enforcement will take place. A number of factors influence police discretion; they are discussed in Chapter 10.

TABLE 1.1 Selected Amendments to the U.S. Constitution

Fourth Amendment

The right of the people to be secure in their persons, houses, papers, and effects, against unreasonable searches and seizures, shall not be violated, and no warrants shall be issued but upon probable cause, supported by oath or affirmation, and particularly describing the place to be searched and the persons or things to be seized.

Fifth Amendment

No person shall be held to answer for a capital, or otherwise infamous crime, unless on a presentment or indictment of a grand jury, except in cases arising in the land or naval forces, or in the militia, when in actual service in time of war or public danger; nor shall any person be subject for the same offense to be twice put in jeopardy of life or limb; nor shall be compelled in any criminal case to be a witness against himself, nor be deprived of life, liberty, or property, without due process of law; nor shall private property be taken for public use without just compensation.

Sixth Amendment

In all criminal prosecutions, the accused shall enjoy the right to a speedy and public trial, by an impartial jury of the State and district wherein the crime shall have been committed, which district shall have been previously ascertained by law, and to be informed of the nature and cause of the accusation; to be confronted with the witnesses against him; to have compulsory process for obtaining witnesses in his favor, and to have the assistance of counsel for his defense.

Eighth Amendment

Excessive bail shall not be required, nor excessive fines imposed, nor cruel and unusual punishments inflicted.

Police, Terrorism, and Homeland Security

Perhaps there is no greater test of our commitment to freedom, democracy, and the rule of law than the challenge of policing in the post-9/11 era. The events of September 11, 2001, at the World Trade Center, the Pentagon, and in western Pennsylvania suddenly created new top priorities for American law enforcement—**counterterrorism** and **homeland security.** To achieve these new priorities, the U.S. national government considered and/or adopted a range of responses, including the USA Patriot Act, that impinge on traditional American views about privacy, freedom of movement, and the rights of people accused of crimes. Who is asked to carry out these controversial new responses? The police, of course.

The post-9/11 situation is challenging for police in several respects. For example, terrorists operate with a different type of motivation than traditional criminals and often are willing to die to further their causes. Terrorists may employ tools (chemical, biological, or radiological) or explosive weapons of mass destruction that local and state police are ill equipped to resist. When local and state police engage in counterterrorism activities, they often work with national-level agencies that they have not traditionally had much interaction with, such as the Central Intelligence Agency (CIA) and the National Security Agency (NSA). Homeland security engages the police with the military in a way that has historically been discouraged in America (the military has generally been very restricted in its role within the borders of the United States). Overall, the counterterrorism and homeland security missions tend to thrust federal agencies into the forefront; this is awkward because local and state police have always had the primary responsibility for law enforcement and crime control in the United States.

We will have more to say about the specific challenges of post-9/11 policing in Chapter 15. In the big picture, these challenges go to the core issues of democracy and law—how best to ensure safety and order while protecting individual freedoms. Institutions such as Congress, the president, and the courts are responsible for making and reviewing laws and programs designed to support safety with freedom. But there is no more crucial institution than the police when it comes to constructing the reality of safety and freedom on the streets and in our communities. In Voices from the Field, Philadelphia Police Commissioner Charles Ramsey provides his perspective on balancing policing and freedom in the post-9/11 era.

Police Systems

At a fundamental level, there are three basic types of police in the United States: citizen-police, private police, and public police. This book is primarily about public police officers.

It is not uncommon for people in a democracy to participate in the policing process. As citizen-police we may make arrests when a felony is committed in our presence (in some states citizens may also arrest for breaches of the peace). When we report a crime and cooperate in the subsequent investigation, we are participating in the policing process. Another type of citizen involvement is related to the legal doctrine of *posse comitatus,* in which individuals can be required to assist police officers. This conjures up the image of the sheriff's or marshal's posse in Western movies, but it also includes the possibility that any of us, if requested, would be required to aid a police officer.

Vigilantism is another example of citizen participation in law enforcement. Historically, vigilantes were community members (e.g., civic, business, or religious leaders) or mobs who took the law into their own hands. These groups developed as the result of a public perception that the existing law enforcement system was inadequate and corrupt or that it did not serve the interests of the vigilantes (Walker 1977, 30–31). Although more common in the nineteenth century, this type of citizen involvement in law enforcement still occurs.

There are also both public and private police. **Public police** are employed, trained, and paid by a government agency; their purpose is to serve the general interest of all citizens. **Private police** are those police employed and paid to serve the specific purposes, within the law, of an individual or organization. A municipal police officer is a public police officer; a guard at a bank or department store is a private police officer. Public police may also serve in a private capacity. It is common for public police officers to work part-time in a private capacity, such as at a nightclub or shopping center.

Public police agencies fit into the governmental structure in different ways. Most police chiefs report to an elected official (mayor) or appointed official (city manager) within the executive branch of government, although a few report directly to a city council or quasi-independent police commission. Sheriffs, on the other hand, are elected by the voters and generally report only to them. There is one important caveat to this, however—sheriffs usually must apply to a county council for a portion of their annual budget. Thus, while sheriffs are independent elected officials, they are typically dependent on other elected officials for the resources they need to operate. This is another example of checks and balances.

VOICES FROM THE FIELD

Charles H. Ramsey
Police Commissioner, Philadelphia, Pennsylvania

Question: How do you see the role of the police in a free society?

Answer: When I was Chief of the Metropolitan Police Department in Washington, DC, I partnered with the United States Holocaust Memorial Museum and the Anti-Defamation League to build an experiential training program called "Law Enforcement and Society: Lessons from the Holocaust."

With the Holocaust as the historical backdrop, police officers are asked to examine their role in a democratic and pluralistic society. The program, now in its 10th year, gains access to some of the most critical issues facing police officers and law enforcement agencies today—issues such as racial profiling, biased policing, equal treatment under the law, and, perhaps most importantly, the role of police officers in upholding the rights of all citizens.

What followed from the state-sanctioned policies in Nazi Germany 70 years ago was nothing short of the denial of the most basic of human rights and individual freedoms. And almost from the beginning, local police were intimately involved in this process. Whether it was providing intelligence information to invading army troops or harassing people who violated Nazi taboos, arresting political opponents or being the foot soldiers in the mobile killing squads, local police soon became integrated into the Nazi reign of repression and brutality. The Holocaust, however, did not just happen overnight. It occurred along a continuum that started with the use of inappropriate language separating people along the lines of religion and nationality and ended with the absolute denial of a person's constitutional rights.

The Law Enforcement and Society program is a critical part of teaching law enforcement officers our core values of Democracy—fairness, equality, and compassion. In that moment where a police officer encounters a victim of crime, or is arresting an offender, or is answering a request for directions, or on routine patrol, she has a choice about how to treat the person standing before her. Does she treat him with dignity and respect? Or does she see him simply as the "other," based on a label such as race, gender, sexual orientation, religion, class, ability, nationality, or ethnicity?

The lesson in the Law Enforcement and Society training is straightforward, but powerful: When police officers violate their oath and their code of ethics, there are consequences—devastating consequences. We cannot close our eyes and divorce ourselves from our own sense of morality. We cannot think of ourselves, as we are so often portrayed, as the "thin blue line" between right and wrong or good and evil. I believe that is an inadequate metaphor and that true "community policing" does not define police officers as a line—thin, blue, or otherwise. We are not now—nor should we ever be—something that divides and separates our communities.

Rather, I like to think of the police as a thread—a thread that is woven throughout the communities we serve and that holds together the very fabric of democracy and freedom in our communities. If the police begin to unravel, then our very democracy begins to unravel as well. That image, much more so than the thin blue line concept, captures the true role of the police in protecting and preserving a free society.

Before his appointment as Police Commissioner in Philadelphia, Charles Ramsey came up through the ranks in the Chicago Police Department and then served as Chief of the Metropolitan Police Department in Washington, DC. In addition, he currently serves as President of the Board of Directors of the Police Executive Research Forum.

Public police organizations are part of the **criminal justice system,** which includes the courts and correctional institutions. The police function as the "gatekeepers" of the criminal justice system because they determine who will be cited or arrested. The judicial branch and its representatives, including prosecutors, defense attorneys, and judges, process the accused to determine guilt or innocence and to sentence those who are convicted. The correctional part of the system (e.g., probation, community treatment programs, jails, prisons, parole) supervises, rehabilitates, and/or punishes convicted criminals.

Around the world, police systems vary greatly. One feature that varies is the extent to which they are unitary or fragmented. Some countries have just one police institution for the entire nation—these are unitary systems. Many other countries have more than one police institution, but still only a few, such as a national police plus a gendarmerie for rural areas, or a preventive police, an investigative police, and a border police. At the other end of the spectrum are countries that have many separate police institutions, often dispersed among national, state, and local levels of government. Mexico, India, Brazil, Germany, Canada, and England are some countries with relatively fragmented police systems.

A second important feature of police systems in different countries is their connection to the military. The modern trend has been toward a clear separation of the police and the military, partly in the spirit of checks and balances on government authority, but mainly because the use of military power against a country's own citizens is considered repressive except in the gravest emergencies. In some countries, however, the police and the military are largely indistinguishable or the police are subservient to the military.

The police system in the United States is distinctive with regard to both of these comparative features. U.S. police are clearly separate from, and independent of, the military. Even at the federal (national) level, where most military resources and assets are situated, the military is in the Department of Defense while law enforcement agencies are mainly in the Department of Justice and the Department of Homeland Security. As described in the following section, when it comes to unitary versus fragmented policing systems, ours is the most fragmented in the world, by far.

The U.S. Police System

The most distinctive feature of American policing is that it is fragmented and local. There are almost 18,000 public police agencies in the United States (Reaves 2007), far more than can be found in any other country. Almost 90 percent of these (15,833 agencies) are local (city, town, township, village, borough, parish, county, etc.), while the rest are federal, state, or special-purpose law enforcement agencies.

The organization of the U.S. police tends to follow the geographical and political structure of the U.S. government. Each of the levels of government—federal, state, county (or parish in Louisiana), and municipal—has police powers and may have its own police forces. The federal and state levels of government tend to have multiple police forces that specialize in specific types of law enforcement. County and municipal (collectively called local) governments each tend to have just one police force that provides a wide range of police services.

Law enforcement organizations differ, in part, by their legal **jurisdiction,** including the criminal matters over which they have authority. For example, the jurisdiction of the Internal Revenue Service (IRS) Criminal Investigation Division is limited to violations of federal tax laws. The Federal Bureau of Investigation (FBI) is the most generalist law enforcement agency of the federal government. It is charged with the investigation of all federal laws not assigned

TABLE 1.2 Ten Largest Federal Agencies With the Authority to Carry Firearms and Make Arrests

AGENCY	FULL-TIME OFFICERS
U.S. Customs and Border Protection	27,705
Federal Bureau of Prisons	15,214
Federal Bureau of Investigation	12,242
U.S. Immigration and Customs Enforcement	10,399
U.S. Secret Service	4,769
Drug Enforcement Administration[a]	4,400
Administrative Office of the U.S. Courts[b]	4,126
U.S. Marshals Service	3,233
U.S. Postal Inspection Service	2,976
Internal Revenue Service, Criminal Investigation	2,777

Note: Table 1.2 excludes employees based in U.S. territories or foreign countries.

[a]Data are estimates based on information provided by the agency.
[b]Includes all Federal probation officers employed in Federal judicial districts that allow officers to carry firearms.
[c]Includes 1,536 Park Rangers and 612 U.S. Park Police officers.
Source: B. A. Reaves, *Federal Law Enforcement Officers, 2004* (Washington, DC: Bureau of Justice Statistics, 2006), 2.

to some other agency (e.g., the Postal Service or the IRS). By contrast, local police enforce all laws that are applicable, including state laws and local ordinances, within the legally incorporated limits of their city or county. Their jurisdiction is defined mostly by geography, whereas federal agency jurisdictions are nationwide, but limited to specific federal statutes.

The federal government has more than 60 agencies with law enforcement and investigative powers (see Table 1.2 for a list of the 10 largest federal law enforcement agencies). State governments, in addition to having a state police or highway patrol department (e.g., the Alaska Department of Public Safety or the New York State Police), often have other agencies with police powers to deal with such matters as revenue collection, parks and recreation, and alcoholic beverage control. At the county level, the most common type of law enforcement agency is the sheriff's office, but some counties also have investigators who work for prosecuting attorneys and public defenders. In addition, some counties have police departments (e.g., Miami–Dade County). In such situations, the sheriff's department is usually responsible for operating the county jail and for assisting the courts but does not engage in extensive policing activities. Finally, most municipal governments also have their own police force (e.g., the Los Angeles Police Department [LAPD]). County sheriffs and local police are generally involved in patrolling, responding to calls for service, and conducting investigations; however, sheriff's departments also invest substantial resources in managing jails and providing court services.

Table 1.3 presents information on state and local law enforcement agencies by size of the organization. Clearly, small police departments are most common. Over one half of all U.S. police agencies have fewer than 10 full-time sworn officers. About 75 percent have fewer than 25 officers, and over 90 percent have fewer than 100 officers. This feature of American law enforcement is very important to keep in mind. Although most of us conjure up images

TABLE 1.3 State and Local Law Enforcement Agencies by Size of Agency

NUMBER OF FULL-TIME SWORN PERSONNEL	NUMBER OF AGENCIES	PERCENTAGE OF AGENCIES
All sizes	17,876	100.0
1,000 or more	79	0.4
250–999	306	1.7
100–249	714	4.0
25–99	3,563	19.9
10–24	4,213	23.6
2–9	6,799	38.1
0–1	2,202	12.3

Source: B. A. Reaves, *Census of State and Local Law Enforcement Agencies, 2004* (Washington, DC: Bureau of Justice Statistics, 2007), 2.

of the FBI, New York Police Department (NYPD), or LAPD when we think of police organizations, Mayberry RFD is more typical.

The most common type of local law enforcement agency is the municipal (city, town, village, borough) police force. There were 12,766 municipal police departments in the year 2004, the latest census of law enforcement agencies (Reaves 2007). The next most common type is the county sheriff's department (3,067). Other common types of local law enforcement agencies are the tribal police department (154), county police department (56), multijurisdictional regional agency (63), and locally elected constable's office (513).

While the typical police department in the United States is small, there are some very large law enforcement agencies in the country (see Table 1.4). Fourteen federal law enforcement agencies have 1,000 or more sworn personnel. Each state except Hawaii has a state police or highway patrol agency, all with at least 100 sworn personnel (North Dakota is the smallest, with 135 full-time sworn officers, and California is the largest, with 7,085). In addition, there are 47 local agencies with 1,000 or more sworn police personnel. The largest municipal police department is in New York City, with 36,118 full-time sworn personnel. The largest sheriff's department is in Los Angeles County, with 8,239 sworn personnel (Reaves 2007).

Police agencies are one important aspect of the structure of policing in America—another is *police employment*. Consistent with what has been described above, most police officers work at the local level. About 74 percent of America's 837,000 sworn law enforcement officers work for local agencies, 12 percent for federal agencies, 7 percent for primary state agencies, and 6 percent for special-purpose agencies (Reaves 2006; 2007). The proportion of all officers who work for large agencies might be surprising, however, given the preponderance of small police departments. The reason, of course, is that small agencies are just that—small. There are a lot of them (more than 16,000 with fewer than 100 officers), but by definition they do not employ very many personnel. Thus, although about 90 percent of American law enforcement agencies have fewer than 100 officers, those agencies employ only about 36 percent of all sworn police officers in the country. To put it another way, 64 percent of all police *officers* in the United States (including federal, state, and local) work for agencies with more than 100 sworn officers.

TABLE 1.4 Thirty Largest State and Local Law Enforcement Agencies by Number of Full-Time Sworn Personnel

AGENCY	FULL-TIME SWORN PERSONNEL
New York (NY) Police	36,118
Chicago (IL) Police	13,129
Los Angeles (CA) Police	9,099
Los Angeles County (CA) Sheriff	8,239
California Highway Patrol	7,085
Philadelphia (PA) Police	6,832
Cook Co. (IL) Sheriff	5,555
Houston (TX) Police	5,092
New York State Police	4,667
Pennsylvania State Police	4,200
Washington (DC) Metropolitan Police	3,800
Detroit (MI) Police	3,512
Texas Department of Public Safety	3,437
Broward County (FL) Sheriff	3,190
Baltimore (MD) Police	3,160
Miami–Dade County (FL) Police	3,094
Dallas (TX) Police	2,935
Phoenix (AZ) Police	2,858
New Jersey State Police	2,768
Suffolk County (NY) Police	2,692
Las Vegas (NV) Metropolitan Police	2,674
Nassau County (NY) Police	2,574
Harris County (TX) Sheriff	2,545
Massachusetts State Police	2,200
San Francisco (CA) Police	2,167
Orange County (CA) Sheriff	2,119
San Diego (CA) Police	2,103
San Antonio (TX) Police	2,054
Memphis (TN) Police	2,017
Illinois State Police	2,008

Source: B. A. Reaves, *Census of State and Local Law Enforcement Agencies, 2004* (Washington, DC: Bureau of Justice Statistics, 2007), 9.

The pattern of police agencies and police employment varies substantially around the United States (Reaves 2006, 2007; Cordner 2011). In general, western states have fewer law enforcement agencies and fewer police officers in proportion to their population than midwestern or eastern states. Hawaii and California have the fewest police agencies per population and South Dakota and North Dakota have the most. Washington and Vermont have the fewest police officers per population and Louisiana and New York have the most. Rural states tend to rely more on state police than urbanized states—the most "state police-dependent" states are Delaware, Vermont, West Virginia, and Alaska. Sheriff's departments play a big role in law enforcement in some states and a negligible role in others. The states in which sheriff's departments represent the biggest portion of police employment are Louisiana, Wyoming, Florida, and Idaho. At the other end of the spectrum, the least "sheriff-dependent" states (not counting Alaska and Hawaii, which have no counties and therefore no sheriff's departments at all) are Delaware, Connecticut, New Hampshire, Pennsylvania, and Rhode Island.

Other Types of Law Enforcement Agencies

In addition to the basic structure of policing described above, there are several other forms of public policing, including tribal police, public safety agencies, consolidated agencies, regional police, special-jurisdiction police, contract law enforcement, and task-forces.

Tribal police are law enforcement agencies created and operated by Native Americans. Their jurisdiction is usually, but not always, limited to reservation land. These types of police agencies are separate from those law enforcement organizations operated by the Bureau of Indian Affairs, which is a federal agency.

Public safety agencies represent the integration of police and firefighting services (and possibly other services like disaster preparedness, hazardous waste disposal, and emergency medical services). This integration can be limited to administrative matters or may include the joint performance of both firefighting and police duties. When the duties or work are integrated, employees are trained to perform both police and firefighting activities.

Consolidated agencies represent the integration of two or more police departments. This integration can be either by function or by organization. Functional, or partial, integration involves the combining of the same activity, perhaps communications or training. For example, two or more police departments may decide to share the same communication system or develop a common training program. Organizational integration involves two or more departments becoming one. This is usually a county and a city department, as in Clark County–Las Vegas, Nevada, or Duval County–Jacksonville, Florida, but it could also involve two or more cities.

Historically, it has been common for communities to consider the consolidation of police departments, particularly in urban areas. Supporters of consolidation argue that a larger police force can provide better service at lower cost. Although this argument is not always accurate, it does tend to generate some support for consolidation. Opponents of consolidation argue that if the community maintains control of its own police force, it will be more responsive to the needs of that community. Citizens often want to maintain direct control over the use of police power in their community. Although functional consolidation of police departments is commonplace in urban areas, the complete consolidation of two or more police departments is rare.

Regional police can result from full-fledged consolidation, but generally the term refers to a situation in which two or more local governments decide to jointly operate a police agency across their jurisdictions. The regional police agency is often overseen by a board or commission with representation from all participating jurisdictions, and funding is provided by each on a proportional basis. Pennsylvania is distinctive in having several of these types of agencies, such as the Berks–Lehigh Regional Police Department that serves four municipalities spread over two counties.

Special-jurisdiction police usually have the same police powers as those officers employed in other police departments, but they tend to have jurisdiction in a tightly specified area. Colleges and universities often have their own campus police force (e.g., the San Jose State University Police Department). Other examples include transit police (e.g., the Bay Area Rapid Transit in California), park or recreation area police, and public school police. Table 1.5 provides data on the number and types of special-jurisdiction police.

Contract law enforcement, or contract policing, involves a contractual arrangement between two units of government in which one agrees to provide law enforcement services for the other. For example, a county sheriff's department might enter into a contract with a municipality to provide a given level of police service for a certain amount of money. The municipality might not wish to pay to establish its own police department or it might believe it would receive better services from the larger organization. Although it is possible to have a contractual relationship between any two governmental units, the most common one is between a county and a city. Contract law enforcement is quite common in many urban areas.

Task forces are a form of functional consolidation but tend to be temporary (i.e., from a few weeks to years) rather than permanent. Some task forces, however, have lasted more than 20 years. Two or more departments may decide to create a task force to respond to crimes such as auto theft, drugs and related problems, serial rape, or serial murder. Cooperative arrangements can exist at the local level (e.g., several municipal police departments and the county sheriff) or between local and state, or local and federal, law enforcement agencies (e.g., a drug, gun, or gang violence task force). A task force may also include representatives from other criminal justice agencies (e.g., probation and parole) or other governmental and community organizations (e.g., social services). What is unique about this arrangement is that it involves the joint efforts of two or more police departments directed toward common problems.

Similarities and Differences

Local police, when compared with state and federal law enforcement, have the most employees, cost the most money, deal with most reported crime, respond to the majority of other police-related problems that occur (traffic accidents, domestic disputes, barking dogs), and tend to have a closer relationship with citizens. State police, naturally, are spread farther apart, tend not to be as closely connected to local communities, and often have their primary focus on traffic safety. Federal law enforcement agencies, with a few exceptions (such as the U.S. Park Police), are mainly investigative and are least connected to local communities.

There are substantial differences within these categories, however. Some local agencies are large and have many personnel who perform specialized duties (investigation, traffic, juvenile, etc.), while others are small with no specialization whatsoever. State law enforcement agencies vary, especially between state police and highway patrol and depending on whether the state has a separate Bureau of Investigation or whether that function is incorporated within the state police. Even federal agencies that might seem similar have significant differences. For example, the FBI has traditionally emphasized reactive (after the fact) investigation (although that has shifted to some degree since 9/11), whereas the Drug Enforcement Agency (DEA) has long emphasized proactive and instigative methods

TABLE 1.5 Special-Jurisdiction Law Enforcement Agencies by Type of Jurisdiction and Number of Full-Time Sworn Personnel

TYPE OF SPECIAL JURISDICTION	AGENCIES	FULL-TIME SWORN PERSONNEL
Total	1,481	49,398
College/university/school	925	16,122
Other public buildings/facilities	86	3,125
Natural resources/parks and recreation	205	14,332
Transportation systems/facilities	130	9,073
Criminal investigations	103	4,739
Special enforcement	32	2,007

Source: B. A. Reaves, *Census of State and Local Law Enforcement Agencies, 2004* (Washington, DC: Bureau of Justice Statistics, 2007), 7.

of investigation (Wilson 1978). A significant amount of Secret Service work involves executive protection rather than investigation.

Local jurisdictions vary greatly between urban, suburban, and rural, from New York City to rustic West Virginia, remote Alaska, or the Mississippi Delta. Although urban crime rates tend to be higher than rural crime rates, crime associated with urban areas is often exported to rural areas; for example, urban drug trafficking is a driving force behind the spread of drug use and the development of gangs in rural areas. Some of the crimes that tend to be associated with rural areas include growing marijuana and manufacturing methamphetamine; theft of crops, timber, and animals; and poaching. Some crimes in rural areas are more easily solved (i.e., an arrest is made) because homicide, rape, and assault are more likely to occur among acquaintances than in urban areas. Also, rural witnesses may be better able to personally identify observed suspects. By contrast, a witness in an urban area is more likely to be describing someone who is a total stranger to them.

Sims describes other differences that exist between urban and rural police:

Urban police tend not to live where they work, while rural officers do.... [R]ural law enforcement is personalistic and nonbureaucratic, in contrast to the formality, impersonality and bureaucratization of urban police. Rural law enforcement involves...more face-to-face interaction and communication. [It also]...includes a greater...percentage of police–acquaintance contacts and...[fewer] police–stranger contacts. *(1996, 45)*

In addition, rural law enforcement officers, more than their urban counterparts, often work with lower budgets, fewer staff, less equipment, and fewer written policies. But they also appear to be more efficient than urban police and more respected by the public. The context in which rural police work takes place also affects their activities. Rural citizens may be more likely to rely on informal social controls (i.e., take care of the problem themselves) rather than report a "private" matter to the police. In addition, rural residents may be more likely to mistrust government and, therefore, may be more reluctant to share information (Weisheit, Falcone, and Wells 1994; McDonald, Wood, and Pflug 1996). Inside Policing 1.1 presents several comments by rural police officers concerning differences between rural and urban police.

INSIDE POLICING 1.1 Rural Police Work

Former Rural Police Officer

"The small town police officers are more in tune with the fact that if I'm a member of the Kiwanis, Lions Club or the Jaycees, these people can help me....[In] New York [if]...you get into a bind they aren't going to help you as much. [Rural]...police are very active...in these types of organizations." (81)

Rural Police Officer

"[When arresting someone]...you can't act overly high and mighty with them, you won't get any cooperation. In big cities, that's what you do, you come on strong, 'I'm the boss.' That's often a very effective method there but not out here in the rural areas." (82)

Rural Police Officer

"[M]ost...training academies are geared for large, urban departments. I used to send somebody to the academy and when they came back I would have to ride herd on them for two months to get the academy out of them. At the academy, everything is treated very, very serious. All traffic stops are felonies unless proven otherwise....In a small town, [citizens] are people first and suspects second. In a large town...[it is the reverse]." (84)

Rural Police Officer

"Their [police and citizen's] kids go to the same school. You see [people]...on the street,...in the grocery store. (Big-city cops) the officers are cold. They treat...[the good and the bad people]...the same way." (86)

Small-Town Chief of Police

"I've had people in here to counsel...[them] on their sex life because they think I'm the almighty, and can do that. I've had people come in here who are having trouble making ends meet, and we [help them]...get welfare. Somebody needs a ride, like an elderly lady needs a ride to the doctor. We'll take her to the doctor and go get her groceries for her." (87)

SOURCE: R. A. Weisheit, D. N. Falcone, and L. E. Wells, *Crime and Policing in Rural and Small-Town America* (Prospect Heights, IL: Waveland Press, 1996).

Police Role and Purpose

Egon Bittner (1970, 46) famously described the core of the police role as "the distribution of non-negotiably coercive force employed in accordance with the dictates of an intuitive grasp of situational exigencies." The police are who we call when something really bad is happening right now, and we give them the authority to deal with it forcefully, if necessary. Moreover, police have discretion in deciding what to do and how to do it. None of this authority or discretion is unlimited, of course, but the reality is that society needs a mechanism for handling trouble, including trouble that has to be dealt with immediately. That mechanism is the police.

The police are the major representatives of the legal system in their transactions with citizens. The police "adapt the universal standards of the law to the requirements of the citizen and the public...through their right to exercise discretion." They are also the "major emergency arm of the community in times of personal and public crisis." In carrying out their mandate, the police "possess a virtual monopoly on the legitimate use of force" (Reiss 1971, 1–2).

Although using force may be at the core of the police role, the police also provide a variety of more mundane governmental and social services. In doing their job, the police have intimate contact with a wide variety of citizens in a wide variety of situations:

> Police officers deal with people when they are both most threatening and most vulnerable, when they are angry, when they are frightened, when they are desperate, when they are drunk, when they are violent, or when they are ashamed. Every police action can affect in some way someone's dignity, or self-respect, or sense of privacy, or constitutional rights. *(President's Commission 1967, 91–92)*

The police role is the part that police are expected to play in a democratic society. There are several major sources of expectations concerning what the police should do and how they should do it, including the law, the police organization, the community, and the individual (Roberg, Kuykendall, and Novak 2002). The extent of role-related conflict over the police either increases or decreases depending on the degree to which these expectations are shared. When expectations from different sources are compatible, there is minimal difficulty in deciding what the police should do and how they should do it. When expectations differ, however, conflict can arise over the police role.

1. **Legal expectations**. Laws provide the basic framework in which the police are supposed to function. Although the police do not always follow the law, legal expectations have a substantial influence on what they do and how they behave. Police do not enforce all laws all the time, however; rather, they exercise discretion in deciding what laws to enforce and how to enforce them. These discretionary decisions may not always be compatible with what either the formal organization or the community expects.

2. **Organizational expectations**. The formal and informal aspects of a police department produce organizational expectations. Formal expectations are derived from leaders, supervisors, training programs, and the goals, objectives, policies, procedures, and regulations of the police department. Informal expectations are derived from officers' peers, the work group, and the police culture (Crank 1998; Paoline 2001). Officers are strongly influenced by their work experiences and the way in which they adjust to the emotional, psychological, intellectual, and physical demands of police work. They must attempt to do their job in a manner that is acceptable to both the police department and their peers, while trying to stay safe and not provoke citizen complaints.

3. **Community expectations**. Societal trends and problems, in general and in each community, create an environment of community expectations. Individual citizens and subgroups—women and men, youth, rich and poor, traditionalists and cosmopolitans, members of minority groups, immigrants—all have their own opinions about police and their own priorities and preferences. In some communities there can be a reasonable degree of consensus about the role that the police should play, but in many communities there are divergent expectations. To add one additional complication, these expectations often change over time, in response to specific events, evolving conditions, or changes in the composition of the community.

4. **Individual expectations**. Police employees' individual expectations refer to their perspectives concerning the degree to which their needs are met by the organization and their working environment. All employees expect to be treated fairly and adequately rewarded. They also have their own beliefs about police work and how the police role should be carried out. Those beliefs may be affected by peers and the police culture, but they can also be quite individualistic (Linn 2008).

Law Enforcement or Politics?

What is the most effective way to integrate the role of police into a democratic society? At the extremes there are two alternatives: a rule-oriented way or one that is responsive and individualized. The former is a legalistic (or bureaucratic, quasi-military, professional, or reform) approach; the latter is a political approach. The concept of a law enforcement or legalistic approach assumes that justice is a product of consistent application of laws and departmental policies and procedures. Ideally, these laws, policies, and procedures are rationally developed and free of any bias that would be inconsistent with the fundamental principles of the society.

There are two different variations of the political view of the police role. One is that laws and the police primarily serve the interest of the most influential persons in a community. Such individuals are considered above the law, whereas others are treated more harshly. This view leads to politics of preference and discrimination. The second view focuses on responsiveness and individualization. Its advocates argue that strict enforcement of the rules does not take into account the uniqueness of the problems and needs of individuals and neighborhood groups in the community. Complete consistency is not required, and preferential treatment and discrimination are not inevitable if police officers are professional. The police response should be lawful and a function of the situational context and community values as these relate to community problems.

This debate between the legalistic and the political approach emphasizes a long-standing tension in democratic societies—the rule of law versus community expectations. At the one extreme is the uncaring bureaucrat who never deviates from the rules and does not seek opinions about which rules are important and when and how they should be applied. At the other extreme is the tyranny of the majority. However much we subscribe to the rule of law, those who provide government service are often called upon to tailor that service to the needs of a particular community. But how can they do this without providing preferential treatment for some (individuals, groups, neighborhoods) while discriminating against others? The answer to this question remains elusive and varies concerning how, or even if, it can be done.

The legalistic approach and the two variants of the political approach to the role of the police identify three possible types of police–community relationships. The *political model* refers to a police–community relationship that is plagued by problems of preferential treatment, discrimination, and corruption. The *legalistic or reform/professional model* is based on the assumption that political influence has a corrupting influence on policing; therefore, the police–community relationship must be more structured or bureaucratic. The *community policing model* is based on the desirability of the police being responsive to individuals and groups without engaging in preferential treatment or discrimination.

Crime Fighting or Social Service?

The debate about whether the police should only fight crime or should also provide social services influences the priority given to police activities, the type of personnel selected, the way officers are trained, and the styles that officers adopt. Officers who consider themselves crime fighters believe that crime is a function of a rational choice made by criminals and that the primary police purpose is to patrol and conduct investigations to deter crime and apprehend offenders. Officers who consider themselves social service providers believe that crime results from a variety of causes and that there are other police activities like crime prevention education and community building that may also reduce the crime rate. The social service orientation tends to result in more police–community involvement and a less aggressive and authoritarian approach to policing.

There are, of course, no "pure" crime fighters or social service providers; however, the belief that police are, or should be, one or the other influences how the police role in a community will be constructed. Often the role expectations vary by source. Some communities, neighborhoods, or groups may expect police to be crime fighters, whereas others may want a social service orientation. Often, police officers themselves prefer to think of themselves as crime fighters.

Proactive or Reactive?

Proactive police work emphasizes police-initiated activities by the individual officer and the department. **Reactive** police work is more in the form of responses to incidents when assistance is specifically requested by citizens. Giving a traffic ticket or other citation or conducting a field interrogation is proactive. Developing a solution to a crime or other problem that is designed to keep it from occurring is also proactive. For example, undercover decoy programs are proactive, as are "stakeouts" (following suspected career criminals) and picking up truants (who may be committing burglaries when absent from school). Responding to specific incidents based on citizen requests and following up on those incidents are reactive responses.

What can be problematic about proactive responses is that they make the police more intrusive in the community—that is, police are more likely to initiate contacts or tactics without being asked, and some proactive efforts are potentially dangerous (e.g., stakeout and decoy programs). Being proactive can be associated with good management, but it may also be intrusive and risky.

Which is more compatible with democracy—a police force that is primarily reactive or one that is more proactive? Passive reactive policing interferes with our freedom the least, but probably also protects us the least. In trying to strike the right balance, it may be important to distinguish the degree to which proactive police work is in response to community expectations versus merely the expectations of the police department or individual police officers. What is clear, however, is that the more proactive and intrusive the police are, the greater the risk to police officers, citizens, and democracy.

Police Activities and Workload

As these debates about the role of the police suggest, police officers perform a variety of different kinds of tasks and activities. Since the 1960s, many studies have attempted to summarize the nature of police work by categorizing different measures of reactive and proactive police work, such as calls to the police, calls dispatched, time consumed, and encounters with citizens (see Cordner 1989 for one review of many of these studies). By the 1980s, it had become widely accepted that actual police work, as contrasted with its depiction in the media, was a rich and varied blend of several types of activities, including crime control (taking crime reports, investigating crimes, inquiring into suspicious circumstances), law enforcement (making arrests, issuing traffic citations), order maintenance (handling disputes, keeping the peace), and service (everything from finding lost children to helping disabled motorists). The actual mix of these different types of activity varies between different jurisdictions (such as between a city and an affluent suburb) and between different patrol beats within a jurisdiction.

The most comprehensive study of patrol work was the Police Services Study (Whitaker 1982). This study examined patrol work in 60 different neighborhoods, with observers accompanying patrol officers on all shifts in 24 police departments (including 21 municipal and 3 county sheriff's departments). The observers collected information on each encounter between a police officer and a citizen, detailing nearly 6,000 encounters in all. The fact that this study included so many different police departments and police-initiated as well as citizen-initiated activity makes it very persuasive. In a sophisticated re-analysis of the Police Services Study, Mastrofski (1983) looked at the most frequent incidents encountered by patrol officers. He found the following breakdown:

- 29.1%—Crime-related incidents
- 24.1%—Traffic regulation and enforcement
- 22.7%—Nuisances, disputes, and dependent persons
- 24.1%—Services and other miscellaneous incidents

The Police Services Study also examined the specific actions that police officers took during their 6,000 encounters with the public. The figures below indicate the proportion of all encounters in which police officers took each kind of action. (These figures add up to more than 100 percent because officers often took more than one type of action in an encounter.

57%	Interviewed a witness or person requesting service
40%	Interrogated a suspect
29%	Conducted a search or inspection
28%	Lectured or threatened (other than threat of force)
27%	Gave information
23%	Gave reassurance
14%	Used force or threat of force
11%	Gave assistance
9%	Gave a ticket
8%	Used persuasion
5%	Made an arrest
2%	Gave medical help

The police invoked the law relatively rarely, making arrests in only 5 percent of the encounters and issuing tickets in fewer than 1 of 10 encounters. Officers used force or the threat of force in 14 percent of the encounters (with force actually used in 5 percent and most of this amounting only to handcuffing or taking a suspect by the arm). The use of force or its threat was about equally likely in situations involving crime, disorder, and traffic encounters, but very rare in service situations.

Perhaps the most interesting characteristic of police work revealed by these figures is the importance of communication skills. Five of the six most common actions taken by officers consisted entirely of talking and listening. These five were interviewing, interrogating, lecturing or threatening, giving information, and giving reassurance. It is primarily by communicating that police officers determine what is going on in any given situation, and it is primarily through communicating that an amicable solution is reached. Enforcing the law and using force often come into play only after communication tactics and informal solutions prove unsuccessful, although it should be noted that serious law violations sometimes require immediate enforcement, and very dangerous suspects may warrant immediate use of force.

The traffic function of policing accounts for a sizable portion of all police–citizen encounters and has a significant impact on how the public views the police. According to a study based on a large sample of U.S. residents, vehicle stops (which may be precipitated by traffic violations or suspicion of a crime) accounted for 56% of all public contacts with police in 2005 (Durose, Smith, and Langan 2007). An estimated 18 million drivers were pulled over by the police during that year. Of the drivers stopped, 57 percent were ticketed, 4.8 percent were searched, 2.4 percent were arrested, and 0.8 percent had some type of force used against them (most of whom felt that the force used had been unnecessary or excessive).

Police officers typically have a great deal of discretion in making traffic stops and issuing citations, and the level of traffic enforcement varies greatly among individual officers and between different departments. Some departments have no formal policies regarding traffic enforcement, although there are often informal policies and expectations. For example, specialized traffic units may have policies requiring officers to generate at least one citation per hour, whereas regular patrol officers may be expected to write one or two citations per shift. Of course, such policies or expectations can lead to unequal traffic enforcement, with officers scrambling at the end of shifts or at the end of the month to "keep their numbers up" or "meet their quotas." We will have a great deal more to say about police behavior and police use of force in Chapters 9 and 10.

Police Goals and Strategies

In this section we have discussed several different ways of thinking about the role of the police in a free society and also some information about what police officers actually do. To complete the discussion, we will consider what police officers and entire police agencies are supposed to accomplish (their purpose or goals) and we will briefly touch on the strategies that police agencies use to try to accomplish their goals.

A particularly useful listing of police goals is provided in Table 1.6. Moore and Braga (2003) present these goals as the "bottom line" of policing. This framework illustrates that the police bottom line (i.e. the measuring stick that we should use to determine how well a police agency [or individual officer] is performing) is actually multidimensional. This is another way of saying that we expect the police to accomplish several different things, more or less simultaneously. This helps explain why policing is complex and also why different members of the community might have different opinions about how good a job their police are doing—which goals are most or least important varies from person to person and also over time.

TABLE 1.6 Dimensions of Police Performance

- Reduce crime and victimization
- Call offenders to account
- Reduce fear and enhance personal security
- Ensure civility in public spaces (ordered liberty)
- Use force and authority fairly, efficiently, and effectively
- Use financial resources fairly, efficiently, and effectively
- Quality services/customer satisfaction

Source: M. H. Moore and A. Braga, *The "Bottom Line" of Policing: What Citizens Should Value (and Measure) in Police Performance* (Washington, DC: Police Executive Research Forum, 2003), p. 18.

Individual officers who give highest priority to the goal of calling offenders to account tend to perceive the police role as mainly law enforcement, in contrast to officers who put more priority on maintaining order (ensuring civility in public places) or reassuring the public (reducing fear). An emphasis on reducing crime reflects the crime fighter role, whereas the social service role tends to focus somewhat more on satisfying the public by providing quality services. A proactive approach to policing might promise more success in reducing crime or holding offenders accountable, but at the risk of inefficient or unfair use of police power and authority. The interplay among these different dimensions of police performance helps explain the different ways that police officers (and the public) perceive the police role.

At the police agency level, we can see the same thing. Some police departments put their highest priority on reducing crime, perhaps because their jurisdiction has a high crime rate or just because the police chief adheres to the crime fighter role. Other police departments seem to focus more on maintaining order or providing services, whether because crime rates are lower in their jurisdictions or in response to different community and political expectations (Wilson 1968). Certain agencies, especially federal and some special-jurisdiction agencies, clearly put their greatest emphasis on calling offenders to account—in these agencies, investigation is the dominant activity and success is measured almost entirely in terms of cases solved.

Efficient use of financial resources has always seemed to be a high priority for taxpayers, but it has definitely come to the forefront in recent years. Tax limitation measures adopted over the past 20–30 years have significantly reduced public funds in many states and local jurisdictions. On top of that, the current economic downturn has caused many police agencies to cut back on services and even lay off sworn personnel. After 1 or 2 decades during which police agencies seemed to have favored status with taxpayers, city managers, and mayors at budget time, finances have gotten very tight and police chiefs are having to find places to make cuts in their budgets.

One other thing that has been learned in recent years is that the public tends to put a high priority on the "using force and authority fairly" and "quality services" dimensions. If a community believes that its police officers do not treat people fairly or if citizens have unpleasant contacts with officers, public trust and confidence are easily compromised. This seems to be true even if, at the same time, the police department can demonstrate success in achieving other goals, such as reducing crime and holding offenders to account. This characteristic of police performance is now sometimes referred to as procedural justice (Sunshine and Tyler 2003); the lesson is that process can be as important as outcome in judging the effectiveness of the police and maintaining the legitimacy of the police institution, a point to which we will return in Chapter 5.

Another implication of procedural justice and police legitimacy is that *how* the police try to accomplish their goals can be as important as whether they accomplish them. This brings strategies and tactics into the discussion. *Strategies* refers to the broad approaches that police agencies take in trying to accomplish their multiple goals, while *tactics* refers to narrower and more specific programs and activities. Community policing is an example of a strategy, whereas foot patrol is a tactic.

Major police strategies can be differentiated in two ways: (1) according to the specific methods that they employ, as noted above, and (2) according to how much priority they place on the various goals of policing. In later chapters we discuss several police strategies, including the reform/professional model, community policing, problem-oriented policing, and intelligence-led policing. In a nutshell, professional policing emphasizes reducing crime and holding offenders to account, relying mainly on police presence and strict enforcement of the law. Community policing tends to put more emphasis on the goals of customer satisfaction and fear reduction than the other strategies and relies more on personalized policing, community education, and community engagement. Problem-oriented policing emphasizes reducing the harm that is caused by crime and other types of problems, mainly by taking an analytical and preventive approach to identify tailor-made solutions to specific problems. Intelligence-led policing is the newest and least developed strategy; it seems to focus mainly on crime reduction aided by high-tech approaches to prediction, prevention, and suppression.

Looking Ahead

The aim of this chapter has been to lay a brief foundation for your study of police and society. The next three chapters continue in that same vein. Chapter 2 presents the history of police, to help you understand when and why modern police departments developed and how they have evolved, as well as what societies did before they had police departments as we know them today. Chapter 3 provides the legal framework of policing, including concepts from constitutional, criminal, and civil law that define the parameters or "guardrails" within which police are allowed to use their power and authority. Chapter 4 focuses exclusively on community policing, the police strategy that came to prominence in the 1990s but is struggling today in the face of financial pressures and competing perspectives on how best to deal with crime and terrorism.

The second section of the book shifts to the organizational or administrative perspective on policing. This is an important approach, because police officers are members of police *organizations*, and society looks to police *organizations* to make their communities safe and free. Chapter 5 discusses police management, including how police agencies are structured and how police officers are managed and led. Chapter 6 looks at organizational change, a key perspective for improving policing and making sure that police departments keep up with changing times. Chapter 7 targets three specific police administrative processes related to acquiring and developing the right kinds of people to do police work—recruitment, selection, and training. Chapter 8 focuses on the operational strategies, tactics, and programs that police use in the field to try to reduce crime and achieve their other important organizational goals.

The third section of the book concentrates on police behavior, in other words, what police officers do, why they do it, and how best to control it. Chapter 9 discusses a variety of types of police behavior and misbehavior, along with theories that aim to explain the behavior. Chapter 10 focuses specifically on the core of the police role, force and coercion. Chapter 11 then presents information on the many internal and external methods that are used to try to hold both individual police officers and police agencies accountable for their behavior and their use of power and authority. It has been said that power corrupts, and absolute power corrupts absolutely. Police definitely have power, but quite a few mechanisms are in place to control that power and hold police accountable when they misuse it.

The fourth and final section of the book discusses a variety of important contemporary issues affecting police and society. Chapter 12 reviews the experience of women and minorities in policing and explains why it is so important for police agencies to reflect the diversity of their communities. Chapter 13 looks at the effects of stress on police officers and considers the highly important topic of police officer safety, including the surprising fact that fewer police die in the line of duty today than in the past. Chapter 14 assesses the role of higher education in policing; the necessity of college for police officers is an issue that has been vigorously debated since the 1960s. Chapter 15 then discusses a number of different current and emerging issues in society and within policing, such as the aging population, racial profiling, the privatization of policing, the impact of modern technologies, and the continuing evolution of police strategies.

As previously noted, that's a lot of information. Each chapter is full of many important details, but as you digest them, try to keep the big picture in mind as well—policing foundations, police administration, police behavior, and contemporary issues. You might want to use that framework, along with the chapter titles, as a kind of outline or mental filing system to help you keep so much information organized in a coherent and understandable format.

Summary

The type of police a society has is determined by its history, culture, and form of government—totalitarian or democratic. In free and democratic societies police fill an anomalous and conflicted function. The rule of law is one of the most important means for dealing with this conflict. Laws represent rules that citizens are required to follow, of course, but also rules that the police are supposed to follow in their interactions with citizens. In today's world, terrorism has introduced another new challenge for the relationship among democracy, law, and the police.

Police are defined as those nonmilitary individuals or organizations that are given the general right by government to use force to maintain the law, and their primary purpose is to respond to problems of individual and group conflict that involve illegal behavior. The police role and what is considered appropriate or inappropriate police behavior are influenced by legal, organizational, and community expectations as well as the personal values and beliefs of individual police officers. When the expectations arising from these different quarters all line up nicely, policing can operate from consensus and things should go fairly smoothly. Often in a democratic society, however, expectations clash, creating conflict over the police role and the specific actions that police take when dealing with crime, disorder, and other issues.

Another challenge faced in policing is a multidimensional "bottom line." Society expects police to accomplish several different ends, including reducing crime but also providing quality services, making public places orderly, and reassuring people that they are safe. On top of that, police are expected to treat people fairly and equitably and to accomplish their multifaceted bottom line without expending any more tax dollars than absolutely necessary. Several different police strategies currently compete for popular and professional acceptance as the most effective way to deliver policing in the twenty-first century.

Critical Thinking Questions

1. How is policing different in a free and democratic society as opposed to a totalitarian society?

2. It has been said that "democracy is always hard on the police." Why do you think this is the case?

3. Why is the rule of law important for policing in a democracy?

4. Discuss the ramifications of the multidimensional police bottom line. If you were a mayor, how would you use this bottom line to determine how good your town's police department was and what it should do to improve?

5. The police system in the United States is very fragmented. Do you think this is a positive or a negative feature? Why?

6. What would a police department that was proactive and emphasized crime fighting be like? What would be some pros and cons to this approach to policing?

References

Begin, B. 2010. "SFPD Drops Drug Testing from Crime Lab," *San Francisco Examiner*, May 6. On-line at http://www.sfexaminer.com/local/SFPD-drops-drug-testing-lab-92910809.html.

Berkeley, G. E. 1969. *The Democratic Policeman.* Boston: Beacon Press.

Bittner, E. 1970. *The Functions of Police in Modern Society.* Washington, DC: U.S. Government Printing Office.

Cordner, G. W. 1989. "The Police on Patrol." In D. J. Kenney (ed.), *Police & Policing: Contemporary Issues.* New York: Praeger, pp. 60–71.

———. 2011. "The Architecture of U.S. Policing: Variations Among the 50 States," *Police Practice & Research: An International Journal* 12, 2 (forthcoming).

Crank, J. P. 1998. *Understanding Police Culture.* Cincinnati, OH: Anderson Publishing Company.

Durose, M. R., Smith, E. L., and Langan, P. A. 2007. *Contacts Between Police and the Public, 2005.* Washington, DC: Bureau of Justice Statistics.

Goldstein, H. 1977. *Policing a Free Society.* Cambridge, MA: Ballinger Publishing Company.

Gurman, S. 2010. "Police Cite Value of Plainclothes Details," *Pittsburgh Post-Gazette*, February 8. On-line at http://www.post-gazette.com/pg/10039/1034313-53.stm.

Harris, M. 2009. "Baltimore Police Won't Release Crime Lab Analysis," *Baltimore Sun*, January 9. On-line at http://www.baltimoresun.com/news/maryland/baltimore-city/bal-md.ci.lab09jan09,0,5815732.story.

High Point Police Department. 2006. "Eliminating Overt Drug Markets in High Point, North Carolina." Nomination for the Herman Goldstein Award for Excellence in Problem-Oriented Policing. On-line at http://www.popcenter.org/library/awards/goldstein/2006/06-20(F).pdf.

Hunt, A. 2010. "Cops Prowl Detroit for Guns," *Detroit Free Press*, June 6. On-line at http://m.freep.com/news.jsp?key=663791&rc=ne.

Kahn, C. 2007. "L.A. Police Dept. Moves Quickly to Discipline Officers," *National Public Radio,* May 8. On-line at http://www.npr.org/templates/story/story.php?storyId=10080648.

Linn, E. 2008. *Arrest Decisions: What Works for the Officer?* New York: Peter Lang Publishing.

Mastrofski, S. 1983. "The Police and Noncrime Services." In G. Whitaker and C. Phillips (eds.), *Evaluating the Performance of Crime and Criminal Justice Agencies.* Beverly Hills, CA: Sage, pp. 33–61.

McDonald, T. D., Wood, R. A., and Pflug, M. A. (eds.). 1996. *Rural Criminal Justice.* Salem, WI: Sheffield Publishing.

Megerian, C. 2010. "N.J. Police Looks the Other Way After Fellow Trooper Drinks and Drives," *Newark Star-Ledger*, April 25. On-line at http://www.nj.com/news/index.ssf/2010/04/state_police_look_the_other_wa.html.

Mendoza, M., and Olson, B. 2009. "Major, Costly Overhaul Likely in HPD Fingerprint Unit," *Houston Chronicle*, December 2. On-line at http://www.chron.com/disp/story.mpl/metropolitan/6747074.html.

Moore, M. H., and Braga, A. 2003. *The "Bottom Line" of Policing: What Citizens Should Value (and Measure) in Police Performance.* Washington, DC: Police Executive Research Forum.

Paoline, E. A. 2001. *Rethinking Police Culture: Officers' Occupational Attitudes.* El Paso, TX: LFB Scholarly Publishing.President's Commission on Law Enforcement and Administration of

Justice. 1967. *The Challenge of Crime in a Free Society*. Washington, DC: U.S. Government Printing Office.

Reaves, B. A. 2006. *Federal Law Enforcement Officers, 2004*. Washington, DC: Bureau of Justice Statistics.

———. 2007. *Census of State and Local Law Enforcement Agencies, 2004*. Washington, DC: Bureau of Justice Statistics.

——— and Goldberg, A. L. 2000. *Law Enforcement Management and Administrative Statistics, 1997*. Washington, DC: Bureau of Justice Statistics.

Reiss, A. J., Jr. 1971. *The Police and the Public*. New Haven, CT: Yale University Press.

Reith, C. 1938. *The Police Idea*. London: Oxford University Press.

Roberg, R. R., Kuykendall, J., and Novak, K. 2002. *Police Management*, 3rd ed. Los Angeles: Roxbury Publishing Company.

Royal Commission on the Police. 1962. *Report*. London: Her Majesty's Stationery Store.

Scolforo, M. 2007. "State Trooper Praised at Amish Shooting," *Associated Press*, September 21. On-line at - http://www.thefreelibrary.com/State+trooper+praised+at+Amish+shooting-a01611392411.

Sims, V. H. 1996. "The Structural Components of Rural Law Enforcement: Roles and Organizations." In T. D. McDonald, R. A. Wood, and M. A. Pflug (eds.), *Rural Criminal Justice*. Salem, WI: Sheffield Publishing, pp. 41–54.

Smalley, S. 2009. "Always on My Mind," *Newsweek*, January 31. On-line at http://www.newsweek.com/2009/01/30/always-on-my-mind.html.

Sunshine, J., and Tyler, T. R. 2003. "The Role of Procedural Justice and Legitimacy in Shaping Public Support for Policing," *Law & Society Review* 37: 513–548.

Tuohy, J. 2010. "Chief Questions Use of Taser on 10-Year-Old Boy," *Indianapolis Star*, April 2. On-line at http://www.indy.com/posts/chief-questions-use-of-taser-on-10-year-old-boy.

Walker, S. 1977. *History of Police Reform*. Lexington, MA: Lexington Books.

Weisheit, R. A., Falcone, D. N., and Wells, L. E. 1994. "Rural Crime and Rural Policing." *National Institute of Justice: Research in Action*. Washington, DC: U.S. Government Printing Office.

Whitaker, G. P. 1982. "What Is Patrol Work?" *Police Studies* 4: 13–22.

Wilson, J.Q. 1968. *Varieties of Police Behavior: The Management of Law and Order in Eight Communities*. Cambridge, MA: Harvard University.

———. 1978. *The Investigators: Managing FBI and Narcotics Agents*. New York: Basic Books.

CHAPTER 2

Police History

CHAPTER OUTLINE

- Foundations of Policing
    Early Policing
    Policing in Nineteenth-Century England
- The Emergence of Modern Policing in the United States
    The First City Police Forces
    The County Sheriff
- Vigilance Committees
- Modern American Policing
    The Political Era
    Police Development
    Criticism in the Political Era
    The Reform Era
    Minority Perspective on the Development
        of American Police
- State Police
    Texas and Massachusetts
    Pennsylvania
    Highway Patrol

CHAPTER OUTLINE   (continued)

- Federal Law Enforcement
  The Revenue Cutter Service and the U.S. Marshal Service
  Postal Inspectors
  The Secret Service
  The Federal Bureau of Investigation
- Summary
- Critical Thinking Questions
- References

KEY TERMS

- class-control theory
- constable
- constable–nightwatch system
- crime-control theory
- disorder-control theory
- frankpledge system
- highway patrol
- kin policing
- marshal
- nightwatch
- patronage system
- political era
- *posse comitatus*
- professionalization
- reform era
- sheriff
- state police
- thief catcher
- urban-dispersion theory
- vigilantes

IT IS IMPORTANT TO understand the history of policing for several reasons. Possessing an understanding and appreciation for the history of the police allows one to identify enduring aspects of the police. It also allows for an evaluation of prior police reform efforts. Using this, it provides a basis for anticipating future policing developments (Walker and Katz 2011). Yet despite extensive research into policing since the 1960s, there are still no definitive answers as to what the police role should be or what particular activities are consistently more effective in reducing crime while maintaining widespread community support, particularly among the poor and minority members of society. Is it even possible for the police to be effective in reducing crime without providing preferential treatment for some while discriminating against others?

This question identifies the fundamental police problem in a democracy. The modern approach in responding to this problem is community policing, which is discussed in Chapter 4. Prior to community policing there were other approaches to making police compatible with democracy. These approaches, called models of policing, are briefly discussed in this chapter.

Foundations of Policing

The history of policing begins with a consideration of kin police, Greek and Roman police, and the development of policing in Europe, particularly in England, because of that country's influence on the formation of modern police departments in the United States.

Early Policing

One of the earliest methods of policing is known as **kin policing,** in which the family, clan, or tribe enforced informal and customary rules, or norms, of conduct. Often the response to a deviation from group norms was brutal (e.g., a hand cut off for stealing or a brand on the forehead for being a criminal). In effect, each member of the group had at least some authority to enforce the informal rules (Berg 1992, 15–16).

The kin policing of clans and tribes began to change during the rise of the Greek city-states and Rome. Until about 594 B.C. in Greece and the third century B.C. in Rome, public order was the responsibility of appointed magistrates, who were unpaid, private individuals. The first paid, public police officer was the *praefectus urbi,* a position created in Rome about 27 B.C. By 6 A.D., Rome had a large public police force that patrolled the streets night and day. After the fall of the Roman Empire, anarchy tended to prevail on the European continent until the twelfth and thirteenth centuries, when kings began to assume the responsibility for legal administration.

Their approach included strengthening the **nightwatch,** a group of citizens who patrolled at night looking for fires and other problems, and appointing individuals to conduct investigations, make arrests, and collect taxes. In some countries, such as France, mounted military patrols were also employed.

In the twelfth century in England, **sheriffs** were appointed by the king to levy fines and make sure that the **frankpledge system** worked. This system for keeping order had existed for centuries and was based on an organization of tithings (10 families) and hundreds (10 tithings). Eventually these hundreds became known as parishes, and several hundreds became known as a shire. The area made up of several hundreds was similar to a contemporary county.

In this system, men over the age of 15 formed a **posse comitatus**, a group called out to pursue fleeing felons. In 1285 the Statute of Westminster mandated that every hundred citizens appoint two constables to assist the sheriff. Like the sheriff, the **constable** inquired into offenses (conducted investigations), served summonses and warrants, took charge of prisoners, and supervised the nightwatch. By the thirteenth century, law was administered by magistrates, who were appointed by the king, and by sheriffs and constables. In the late 1200s, the office of justice of the peace was established in England. The county sheriff was responsible for policing a county and was assisted by the justice of the peace, who in turn was assisted by constables.

This arrangement was the foundation for a system of law enforcement that was to stay in place until the 1800s. Much of the work of these individuals, however, except the sheriffs, was voluntary and not popular, so the practice of paying for substitutes became commonplace. In many instances, the same person was paid year after year to do the work of those who were appointed to the position but did not wish to serve. Often the substitutes were inadequately paid, elderly, poorly educated, and inefficient. These deficiencies did not help the image or effectiveness of policing in the eyes of the community.

At the end of the 1700s, families by the thousands began to move to newly established factory towns to find work. Patterns of lives were disrupted and unprecedented social disorder resulted. Existing systems of law enforcement, primarily the justice of the peace and the constable, were inadequate to respond to the problems associated with these changes.

In the **constable–nightwatch system** of policing, the constables, who were appointed by the local justices, patrolled their parishes during the day. The constables had limited power, and when they tried to obtain citizen assistance by raising the "hue and cry" to capture a fleeing criminal, they were more likely to be ridiculed than helped. At night, men of the watch were charged with patrolling deserted streets and maintaining street lamps. These individuals, however, were more likely to be found sleeping or in a pub than performing their duties.

In London, criminals had little to fear from this system of law enforcement, and they moved freely about the city streets. Victims of crime, if well to do, were protected by their servants and retainers (who formed a bodyguard or type of private police). Poorer citizens had no such protection. When property crimes were committed, the usual procedure was for the victim to employ a **thief catcher.** This person, usually an experienced constable familiar with the criminal underworld, would attempt, for a fee, to secure a return of all or part of the stolen property. Often the thief catcher would supplement his fee by keeping part of the stolen property for himself. Thief catchers were not interested in apprehending and prosecuting criminals but in getting paid and returning all or part of the stolen property.

Policing in Nineteenth-Century England

It is important to focus on the early policing models of nineteenth-century London because this system became a model for policing in England and to some degree for the United States (President's Commission 1967, 3–5). Henry Fielding, the magistrate for Middlesex and Westminster, was among the first to believe police action could prevent crime. From 1754 to 1780, he assisted in the organization of the Bow Street station and is credited with developing the first police investigators. This station was organized into three groups that performed specific crime control functions. Men engaged in foot patrol in the inner areas of the city. Additionally, men on horseback allowed for patrol up to 15 miles away from the Bow Street station. Finally, a group of men were responsible for responding to crime scenes to engage in investigations. These plain-clothed men became known as the *Bow Street Runners,* or *"Thief Takers,"* and as such represented the first detective unit (Germann, Day, and Gallati 1978).

In 1822, Sir Robert Peel, the British home secretary, criticized the poor quality of police in London. In 1829 he was able to pass the Act for Improving the Police in and Near the Metropolis, also known as the Metropolitan Police Act. This measure resulted in the creation of the first organized British metropolitan police force and the creation of modern-day police (Germann, Day, and Gallati 1978).

Initially, Charles Rowan and Richard Mayne were appointed to develop the force. They adopted a military structure and sought to employ the most competent personnel possible. There was considerable resistance, however, to this new type of police among the British populace. They feared the abuse of governmental authority, the kind of secret police that existed in other countries such as France, and limitations on individual freedom. Historically, Britain, like other countries, had many problems in this regard. Eventually the police became accepted, largely because Rowan and Mayne were selective about who they employed and how officers were to behave. By the 1850s, every borough and county in England was required to develop its own police force. Inside Policing 2.1 provides brief descriptions of the contributions of Peel, Rowan, and Mayne to the development of the British police.

One of the most important principles of the Peelian approach was to emphasize the preventive aspects of law enforcement. This attitude resulted in police officers being distributed throughout the city to prevent crimes or to be close by when crimes occurred so that officers could make arrests and help victims. This idea was to become an important part of the development of police in the United States. Other principles were also implemented to guide the development of the new police force. Originally there were 12 principles;

however, some of them dealt with the same issues. The Peelian Principles include the following:

1. The police must be under the control of government.
2. The police must be organized along military lines to ensure stability and efficiency.
3. Police buildings should be located so they are easily accessible to citizens.
4. The public should be informed about the extent and nature of crime. The most appropriate method of evaluating the police is the amount of crime in a community.
5. Police officers should be distributed by time and area. To do this, it is important to keep records of police activities.
6. If a police organization is to be effective, its selection process and training program must be of high quality. New officers should be employed in a probationary status.
7. Police officers who have a good appearance will be more respected by the public.
8. Police officers should be able to control their temper and should emphasize a quiet, determined manner, rather than violent action, in dealing with citizens.
9. To ensure public confidence in the police, all officers must be easily identified; therefore, all officers should be given a number (Kirkham and Wollan 1980).

INSIDE POLICING 2.1   Founders of the British Police

Sir Robert Peel

In 1822 Robert Peel was appointed home secretary, the person responsible for internal security in England. One of his most important objectives was to establish an effective police force to respond to riots and crime problems. It took him 7 years—until 1829—before he was successful. Because the idea for a new approach to policing was so controversial, Peel initially asked that the new police be established only in metropolitan London. He intended, however, that eventually a similar type of police organization would be established for all of Great Britain. Peel was a strong advocate of the concept of a civilian (rather than a military) police force that did not carry guns and that was put out in the community to patrol to prevent crime. The new police became known as Bobbies, after the founder of the department.

Colonel Charles Rowan

Charles Rowan was one of the first commissioners of the new police in London. He served in that capacity until 1850, when he retired. Rowan had a military background that prepared him for such service. Early in the nineteenth century he served under Major General Sir John Moore, whose approach to dealing with his soldiers probably had a strong influence on how Rowan thought the police should relate to the public. Moore believed that officers should show respect for soldiers and treat them firmly and justly. Rowan wanted the same type of relationship to exist between police officers and citizens. Both he and Mayne encouraged officers to listen to citizen complaints and to be tolerant of verbal abuse by citizens.

Richard Mayne

Richard Mayne, an Irish barrister, served as a police commissioner until 1868. His extended service enabled the London police to develop a force that was well respected by citizens. Together with Rowan, he organized the force into numerous divisions that varied in size depending on

(Continued)

INSIDE POLICING 2.1 Founders of the British Police (*Continued*)

the amount of crime in a division's area. Each division had a superintendent in charge, with inspectors, sergeants, and constables, in descending order of rank. Constables were placed in a blue uniform and armed with a short baton and a rattle (for raising an alarm). The uniform was designed so that it would not be similar to military dress. Mayne and Rowan were both concerned that a military-style police would have more difficulty in being accepted by the public.

SOURCES: Adapted from H. A. Johnson, *History of Criminal Justice* (Cincinnati: Anderson Publishing Company, 1988), 173–175; D. R. Johnson, *American Law Enforcement: A History* (St. Louis: Forum Press, 1981), 20–21.

The remainder of this chapter is divided into three sections: the development of modern policing at (1) the local (county and municipal) level of government, (2) the state level, and (3) the federal level. The historical discussion of modern policing in this chapter ends in the 1960s, but continues in Chapter 4 with a discussion of the development of community policing between the 1970s and 1990s.

The Emergence of Modern Policing in the United States

In the 1600s and 1700s, the English colonists in America brought with them the system of policing that existed in England. This system included the offices of justice of the peace, sheriff, constable, and nightwatch. Over time, the basic responsibility for law enforcement gradually shifted from volunteer citizens to paid specialists. This process of role specialization was the result of a growing and increasingly complex society attempting to master the physical environment and cope with human problems. One consequence of these economic, social, and technological changes was an increasing public concern about deviant and disruptive behavior.

Initially, the constable–nightwatch system of policing evolved as a response to the problems of maintaining order and enforcing the law. The system included a limited number of constables who had civil and criminal responsibilities and a patrolling nightwatch staffed with persons who were required to serve as a community obligation. As in England, this obligation was unpopular, and paid substitutes, who were often incompetent, were used until finally the nightwatch became a full-time, paid occupation.

The First City Police Forces

Between the 1830s and the 1850s, a growing number of cities decided that the constable–nightwatch system of law enforcement was inadequate. As a result, paid daytime police forces were created. Eventually the daytime force joined with the nightwatch to create integrated day–night, modern-type police departments. In 1833, an ordinance was passed in Philadelphia that created a 24-person day force and a 120-person nightwatch, all of whom were to be paid. In 1838, Boston created a daytime force to supplement the nightwatch, and soon other cities followed. This arrangement provided the foundation for the emergence of modern policing: a force of officers in one department available 24 hours a day to respond, often through patrolling, to problems of crime and disorder (Lane 1967; Miller 1977; Johnson 1981).

Four theories have been suggested to explain the development of police departments. The **disorder-control theory** explains development in terms of the need to suppress mob violence. For example, Boston had three major riots in the years preceding the establishment of its police department (Lane 1967). Mob violence also occurred in other cities in the 1830s and 1840s. The **crime-control theory** suggests that increases in criminal activity resulted in a perceived need for a new type of police. Threats to social order, such as highway robbers and violent pickpockets, created a climate of fear. Concern about daring thieves and property offenses was also widespread in cities during this time (Johnson 1981).

The **class-control theory** regards the development of the police as a result of class-based economic exploitation. Its advocates note that urban and industrial growth coincided with the development of the new police. During this period, many persons of different social and ethnic backgrounds competed for opportunities that would improve their economic status. The resulting disruption prompted the middle and upper classes, usually white Anglo-Saxon Protestants, to develop a means to control the people involved, usually poor immigrants, sometimes not Anglo and often not Protestant. This theory holds that modern police forces were merely tools created by the industrial elite to suppress exploited laborers who were being used as fuel for the engine of capitalism (Cooper 1975; Johnson 1981). The last view, **urban-dispersion theory**, holds that many municipal police departments were created because other cities had them, not because there was a real need. Police forces were considered an integral part of the governmental structure needed to provide a stabilizing influence in communities (Monkkonen 1981).

No single theory provides an adequate explanation. Although some cities had major urban disturbances before they established new police departments, others did not. Although there was also a public concern about crime, the degree of concern varied among communities. Some cities established after the 1830s and 1840s did not have mob violence or serious crime. Yet police departments were created because a governmental structure was assumed to include a police component similar to the ones that existed in older, larger cities. Police were also used to control class-based economic unrest, but since many police officers came from the dissident groups or had friends or family members who were participants, some police officers and departments resisted brutal or excessive responses.

The police departments established from the 1830s to 1850s—Boston in 1837, New York in 1844, Philadelphia in 1854—were loosely based on the Peelian model of the London police. As noted above, this model emphasized prevention more than apprehension. **Prevention** was to be accomplished by dispersing police throughout the community to keep crime from occurring and to intervene when it did. Apprehension, or arrest, was not stressed because it was associated with secrecy, deceit, incitement, and corruption. Chapter 8 discusses the historical development of both the patrol and the investigation functions in law enforcement.

The London model also included an elaborate structure based on military principles, strict rules of conduct, and well-defined management practices. Great care was taken in the selection and retention of police officers. Since the creation of a new police force in England was controversial, the most important consideration was control of officer behavior. Community expectations and acceptance were the overriding concerns in the development and management of police.

In the United States, however, the establishment of the new police was not as controversial. Departments were generally based on the Peelian prevention concept, but there were minimal similarities beyond that point. Differences were essentially the result of three factors: social context, political environment, and law enforcement policies. The United States was more violent than Britain, politicians were more meddlesome, and the police were more decentralized and were expected to be locally responsive (Johnson 1981).

INSIDE POLICING 2.2 The County Sheriff

The office of sheriff was first established in the eighth century in England. Individuals who occupied this position were both powerful and influential. They served as the chief magistrates of the courts under their jurisdiction, collected taxes, and attempted to apprehend criminals. American colonists adopted the idea of the county sheriff, but by the time all the colonies were settled, the duties of the office had been limited primarily to civil matters in the county and criminal law enforcement in areas where municipal police had no jurisdiction.

The sheriff became an elected official in the United States and, for many years, was paid based on fees received for serving summonses, subpoenas, and warrants and for looking after prisoners at the county jail. The sheriff became an important figure in Western states where local law enforcement was the responsibility of the sheriff and of town or city police officers, called marshals. Sheriffs usually were elected to office as representatives of the most influential groups in the county. Only a small portion of the sheriff's time was spent pursuing criminals. Other duties, such as tax collecting, inspecting cattle brands, punishing convicted felons, and serving court orders, proved to be more time consuming.

In 2004 there were 3,067 sheriff's departments in the United States, with 326,531 employees, of which 175,018 were sworn officers. Sheriff's departments have experienced considerable growth recently. Since 1992, the number of employees within sheriff's departments has grown 44.9 percent (compared with 19.8 percent growth in municipal police departments). Sworn personnel in sheriff's departments have increased 28.1 percent (compared with 19.3 percent in police departments). Although the typical sheriff's department is relatively small, 12 departments employ over 1,000 sworn officers. The largest sheriff's department is in Los Angeles County (8,239 sworn officers).

Although the primary responsibilities of the modern sheriff vary somewhat by department, the most typical include the following: (1) collect some types of taxes (in some but not all counties) and serve civil processes; (2) provide personnel (bailiffs) and security for the court system; (3) operate jails and other correctional facilities (such as prison farms); (4) maintain peace and order; (5) provide general law enforcement service in unincorporated areas (that is, those areas not in legally incorporated cities and towns); and (6) in some counties provide contract law enforcement services.

SOURCES: B. A. Reaves, *Census of State and Local Law Enforcement Agencies, 2004* (Washington, DC: Bureau of Justice Statistics, 2007); R. D. Pursley, *Introduction to Criminal Justice,* 5th ed. (New York: Macmillan, 1991), 132–135; D. R. Johnson, *American Law Enforcement: A History* (St. Louis: Forum Press, 1981), 100–101; H. Abadinsky, *An Introduction to Criminal Justice* (Chicago: Nelson–Hall, 1987), 155–159.

The County Sheriff

By the 1870s, most cities had a police department, even if it consisted of only one person. In more rural areas, the county sheriff was the dominant law enforcement officer. Inside Policing 2.2 describes the development and role of the sheriff.

Vigilance Committees

Another form of policing that was important during the nineteenth century was the private, organized group known as a vigilance or vigilante committee. The word *vigilante* is of Spanish origin and means "watchman" or "guard." Although the term **vigilante** has several possible meanings, one definition of a vigilante group is a voluntary association of men (they rarely included women) who organized to respond to real or imagined threats to their safety, to protect their property or power, or to seek revenge.

The behavior associated with vigilante movements ranges from attempts to provide reasonable due process to individuals suspected of criminal acts to arbitrary, discriminatory, and brutal acts of revenge. The term *lynching* was originally used to describe public whippings carried out by a Colonel Lynch, head of a vigilante movement in the late 1700s in Virginia. Later this term was used to mean hanging. In southern states between 1882 and 1951, approximately 4,700 persons were lynched by unorganized mobs, a form of vigilantism. Most of the victims were black (Karmen 1983, 1616–1618).

Vigilante movements were most common in the American West during the nineteenth century. This was in large part because the western frontier was undeveloped; hence the need for an established police to engage in social control was not efficient. Vigilantes would form episodically as needed. Yet it is important not to confuse vigilantes with lawless mobs. Often the vigilante was composed of the social elite from that society, with the purpose of enforcing conservative values of life, property, and law and order. Prominent figures who were either part of vigilantes or supported their actions included two U.S. presidents (Andrew Jackson and Theodore Roosevelt), five U.S. senators, and eight governors (Brown 1991).

Interestingly, vigilante movements continue to exist to this day. The Guardian Angels are an example of a vigilante movement that started in New York City in the 1970s and subsequently spread to more than 60 cities. This is a group of teenagers and young males, including college students in some cities, who provide citizen patrols in high-crime areas (Berg 1992, 225). Initially, the police in many cities did not welcome the assistance of the Guardian Angels, but eventually a more cooperative relationship developed.

Modern American Policing

The next sections identify and describe two models of policing: the political and the reform (also called the reform, bureaucratic, or quasi-military model). Kelling and Moore (1988) noted that American policing evolved over the twentieth century across seven different dimensions: authorization (where the police derive their power and legitimacy within society), function (the role police play within society and the goals they have), organizational design (how the police are bureaucratically structured), relationship to environment (social distance from the public the police control), demand (how police services and activities are managed), tactics (programs, activities, and output the police use to achieve their goals), and outcomes (measures of success and failure). They argue that by utilizing this framework it is possible to identify distinct eras of policing.

The Political Era

From about the middle of the eighteenth century to the 1920s, local policing was dominated by politics; consequently, this era saw the development of what was essentially a **political model** of policing oriented to special interests. Politics influenced every aspect of law enforcement during this period: who was employed, who was promoted, who was the chief of police, and who was appointed to the police commission, a group of citizens appointed to "run" the police department in a manner approved by elected officials. To some degree even police arrest practices and services were determined by political considerations (Kelling and Moore 1988). An example of the political model is presented in Inside Policing 2.3.

Police Development

Political and economic corruption was commonplace in police departments during this period. Although some officers were honest and responsible, a large number were neither.

Police work during this period became decentralized and neighborhood oriented. Individual officers had a great deal of discretion and tended to handle minor violations of the law on a personal basis. The nature of the offense, whether the suspect treated the officer with "respect," what was known about the person's family, and prior activities were all taken into consideration. Standards of enforcement often varied within cities, and local politicians played a more important role in determining enforcement priorities than did the chief of police.

INSIDE POLICING 2.3 **Political Era Policing**

An example of political era policing can be found by examining the history of the Kansas City (Missouri) Police Department. Thomas Pendergast ran the Democratic political machine in Kansas City between the 1880s and 1930s. "Boss Tom" levied great power and influence among local politicians, although he was elected as a city alderman only once, and his official occupation was as an owner of a concrete business. This influence enabled him to not only secure government contracts for his business, but also to ensure protection for his other interests: gambling, prostitution, and bootlegging.

Pendergast did many favors for government officials and over time was able to place allies in key positions. Pendergast supporters occupied offices such as county prosecutor, mayor, and governor. One supporter was a relatively unknown named Harry S Truman who (with Pendergast's support) became a county judge during this era. But controlling the Kansas City Police Department was critical to his operation. Only with the assistance of the police department would he be able to operate his illegal activities. By 1900, Pendergast had named 123 of the 173 officers within the police department, and later he would also have influence over the majority of the Board of Police Commissioners. Because officers literally owed him their livelihood, Pendergast would routinely use the police to forward his interests. For example, during elections officers would engage in intimidation and illegal arrests to ensure that supporters of anti-Pendergast candidates did not vote on Election Day. Police officers would not investigate gambling, prostitution, and bootlegging operations affiliated with Pendergast, instead focusing their efforts on his rivals.

Pendergast's primary liaison to the police department was a gangster named Johnny Lazia. He too was a bootlegger and a gambler and would routinely provide police officers with portions of his profits in exchange for their protection. Because of their control of the police, Kansas City had a reputation for being a safe place for out of town criminals. These criminals were required to pay Lazia for the right to hide out in Kansas City, and officers were directed to arrest those who did not pay him off.

During this time, Pendergast's concrete business built many city structures including city hall, the county courthouse, the municipal auditorium, and a police station. But eventually support for the political machine waned, and in 1939 the state of Missouri took control of the Kansas City Police Department, eliminating "home rule." A newly appointed police chief discovered rampant corruption within the department, and half of the officers were dismissed. This arrangement, which is still in place today, permits the governor to appoint members of the Board of Police Commissioners.

Subsequent investigations into Pendergast's business practices revealed he engaged in tax evasion between 1927 and 1937, for which he was sent to prison for 15 months. Vice President Truman was among those who attended Pendergast's funeral when he died in 1945. Truman was sworn in as the 33rd President of the United States several weeks later.

SOURCE: Adapted from http://www.kcpolicememorial.com/history/.

Several trends converged in the mid-1800s that resulted in the creation of political machines that controlled cities, including the police department. As cities grew, there was an increasing need for municipal services, such as police, fire protection, and collection of garbage. Upper-class and middle-class citizens had the political influence to ensure that their needs were met, but many newly arriving immigrants, both native (from rural areas) and foreign born, did not. As the numbers of new arrivals increased, those with political ambition began to try to gain the political support of other newcomers. Often the leaders of these groups were successful and they took political control of many cities. Of course, upper-class and middle-class citizens in these cities did not give up their attempts to influence the political process or get elected to office. Even after they lost power, they played the role of critic of the political machines that emerged (Johnson 1981, 17–55).

To be elected to public office, a candidate had to make promises to citizens. One of the most important promises was related to employment. Public jobs served as rewards for some individuals who supported the political party in power. Police jobs became an important part of this political **patronage system**. These types of jobs were popular because they required little or no skill and paid well compared with other jobs that also required minimal ability. Moreover, many officers did little but frequent bars and pool halls when they were supposed to be working. These officers considered a police job a reward for supporting the political machine more than a real job.

Police departments were also of vital importance to the political machine's boss in his ability to maintain political control. The police were particularly useful during elections because they maintained order at polling booths and were able to determine who voted and who did not. Individuals who became police officers were often avid supporters of the political machine and would do anything to help keep it in power. After all, their jobs depended upon it. But they also supported it because the machine often represented a point of view that was consistent with their own.

The upper class and middle class often criticized the morality of ethnic immigrants and the poor, and they periodically tried to get the police to enforce a white, middle-class standard of morality by supporting legislation that attempted to control drinking, gambling, and prostitution. Nevertheless, even when criminal laws and ordinances were enacted in an attempt to regulate these activities, they were not always enforced, because by the late nineteenth century, many immigrants, particularly the Irish, were working as police officers, and many police officers were tolerant of such "vices" and even participated in them, on and off duty (Johnson 1981, 17–55).

From the discussion above it is possible to summarize the political era utilizing the seven distinguishing features in Kelling and Moore's (1988, 2–4) framework. In this era the police *derived their authority* from powerful local politicians who utilized the police to maintain the status quo and retain political power (like Pendergast). The police engaged in a variety of *functions* that included crime control, but arguably providing social services was critical for the police to maintain legitimacy. A geographically decentralized *organizational structure* was necessary during this era to ensure the police were able to satisfy the needs of local politicians. These characteristics led to a close and personal *relationship to citizens*. *Demands for police services* were channeled through local politicians as well as personal contacts with citizens. These services were through *tactics* that included foot patrol and rudimentary investigations. The police were *evaluated* mostly by the level of satisfaction of citizens and local politicians and not necessarily by their ability to engage in crime prevention.

Criticism in the Political Era

By the 1890s, as cities began to grow larger and become more difficult to manage, the politically dominated, often corrupt, police departments came under increasing criticism. This criticism applied not only to the police but also to all city services. All problems attendant to large cities appeared to become important during this period: an increase in crime, population congestion, inadequate housing, health problems, waste disposal, and so on. The period from the mid-1890s to the mid-1920s became known as the Progressive Era in the United States because many of these types of problems, including poor working conditions and child labor, began to be addressed, not only in the public sector but also in private enterprise.

Social critics began to argue that political power should change hands. These reformers were made up of religious leaders and civic-minded upper-class and middle-class business and professional people. They argued that government should be managed efficiently, public officials should be honest, and there should be one standard of conduct for everyone. The recommended reform model was based on the principles of industrial management because these principles were given credit for making the United States an economic success. Efficiency meant providing the highest quality service at the lowest cost. To become efficient, organizations had to have centralized control under a well-qualified leader, develop a rational set of rules and regulations, and become highly specialized, with duties and performance requirements specified for each specialized position.

The Progressive Era movement touched all aspects of American life. As it applied to government, it was based on three basic ideas: (1) honesty and efficiency in government, (2) more authority for public officials (and less for politicians), and (3) the use of experts to respond to specific problems. This movement and these ideas gained more and more credence as the United States moved into the twentieth century. These changes also applied to police departments; gradually they began to shift away from a political orientation to more of a bureaucratic, legalistic, or reform approach to policing (Johnson 1981, 17–55; Kelling and Moore 1988).

The Reform Era

By the 1920s, attempts to reform local policing, and, to some degree, state and federal law enforcement, were beginning to have an impact. From the 1920s to the 1960s was probably the most significant period in the development of policing in the United States because it established the foundations for the professionalization of law enforcement. **Professionalization** has a number of possible definitions. As used here it means an attempt to improve police behavior and performance by adopting a code of ethics and improving selection, training, and management of police departments. It also means the police, like other professions, would focus on a single core strategy rather than performing a kaleidoscope of loosely coupled services. For the police this core strategy would become crime control. Professionalism is discussed in more detail in Chapter 11.

During this period a **reform model** (also called the professional, bureaucratic, legalistic, quasi- or semi-military model) of policing began to dominate thinking about police work. Essentially, it means that the police–community relationship should be based on law and departmental policy because police (both as organizations and as individuals) should not be unduly influenced by politics or personal considerations when making decisions. One of the most important aspects of the legalistic model is related to the mission of the police. Advocates of this model thought that crime fighting should be the primary purpose of the police. They used this idea to mobilize support for their reforms and to improve the public image of the police (Kelling and Moore 1988). The police, in effect, began to emphasize the most dramatic aspects of their work (Johnson 1981, 105–189).

Between about 1920 and the mid-1960s, many police departments changed dramatically in the United States. Political meddling was substantially, but not entirely, replaced by efficient and centralized management and a commitment to professionalism. This change was the result of (1) European developments in criminalistics, (2) changes in American society and politics, and (3) the growth of the police reform movement.

American society and politics also began to change in ways that affected the development of policing. As the economy put more emphasis on industrial and consumer goods and rail and automobile transportation improved, more and more people moved to the suburbs. Many of them were white and middle class. The population of cities began to change as increasing numbers of Spanish-speaking immigrants and blacks from the rural South arrived. Many of these newcomers were unskilled, poor, powerless, and in great need of city services (Johnson 1981, 105–189).

The Spanish-speaking and black neighborhoods were often plagued by extensive crime problems. Many police officers began to think of these neighborhoods as dangerous and troublesome areas in which to work. Given the fact that police forces, beginning with the slave patrols, had a long history of racist behavior, the tension between minority groups and the police increased and became an important factor in the numerous urban riots of the twentieth century. These riots began in East St. Louis in 1917 and were followed by several in 1919, at least 7 during World War II, and numerous riots in the 1960s. There were 42 major to serious disorders in 1967 alone (National Advisory Commission 1968, 35–206). Although there were many reasons for these riots, a significant factor was the behavior of police officers in minority neighborhoods.

In the newly established suburban communities, the mostly white, middle-class inhabitants expected that government services would be based on the principles of efficiency and quality. The police were expected to be well trained and courteous, use the best equipment, and employ the latest management techniques. Many of the reform ideas of the Progressive Era and the legalistic model of policing had a positive impact on these communities before they gained influence in larger, older cities, where a tradition of political interference was difficult to change.

Among the more important developments during this period was the emergence of the commission approach to reform. When there was sufficient concern about police behavior in a community, prominent citizens and experts were appointed to commissions to conduct investigations and to make recommendations for change. Commissions were formed at both the local and the national level.

In 1919, the Chicago Crime Commission was established to supervise the criminal justice system in Chicago. Unlike most other commissions created during the following decade, the one in Chicago became permanent. By 1931, 7 local, 16 state, and 2 national crime commissions had been established to investigate the police. Perhaps the best known of these was the National Commission on Law Observance, established by President Herbert Hoover in 1929. It was also known as the Wickersham Commission, for the man who headed the investigation. In 1931 the commission published 14 volumes, 2 of which were about the police. The 12 other volumes were concerned with other aspects of crime and the criminal justice system. August Vollmer was the principal police consultant to the Wickersham Commission and author of the major report on the police (Walker 1977, 125–134).

Vollmer's report identified what he thought were the most important problems in law enforcement: excessive political influence, inadequate leadership and management, ineffective recruitment and training, and insufficient use of the latest advances in science and technology. By 1931, it was widely accepted that these were the problems that needed to be addressed in police work. However, another report by the commission, on police lawlessness, overshadowed Vollmer's recommendations. The report identified widespread police abuses, including the use of brutality, to secure confessions (Walker 1977, 128–134).

After the Wickersham Commission published its reports, there was at least the beginning of a national consensus on the direction for the professionalization of the police, essentially toward a legalistic model in which laws and rules were enforced without regard to politics by well-trained and scientifically proficient, dedicated, honest employees who worked in a centralized department that was primarily concerned with crime fighting. Many police departments, however, remained substantially political well into the 1960s.

One of the most significant events of the twentieth century—the Great Depression of the 1930s—actually made police reform easier. With reduced funds available, there was less opposition to centralizing the police, and in many cities some local precinct stations were closed to save money. Centralization made it easier for chiefs of police to control their officers and also resulted in less meddling by politicians. In addition, for the first time, well-educated, middle-class Americans became interested in police work as a career because it offered job security (Johnson 1981, 105–189).

INSIDE POLICING 2.4 Founders of the U.S. Police

August Vollmer

August Vollmer served first as town marshal and then as chief of police in Berkeley, California, from 1905 until 1932. He became one of the leading spokesmen for police professionalism in the first few decades of the twentieth century. He advocated the principles of merit associated with the Progressive Era, as well as more education and training, adoption of the latest management techniques, and the use of science and technology. Vollmer was an advocate of the police officer as social worker, in the sense that he believed police should act to prevent crime by intervening in the lives of potential criminals, particularly juveniles.

Vollmer is often called the father, or dean, of modern police administration. Some of his important contributions include the early use of motorized patrol and the latest advancements in criminalistics. He suggested the development of a centralized fingerprint system that was established by the FBI; he established the first juvenile unit and was the first to use psychological screening for police applicants and the first to emphasize the importance of college-educated police officers.

In the area of education Vollmer was instrumental in the establishment of police-training classes and later a criminology degree program at the University of California at Berkeley. He became a professor of police administration at Berkeley in 1929. He helped develop the first degree-granting program in law enforcement at San Jose State College (now San Jose State University) in 1930. As a result of his efforts, higher education programs became increasingly acceptable.

After he retired as chief of the Berkeley Police Department he continued to serve as a consultant and write about the police. He also kept in touch with many former employees. He died in 1955.

Orlando Winfield Wilson

O. W. Wilson worked in Berkeley, California, for August Vollmer from 1921 to 1925. At the same time, he completed his degree at the University of California. With Vollmer's recommendation he became chief of police in Fullerton, California, in 1925 but lasted only until 1926 because his ideas about modern law enforcement were not acceptable to many citizens in the community.

Wilson was considering another career when Vollmer recommended him as a possible chief for the Wichita, Kansas, police department in 1928. Wilson was selected for that position and over the next 11 years turned what was considered an inefficient and corrupt department into what some called the West Point of law enforcement. He left Wichita in 1937 because his strict enforcement of vice laws had alienated too many powerful citizens. He resigned under pressure, but not before creating what became a model for other police departments. Visiting dignitaries from other countries who expressed a desire to visit a police department were taken to Wichita by the U.S. State Department.

After Wilson left Wichita, he became a professor in the School of Criminology at the University of California at Berkeley from 1939 to 1960. His service was interrupted during World War II when he became a colonel in the U.S. Army. His job was to develop plans to rebuild police departments in countries that had been occupied by Axis Powers. After he left the army he returned to his teaching position.

In 1950 Wilson published the first edition of *Police Administration,* arguably one of the most influential books ever written about police in the United States. It describes in detail how police departments should be organized and managed. It was widely used in training programs, colleges, and universities and as a basis for organizing and managing police departments in the United States and other countries until the 1970s, when Wilson's ideas began to be criticized. Nevertheless, the basic structure of many present-day police departments is the result of Wilson's ideas.

In 1960, while still teaching at Berkeley, Wilson agreed to serve on the committee to select a new police commissioner in Chicago. When the committee could not find an acceptable candidate, they offered the job to Wilson. He agreed and served until 1967; during that time he made many important changes that received widespread publicity and made Chicago a model of modern policing. One year after he retired, however, the Chicago police performed poorly in their attempts to manage the demonstrations at the 1968 Democratic Convention. This failure raised important questions about Wilson's effectiveness and the difficulty of changing police organizations. After his retirement Wilson moved to California and spent his time writing and traveling until his death in 1972.

Wilson typified police leadership and management during the legalistic era. He believed politics had no place in policing; he was a strong advocate of centralized police management and strict discipline. He was also an articulate spokesman for police professionalism as it related to more training and education, better salaries and benefits, and his definition of police management.

SOURCES: S. Walker, *A Critical History of Police Reform* (Lexington, MA: D. C. Heath, 1977), 21–165; G. E. Caiden, *Police Revitalization* (Lexington, MA: D. C. Heath, 1977), 210–217; G. F. Cole, *The American System of Criminal Justice,* 5th ed. (Pacific Grove, CA: Brooks/Cole Publishing Company, 1989), 178; adapted from W. Bopp, *O. W. Wilson and the Search for a Police Profession* (Port Washington, NY: Kennikat Press, 1977).

By the 1930s, the reform themes—centralization, standardization of behavior through the development of policies and procedures, more education and training, selection and promotion based on merit, commitment to the goal of fighting crime, and use of the latest advances in science and technology—were well established.

The police in America had undergone a dramatic transformation during the twentieth century. In the reform era the police *derived their authority* from the law and professionalism, which was critical to wrestle influence away from local politicians. Their *primary function* became crime control, and delivery of police services common in the political era became less frequent and devalued. The *organizational design* became centralized, which was necessary to manage police tasks in a consistent and evenhanded fashion. The *relationship the police had to the public* became more distant since close ties were seen as unnecessary or even counterproductive to their core strategy of crime control. *Demand* for police activities was guided from centralized dispatchers. The core *tactics* of the police were routine patrol, rapid response, and reactive investigations. *Success and failure was measured* by the ability of the police to control crime, particularly those serious crimes as defined by the FBI's Uniform Crime Reports (Kelling and Moore 1988, 4–7).

By the 1960s, however, these reform ideas began to be questioned as a result of three important developments: urban riots, the civil rights movement, and the perception of an increasing crime rate. As minorities, and later women, became increasingly active in trying to change their status in society and as people began to be more concerned about crime, the police became one focal point for criticism. By the mid-1960s, this concern was so great that two other national commissions were established, in part to address problems concerning the police. These were the President's Commission on Law Enforcement and Administration of Justice (hereinafter called the Crime Commission), established by President Lyndon Baines Johnson in 1965, and the National Advisory Commission on Civil Disorders (hereinafter called the Riot Commission), established in 1967.

Like its predecessor the Wickersham Commission, the Crime Commission focused on crime and the entire criminal justice system. The Riot Commission examined not only the criminal justice system, but also many aspects of civil disorders such as poor housing and unemployment. The recommendations of these two commissions concerning the police were a blend of previous reform suggestions plus new ones intended to make the police more responsive to the community. In effect, the legalistic model of policing that had been the basis of reform for several decades began to be challenged. However, this does not mean that its tenets were abandoned; only that some were debated and gradually began to be replaced with new ideas about the role of the police.

Three of the most prominent spokesmen for police reform were August Vollmer, O. W. Wilson (see Inside Policing 2.4), and J. Edgar Hoover (see Inside Policing 2.8). They were controversial during their careers and have remained so as historians have provided examples of their abuses of authority and their racist and sexist behaviors. Despite this criticism, their ideas about the police role and police management remain influential and have resulted in improved police performance in many areas.

Voices From the Field presents a brief historical and personal account of police history from Chief of Police (Ret.) David C. Couper, who was an integral force in implementing quality management and problem solving in Madison, Wisconsin.

The political era of often corrupt and inefficient policing was somewhat changed by the reform era, which, in turn, met criticism. The civic problems of the 1960s brought a new set of critics who wanted to overcome the isolation of a professionalized police force from citizen concerns and develop new strategies and methods to respond to crime and order-maintenance problems. These subsequent changes, along with others, resulted in the emergence of what is now called community policing.

About the same time (the mid-1970s) that the reforms began to be implemented, the crime rate began a decline that, so far, has lasted about 30 years. In Chapter 4, the development of and controversies about community policing and the extent to which it contributed to a decline in crime are discussed. The next two sections of this chapter briefly trace the development of law enforcement at the state and federal levels.

VOICES FROM THE FIELD

David C. Couper
Chief of Police (Ret.), Madison Police Department

Question: How has policing changed since the 1960s?

Answer: In the spring of 1960, after serving 4 years with the Marines, I enrolled at the University of Minnesota and started to look for a night job. That's how I began my police career. When I retired, a good friend of mine, who spent most of her life researching the police, commented on how far the police had come in society. I remember saying, "Improving the police is like stretching a big rubber band. When you let go, it snaps right back to the way it was before you started." I think that statement is still true.

When Sir Robert Peel founded the Metropolitan Police Department in London, his basic principle for policing was that, in order for the police to perform their duties, they had to have public approval and that approval would be diminished proportionally by their use of physical force. To Peel, "the police are the public and the public are the police." Even then, 150 years ago, someone knew that if the police were to be successful in preventing crime and disorder, they had to have the goodwill of the people—all the people.

I joined a large-city urban police department in the 1960s. Luckily, I had a 4-week recruit academy taught by a police commander who was an unusual cop—he had a college degree. When I began police work by walking a beat, there were no portable radios; I "pulled," or checked in with, the dispatcher every hour on our beat. Many of us in that era saw (and often silently condoned) discrimination against blacks and other minorities. It nevertheless impacted us. When our colleges and universities shut down during the days of the Vietnam War protest, we found ourselves on a police line facing our fellow students. And it changed us.

As chief of police of a medium-sized city in 1972, I found myself in the forefront of police change. My city found itself in a "war at home"; there was extreme tension not only with university students

but with the minority community as well. Many young, college-educated chiefs were able to implement community and problem-oriented policing, total quality management, a "softer" and negotiated approach to public demonstrations and civil disobedience, and effective controls on the use of deadly force. We committed ourselves to bringing women, minorities, and college-educated young people into policing.

Today, in a "post-9/11" world, I see the police in a very precarious position. Yes, they have compact portable radios, cell phones, computers, DNA identification methods, and lightweight body armor, but I believe they have lost the vision that sustained many of us before September 11. What I believe sustained the police from the 1960s to the 1990s was the understanding that they are the gatekeepers of a great democracy, that they are first and above all things "constitutional officers" committed to preserving and defending, on a daily basis, the Bill of Rights. It is easy to stray from a noble vision and to think that police work is about a life-and-death battle between "them" and "us." Fear has not only permeated our nation, but our nation's police as well. And a police department that is fearful of the public is a dangerous organization.

In the past the police were uneducated, corrupt, and abusive. They did not have the goodwill or cooperation of the public because of their lack of education, corruption, and use of brutality. This led to calls for police reform. Today, the police are better educated (yet a college degree is not universally required for employment), corruption is less a problem (but it still exists), and the use of deadly force has been constrained (although deadly mistakes still occur and police pursuit of fleeing motor vehicles remains a critical issue). But I will contend that the goodwill and cooperation of the public, especially among racial minorities and immigrants, is still severely lacking.

David C. Couper served as the Chief of Madison (WI) Police Department for 20 years (1973–1993). During his tenure, Chief Couper instituted a 15-year review of the departments' organizational change.

Minority Perspective on to the Development of American Police

There is a tendency to focus exclusively on the American history of the police as it developed in the northern colonies, but it is important to highlight other areas where different approaches to law enforcement emerged. Two particular areas included the southern colonies and the western American frontier. In the southern colonies, slave patrols represented the first form of modern policing, existing as early as the mid-1700s. Slave patrols were created to apprehend runaway slaves and to ensure that slaves did not revolt against their masters. The need for slave patrols was premised on the fact that slaves represented a dangerous class that the economic elite (e.g., plantation owners) desired to control. Eventually all southern states had statutes that created and legitimized slave patrols (Williams and Murphy 1990). Further, slave patrols relied on private citizens to carry out their duties. Participation in slave patrols was part of a citizen's civic responsibility. This structure often led to great difficulties in accountability to the central government, as well as great variation in the behavior of the various "policing" functions. When disorderly or runaway slaves were encountered, they were often immediately punished by the patrol; thus, recognizable due process was absent from this style of policing. Reichel (1999, 85) commented, "[I]n an ironic sense the resistance by slaves should have been completely understandable to American Patriots. Patrols were allowed search powers that the colonists later found so objectionable in the hands of British authorities." The level of fear and resentment on the part of slaves toward these patrols was great.

Some argue that within urban environments, the development and function of the police was guided by a desire to maintain racial segregation and discrimination. The police are agents of governmental social control and legal order, and this was differentially applied toward minorities. For example, influential politicians within the political era were typically white males and they utilized the police to maintain the status quo, often by controlling "outsiders" who were most likely to be black. Minority groups were politically powerless and thus had less influence on policing than their white counterparts. During the reform era, under the guise of equal application of the law, the police differentially applied the law within predominately black urban communities. At the same time, minority representation within police departments was stalled during this period. Civil service requirements that were designed to professionalize the police and remove political influence from hiring and firing officers became roadblocks for integration of minorities. As late as the 1960s, at the peak of the reform era, minorities who became part of the policing establishment were relegated to policing "black neighborhoods" or not given full police power. In short, the policing experience in America varied considerably for people of different races and ethnicities (Williams and Murphy 1990). With this in mind, cultural diversity within police organizations will be more fully examined in Chapter 12.

State Police

Texas and Massachusetts

Prior to 1900, only Texas and Massachusetts had formed a state police force. The idea was slow to catch on, and not until the 1960s did all states have some form of state police. In early Texas many inhabitants lived in rural isolation and faced dangerous problems such as widespread Indian raids. Consequently, the citizens decided to create a quasi-military force, called the Texas Rangers, to protect themselves. After Texas declared its independence from Mexico in 1836, the Rangers were well established. Originally designed for community defense, by the 1850s they were doing general police work. They pursued robbers, runaway slaves, and illegal immigrants from Mexico. Rangers tended to take the law into their own hands and to be brutal in their treatment of prisoners, particularly minorities. Such behavior was commonplace well into the twentieth century. In 1935 Texas created a larger state police, the Department of Public Safety, which was given the responsibility of supervising Ranger activity, and their behavioral excesses were gradually reduced (Johnson 1981, 161–162).

Massachusetts' experiment with a state police force was controversial. Rural residents and prohibitionists were disenchanted with the failure of city police to enforce laws against drinking, so the state legislature created a state police force and gave it general law enforcement responsibilities. Its primary task, however, was to enforce laws against vice. That was what it did in large cities, but in other areas it gradually won a reputation for effective detective work in robbery and murder cases. Nevertheless, controversy about its activities in cities continued, and the state police force was disbanded in 1875. A few state investigators were retained to work in rural areas.

Pennsylvania

The next appearance of a state police force was in 1905, with the establishment of the Pennsylvania State Police. In the Midwest and Northeast, as early as the 1860s, certain problems arose that proved difficult for local police to resolve. These problems were related to economic development, particularly in the areas of mining and industrialization. A combination of an increasing crime problem in affluent rural areas coupled with the exploitation of workers and the workers' demands that such treatment stop resulted in levels of conflict and violence that were difficult to control.

Western Pennsylvania had more than its fair share of such problems. As a major mining region that attracted immigrant labor, it suffered ethnic and labor violence in the latter part of the nineteenth century. The violence became so extensive that President Theodore Roosevelt appointed a commission to look into a major coal strike in 1902. The result was the creation of the Pennsylvania State Police in 1905. This police force was unlike any other in the United States because it emphasized a military approach. All officers had either National Guard or Army experience. The state police proved to be evenhanded in handling labor conflict, and the levels of violence began to decline. Like the Texas Rangers, however, state police officers tended to discriminate against "foreigners." In fact, officers were chosen, in part, because they had contempt for foreigners.

Gradually, the Pennsylvania State Police began to expand its duties, and it began to do routine police work in rural areas throughout the state. Between 1908 and 1923, 14 states, mostly in the North, created state police forces based on the Pennsylvania model. Not all state police, however, were as evenhanded as those in Pennsylvania when it came to labor strife. In Nevada, Colorado, and Oregon the state police tended to side with organized business interests (e.g., mining). This bias became such a problem in Colorado that in 1923 the state police were disbanded (Johnson 1981, 161–164).

Highway Patrol

Between the 1920s and the 1960s, state police forces began to take on new responsibilities. One of the most important was enforcement of traffic laws. With the increasing use of automobiles, the number of related problems—the violation of traffic laws, accidents, and the regulatory requirements associated with the registration of vehicles and the licensing of drivers—also increased. As the highway system grew, there was need for a statewide authority because many of the roads were outside the jurisdiction of cities. The automobile also gave criminals more flexibility: They could come and go more easily and avoid capture more readily.

This situation resulted in two approaches to the development of state law enforcement: a **state police** and a **highway patrol.** The former had broad law enforcement powers (similar to municipal police departments), whereas the latter was generally limited to traffic enforcement. The highway patrol approach became more common. For example, in the 1920s, eight state police departments and six highway patrol units were established. In the 1930s, 18 units were created to deal with traffic, but only 8 to deal with general law enforcement (Johnson 1981, 161–164). The differences between state police forces and state highway patrols are important. State police have their own criminal investigators, may have their own patrol force, gather criminal intelligence, and usually have a forensic science laboratory. State highway patrols concentrate on traffic and accidents on the state's roads and highways (Borkenstein 1977, 1131–1134).

By the 1960s, nearly all states had some type of state police or highway patrol or a combination of the two. They are usually responsible for traffic regulation on state roads and highways, and about two thirds also have general police powers. State police often fill a void in rural law enforcement because they provide services where there are none, or their assistance is requested by other law enforcement units (Cole 1989, 120). Inside Policing 2.5 briefly describes the development of the state police in Oregon, which was typical of other states during the 1920s and 1930s. Inside Policing 2.6 describes the evolutionary process of the Missouri State Highway Patrol.

INSIDE POLICING 2.5 The Oregon State Police

Discussions about the possibility of creating a state police force in Oregon began in 1918. During World War I the state had created an Oregon Military Police to protect shipbuilding plants, but it was disbanded after the war ended. Concern about problems associated with state policing continued because responsibilities were fragmented among several state departments. The State Traffic Department had already been established, but it was having a difficult time coping with the increasing number of automobiles on state highways. In 1929 it had only 50 officers to patrol the entire state. Prohibition was also proving to be a difficult problem. Increasingly, criminals were using cars and were able to avoid local police, who had jurisdiction only within city limits.

In response to these concerns, the state senate established the state police force on March 1, 1931. The force was designed by a committee that examined the Royal Canadian Mounted Police, the Texas Rangers, and the state police of New Jersey, Pennsylvania, and Michigan. The new force began operations on August 1. It was given the law enforcement responsibilities of several older state agencies, including the State Highway Commission (which governed the State Traffic Department), the Secretary of State, the Fish and Game Commission, the State Fire Marshals, and the Prohibition Commissioner. The responsibilities of this new police force included the enforcement of traffic laws, game and fish codes, all laws relating to arson and fire prevention, and laws against illegal liquor and drugs. In addition, the department was given law enforcement responsibilities throughout the state so the department could serve as a rural patrol force and assist local police.

The state police were given additional responsibilities in 1939 and 1941. In 1939 a crime detection laboratory was established at the University of Oregon Medical School; it was subsequently relocated in Portland. By 1989 there were six regional crime detection laboratories, which provided assistance to local police. In 1941 all fingerprint records and criminal photographs were transferred from the state penitentiary to the state police.

In the late 1970s the state police force was reorganized into the present five districts. By 1989 the number of patrol stations had increased from 31 to 45. By 1996, the number of personnel had increased from the original 95 to over 1,200.

SOURCE: Oregon Department of State Police. *Memorandum.* March 15, 1989.

INSIDE POLICING 2.6 Missouri State Highway Patrol

The Missouri State Highway Patrol (MSHP) was officially created in 1931, although it took 6 years of political compromises to do so. While some states were comfortable with the creation of a state policing agency, the creation of state-level law enforcement was difficult in Missouri because of the general skepticism on the part of local politicians to relinquish control to the state government. State police agencies, in many ways, act in direct competition with lower levels of government, particularly county sheriffs. Yet there was a recognized need for a state-level department in Missouri at the beginning of the twentieth century. This was in part because of the creation of an expanded highway system throughout the largely rural state, the difficulty associated with enforcing Prohibition's bootlegging laws, labor disputes in rural areas, and the decentralization of local law enforcement in the state. Thus the creation of the MSHP represented a significant compromise between local and state politicians: the MSHP would have jurisdiction limited to the enforcement of traffic offenses and not be empowered to have general policing duties (such as search and seizure). Thus the MSHP had a narrowly defined mission. Slowly, over time, the MSHP did evolve into a full-service state police agency, although their name remained "highway patrol." This evolutionary process was also experienced in other states, including Mississippi, Nebraska, Ohio, and Washington.

Missouri's experience demonstrates another type of state law enforcement evolution. Recognizing the rivalry between state- and county-level law enforcement, the state initially resisted creating a full-service state police agency. Thus the only way the state was to create a much-needed state-level agency was to limit its power. As social and political conditions changed over time, the mission of the highway patrol was broadened to reflect the general services department it is today.

SOURCE: D. N. Falcone, "The Missouri State Highway Patrol as a Representative Model," *Policing: An International Journal of Police Strategies and Management,* 2001 24: 585–594.

Some states also have other types of law enforcement agencies. Just as with the federal government, any state agency that regulates behavior that is punishable by fine or imprisonment may have a law enforcement component. States that have a park system or environmental laws, any form of legalized gambling, or state income taxes will usually have law enforcement officers associated with that activity. Many states also have an agency whose responsibility is to regulate the selling and distribution of liquor. A few states even have agencies that respond primarily to drug-related problems.

In addition to state police, state highway patrols, and the other types of agencies noted above, many states also provide law enforcement services to local jurisdictions—for example, special investigation assistance and crime labs for the analysis of physical evidence. There may also be a statewide computer system to provide information about wanted persons and stolen property. Many states also gather and analyze crime-related information and provide the results to local police. All states now have some type of organization to set standards for the selection and training of police—for example, the California Commission on Peace Officers Standards and Training (POST).

Federal Law Enforcement

The development of federal agencies tended to lag behind those at the local level because the constitutional mandate for federal law enforcement is not clear. Prior to the Civil War there were three types of federal law enforcement activities.

The Revenue Cutter Service and the U.S. Marshal Service

In 1789 the Revenue Cutter Service was created to respond to problems of smuggling. In that same year the U.S. Marshal Service was established so that the federal courts would have officers to perform police duties. **Marshals** investigated cases of mail theft and crimes against the railroad. They also investigated murders on federal lands, but the majority of their responsibilities were civil. One of the more interesting aspects of the marshal's role was law enforcement in the West, described in Inside Policing 2.7.

Postal Inspectors

Crimes involving the mail were a significant problem in the nineteenth century. Often these crimes were committed by postal employees because many people sent money through the mail. Swindlers and confidence men also used the mail. Lotteries were a popular "scam" in which people were asked to send a small amount of money to be eligible for an expensive prize; of course, those who sent in money never heard from the lottery sponsors again. In the states, the post office assumed responsibility for all mail-related crimes. At first the postmaster used assistants to investigate crimes, but in 1836 the position of postal inspector was established. By the Civil War, postal inspectors were investigating robberies, embezzlements, and the counterfeiting of stamps, as well as post office employees involved in criminal activities.

The Secret Service

Although counterfeiting money had always been a problem at local and state levels of government, it became a very serious problem nationally when the federal government decided to issue a standard paper currency in 1861, at the time of the Civil War. The first attempts to suppress counterfeiting of national currency occurred in 1864, when the secretary of the treasury employed a few private detectives. In June 1865 the Secret Service was established. The first director, William Wood, distributed his agents among 11 cities and instructed them to work undercover to penetrate counterfeiting rings.

By the late nineteenth century, the Secret Service provided investigative services to other agencies of government that needed them, including the postal service, customs service, and Bureau of Immigration. In 1901 the task of protecting the president was added to the Secret Service's responsibility. In 1908 its role was limited to two major activities: protective services and counterfeiting (Johnson 1981, 73–88).

The Federal Bureau of Investigation

To take over some of the duties the Secret Service had been performing for other agencies, the Bureau of Investigation was created within the Justice Department in 1908. This office began its work when the Secret Service transferred eight agents to the new bureau. It later became the FBI, the general investigative law enforcement agency of the federal government.

The primary reason the FBI eventually became so highly regarded was the publicity surrounding its crime-fighting role in the 1930s. The two most important crimes involving the FBI were the kidnapping of the baby of ace flier Charles Lindbergh and the ambush murders of five people, including one FBI agent, which became known as the Kansas City Massacre. The Lindbergh incident was only one of several such cases in the late 1920s and

1930s. During this period criminals abducted several wealthy individuals or members of their families and held them for ransom. However, the Lindbergh case received the most publicity, and the FBI was successful in identifying a suspect who was convicted and executed. In Kansas City, Pretty Boy Floyd and two companions tried to rescue a friend being taken to prison. Four police officers and one federal agent were killed. One of the criminals was captured, convicted, and executed. Floyd was killed by the FBI in a shoot-out, and the third was killed by other criminals.

INSIDE POLICING 2.7 Federal Marshals in the American West

U.S. marshals were among the first law enforcement officials in the West. In federal territories they were often the only officials available to deal with criminals. Once a territory became a state, other law enforcement officials, such as the sheriff, town marshal, or city police, assumed responsibility for most law enforcement problems. However, because these local police officers had authority only in one jurisdiction, the U.S. marshal appointed some of them to be deputy marshals, which allowed them to pursue criminals outside the town or county.

Marshals usually had no law enforcement experience but were appointed because of their political connections. Often they were criticized for being inefficient and corrupt, much like city police of the nineteenth century. Their payment—rewards and fees—strongly influenced their priorities. Because rewards for catching criminals were rare, most of a marshal's salary was determined by fees collected from serving civil processes. This system of payment lasted until 1896.

Marshals usually dealt with liquor smugglers, gun runners, and individuals who committed crimes involving the mail. The most infamous criminals were the train robbers. The railroads may well have been the most disliked industry in the nineteenth century. Although railroads played an important role in the development of the United States, the owners treated many citizens in a callous and indifferent manner. Consequently, train robbers were considered "heroes" by some people. This status contributed to the rise of romantic legends about outlaws such as the James, Younger, and Dalton brothers and Bill Doolin. But train robbers were hardly heroes. Jesse James initiated the idea of wrecking a train to rob it. Or they might ambush a train at a water stop and use dynamite or gunfire to steal the money or gold it carried.

After a robbery the outlaws would escape to some hideaway and then disperse. U.S. marshals might pursue them with a posse, but full-scale battles between a posse and gang were rare. More often, the outlaws were tracked down individually. Paid informants were very useful in this regard. They resulted in the demise of Bill Doolin and the Wild Bunch, who committed train robberies and bank holdups in the Oklahoma Territory in the early 1890s. Using informants, the local U.S. marshal was able to acquire enough information to track down each member of the gang. Most of the Wild Bunch died in shoot-outs with marshals, their deputies, and members of a posse. These shoot-outs were not in the open but usually during an ambush in which the outlaw was outnumbered and outgunned. Marshals were more inclined to use a shotgun than a "six shooter." When Doolin was finally located, he was killed by a shotgun blast fired by a deputy marshal, one of six hidden posse members who waited for Doolin to walk down the street.

Marshals played an important role in the American West. They were effective in developing informants and isolating outlaws. Perhaps their most important contribution was developing a basis for cooperation between different law enforcement bodies (i.e., town marshal and police, county sheriff) as federal territories became states.

SOURCE: D. R. Johnson, *American Law Enforcement: A History* (St. Louis: Forum Press, 1981), 96–100.

Another event that added to the prestige and power of the FBI was the election of Franklin Roosevelt as president. He became a strong supporter of J. Edgar Hoover and the FBI and assisted in expanding the Bureau's powers. The most important expansion was its responsibility to investigate cases of domestic espionage, counterespionage, and sabotage (Johnson 1981, 172–181). The federal responsibility for enforcement of laws against drugs began in 1914, when the Harrison Narcotic Act was signed into law. The Bureau of Internal Revenue was given the responsibility for enforcing this act. It created a Narcotics Section, which within a few years became a major division. In 1930 the Federal Bureau of Narcotics was created; it became the Drug Enforcement Administration (DEA) in 1973.

INSIDE POLICING 2.8 J. Edgar Hoover

J. Edgar Hoover was director of the FBI from 1924 until his death in 1972. He first entered the Department of Justice in 1917, while attending law school. When he took over the Bureau in 1924, it had just experienced a scandal and Hoover set out to reform the organization. Like O. W. Wilson and William Parker, Hoover believed in a centralized command structure and improved recruitment and training. Interestingly, Wilson and Parker did not have a high regard for Hoover and vice versa. This mutual disdain was the result of competition over leadership in the police reform movement and the fact that the FBI under Hoover looked down on local law enforcement.

The FBI began to receive national attention during the 1930s in its well-publicized campaign to catch infamous criminals such as John Dillinger. After some successes, the FBI became a national symbol of effective crime fighting. Hoover enhanced the bureau's reputation by establishing a national fingerprint file, providing assistance to local departments in training their personnel, and providing criminalistics services in some important criminal cases. In the 1960s the bureau also established a national computer system that included important crime-related information.

Perhaps the most important contribution to local law enforcement was the development of the FBI National Academy, which trained police managers from all over the United States. For many years this program was considered, and is still considered by some, the most prestigious in law enforcement. Another contribution to policing included the creation of the Uniform Crime Reports. These crime statistics were compiled annually by the FBI and were used as a method to evaluate the effectiveness of local police departments. This represented the first systematic attempt to evaluate how effective police were at reducing crime, and the UCR continues to be used for this purpose today.

Hoover enhanced his reputation during World War II as the Bureau pursued and arrested several spies. A fervent anticommunist, Hoover was criticized after the war for his involvement with Senator Joseph McCarthy and in the 1950s and 1960s for his failure to respond effectively to the problems of organized crime. He was also criticized for his tactics in responding to civil rights issues. After Hoover's death it was discovered that the FBI often used illegal methods (e.g., wiretaps) to secure information about such civil rights leaders as Martin Luther King and to gather intelligence on activist groups. Hoover believed that communists had infiltrated the civil rights movement with the intent of using the race issue to destabilize the country.

Hoover is a good example of how a person in law enforcement can become very powerful. As a result of the investigations of his agents, he had access to a large amount of information about many important people in Washington and throughout the United States. Some critics have suggested that such knowledge was a significant factor in his being able to stay in office until his death at the age of 77. Some critics have even suggested that some presidents were fearful of Hoover's power. Nevertheless, despite these criticisms, Hoover did make important contributions to law enforcement in developing the FBI.

SOURCES: D. R. Johnson, *American Law Enforcement: A History* (St. Louis: Forum Press, 1981), 171–180; G. E. Caiden, *Police Revitalization* (Lexington, MA: D.C. Heath, 1977), 242, 286, 333.

INSIDE POLICING 2.9 The Federal Bureau of Investigation

Founded in 1908, the FBI is part of the United States Department of Justice. In 1997, it employed more than 11,000 special agents and 16,000 support personnel. The mission of the FBI is to uphold the law through the investigation of violations of federal criminal law; protect the United States from foreign intelligence and terrorist activities; provide leadership and law enforcement assistance to federal, state, local, and international agencies; and perform these tasks in a manner that is responsive to the needs of the public and is faithful to the Constitution of the United States.

The Bureau's criminal investigation priorities include public corruption, civil rights issues, organized crime, white collar crime, and major thefts/violent crime. Examples of investigations involving violent crimes and major offenders include searching for fugitives and escaped prisoners involved in FBI investigations; crime on Indian reservations; assaulting, kidnapping, or killing the president, vice president, and members of Congress; kidnapping and extortion; sexual exploitation of children; and tampering with consumer products. The FBI's national security priorities include counterterrorism, counterintelligence, and cyber crime.

The headquarters of the FBI is in Washington, DC. In addition, there are field offices in 56 major cities, including 1 in Puerto Rico. There are also 400 satellite offices, known as resident agencies, which house from 1 to 12 special agents. Both field offices and resident agencies are located according to crime trends and available resources. The FBI's role in international investigations (e.g., drugs, terrorism, financial crimes) has resulted in the establishment of 60 legal attaché offices in embassies around the world.

The FBI is also involved in numerous other activities, including managing several computer crime–related data bases, providing crime laboratory services to agents and other law enforcement organizations, and training programs for FBI agents and employees and officers from state and local police.

SOURCE: http:www.fbi.gov.

By the 1920s, the U.S. Marshals Service, the FBI, the Postal Inspectors, the Secret Service, and the Narcotics Division of the Internal Revenue Service were the established federal law enforcement agencies. The one that received the most attention was the FBI. Between the 1930s and the 1960s, the FBI became the premier law enforcement body in the United States. J. Edgar Hoover was appointed to serve as director in 1924. He became a national law enforcement leader and advocate of police reform in the 1930s and maintained this role into the 1960s. He is profiled in Inside Policing 2.8. Information about the current role and selected activities of the FBI is presented in Inside Policing 2.9.

By the 1990s there were many different types of federal law enforcement agencies and agencies that had a law enforcement component, that is, had some employees responsible for law enforcement, investigation, and/or compliance activities. Federal law enforcement agencies are organized within a variety of federal departments, including the Department of Justice (FBI, DEA, Alcohol, Tobacco, Firearms, and Explosives, and U.S. Marshal's Service), the Department of Homeland Security (Immigration and Customs Enforcement, Secret Service), and the Department of Treasury (Internal Revenue Service).

Summary

The police heritage in the United States can be traced to classical Greece and Rome and to developments in Europe, particularly England. The first form of policing in U.S. cities was the constable–nightwatch system, which existed from the 1600s to the 1930s. When this system proved to be inadequate, it was replaced by modern, integrated day–night police departments. Modern police departments at the local level have moved through three distinct periods of development, each dominated by a different model of policing. These models are political, reform, and community policing. Each model has a different conception of the police role and how police officers should interact with members of the community. Two of the models—the political and the reform—are discussed in this chapter.

State and federal police forces also have an interesting history. State police forces were created to respond to both law enforcement and traffic problems and to provide related services to local police. Federal law enforcement agencies have existed since the eighteenth century but were not well established until the middle of the nineteenth century. Today there are numerous federal law enforcement agencies and agencies with investigators working in a law enforcement capacity.

Critical Thinking Questions

1. In what way did Sir Robert Peel and his ideas about policing influence the development of policing in the United States? How did English policing differ from early policing in the northern colonies?

2. Identify and explain the characteristics of political policing. Why did political policing develop in the United States?

3. Identify and explain the characteristics of reform policing. Why did reform era policing develop in the United States?

4. Discuss the contributions of August Vollmer and O. W. Wilson to the development and evolution of law enforcement.

5. Briefly discuss the evolution of policing in America, including slave patrols and frontier/vigilante policing.

6. How was it that state and federal law enforcement was able to emerge, when historically in America there was a desire for local rule?

References

Abadinsky, H. 1987. *An Introduction to Criminal Justice.* Chicago: Nelson–Hall.

Berg, B. L. 1992. *Law Enforcement: An Introduction to Police in Society.* Boston: Allyn and Bacon.

Bopp, W. J. 1977. *O. W. Wilson and the Search for a Police Profession.* Port Washington, NY: Kennikat Press.

Borkenstein, R. 1977. "State Police." In S. H. Kadish (ed.), *Encyclopedia of Crime and Justice,* pp. 1131–1135. New York: The Free Press.

Brown, R. M. 1991. "Vigilante Policing." In C. B. Klockars and S. D. Mastrofski (eds.), *Thinking About Police: Contemporary Readings,* 2nd ed., pp. 58–73. New York: McGraw–Hill.

Caiden, G. E. 1977. *Police Revitalization.* Lexington, MA: D. C. Heath.

Cole, G. F. 1989. *The American System of Criminal Justice,* 5th ed. Pacific Grove, CA: Brooks/Cole Publishing Company.

Cooper, L. 1975. *The Iron Fist and the Velvet Glove.* Berkeley: Center for Research on Criminal Justice.

Falcone, D. N. 2001. "The Missouri State Highway Patrol as a Representative Model." In *Policing: An International Journal of Police Strategies and Management* 24: 585–594.

Germann, A. C., Day, F. D., and Gallati, R. R. 1978. *Introduction to Law Enforcement and Criminal Justice.* Springfield, IL: Charles C. Thomas.

Johnson, D. R. 1981. *American Law Enforcement: A History.* St. Louis: Forum Press.

Johnson, H. 1988. *History of Criminal Justice.* Cincinnati: Anderson Publishing Company.

Kansas City Police Officers Memorial. http://www.kcpolicememorial.com/history/

Karmen, A. A. 1983. "Vigilantism." In S. H. Kadish (ed.), *Encyclopedia of Crime and Justice,* 4: 1616–1618. New York: Free Press.

Kelling, G. L., and Moore, M. H. 1988. "The Evolving Strategy of Policing." Perspectives on Policing: National Institute of Justice, Washington, DC.

Kirkham, G. L., and Wollan, L. A. 1980. *Introduction to Law Enforcement.* New York: Harper & Row.

Lane, R. 1967. *Policing the City: Boston 1822–1882.* Cambridge, MA: Harvard University Press.

Miller, W. 1977. *Cops and Bobbies.* Chicago: University of Chicago Press.

Monkkonen, E. 1981. *Police in Urban America.* Cambridge: Cambridge University Press.

National Advisory Commission on Civil Disorders. 1968. *Report.* New York: New York Times Company.

Oregon Department of State Police. *Memorandum.* March 15, 1989.

President's Commission on Law Enforcement and Administration of Justice. 1967. *Task Force Report: The Police.* Washington, DC: U.S. Government Printing Office.

Pursley, R. D. 1991. *Introduction to Criminal Justice.* 5th ed. New York: Macmillan.

Reaves, B. A. 1992. *Sheriff's Departments, 1990.* Washington, DC: Bureau of Justice Statistics.

Reaves, B. A. 2007. *Census of State and Local Law Enforcement Agencies, 2004.* Washington, DC: Bureau of Justice Statistics.

Reichel, P. L. 1999. "Southern Slave Patrols as a Transitional Police Type." In L. K. Gaines and G. W. Cordner (eds.), *Policing Perspectives: An Anthology,* pp. 79–92. Los Angeles: Roxbury.

Walker, S. 1977. *A Critical History of Police Reform.* Lexington, MA: D. C. Heath.

Walker, S., and Katz, C. M. 2011. *The Police in America: An Introduction.* 7th ed. New York: McGraw-Hill.

Williams, H., and Murphy, P. V. 1990. "The Evolving Strategy of Police: A Minority Perspective." Perspectives on Policing: National Institute of Justice, Washington, DC.

CHAPTER 3

Legal Issues

CHAPTER OUTLINE

- Criminal Procedure
    Searches and Seizures of Persons
    Searches and Seizures of Property
    Interrogations and Confessions
- Civil Liability
    Costs of Liability in Policing
    Avenues of Liability
    Civil Liability in State Courts
    Civil Liability in Federal Courts
    Emerging Liability Issues for the Twenty-
       First Century
    Use of Force
    Impact on Officers
- Summary
- Critical Thinking Questions
- References

- affidavit
- arrest
- bright-line rule
- Carroll Doctrine
- color of law
- constitutional or federally protected rights
- criminal procedure
- custody

- depolicing
- exclusionary rule
- fruit of the poisonous tree doctrine
- hot pursuit exception
- intentional torts
- interrogations
- Miranda warnings
- negligent torts

- open fields doctrine
- plain view doctrine
- pretextual stops
- probable cause
- protective sweep
- reasonable suspicion
- stop and frisk

LAW ENFORCEMENT IS AMONG the core roles of the police in America. The police are the primary government agent responsible for enforcing criminal law, initiating the formal criminal justice system, and assisting in the prosecution of law violators. However, the police are also accountable to the rule of law, and the law acts as a mechanism to control and guide police behavior. This is because the police are responsible for both public safety and protecting civil liberties. Legal issues identify what actions by the public are forbidden and provide the police with a basis to engage in law enforcement; however, the law also provides guard rails in which the police must operate while enforcing the law. Thus criminal procedure and civil liability are mechanisms to ensure that police operate in such a way as to not compromise citizens' individual liberties while engaging in law enforcement and also provide remedies for citizens when these liberties are compromised. This chapter will explore each of these legal aspects of policing.

Criminal Procedure

Criminal procedure is the process by which a person accused of a crime is processed through the criminal justice system (Worrall 2010). It also consists of rules that the government must abide by to ensure that certain rights enjoyed by the public are not violated and ensures fairness in the processing of people accused of crimes. The most common rights related to policing addressed by the courts include arrest, searches, seizures, and interrogations. Criminal procedure is also related to the adjudication process, such as ensuring a fair trial, right to retain counsel, and various pretrial procedures.

Prior to 1937, there were few important procedural rulings by the U.S. Supreme Court. The individual safeguards found in the Bill of Rights had not yet been applied to the states. Between the 1930s and 1960s, the Court began to selectively incorporate some of these safeguards into the procedural requirements that local police had to follow. Not until the 1960s did the "due process revolution" begin. During this decade, the Supreme Court increasingly applied provisions of the Bill of Rights to the states. The 1960s were characterized by widespread support for the protection of the civil rights of individuals. The Warren Court of this period, named for Chief Justice Earl Warren, was associated with a liberal political philosophy because the majority of judges supported more legal restrictions on the police. From a politically conservative point of view (which included the views of a majority of police officers), the police were "handcuffed" in their ability to fight crime. Hence, the process of criminal procedure is concerned with two competing values: the need to protect the freedom of citizens from government tyranny while simultaneously ensuring a civil and ordered society that is free from disorder and crime.

A comprehensive overview of case law related to criminal procedure is beyond the scope of this chapter, although Inside Policing 3.1 provides capsules of benchmark and contemporary decisions related to criminal procedure and police civil liability. Instead, we provide a description of laws and procedures related to common police practices of street level officers. This chapter will present an overview of rights related to searches and seizures of persons and property and rights citizens enjoy during custodial interrogations.

Searches and Seizures of Persons

The Fourth Amendment provides safeguards from unreasonable searches and seizures. Thus, it is this amendment that guides the Court in creating guidelines for when officers may stop or arrest citizens, because these actions constitute a seizure of that person. The two most common forms of seizure of a person are stops (and often "frisks" associated with the stop) and arrests, and the Court has provided roadmaps to ensure that these seizures are not unreasonable in scope or duration.

Before discussing stops and frisks or arrests, it is first important to understand the degree of certainty an officer must possess to avoid an unreasonable action. Stops and frisks must at a minimum be based on the legal standard of reasonable suspicion. This standard is difficult to quantify and perhaps explain, but del Carmen (2001) describes **reasonable suspicion** as that which is based on objective facts and logical conclusions that a crime has been or is about to be committed, and this is based on the circumstances at hand. Although the Court has not clearly defined this standard, in *Alabama v. White* (1990) it acknowledged that reasonable suspicion is a lower standard than probable cause and may arise from information that itself has questionable reliability. Since reasonable suspicion is somewhat less rigorous than other standards, the scope of officer behavior is necessarily limited to actions such as stopping a suspect or frisking a suspect. On the other hand, arrests must be based on the standard of **probable cause.**

Probable cause "exists where the facts and circumstances within the officers' knowledge, and of which they have reasonably trustworthy information, are sufficient in themselves to warrant a belief by a man of reasonable caution that a crime is being committed" (*Brinegar v. U.S.* 1949). Hence, the officer has reason to believe that a particular individual has "more likely than not" committed a certain crime. Probable cause is the minimum legal standard necessary to make a custodial arrest of a person, and it is a more rigorous standard than reasonable suspicion. In sum, the degree of certainty the officer has that criminal activity is afoot is inversely related to the scope, length, and intensity of the detention of the suspect.

While the Fourth Amendment provides a right to be free from unreasonable searches and seizures, it does not address how this right should be enforced. The most recognized method for enforcing the reasonableness standard of the Fourth Amendment is called the **exclusionary rule.** This holds that evidence obtained by the government in violation of the Fourth Amendment's guarantee against unreasonable searches and seizures is not admissible in criminal prosecution to demonstrate guilt. This rule is premised on the belief that excluding illegally seized evidence from court will deter police officers from acting improperly. While the birth of the exclusionary rule can be traced back to *Weeks v. U.S.* (1914), it was not until the decision in *Mapp v. Ohio* (1961) that the Court incorporated this rule to govern evidence collected by state and local police officers. Justice Clark, writing for the majority, stated that the Court previously acknowledged that the "criminal is to go free because the constable has blundered," but also noted, "The criminal goes free, if he must, but it is the law that sets him free. Nothing can destroy a government more quickly than its failure to observe its own laws, or worse, its disregard of the charter of its own existence."

INSIDE POLICING 3.1 Selected Supreme Court Cases (1960 to the Present)

Mapp v. Ohio, 367 U.S. 643 (1961): The "exclusionary rule" used in federal trials is applied to the states. Evidence obtained illegally cannot be used in a trial or in subsequent proceedings.

Miranda v. Arizona, 384 U.S. 436 (1966): To prevent police from coercing confessions, the court established a rule that a defendant must be informed of Fifth and Sixth Amendment rights and that the defendant must waive those rights prior to any police interrogation.

Katz v. United States, 389 U.S. 347 (1967): Fourth Amendment requirements for search and seizure apply to electronic surveillance even if there is no actual physical intrusion into the property of a defendant.

Terry v. Ohio, 468 U.S. 1 (1968): Police officers are authorized to "stop and frisk" suspicious persons to conduct a proper investigation and to protect the officer from possible harm.

Chimel v. California, 395 U.S. 752 (1969): When making arrests, police officers are allowed to search the defendant and the immediate area under the defendant's control (which, in effect, means that only the area within an "arm's length" distance could be searched).

U.S. v. Ross, 456 U.S. 798 (1982): Where probable cause exists to believe that an automobile contains evidence in a criminal case, police may conduct a warrantless search, including searching any closed containers that may be in the automobile (e.g., luggage).

New York v. Quarles, 467 U.S. 649 (1984): Miranda warnings do not apply when circumstances dictate to the police that "public safety" is an important and "immediate necessity." This means that under certain circumstances the police can ask incriminating questions of suspects prior to giving the suspect the Miranda warning. This is the "public safety" exception to the exclusionary rule.

Nix v. Williams, 467 U.S. 431 (1984): Illegally obtained evidence will not be excluded from a trial if it is "inevitable" that the evidence will be "discovered" anyway. This is the "inevitability of discovery" exception to the exclusionary rule.

U.S. v. Leon, 468 U.S. 897 (1984): Evidence obtained using a search warrant that a police office obtained from a "detached and neutral" judge can be used at trial even if it is later discovered that there was no probable cause to issue the warrant. This is one example of the good-faith exception to the exclusionary rule.

Moran v. Burbine, 475 U.S. 412 (1986): A request for an attorney must come from the defendant. If another party calls an attorney and the attorney contacts the police about the defendant, the police are not obligated to delay or stop an interrogation of the defendant. This attempted contact has no bearing on the admissibility of the defendant's statement if the defendant waived his or her right to an attorney.

U.S. v. Sokolow, 490 U.S. 1 (1989): Sokolow was stopped by police as a possible "drug courier" when trying to smuggle drugs through the Honolulu airport. The Court ruled that probabilistic information describing characteristics of drug couriers provided a basis for an investigative detention in accordance with principles of reasonable suspicion.

(Continued)

INSIDE POLICING 3.1 Selected Supreme Court Cases (1960 to the Present) (*Continued*)

Michigan Department of State Police v. Sitz, 496 U.S. 444 (1990): Vehicles may be stopped at highway sobriety checkpoints even though there is no individualized suspicion the driver is committing a crime.

Florida v. Bostick, 501 U.S. 429 (1991): This case expanded the meaning of "consent" in consensual searches. If an officer's request is not coercive and the passenger was free to refuse, the search satisfies consent, even if the passenger—Bostick, in this case, being on a bus—is not free to leave.

Whren v. U.S., 517 U.S. 806 (1996): Does a pretextual stop (a stop made for a legally valid reason such as a taillight violation but whose underlying purpose was altogether different, such as to examine the vehicle for drugs) made by a police officer invalidate a subsequent legal vehicular search for drugs? The Court ruled that the subjective intentions of police officers do not invalidate an objectively reasonable action.

County of Sacramento v. Lewis, 523 U.S. 883 (1998): The Supreme Court held that, in a high-speed chase, a police officer does not deprive an individual of substantive due process by causing death through actions that indicate a deliberate disregard or a reckless disregard for the rights of others. Only arbitrary conduct is actionable.

Atwater v. Lago Vista, 532 U.S. 318 (2001): Texas law indicates failure of front seat passengers to wear a seat belt or properly secure children riding in the front seat to be a misdemeanor, punishable by only a fine. Officers who take citizens into physical custody pursuant to this law do not violate the Fourth Amendment's safeguard from unreasonable search and seizure.

Kyllo v. U.S., 533 U.S. 27 (2001): A search warrant must be obtained in advance if officers want to use thermal imaging devices to scan homes for heat sources consistent with growing marijuana. Such devices may not be used to gather probable cause.

Illinois v. McArthur, 531 U.S. 326 (2001): Police officers may detain an individual from reentering his home to secure a search warrant if there is probable cause to believe he had hidden marijuana in the home and would destroy it upon reentry.

Maryland v. Pringle, 540 U.S. 366 (2003): Discovery of drugs from the back seat of an automobile is probable cause to arrest all occupants of the vehicle even if all occupants deny ownership of the drugs.

Missouri v. Seibert, 542 U.S. 600 (2004): Strategically withholding Miranda warnings during a custodial interrogation may render a subsequent post-Miranda confession unconstitutional.

Illinois v. Caballes, 543 U.S. 405 (2005): Drug-sniffing dogs may "search" a vehicle stopped during a routine traffic stop even if there is no reasonable suspicion the vehicle contains drugs.

Hudson v. Michigan, 547 U.S. 586 (2006): Although officers are required to knock and announce their presence during the execution of a typical search warrant, failure to properly knock and announce will not result in exclusion of evidence seized pursuant to the warrant.

Georgia v. Randolph, 547 U.S. 103 (2006): All on-location cohabitants of a residence must provide consent for officers to search to make the search reasonable.

Brendlin v. California, 551 U.S. 249 (2007): A passenger of a motor vehicle is considered "seized" under the meaning of the Fourth Amendment. A reasonable person would believe they are not free to leave when the car they are traveling in is stopped by the police.

Herring v. U.S., 555 U.S. ____ (2009): Evidence discovered pursuant to an arrest warrant is admissible in court even if it was later determined that the officer was misinformed by the warrant clerk and in fact a valid warrant did not exist.

> *Florida v. Powell*, 559 U.S. ___ (2010): The Miranda requirement is satisfied when the police advise someone they have the right talk with a lawyer before answering any questions and may invoke this right at any time during questioning. The police do not have to explicitly advise the person of the right to have an attorney present during questioning.
>
> *Berghuis v. Thompkins*, 560 U.S. ___ (2010): Suspects in a custodial interrogation must explicitly exercise their right to be silent. Statements made at the end of an interrogation where the suspect was uncommunicative (but did not state they wished to exercise their rights) are admissible in court.

An extension of the exclusionary rule is the **fruit of the poisonous tree doctrine,** which indicates that not only evidence seized improperly must be excluded from criminal court, but also any additional evidence seized after that police action. For example, assume the police improperly obtained a confession to a crime and that during the confession the suspect told the police where to find evidence (such as a knife). When the police locate the evidence, they find additional evidence (such as a handgun) of a different crime. In this hypothetical scenario, the confession and the knife would be excluded from court pursuant to the exclusionary rule. The handgun would also be excluded, because it was the "fruit" that was obtained from an initial improper confession.

American police interact with citizens hundreds of thousands of times each day. Issues of liability become important when officers wish to detain citizens against their wishes. To detain citizens, officers are required to have a certain level of proof a crime has been committed or that the citizen was involved in criminal activity. In *U.S. v. Seslar* (1993) three different types of police–citizen encounters were identified:

1. Consensual encounters. These involve *voluntary interactions* between the police and the public, and the questioning by the officer is typically noncoercive. There is *no legal justification needed* in these encounters, and because the encounter is consensual the citizen is free to terminate the encounter at any time. Thus there is no seizure under the meaning of the Fourth Amendment.

2. Investigative detentions. These encounters involve a *temporary detention* of the citizen's movement by the police. Officers may detain citizens for questioning when there is *reasonable suspicion* to believe the citizen has committed, is committing, or is about to commit a crime. This type of temporary detention has also been referred to as a "Terry Stop" after the landmark Court decision (*Terry v. Ohio* 1968).

3. Arrests. Arrests involve a *seizure of the citizen* by the police that are characterized as lengthy and highly intrusive, in which there is likelihood that the intent of the detention is to subject the citizen to criminal prosecution. To make an arrest, officers are required to have *probable cause* that a crime has been or is being committed (Klotter 1999).

Officers must understand these basic typologies of encounters to avoid exposing themselves and police organizations to civil liability and must be prepared to articulate the facts and circumstances available to justify a level of proof. Indeed, officers may consider the totality of circumstances when determining reasonable suspicion or probable cause. If an officer detains a citizen beyond his or her will without the requisite level of proof, then an illegal seizure under the Fourth Amendment may occur or the intentional tort of false arrest.

Stop and Frisk. An officer may *stop* a person, temporarily depriving him or her of freedom of movement, if the officer has reasonable suspicion that the person is involved in a crime. Furthermore, the officer may *frisk* the person if there is reasonable suspicion to believe the citizen is armed and poses a threat to the officer for the duration of the stop. The landmark case that outlined the parameters for stops and frisks was Terry v. Ohio (1968). In that case, the suspect (Terry) was observed by a seasoned police officer engaging in suspicious behavior in front of a store in downtown Cleveland with others. Based on the officer's experience, he indicated it was reasonable to believe they were casing the store for a robbery. Upon stopping the suspects to inquire of their intentions, the officer indicated that the suspects' mumbled responses to his questions led him to believe that the suspects were armed. He discovered a firearm on Terry after patting down his upper torso, and Terry was charged with carrying a concealed weapon.

Although the officer did not have enough information to elevate the legal standard to probable cause, he indicated there was reasonable suspicion to believe Terry was about to commit a crime and was armed at the time of the encounter. The Court indicated that a temporary stop of Terry, based on reasonable suspicion, did not violate the Fourth Amendment and that a limited patdown or frisk of his outer garments was reasonable based on the circumstances. Since stops and frisks represent a limited intrusion on the citizen's liberty, these practices are permissible even if the officer does not have probable cause to believe a crime is about to be committed.

A recent case further illustrates the scope of a stop and frisk. Lemon Johnson was a passenger in a vehicle that was properly stopped for traffic violations. Officers questioned the occupants of the vehicle regarding gang activity in the area and requested Johnson exit the vehicle, which he did. Suspecting Johnson was involved with gangs and armed, officers conducted a patdown of his clothing and discovered a handgun and drugs. Johnson argued that the conversation was consensual and not a "stop," as required under Terry. Further, he argued that officers did not have probable cause to believe he was involved with gang activity so they were unjustified in their frisk. A unanimous Court rejected his argument. They indicated that indeed Johnson was lawfully seized because he was a passenger in a lawfully detained vehicle. Further, the Court said officers had suspicion to believe he was affiliated with a violent street gang, and thus the limited frisk of his clothing was reasonable to ensure officer safety (*Arizona v. Johnson* 2008).

Unprovoked flight from police officers may also constitute reasonable suspicion that legitimizes a temporary stop of the individual. The Court held in *Illinois v. Wardlow* (2000) that unprovoked flight from the police provides an officer with ample reasonable suspicion to temporarily detain that suspect. Further, the Court indicated that this behavior, coupled with the fact that the encounter took place in a high-crime area, produced legal justification to stop and detain the citizen. Mere presence in a high-crime area would not substantiate reasonable suspicion; however, flight coupled with the environmental characteristics of where the encounter took place provides additional rationale for suspicion. Suspicion may be formed by taking both behavior and location into consideration.

It is also important to understand that not all stops necessitate a frisk and that these are separate activities (although the term stop and frisk often is confused so that people believe they are one continuous act). Frisks may only be conducted if there is reasonable suspicion to believe the suspect is armed and may pose a physical threat to the officer during the encounter (del Carmen 2001). Hence, the officer must articulate separately which factors led to the stop and which factors led to a frisk.

The purpose of the frisk is limited in scope to weapons or instruments that can injure the officer and may not be used as a "fishing expedition" for evidence or other contraband. For example, in *Minnesota v. Dickerson* (1993) the Court indicated that drugs found during a frisk must be excluded as evidence from trial. Dickerson was observed leaving a known "crack house," and he was frisked by an officer pursuant to a stop. The officer felt a small object in Dickerson's pocket and, by manipulating it with his hands, believed it to be crack cocaine wrapped in cellophane. The officer retrieved the object and confirmed it was drugs. This procedure went beyond the scope of a *Terry* frisk. The evidence was not admissible in court because the purpose of the frisk was to discover weapons, and since the officer had to manipulate the object to determine what it was, this manipulation constituted a second search that was beyond what was reasonable.

In summary, stops and frisks are separate activities that must require reasonable suspicion. The purpose of a stop is to prevent criminal activity or to determine whether a crime has taken place; the purpose of a frisk is to ensure officer safety. The extent of intrusion permissible in a frisk is limited to a patdown of the suspect's outer clothing for weapons. The duration of the encounter is to be no longer than permitted to achieve its purpose, and no physical force is permitted, beyond that of the patdown (del Carmen 2001).

Arrest. An arrest is the act of depriving a person of his or her liberty by legal authority and is performed for the purposes of interrogation or criminal prosecution (Zalman and Seigel 1997). Laws related to the reasonableness of an arrest also fall under the rubric of the Fourth Amendment, because arrest is the seizure of a person against his or her will by an agent of the government. Arrests are among the most critical activities police officers perform within the criminal justice system, because an arrest must typically be made before other components of the system may act. Following an arrest, administrative procedures are conducted, including fingerprinting, photographing, or "booking" the person into jail. Unfortunately, the public does not completely understand when and under what circumstances an arrest can be made or the legal guidelines officers must follow when conducting a search for evidence during an arrest.

Officers must have probable cause to believe that a particular person has committed a specific crime to make an arrest. Since arrests are more intrusive than stops, it is necessary that the officer have a higher legal justification to deprive a person of his or her liberty. There is also a preference that arrests be made on issuance of an arrest warrant issued by a neutral and detached magistrate. In reality, however, the vast majority of arrests are made without an arrest warrant. Obtaining a warrant to make arrests in many situations would unduly limit the crime-control function of the police. The courts have indicated that routine felony arrests made in public do not require a warrant, even if officers have ample opportunity to obtain one (*U.S. v. Watson* 1976). However, if officers wish to make a felony arrest in a private home, they must first secure a warrant if there is opportunity to do so or if exigent (emergency) circumstances are absent (*Payton v. New York* 1981). This demonstrates the expectation of privacy an individual enjoys in private places over public places.

It is not necessary to have reasonable suspicion to frisk an individual if that person is under arrest and taken into custody. Upon arrest, officers may perform a comprehensive search of the suspect and the possessions in their immediate control. This search incident to arrest may be for weapons, but can also include any contraband discovered during the search. Further, officers may search the area in the suspect's immediate control to discover evidence or weapons without a search warrant (*Chimel v. California* 1969). The area in someone's "immediate control" has been understood to consist of the area within the person's wingspan or their "lunge-and-reach" area. The purposes of the *Chimel Rule* are to ensure officer safety and to prevent the destruction of evidence.

It is also permissible for officers to perform a limited **protective sweep** of a home to determine whether there are others who could pose a safety risk for officers (*Maryland v. Buie* 1990). Buie and an accomplice were wanted for armed robbery, during which one of the men was wearing a red running suit. Officers obtained an arrest warrant for Buie, entered his house, and saw Buie emerge from the basement. After placing him under arrest, officers proceeded to the basement to determine whether anyone else was there who could pose a threat to officer safety. Once in the basement, officers observed a red running suit that matched the description of the one used during the course of the robbery. This running suit was seized (without a warrant) and used against Buie in court. The Supreme Court indicated that the search of Buie's basement was reasonable and that officers had reason to perform a cursory search of the area for protective purposes. However, a protective sweep is different from a full-blown search for evidence. This allows for only a cursory inspection of spaces where a person may be located. In this regard, protective sweeps are similar to frisks in that they must be limited in nature to discovery of weapons or people who could harm the officer and not to evidence of a crime. In contrast to frisks, evidence of a crime discovered during a protective sweep is permissible in court.

Searches and Seizures of Property

Similar to searches and seizures of persons, the courts have attempted to balance the need for public safety with adhering to expectations of privacy in regard to searches and seizures of property. Also, there is a preference for searches and seizures of property to be conducted pursuant to a search warrant. A *search warrant* is a "written order, issued by a magistrate, directing a peace officer to search for property connected with a crime and bring it before the court" (del Carmen 2001, 181). Search warrants must demonstrate that there is probable cause that evidence of a crime exists in a particular place and must fully describe the place to be searched, thus eliminating the possibility of a "general warrant." Probable cause must be supported under oath or affirmation, typically by a police officer, before a neutral and detached judge. During this oath (often called an **affidavit**, which is the same as an oath except that it is written), the officer describes exactly what is to be seized and exactly what is to be searched. The judge may then issue a search warrant commanding law enforcement to conduct a search by signing the warrant (del Carmen 2001).

There are many circumstances where searches without a warrant are reasonable in their scope. For example, the **plain view doctrine** falls beyond the warrant requirement. It is not unreasonable for the police to seize evidence of a crime if the evidence is in view of the officer. But the plain view doctrine contains several important caveats. First, the police must have prior justification for being present at the scene, or, stated differently, the initial police intrusion must be lawful. Second, the evidence seized must be in plain view, and police may not take actions that expose to view concealed portions of the premises or its contents. Third, the objects seized must be immediately apparent as evidence or contraband.

The facts and circumstances in *Arizona v. Hicks* (1987) are instructive and provide an example of the plain view doctrine in action. The police responded to Hicks's apartment after a neighbor called complaining that someone had fired a bullet through the floor of the apartment. On arrival, the police entered the apartment and discovered several guns and a stocking mask. However, while in the apartment, an officer observed several new pieces of expensive stereo equipment that appeared out of place in the otherwise squalid apartment. Having reasonable suspicion that these stereos were stolen, the officer moved the pieces, recorded the serial numbers, and confirmed via radio that, indeed, the equipment was stolen. Hicks was charged and convicted of receiving stolen property. Later, the Supreme Court indicated the stereo equipment could not be used as evidence to prosecute Hicks because the act of moving the stereo constituted a second search in which the officers did not have probable cause. While the officers were legally present in the apartment and the stereo equipment was in plain view, it was not immediately apparent as evidence or contraband. Hence, the third criterion for the plain view doctrine was not present.

Another exception to the warrant requirement is items observed in open fields. The **open fields doctrine** indicates that "items in open fields are not protected by the Fourth Amendment's guarantee against unreasonable searches and seizures, so they can properly be taken by an officer without a warrant or probable cause" (del Carmen 2001, 259). In other words, people who leave items in public view do not enjoy a right to privacy; thus the Fourth Amendment does not apply to these places. In *Oliver v. U.S.* (1984), the police were acting on a tip that marijuana was being grown in a field on Oliver's farm. The police ignored the "No Trespassing" sign at the edge of the property and, without probable cause, entered the field to observe the marijuana. The Court indicated that this type of trespass was permissible and that the marijuana could be used as evidence to convict Oliver.

Similarly, warrants are not required for property that is abandoned (such as garbage left on private premises). The police may seize garbage bags left for removal and search these bags for contraband (often receipts of illegal activity or drug paraphernalia). Once a person abandons property and makes it available for public scrutiny, that person no longer enjoys an expectation of privacy in relation to that property (*California v. Greenwood* 1988).

Another common exception to the warrant requirement is the **hot pursuit exception.** Police may follow a felon or otherwise dangerous criminal into a place typically protected by the Fourth Amendment, such as a home, or may cross jurisdictional boundaries. Hot pursuits must be based on probable cause, but the officer may develop probable cause via hearsay or direct observation. The gravity of the offense must be taken into consideration, and relatively minor offenses may not provide justification for warrantless pursuits. Once in a constitutionally protected area, the officer may search for the suspect and for weapons or evidence, but once the suspect is found, the search must cease. At this point, any search without a warrant must be based on other factors, such as those described previously in *Chimel* or *Buie*.

Another exception to the warrant requirement is when the citizen provides officers with *consent* to search. Officers may search a person or property if a person *voluntarily* consents to the search; consent searches therefore do not require a warrant, and any evidence that is obtained during a consent search is permissible in court. Furthermore, officers do not need to advise citizens of their right to refuse consent (*Schneckloth v. Bustamonte* 1973); it must merely be demonstrated that consent was voluntarily given and not coerced by the officer.

Vehicle Searches. Court doctrines related to search and seizure often rely on an individual's expectation of privacy when determining the reasonableness of police action. Generally, people enjoy a greater level of privacy in homes and private places than they do in public. But the lines between public and private spheres become difficult to disentangle when confronted with stops of citizens in motor vehicles. Are motor vehicles private places? Or because they are operated in public, do citizens enjoy a diminished expectation of privacy in vehicles? What can police do when making a traffic stop? Because of the unique nature of motor vehicle searches, it is important to consider these searches and seizures separately from those conducted in other types of places.

The courts have recognized motor vehicles as having substantially fewer Fourth Amendment protections than fixed premises. This is because motor vehicles are highly mobile, allowing for evidence to be moved and suspects to flee police custody. The contents of motor vehicles (including drivers and passengers) travel in plain view, thus exposing them to public review. Furthermore, motor vehicles are highly regulated by the government (e.g., driver's licenses, vehicle registration, and insurance). Together, these characteristics have led the courts to adopt relaxed standards regarding searches and seizures and the necessity of obtaining warrants for searches of motor vehicles.

Police officers may stop motor vehicles if they have reasonable suspicion that a crime has been committed. Upon stopping a vehicle, officers may investigate to determine whether there is probable cause to arrest a driver (or passengers) or issue a summons/ticket. In fact, officers have a great deal of discretion pursuant to traffic stops. Inside Policing 3.2 provides an overview of what officers may do during traffic stops.

May an officer stop a vehicle for a traffic violation under the pretext that the stop may elicit another, more serious violation? This was the question posed before the Court in *Whren v. U.S.* (1996). Two plainclothes officers observed Whren and another occupant driving a vehicle with temporary tags in an area of high drug activity. The vehicle was stopped at an intersection for an unusually long period of time, and the driver was staring at the lap of the passenger. Suspecting the occupants to be involved with drug sales, the officers approached the vehicle at a red light, stopping them for a traffic violation. Whren was observed to be holding a bag of crack cocaine, for which he was arrested and subsequently convicted. Whren argued that the officers would not normally engage in traffic enforcement and were using the traffic violation merely as a pretext to determine whether he was involved with drugs. The Supreme Court determined this practice to be permissible and that seizures incident to *pretextual stops* of vehicles are not unreasonable.

INSIDE POLICING 3.2 What May an Officer Do After a Vehicle Is Stopped?

1. **Order driver and passengers to get out of the vehicle.** Officer safety is often cited as a primary rationale for having occupants exit the vehicle.

2. **Ask driver to produce driver's license and other documents (as required by state law).**

3. **Ask questions of driver and passengers.** This may be done without providing Miranda warnings, and while occupants have the constitutional right not to respond, nonresponse may be taken into consideration when determining probable cause.

4. **Search passengers' belongings, if there is probable cause.** This is because passengers have a diminished expectation of privacy in a vehicle and the government's interest in effective law enforcement would be impaired because of the mobility of the vehicle.

5. **Require drunk driving suspects to take a breathalyzer test.** These tests may not be administered to all drivers, only to ones suspected of drunk driving.

6. **Locate and examine Vehicle Identification Number (VIN).** Officers may compare the VIN to the one registered to the plates of the vehicle or to determine whether the car is stolen. A VIN is conveniently located on the dashboard on the driver's side and is visible from outside the vehicle.

7. **Search vehicle if probable cause develops.**

8. **Search vehicle if consent is given.** If a person intelligently and voluntarily gives consent to search a vehicle, probable cause is not required.

9. **Search the passenger compartment for weapons if there is reasonable suspicion of a threat to officer safety.**

10. **Seize items in plain view.**

11. **Arrest with probable cause.**

SOURCE: Adapted from R. V. del Carmen, *Criminal Procedure: Law and Practice* (Stamford, CT: Wadsworth, 2001), 221–225.

Circumstances exist where police officers may stop vehicles without reasonable suspicion. **Sobriety checkpoints** permit police officers to systematically stop vehicles without reasonable suspicion, because the nature of the stop is limited. This issue was addressed in *Michigan Department of State Police v. Sitz* (1990). The sobriety checkpoint in question was highly publicized prior to initiation, and officers' actions were set by guidelines developed by the Checkpoint Advisory Committee. Officers stopped 126 vehicles passing a set location over the course of 75 minutes. Motorists were stopped, on average, for 25 seconds so those officers could conduct preliminary investigations for intoxication. The Court determined that the stops were not unreasonable by adopting a balancing test of three factors: "the gravity of public concerns served by the seizure, the degree to which the seizure advances the public interest, and the severity of the interference with individual liberty" (del Carmen 2001, 221). *Sitz* does not permit random stops for sobriety checks, and such stops absent reasonable suspicion are restricted to fixed checkpoints.

While officers may stop motorists at sobriety checkpoints without individualized suspicion of criminal behavior, the same rules do not apply for ordinary criminal wrongdoing. The City of Indianapolis conducted vehicle checkpoints to determine whether drivers were in possession of illegal drugs. Drivers were temporarily detained, similar to the process described in *Sitz*, but here the Court felt there was not a compelling state interest to engage in drug interdiction that permitted such suspiciousness stops. Determining whether a driver is in possession of drug does not represent the same level of immediate public safety risk as demonstrated in *Sitz*, thus this practice is unconstitutional (*Indianapolis v. Edmond* 2000). But later the Court did permit checkpoints designed to gather information about a specific crime. In Lombard, Illinois, a 70-year-old bicyclist was struck and killed by an unknown motorist. Shortly thereafter the police set up a checkpoint where motorists were stopped and asked whether they knew anything about the hit-and-run accident, and police provided motorists with a flyer containing information about the crime and ways to contact the police to share information. During the course of this checkpoint, Robert Lidster lost control of his vehicle, hitting an officer, and was later determined to be driving while intoxicated. He contested this charge, indicating he was stopped at a checkpoint without reasonable suspicion and that the purpose of the checkpoint was to detect ordinary criminal wrongdoing (which was determined in *Edmond* to be unconstitutional). The Court disagreed, stating it was a reasonable investigatory tool to gather information regarding a death. Here the Court recognized that the public interest of a death investigation outweighed any minor inconvenience or privacy concern experienced by individual drivers, making suspicionless stops reasonable (*Illinois v. Lidster* 2004).

The *Carroll Doctrine* provides for warrantless searches of motor vehicles if the vehicle is, in fact, mobile and if there is probable cause. The Court's rationale in *Carroll v. U.S.* (1925) is that the inherent mobility of a vehicle may permit destruction of evidence, allow the occupants to flee the jurisdiction, and make obtaining a warrant in this situation impractical for law enforcement. The scope of the search may extend to the entire car, including the trunk and closed containers, if there is probable cause to believe these locations contain evidence or contraband (*U.S. v. Ross* 1982). The Court also determined that searches of passengers' belongings with probable cause are reasonable (*Wyoming v. Houghton* 1999).

Traditionally officers may search and seize evidence from the passenger's compartment of the vehicle incident to a valid arrest. In *New York v. Belton* (1981) the Court held that the passenger compartment of a vehicle may be searched if the occupant is under arrest. This is similar to the *Chimel* rule discussed earlier—the search of the vehicle is permissible when done contemporaneously with an arrest, and officers were not required to articulate probable cause for the search. The ruling in Belton is considered a **bright-line rule**, which is a clear, easily understood, and easily applied standard in a specific situation. The search incident to arrest rule was revisited in *Thorton v. U.S.* (2004). In this case the officer was in the process of stopping a motor vehicle when the driver parked and exited the vehicle. Unlike most police–public contacts involving motor vehicles, the initial contact was after the driver had exited the car and closed the door behind him. The officer discovered drugs in Thorton's pocket and placed him under arrest. Then, pursuant to the arrest that occurred outside the vehicle, the officer used the Belton rule to search the vehicle, eventually finding a firearm that petitioner Thorton was not permitted to possess because of a prior felony conviction. The Court ruled that this search was permissible, and the evidence discovered pursuant to the search was admissible in court. The majority relied on the fact that the petitioner was under arrest and that a search pursuant to the arrest was reasonable to protect officer safety and preserve evidence.

But recently the Court has limited the scope of the *Belton* rule in *Arizona v. Gant* (2009). Officers learned Rodney Gant did not possess a valid license and further observed him driving a motor vehicle. Gant was arrested, handcuffed, and placed in the back of a police car. Then officers conducted a search of his vehicle consistent with the *Belton* rule. The search of the vehicle produced drugs and drug paraphernalia in his vehicle. In a 7–2 ruling, the majority found the scope of the search in *Gant* to be unreasonable. They reasoned that search of a vehicle pursuant to arrest is not necessarily automatic—officers must reasonably believe that the search will produce evidence related to the crime for which the person was arrested, or the person under arrest must be in close proximity to the passenger compartment where a weapon could be obtained or evidence destroyed. In this case, Gant was arrested for driving under a suspended license, so officers could not reasonably justify searching for physical evidence related to that offense. Further, Gant was secured in a police car so he was in no position to procure a weapon or destroy evidence. This recent ruling places real limitations on vehicle searches.

Interrogations and Confessions

Policing, at its core, involves personal contact between the officer and the public. Although these contacts occur millions of times a year, there are certain circumstances in which the police must advise citizens of their constitutional rights regarding answering questions. These procedures stem from perhaps one of the best known cases in the history of the Supreme Court, namely *Miranda v. Arizona* (1966). While most people can recite these *Miranda warnings* verbatim (largely from their popularized use in television dramas), certainly far fewer people appreciate how these rights came about, when they must be used by police, and whether exceptions exist.

Ernesto Miranda, a poor Mexican immigrant, was arrested for rape and kidnapping. Police officers interrogated Miranda for 2 hours while he was in custody, during which time he confessed to the crimes. After conviction, Miranda appealed, claiming his Fifth Amendment privilege from self-incrimination was violated. The U.S. Supreme Court agreed and indicated that the police must take appropriate safeguards to ensure that a defendant's rights are not violated during such procedures. Specifically, police must advise defendants that (1) they have the right to remain silent, (2) any statement made may be used against the defendant in court, (3) the defendant has the right to have an attorney present during questioning, and (4) if a defendant cannot afford an attorney, then the state will appoint one prior to questioning. The defendant must intelligently and voluntarily waive these rights prior to questioning, and while this waiver does not have to be written, many police organizations require a written waiver by the defendant.

The Court said that the police must advise defendants of these rights during all custodial interrogations. *Custody* occurs when a person is deprived of his or her freedom in a significant way, such as during an arrest. *Interrogations* are those circumstances when the police ask questions that tend to incriminate the citizen (del Carmen 2001). The Court required giving this advice because it recognized that custodial interrogations could be so psychologically coercive that responses during these encounters may not be completely voluntary. What makes this case so unique (and perhaps so memorable) is that the Court created active procedural safeguards for the police to follow, which are similar to a recipe for ensuring that a person's rights are not violated. But it is interesting to note that Miranda warnings are not constitutional rights per se and that it is possible for a law to be created that would make these familiar rights a thing of the past. As the author of the majority opinion, Chief Justice Warren indicated,

> We encourage Congress and the States to continue their laudable search for increasingly effective ways of protecting the rights of the individual while promoting efficient enforcement of our criminal laws. However, unless we are shown other procedures which are at least as effective in apprising accused persons of their right of silence and in assuring a continuous opportunity to exercise it, the following safeguards must be observed.

Congress appeared to rise to Chief Justice Warren's challenge and 2 years after the *Miranda* decision enacted 18 USC § 3501, which held in part that any voluntary confession may be admissible in evidence against the defendant. This statute went largely unutilized until the Court considered *Dickerson v. U.S.* (2000). Charles Dickerson made presumably voluntary incriminating statements to the FBI during a custodial interrogation prior to being advised of the Miranda warnings and argued that because of this his statements were inadmissible as evidence against him at criminal trial. The government argued that these voluntary statements were admissible as evidence pursuant to 18 USC § 3501. Chief Justice Rehnquist, writing for the majority, held that in fact the Miranda procedure had become an "embedded" police practice and has become a "part of our national culture"; further, "Miranda announced a constitutional rule that Congress may not supersede legislatively." Despite 18 USC § 3501, the *Dickerson* decision reaffirmed the Miranda requirement during custodial interrogations.

Once someone has exercised their desire to speak with an attorney, all questioning of the accused must stop. However, if there is a significant break between requesting an attorney and re-questioning, then statements made may be admissible in trial court. In *Edwards v. Arizona* (1981) the suspect exerted his desire to speak with an attorney. The next day the police re-initiated questioning, and this time the defendant waived his rights and made incriminating statements. The Court held that this waiver during the second interrogation was invalid and that he could not voluntarily waive his rights so soon after exerting them. But more recently, the Court said that a significant lapse in time between interrogations could create a situation where a waiver during the subsequent interrogation was considered voluntary. In *Maryland v. Shatzer* (2010) the Court held that a break of more than 2 weeks created a presumption of voluntariness in the second interrogation. The Court has subsequently outlined several exceptions to the Miranda requirements.

Public Safety Exception. The police may ask questions of a suspect who is in custody if there is a concern for public safety, and this exception to the Miranda warnings was outlined in *New York v. Quarles* (1984). In this case, officers were approached by a woman who claimed that she had just been raped by a man fitting the description of Quarles and that the man had a firearm. Officers found Quarles in a supermarket, placed him under arrest, and found him in possession of an empty holster. Before he was advised of his Miranda warnings, the officer asked him where the gun was, to which Quarles responded by leading the officer to the gun. The Court indicated that while Quarles was clearly in custody and while the officer's questions constituted an interrogation, there existed a significant, immediate threat to public safety that permitted the officer to ask these questions without first issuing Miranda warnings. The rationale was that the threat to public safety outweighed the suspect's right to be free from self-incrimination.

Inevitable Discovery. If the police do not advise suspects of their Miranda warnings during custodial interrogations, then the information given during an interrogation may not be used in criminal court, according to the exclusionary rule. Furthermore, if the suspect provides information during the interrogation that leads to the recovery of physical evidence, this evidence, too, may not be used in court—unless the police can demonstrate that the physical evidence would have been inevitably discovered without the benefit of the information provided during the improper interrogation.

This exception was outlined in a series of cases before the Court. First, in *Brewer v. Williams* (1977), the Court indicated that the admission by the defendant would be excluded from court because the police engaged in what amounted to a functionally equivalent interrogation. On December 24, 1969, officers were driving the suspect (Williams, a religious man under arrest for kidnapping a little girl) to meet his attorney, and the suspect had previously indicated he wished to remain silent until speaking with his attorney. The officers engaged in what has been known as the "Christian Burial Speech," telling Williams that it would be nice if the girl's body could be recovered before Christmas so that the family could provide her with a proper Christian burial. Williams then led the police to the body, which happened to be only a few miles away from where a search party was actively looking for evidence of the crime.

Initially, the Court indicated that the admission was inadmissible in court, as the "speech" was likely to elicit an incriminating response from Williams, in violation of his Miranda warnings. Since the discovery of the body was a "fruit" produced by an improper police action, it, too, must be eliminated from court. However, it was later argued in *Nix v. Willams* (1984) that the search party would inevitably have discovered the body, even if Williams had not led the police to the crime scene. The Supreme Court agreed, indicating that evidence that would have inevitably been discovered by the police is admissible in court. It is important to understand that the fact that an active search party was close to discovering the body was an integral component of the Court's rationale. Had the search party not been so close to the evidence, the ruling might have been different.

This chapter has thus far concentrated on issues related to criminal procedure, while highlighting current legal doctrines related to searches and seizures of persons, property, and the rights of the accused during police interrogations. To ensure compliance with criminal procedure, improperly obtained evidence is excluded from criminal court. However, there are other legal remedies available to ensure police compliance with criminal procedure as well as compliance with the substantive law or organizational procedure. A common remedy is civil liability.

Civil Liability

America is a litigious society, and certainly the police are not completely immune from such action. Civil liability is a growing concern in American policing, and this trend will not change in the foreseeable future. In many ways civil liability is inherent in the awesome power that police have in a democratic society, and civil lawsuits often arise when police officers abuse this power, engage in negligent behavior, or otherwise violate the civil rights of a citizen. The risk of being sued is part of the police presence, and officers, supervisors, managers, and other agents of government understand this. However, exactly *how, why,* and *under what circumstances* they may be held liable are not always as clear.

This section offers an overview of the laws that govern civil liability for police officers. It includes the actual (and potential) costs and pervasiveness of civil lawsuits against the police, various avenues for civil litigation (including state law and federal laws), emerging trends in police liability, and the unintentional cost litigation may have on officers. Police administrators must be cognizant of the law as it relates to policing innovation and, ultimately, "police executives of the future will have to sift innovations through a civil liability filter" (Kappeler 2001, 200).

Reginald T. Shuford, the American Civil Liberties Union Foundation's chief litigator in challenges to racial profiling, provides a discussion on how civil litigation has impacted policing in Voices From the Field. Shuford is leading national litigation efforts and consulting with state ACLU affiliates in cases of "driving while black or brown," airport profiling, and profiling related to the war on terror.

Costs of Liability in Policing

Many different costs are associated with police civil liability. Beyond the obvious monetary costs, there are often other ancillary costs associated with retraining officers and purchasing new equipment, as well as personal costs for officers and supervisors who are targets of litigation. Civil litigation has increased, both in the frequency of lawsuits and in the amount of money paid to plaintiffs.

The number of civil lawsuits against the police continues to grow, and this trend will likely continue. An early report by the International Association of Chiefs of Police indicated there were 1,741 civil suits against the police in 1967. This estimate grew to 3,897 in 1971, an increase of 123 percent. By 1975, the number of suits nearly doubled again (del Carmen 1991). The frequency of such suits has continued to escalate since that time. Silver (1996) estimated that police face more than 30,000 suits per year. However, the true number of civil lawsuits filed against the police is largely unknown, and this has led some to call for the creation of a national, systematic data set to fully understand the dimensions of civil liability (Vaughn, Cooper, and del Carmen 2001). Kappeler (2001) estimated that the costs of liability could be as high as $780 billion annually.

Reginald T. Shuford, J. D.

American Civil Liberties Union Foundation

Question: How has court litigation impacted policing in America?

Answer: At a general level, litigation against police departments has had a manifold effect. First, litigation helps to clarify the parameters of policing such that the balance between public safety and civil rights and liberties can be maintained. Court decisions and settlements provide officers with a roadmap of the boundaries within which they must operate to avoid running afoul of the Constitution and other laws. This result is beneficial to police officers and civilians alike. Officers who adhere to these rulings are more likely to avoid being sued or disciplined, protecting their reputations and careers while at the same time saving their departments a significant amount of money and resources. The benefit to civilians is that they learn what their rights are and are therefore more empowered to ensure that those rights are protected and respected. Second, litigation—and the threat of litigation—promotes accountability. Litigation can be extraordinarily expensive and time-consuming. Accordingly, most responsible police agencies will seek to avoid litigation—or, if sued, will settle the case—by ensuring that their officers are trained to act within the bounds of the law and are disciplined when they do not; will devise systems to ensure that citizen complaints are properly processed and which provide managerial oversight; and will collect data to make sure that their officers are acting evenhandedly and not on account of an individual's race, national origin, or some other protected characteristic.

The case of *NAACP et al. v. Maryland State Police* is instructive. Filed by the American Civil Liberties Union (ACLU) in 1998 on behalf of the National Association for the Advancement of Colored People (NAACP) of Maryland and a number of individuals, the lawsuit alleged that the Maryland State Police maintained a policy and practice of racial profiling carried out by some of its troopers. After years of contentious and costly litigation, the parties reached partial settlement of the case in May 2003, resolving everything but money damages for individual plaintiffs. The settlement includes a general prohibition against racial profiling; ongoing data collection, with personal data assistants and video and audio recording equipment in most cars; the creation of a Police–Citizen Advisory Committee; the appointment of a consultant who will oversee implementation of the settlement and issue regular progress reports; creation of a brochure with information about how to lodge a complaint or commendation; and development of new guidelines on the use of canines and consent searches. The settlement also contains oversight and monitoring mechanisms requiring the Maryland State Police to review information about racial profiling on a consistent basis and to investigate and take appropriate action in response to "red flags" that troopers may be profiling.

Reginald Shuford is a senior staff attorney for the ACLU Racial Justice Program and has authored petitions, articles, and U.S. Supreme Court briefs concerning discrimination, the Equal Protection Clause, and First and Fourth Amendment rights.

What has changed in policing over the past 3 decades to warrant such profound increases in civil liability? One possible answer is "nothing"; instead, the propensity of the public and its lawyers to sue officers for their actions during encounters may have increased. The increase in lawsuits may be more a function of the public's view of the police (and government in general) as having abundant resources with which to compensate citizens for even the most meager of transgressions. And there may be some truth to this perception. Kappeler (2001) reported that the average jury award for litigation against municipal government is around $2 million. Awards resulting from civil litigation involving the police tend to be somewhat lower than this estimate. Ross (2000) conducted an analysis of federal lawsuits alleging failure to train between 1989 and 1999. He reported that the average award for the plaintiff was around $492,794, with an additional average of $60,680 in attorneys' fees. A survey of Texas police chiefs found the typical award in police civil liability cases was around $98,100; however, these amounts are often significantly reduced on appeal (Vaughn, Cooper, and del Carmen 2001).

Of course, many of these cases are settled prior to court. Often the decision to settle out of court is a tactical decision designed to avoid potentially paying more money in a jury-awarded decision. In their survey of Texas police chiefs, Vaughn and colleagues (2001) asked chiefs about their motivations to settle. Sixty percent reported that the decision was motivated by the desire to avoid paying more money later. Indeed, there was some truth to this motivation, in that the average settlement was around $55,411 per case (compared with $98,100 awarded by a jury). Other motivations included wanting to make the case go away (56 percent), to avoid losing in court (38 percent), to avoid embarrassment (37 percent), and to compensate for police wrongdoing (22 percent). Only 17 percent of police chiefs indicated that their decision to settle was in part to compensate the plaintiff for some wrongful act by the police officer. In addition to paying less than if the case proceeded to court, the municipality would not have to devote scarce resources to other costs associated with the litigation, including attorney costs, costs associated with expert testimony, and officers' time testifying in court.

Although the number of lawsuits filed for improper police behavior has increased, what is seldom reported is the success rate for plaintiffs in their quests for compensation. The fact is, most police lawsuits are decided in favor of the officers, although the exact number varies considerably. Early research indicated that only about 4 percent of all claims against the police were found in favor of the plaintiff. More recent research places this figure at about 8 percent (Kappeler, Kappeler, and del Carmen 1993). In their survey of Texas police chiefs, Vaughn, Cooper, and del Carmen (2001) found that chiefs reported losing about 22 percent of all civil suits. In his examination of federal lawsuits decided in federal district courts between 1980 and 2000, Kappeler (2001) reported that plaintiffs prevailed in between 45.7 and 53.4 percent of all cases. However, "prevail" does not necessarily mean the police were found liable, only that there were sufficient grounds to warrant a jury trial, since there was found to be a substantive issue before the court. Nonetheless, these civil suits can cause significant damage to the reputations of police officers and the police departments involved. Further, the cost associated with protecting officers and departments from lawsuits can be quite high, regardless of the final determination.

Avenues of Liability

Police may be defendants in two different ways: They may be sued in state courts for violations of state laws, or they may be sued in federal court for violations of constitutional or federally protected rights. However, it is important to understand that defendants may be held liable simultaneously in both arenas for the same action if the action violates both state torts and civil liberties. Recall that this discussion revolves around civil law; therefore, double jeopardy claims are irrelevant. In other words, if the officer's actions are negligent under state tort laws and are at the same time a violation of federal civil rights, the plaintiff may seek relief in both state courts and federal courts. To make matters more confusing, if the action by the officer is also in violation of criminal law, then prosecutors may seek indictments in criminal court as well. To understand these different procedures, we will now explore the basics of state tort law and federal liability, with particular emphasis on Title 42, Section 1983, of the U.S. Code.

Civil Liability in State Courts

Officers and supervisors may be defendants in state courts when state torts are violated. Most suits in state court allege wrongful police conduct in which a person is injured because of actions conducted by another person. Generally there are three classifications of state tort laws: strict liability torts, intentional torts, and negligent torts. Strict liability torts involve the creation of some condition that is so hazardous that the person engaging in such an activity can be reasonably certain a result of injury or damage will occur (Kappeler 2001). Strict liability torts rarely involve the police and thus will not be discussed in detail here.

Intentional Torts. *Intentional torts* involve behavior specifically designed to cause some type of injury or harm. The key to intentional torts is the *culpable state of mind of the officer,* in that his or her actions were purposive and designed to bring about some type of injury or property loss. While numerous different activities may be classified as intentional torts, among the most common for police officers are excessive use of force, wrongful death, assault, battery, and false arrest.

Excessive use of force entails the application of physical force that is not in line with the level of resistance faced by the officer. In other words, the application of force was unreasonable. Officers are trained to match resistance by citizens with a certain level of force, but this must be *proportional* to the level of resistance by the citizen. If officers use force that is not proportional, they may be sued for intentional use of excessive force. Effective training, supervision, and documentation of use-of-force encounters between the police and the public are essential to reduce exposure to civil liability. Similarly, **wrongful death** suits may arise when an unjustified police action results in the death of a citizen. The victim's family levies a civil suit, and compensation is sought for pain and suffering, medical and funeral expenses, and loss of future earnings (del Carmen and Smith 2001).

Assault involves the "intentional causing of an apprehension of harmful or offensive conduct; it is the attempt or threat, accompanied by the apparent ability, to inflict bodily harm on another person" (del Carmen 1991, 18). Assault occurs when officers intentionally cause a person to fear for his or her safety. An example of this may be that during a custodial investigation, the officer grabs and threatens the suspect with serious physical injury, such as throwing him or her out the second floor window (Kappeler 2001). In contrast, **battery** is harmful or offensive body contact between two people, such as when an officer applies any force to an individual without justification. The basic difference between the two is that assault involves menacing conduct, whereas battery must involve actual contact (del Carmen 1991).

Claims of *false arrest* arise from intentional, illegal detention of an individual for prosecution. Typically, these suits arise from warrantless arrests, a common event in modern policing. The legal standard for making an arrest is probable cause; that is, the facts and circumstances would lead a reasonable person to believe a specific person has committed a criminal act. If officers detain a person without sufficient probable cause, this may give rise to an allegation of false arrest.

Police officers, supervisors, organizations, and municipalities are often the targets of intentional tort violations, perhaps because of their very nature. The police occupy a unique role in society, whereby they are among the few government entities sanctioned to exercise control over the public through the use of force. Given the sheer number of encounters between the police and the public, coupled with the legitimate right to use coercion, it is not surprising that these civil suits occur with some frequency. However, actions only become problematic under intentional tort laws when the action is unreasonable.

Negligent Torts. Whereas intentional torts focus on the mental state of an individual, negligent torts only require *inadvertent and unreasonable behavior resulting in damage or injury* (Kappeler 2001). Negligence is injury that is the result of a lapse of due care where the ingredients for injury were the result of some action or inaction on the officer's part. Thus, negligence provides liability for unreasonably creating a risk (Levine, Davies, and Kionka 1993). To prove negligence, four criteria must be satisfied. First, there is *legal duty*, which involves those actions on the part of the defendant as prescribed by the courts that require some action. Thus, there must be a legal basis for the requirement of certain behavior or activity. Second, **breach of duty** (or failure to conform with duty) is more complex. It must be demonstrated that a reasonably prudent person would believe the officer breached his or her duty to a plaintiff. Third, this breach of duty must **cause** some type of injury, or, in other words, but for the actions of the officer, the plaintiff would not have been injured or damaged. Finally, **actual damage or injury** must have resulted from this action, including mental, physical, or economic injury (del Carmen 1991; Hughes 2001a; Kappeler 2001).

Failure to arrest may be negligent behavior if the plaintiff can prove the *officer's inaction caused injury or damage.* Discretion involves the ability to choose between a course of action or inaction. Officers often do not make arrests even when there are sufficient legal grounds to do so. Whether discretion is a virtue or a vice is beyond the parameters of the current discussion; however, officers and supervisors should recognize liabilities associated with inaction. An example of negligence may be illustrated by the circumstances surrounding *Thurman v. City of Torrington* (1985). The plaintiff, Tracey Thurman, alleged that Torrington police officers failed to arrest her estranged husband for a pattern of domestic abuse, even though officers observed the abuse in question. After failing to arrest the suspect, Thurman sustained significant and debilitating injuries that persist to this day. Although this case was settled in federal court, the ingredients for negligent failure to arrest were also present. The *Thurman* case, along with other factors, gradually led to police departments taking a more legalistic approach to domestic abuse (Sherman 1992).

Civil Liability in Federal Courts

Recently, there has been a tremendous increase in the number of civil liability filings against the police in federal courts. The most typical avenue for redress has come through the "resurrection" of Title 42 of the U.S. Code, §1983 (Barrineau 1994). In §1983, citizens can seek relief from officials who violate their constitutional rights under the guise of their governmental positions. Title 42 USC §1983 reads in part,

> Every person who, under color of any statute, ordinance, regulation, custom, or usage, of any State or Territory or the District of Columbia, subjects, or causes to be subjected, any citizen of the United States or other person within the jurisdiction thereof to the deprivation of any rights, privileges, or immunities secured by the Constitution and laws, shall be liable to the party injured in an action at law, suit in equity, or other proper proceeding for redress.

As such, 42 USC §1983 does not create any substantive rights. Instead, it outlines a procedure individuals can follow to seek compensation for violations of their constitutional rights. There are two essential components of §1983; namely (1) the defendant must be acting under the color of law and (2) there must be a violation of a constitutional or federally protected right.

Color of Law. *Color of law* translates into the misuse of power possessed by an individual who is a "state actor" and derives his or her power from the government. Police officers are given authority and power by the state. Thus, if officers are performing typical police duties (e.g., making arrests, enforcing traffic regulations, or conducting searches and seizures of property), they are, for the purposes of liability, acting under the color of law (Kappeler 2001). Worrall (1998) indicated that the courts often define the color of law by asking, "Was police power used?" or "Did the department authorize the act?"

Is an officer who is working off-duty security acting under the color of law for the purposes of liability? Can police organizations be liable under §1983 for their actions? In other words, are there circumstances in which police officers may not act under the color of law? Vaughn and Coomes (1995, 398) noted several important exceptions and caveats to this prong of §1983 requirements for liability. In their review of contemporary case law on the topic, they concluded that officers act "under the color of law if they invoke police power, if they discharge duties routinely associated with police work, or if they use their authority to lure potential plaintiffs into compromising positions." Officers are acting under the color of law if they perform certain activities typically associated with policing, including wearing a uniform, identifying themselves as police officers, placing people under arrest, and filing reports. This is subjective from the plaintiff's point of view and depends on whether the plaintiff believed the defendant was acting as a public official.

However, if an officer, even if in uniform, acts as a private citizen and does not invoke his or her police powers, then he or she is not acting under the color of law for liability purposes. To answer the question posed above, if the officer is working an off-duty assignment under the auspices and direction of the police department, then his or her actions may be carried out under the color of law. In contrast, if the officer is working off-duty security through a private contract with a private security firm, then he or she is not acting under the color of law. Table 3.1 provides a series of situations where officers are considered acting under the color of law as well as when they are not doing so.

Violations of Constitutional or Federally Protected Rights. The second prong of §1983 involves rights protected by **constitutional** or federally **protected rights**. Therefore, rights provided by the states are not covered in §1983 actions. Typically, plaintiffs will seek redress for violations in one of the amendments outlined in the Bill of Rights or the equal protection clause of the Fourteenth Amendment.

An example of §1983 in action may be instructive. In *Graham v. Connor* (1989), the plaintiff (Graham) asked a friend to drive him to a store to obtain orange juice for his diabetic condition. Upon arriving at the store, Graham observed too many people in line, so he hurried out and asked his friend to drive him to a friend's house instead. A police officer, observing Graham's suspicious behavior, stopped the car driven by Graham's friend and detained the plaintiff until he could determine what had happened in the store (even though Graham explained his medical condition). After the officer determined that no crime had been committed, he released Graham. However, while Graham was in police custody, he was denied access to treatment for his medical condition and sustained injuries as a result.

TABLE 3.1 Factors to Determine Whether an Officer Acted Under the Color of Law

OFFICERS ACT UNDER THE COLOR OF LAW IF...	OFFICERS DO NOT ACT UNDER THE COLOR OF LAW IF...
They identify themselves as a law enforcement agent.	They do not invoke police power.
They perform duties of a criminal investigation.	Their inaction does not constitute state action.
They file official police documents.	They commit crimes in a personal dispute without invoking police power.
They attempt or make an arrest.	They act as federal agents.
They invoke their police powers outside their lawful jurisdiction.	They report the details of alleged crimes as private citizens.
They settle a personal vendetta with police power.	
They display or use police weapons/equipment.	They work for a private security company and do not identify themselves as law enforcement personnel.
They act pursuant to a statute or ordinance.	The department removes the officers' lawful authority.
The department policy mandates they are "always on duty."	
They intimidate citizens from exercising their rights.	
The department supports, facilitates, or encourages the off-duty employment of its officers as private security personnel.	

Source: Adapted from M. S. Vaughn and L. F. Coomes, "Police Civil Liability Under Section 1983: When Do Police Officers Act Under the Color of Law?" *Journal of Criminal Justice* (1995) 23, 409.

Graham sued the officer for violating his Fourth Amendment rights that protected him from excessive use of force. The Court held that officers might be liable pursuant to §1983 for excessive use of force. In doing so, they determined a standard of *objective reasonableness* is to be used in such cases, indicating the force must be considered from the view of the officer at the time of the event and not in 20/20 hindsight.

Defenses to §1983. There are four instances when, confronted with suits under §1983, defendants can offer defenses for their actions, thus negating the federal lawsuit. First, *absolute immunity* is when a civil action is brought against those protected by this form of immunity that will be dismissed by the court. However, this form of immunity has little application to liability for police officers, and it is typically reserved for the judiciary. The lone exception to this rule is when an officer commits perjury in court. If the officer, while testifying in criminal court, gives incorrect information that violates a person's right, the officer may seek absolute immunity from lawsuits from §1983 lawsuits. However, although immune from civil lawsuits, the act of perjury is a criminal offense with which officers may be charged and convicted in criminal courts (Kappeler 2001). Second, **qualified immunity** extends to police officers performing duties that are discretionary in nature. This immunity analysis hinges on two questions posed in *Saucier v. Katz* (2001). First, did the officer's conduct violate a constitutional or a federally protected right? Second, was this right clearly established at the time of the action? According to Kappeler (2001, 62), "If a court determined that the law was not clearly established or that the officer's conduct was reasonable, the officer is to be afforded immunity from liability."

Qualified immunity is explored in *Groh v. Ramirez* (2004), and that case may be illustrative of how this defense is exercised in practice. Groh, acting as a Special Agent for the Bureau of Alcohol, Tobacco, and Firearms, prepared a warrant to search Ramirez's home for firearms and other contraband. The warrant was approved by a federal judge; upon executing the warrant, agents indeed discovered firearms. Search warrants, as described earlier in this chapter, are required to contain four separate elements: probable cause, support by oath or affirmation, a description of what will be searched, and a description of what will be seized. The warrant in *Groh* failed to indicate exactly what was to be seized. Based on this omission, Ramirez sought civil damages against Groh and other agents who executed the warrant, reasoning that the agent (while acting under color of law) violated his right to be free from unreasonable searches and seizures. Special Agent Groh sought qualified immunity, reasoning the omission in the warrant was merely a negligent oversight. The Court agreed with Ramirez, noting that the warrant was so deficient that a reasonable officer should have known that it was invalid. The fact that a judge approved the warrant does not absolve the officer from civil liability. The Court applied *Saucier*, indicating that the agent's behavior violated a federally protected right and that this right was clearly established at the time. The special agent was not entitled to qualified immunity from civil liability.

Third, police officers may defend themselves from federal litigation if they can claim there was **probable cause** to believe their action was legal. This is particularly important for defenses of false arrest or improper searches and seizures. For example, if officers can demonstrate probable cause was present either that a person had committed a crime or that probable cause existed that justified a search, then redress in federal court is barred (*Hunter v. Bryant* 1991; Kappeler 2001). Even if it is later determined that probable cause did not exist, but the officer was acting on good faith, the officer is immune from liability. "Probable cause is so strong a defense in arrest and search and seizure cases that some courts have held that if probable cause is present, the officer is not liable even if malice is involved in the officer's act" (del Carmen 1991, 57). Finally, officers may be free from civil liability if they can demonstrate their actions were conducted in **good faith**. This means the officers could not have reasonably known that their actions were in violation of law or the Constitution, such as executing a warrant that they believed to be valid. The factors the court will consider regarding good faith actions include the following:

1. The officer acted in accordance with agency rules and regulations,
2. The officer acted pursuant to a statute that was reasonably believed to be valid, but was later declared unconstitutional,
3. The officer acted in accordance with orders from a superior that were reasonably believed to be valid, or
4. The officer acted in accordance with advice from a legal counsel that was reasonably believed to be valid. (del Carmen 1991, 55–56)

Emerging Liability Issues for the Twenty-First Century

Policing in the twenty-first century may present new challenges to police officers, supervisors, and municipalities in the civil liability arena. Changes in technology, information systems, data analysis, and society provide a dynamic environment to which police officers must adapt. As stated earlier, people may become plaintiffs in civil liability suits for violating constitutional or federally protected rights. As such, it is important for officers and police managers to remain current on changes in criminal procedure. This section does not present an exhaustive discussion of these issues, but provides an overview of contemporary issues confronting modern police organizations.

Community Policing and Zero-Tolerance Policing. Community policing is designed to increase the level of discretion of the line officer as well as the frequency of officer–citizen encounters. Officers will have more ability to make decisions, engage in problem-solving activities, and facilitate partnerships with citizens. The changing role of the police has caused some to wonder whether community policing may alter the exposure of police officers and police managers to civil liability. Interestingly, Worrall (1998) found that an organization's level of commitment was related to fewer civil liability lawsuits. Recalling the characteristics of community policing, the idea that it may decrease liability makes sense theoretically, and Vaughn, Cooper, and del Carmen (2001) outlined these arguments: (1) there is an increase in women's and minority voices in police organizations designed to reduce citizens' complaints, (2) there are improvements in attitudes toward the police, and (3) there are improvements in confidence in the police and the criminal justice system. In short, because the police and the public are working in partnership, there may be less antagonism and misunderstanding between them.

On the other hand, there are several reasons to believe community policing may increase civil liability for police. First, the number of contacts between the police and the public should increase; this may lead to more opportunities for civil liability. Community policing also exposes police to areas that were, prior to the community policing model, not considered public matters. Hughes (2000), for instance, argues that increased contact with the public in new and diverse matters will logically lead to more opportunities for civil suits against the police.

Second, discretion and policy creation are shifted to the lowest level of the organization. Therefore, officers will have more opportunity and responsibility for creating and implementing policies or customs on behalf of the organization "under the color of law." This may suggest that control and accountability of police officers will decrease and make direct supervision of these officers more difficult. Indeed, direct supervision and control of officers is counter to the community policing philosophy. Similarly, police departments may have to relax the number of policies influencing the behavior of officers.

Increased liability may be demonstrated by considering New York City's experience with its **Compstat** (Compare Statistics) procedure. The NYPD has realized reductions in crime, and at least some of these benefits can be attributed to their aggressive zero-tolerance model of police services. This style encourages officers to be proactive in their problem solving and make arrests for relatively minor violations of the law. However, Greene (1999) also noted that the number of legal filings alleging violations of civil rights has increased dramatically during the same time period. Many of these complaints involved police abuse of authority or brutality.

Use of Force

Officers expose themselves and police organizations to civil liability when excessive physical force is used during interactions with the public. Excessive use of force is considered an unreasonable seizure of an individual and therefore a violation of the Fourth Amendment, which creates the potential for §1983 action. This was introduced earlier in this chapter (*Graham v. Connor*, 1989), and the use of force will be more fully explored in Chapter 10. However, an increasingly popular form of less lethal force being adopted by police departments is conducted energy devices (CEDs), also known as Tasers. The Court has yet to fully examine under what conditions the application of CEDs is considered unreasonable, creating a potential for an emerging source of liability for police in America.

CEDs provide an attractive option for officers who are confronted with active resistance by citizens. CEDs release an electrical charge that temporarily incapacitates the suspect. Unlike other forms of less lethal force like batons, PR-24s, or oleoresin capsicum spray (OC spray, Mace, or pepper spray), CEDs can be applied at a distance, reducing the necessity for officers to be in close proximity with the citizen, and thus it is a safer use of force alternative for officers. The availability of CEDs may also decrease the frequency of firearm use, and this creates fewer lethal force incidents. Because of this, many police departments have recently adopted CEDs into their use of force options for officers (White and Ready 2008).

However, there exists debate regarding whether CEDs are truly safe alternatives during less than lethal police–public encounters. Amnesty International (2008) noted an unacceptable frequency of in-custody deaths during CED applications and called for police departments to discontinue their use or significantly limit when they can be used. Research by Lee et al. (2009) found that in-custody deaths increased 6.4-fold in police departments in the year following use of CEDs, while firearm use decreased 2.3 times. However, in-custody deaths and firearm use returned to "normal" levels in 2–5 years, essentially regressing to the mean. No change in officer injuries was reported in the 5-year follow up. The researchers concluded that given the significant potential for death associated with CEDs, it may not be an appropriate less lethal force alternative. The dilemma for police is how to properly train officers on when CEDs should be used during interactions with resistant suspects and where in the use of force continuum it is appropriate to place CEDs. Some recommend CEDs are properly placed below intermediate on the continuum (Hough and Tatum 2009). However, given the potential for unintended injury or death, it may be more appropriate to reserve CED application for more resistant suspects or when there is an immediate threat to officers or others and less intrusive tactics are unavailable.

A 2009 case from the Ninth Circuit Court of Appeals addresses the issue of civil liability and CED application. The case considered whether Officer McPherson was entitled to qualified immunity during a use of force encounter when applying a CED. Carl Bryan was pulled over for a seatbelt violation. Bryan, reported to be quite agitated and clothed only in boxer shorts and tennis shoes, exited his vehicle despite Officer McPherson's directions to remain in the vehicle. Bryan was resistant in that he was not following verbal commands; however, he was neither assaultive nor attempting to flee. Officer McPherson discharged a CED without warning when Bryan was 20 feet from the officer, facing the opposite direction. The CED immobilized Bryan, and his subsequent fall caused facial contusions and fractured four teeth. Bryan filed for civil damages under 42 USC §1983. The Court of Appeals held that use of the CED in this circumstance was unconstitutionally excessive and denied Officer McPherson's request for qualified immunity. The Appellate Court reasoned that this was a minor offense, there was no immediate threat to the officer, and less intrusive tactics were more appropriate. The officer should have recognized the significant potential for unintended harm associated with using a CED under these circumstances and a reasonable officer should have known that it was unreasonable to deploy this level of force during the encounter. The fact that the officer did not intend to cause the level of harm that was actually inflicted is irrelevant. The Appellate Court, in denying qualified immunity, concluded that law was clearly established and that the officer should have realized the application of force was excessive (*Bryan v. McPherson* 2009). CEDs are an emerging civil liability threat in American policing since they are becoming increasingly popular but there is a lack of consensus among citizens, police administrators, and the legal community as to appropriate application.

Impact on Officers

The potential for civil liability is a part of policing that officers and supervisors must accept. In a survey of police officers, Hughes (2001b) found that 18.5 percent of officers had been sued for a job-related matter and 74.8 percent of officers personally knew of an officer who had been named in a lawsuit for a job-related matter. At the same time, 86.4 percent felt that officers are sued even when acting properly. This has led some officers to view public complaints and lawsuits as just another part of policing.

INSIDE POLICING 3.3 The Civil Lawsuit Experience

Civil lawsuits impact officers in significant ways, regardless of the outcome. Joan C. Barker conducted extended research with the LAPD that gave her unprecedented access to conversations and observations into the lives of police officers. Below is one officer's experience of being sued.

> We were on loan to Hollywood because they were having the Christmas parade. So we were working the crowd, people were just arriving and everyone was in a good mood. Lots of people. Families and such. And everything was fine when this citizen came over and told us that there was a man down and bleeding. We went to see this guy, and he was down and out. All bloody. He was passed out, and when I leaned over to talk to him, he woke and said he'd been in a bar and got in a fight and got himself beat up; and then he saw who we were, that we were police, and became all combative. Calling us "pigs" and that sort of thing. He was drunk and not hearing at all what we had to say. He was swearing and spitting at the [pedestrians]. And now there were lots of people, mothers and their children, all coming to this parade.
>
> Here's this beat-up drunk swearing and carrying on. This guy was saying real foul things, bad language and spitting at the people...and we told him to "shut up," but we said it nicer at the time. The first time we did, then later it was just "shut up." But we handcuffed him, and he was spitting and kicking out at people, so we thought, "We can't have this." So we got out the restraints and tied him so he couldn't kick anymore. Had to pick him up and carry him to where we could get a car for transport. And the sergeant said we should take him to county and get him [treated] and absentee to book him, and we did. Eight hours, eight hours of paperwork because of this guy.
>
> And that was it. We thought that was it, and then we get summonses. [His partner] and I got the summonses and we didn't even know what they were talking about. It had been five years since the incident. We didn't even recognize the name. It wasn't

(Continued)

---

even familiar to me; I had to go through my officer's notebook to find out what had happened, and then I remembered the guy and what happened. Now, this is what he alleges. He alleges that my partner and I went into this gay bar, and pulled him out and beat him up, because he was gay, and then arrested him. He didn't even know what had happened to him, but that was his story. I actually think he really believes that we did it. I think he really didn't remember what really happened and thought we did it. He alleged this, brought this to a lawyer five years later. Five years! Half a decade. Where are you going to get the witnesses [even] three years later? Just [his partner] and me and the sergeant.

It was the worst time of my life, to be accused of something and not be able to prove myself innocent. To not even have the opportunity to prove myself because the city was busy covering its ass. [very agitated] I didn't do anything, and everybody knew it. I had a partner and a sergeant, and they took the deposition of [his partner], but didn't even call the sergeant in. They didn't even need us because they'd already decided. They just paid the fucker thirty-five hundred dollars, and it goes in my package that there was an action against me and the city paid. How does that look?

When the partner was interviewed, he stated:

After that time I did as little as I could and had as little contact with citizens as possible. I used to work the L car [a one-officer unit that handles reports most of the time], so I was only there if they asked me to be there. And there was a record of that. I didn't do anything else if I could help it. It didn't make any sense to do anything—any real police work. Not patrol. I didn't want to go through that again.

Based on this description, it is apparent the officers harbored resentment toward the city for settling the lawsuit. By settling out of court the city avoided additional costs associated with the lawsuit, but it sent a message to the officers (and perhaps other officers in the department) that they had done something wrong. This also led to one officer seeking assignments not involving contact with citizens to avoid similar situations. It is important to recognize that civil lawsuits are stressful events for officers and that these lawsuits (regardless of the outcome) may increase the level of officer cynicism and stress.

SOURCE: Adapted from J. C. Barker. *Danger, Duty and Disillusion* (Prospect Heights, IL: Waveland Press, 1999), 128–129.

While the media tend to focus on plaintiff experiences, it is also important to consider the impact of a lawsuit from the officer's perspective. When officers and supervisors are sued for wrongdoing, there may be effects beyond the obvious loss of monetary resources. When named as a defendant in a civil lawsuit, an officer may experience heightened levels of stress and anxiety. Pursuant to citizen complaints or civil litigation, officers are often interrogated regarding not only the act in question, but also past behavior and disciplinary records. Previously, we discussed the fact that officers often report administrative policies, discipline, and a perceived lack of support as important sources of stress. However, these organizational responses, at least in part, may be reactions by supervisors and municipalities to insulate themselves from litigation. Still, officers may interpret these reactions as the organization not "backing" them, citizens being out to "get rich" at the expense of officers, and "no one respecting what the police do." Not only does the stress of many officers increase, but these problems may also lead to increased cynicism among officers. Inside Policing 3.3 provides one officer's account of being the subject of a civil lawsuit.

Even when not identified as defendants, civil lawsuits can impact other officers in the police organization. In the wake of a lawsuit, officers may feel the need to engage in fewer interactions with the public, particularly officer-initiated encounters. Officers rationalize this as a normal response to what they feel is an unjust situation and rationalize that their own likelihood of being named as a defendant in a lawsuit decreases if they interact with fewer citizens. This phenomenon has been called **depolicing**.

There is some evidence that depolicing may have recently occurred in Cincinnati. In April 2001, a white Cincinnati police officer shot and killed an unarmed young, black male. This shooting sparked several days of rioting, resulting in injuries sustained by citizens and officers alike. In the months that followed, the officer was indicted and a civil lawsuit was filed in federal court alleging the police department engaged in racial profiling. After the riots, indictment, and lawsuit, there was evidence that officers engaged in a department-wide slowdown in activity. For example, in June 2000, officers made 5,063 arrests for nonviolent crimes (such as disorderly conduct and weapons violations). In June 2001 (after the riots, indictment, and lawsuit), the department made half as many arrests (2,517). Additionally, arrests for violent crimes (such as murder and arson) declined to 487 from 502. This was despite a 20 percent increase from June 2000 in these crimes. Furthermore, traffic citations were down 35 percent. One police officer stated that officers were frustrated with the increase in crime rates, but also afraid of being labeled racial profilers whenever they arrested someone (Cloud 2001; McLaughlin and Prendergast 2001).

Depolicing has implications for police managers. The most effective way to avoid this phenomenon is to maintain an environment that does not allow it to occur in the first place. Police managers who are confronted with subordinates engaged in depolicing will need to take additional steps to explain to officers that avoiding encounters with the public is not in line with organizational goals and is unethical behavior. Effective policing involves maintaining a healthy relationship with citizens. By engaging in depolicing, officers not only alienate citizens who are frustrated with the police, but also alienate citizens who support the police. Over time, it is likely depolicing will fade away and police officer activity will regress to the mean (or return to previous levels). In the meantime, the department may sustain irreparable damage to public trust, public support, and the department's reputation.

Recent empirical research suggests that the phenomenon of depolicing may be limited to posttraumatic events, such as those described above. Novak, Smith, and Frank (2003) examined whether officers who had experienced civil liability claims behaved differently than other officers. Their basic hypotheses were that officers will behave less aggressively (e.g., fewer proactive encounters with citizens, arrests, use of force, and searches) if they have previously been sued, known officers who have been sued, or are highly cognizant of liability during the course of their activities. In other words, officers who have more experience with litigation will subsequently avoid situations that increase their exposure to liability. However, the data did not support these hypotheses. It appeared that an officer's aggressive behavior was largely unaffected by that officer's experience with litigation. While it is important to not confuse aggressive and proactive behavior with improper behavior, it appears that officers may not allow fear of litigation to hamper them from engaging in proactive law enforcement activities. Relatedly, Hickman, Piquero, and Greene's (2000) analysis of officers in Philadelphia indicated that officers assigned to community policing roles performed at parity with officers assigned to more traditional police roles regarding generation of citizen complaints. They found no difference between officers in proportion, type, or frequency of citizen complaints filed against them.

Summary

Criminal procedure is the process by which a person accused of a crime is processed through the criminal justice system and outlines the rules that the government must follow to ensure the civil liberties of citizens. Police officers may stop a citizen only if there is reasonable suspicion to believe criminal activity is afoot and may frisk that citizen only if there is reasonable suspicion to believe that the person is armed, posing a threat to officer safety. Arrests can only occur if the legal threshold is elevated to probable cause. Pursuant to an arrest, officers may search the person and the area within his or her immediate control or may perform a protective sweep for others who may pose a threat to officer safety. Like arrests, searches of property must be conducted only with probable cause. While there is a preference for obtaining a search warrant prior to engaging in a search of property, notable exceptions to this requirement include the plain view doctrine, the open fields doctrine, and the hot pursuit exception. The courts have indicated that persons in motor vehicles enjoy a diminished expectation to privacy, and searches of motor vehicles are more relaxed than those of private homes. Before questioning suspects who are in custody, officers must advise them of their Miranda warnings, and these rights must be intelligently and voluntarily waived prior to questioning. Notable exceptions to the Miranda requirement include the public safety exception and inevitable discovery.

Civil litigation regarding police behavior has increased over time, both in the number of suits filed and in the amount of money paid for damages or injury. People who initiate lawsuits (called plaintiffs) against the police (called defendants) may do so in either state courts or federal courts. In state courts, torts may be brought for intentional as well as negligent behavior. In federal courts, plaintiffs may bring lawsuits against the police if there is a violation of constitutional rights or federally protected rights. Often, these lawsuits are filed under 42 USC §1983. To be successful in a §1983, the plaintiff must demonstrate that the officer acted under the color of law and that the act violated his or her civil rights. Acceptable defenses to §1983 lawsuits include absolute immunity, qualified immunity, probable cause, and good faith. While community policing may decrease the incidence of civil liability in policing, there is an equal chance that civil liability will increase. Regardless of whether plaintiffs prevail in their lawsuits against the police (and most do not), the process can cause negative consequences for police officers, including increased stress and cynicism.

Critical Thinking Questions

1. Discuss the difference between reasonable suspicion and probable cause as well as the permissible behaviors associated with these legal thresholds.

2. Compare and contrast the criminal justice system to the civil system of justice.

3. Discuss the ways in which the police must balance the need for public safety with the need to ensure the civil liberties of citizens.

4. Does requiring the police to advise suspects of their Miranda warnings unduly handcuff the police? Support your answer.

5. What is more effective at controlling police behavior: the exclusionary rule or civil litigation? Why?

6. What types of claims may plaintiffs seek in state courts? In federal courts?

7. Describe 42 US §1983. What key components are necessary for a claim under §1983?

8. Under what circumstances do officers act "under the color of law," and why is it important to understand this?

9. Will community policing increase or decrease the number of civil liability claims? Support your answer.

References

Alabama v. White, 496 U.S. 325 (1990).

Amnesty International. 2008. "'Less than Lethal'? The Use of Stun Weapons in US Law Enforcement." London: Amnesty International Publications.

Atwater v. Lago Vista, 532 U.S. 318 (2001).

Arizona v. Gant, 556 U.S. ___ (2009).

Arizona v. Hicks, 480 U.S. 321 (1987).

Arizona v. Johnson, 555 U.S. ___ (2008).

Barker, J. C. 1999. *Danger, Duty and Disillusion.* Prospect Heights, IL: Waveland.

Barrineau, H. E. 1994. *Civil Liability in Criminal Justice,* 2nd ed. Cincinnati, OH: Anderson Publishing.

Brendlin v. California, 551 U.S. 249 (2007).

Berghuis v. Thompkins, 560 U.S. ___ (2010).

Brewer v. Williams, 430 U.S. 387 (1977).

Brinegar v. U.S., 338 U.S. 160, 176 (1949).

Bryan v. McPherson, No. 08-55622, U.S. Ninth Circuit (2009).

California v. Greenwood, 486 U.S. 35 (1988).

Carroll v. U.S., 267 U.S. 132 (1925).

Chimel v. California, 395 U.S. 752 (1969).

Cloud, J. 2001, July 30. "What's Race Got to Do With It? Despite a Crime Wave, Cincinnati's Cops Pull Back, Underscoring Stakes in the Conflict Over Racial Profiling." Retrieved August 16, 2001, from http://www.time.com/time/covers/1101010730/cover.html.

County of Sacramento v. Lewis, 523 U.S. 883 (1998).

del Carmen, R. V. 1991. *Civil Liabilities in American Policing: A Text for Law Enforcement Personnel.* Englewood Cliffs, NJ: Prentice Hall.

———. 2001. *Criminal Procedure: Law and Practice,* 5th ed. Belmont, CA: Wadsworth.

del Carmen, R. V., and Smith, M. R. 2001. "Police, Civil Liability, and the Law." In Dunham, R. G. and Alpert, G. P. (eds.), *Critical Issues in Policing,* 4th ed, pp. 181–198. Prospect Heights, IL: Waveland.

Dickerson v. U.S., 530 U.S. 428 (2000).

Edwards v. Arizona, 451 U.S. 477 (1981).

Florida v. Powell, 559 U.S. ___ (2010).

Georgia v. Randolph, 547 U.S. 103 (2006).

Graham v. Connor, 490 U.S. 397 (1989).

Groh v. Ramirez, 540 U.S. 551 (2004).

Greene, J. A. 1999. "Zero Tolerance: A Case Study of Police Policies and Practices in New York City." *Crime and Delinquency* 45: 171–187.

Herring v. U.S., 555 U.S. ____ (2009).

Hickman, M. J., Piquero, A. R., and Greene, J. R. 2000. "Does Community Policing Generate Greater Numbers and Different Types of Citizen Complaints Than Traditional Policing?" *Police Quarterly* 3: 70–84.

Hough, R. M., and Tatum, K. M. 2009. "Examining the Utility of the Use of Force Continuum: TASERs and Potential Liability." *Law Enforcement Executive Forum* 9: 37–50.

Hudson v. Michigan, 547 U.S. 586 (2006).

Hughes, T. 2000. Community Policing and Federal Civil Liability Under 42 USC §1983. Unpublished doctoral dissertation: University of Cincinnati.

———. 2001a. "*Board of the County Commissioners of Bryan County, Oklahoma v. Jill Brown:* Municipal Liability and Police Hiring Decisions." *Justice Professional* 13: 143–162.

———. 2001b. "Police Officers and Civil Liability: 'The Ties That Bind'?" *Policing: An International Journal of Police Strategies and Management* 24: 40–262.

Hunter v. Bryant, 502 U.S. 224, 112 S. Ct. 634 (1991).

Illinois v. Caballes, 543 U.S. 405 (2005).

Illinois v. Lidster, 540 U.S. 419 (2004).

Illinois v. McArthur, 531 U.S. 326 (2001).

Illinois v. Wardlow, 528 U.S. 119 (2000).

Indianapolis v. Edmond, 531 U.S. 32 (2000).

Kappeler, V. E. 2001. *Critical Issues in Police Civil Liability,* 3rd ed. Prospect Heights, IL: Waveland.

Kappeler, V. E., Kappeler, S. F., and del Carmen, R. V. 1993. "A Content Analysis of Police Civil Liability Cases: Decisions in the Federal District Courts, 1978–1990." *Journal of Criminal Justice* 21: 325–337.

Katz v. United States, 389 U.S. 347 (1967).

Klotter, J. C. 1999. *Legal Guide for Police: Constitutional Issues,* 5th ed. Cincinnati, OH: Anderson Publishing.

Kyllo v. U.S., 533 U.S. 27 (2001).

Lee, B. K., Vittinghoff, E., Whiteman, D., Park, M., Lau, L. L., and Tseng, Z. H. 2009. "Relation of Taser (Electrical Stun Gun) Deployment to Increase in In-Custody Sudden Deaths." *The American Journal of Cardiology* 103: 877–880.

Levine, L., Davies, J., and Kionka, E. 1993. *A Torts Anthology.* Cincinnati, OH: Anderson Publishing.

McLaughlin, S., and Prendergast, J. 2001, June 30. "Police Frustration Brings Slowdown: Arrests Plummet From 2000; Officers Seek Jobs in Suburbs." Retrieved August 16, 2001, from http://enquirer.com/editions/2001/06/30/loc_police_frustration.html.

Mapp v. Ohio, 367 U.S. 643 (1961).

Maryland v. Buie, 494 U.S. 325 (1990).

Maryland v. Pringle, 540 U.S. 366 (2003).

Maryland v. Shatzer, 599 U.S. ___ (2010).

Michigan Department of State Police v. Sitz, 496 U.S. 444 (1990).

Minnesota v. Dickerson, 508 U.S. 366 (1993).

Miranda v. Arizona, 384 U.S. 436 (1966).

Missouri v. Seibert, 542 U.S. 600 (2004).

Moran v. Burbine, 475 U.S. 412 (1986).

NAACP et al. v. Maryland State Police, No. CCB-98-1098, U.S. District Court of Maryland (1998).

New York v. Belton, 453 U.S. 454 (1981).

New York v. Quarles, 467 U.S. 649 (1984).

Nix v. Williams, 467 U.S. 431 (1984).

Novak, K., Smith, B., and Frank, J. 2003. "Strange Bedfellows: Civil Liability and Aggressive Policing." *Policing: An International Journal of Police Strategies and Management* 26: 352–368.

Oliver v. U.S., 466 U.S. 170 (1984).

Payton v. New York, 445 U.S. 573 (1981).

Ross, D. L. 2000. "Emerging Trends in Police Failure to Train Liability." *Policing: An International Journal of Police Strategies and Management* 23: 169–193.

Saucier v. Katz, 533 U.S. 194 (2001).

Schneckloth v. Bustamonte, 412 U.S. 218, 219 (1973).

Sherman, L. W. 1992. *Policing Domestic Violence.* New York: Free Press.

Silver, I. 1996. *Police Civil Liability.* New York: Mathew Bender.

Thorton v. U.S., 541 U.S. 615 (2004).

Terry v. Ohio, 392 U.S. 1, (1968).

Thurman v. City of Torrington, 595 F.Supp. 1521 (1985).

U.S. v. Leon, 468 U.S. 897 (1984).

U.S. v. Ross, 456 U.S. 798 (1982).

U. S. v. Seslar, 996 F 2d. 1058 (10th Cir.) (1993).

U.S. v. Sokolow, 490 U.S. 1 (1989).

U.S. v. Watson, 423 U.S. 411 (1976).

Vaughn, M. S., and Coomes, L. F. 1995. "Police Civil Liability Under Section 1983: When Do Police Officers Act Under the Color of Law?" *Journal of Criminal Justice* 23: 395–415.

Vaughn, M. S., Cooper, T. W., and del Carmen, R. V. 2001. "Assessing Legal Liabilities in Law Enforcement: Police Chiefs' Views." *Crime and Delinquency* 47: 3–27.

Weeks v. U.S., 232 U.S. 383 (1914).

White, M. D., and Ready, J. 2007. "The TASER as a Less Lethal Force Alternative: Findings on Use and Effectiveness in a Large Metropolitan Agency." *Police Quarterly* 10: 170–191.

Whren v. U.S., 517 U.S. 806 (1996).

Worrall, J. L. 1998. "Administrative Determinants of Civil Liability Lawsuits Against Municipal Police Departments: An Exploratory Analysis." *Crime and Delinquency* 44: 295–313.

Worrall, J. L. 2010. Criminal Procedure: From First Contact to Appeal, 3rd ed. Boston: Pearson Prentice Hall.

Wyoming v. Houghton, 526 U.S. 295 (1999).

Zalman, M. 2006. *Essentials of Criminal Procedure.* Upper Saddle River, NJ: Pearson Prentice Hall.

Zalman, M., Siegel, L. 1997. Criminal Procedure: Constitution and Society, 2nd Edition. Belmont, CA: West/Wadsworth.

CHAPTER 4

Community Policing

CHAPTER OUTLINE

- Evolving Strategies of Policing
- Early Forms of Community Policing
    - Police–Community Relations
    - Crime Prevention
    - Team Policing
    - Foot Patrol and Broken Windows
- Community Policing
- Elements of Community Policing
    - The Philosophical Dimension
    - The Strategic Dimension
    - The Tactical Dimension
- Implementing Community Policing
    - Positive Indications
    - Questions and Doubts
- Evaluating Community Policing
- Community Policing Today
- Summary
- Critical Thinking Questions
- References

- broad police function
- broken windows
- citizen input
- community crime prevention
- community policing (COP)
- crime prevention through environmental design (CPTED)
- geographic focus
- partnerships
- personalized service
- police–community relations
- positive interaction
- prevention emphasis
- problem analysis triangle
- problem-oriented policing (POP)
- problem solving
- reoriented operations
- SARA model
- situational crime prevention
- target hardening
- team policing

COMMUNITY POLICING BECAME THE dominant model of policing in the 1990s and remains influential today. This chapter explains how and why community policing developed and provides a general framework for understanding community policing. Part of the discussion revolves around precursors to community policing, including police–community relations, team policing, and foot patrol. Definitions and philosophy of community policing are presented, as well as research on the current status of community policing and its effectiveness.

Evolving Strategies of Policing

The problems of the 1960s and the influence of the reform model of policing, especially its legalistic orientation as discussed in Chapter 2, continued to be of concern to many police, political leaders, and academics in the 1970s and 1980s. These concerns tended to focus heavily on unsatisfactory relationships between police and their communities, especially minority communities. At the same time, crime rates increased steadily throughout the 1970s, suggesting that prevailing methods of policing were failing on two important counts, both public trust and crime control. These issues, together with new information from police research and trial-and-error experience with police tactics and strategies, help account for the experimentation with community policing in the 1980s and then its dramatic increase in popularity in the 1990s.

In regard to research, key studies in three areas shook the foundations of the reform model of policing. Starting in the 1970s, studies cast doubts on the effectiveness of reactive motorized patrol in controlling crime, the need for a rapid response to most citizens' reports of crime and requests for services, and the effectiveness of criminal investigation (these studies are discussed in Chapter 8). Although these studies had limitations, the research raised significant questions about whether the police were using the best methods to control crime. This inquisitive and questioning approach has become ingrained in modern policing, leading to continuous efforts to develop more effective tactics and strategies.

The police were also encouraged to broaden their use of research and the analytical process to solve problems. Goldstein (1990), for example, recommended that the police begin to think in terms of problems rather than incidents; that is, they should change from an incident-based response strategy to a problem-oriented strategy (e.g., viewing a group of incidents as a potential problem). Goldstein argued that officers should not only try to determine the relationship between incidents that might be occurring in the same family, building, or area, but also consider alternatives other than law enforcement to try to solve problems. The key to problem-oriented policing (described later in this chapter) is the use of data to analyze problems to discover exactly what they are, why they are occurring, why they are occurring where they are occurring (and not somewhere else), and so forth.

Early Forms of Community Policing

Even before questions were raised about the reform model's effectiveness in controlling crime, there was concern about public trust. Some police agencies began searching for ways of improving their relationships with the public as early as the 1950s. These efforts largely began as public relations, broadened to police–community relations, and then branched into crime prevention, team policing, and foot patrol. All of these paths eventually led to community policing.

Police–Community Relations

Historically, one of the most persistent and compelling problems confronting the police has been their relationship with minority groups. Depending on the time period, a minority group could consist of Irish Americans, Italian Americans, Hispanics or Latinos, African Americans, Asian Americans, Native Americans, gays and lesbians, or other groups. The police have had a long history of discriminating against members of minority groups because of their own prejudice, ignorance, or official responsibility for enforcing laws that restricted the civil rights of some people (such as segregation laws). Numerous civil disturbances in the United States have been precipitated by police behavior considered inappropriate by minority groups.

In addition, changes in society and in the routine nature of police work have tended to create more "distance" between the police and the public. The advent of police cars, for example, and later air conditioning in those cars led to police officers having bigger patrol beats and less informal contact with citizens. Similarly, the development of 911 telephone systems made it easier for the public to summon the police in an emergency, but also made police patrol units much busier and more closely tethered to their patrol cars, further reducing informal police–public contact. Of course, the police are not alone in having grown busier and more dependent on the automobile over the years—most Americans have had the same experience. Consequently, not only are the police and the community less familiar with each other today, but also neighbors do not know each other.

The reform model of policing that developed in the United States during the middle part of the twentieth century essentially saw the relationship with the community as a matter of legal and bureaucratic considerations. As tensions developed, this model attempted to be more responsive to the public by diversifying the police force and establishing community-relations programs. In the 1950s and 1960s, many police departments established community relations units in response to perceived problems in police–community relations. Initially, these community relations units engaged mostly in public relations by presenting the police point of view to the community. This one-side approach was soon recognized as inadequate, however, and was expanded to provide the community with a forum for expressing its views to the police. The two-way **police–community relations** philosophy emphasized the importance of communication and mutual understanding. Police departments often formed advisory groups of citizens, held neighborhood meetings, started programs designed to improve relations with youth, and generally tried to reach out to the community.

In the 1970s it became apparent that a few police–community relations officers or a small unit were not effective in guaranteeing smooth relations between a community and its police department. It was recognized that a community experiences its police department through the actions of patrol officers and detectives more than through the speeches made by a few community relations specialists. Efforts were then undertaken to train regular patrol officers in community relations and crime prevention techniques and to make them more knowledgeable about community characteristics and problems (Boydstun and Sherry 1975).

In the 1970s and 1980s, the public became increasingly fearful of crime, especially violence, gang activity, and drug use, all of which were alarmingly portrayed by the media. Many police departments became more legalistic, proactive, and assertive in an effort to deal with these problems and to satisfy public and political pressure. They tended to rely on aggressive patrol, field interrogations, citations, arrests, and increased undercover activities. These approaches, while applauded by many minority leaders (because crime victimization tends to be disproportionately experienced by minority citizens), also increased the tension between police and minority citizens, particularly African Americans and Hispanics. The perception that some police officers were discriminating against minority citizens became widespread. In fact, this perception was often accurate, particularly as it applied to police use of excessive force. However, the degree to which such behavior was racially motivated or willful was much more difficult to determine. These issues, and how best to deal with them, continue today in the context of racial profiling (Fridell et al. 2001).

Crime Prevention

Early police efforts at public relations and community relations naturally evolved toward crime prevention, in part because of the public's thirst for information about how to protect themselves and their families. This was ironic in the sense that police efforts to improve community relations led the public to ask for information about how best to control crime. Because of this history, crime prevention as a police strategy refers not so much to preventive patrol as to special programs designed to make citizens, homes, and businesses more difficult to victimize. Organizationally, crime prevention units are often combined with community services and community relations units rather than with patrol or investigations.

Some police departments assign one or more officers to crime prevention duties. These officers then specialize in performing security surveys, giving public crime prevention lectures and presentations, and organizing community participation in crime prevention programs. Other departments have chosen to assign crime prevention duties to all patrol officers. Under this model, each officer is responsible for crime prevention duties on his or her beat.

One method, called **target hardening**, seeks improvements in doors, windows, locks, alarms, lighting, and landscaping that make illegal entry into homes and businesses more difficult and time-consuming. Another method is to train citizens to avoid threatening situations and to react correctly when attacked or threatened. Still other methods encourage citizens to watch out for their neighbors' property and even to patrol their own neighborhoods.

Early crime prevention efforts evolved into **crime prevention through environmental design (CPTED)**, which includes target hardening as well as territorial reinforcement, where a sense of security is increased in settings where people live and work through activities that encourage informal control of the environment. CPTED overlaps with the modern strategies of community policing and problem-oriented policing by localizing police services, collaborating with other city agencies (e.g., parks or utility departments) to resolve problems, and maintaining regular police–citizen communication about neighborhood problems. Inside Policing 4.1 describes some of the strategies that may be applied through CPTED.

In trying to build a more crime-free environment, some cities are requiring police input regarding building designs. In Tempe, Arizona, for example, an ordinance was passed that requires police approval of any commercial building, park, or residential housing development built in the city. Tempe police officers review construction blueprints and visit building sites to ensure that crime prevention features are built into the designs; officers address issues such as parking lot locations, lighting, and the placement of plants and counters in stores. The goal is to provide employees and residents with a better view of their surroundings and to reduce places where criminals may hide. Getting police involved in building designs for crime prevention is similar to the long-established practice of the city's relying on fire department officials to help determine building codes for fire prevention purposes ("Building a More Crime-Free Environment" 1998).

Yet another approach is **community crime prevention**, which is based on the assumption that if a community can be changed, so can the behavior of those who live there. Attempts to change communities often include: (1) organizing the community to improve and strengthen relationships among residents to encourage them to take preventive precautions and to obtain more political and financial resources; (2) changing building and neighborhood design to improve both public and police surveillance, which improves guardianship; (3) improving the appearance of an area to decrease the perception that it is a receptive target for crime; and (4) developing activities and programs that provide a more structured and supervised environment (e.g., recreation programs).

The evidence is mixed regarding the overall effects of crime prevention programs. Target hardening and increased community participation in crime prevention certainly may contribute to crime reduction, and evidence is available that crime prevention programs sometimes make citizens feel safer and more willing to report suspicious activity (Rosenbaum 1987). For example, when used properly, street lighting has been shown to reduce crime (Welsh and Farrington 2004). The Neighborhood Watch program is also associated with modest reductions in crime (Holloway, Bennett, and Farrington 2008). However, the current tendency is to oversell community crime prevention as *the* solution to every community's crime and fear of crime problems. Yet some communities may not be receptive to such programs; citizen participation is frequently difficult to maintain over extended periods, and some programs may have unintended side effects such as increased fear among some participants.

An increasingly popular approach to crime prevention that closely parallels problem-oriented policing is **situational crime prevention** (Clarke 1997). This approach emphasizes the necessity of tailoring crime prevention responses to the specific characteristics of the crime problem being addressed—it rejects any one-size-fits-all thinking. Rather than looking for a solution to all robberies, for example, situational crime prevention

INSIDE POLICING 4.1 CPTED: Strategies and Trends

What Police and Residents Can Do

Police departments, community residents, and local officials all have roles to play in implementing a comprehensive CPTED and community policing strategy to promote public safety in private neighborhoods, business areas, and public housing.

Police can do the following:

- Conduct security surveys for residents and provide security improvements such as adequate lighting and locks.
- Conduct patrols of parks and other public spaces to eliminate crime and drug use.
- Use their substations to inform residents of high-risk locations in the neighborhood.
- Work with urban planners and architects to review the designs and plans to enhance community security.
- Prepare educational materials for building owners and managers to deal with problem tenants and improve the livability and security of rental units.
- Control traffic flow to reduce the use of streets by criminals and increase neighborhood cohesion and resident interaction.

Residents can do the following:

- Engage in clean-up programs to remove trash or graffiti.
- Carry out programs to improve the appearance, safety, and use of public spaces.
- Conduct their own patrols to identify neighborhood problems.
- Join an organized block watch program.

Specific crime prevention activities include the following:

- Security in parks. Parks can be refurbished, lighting can be installed, and opening and closing times can be scheduled to improve security. Adopt-a-park programs can be used to involve residents in cleaning up trash and litter and providing information to police about illegal activities being carried out in recreational areas. Recreational events can be scheduled to increase the community's informal social control of these places.
- Building regulations. Local government can be encouraged to use building codes as well as inspection and enforcement powers to increase environmental security. The owners of deteriorated or abandoned buildings can be required to repair, secure, or demolish them. Provisions related to security can also be incorporated into the city building code.

Civil Remedies

Civil actions can be used against building owners or tenants to control criminal activity or the inappropriate use of property. These actions may include the following:

- Obtaining title to abandoned property by community-improvement associations.
- Using nuisance abatement, along with inspections by public works, building, fire, housing, or utility authorities, to control criminal behavior or drug use in specific buildings or settings.
- Encouraging leases that contain language that controls illegal activities of tenants.
- Using anti-trespassing laws to control unwanted loitering.
- Enforcing liquor laws to control violence and disorderly behavior around bars or liquor stores (especially at closing times).

SOURCE: Adapted from D. Fleissner and F. Heinzlemann, "Crime Prevention Through Environmental Design and Community Policing," *Research in Action* (Washington, DC: National Institute of Justice, 1996) 3–4.

might focus particularly on robberies at ATM machines or robberies of taxicab drivers. It also focuses primarily on reducing opportunities for crime by increasing the effort required to commit offenses, increasing the risk of being detected, and reducing the reward should the offense be consummated. Situational crime prevention has achieved substantial success when targeted at a wide variety of types of offenses, including auto theft, shoplifting, thefts from vending machines, assaults at bus stops, and robberies at convenience stores.

Team Policing

The decade of the 1960s was a tumultuous era in the United States, with riots breaking out in many cities. As noted above, in some instances the police actually provided the spark that precipitated these riots. Out of this crisis came the growing recognition that the police lacked responsiveness to, and understanding of, community expectations. Following this urban unrest, it became clear that a different style of police force would be necessary—one that could be more responsive to community needs. Thus, a major reorganization effort toward decentralization and increased community participation, known as **team policing**, was attempted in the early 1970s.

Team policing was first used by the Syracuse Police Department in 1968, and by 1974 as many as 60 departments across the country had attempted some form of team policing (Schwartz and Clarren 1977). According to Sherman, Milton, and Kelley (1973), in theory, team policing was based on reorganizing the patrol force to include one or more quasi-autonomous teams, with a joint purpose of improving police services to the community and increasing job satisfaction of the officers. The team was normally stationed in a particular neighborhood and was responsible for all police services in that neighborhood. It was expected to work as a unit and maintain a close relationship with the community to prevent crime and maintain order.

Sherman and his associates conducted a thorough evaluation of team policing in seven cities. Although team policing had different meanings in each city, six of the seven programs attempted to implement three common operational elements: (1) geographic stability of patrol, that is, permanent assignment of teams of police to small neighborhoods; (2) maximum interaction among team members, including close internal communication among all officers assigned to an area during a 24-hour period, 7 days a week; and (3) maximum communication among team members and the community.

The departments that were the most successful in implementing these three operational elements also had certain organizational supports in common, including (1) unity of supervision (i.e., one supervisor responsible for a given area at all times), (2) lower-level flexibility in policy making, (3) unified delivery of services, and (4) combined investigative and patrol functions. There was wide variation by city in planning and implementing the various elements. Some programs achieved overwhelming success in certain areas. For example, the Venice (Los Angeles) team developed hundreds of block captains, who exchanged crime information with police on a regular basis; one team in Holyoke virtually abandoned preventive patrol since the citizenry informed them almost immediately of many crimes in progress. In both Dayton and Holyoke, community boards composed of representatives chosen by local groups (e.g., Parent–Teacher Associations, civic associations, tenant organizations) participated in police policy making; the Dayton team also used medical and welfare agencies for referrals most frequently instead of making arrests (Sherman, Milton, and Kelley 1973).

On the whole, however, most programs differed little from the traditional policing of the past. For instance, in none of the cities studied was a decentralized patrol style realized (i.e., authority and decision making were not delegated down to street officers). There appeared to be three major reasons why team policing either failed or reached only partial success:

1. Departmental middle management, which saw team policing as a threat to their power, subverted and, in some cases, actively sabotaged the plans.

2. The dispatching technology did not permit the patrols to remain in their neighborhoods, despite stated intentions about adjusting that technology to projects.

3. The patrols never received a sufficiently clear definition of how their behavior and role should differ from those of a regular patrol; at the same time, they were considered an elite group by their peers, who often resented not having been chosen for the project (Sherman, Milton, and Kelley 1973, 107–108).

Although it is apparent that team-policing experiments, to a large extent, failed owing to a lack of proper planning and training, it is also true that the amount of change required in switching from a highly bureaucratic, authoritarian structure to a decentralized, democratic one was simply too great—especially in a relatively short period of time. Another hurdle facing those departments attempting such a significant change was that no attempt had been made to establish a departmental climate of innovation. As will be noted in Chapter 6, all these hurdles also confront police departments attempting to move to community policing.

Furthermore, because team policing was based on decentralized decision making for patrol officers, some police managers became concerned with the problem of accountability. For example, in another well-documented study in Cincinnati, Ohio, known as COMSEC (Community Sector Team Policing Experiment), top administrators had second thoughts about the program as it progressed. Although they wanted the teams to be responsive to the community, they "feared that with the promised autonomy and reduction in central control, their officers might become less productive or even corrupt" (Schwartz and Clarren 1977, 7). Of course, that is precisely why strong, bureaucratic, central control had become a mainstay in police administration over past decades (see Chapter 5). The dilemma with such centralized control, however, is not only lack of community responsiveness, but also reduction of morale among officers (who have fewer decision-making responsibilities).

Team policing was the fad of the 1970s, but it was a "flash in the pan"—by the 1980s it had disappeared. Other developments, however, helped it reappear a decade or so later in the form of community policing.

Foot Patrol and Broken Windows

Many observers now believe that the abandonment of foot patrol by most American police departments by the mid-1900s changed the nature of police work and negatively affected police–citizen relations. Officers assigned to large patrol car beats do not develop the intimate understanding of and cordial relationship with the community that foot patrol officers assigned to small beats develop. Officers on foot are in a position to relate more intimately with citizens than officers driving by in cars.

The results of two research studies, together with the development of small portable police radios, gave a boost to the resurgence of foot patrol starting in the 1980s. Originally, the police car was needed to house the bulky two-way radio. Today, foot patrol officers carry tiny, lightweight radios that enable them to handle calls promptly and to request information or assistance whenever needed. They are never out of touch and they are always available.

An experimental study conducted in Newark, New Jersey, was unable to demonstrate that either adding or removing foot patrol affected crime in any way (Police Foundation 1981). This finding mirrored what had been found 7 years earlier in Kansas City regarding motorized patrol. Citizens involved in the foot patrol study, however, were less fearful of crime and more satisfied with foot patrol service than with motor patrol. Also, citizens were aware of additions and deletions of foot patrol in their neighborhoods, a finding that stands in stark contrast to the results of the Kansas City study, in which citizens did not even notice changes in the levels of motorized patrol. A second major foot patrol research program in Flint, Michigan, reported findings that were similar to the Newark findings, except that crime too decreased (Trojanowicz 1982).

These studies were widely interpreted as demonstrating that, even if foot patrol did not decrease crime, at least it made citizens feel safer and led to improvements in police–community relations. Why the difference between motorized patrol and foot patrol? In what has come to be known as the **broken-windows** thesis, foot patrol officers pay more attention to disorderly behavior and minor offenses than do motor patrol officers (Wilson and Kelling 1982). Also, they are in a better position to manage their beats, to understand what constitutes threatening or inappropriate behavior, and to observe and correct it. Foot patrol officers are likely to pay more attention to derelicts, petty thieves, disorderly persons, vagrants, panhandlers, noisy juveniles, and street people, who, although not committing serious crimes, cause concern and fear among many citizens. Failure to control even the most minor aberrant activities on the street contributes to neighborhood fears. Foot patrol officers have more opportunity than motor patrol officers to control street disorder and reassure ordinary citizens (see Figure 4.1 for a tool that can be used to discuss neighborhood problems with residents).

Geography plays a large role in determining the viability of foot patrol as a police strategy, of course. The more densely populated an area, the more the citizenry will travel on foot and the more street disorder there will be. The more densely populated an area, the more likely that foot patrol can be effectively used as a police strategy. Although foot patrol may never again become the dominant police strategy it once was, it can play a large role in contributing police services to many communities.

Community Policing

Starting in the 1980s, an even broader approach than community relations and foot patrol began developing. More and more police departments began employing foot patrol as a central component of their operational strategy, rather than as a novelty or an accommodation to downtown business interests. Crime prevention programs became more and more reliant on community involvement, as in neighborhood watch, community patrol, and "crimestoppers" programs. Police departments began making increased use of civilians and volunteers in various aspects of policing and made permanent geographic assignment an important element of patrol deployment. This all came to be called **community policing**, entailing a substantial change in police thinking,

Community Foot Patrol Program	PROBLEM IDENTIFICATION INTERVIEW	DATE / / .

RESPONDENT'S PROFILE

☐ Business   ☐ Residence   Community Name _____

Address: _____   No. of Persons Interviewed _____

Years in Neighborhood: ☐ Less Than 1   ☐ 1 to 2   ☐ 3 to 5   ☐ Over 5

Age Group: ☐ Less Than 18   ☐ 18 – 29   ☐ 30 – 39   ☐ 40 – 49
☐ 50 – 59   ☐ Over 60

Sex: ☐ Male   ☐ Female

Race: ☐ White   ☐ Black   ☐ Oriental   ☐ Hispanic   ☐ Other

INTERVIEW QUESTIONS

1. When you think of neighborhood problems or crime, what are your concerns? _____

2. How often does this problem occur?
☐ Periodically   ☐ Isolated Incident   ☐ Constantly   ☐ Frequently

3. How has this problem inconvenienced you or changed your daily life? _____

4. What do you feel is the cause of the problem? _____

5. What do you feel could be done to correct the problem? _____

6. Do you feel the police department is responsive to the needs of your neighborhood. (i.e. have the police services been adequate in your neighborhood ?) If not, explain. _____

7. Do you feel the county government has been responsive to your neighborhood's needs? (Do not restrict to crime.) If not, explain. _____

8. _____
9. _____
10. _____

FIGURE 4.1 Problem-Identification Interview.

SOURCE: From J. Scannell, *Community Foot Patrol Officer (CFPO) Guidelines and Procedures*, 1998, 36–37. Reprinted by permission of Baltimore County Police Department, Towson, Maryland.

one where police strategy and tactics are adapted to fit the needs and requirements of the different communities the department serves, where there is a diversification of the kinds of programs and services on the basis of community needs and demands for police services and where there is considerable involvement of the community with police in reaching their objectives. *(Reiss 1985, 63)*

Community policing is the logical combination of more than 30 years of police effectiveness research and decades of experimentation with police–community relations programs, crime prevention strategies, and team policing. It can be thought of as an attempt to harness the advantages of foot patrol and generalize them throughout all police field services, with an emphasis on broken-windows theory and its focus on minor crime, disorder, and fear of crime. In Voices from the Field, former Police Chief Darrel Stephens from Charlotte–Mecklenburg, North Carolina, presents his perspective on the impact of community policing as well as problem-oriented policing.

The Office of Community Oriented Police Services (2009), formed in the U.S. Department of Justice in the 1990s, defines community policing as "a philosophy that promotes organizational strategies, which support the systematic use of partnerships and problem-solving techniques, to proactively address the immediate conditions that give rise to public safety issues such as crime, social disorder, and fear of crime." This definition includes several important components that have come to characterize modern community policing—philosophy, organizational strategy, partnerships, and problem solving.

Still, community policing remains many things to many people. A common refrain among proponents is, "Community policing is a philosophy, not a program." Two equally common refrains among police officers are, "This is what we've always done" and "Just tell me exactly what you want me to do differently." Some critics, echoing concerns similar to those expressed by police officers, argue that if community policing is nothing more than a philosophy, it is merely an empty shell (Goldstein 1987).

Elements of Community Policing

It would be easy to list dozens of common characteristics of community policing, starting with foot patrol and mountain bikes and ending with the police as organizers of, and advocates for, the poor and dispossessed. Instead, it may be more helpful to identify three major dimensions of community policing and some of the most common elements within each (Cordner 1999). These three dimensions of community policing are as follows:

- The philosophical dimension.
- The strategic dimension.
- The tactical dimension.

The Philosophical Dimension

Many of its most thoughtful and forceful advocates emphasize that community policing is a new philosophy of policing, perhaps constituting even a paradigm shift away from reform/professional-model policing. The philosophical dimension includes the central ideas and beliefs underlying community policing. Three of the most important of these are citizen input, broad function, and personalized service.

Citizen Input. Community policing takes the view that, in a free society, citizens should have open access to police organizations and input to police policies and decisions. Access and input through elected officials are considered necessary but not sufficient. Individual neighborhoods and communities should have the opportunity to influence how they are policed, and legitimate interest groups in the community should be able to discuss their views and concerns directly with police officials. Police departments, like other agencies of government, should be responsive and accountable.

Mechanisms for achieving greater **citizen input** are varied. Some police agencies use systematic and periodic community surveys to elicit citizen input (Bureau of Justice Assistance

VOICES FROM THE FIELD

Darrel Stephens
Director of State and Local Initiatives, Public Safety Leadership Program, Johns Hopkins University

Question: What difference has community policing and problem-oriented policing made in American policing?

Answer: Policing in America has changed over my 40-year career. It is not the same institution that was chronicled in the series of Presidential Commission reports on crime and the administration of justice in the late 1960s and early 1970s—it is much better. A great deal more is known about the impact of the fundamental strategies the police have used for many years to address crime problems. We know more about the limitations of the police and how they might be more effective. Police departments are more diverse, educational levels of police officers have significantly increased, and both citizen oversight and community engagement are stronger.

This change has come about for a number of reasons, but two are particularly significant. The first is the advancement of the ideas of community and problem-oriented policing over the past 20 years as better ways of delivering police services to the community. The second is the research that provided the foundation for these ideas to ride the crest of the political wave that invested unprecedented levels of federal funding into local policing.

Prior national efforts to improve the police and address concerns with crime had accepted the basic premise on which the police and criminal justice system rested. Most people believed the best way to deal with crime was to increase the number of police, improve training and equipment, develop systems to reduce response time, build more prison beds, issue harsher sentences, and federalize more crimes that had historically been the responsibility of the states and local government.

The community and problem-oriented policing initiatives took a different approach. These ideas called for a fundamental change in the way the police related to citizens and stakeholders. Citizens are more than the "eyes and ears" of the police to feed the criminal justice system—they are viewed as partners who have ideas, resources, and the ability to do things that can prevent crime as well as solve it. The police use problem-solving techniques to gain deeper insight into the issues that they are called on to address and to develop tailored solutions that have a longer-lasting impact on the problem. Moreover, these solutions are not confined to a law enforcement response. The response might be aimed at prevention or engaging other community or governmental resources that are in a better position to deal with the problem than the police could.

Community and problem-oriented policing have touched most police agencies in America and have significantly improved the quality of policing. But things have changed in recent years—the status of community and problem-oriented policing is currently a bit unsettled. September 11 added additional responsibilities to police and local government as they work to prevent an attack and, at the same time, improve response capabilities. Many new ideas compete for the attention of the police—Compstat, Intelligence-Led Policing, Evidence-Based Policing, Predictive Policing—that create confusion over how these ideas fit together and their actual operational focus. The economy has also caused personnel reductions that have forced some departments to back away from engaging the community in problem-solving in place of just responding to calls and assigning tactical units to hot-spots where they rely on aggressive patrol tactics and visibility.

The next few years will reveal how community and problem-oriented policing fit in the policing strategies of the future. They have clearly played an important and productive role over the past 25 years—hopefully they will continue as a prominent feature of future policing models

Darrel Stephens served as police chief in Charlotte–Mecklenburg, North Carolina, St. Petersburg, Florida, and Newport News, Virginia. He was also the Executive Director of the Police Executive Research Forum.

1994a). Others rely on open forums, town meetings, radio and television call-in programs, and similar methods open to all residents. Some police officials meet regularly with citizen advisory boards, ministry alliances, minority group representatives, business leaders, and other formal groups. These techniques have been used by police chief executives, district commanders, and ordinary patrol officers; they can be focused as widely as the entire jurisdiction or as narrowly as a beat or a single neighborhood.

Today, police departments are moving quickly to use websites, blogs, social networking, and social media (including Twitter and Facebook) to further enhance their communication with the public (Barnes and Sipes, 2010). The techniques used to achieve citizen input are really less important than the end result, however. Community policing emphasizes that police departments should seek and carefully consider citizen input when making policies and decisions that affect the community. Any other alternative would be unthinkable in an agency that is part of a government "of the people, for the people, and by the people."

Broad Police Function. Community policing embraces a broad view of the police function rather than a narrow focus on crime fighting or law enforcement (Kelling and Moore 1988). Historical evidence is often cited to show that the police function was originally quite broad and varied and that it narrowed only in recent decades, perhaps because of the influence of the reform/legalistic model and popular media representations of police work. Social science data are also frequently cited to show that police officers actually spend relatively little of their time dealing with serious offenders or investigating violent crimes.

This broader view of the police function recognizes the kinds of nonenforcement tasks that police already perform and seeks to give them greater status and legitimacy. These include order maintenance, social service, and general assistance duties. They may also include greater responsibilities in protecting and enhancing "the lives of those who are most vulnerable—juveniles, the elderly, minorities, the poor, the disabled, the homeless" (Trojanowicz and Bucqueroux 1990, xiv). In the bigger picture of the **broad police function**, the police mission is seen to include resolving conflict, helping victims, preventing accidents, solving problems, and reducing fear, as well as reducing crime through apprehension and enforcement.

Personal Service. Community policing supports tailored policing based on local norms and values and individual needs. An argument is made that the criminal law is a very blunt instrument and that police officers inevitably exercise wide discretion when making decisions. Traditionally, individual officers have made arrests and other decisions based on a combination of legal, bureaucratic, and idiosyncratic criteria, while the police department maintained the myth of full or at least uniform enforcement (Goldstein 1977). Under community policing, officers are asked to consider the "will of the community" when deciding which laws to enforce under what circumstances, and police executives are asked to tolerate and even encourage such differential and personalized policing.

Differential or tailored policing primarily affects police handling of minor criminal offenses, local ordinance violations, public disorder, and service issues. Some kinds of behavior proscribed by state and local law, and some levels of noise and disorder, may be seen as less bothersome in some neighborhoods than in others. Similarly, some police methods, including such aggressive tactics as roadblocks as well as more prevention-oriented programs such as landlord training, may coincide with norms and values in some neighborhoods but not others.

Even the strongest advocates of community policing recognize that a balance must be reached between differential neighborhood-level policing and uniform jurisdiction-wide policing. Striking a healthy and satisfactory balance between competing interests has always been one of the central concerns of policing and police administration. Community policing simply argues that neighborhood-level norms and values should be added to the mix of legal, professional, and organizational considerations that influences decision making about policies, programs, and resources at the executive level as well as at the enforcement level on the street.

This characteristic of community policing is also aimed at overcoming one of the most common complaints that the public has about government employees in general, including police officers—that they do not seem to care and are more interested in "going by the book" than in providing quality, **personalized service**. Many citizens seem to resent being subjected to "stranger policing" and would rather deal with officers who know them and whom they know. Of course, not every police–citizen encounter can be amicable and friendly. But officers who generally deal with citizens in a friendly, open, and personal manner may be more likely to generate trust and confidence than officers who operate in a narrow, aloof, and/or bureaucratic manner.

The Strategic Dimension

The strategic dimension of community policing includes the key operational concepts that translate philosophy into action. These strategic concepts are the links between the broad ideas and beliefs that underlie community policing and the specific programs and practices by which it is implemented. They ensure that agency policies, priorities, and resource allocation are consistent with a community-oriented philosophy. Three strategic elements of community policing are reoriented operations, geographic focus, and prevention emphasis.

Reoriented Operations. Community policing recommends less reliance on the patrol car and more emphasis on face-to-face interactions through reoriented operations. One objective is to replace ineffective or isolating operational practices (e.g., motorized patrol and rapid response to low-priority calls) with more effective and more interactive practices. A related objective is to find ways of performing necessary traditional functions (e.g., handling emergency calls and conducting follow-up investigations) more efficiently to save time and resources that can then be devoted to more community-oriented activities.

Many police departments today have increased their use of foot patrol, directed patrol, door-to-door policing, and other alternatives to traditional motorized patrol (Cordner and Trojanowicz 1992). Generally, these alternatives seek more targeted tactical effectiveness, more attention to minor offenses and "incivilities," a greater "felt presence" of police, and/or more police–citizen contact. Other police departments have simply reduced their commitment to any form of continuous patrolling, preferring instead to have their patrol officers engage in problem solving, crime prevention, and similar activities when not handling calls and emergencies.

Many police agencies have also adopted differential responses to calls for service (McEwen, Connors, and Cohen 1986; McEwen et al. 2003). Rather than attempting to immediately dispatch a sworn officer in response to each and every notification of a crime, disturbance, or other situation, these departments vary their responses depending upon the circumstances. Some crime reports may be taken over the telephone, some service requests may be referred to other government agencies, and some sworn officer responses may be delayed. A particularly interesting alternative is to ask complainants to go in person to a nearby police mini-station or storefront office, where an officer, a civilian employee, or even a volunteer takes a report or provides other in-person assistance. Use of differential responses helps departments cope with the sometimes overwhelming burden of 911 calls and frees up patrol officer time for other activities, such as patrolling, problem solving, and crime prevention (Fleming and Grabosky 2009).

Traditional criminal investigation has also been reexamined by research (Eck 1992). Some departments have despecialized the activity, reducing the size of the detective unit and making patrol officers more responsible for follow-up investigations. Many have also eliminated the practice of conducting an extensive follow-up investigation of every reported crime, focusing instead on the more serious offenses and on more "solvable" cases. Investigative attention has also been expanded to include a focus on offenders as well as on offenses, especially in the form of repeat offender units that target high-frequency serious offenders. A few departments have taken the additional step of trying to get detectives to expand their case-by-case orientation to include problem solving and crime prevention. In this approach, a burglary detective would be as concerned with reducing burglaries through problem solving and crime prevention as he or she was with solving particular burglary cases.

Not all contemporary alternatives to motorized patrol, rapid response, and criminal investigation are closely allied with community policing. Those specific operational alternatives, and those uses of the freed-up time of patrol officers and detectives, that are consistent with the philosophical and strategic foundations of community policing can be distinguished from those that conform to other philosophies and strategies of policing (Moore and Trojanowicz 1988).

Geographic Focus. Community-policing strategy emphasizes the geographic basis of assignment and responsibility by shifting the fundamental unit of patrol accountability from time of day to place. That is, rather than holding patrol officers, supervisors, and shift commanders responsible for wide areas, but only during their 8- or 10-hour shifts, community policing seeks to establish 24-hour responsibility for smaller areas.

Of course, no single officer works 24 hours a day, 7 days a week, week in and week out. Community policing usually deals with this limitation in one or a combination of three ways: (1) community-police officers assigned to neighborhoods may be specialists, with most call handling relegated to a more traditional patrol unit; (2) each individual patrol officer may be held responsible for long-term problem solving in an assigned neighborhood, even though he or she handles calls in a much larger area and, of necessity, many of the calls in the assigned area are handled by other officers; or (3) small teams of officers share both call-handling and problem-solving responsibility in a beat-size area.

A key ingredient of this **geographic focus**, however it is implemented, is permanency of assignment. Community policing recommends that patrol officers be assigned to the same areas for extended periods of time to increase their familiarity with the community and the community's familiarity with them. Ideally, this familiarity will build trust, confidence, and cooperation on both sides of the police–citizen interaction. Also, officers will simply become more knowledgeable about the community and its residents, aiding early intervention and timely problem identification and avoiding conflict based on misperception or misunderstanding.

It is important to recognize that most police departments have long used geography as the basis for daily patrol assignment. Many of these departments, however, assign patrol officers to different beats from one day to the next, creating little continuity or permanency. Moreover, even in police agencies with fairly steady beat assignments, patrol officers are held accountable only for handling their calls and maintaining order (keeping things quiet) *during their shift*. The citizen's question, "Who in the police department is responsible for my area, my neighborhood?" can then only truthfully be answered "the chief" or, in large departments, "the precinct commander." Neither patrol officers nor the two or three levels of management above them can be held accountable for dealing with long-term problems in specific locations anywhere in the entire community. Thus, a crucial component of community policing strategy is to create some degree of geographic accountability at all levels in the police organization but particularly at the level of the patrol officer, who delivers basic police services and is in a position to identify and solve neighborhood problems.

Prevention Emphasis. Community-policing strategy also emphasizes a more proactive and preventive orientation, in contrast to the reactive focus that has characterized much of policing under the reform/legalistic model. This proactive, preventive orientation takes several forms. One is simply to encourage better use of police officers' time. In many police departments, patrol officers' time not committed to handling calls is either spent simply waiting for the next call or randomly driving around. Under community policing, this substantial resource of free patrol time is devoted to directed enforcement activities, specific crime prevention efforts, problem solving, community engagement, citizen interaction, or similar kinds of activities.

Another aspect of the **prevention emphasis** overlaps with the substantive orientation of community policing and problem-oriented operations. Officers are encouraged to look beyond the individual incidents that they encounter as calls for service and reported crimes to discover underlying problems and conditions (Eck and Spelman 1987). If they can discover such underlying conditions and do something to improve them, officers can prevent the future recurrence of incidents and calls. While immediate response to in-progress emergencies and after-the-fact investigation of crimes will always remain important functions of policing, community policing seeks to elevate before-the-fact prevention and problem solving to comparable status.

Closely related to this line of thinking, but deserving of specific mention, is the desire to enhance the status of crime prevention within police organizations. Most police departments devote the vast majority of their personnel to patrol and investigations, primarily for the purposes of rapid response and follow-up investigation *after* something has happened. Granted, some prevention of crime through the visibility, omnipresence, and deterrence created by patrolling, rapid response, and investigating is expected, but the weight of research over the past 2 decades has greatly diminished these expectations (Kelling et al. 1974; Greenwood and Petersilia 1975; Spelman and Brown 1982). Despite these lowered expectations, however, police departments still typically devote only a few officers specifically to crime prevention programming and do little to encourage regular patrol officers to engage in any kind of crime prevention activity beyond routine riding around.

Moreover, within both informal and formal police cultures, crime solving and criminal apprehension are usually more highly valued than crime prevention. An individual officer is more likely to be commended for arresting a bank robber than for initiating actions that prevent such robberies. Detectives usually enjoy higher status than uniformed officers (especially in the eyes of the public), whereas within many police agencies crime prevention officers are seen as public relations functionaries, kiddie cops, or worse. To many police officers, crime prevention work is simply not real police work.

The preeminence of reactive crime fighting within police and popular cultures is under-standable, given the dramatic nature of emergencies, crimes, and investigations. Much of police work is about responding to trouble and fixing it, about the contest between good and evil. Responding to emergencies and fighting crime have heroic elements that naturally appeal to both police officers and citizens. Given the choice, however, almost all citizens would prefer not being victimized in the first place to being dramatically rescued. Most citizens would agree that "an ounce of prevention is worth a pound of cure." This is not to suggest that police should turn their backs on reactive handling of crimes and emergencies, but only that before-the-fact prevention should be given increased consideration.

A final element of community policing's preventive focus takes more of a social wel-fare orientation, particularly toward juveniles. An argument is made that police officers, by serving as mentors and role models and by providing educational, recreational, and even counseling services, can affect people's behavior in positive ways that ultimately lead to reductions in crime and disorder. In essence, police are asked to support and augment the efforts of families, churches, schools, and social service agencies. This kind of police activity is seen as particularly necessary by some to offset the deficiencies and correct the failures of these other social institutions in modern America.

The Tactical Dimension

The tactical dimension of community policing ultimately translates ideas, philosophies, and strategies into concrete programs, practices, and behaviors. Even those who insist that "community policing is a philosophy, not a program" must concede that unless community policing eventually leads to some action, some new or different behavior, it is all rhetoric and no reality (Greene and Mastrofski 1988). Indeed, many commentators have taken the view that community policing is little more than a new police marketing strategy that has left the core elements of the police role untouched (see, e.g., Klockars 1988; Manning 1988; Weatheritt 1988). Three of the most important tactical elements of community policing are positive interaction, partnerships, and problem solving.

Positive Interaction. Policing inevitably involves some negative contacts between officers and citizens—arrests, tickets, stops for suspicion, orders to halt disruptive behav-ior, inability to make things much better for victims, and so forth. Community policing recognizes this fact and recommends that officers offset it as much as they can by engaging in positive interactions whenever possible. Positive interactions have further benefits as well, of course: they generally build familiarity, trust, and confidence on both sides; they remind officers that most citizens respect and support them; they make the officer more knowledge-able about people and conditions on the beat; they provide specific information for criminal investigations and problem solving; and they break up the monotony of motorized patrol.

Many opportunities for **positive interaction** arise in the course of call handling. Too many officers rush to clear their calls, however, often in response to workload concerns and pressure from their superiors, peers, and dispatchers. As a result, they typically do a medio-cre job of handling the immediate incident and make little or no attempt to identify under-lying conditions, secure additional information, or create satisfied customers. The prime directive seems to be to do as little as possible to clear the call quickly and get back in the car and on the radio, ready to go, to do little or nothing at the next call. Getting there rap-idly and then clearing promptly take precedence over actually delivering much service or accomplishing anything. Community policing suggests, instead, that officers should look at calls as opportunities for positive interaction, quality service, and problem identification.

Even more opportunities for positive interaction can be seized during routine patrol if officers are willing to exit their vehicles and take some initiative. Officers can go in and out of stores and in and out of schools, talk to people on the street, knock on doors, and so forth. They can take the initiative to talk not only with shopkeepers and their customers but also with teenagers, apartment dwellers, tavern patrons, and anybody else they run across in public places or who is approachable in private places. Police should insert themselves wherever people are and talk to those people, not just watch them.

Partnerships.   Participation of the community in its own protection is one of the central elements of community policing (Bureau of Justice Assistance 1994c). This participation can run the gamut from watching neighbors' homes to reporting drug dealers to patrolling the streets. It can involve participation in problem identification and problem-solving efforts, in crime prevention programs, in neighborhood revitalization, and in youth-oriented educational and recreational programs. Citizens may act individually or in groups, they may collaborate with the police, and they may even join the police department by donating their time as police department volunteers, reserves, or auxiliaries.

Under community policing, police agencies are expected not only to cooperate with citizens and communities but also to actively solicit input and participation and build **partnerships** (Bureau of Justice Assistance 1994b). The exact nature of this participation can and should vary from community to community and from situation to situation, in keeping with the problem-oriented approach. As a general rule, however, police should avoid claiming that they alone can handle crime, drug, or disorder problems, and they should encourage individual citizens and community groups to shoulder some responsibility for dealing with such problems (Scott and Goldstein 2005).

Police have sometimes found it necessary to engage in community organizing as a means of accomplishing any degree of citizen participation in problem solving or crime prevention. In disorganized and transient neighborhoods, residents are often so distressed, fearful, and suspicious of each other (or just so unfamiliar with their neighbors) that police have literally had to set about creating a sense of community where none previously existed. As difficult as this kind of community organizing can be, and as far from the conventional police role as this may seem, these are often the very communities that most need both enhanced police protection and a greater degree of citizen involvement in crime prevention, order maintenance, and general watchfulness over public spaces.

One vexing aspect of community organizing and community engagement results from the pluralistic nature of our society. Differing and often conflicting interests are found in many communities, and they are sometimes represented by competing interest groups. Thus, the elders in a community may want the police to crack down on juveniles, whereas the youths themselves complain of few opportunities for recreation or entertainment. Tenants may seek police help in organizing a rent strike, whereas landlords want police assistance in screening or managing the same tenants. Finding common interests around which to rally entire communities, or just identifying common interests on which to base police practices, can be very challenging and, at times, impossible.

It is important to recognize that this inherent feature of pluralistic communities does not arise because of community policing. Police have long been caught in the middle between the interests of adults and juveniles, landlords and tenants, and similar groups. Sometimes the law has provided a convenient reference point for handling such conflicts, but just as often police have had to mediate, arbitrate, or just take the side of the party with the best case. Moreover, when the law has offered a solution, it has frequently been a temporary or unpopular solution and one that resulted in the police taking sides, protestations of "we're just enforcing the law" notwithstanding.

Fortunately, nearly all citizens want to be safe from violence, want their property protected, and want some level of orderliness in their neighborhoods. Officers can usually find enough consensus in communities upon which to base cooperative efforts aimed at improving safety and public order. Sometimes, apparently deep conflicts between individuals or groups recede when attention is focused on how best to solve specific neighborhood problems. It would be naive to expect overwhelming community consensus in every situation, but it is equally mistaken to think that conflict is so endemic that widespread community support and participation cannot be achieved in many circumstances.

Problem Solving. Supporters of community policing are convinced that the very nature of police work must be altered from its present incident-by-incident, case-by-case orientation to one that is more problem oriented (Goldstein 1990). Certainly, incidents must still be handled and cases must still be investigated. Whenever possible, however, attention should be directed toward underlying problems and conditions. Following the medical analogy, policing should address causes as well as symptoms and should adopt the epidemiological public health approach as much as the individual doctor's clinical approach.

This **problem-solving** approach should be characterized by several important features: (1) it should be the standard operating method of policing, not an occasional special project; (2) it should be practiced by personnel throughout the ranks, not just by specialists or managers; (3) it should be empirical, in the sense that decisions are made on the basis of information that is gathered systematically; (4) it should involve, whenever possible, collaboration between police and other agencies and institutions; and (5) it should incorporate, whenever possible, community input and participation, so that it is the community's problems that are addressed (not just the police department's) and so the community shares in the responsibility for its own protection.

The problem-solving process consists of four steps (see Inside Policing 4.2): (1) careful identification of the problem; (2) careful analysis of the problem; (3) a search for alternative solutions to the problem; and (4) implementation and assessment of a response to the problem. Community input can be incorporated within any or all of the steps in the process. Identification, analysis, and assessment should rely on information from multiple sources. A variety of alternative solutions should be considered, including, but not limited to, traditional enforcement methods. Typically, the most effective solutions are those that combine several different responses, including some that draw on more than just the police department's authority and resources.

A crucial characteristic of the problem-oriented approach is that it seeks solutions tailored to specific community problems. Arrests and law enforcement are not abandoned—rather, an effort is made in each situation to determine which alternative responses best fit the problem. Use of criminal law is always considered, as are civil law enforcement, mediation, community mobilization, referral, collaboration, alteration of the physical environment, public education, and a host of other possibilities (see Inside Policing 4.3). The common-sense notion of choosing the tool that best fits the problem, instead of simply grabbing the most convenient or familiar tool in the toolbox, lies close to the heart of the problem-solving method. A carpenter would not use a hammer when a saw would be more effective. Similarly, police should use the criminal law when it is the most effective tool for the situation, but not when some other tool would actually work better.

INSIDE POLICING 4.2   The SARA Model

A commonly used problem-solving method is the **SARA model** (scanning, analysis, response, and assessment). The SARA model contains the following elements:

Scanning:
- Identifying recurring problems of concern to the public and the police.
- Identifying the consequences of the problem for the community and the police.
- Prioritizing those problems.
- Developing broad goals.
- Confirming that the problems exist.
- Determining how frequently the problem occurs and how long it has been taking place.
- Selecting problems for closer examination.

Analysis:
- Identifying and understanding the events and conditions that precede and accompany the problem.
- Identifying relevant data to be collected.
- Researching what is known about the problem type.
- Taking inventory of how the problem is currently addressed and the strengths and limitations of the current response.
- Narrowing the scope of the problem as specifically as possible.
- Identifying a variety of resources that may be of assistance in developing a deeper understanding of the problem.
- Developing a working hypothesis about why the problem is occurring.

Response:
- Brainstorming for new interventions.
- Searching for what other communities with similar problems have done.
- Choosing among the alternative interventions.
- Outlining a response plan and identifying responsible parties.
- Stating the specific objectives for the response plan.
- Carrying out the planned activities.

Assessment:
- Determining whether the plan was implemented (a process evaluation).
- Collecting pre- and postresponse qualitative and quantitative data.
- Determining whether broad goals and specific objectives were attained.
- Identifying any new strategies needed to augment the original plan.
- Conducting ongoing assessment to ensure continued effectiveness.

SOURCE: http://www.popcenter.org/about-SARA.htm.

We have used the terms *problem solving* and *problem-oriented policing* somewhat interchangeably, but they can and should be differentiated. Problem solving refers to small-scale, officer-level activity within the context of community policing. For example, if an officer is trying to resolve a landlord–tenant dispute, she or he should first analyze the situation and then, based on what was found, possibly arbitrate the dispute, or refer the tenant to legal aid, or help the landlord develop a better and more binding rental contract, or all of the above. In any event, the response should be tailored to the specifics of the situation and should take advantage of handlers, guardians, and place managers whenever possible, instead of relying solely on police authority and the criminal law.

INSIDE POLICING 4.3 **The Problem Analysis Triangle**

While the SARA model is useful as a way of organizing the approach to recurring problems, it is often very difficult to figure out just exactly what the real problem is. The **problem analysis triangle** (sometimes referred to as the crime triangle) provides a way of thinking about recurring problems of crime and disorder. This idea assumes that crime or disorder results when (1) likely offenders and (2) suitable targets come together in (3) time and space in the absence of capable guardians for that target. A simple version of a problem analysis triangle looks like this:

Offenders can sometimes be controlled by other people: those people are known as handlers. Targets and victims can sometimes be protected by other people as well: those people are known as guardians. And places are usually controlled by someone: those people are known as managers. Thus, effective problem solving requires understanding how offenders and their targets/victims come together in places and understanding how those offenders, targets/victims, and places are or are not effectively controlled. Understanding the weaknesses in the problem analysis triangle in the context of a particular problem will point the way to new interventions. A complete problem analysis triangle looks like this:

Problems can be understood and described in a variety of ways. No one way is definitive. They should be described in whichever way is most likely to lead to an improved understanding of the problem and effective interventions. Generally, incidents that the police handle cluster in four ways:

- Behavior. Certain behavior(s) is (are) common to the incidents—for example, making excessive noise, robbing people or businesses, driving under the influence, crashing vehicles, dealing drugs, stealing cars. There are many different behaviors that might constitute problems.
- Place. Certain places can be common to incidents. Incidents involving one or more problem behaviors may occur at, for example, a street corner, a house, a business, a park,

a neighborhood, or a school. Some incidents occur in abstract places such as cyberspace, on the telephone, or through other information networks.

- Person. Certain individuals or groups of people can be common to incidents. These people could be either offenders or victims. Incidents involving one or more behaviors, occurring in one or more places, may be attributed to, for example, a youth gang, a lone person, a group of prostitutes, a group of chronic inebriates, or a property owner. Or incidents may be causing harm to, for example, residents of a neighborhood, senior citizens, young children, or a lone individual.
- Time. Certain times can be common to incidents. Incidents involving one or more behaviors, in one or more places, caused by or affecting one or more people may happen at, for example, traffic rush hour, bar closing time, the holiday shopping season, or during an annual festival.

There is growing evidence that, in fact, crime and disorder do cluster in these ways. It is not evenly distributed across time, place, or people. Increasingly, police and researchers are recognizing some of these clusters as:

- Repeat offenders attacking different targets at different places.
- Repeat victims repeatedly attacked by different offenders at different places.
- Repeat places (or hot spots) involving different offenders and different targets interacting at the same place.

SOURCE: http://www.popcenter.org/about/?p=triangle.

Problem-oriented policing, as contrasted with problem solving, is simply broader in scope with deeper analysis and more wide-ranging solutions. For example, the officer handling the landlord–tenant dispute might suspect that it is a recurring problem, not just at one location but at many rental properties throughout the city. Further analysis by this officer or someone else in the police department would reveal the actual size of the whole problem, where it occurs (and where it does not), and so on. If it is a big problem, then city-wide responses tailored to the nature of the problem would be devised and implemented. One possibility might be landlord training. The process of scanning, analysis, response, and assessment would the same as in smaller-scale problem solving; it would just be addressed to a bigger and broader problem. Similarly, attention would be focused on offenders and their handlers, victims and their guardians, and places and their managers, just as in problem solving. Hopefully, however, broader-scale problem-oriented policing would result in a bigger impact on the whole problem city-wide compared with smaller-scale problem solving at just one location.

Problem-oriented policing is very consistent with community policing, but conceptually separate. The principal aim of problem-oriented policing is to identify and reduce all kinds of chronic crime and disorder problems, whereas the principal aim of community policing is to repair and improve one particular type of problem, police–community relations. They are both very important developments in modern policing, and they are quite complementary.

A great deal of information about community policing is available from the Office of Community Oriented Policing, found on-line at http://www.cops.usdoj.gov. The best source of information about problem-oriented policing is the Center for Problem-Oriented Policing, found online at http://www.popcenter.org. One of the most practical and beneficial resources offered at this site is the *Problem-Specific Guides for Police* on topics such as false burglar alarms, drive-by shootings, rave parties, and prescription fraud (see Inside Policing 4.4). Each of these guides briefly summarizes research about the problem itself and various responses that have been used to deal with the problem around the world and then offers realistic options tailored to the specific characteristics of the problem. There are currently 58 of these guides. They are short, practical, and periodically updated.

Implementing Community Policing

The evidence today about the implementation of community policing is mixed and somewhat contradictory. This is not really surprising. Because community policing is such a broad and flexible concept, it has been implemented differently in different places. In fact, what one jurisdiction calls community policing another jurisdiction committed to community policing might not even recognize. This has been both the greatest strength and the greatest weakness of community policing.

INSIDE POLICING 4.4 **Problem-Specific Guides for Police**

The *Problem-Specific Guides for Police* summarize knowledge about how police can reduce the harm caused by specific crime and disorder problems. The guides are available in print versions and web versions. Guides are updated periodically on the basis of new research and police practice.

1. Assaults in and Around Bars, 2nd ed. (2006)
2. Street Prostitution, 2nd. ed. (2006)
3. Speeding in Residential Areas, 2nd. ed. (2010)
4. Drug Dealing in Privately Owned Apartment Complexes (2001)
5. False Burglar Alarms, 2nd ed (2007)
6. Disorderly Youth in Public Places (2001)
7. Loud Car Stereos (2001)
8. Robbery of Automated Teller Machines (2001)
9. Graffiti (2002)
10. Thefts of and From Cars in Parking Facilities (2002)
11. Shoplifting (2002)
12. Bullying in Schools (2002)
13. Panhandling (2002)
14. Rave Parties (2002)
15. Burglary of Retail Establishments (2002)
16. Clandestine Methamphetamine Labs (2006)
17. Acquaintance Rape of College Students (2002)
18. Burglary of Single-Family Houses (2002)
19. Misuse and Abuse of 911 (2002)
20. Financial Crimes Against the Elderly (2003)
21. Check and Card Fraud (2003)
22. Stalking (2004)

23. Gun Violence Among Serious Young Offenders (2004)
24. Prescription Fraud (2004)
25. Identity Theft (2004)
26. Crimes Against Tourists (2004)
27. Underage Drinking (2004)
28. Street Racing (2004)
29. Cruising (2004)
30. Disorder at Budget Motels (2005)
31. Drug Dealing in Open-Air Markets (2005)
32. Bomb Threats in Schools (2005)
33. Illicit Sexual Activity in Public Places (2005)
34. Robbery of Taxi Drivers (2005)
35. School Vandalism & Break-ins (2005)
36. Drunk Driving (2006)
37. Juvenile Runaways (2006)
38. Exploitation of Trafficked Women (2006)
39. Student Party Riots (2006)
40. People with Mental Illness (2006)
41. Child Pornography on the Internet (2006)
42. Witness Intimidation (2006)
43. Burglary at Single-Family House Construction Sites (2006)
44. Disorder at Day Labor Sites (2007)
45. Domestic Violence (2007)
46. Thefts of and From Cars on Residential Streets & Driveways (2007)
47. Drive-by Shootings (2007)
48. Bank Robbery (2007)
49. Robbery of Convenience Stores (2007)
50. Traffic Congestion Around Schools (2007)
51. Pedestrian Injuries & Fatalities (2007)
52. Bicycle Theft (2008)
53. Abandoned Vehicles (2008)
54. Spectator Violence in Stadiums (2008)
55. Child Abuse and Neglect in the Home (2010)
56. Homeless Encampments (2010)
57. Stolen Goods Markets (2010)
58. Theft of Customers' Personal Property in Cafes and Bars (2010)

SOURCE: http://www.popcenter.org/problems/.

Positive Indications

Specific illustrations of successful community policing implementation are readily available. The Chicago Alternative Policing Strategy, which began in 1993, remains the best big-city example of department-wide community policing, with sustained implementation for well over a decade and measurable effects on crime, public opinion, citizen involvement, problem solving, and African Americans' views about neighborhood problems (Chicago Community Policing Evaluation Consortium 2003; Skogan and Steiner 2004; Skogan 2006). Successful implementation in many smaller jurisdictions has also been documented (Office of Community-Oriented Policing Services 2002). Descriptions of award-winning community policing and problem-oriented policing efforts can be found on the Internet (International Association of Chiefs of Police 2010; Center for Problem-Oriented Policing Center 2010; see also Sampson and Scott 2000).

National surveys have consistently found a high level of community policing implementation among police departments around the country. For example, in 2002 the Police Executive Research Forum (Fridell and Wycoff 2003) surveyed a sample of 282 police departments that had also been surveyed in 1993 and 1997. The 16 *most common* community policing activities (of a total of 56 choices offered by the survey), claimed by at least 75 percent of responding agencies on the 2002 survey, are listed below:

- Citizens attend police–community meetings.
- Citizens participate in neighborhood watch.
- Citizens help police identify and resolve problems.
- Citizens serve as volunteers within the police agency.
- Citizens attend citizen–police academies.
- Police hold regularly scheduled meetings with community groups.
- Police have interagency involvement in problem solving.
- Police have youth programs.
- Police have victim-assistance programs.
- Police use regulatory codes in problem solving.
- Police work with building-code enforcement.
- Agencies use fixed assignments to specific beats or areas.
- Agencies give special recognition for good community policing work by employees.
- Agencies classify and prioritize calls.
- Agencies do geographically based crime analysis.
- Agencies use permanent neighborhood-based offices or stations.

These most common community policing activities paint a fairly positive picture of citizen participation, partnerships, outreach, problem solving, and organizational change in place in American policing in 2002. Over half of these activities had registered below the 75 percent implementation threshold on the first survey in 1993, indicating that real progress had been made over the decade in the implementation of community policing.

As a measure of that progress, the individual community policing activities listed below are those that showed a 10 percent or greater increase in implementation between 1993 and 2002 (or between 1997 and 2002, if the item was not included on the 1993 survey). The nature of these community policing activities, which became more widely adopted over the decade, lends solid support to a positive interpretation of community policing progress since 1993. (None of the 56 COP activities showed a 10 percent or greater decrease in adoption between 1993 and 2002.)

- Citizens participate in citizen patrols.
- Citizens attend citizen–police academies.
- Police engage in interagency code enforcement.
- Police work with community corrections.
- Police work with alternative dispute resolution.
- Police use regulatory codes in problem solving.
- Police work with building-code enforcement.
- Agencies have a disciplinary system to support problem solving.
- Agencies have a specialized problem-solving unit.
- Agencies have landlord-training programs.
- Agencies provide citizen training in problem solving.
- Agencies classify and prioritize calls.
- Agencies do geographically based crime analysis.
- Agencies have job descriptions that include community policing.
- Agencies do citizen surveys to determine needs and priorities.
- Agencies do citizen surveys to evaluate police services.
- Agencies use fixed shifts.
- Agencies have physical decentralization of field services.
- Agencies use permanent neighborhood-based offices or stations.
- Agencies use employee evaluations to reinforce community policing.

Questions and Doubts

As positive as this picture seems, there is also evidence that community policing is sometimes more rhetoric than reality (Mastrofski 2006). For example, the seven *least common* community policing activities, claimed by less than 25 percent of the responding agencies on the 2002 survey, were as follows:

- Citizens help prepare work agreements for problem solving.
- Citizens participate in the police promotional process.
- Citizens participate in a court-watch program.
- Citizens help review complaints against the police.
- Citizens participate in the selection process for new officers.
- Citizens help evaluate officers' performance.
- Agencies have decentralized crime analysis.

These least common COP activities illustrate the limited role that the community has thus far taken in police administration and policy making. Apparently, it has become common for citizens to participate in neighborhood watch and neighborhood problem solving, attend meetings with the police, attend citizen–police academies, and do volunteer work within the police agency. It has *not* become common for citizens to play a role in evaluating their neighborhood police officers, selecting and promoting police officers, or reviewing complaints against the police. It would seem that police agencies have tended to adopt a relatively modest version of community policing, according to the surveys. Few police agencies have shown much interest in the most "radical" component of community policing—real power sharing with the community (Brown 1985).

Information from other sources tends to corroborate the sometimes limited or modest nature of community policing as implemented. For example, community-police officers in cities seem to spend relatively little time actually interacting with or engaging citizens (Parks et al. 1999). Instead, they spend considerable time in the office doing administration and paperwork, and like their regular patrol colleagues, they spend considerable time on routine patrol and conducting personal business. This pattern of time utilization also holds true for small-town and rural officers (Frank and Liederbach 2003). Similarly, while community-police officers often develop higher job satisfaction and a more positive outlook toward the community than their patrol officer peers, many other basic attitudes and beliefs related to traditional law enforcement practices remain unchanged (Pelfrey 2004). This suggests that the experience of doing community policing has a strong but not necessarily life-changing impact on officers, perhaps because of the countervailing influence of the traditional police culture.

It has also been found that everyday problem solving by police officers typically does not conform very closely to the analytical and collaborative problem-solving model promoted by the advocates of problem-oriented policing (Cordner and Biebel 2002). Typical street-level problem solving tends to focus on problems that are small in scope; officers analyze those problems primarily through personal observation and tend to draw on personal experience for responses, which almost always include enforcement, often in concert with one or two other responses (see Figure 4.2). The reality of street-level problem solving seems to be that it is often more thoughtful, analytical, collaborative, and creative than mere knee-jerk enforcement, but it is still a far cry from the ideal model of problem-oriented policing (also see Scott 2000).

Another limitation of community policing is that there is little evidence that it enhances community processes in ways that would be expected to subsequently reduce fear, disorder, and crime (Kerley and Benson 2000). This is probably because most community policing is still *police centered,* with the police more often doing things directly to try to reduce crime and disorder rather than working to strengthen the community so that it might more successfully protect itself. This is not to say that many police agencies have not tried to increase public participation in crime prevention and other activities, but the ideal of police and citizen *coproduction of public safety* has not generally been realized to any significant degree. On a related issue, community policing has clearly helped the police work more closely with some parts of the community, but other segments of the community have been more resistant or simply harder to engage (Skogan 2006).

Of equal concern is that the adoption of community policing *strategies* at the managerial level does not always lead to the utilization of community-based *tactics* in the field (Bennett 1998). Implementation of any new program in a complex organization is a management challenge—implementation of such a far-reaching philosophical and strategic change as community policing requires careful planning, systematic attention to detail, leadership, and patience (see Chapter 6). These capabilities are not always in great supply in police agencies, especially when agencies are buffeted by political pressures and/or

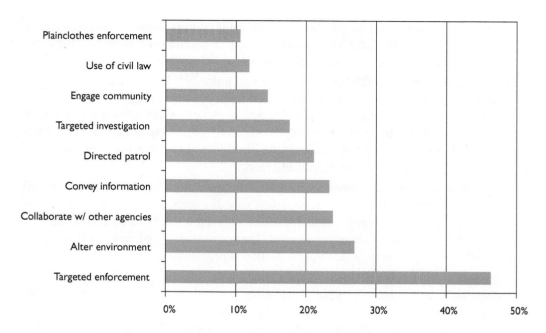

FIGURE 4.2 **Response Strategies Utilized in Problem-Oriented Policing Projects in San Diego (Top Nine Responses).**

Source: G. Cordner and E. P. Biebel, *Problem-Oriented Policing in San Diego: A Study in POP in Practice in a Big-City Police Department.* Report submitted to the National Institute of Justice, Washington, DC, 2002. Available at—http://www.ncjrs.gov/pdffiles1/nij/grants/200518.pdf.

frequent changes in top management, both of which are common. Consequently, many police departments have a much stronger commitment to community policing at the top than at the street level.

One of the logical methods for enhancing community policing implementation is training. A substantial amount of community policing training has been made available over the past 15 years by police academies, Regional Community Policing Institutes (see http://www.cops.usdoj.gov/Default.asp?Item=115), and others. Studies have indicated that this training is often successful in conveying knowledge about community policing, developing skills, and changing attitudes (see, for example, Scarborough et al. 1998). However, research also indicates that the effects of community policing training do not survive once the officer leaves training and enters (or reenters) the police culture, where traditional values and practices tend to be held supreme (Haarr 2001). One step that many police agencies have overlooked is the necessity of revising their performance evaluation systems to incorporate community policing and problem-solving activities (Lilley and Hinduja 2006). A common refrain in many organizations, including police departments, is "if you don't measure it, it won't happen."

Evaluating Community Policing

The *effectiveness* of community policing has been extremely difficult to determine for several interrelated reasons:

- **Programmatic complexity**—there is no single definition of community policing or any universal set of program elements. Police agencies around the country (and around the world) have implemented a wide array of organizational and operational innovations under the label "community policing." Because community policing is not one consistent "thing," it is difficult to say whether "it" works.

- **Multiple effects**—the number of intended and unintended effects that might accrue to community policing is considerable. Community policing might affect crime, fear of crime, disorder, community relations, and/or police officer attitudes, to mention just a few plausible impacts. The reality of these multiple effects, as opposed to a single bottom-line criterion, severely reduces the likelihood of a simple yes or no answer to the question, "Does community policing work?"

- **Variation in program scope**—the scope of community policing projects has varied from single-officer assignments to department-wide efforts. Some of the most positive results have come from projects that involved only a few specialist officers, small special units, or narrowly defined target areas. The generalizability of these positive results to full-scale department-wide implementation is problematic.

- **Research design limitations**—despite impressive efforts by police officials and researchers, most community policing studies have had serious research design limitations. These included lack of control groups, failure to randomize treatments, and a tendency to measure only short-term effects. Consequently, the findings of many community policing studies do not have as much credibility as we might hope.

It is difficult, if not impossible, to assess the implementation and effectiveness of community policing without taking into account the impact of over $9 billion in federal government support for community policing starting in 1994, in the form of the Office of Community Oriented Policing Services and the promise of an additional 100,000 "Clinton cops." The *Attorney General's Report to Congress* in the year 2000 claimed that over 105,000 new community policing officers had been funded during the first 6 years of the Crime Control Act. An independent evaluation estimated that the actual number of new officers on the street was closer to about 75,000, and some of these were not newly created and filled positions but rather existing sworn personnel who had been "redeployed" to community policing duties through creative utilization of technology and civilian (nonsworn) personnel (Roth and Ryan 2000).

The attorney general's report also noted that crime had reached its lowest level since 1968, and a COPS office-funded evaluation similarly credited community policing with making a substantial contribution to crime decreases during the 1990s (Zhao, Scheider, and Thurman 2002). That evaluation has subsequently been sharply criticized on methodological grounds, however (Ekstrand 2003; Muhlhausen 2003). It is difficult to say at this point how much of the crime decrease was the result of community policing versus other police initiatives (such as aggressive enforcement), greatly expanded incarceration of offenders, the waning of the crack cocaine epidemic, economic factors, or demographic changes in society.

At the level of particular jurisdictions and police agencies, as opposed to the national level, the scientific evidence on whether community policing reduces crime is weak (Skogan and Frydl 2004). Systematic reviews of the best, most rigorous studies have concluded that diffuse police strategies such as community policing have not been shown to reduce crime, whereas more specific strategies (like neighborhood watch and targeted hot spots policing) do consistently lead to crime reductions (Weisburd and Eck 2004; Braga 2008). Notably, however, problem-oriented policing is also one of those targeted approaches that has been found to be effective in reducing crime (Weisburd et al. 2008). Logically, then, it would seem to follow that when community policing includes a strong problem-solving component it is more likely to be effective in reducing crime than when it lacks such a focus.

But remember, crime reduction is not the only objective of the police or the sole criterion by which they are judged. Evaluations have generally found that sincere community policing efforts lead to improved public trust in the police, which is a very important outcome in a free society. In addition, community policing has often led to public reassurance and reductions in fear of crime (Cordner 2010). These, too, are important outcomes with real consequences for individuals and communities. Clearly, then, community policing has been quite successful in several respects and holds the promise of effectiveness in crime reduction too, as long as it is paired closely with problem-oriented policing.

Community Policing Today

In Chapter 2 we discussed the development of modern policing in America, including the political era and the reform era. Kelling and Moore (1988) utilized a corporate framework for understanding this development and further argued that the police have evolved into a third era: the community problem-solving era.

The current chapter has discussed community policing and problem-oriented policing more fully. The community policing philosophy is distinctive from the previous eras of American policing in several ways. The police derive their authority from community support, in addition to law and professionalism. Crime prevention and problem solving become more important functions of the police. The organizational structure required to accomplish this is necessarily decentralized to strategically tailor police services to unique problems in varying environments. In other words, police activity is not one size fits all (as suggested in the reform era). The police enjoy a closer relationship to the public; however, this relationship is more consultative than in previous eras. Demand for police services is influenced by the nature of local problems and channeled through citizens with whom officers consult on a regular basis. To this end, 9-1-1 and dispatch-directed activities are reserved for emergencies and comprise a lower proportion of the day-to-day demands on officers. Problem solving includes a variety of tactics beyond law enforcement and necessarily must be adapted from place to place. The overall outcome of success is measured by citizens' quality of life and satisfaction with police services. Crime rates are merely one of many indicators of quality of life (Kelling and Moore 1988).

As mentioned in the beginning of this chapter, community policing became the dominant policing model in the 1990s. Even then, however, it had to compete with more targeted, aggressive, and legalistic methods like zero-tolerance policing and hot-spot policing that promised more immediate effects on street crime and disorder. These methods became allied with an extremely popular new management model called Compstat (discussed in Chapter 5) that was developed in New York and given credit for dramatic crime decreases in that city. Then, the events of September 11 occurred. That terrorist attack naturally caused many to quickly conclude that police needed to become more militaristic to confront such a vicious enemy. Community policing seemed anything but the tough, hard-nosed strategy that would be needed to win the War on Terror.

Since that time, however, a different line of thinking has also emerged. Even in the fight against terrorism, police are unlikely to find out about attacks in advance unless someone (some member of the community) steps forward with information. Also, who is more likely to notice a dangerous new person in the neighborhood or a local youth becoming radicalized—an officer who works there occasionally or an officer who works there every day? It has dawned on police, counterterrorism strategists, and political leaders that if a police department has a good and trusting relationship with its community and intimate knowledge of its own about the people in the community, it has a much better chance of playing the role of "first preventer" and not just first responder after a deadly attack has already occurred (Kelling and Bratton 2006). In other words, community policing is a promising strategy for dealing with terrorism too, not only crime, disorder, and public trust.

Community policing remains in the mix of popular and viable police strategies today. A generation of police has been hired since it became commonplace, and a generation of community residents has experienced its benefits. In fact, one reason why community policing is not discussed quite as much today is that many people basically now take it for granted. Who would disagree that the police need the public's cooperation to control crime and disorder? Who would disagree that a police department that loses the public's trust finds itself in difficult straits?

That said, it is also true that many police agencies implemented community policing only half-heartedly, federal financial support for community policing is greatly diminished from the levels seen in the 1990s, and the current recessionary times are tightly squeezing local governments and their police departments. Many police agencies are now cutting back on the very tactics and programs that won so much public approval and trust over the past 15–20 years, not because they want to but because their budgets are decimated; others never really got started, even though they may have adopted the rhetoric of community policing. In this scenario, those police officials whose support for community policing always was lukewarm, and those who favor more aggressive and legalistic tactics, have an opportunity to seize the upper hand. It will be interesting in these challenging times to see whether community policing will survive and thrive or whether its stature will be reduced.

Summary

One of the important objectives of police departments is the establishment of good relations with the community. Good police–community relations are desirable in their own right in an open society, and they are also desirable because they help the police obtain the public's cooperation in controlling crime, disorder, and fear. As of the 1960s, if not before, police in America began to recognize that they had police–community relations problems, especially, but not exclusively, with minority groups. Police tried a series of programs and strategies, including police community relations programs, crime prevention programs, team policing, and foot patrol, in an effort to bridge the gap with the community. In the 1980s and 1990s these efforts led to the development and popularity of community policing, which can be understood in terms of a variety of philosophical, strategic, and tactical elements.

During its short history, community policing has proven difficult to measure and evaluate. Clearly, many police departments have implemented some aspects of community policing, but overall the degree of implementation should be considered modest. Although some police officers have embraced community policing wholeheartedly, there is still much resistance at the street level. Evaluations of community policing have been quite promising, especially on the issue of improving police–community relations. However, when serious crime problems arise, both the police and the community still seem more inclined to resort to traditional enforcement responses than to full-fledged community policing. In addition, when police budgets get tight, it sometimes seems that components of community policing are among the first to be cut back or eliminated. Despite these concerns, however, it is also true that an entire generation of Americans, and American police, has experienced some of the tangible benefits of community policing and is unlikely to forsake them easily.

Critical Thinking Questions

1. The relationship between the police and the community, and especially minority communities, seems to be a chronic problem. Why do you think that is the case?

2. The public seems to react positively to foot patrol. Citizens feel safer and rate the police more highly when served by officers on foot. Why do you think this is the case?

3. A key element of community policing is citizen input. What methods would you suggest the police use to get citizen input about priorities and policies? Who needs citizen input the most—the police chief or the beat patrol officer?

4. Getting police officers and police departments to really emphasize crime prevention, as opposed to law enforcement and criminal investigation, has proven to be difficult. Why do you think this is the case?

5. The partnerships element of community policing has been criticized as a mere public relations campaign—an effort to get the public to like the police better. How would you go about establishing meaningful partnerships that accomplish more than just good public relations?

6. Many police departments have encountered difficulties in implementing community policing. Why do you think it has been so difficult to translate the rhetoric of community policing into reality?

7. The federal government provided several billion dollars in support of community policing starting in 1994, but that support has waned since 2001. Do you think community policing will survive without federal financial support? Do you think it should, especially in the post-9/11 era? What do you think the federal government should do at this point to help improve American policing?

References

Attorney General. 2000. "Attorney General's Report to Congress: Office of Community Oriented Policing Services." Available at http://www.cops.usdoj.gov/Default.asp? Open=True&Item=289.

Barnes, T. and Sipes, L. 2010. "Three Years of Social Media: Lessons Learned." *Community Policing Dispatch* 3 (January). Available at http://cops.usdoj.gov/html/dispatch/January_2010/social_media.htm.

Bennett, T. 1998. "Police and Public Involvement in the Delivery of Community Policing." In J. P. Brodeur (ed.), *How to Recognize Good Policing: Problems and Issues,* pp. 107–122. Thousand Oaks, CA: Sage Publications.

Boydstun, J. E., and Sherry, M. E. 1975. *San Diego Community Profile: Final Report.* Washington, DC: Police Foundation, 1975.

Braga, A. 2008. *Police Enforcement Strategies to Prevent Crime in Hot Spot Areas: Crime Prevention Research Review* No. 2. Washington, DC: Office of Community Oriented Policing Services.

Brown, L. P. 1985. "Police-Community Power Sharing." In W. A. Geller (ed.), *Police Leadership in America: Crisis and Opportunity,* pp. 70–83. New York: Praeger.

"Building a More Crime-Free Environment." 1998. *Law Enforcement News.* November 15: 5.

Bureau of Justice Assistance. 1994a. *A Police Guide to Surveying Citizens and Their Environment.* Washington, DC: Author.

Bureau of Justice Assistance. 1994b. *Neighborhood-Oriented Policing in Rural Communities: A Program Planning Guide.* Washington, DC: Author.

Bureau of Justice Assistance. 1994c. *Understanding Community Policing: A Framework for Action.* Washington, DC: Author.

Caiden, G. E. 1977. *Police Revitalization.* Lexington, MA: D. C. Heath.

Center for Problem-Oriented Policing. 2010. See http://www.popcenter.org/library/awards/goldstein/ for winners of the Herman Goldstein Problem-Oriented Policing Awards since 1993.

Chicago Community Policing Evaluation Consortium. 2003. *Community Policing in Chicago, Years Eight and Nine: An Evaluation of Chicago's Alternative Policing Strategy and Information Technology Initiative.* Springfield, IL: Illinois Criminal Justice Information Authority.

Clarke, R. V. (ed.). 1997. *Situational Crime Prevention: Successful Case Studies,* 2nd ed. New York: Harrow and Heston.

Cordner, G. 1999. "Elements of Community Policing." In L. K. Gaines and G. Cordner (eds.), *Policing Perspectives: An Anthology,* pp. 137–149. Los Angeles: Roxbury.

———. 2010. *Reducing Fear of Crime: Strategies for Police.* Washington, DC: Office of Community Oriented Policing Services. Available at http://www.cops.usdoj.gov/files/RIC/Publications/ e110913242-ReducingFear.pdf.

Cordner, G., and Biebel, E. P. 2002. *Problem-Oriented Policing in San Diego: A Study of POP in Practice in a Big-City Police Department.* Report submitted to the National Institute of Justice, Washington, DC. Available at http://www.ncjrs.org/pdffiles1/nij/grants/200518.pdf.

Cordner, G., and Trojanowicz, R. C. 1992. "Patrol." In G. Cordner and D. C. Hale (eds.), *What Works in Policing? Operations and Administration Examined,* pp. 3–18. Cincinnati, OH: Anderson.

Eck, J. E. 1992. "Criminal Investigation." In G. Cordner and D. C. Hale (eds.), *What Works in Policing? Operations and Administration Examined,* pp. 19–34. Cincinnati, OH: Anderson.

Eck, J. E., and Spelman, W. 1987. *Problem-Solving: Problem-Oriented Policing in Newport News.* Washington, DC: Police Executive Research Forum.

Ekstrand, L. E. 2003. "Technical Assessment of Zhao and Thurman's 2001 Evaluation of the Effects of COPS Grants on Crime." Washington, DC: U.S. General Accounting Office, GAO-03–867R. Available at http://www.gao.gov/new.items/d03867r.pdf.

Fleissner, D., and Heinzelmann, F. 1996. "Crime Prevention Through Environmental Design and Community Policing." *Research in Action.* Washington, DC: National Institute of Justice.

Fleming, J., and Grabosky, P. 2009. "Managing the Demand for Police Services, or How to Control an Insatiable Appetite. *Policing: A Journal of Policy and Practice* 3: 281–291.

Frank, J., and Liederbach, J. 2003. "The Work Routines and Citizen Interactions of Small-town and Rural Police Officers." In Q. C. Thurman and E. F. McGarrell, eds., *Community Policing in a Rural Setting,* pp. 49–60. Cincinnati, OH: Anderson.

Fridell, L., Lunney, R., Diamond, D., and Kubu, B. 2001. *Racially Biased Policing: A Principled Response.* Washington, DC: Police Executive Research Forum.

Fridell, L., and Wycoff, M. A. 2003. "The Future of Community Policing." Washington, DC: Police Executive Research Forum. Mimeo.

Goldstein, H. 1977. *Policing a Free Society.* Cambridge, MA: Ballinger.

———. 1987. "Toward Community-Oriented Policing: Potential, Basic Requirements and Threshold Questions." *Crime & Delinquency* 33: 6–30.

Goldstein, H. 1990. *Problem-Oriented Policing.* New York: McGraw–Hill.

Greene, J., and Mastrofski, S. (eds.). 1988. *Community Policing: Rhetoric or Reality?* New York: Praeger.

Greenwood, P. W., and Petersilia, J. 1975. *The Criminal Investigation Process, Volume I: Summary and Policy Implications.* Santa Monica, CA: Rand Corporation.

Haarr, R. N. 2001. "The Making of a Community Policing Officer: The Impact of Basic Training and Occupational Socialization on Police Recruits." *Police Quarterly* 4: 402–433.

Holloway, K., Bennett, T., and Farrington, D.P. 2008. *Does Neighborhood Watch Reduce Crime? Crime Prevention Research Review* No. 3. Washington, DC: Office of Community Oriented Policing Services.

International Association of Chiefs of Police. 2010. Community Policing Award. Available at http://www.theiacp.org/About/Awards/CommunityPolicingAward/tabid/614/Default.aspx.

Kelling, G. L., Pate, T., Dieckman, D., and Brown, C. E. 1974. *The Kansas City Preventive Patrol Experiment: A Summary Report*. Washington, DC: Police Foundation.

Kelling, G. L., and W. J. Bratton. 2006. "Policing Terrorism." *Civic Bulletin* No. 43. New York: Manhattan Institute for Policy Research.

Kelling, G. L., and Moore, M. 1988. "The Evolving Strategy of Policing." *Perspectives on Policing*. Washington, DC: National Institute of Justice.

Kerley, K., and Benson, M. 2000. "Does Community-Oriented Policing Help Build Stronger Communities?" *Police Quarterly* 3: 46–69.

Klockars, C. B. 1988. "The Rhetoric of Community Policing." In J. Greene and S. Mastrofski (eds.), *Community Policing: Rhetoric or Reality?*, pp. 239–258. New York: Praeger.

Lilley, D., and Hinduja, S. 2006. "Organizational Values and Police Officer Evaluation: A Content Comparison Between Traditional and Community Policing Agencies." *Police Quarterly* 9: 486–513.

Manning, P. K. 1988. "Community Policing as a Drama of Control." In J. Greene and S. Mastrofski (eds.), *Community Policing: Rhetoric or Reality?*, pp. 27–46. New York: Praeger.

Mastrofski, S. 2006. "Community Policing: A Skeptical View." In D. Weisburd and A. A. Braga, (eds.), *Police Innovation: Contrasting Perspectives*. Cambridge: Cambridge University Press.

McEwen, J. T., Connors, E. F., and Cohen, M. I. 1986. *Evaluation of the Differential Police Responses Field Test*. Washington, DC: National Institute of Justice.

McEwen, T., Spence, D., Wolff, R., Wartell, J., and Webster, B. 2003. *Call Management and Community Policing: A Guidebook for Law Enforcement*. Washington, DC: Office of Community Oriented Policing Services.

Moore, M. H., and Trojanowicz, R. C. 1988. "Corporate Strategies for Policing." *Perspectives on Policing*. Washington, DC: National Institute of Justice.

Muhlhausen, D. B. 2003. "GAO Critiques Research Touting COPS Program Effectiveness," WebMemo 313. Washington, DC: Heritage Foundation. Available at http://www.heritage.org/Research/Crime/wm313.cfm.

Office of Community-Oriented Policing Services. 2002. *Community Policing in Smaller Jurisdictions*. Washington, DC: Authors.

———. 2009. *Community Policing Defined*. Washington, DC: Authors. Available at http://www.cops.usdoj.gov/RIC/ResourceDetail.aspx?RID=513.

Parks, R., Mastrofski, S., DeJong, C., and Gray, K. 1999. "How Officers Spend Their Time With the Community." *Justice Quarterly* 16, 3: 483–518.

Pelfrey, W. V., Jr. 2004. "The Inchoate Nature of Community Policing: Differences Between Community Policing and Traditional Police Officers." *Justice Quarterly* 21: 579–601.

Police Foundation. 1981. *The Newark Foot Patrol Experiment*. Washington, DC: Police Foundation.

Reiss, A. J., Jr. 1985. "Shaping and Serving the Community: The Role of the Police Chief Executive." In W. A. Geller (ed.), *Police Leadership in America: Crisis and Opportunity*, pp. 61–69. New York: Praeger.

Rosenbaum, D. P. 1987. "The Theory and Research Behind Neighborhood Watch: Is It a Sound Fear and Crime Reduction Strategy?" *Crime & Delinquency* 33: 103–134.

Roth, J. A., and Ryan, J. F. 2000. "The COPS Program After 4 Years—National Evaluation," Research in Brief. Washington, DC: National Institute of Justice. Available at http://www.urban.org/pdfs/COPS_summary.pdf.

Sampson, R., and Scott, M. 2000. *Tackling Crime and Other Public-Safety Problems: Case Studies in Problem-Solving*. Washington, DC: Office of Community Oriented Policing Services.

Scarborough, K. E., Christiansen, K., Cordner, G., and Smith, M. 1998. "An Evaluation of Community Oriented Policing Training." *Police Forum* 8: 11–15.

Schwartz, A. T., and Clarren, S. N. 1977. *The Cincinnati Team Policing Experiment: A Summary Report.* Washington, DC: Police Foundation.

Scott, M. 2000. *Problem-Oriented Policing: Reflections on the First 20 Years.* Washington, DC: Office of Community Oriented Policing Services.

Scott, M. and Goldstein, H. 2005. *Shifting and Sharing Responsibility for Public Safety Problems: Response Guide No. 3.* Washington, DC: Office of Community Oriented Policing Services. Available at http://www.popcenter.org/responses/responsibility/.

Sherman, L. W., Milton, C. H., and Kelley, T. V. 1973. *Team Policing: Seven Case Studies.* Washington, DC: Police Foundation.

Skogan, W.G. 2006. *Police and Community in Chicago: A Tale of Three Cities.* New York: Oxford University Press.

Skogan, W., and Frydl, K. 2004. *Fairness and Effectiveness in Policing: The Evidence.* Washington, DC: The National Academies Press, National Research Council of the National Academies.

Skogan, W. G., and Steiner, L. 2004. *CAPS at Ten: Community Policing in Chicago.* Chicago: Criminal Justice Information Authority.

Spelman, W., and Brown, D. K. 1982. *Calling the Police: Citizen Reporting of Serious Crime.* Washington, DC: Police Executive Research Forum.

Trojanowicz, R. C. 1982. *An Evaluation of the Neighborhood Foot Patrol Program in Flint, Michigan.* East Lansing, MI: School of Criminal Justice, Michigan State University.

Trojanowicz, R., and Bucqueroux, B. 1990. *Community Policing: A Contemporary Perspective.* Cincinnati, OH: Anderson.

Weatheritt, M. 1988. "Community Policing: Rhetoric or Reality?" In J. Greene and S. Mastrofski, eds., *Community Policing: Rhetoric or Reality?*, pp. 153–176. New York: Praeger.

Weisburd, D. and Eck, J. E. 2004. "What Can Police Do to Reduce Crime, Disorder, and Fear?" *The Annals of the American Academy of Political and Social Science* 593: 42–65.

Weisburd, D., Telep, C. W., Hinkle, J. C., and Eck, J. E. 2008. "The Effects of Problem-Oriented Policing on Crime and Disorder." *Campbell Systematic Reviews 14.* Oslo, Norway: The Campbell Collaboration.

Welsh, B., and Farrington, D. 2004. "Surveillance for Crime Prevention in Public Space: Results and Policy Choices in Britain and America." *Criminology and Public Policy* 3: 497–526.

Wilson, J., and Kelling, G. 1982. "Broken Windows: The Police and Neighborhood Safety." *Atlantic Monthly* 249: 29–38.

Zhao, J., Scheider, M. C., and Thurman, Q. 2002. "Funding Community Policing to Reduce Crime: Have COPS Grants Made a Difference?" *Criminology and Public Policy* 2: 7–32.

Part II

Police Administration

CHAPTER 5

Police Management

CHAPTER OUTLINE

- The Managerial Process
- The Development of Police Management
    Classical Police Management
    Behavioral Police Management
    Contemporary Police Management
- Organizational Design
    Restructuring and Community Policing
    Implementation: Fact or Fiction?
    Criticisms of the Paramilitary Design
    Increasing Influence of Police Paramilitary Units
    Broken-Windows and Zero-Tolerance Policing
    Compstat, Police Legitimacy, and Procedural
      Justice
- Police Goals and Organizational Performance
    Impact of Supervisory Styles on Officer Behavior
    Measuring Police Performance
    Changing Performance Measures

CHAPTER OUTLINE (continued)

- Managing Group Behavior
    - Police Subcultures
    - Employee Organizations
    - Police Unions
- Media Relations
- Summary
- Critical Thinking Questions
- References

KEY TERMS

- broken windows theory
- centralization
- chain of command
- classical principles
- Compstat
- contingency theory
- controlling
- decentralization
- disorder index
- generalists
- goals

- leading
- management
- National Incident-Based Reporting System (NIBRS)
- organization design
- organizing
- paramilitary model
- Public Information Officer (PIO)
- planning

- police legitimacy
- police paramilitary units (PPU)
- procedural justice
- specialization
- systems theory
- total quality management (TQM)
- zero-tolerance policing

THE PROCESS OF POLICING a democratic society is complex. Indeed, because of this complexity, a police department is probably one of the most difficult public institutions to manage effectively. Consequently, it is important to have a fundamental understanding of both the historical and the present-day processes used in managing police departments. Not only are these processes critical to how the police operate and behave in society, but also they contribute to the type of individuals selected to become officers—the subject of Chapter 7.

Management is directing individuals to achieve organizational goals in an efficient and effective manner. The functions carried out by police managers include organizing, leading, planning, and controlling; how well these functions are performed determines, to a large degree, how successful a department will be.

The Managerial Process

Although managers perform each of the functions described above, the time involved in each one varies according to the manager's level in the department. For instance, people at higher levels, such as assistant chiefs, spend a greater proportion of their time in organizing and planning; those at lower levels, such as sergeants, spend more time on *supervision,* which focuses primarily on leading and controlling. The time spent in various functions is also influenced by the size of the department. In a small police department, for instance, a sergeant may function both as an assistant chief and as a supervisor. The four steps of the managerial process, organization, leading, planning, and controlling, are briefly described below.

Organizing is the process of arranging personnel and physical resources to carry out plans and accomplish goals and objectives. Organizational design or structure, job design, group working arrangements, and individual work assignments are subject to the organizing process. Although all managers are involved in organizing, once again the degree and scope differ, depending on their level within the department. While the patrol supervisor is more concerned with work assignments, the chief is more concerned with the overall distribution of personnel and physical resources.

Leading is motivating others to perform various tasks that will contribute to the accomplishment of goals and objectives. Motivating others is a difficult and complex process, especially in civil service organizations, where managers have far less control over salaries and pay incentives than in the private sector. Accordingly, police managers must rely more on internal rewards to motivate employees, such as job satisfaction and feelings of accomplishment. This situation suggests that job design is a key ingredient in motivating police personnel (more on this later). It should be noted that the leadership role for top-level managers can also encompass managing the relationship between the police and the community, as well as other important organizations, including criminal justice and government agencies.

Planning is the process of preparing for the future by setting goals and objectives and developing courses of action for accomplishing them. The courses of action involve such activities as determining mission and value statements, conducting research, identifying strategies and methods, developing policies and procedures, and formulating budgets. Although all managers engage in planning, once again the scope and nature of the activity differ considerably, depending on the managerial level within the department. For instance, whereas a patrol supervisor may develop work schedules and operating activities for the upcoming week, police chiefs may plan activities and changes for the upcoming year. In general, the higher the managerial level, the broader the scope of planning and the longer the time frame for the plan.

Controlling is the process by which managers determine how the quality and the quantity of departmental systems and services can be improved, whether goals and objectives are being accomplished, whether operations are consistent with plans, and whether officers follow departmental policies and procedures. Both *efficiency* (relationship between resources and outputs) and *effectiveness* (degree to which goals and objectives are accomplished) are key concepts in this phase of management. If goals or objectives are not realized or plans, policies, and procedures are not being followed, managers must determine why and take action. Controlling may be the most troublesome managerial function because it may be difficult to determine why performance failures occur and what action to take to improve or correct them. For example, police corruption and brutality continue to be serious problems, despite frequent attempts to determine their causes and correct them.

As noted above, managers at various levels in the department perform their functions differently. Figure 5.1 depicts the various hierarchical levels found in medium to large police departments. Such organizational structures are termed pyramids because the number of personnel decreases as one goes up in the hierarchy (i.e., there are fewer at the top). At the same time, this diminishing group receives increased power, authority, and rewards.

In general, as depicted in Figure 5.1, four separate hierarchical levels of activities exist in larger organizations; smaller organizations (which generally have fewer managerial levels) may have only two or perhaps three levels of hierarchy. This pyramidal structure is known

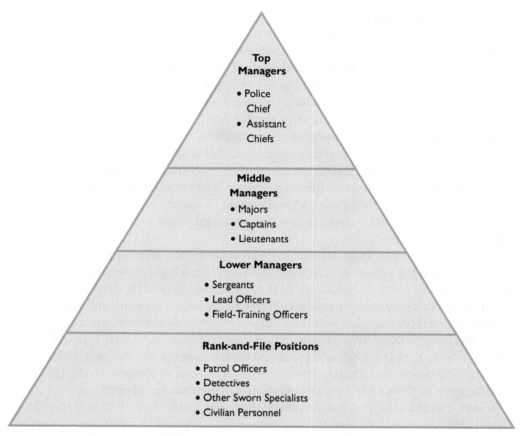

FIGURE 5.1 Organization Pyramid With Levels of Hierarchy.

as the **chain of command**, where the higher the position, the greater the power, authority, and influence. In addition, formal communication in traditional paramilitary structures strictly adheres to the chain of command, emanating from the top of the hierarchy down through the lower levels and back up (it should be noted that strict adherence to the chain regarding communication can create problems with respect to both timeliness of decision making and accuracy of communication). The activities of personnel at each level are as follows: *top managers* conduct overall goal formulation and make policy decisions regarding allocation of resources; *middle managers* formulate objectives and plans for implementing decisions from above and coordinate activities from below; *lower managers* implement decisions made at higher levels and coordinate and direct the work of employees at the lowest level of the organization; and *rank-and-file personnel* carry out specific tasks.

The following discussion of the development of police management theory has relevance to how police departments have been traditionally structured and managed and what impact contemporary developments are having on police management.

The Development of Police Management

The theory and practice of police management have evolved through three major developmental perspectives—classical, behavioral, and contemporary. Each of these perspectives and its impact on police management are described below.

Classical Police Management

The early writers on police management emphasized what is known as a classical approach to organization, including a rigid hierarchical structure, strong centralized control, and authoritarian leadership styles. A cornerstone of this approach was Max Weber's concept of *bureaucracy,* a term he coined at the end of the nineteenth century to identify characteristics that organizations needed to operate on a rational basis. Following the introduction of the bureaucratic model, a number of writers started to develop what have become known as **classical principles** of organization, which were believed to be universal. Some of Weber's administrative principles that reflect this approach include *specialization* (division of work); *authority and responsibility* (right to command and require obedience); *discipline* (necessary for effectiveness); *unity of command* (employees are to receive orders from only one superior); *scalar chain* (hierarchy of authority); and *centralization* (the extent to which decision making is retained by the top organizational levels; Gerth and Mills 1946).

Early police theorists, in an attempt to create a more professional police force, placed great emphasis on the classical principles. The result was a highly bureaucratic structure, managed and organized along military lines in an attempt to insulate the police from partisan politics. This **paramilitary model** emphasized a legalistic approach and authoritarian managerial practices intended to control officers' behavior to improve crime control and lessen corrupt practices. Influential writers promoting these ideals first appeared in the United States in the early 1900s and continued to be influential into the early 1950s. Some editions of the textbooks of these classical writers continued to appear into the 1980s and even the early 1990s and still have an influence on police managerial practices.

A work that had a major impact on police reform was Smith's *Police Systems in the United States* (1940). Smith emphasized that police departments could be significantly improved if they were properly designed and managed according to the "principles of organization," which had won wide acceptance in military and industrial circles. Another significant work that affected police practice was O. W. Wilson's *Police Administration* (1950), followed by later editions with McLaren as coauthor (Wilson and McLaren 1977). The early editions became known as the "bible" of police management, and the prescriptions set forth were, and to some extent still are, followed. Like Smith, Wilson and McLaren suggested that an effective crime-control organization should be designed and managed according to "fundamental" organizational principles, especially with respect to the chain of command and hierarchy of authority.

Behavioral Police Management

Beginning in the early 1970s, police management theorists began attacking the classical approach, with its emphasis on bureaucracy and hierarchical structure, authoritarian managerial practices, and a narrow view of the police role. In line with the increased behavioral research (i.e., the scientific study of human behavior) of the 1950s and 1960s, which placed greater emphasis on worker participation and job satisfaction, these writers stressed a more flexible and democratic organizational model, along with a recognition of the complex nature of the police role.

By the 1960s, a considerable amount of behavioral research had also been completed on what police actually do on the job, indicating that the majority of police work was not directly related to law enforcement, but rather to maintaining order and providing social services (e.g., see Bercal 1970; Cumming, Cumming, and Edell 1965; Goldstein 1968; Parnas 1967; Wilson 1968). Perhaps just as important, it was becoming clear that the police role was broader and more complex than many had originally suspected. This research provided the impetus for a new perspective on police work by suggesting that adherence to a legalistic and technical approach to the job would not be effective. In short, effective policing required qualified personnel who could *use discretion wisely* to deal with a wide range of complex problems and situations.

These findings had serious implications for the well-entrenched paramilitary model. As Bittner noted, "The core of the police mandate is profoundly incompatible with the military posture. On balance, the military bureaucratic organization of the police is a serious handicap" (1970, 51). Bittner viewed the proper use of discretion as central to the professional development of the police role, and he believed that overreliance on regulations and bureaucratic routine seriously inhibited such development. Furthermore, he suggested that although the paramilitary model helped to secure internal discipline, it continued to hinder the development of the police role because "recognition is given for doing well in the department, not outside where all the real duties are located" (54–55). In other words, attention to a neat appearance and conformance to bureaucratic routine were more highly regarded than work methods and performance in the community (i.e., interacting and dealing with the public).

In addition, Goldstein (1977) suggested that the *organizational climate* in police departments must change if the objective is to retain highly qualified (and educated) officers and thus operate effectively in a democratic society. Officers should be more involved in policy making and in determining methods of operation; they should be able to realize their "full potential" in ways other than promotion.

Contemporary Police Management

The increased level of sophistication and findings from behavioral science research led to the development of systems theory and contingency theory and the movement toward private sector influences, including corporate strategy, total quality management, and reinventing government. These developments allowed not only for improved managerial practices, but also for an understanding of the importance of community relationships to the police.

Systems and Contingency Theory. Conceptually, **systems theory** means that all parts of a system (organization) are interrelated and dependent on one another. The importance of applying systems theory to police departments is that it allows managers to understand that any changes made in their unit will have a corresponding impact on other units. Thus, police managers should continually be in contact with one another to make sure that the activities of their units are in agreement with the overall needs and goals of the department.

Police managers should be aware that systems can be viewed as either open or closed. An *open system* interacts with, and adapts to, its environment; a *closed system* does not. In general, all organizations interact with their environment to some degree, but the degree of interaction varies greatly. Essentially, those systems that are more open function more effectively because of their environmental adaptability. The environment for police departments is essentially the community in which they operate; those departments that are relatively more open are more effective because they are aware of community needs and expectations and thus can adapt their practices accordingly. In the past, a lack of interaction with the environment, and thus a lack of understanding of community concerns, has led to serious problems in police–community relations.

If police departments are not managed from an open-systems perspective, they cannot adapt to changing environmental influences and forces and thus will be ineffective, or certainly less effective, in their levels of operation. When this happens, the department will inevitably be forced to change, as external critics make demands that ultimately cannot be ignored. This point has been supported by Zhao's (1996) study of 228 police departments, in which he found that changes toward innovative community policing strategies were more likely to be forced on departments by external environmental demands (e.g., affirmative action programs and community makeup), rather than by consciously chosen internal considerations.

Contingency theory is based on open-systems theory and recognizes that there are many internal and external factors that influence organizational behavior. Because these factors differ according to different organizational circumstances, there is no one "best" way to organize and manage diverse types of police departments. The underlying theme for *contingency management* is that *it all depends* on the particular situation. For example, why does a certain type of leadership work in one type of department but not in other types or in one part of a department but not in other parts? The answer is simply because situations differ. The task for managers, then, is to try to determine in which situations and at what times certain methods and techniques are the most effective.

In the late 1970s, Roberg (1979) applied contingency theory to policing. He emphasized contingency concepts and the necessity of identifying *both* internal and external variables that affect police departmental behavior. Accordingly, such factors as the complex nature of the role, increasing educational levels of employees, and the relatively unstable nature of the environment (e.g., changing laws, cultural diversity, political influences) must be considered in attempting to determine the most effective police management methods. It has become obvious that when such factors are considered, "many of the simplistic classical prescriptions which have been applied to police organization design are clearly inadequate" (Roberg 1979, 190). It was concluded that a less bureaucratic, less centralized design was necessary for police to perform effectively.

Private Sector Influences. Following World War II, a management system focusing on product quality, known as **total quality management (TQM)**, was developed in Japan in an effort to help revitalize Japanese industries. The foundation for this approach lies in *quality-control* techniques and the process of *continuous improvement*. This management process helped turn around the entire Japanese industry, in which "Made in Japan" had become a symbol for inferior products, to become synonymous with the highest-quality products in the world. TQM (also referred to as *quality management*) is a customer-oriented approach that emphasizes human resources and quantitative methods in an attempt to strive toward continuous improvement. To maximize the use of human resources, quality management stresses the importance of employee participation, teamwork, and continuous learning and improvement. The quantitative dimension involves the use of research and statistical techniques to evaluate and improve the processes in an organization and to link those processes to results. First introduced in the private sector, this approach has spread rapidly to the public sector as well—including the police. The first department to utilize quality-management principles was in Madison, Wisconsin. In *Quality Policing: The Madison Experience* (Couper and Lobitz 1991), the police chief of Madison at the time (Couper) and a colleague have written about the experiences of this department's change away from a highly traditional, bureaucratic organization toward a quality-oriented organization. The principles of quality management or "quality leadership" used by this chief in transforming the department are listed in Inside Policing 5.1.

INSIDE POLICING 5.1 Principles of Quality Leadership

1. Believe in, foster, and support teamwork.
2. Make a commitment to the problem-solving process, use it, and let data (not emotions) drive decisions.
3. Seek employees' input before making key decisions.
4. Believe that the best way to improve work quality or service is to ask and listen to employees who are doing the work.
5. Strive to develop mutual respect and trust among employees.
6. Have a customer orientation and focus toward employees and citizens.
7. Manage on the behavior of 95 percent of employees, not on the 5 percent who cause problems; deal with the 5 percent promptly and fairly.
8. Improve systems and examine processes before placing blame on people.
9. Avoid "top-down," power-oriented decision making whenever possible.
10. Encourage creativity through risk taking, and be tolerant of honest mistakes.
11. Be a facilitator and coach; develop an open atmosphere that encourages providing for and accepting feedback.
12. With teamwork, develop with employees agreed-upon goals and a plan to achieve them.

SOURCE: D. C. Couper and S. H. Lobitz, *Quality Policing: The Madison Experience* (Washington, DC: Police Executive Research Forum, 1991), 48.

The process that the Madison Police Department went through in changing to a quality-oriented organization, emphasizing participation and teamwork, was time-consuming and demanding. It took approximately 20 years from the start of the change process in the department to reach a state of general implementation of community policing and quality management (Wycoff and Skogan 1993). If traditional paramilitary departments are to implement similar significant changes, this is the type of long-term sustained effort they must be willing to put forth (see Chapter 6 for further discussion of Madison's change process).

Organizational Design

Organizational design is concerned with the formal patterns of arrangements and relationships developed by police management to link people together to accomplish organizational goals. It was traditionally assumed by the classical school of thought that a pyramidal design was the most appropriate for police departments. Even today, some departments that are moving toward community policing, which requires a less bureaucratic approach, steadfastly cling to a pyramidal design.

The classical design, characterized by many hierarchical levels and narrow spans of control (i.e., a small number of employees per supervisor), allowing for close supervision and control of employees and operations, is known as a *tall structure*. Conversely, a *flat structure* is characterized by few hierarchical levels with wide spans of control (i.e., a large number of employees per supervisor), allowing for greater employee autonomy and less control of operations. These differences between tall and flat structures are shown in Figure 5.2. It is easy to see that the tall structure has two extra levels of hierarchy and narrower spans of control for closer supervision and control over subordinates.

In general, organizations with tall structures attempt to coordinate their activities through **centralization**; that is, authority and decision making are retained by the top organizational levels. In general, organizations with flat structures tend to use **decentralization**, wherein authority and decision making are delegated to lower organizational levels as a mechanism to control their activities. Tall structures also tend to have a greater degree of *specialization* with respect to the division of labor of personnel or the number of activities or tasks each individual performs. In other words, the fewer the number of tasks performed, the greater the level of specialization; conversely, the greater the number of tasks performed, the lower the level of specialization. This means, for example, that patrol officers who perform a greater number of diverse activities beyond traditional policing practices, such as problem solving or investigation, would be referred to as **generalists**.

To make police departments more flexible and to improve decentralized decision making, many departments moving toward community policing are flattening their structures (i.e., reducing hierarchical levels as depicted in Figure 5.2). For example, in Austin, Texas, it was decided to gradually eliminate the rank of deputy chief and one third of the positions of captain. There were several reasons, but for the most part there was a need for more street-level officers to handle calls and be available for the expanded-role concept (i.e., officers as generalists) of the patrol force (Watson, Stone, and DeLuca 1998).

Restructuring and Community Policing Implementation: Fact or Fiction?

As noted above, to implement innovative practices, such as community policing, some restructuring of the traditional paramilitary design is necessary, for example, flattening the

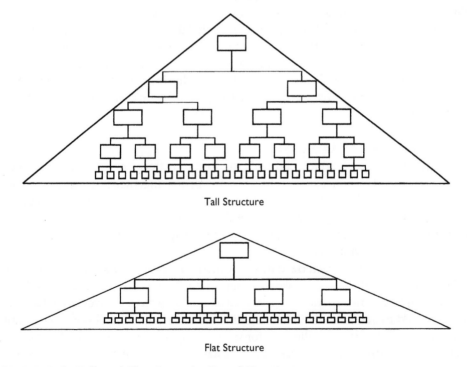

Tall Structure

Flat Structure

FIGURE 5.2 Tall and Flat Organizational Structures.

structure, becoming less specialized, and decentralizing decision making to lower organization levels. However, major organization change in traditional police departments has been difficult to come by. For example, one study by Maguire (1997), which analyzed the structural characteristics of 236 large municipal departments (with 100 or more sworn members), found no significant structural differences among those departments that reported that they had adopted community policing (44 percent), those that reported they were in the planning or implementation stages (47 percent), and those that reported having no plans for community policing (9 percent).A more recent in-depth study by Wilson (2006) using primarily Law Enforcement Management and Administrative Statistics (LEMAS) data on 401 large municipal departments (100 or more sworn employees) from the 1997 and 1999 surveys, found similar results. In general, the results revealed that no relationship existed between organizational structure and community policing; that is, agencies that are more organic in nature (i.e., informal and decentralized with flattened hierarchies) are no more likely to implement community policing than agencies that are mechanistic in nature (i.e., formal and centralized with tall hierarchies).

These findings are contrary to contemporary management thought, which would predict that organic structures are, by their very nature, more likely to be innovative and thus more likely to implement community policing. Thus, these findings draw attention to whether departments that claim to be doing community policing really are. It is one thing, of course, to report in a survey that one's department has implemented (or is implementing) community policing and quite another to structurally change the organization to allow for *sustained adaptation*. For instance, is a department reporting—perhaps even believing—it is implementing community policing to gain professional status, community support, or even federal funding? (2006) findings, for example, rely on LEMAS survey data that do not identify who fills out the surveys (quite possibly a police chief or a close subordinate), and therefore the impartiality of the findings cannot be known.

In addition, during the time frame over which the surveys were distributed and collected, the federal government was providing money to departments to help implement community policing; the author notes that each agency in the survey received $0 to $44,976 per employee, with an average value of $3,287. It would seem logical that agencies receiving federal money for the purpose of implementing community policing would want to promote the idea that the government's money was being well spent.

Based on these findings, it appears that the question remains: Are police departments really changing toward a community policing model or simply reporting that they are for their own purposes (while continuing to operate in a traditional paramilitary fashion)? This is a legitimate question, not only for academics but also for citizens—because their treatment could vary depending on which model their local department is operating under—and will remain unanswered until a valid model of community policing is developed and tested (in an unbiased manner) on a large sample of departments (Maguire 1997).

Criticisms of the Paramilitary Design

The paramilitary design or model has been criticized by police scholars at least since the contemporary police management era. Auten (1981), for instance, suggests that the paramilitary organization treats the patrol officer like a *soldier* and thus is based on inappropriate assumptions about patrol work and democracy. He notes that soldiers work as part of a larger unit; they perform tasks in a prescribed manner; and they must be uniform in appearance, conduct, and behavior. The nature of the police role is quite different from these expectations. First, strict rules cannot be applied to policing because of the nature of the work. Second, orders are rarely required because most of the work by patrol personnel takes place on the street and out of the purview of supervisors. In addition, if the job is to be performed properly, a great amount of initiative and discretion are required. This is particularly true of organizations implementing community policing, where line-level discretion in decision making is seen as a virtue, not a vice. Finally, the managerial philosophy reflected by the paramilitary organization is characterized by an attitude of distrust, control, and punishment. Interestingly, one observer (Cowper 2000) with extensive experience in both policing and the military suggests that military leadership has evolved from strict adherence to the traditional military model (e.g., less reliance on rules, feedback from soldiers), while American police departments continue to adhere more closely to it, with decision making generally more concentrated at the top of the hierarchy. The author's conclusion was that, in some respects, American policing is *more military-like than the military!*

Although such criticisms and charges of ineffectiveness are not new and continue to grow, there has been surprisingly little research conducted either supporting or refuting them. However, a study conducted by Franz and Jones (1987) lends empirical support to the critics' charges. In this study, police officers were compared with employees in other city departments that had not been exposed to the paramilitary design. The researchers found that police employees perceived (1) greater problems with communications, (2) greater amounts of distrust, (3) lower levels of morale, and (4) lower levels of organizational performance. Franz and Jones concluded that "the data presented seriously question the capability of the quasi-military police organizational model to meet today's needs" (p. 161).

Increasing Influence of Police Paramilitary Units

Auten's analogy with the paramilitary model, being based on inappropriate role assumptions about patrol work and the treatment of patrol officers like soldiers, is an interesting perspective when combined with research on the increasing emphasis on highly specialized **police paramilitary units (PPUs)**. PPU is a generic term for units that have traditionally been known as *SWAT* (special weapons and tactics) teams and more recently referred to as *SRTs* (special response teams), *ERUs* (emergency response units), and TACs (tactical action groups) . This section will briefly describe the units, their activities, and how an even stronger paramilitary police culture and community presence may be developing.

These units function as military special-operations teams—often gaining expertise and training from the Navy's Seals and the Army's Rangers—and have as a primary function the threat or use of collective force, not always as a function of last resort. The teams frequently wear full regalia, including black or camouflage battle dress uniforms, with boots, body armor, and helmets; are armed with submachine guns, sniper rifles, percussion grenades, tear gas, pepper gas, and surveillance equipment; and sometimes employ armored personnel carriers. Two separate national surveys provide a developing picture on how these specialized units are increasingly being used. One study by Kraska and Cubellis (1997) consisted of small-locality police departments (municipal and county) with fewer than 100 sworn officers; the second study by Kraska and Kappeler (1997) consisted of medium to large departments with more than 100 sworn officers. The total sample included 473 small-locality departments and 548 medium to large departments.

By combining the data from both surveys, the results indicated that over 77 percent of the police departments had paramilitary units, an increase of 48 percent since 1985 (with a continued growth rate expected). The early formulation of SWAT teams in the 1970s and early 1980s was for the primary purpose of reacting to *emergency situations beyond the scope of patrol,* including civil disturbances, terrorism, hostage situations, and barricaded persons.

However, a much different perspective appears to be developing. The surveys documented 29,962 paramilitary deployments in 1995, a 939 percent increase over the 2,884 call-outs in 1980 (Kraska and Cubellis 1997). The significant increase in PPU call-outs can be attributed to their increasing emphasis on executing search and arrest warrants and to their use as a proactive patrol force (often in full regalia) in high-crime areas. These activities consisted almost exclusively of proactive, no-knock raids, aggressive field interviews, and car stops and searches. Such activities are frequently carried out with a great deal of intimidation and often lead to increased police–community tensions. As one survey respondent described his department's use of SWAT teams,

> We're into saturation patrols in hot spots. We do a lot of our work with the SWAT unit because we have bigger guns. We send out two, two-to-four-men cars, *we look for minor violations* and do jump-outs, either on people on the street or automobiles. After we jump-out the second car provides periphery cover with an ostentatious display of weaponry. We're sending a clear message: if the shootings don't stop, we'll shoot someone.
> (*Kraska and Kappeler 1997, p. 10, italics added*)

The authors conclude that PPUs are thus becoming a *normal part of routine patrol work* by moving away from their more traditional emergency roles and into more routine patrol activities. Several themes appear to be emerging unique to these types of units, including a pronounced military culture, preoccupation with danger, high level of pleasure from engaging in military-type activities, and viewing the PPU team as a group of "elite" officers (Kraska and Paulsen, 1997).

This integration of PPUs into patrol work appears to delineate a parallel trend with, but in opposition to, community policing: from less militaristic to more militaristic, from generalist to specialist, and from service and problem oriented to aggressive crime fighting. While the potential usefulness of PPUs in *bona fide emergencies* is well established, their use in mainstream policing appears unwarranted, especially in small-locality departments, which tend to be oriented toward crime prevention and service.

Countering an argument that this buildup and increased use of PPUs simply reflects a rational response to crime-rate changes, Kraska and Cubellis (1997) compared call-out rates with the rates of violent crimes (i.e., homicide, robbery, and rape) from 1980 through 1995 for each small-locality jurisdiction and found no significant relationship between violent crime and call-outs. Therefore, they concluded that changes in the rate of violent crime were not an important factor in explaining the increased level of PPU activities. Instead, they argue that "the specter of the military model still haunts the real world of contemporary policing, despite the recent rhetoric of democratic reforms" (p. 622).

It is prudent to keep in mind that the significant increase in the use of PPUs and greater push toward militarism in policing occurred prior to the terrorist attacks of September 11, 2001. Consequently, it is likely that such growth will continue to increase, and even flourish, in the near term; the implications for community policing, in general, and civil rights, in particular, appear more important than ever. In this regard, below is a discussion on the increasing use of aggressive police strategies and their impacts, including broken-windows theory, zero-tolerance policing, and Compstat and police legitimacy.

Broken-Windows and Zero-Tolerance Policing

J. Q. Wilson and Kelling (1982) introduced the **broken-windows theory** of law enforcement in the early 1980s. The theory is based on a hypothesis that when low levels of disorder and deviance are not held in check, then more serious types of crime are likely to follow. In other words, when signs of disorder and deviance (i.e., broken windows) are ignored, incidents of violence and delinquency will increase, thus leading to more serious crime problems. Therefore, the theory suggests that for the police to have an impact on serious crime, they should first begin by targeting minor problems. Although the merits of the broken-windows theory have been debated at length by law enforcement officials, researchers, and politicians, little empirical research exists regarding the effectiveness of such strategies to reduce serious crime. The research studies that do exist have mixed results, although the better controlled studies tend not to be supportive. One widely adopted method of policing used to promote broken-windows theory is known as **zero-tolerance policing**, a strategy in which officers "aggressively" (some say "heavy-handedly") target minor crime to send a signal that such behavior will not be tolerated. For example, aggressive-style policing was first studied (prior to the development of broken windows) by Wilson and Boland (1978), who found aggressive traffic enforcement (i.e., increased citations) contributed to a reduction in robbery rates; later research (Sampson and Cohen 1988) also found that aggressive traffic enforcement appeared to reduce robbery rates. However, in a controlled study (Weiss and Freels 1996) comparing a treatment area of increased level of traffic stops with a matched control area (i.e., normal level of traffic stops), no significant differences were found in reported crime for the two areas.

Harcourt (2001) critiques broken-windows theory (and zero tolerance) from empirical, theoretical, and rhetorical perspectives. Although broken-windows theory has existed since the early 1980s, Harcourt argues that the prominent existing data suggest it is false. He suggests that New York City's large drop in crime (see discussion on Compstat below) tells us little about broken-windows theory. For instance, many large cities—including Boston, Houston, Los Angeles, St. Louis, San Diego, San Antonio, San Francisco, and Washington, DC—had experienced significant declines in crime, some proportionately larger than New York's. And many of these cities have not implemented the aggressive, zero-tolerance strategies of New York. Harcourt argues that a large number of factors in combination—such as a large increase in the number of officers hired (approximately 15,000), a shift in drug use patterns away from crack cocaine, favorable economic conditions in the 1990s, a decrease in the number of 18 to 24 year olds, and the arrest of several big drug gangs—have led to the drop in crime in New York City.

Further analysis by Rosenfeld, Fornango, and Baumer (2005) on the effectiveness of the NYPDs Compstat/zero-tolerance strategy on homicide rates further supports Harcourt's analysis. By comparing New York's declining homicide rate during the 1990s, for which the NYPD took credit (e.g., see Bratton 1996; Kelling and Bratton 1998), with that of the 95 largest U.S. cities, while controlling for conditions known to be associated with violent crime rates, the findings indicated that New York's homicide trend did not differ significantly from that of the other large cities. Another critique of broken windows is offered by Herbert (2001), who suggests that broken-windows (zero-tolerance) policing is essentially replacing community policing as the primary reform model of the day, not because it works to reduce crime but because it fits more comfortably within established cultural and political frameworks (see Inside Policing 5.2).

Compstat, Police Legitimacy, and Procedural Justice

From 1990 to 1995, the rate of serious, violent crime declined by about 37 percent in New York City; however, from 1993 to 1996, the number of total arrests rose by 23 percent. Utilizing a zero-tolerance strategy based on broken-windows theory and directed by a

---

INSIDE POLICING 5.2 Broken-Windows Policing Subsuming Community Policing

Part of the explanation for a lack of genuine reform (in policing today) is the unfortunate popular combining of community policing with broken-windows (zero-tolerance) policing, not because it works to reduce crime, but because it's easier for police, citizens, and politicians to understand and accept the *status quo*. This development suggests that we can expect little by way of significant change on the part of police departments. In some cities, like New York, broken-windows policing is merely the professional (legalistic) model on steroids: aggressive, arrest-oriented policing. To embrace this approach is to diminish the potential role of citizens in overseeing police activity, because such oversight is now overshadowed by the energy devoted to disorder. This is important because aggressive policing causes undue harm to far too many citizens. When police too willingly understand themselves as gladiators in a noble fight against crime, they may be too willing to abuse force (and intimidation) in the process. To mandate more and more arrests is to invite officers to cast suspicion on those who may not warrant it and to arrest or abuse those who should be left alone. Such suspicion will inevitably fall disproportionately on minority citizens, further enflaming police–community relations in minority-dominated neighborhoods.

SOURCE: Adapted from S. Herbert. "Policing the Contemporary City: Fixing Broken Windows or Shoring Up Neo-Liberalism?" *Theoretical Criminology,* 2001, 5: 459.

---

process introduced by Police Commissioner William Bratton, known as Compstat, misdemeanor arrests rose by 40 percent—led by drug arrests, which increased by 97 percent during the period. **Compstat**, an acronym for *compare statistics*, was developed as a process that utilizes current crime data to analyze crime patterns and to respond quickly with "appropriate" resources and crime strategies. As aggressive arrests for misdemeanors became more frequent, however, the annual number of complaints of police misconduct filed with the Civilian Complaint Review Board in New York also increased by more than 60 percent from 1992 to 1996 (see Inside Policing 5.3). The increases in arrests in New York were accompanied by nearly a 40 percent increase in the number of sworn police officers between 1990 and 1995. By contrast, San Diego enjoyed a nearly 37 percent reduction in serious, violent crime from 1990 to 1995, while increasing its police force by only about 6 percent.

Significantly, citizen complaints about police misconduct decreased in San Diego by 9 percent from 1993 to 1996. It has been suggested that San Diego was able to accomplish these crime reductions more effectively and far more cost efficiently (i.e., with fewer police hires) than New York by implementing community policing, which emphasized "creating problem-solving partnerships and fostering connections between police and community for sharing information, working with citizens to address crime and disorder problems, and tapping other public and private agencies for resources to help solve them" (Greene 1999, 183). It is noteworthy that because of the increased complaints and publicity by the community over New York's zero-tolerance program, the police commissioner who followed Bratton (Howard Safir) implemented a policy directed at improving officer behavior known as "*courtesy, professionalism, and respect,*" or *CPR*. In the first half year following implementation of the new code, complaints filed against NYPD officers dropped 21 percent compared with the same period a year earlier. More specifically, complaints of police brutality dropped 20 percent (from 1,278 to 1,021) and complaints of abuse of authority fell almost

---

INSIDE POLICING 5.3　NYPD's Zero-Tolerance Policing

Diane Saarinen regularly hosted community forums at which police officials described how they were fighting drug dealers who had sometimes taken over entire blocks. As crime began to drop, she wrote strong letters of support to the local police, thanking them for their work. Now, however, she is writing a different kind of letter, strongly complaining of police abuse. She says she has heard too many stories of overly rough police conduct, including dragging people out of cars at gunpoint, of abusive tactics, of roughing up people who do not speak English, and of shooting civilians. "In the beginning we all wanted the police to bomb the crack houses," she says, "but now it's backfiring at the cost of the community. I think the cops have been given free rein to intimidate people at large."

Are increased complaints an appropriate trade-off for reduced crime? William Bratton, the former New York police commissioner who implemented the aggressive strategy, believes it is not surprising that complaints would increase, because the police are making more arrests and coming into contact with more citizens. He acknowledges that some police go too far, but contends that the reduction in crimes and victimizations is worth it. "In a city of 7.5 million people, 30 million tourists, and 38,000 police, is the level of complaints an appropriate trade-off?" he asked. "I think so, and the people seem satisfied." However, critics wonder if that sort of trade-off is appropriate in a democracy. If there is zero tolerance for lower-level street crimes, why is there not zero tolerance for heavy-handed cops? And the critics are not just from the criminal class or certain neighborhoods. For instance, George Kelling, a professor of criminal justice who coauthored the broken-windows theory and helped Bratton implement it, is worried that his ideas are not being implemented appropriately. "There's an enormous potential for abuse," he says. He criticizes departments that demand IDs from residents or conduct neighborhood drug sweeps, indiscriminately stopping and frisking people, often using excessive force.

SOURCE: Adapted from L. Reibstein, "NYPD Black and Blue." *Newsweek*, June 2, 1997: 66, 68.

---

29 percent (from 1,166 to 829). In addition, charges of discourtesy fell 32 percent, and charges of profanity by police dropped almost 40 percent. Inside Policing 5.3 takes a closer look at the potential problems of this aggressive approach to policing.

In line with the above discussion, even though broken-windows theory has been used as the foundation for Compstat-based zero-tolerance policing, it is worth noting that zero tolerance is an oversimplification of broken-windows theory as described by Wilson and Kelling (1982). Broken-windows theory encourages aggressive enforcement of less serious offenses, as long as they are in line with community standards. Communities are to set thresholds for disorderly public behavior, and the police are responsible for law enforcement in accordance with these norms. Since communities will differ in their tolerance for disorderly behavior, policing strategies will qualitatively differ from community to community. In contrast, the zero-tolerance approach applies the law the same way in all environments in which it is utilized and thus is not a true reflection of broken-windows theory. As Kelling notes in Inside Policing 5.3, the Compstat strategy may not be implementing broken windows appropriately and thus has an "enormous potential for abuse."

Moore (2002) suggests in his analysis of Compstat that while the system picked up one of the important ideas that emerged from community policing,

> ...the focus on disorder offenses as a way of reducing fear, mobilizing forces of informal social control, and reducing serious crime, it left in the background two other big

ideas—the idea that both the *legitimacy* and *effectiveness* of police could be increased by reaching out for effecting working partnerships with community groups, and focusing attention on community-nominated problems that might or might not include serious crime problems. *(p. 159, emphasis added)*

Police legitimacy can be defined as the public's confidence in the police as *fair and equitable*. When police legitimacy is lost by the public, a likely result is a general loss of respect and confidence, which may impact effectiveness through lower levels of crime reporting and cooperation with the police. Sherman (1997) has suggested that the greatest concern for zero-tolerance policing is that while massive arrests for minor crimes may have a short-term impact on crime, over the long term it may actually increase crime (as arrestees—and their social network—may become more defiant and aggressive). In addition, program development to foster greater police legitimacy in the course of making arrests is suggested—for example, providing arrested minor offenders an opportunity to meet with a police supervisor who would explain the program to them, answer questions about why they are being arrested, and give them a chance to express their views. An early study on police field interrogations in San Diego supports this view. Boydstun (1975) discovered that not only did field interrogations have some apparent crime prevention effects, but also, if conducted with civility and an explanation for the reason, there was no adverse impact on citizen attitudes, even in minority communities. Thus, Sherman (1997) suggests that with respect to crime prevention, focusing on police "style" may be as important as focusing on police "substance."

A companion concept to police legitimacy is known as **procedural justice**. In general, procedural justice refers to being treated fairly by the police when acting under authority of the criminal law; that is, being treated in an even-handed manner when performing their law enforcement duties (Skogan and Frydl 2004). Some research has indicated that through the practice of procedural justice, a belief in the legitimacy of the police is fostered (Sunshine and Tyler 2003), which, in turn, tends to inspire greater compliance with the criminal law (Lind and Tyler, 1988; McCluskey, Mastrofski, and Parks 1999). Thus, if citizens believe in both police legitimacy and the criminal law, they are more likely to cooperate with the police and feel a moral obligation to obey the law.

One study by Gau and Brunson (2010) of black and white adolescent males (13 to 19 years of age) living in a disadvantaged St. Louis neighborhood—who often attract unwelcome police attention—tested the impact of procedural justice through police use of aggressive, zero-tolerance tactics. Using surveys and in-depth interviews, the authors discovered that both serious delinquents and non-delinquents in the cohort complained of what they considered frequent and routine harassment by the police, primarily through stop-and-frisk-activities. Even when their activities were law abiding, the young men felt that they we unable to convince officers they were doing nothing wrong. The general conclusion was that relatively unprofessional, aggressive police tactics, even when a formal arrest may not be made, can seriously compromise procedural justice and thus undermine police legitimacy.

These findings support Sherman's (1997) contention with respect to the use of zero-tolerance policing leading to the erosion of police legitimacy. While Gau and Brunson (2010) make several suggestions with respect to alleviating concerns over aggressive stop-and-frisk practices (several of which overlap with those described by Sherman above), perhaps the most straightforward approach would be for police departments to demand that officers always act in a courteous and respectful manner when interacting with the public—poor or rich, urban or rural—whether formally (legally) or informally. To encourage this type of professional behavior, police managers can: (1) establish internal guidelines; (2) reward professional behavior through pay or step increases and internal communications; (3) only promote officers into supervisory and managerial positions who continually behave professionally; and (4) use disciplinary actions or termination that may be necessary to support the principle that unprofessional behavior will never be tolerated.

Police Goals and Organization Performance

Like all organizations, police departments are oriented toward the attainment of goals. In a democracy, it is crucial that police managers, employees, and private citizens have an understanding of what these goals are and how they are to be accomplished (measured). As described in Chapter 1, **goals** are general statements of long-term purpose. Goals are often used to identify the role of the police—for instance, to prevent crime, maintain order, or help solve community problems. They are also often used in mission statements. Goals are important because they help to identify expectations of what the police are doing and their levels of performance. Unrealistic and unreasonable goals make the job of managers and employees more difficult and can even ensure failure. When police overpromise or claim to be able to reduce crime or to solve problems that are largely outside police control, the public is usually disappointed and critical. When employees fail to behave in accordance with unreasonable managerial expectations, managers are often critical, and employees are resentful and may even become less productive. These unreasonable expectations can and often do create an adversarial relationship between the police and the community and between managers and employees (e.g., see the discussion on managers' and street cops' cultures in the next section).

Three major influences affect the development of police goals: community, organizational, and individual. *Community influences* consist of the legal framework in which police function and the community's input into departmental priorities. As previously stressed, however, there is no such thing as a "single" community constituency. Police managers, therefore, must be aware of the various communities they serve and their differing expectations. Thus, departments within a heterogeneous geographic area, or even precincts or units within the same department, may need to establish different goals or use different methods to attain goals. *Organizational influences* are those of powerful members, especially top-level managers, who seek certain goals primarily for the efficiency and perpetuation of the department but also to satisfy its members. Finally, *individual influences* generally benefit members (e.g., job security, pay, or fringe benefits).

Impact of Supervisory Styles on Officer Behavior

It is clear, as the expectation-integration model discussed in Chapter 1 suggests, that the closer police managers come to integrating individual and community goals with those of the organization, the more likely it is that the goals will be accomplished. And organizational goals are more likely to be accomplished if they are aligned with supervisory practices. In a study of the effects of 64 sergeants' supervisory styles on the behavior of 239 patrol officers in the Indianapolis, Indiana, and St. Petersburg, Florida, police departments, Engel (2003) found that the *style* of field supervision can significantly influence patrol officer behavior. Although four supervisory styles were discovered (traditional, innovative, supportive, and active), it was the *active* style that was more likely to have an influence on officer behavior. However, this influence can be either positive or negative; for instance, it can inspire officers to engage in more problem-solving activities, or it can result in more frequent use of force.

The active style was also the most conducive to implementing community policing goals. This research suggests that leading by example is an effective supervisory method, if the example supports the goals of the organization.

Another study found that supervisory styles can have an impact on officer behavior with respect to *integrity violations*. In a study of five regional police organizations in the Netherlands, including over 1,000 officers, Huberts, Kaptein, and Lasthuizen (2007) found that *role modeling* by police supervisors is significant in limiting unethical conduct relating to interpersonal relationships. It appears that employees copy a leader's integrity standards in their daily interactions with one another. In addition, the authors found that leader *strictness* is also important, but appears to be especially effective in controlling fraud, corruption, and the misuse of resources.

With respect to how officers behave during their discretionary time, Famega, Frank, and Mazerolle (2005) conducted an observational study of over 1,300 hours of Baltimore officers while on patrol. It was discovered, on average, that more than three quarters of an officer's time per shift was unassigned; officers primarily self-initiated random patrol or backed up other officers on calls to which they were not dispatched. Only 6 percent of unassigned time activities were directed by supervisors, dispatchers, other officers, or supervisors. The only activities that were more likely to be directed than self-initiated were serving warrants and subpoenas and attempts to locate suspects, witnesses, or informants. Further, only 4 percent of all activities were part of a long-term initiative to deal with a problem. Interestingly, it was noted that Whitaker's (1982) analysis of the Police Services Study (see Chapter 1) found more time was spent on proactive activities over 25 years ago. These findings are somewhat surprising given contemporary research and police practice reforms that emphasize self-initiated tasks during unassigned time and directed activities based on supervisory crime analyses and problem identification (see Chapter 8). The results clearly indicate, given technology advances and time available to do proactive activities, that patrol officers were underutilized. A good part of the problem lies with front-line supervisors, who *provide few directives* (which are not specific in nature) to patrol officers. The researchers suggest that the probable solution lies in holding supervisors and officers more accountable for unassigned time on their beats. Given the Engel (2003) results discussed above, it may also be prudent to encourage and train supervisors to adopt a more *active style*, not only in an attempt to change officer behavior, but also to elicit more directives.

Measuring Police Performance

The performance levels of police departments are, in general, difficult to measure. Performance indicators, such as making arrests, maintaining order, solving problems, providing services, and using discretion, are difficult to define in a meaningful and valid manner. That is, although it may be relatively easy to count the number of arrests that are made by the police *(quantity)*, it is much more difficult to get a handle on how "good" the arrests are *(quality)*. For example, was the arrest necessary? Was there violence prior to the arrest that could have been prevented? Did the arrest lead to a conviction? To date, the police have made very little effort to develop qualitative measures of performance. Therefore, officers may be performing activities that are supported within the department while incurring the wrath of the community.

To properly evaluate a police department's overall effectiveness, both *external* and *internal* goals should be assessed. From an external perspective, the department needs to know the extent to which it is satisfying the community it serves. For instance, are there conflicts between departmental and community goals? If the goals are similar, are the methods used to accomplish the goals acceptable? From an internal perspective, the department needs to know whether its goals are compatible with those of its employees. Is there conflict between what employees think the goals should be and what the department actually stresses, or do conflicts exist between operating units in the department? If they are to be meaningful, these goals need to be honest enough to be achievable and specific enough to be measurable. In general, attainable and generally satisfactory evaluation methods for the police include three major areas:

1. ***Crime and disorder measures.*** Crime and disorder statistics should be compared over time (to establish reliable trends and patterns). Criminal statistics may include the *Uniform Crime Reports* and victimization surveys. Measures of community disorder can be taken from the department's calls for service (e.g., complaints about noise, domestic violence, prostitution, or same-location repeat calls).

2. ***Community measures.*** Community measures may include surveys, interviews, and feedback from community meetings regarding such factors as identifying and solving important community problems relative to crime, fear of crime, and general satisfaction with the police. In addition, representative community boards and police advisory committees that participate in departmental goal setting and performance feedback can be included.

3. ***Individual and team measures.*** Evaluation of individual performance (e.g., performance ratings or evaluations by supervisors) and group performance (e.g., team projects) should be conducted at appropriate intervals—that is, biannually or yearly. In addition, employee opinions regarding operating procedures and policies, or concerns with management, can be measured by surveys and interviews.

With respect to crime and disorder measures, police departments often rely solely on the FBI's *UCRs* (Part I) or index crimes as their crime-rate measure. This crime index is the rate per 100,000 population of eight common violent and property crimes—including murder and nonnegligent manslaughter, forcible rape, robbery, aggravated assault, burglary, larceny or theft, motor vehicle theft, and arson—reported to the police. UCRs, however, are not a very precise measure of actual crime rates, with estimates of less than 50 percent of some criminal acts being reported. The FBI has redesigned the UCR program to form a new program, the **National Incident-Based Reporting System (NIBRS)**, which will help improve the quantity, quality, and accuracy of the statistics (Bureau of Justice Statistics 1997). NIBRS includes 46 crime categories grouped into 22 offense categories in the Part A classification. In addition, there are 11 offenses in a Group B category, for which only arrestee data are to be reported, since most of these offenses come to police attention only when arrests are made (see Figure 5.3).

In addition to providing significantly more crime data, NIBRS (1) distinguishes between attempted and completed crimes, (2) provides additional information on victim/offender relationships and characteristics, and (3) includes the location of crimes. Further, it eliminates the "hierarchy rule" of the UCR, which limits reporting to the most serious offense even though multiple offenses were committed within the course of a single criminal incident (e.g., during a robbery, if a murder and an assault are committed, only the murder is recorded). Thus, those departments that have adopted NIBRS have a much more accurate understanding of crime and disorder in their community and therefore can better plan how to deal with it. As of 2004, a total of 26 states have been "certified" by the FBI to collect and submit NIBRS data. Within these 26 states, 5,271 agencies are submitting all of their crime data to the FBI in the NIBRS format; this represents 16 percent of crime statistics collected by the FBI. In addition, 12 state programs are in various stages of testing NIBRS and 8 other state programs are in various stages of planning and development (FBI n.d.).

Group A Offenses
1. Arson
2. Assault Offenses
   Aggravated Assault
   Simple Assault
   Intimidation
3. Bribery
4. Burglary/Breaking and Entering
5. Counterfeiting/Forgery
6. Destruction/Damage Vandalism of Property
7. Drug/Narcotic Offenses
   Drug/Narcotic Violations
   Drug Equipment Violations
8. Embezzlement
9. Extortion/Blackmail
10. Fraud Offenses
    False Pretenses/Swindle/Confidence Game Credit Card/Automatic Teller Machine Fraud
    Impersonation
    Welfare Fraud
    Wire Fraud
11. Gambling Offenses
    Betting/Wagering
    Operating/Promoting/Assisting Gambling
    Gambling Equipment Violations
    Sports Tampering
12. Homicide Offenses
    Murder and Nonnegligent Manslaughter
    Negligent Manslaughter
    Justifiable Homicide
13. Kidnapping/Abduction
14. Larceny/Theft Offenses
    Pocket-Picking
    Purse-Snatching
    Shoplifting
    Theft From Building
    Theft From Coin-Operated Machine or Device
    Theft From Motor Vehicle
    Theft of Motor Vehicle Parts or Accessories
    All Other Larceny
15. Motor Vehicle Theft
16. Pornography/Obscene Material
17. Prostitution Offenses
    Prostitution
    Assisting or Promoting Prostitution
18. Robbery
19. Sex Offenses, Forcible
    Forcible Rape
    Forcible Sodomy
    Sexual Assault With an Object
    Forcible Fondling
20. Sex Offenses, Nonforcible
    Incest
    Statutory Rape
21. Stolen Property Offenses (Receiving, etc.)
22. Weapon Law Violations

Group B Offenses
1. Bad Checks
2. Curfew/Loitering/Vagrancy Violations
3. Disorderly Conduct
4. Driving Under the Influence
5. Drunkenness
6. Family Offenses, Nonviolent
7. Liquor Law Violations
8. Peeping Tom
9. Runaway
10. Trespass of Real Property
11. All Other Offenses

FIGURE 5.3 **National Incident-Based Reporting System.**

SOURCE: Federal Bureau of Investigation, available on-line at http://www.fbi.gov/ucr/faqs.htm.

Another source of crime data that has become part of many departments' assessment of crime is the use of *victim surveys,* in which scientifically selected samples of the population are asked about being victims of crime. Victimization data tend to provide a more accurate reflection of a community's incidence of crime. Currently the most widely used and extensive victim survey is the *National Crime Victimization Survey (NCVS),* which asks a national sample of approximately 120,000 individuals over 12 years of age specific questions regarding criminal victimizations. Obviously, by combining UCR data or, better yet, NIBRS data, with victimization data, a department will have a more accurate understanding of crime and disorder and what to do about it.

Other performance measures that police departments traditionally use to record crime levels include arrest rates and the crime clearance rate. *Arrest rates* are calculated as the number of persons arrested for all crimes known to the police. Arrest rates are an extremely poor measure of performance for several reasons. For example, they rely on UCR measures of crimes reported and police discretion regarding when to make arrests (officer levels of quality and quantity of arrests vary significantly). A further problem is that police make substantially more arrests for minor violations than for serious violations, whereas the crime index is essentially based on serious crime. A final problem is the fact that the majority of police work does not even involve law enforcement activities, including arrests. The *crime clearance rate* is calculated as the number of Part I crimes reported to the police divided by the number of crimes for which the police have arrested a suspect. The crime clearance rate is another poor indicator of police performance for several reasons. For instance, the police usually consider a case "solved" even if the suspect is acquitted of the crime charged; furthermore, multiple crimes are often "cleared" by associating them with an arrested suspect who has admitted to similar or other crimes.

Changing Performance Measures

With all of their problems, the primary measures of police performance remain the frequency of serious crime (UCRs) and the number of arrests made by the police. However, other important and potentially more valid indicators are being discussed. For example, it has been suggested that the police should consider having a UCR-like **disorder index** as a companion to the crime index on major felonies (National Institute of Justice 1997). By developing a set of *standardized measures for calls for service, over time*, the public's perceptions of community disorder could be measured. As Greene (2000, 359) points out, "these data may more accurately reflect community concerns about crime and disorder or other things that disturb the social fabric." Interestingly, this is precisely what was discovered in the beat meetings in Chicago's community policing program known as CAPS (Chicago Alternative Policing Strategy); that is, what the police thought the major neighborhood problems were (i.e., serious crime) differed substantially from the community's major concerns, which turned out to be relatively minor quality-of-life problems (Skogan and Hartnett 1997). Chapter 6 has an extensive discussion on the development of the CAPS program.

Because problem solving is such an integral part of community policing, being able to adequately respond to community problems becomes a critical criterion for adequate organization performance. According to Goldstein (1990), evaluating police response to problems requires the following:

- A clear understanding of the problem.
- Agreement on the interest(s) to be served in dealing with the problem and their order of interest.

- Agreement on the method used to determine the extent to which these interests (goals) are reached.
- A realistic assessment of what might be expected of the police, that is, solving the problem versus improving the quality of the management of it.
- Determination of the relative importance of short-term versus long-term impact.
- A clear understanding of the legality and fairness of the response, that is, recognizing that reducing a problem through improper use of authority is not only wrong, but likely to be counterproductive.

Goldstein cautions against defining success as the literal solving of a problem, since many police and community problems, by their very nature, are unmanageable because of their magnitude. Instead, he suggests that officers should be involved in identifying the measurable conditions they would like to see changed and attempt to improve these conditions. The bottom line with respect to how successfully a police department handles problem solving can be measured in any of the following ways (Spelman and Eck 1987):

- Total elimination of the problem.
- Reducing the number of incidents the problem creates.
- Reducing the seriousness of the incidents the problem creates.
- Designing methods for better handling of the incidents.
- Removing the problem from police consideration, assuming it can be handled more effectively by another agency.

In his analysis of police performance measurement, Moore (2002) makes a valuable distinction between police *production* (e.g., making arrests, reducing fear of crime) and production *costs* (i.e., how much it costs to produce these things). He suggests two important dimensions with respect to how much it costs for the police to accomplish their goals: first is the fair, efficient, and effective use of *financial resources* (e.g., financial integrity and accountability, equal employment opportunity, fair contracting) and second is the fair, efficient, and effective use of *force and authority* (e.g., fair distribution of services, unbiased operational policies, controlling corruption, reducing force and authority, gaining legitimacy). It is suggested that the police begin to routinely measure and report on their use of force and authority as well as the amount of money they spend. The report should then be audited by an outside agency rather than produced by the agency itself.

Managing Group Behavior

Police managers must be well informed about managing group behavior and possible conflict between and among groups. Because today's police departments tend to be relatively diverse in cultural background and level of skills, it is natural that different groups will have different—often conflicting—demands on management levels.

Police Subcultures

In addition to the formal hierarchical structure of a police department, informal organizational arrangements often have a greater impact on departmental operations. Individual beliefs, values, and norms in police departments are strongly influenced by group behavior, especially by experienced officers. As will be discussed in greater detail in subsequent chapters, *socialization* in policing occurs when recruits learn the values and behavioral patterns of experienced officers. From this early socialization, police officers tend to develop a different view of their job from that of their managers. For example, Reuss-Ianni (1983), in her study of New York police, observed that these divergent views result in two distinct subcultures within the same organization, namely a *manager's culture* and a *street cop's culture*.

This differing perspective of the patrol officer's job develops because the manager's view is often shaped by experiences that remove him or her from the street reality of officers. One example common to police work is the *ends–means dilemma*. Police managers must be concerned with both ends (i.e., results) and means (i.e., how the results are achieved), whereas

> **INSIDE POLICING 5.4   Street Cop's Code**
>
> 1. Take care of your partner first, then the other officers.
> 2. Don't "give up" (inform on) another cop; be secretive about the behavior of other officers.
> 3. Show balls; take control of a situation and don't back down.
> 4. Be aggressive when necessary, but don't go looking for trouble.
> 5. Don't interfere in another officer's sector or work area.
> 6. Do your fair share of work and don't leave work for the next shift; however, don't do too much work.
> 7. If you get caught making a mistake, don't implicate anybody else.
> 8. Other cops, but not necessarily managers, should be told if another officer is dangerous or "crazy."
> 9. Don't trust new officers until they have been checked out.
> 10. Don't volunteer information; tell others only what they need to know.
> 11. Avoid talking too much or too little; both are suspicious.
> 12. Protect your ass; don't give managers of the system an opportunity to get you.
> 13. Don't make waves; don't make problems for the system or managers.
> 14. Don't "suck up" to supervisors.
> 15. Know what your supervisor and other managers expect.
> 16. Don't trust managers; they may not look out for your interests.
>
> SOURCE: Adapted from E. Reuss-Ianni, *Two Cultures of Policing: Street Cops and Management Cops* (New Brunswick, CT: Transaction Books, 1983), 13–16.

officers may be concerned primarily with ends (i.e., making an arrest is more important than protecting constitutional rights). Managers are concerned with departmental priorities, policies, and procedures, whereas officers are concerned with doing the job "according to the street," often acquired not from the department's view of reality but from the officer's perspective, determined by trying to "survive." These differing perspectives can result in an adversarial relationship, where street cops maintain their own "code," which can include the set of rules described in Inside Policing 5.4.

Because both the manager's and the street cop's cultures must relate to the expectations of the communities they serve, there are both public and private worlds of policing. The *public world of policing* is presented to the public as the essence of police work: dedicated public servants performing dangerous work for our safety. Although the managers' and officers' perspectives of police work may differ, neither group tends to be completely candid because both have a vested interest in maintaining an image that avoids controversy. For example, if officers use excessive force to make an arrest, they will probably not admit it because of the street-culture norm to be secretive about illegal or inappropriate behavior. Managers may attempt to uncover inappropriate behavior, but they may not disclose it or they may disclose only parts of it. There may be potentially serious adverse consequences to the department, or they may be willing to disregard illegal tactics if a desirable result is obtained. Police managers, if they are to be effective leaders, however, must be willing to deal with such situations, both formally and informally, as the need arises.

In general, the *private world of policing* has been characterized as politically conservative, closed, or secretive, with a high degree of cynicism and an emphasis on loyalty, solidarity, and respect for authority (Doyle 1980). Undoubtedly, this private world of the patrol officer's culture has the strongest influence on the socialization process throughout the department and most likely the greatest impact on police behavior. A significant problem for managers is when the behavior dictated by the worker's culture conflicts with both departmental and community interests. This conflict is most apparent when a certain degree of deviant behavior (e.g., excessive force, racism, free meals, or gratuities) becomes acceptable, or at least tolerated, at the street level. Police managers must be willing to deal strongly with such behavior from both ethical and legal perspectives. Accordingly, police managers must be aware of group pressures—especially with respect to the street culture—and how they influence officer behavior either positively or negatively.

Employee Organizations

Historically, the best known police employee organization has been the *police union,* which is made up of police officers and is their official representative in collective bargaining with the employer. Because police departments operate on a local level, there is no single national police union. Instead, local departments may belong to one of many national unions. The largest include the Fraternal Order of Police and the International Union of Police Associations, which is affiliated with the American Federation of Labor and Congress of Industrial Organizations AFL-CIO. Other local police unions are affiliated with the Teamsters; the American Federation of State, County, and Municipal Employees; and other smaller national unions.

Although a union is an employee organization, not all employee organizations are unions. As Walker (1992) has pointed out, police officers have historically belonged to *fraternal organizations.* These groups are generally organized along ethnic lines. Nationally, for example, Latino officers are represented by the Latino Police Officers Association and Asian officers by the Asian Police Officers Association. Employee groups may also form their own local organizations. In San Francisco, for example, the African American officers' association is known as Officers for Justice; in San Jose, California, it is known as the South Bay Association of Black Law Enforcement Officers.

As departments become more diverse in their makeup, additional employee organizations develop. For instance, many departments have women's organizations (e.g., the Women's Police Officer Association), and gay and lesbian officers are represented in California by the Golden State Peace Officers Association. Furthermore, police officers and supervisors are often represented by their own associations. It is apparent that if departments are to maintain a healthy work environment, police managers must deal effectively with the diverse needs, expectations, and conflicts of these employee organizations. In general, it is best to establish a working relationship with each group and to share with them the department's expectations. Then, if there are conflicts, they can be dealt with in an open and honest manner.

Police Unions

The police labor movement has gone through several stages. Police associations were evident as early as the 1890s but did not establish themselves until the mid-1960s. Two previous attempts made to unionize police employees failed. The first attempt failed after the Boston police strike of 1919, which created a backlash against police unions throughout the country. The second, between 1943 and 1947, failed because of unfavorable court decisions and strong resistance by police chiefs.

Despite the influence of police unions in understanding policing in America, there exists little systematic information about them. Kadleck (2003) examined 648 police unions from across the country and found that the typical union was founded after 1960 and consists of a voluntary group of police officers headed by an officer who is elected to that position. Leaders of unions also report having influence over policy creation and indicate a general lack of trust among police managers. Commenting on this lack of research, Walker (2008) suggests a research agenda for police scholars to better understand the nature and depth police unions have on the impact of police management, discipline and accountability, police subculture, police–community relations, city or county finances, and finally politics.

The early development of police unionization was controversial and often shrouded in conflict, especially with police management. Once established, unions demanded higher salaries; better fringe benefits; more participation in how, when, and where officers worked; and more elaborate disciplinary procedures to protect employees. They also tended to fight back against the charges of critics. In many police departments, employee organizations have become major obstacles to effecting change. What began as an attempt to improve the lot of the working police officer has often become a barrier to improving standards and performance. Of course, members of police unions may not agree with this perspective; from their point of view, they are simply acting to preserve "hard won" gains. In addition, some unions are vocal proponents of organizational change that will improve performance. In some cases, police unions may be more progressive than police managers.

The issues that are negotiated between police unions and management tend to fall into three categories: salaries and benefits, conditions of work, and grievance procedures.

Salaries and benefits are influenced by a number of factors, including the economic health of a community, the inflation rate, salaries in comparable police departments (or in comparable positions in other occupations), management's resistance, the militancy of the union, and the amount of public support for either labor or management.

Conditions of work include a broad range of possible issues, many of which have traditionally been considered management prerogatives, such as the procedures used for evaluation, reassignment, and promotions; equipment and uniforms; number of officers assigned to a car or section of the community; how seniority and education will be used in assignments and promotions; hours worked and off-duty employment; and training and professional development. Critics argue that this kind of union activity is detrimental to the effective management of the department and the provision of quality services to the community (see Bouza 1985). Others, however, blame the poor management and treatment of employees for promoting such union activity; they view employee influence over management prerogatives in positive terms, potentially leading to improved managerial practices (see Kleismet 1985).

Grievance procedures are concerned with the process to be used in accusing an officer of a violation of departmental policies and procedures of law. Usually, this process involves an identification of officer rights (which may even be codified in state law), how the complaints must be filed, how evidence is obtained and processed, how disciplinary decisions will be made, and what appeals, if any, will be allowed. Quite often, police unions, in an effort to protect employees from arbitrary treatment by managers, will demand elaborate grievance mechanisms that frustrate attempts to respond to almost any type of inappropriate police behavior. However, grievance procedures may also be a useful way of clarifying work rules and of understanding and agreeing on performance expectations.

Significant input in the managerial process by police unions is here to stay. It is important to recognize that union leaders often have a strong informal influence over departmental members. Consequently, these leaders should be treated with respect by police managers, and they should be kept abreast of managerial decisions so they can share this information with the membership. To facilitate this process, union representatives should be encouraged to serve on task forces and participate in management meetings. An open and participative relationship with the union may help to avoid the costly and unpleasant effects that often result from strikes, job actions (i.e., work slowdowns or speedups), refusals to negotiate, and media attention, and, perhaps most important, may result in an improved working environment.

Media Relations

How the police manage their interaction with the media has become increasingly important in the community policing era. The relationship between the media and the police has often been one of uneasiness, with a lack of trust on both sides. In today's environment, police departments must become more transparent with the public they serve; police executives and managers must find ways to communicate in an open and honest way with the media to project their desired departmental image to the public. Of course, this is easier said than done, since the news media tends to focus on dramatic events (and may even sensationalize them), including violent crime and police misconduct, rather than on routine police activities or police improvements. Consequently, it is important for departments to establish good working relationships with the media to "get the word out" on what they are doing to improve community relations and help to reduce community problems and crime. In addition, increased transparency includes dealing forthrightly with the media and the public regarding high-profile events (e.g., police shootings) and problems relating to misconduct (e.g., brutality, corruption), detailing steps that will be taken to correct the problem(s).

One national study (Chermak and Weiss 2006) surveyed 239 law enforcement agencies and 420 media organizations (both television and newspaper) in large cities to determine police–media relationships and the extent to which community policing strategies were being presented and/or covered (96 percent of the surveyed agencies reported some type of community policing program). The results indicated that 80 percent of the departments had at least one full-time **Public Information Officer (PIO)**, who was responsible for managing the agency's public image, disseminating information, and interacting with the media (where a PIO was not designated, some other high-ranking official performed information duties). Both sides agreed that police–media relations were positive (90 percent for the PIOs and 72 percent for the media). In addition, the number of crime stories over a 2-week period was significantly greater than the number of community policing stories over an entire year. These results indicated that police departments and PIOs are not taking full advantage of their access to news organizations to promote community policing. It is suggested that departments should work with the news media in "devising and implementing broader marketing strategies to increase public awareness and involvement in community policing activities" (Chermak and Weiss 2006, 156).

Another area of police–media relations that has not received much attention in the research literature relates to how the police handle crisis events and cases of police misconduct (e.g., misuse of force, questionable shootings, use of tasers). A case study in 2001 (Lachlan et al. 2007) looked at the aftermath of a full-scale riot in Cincinnati when an officer shot and killed an area resident, an apparently unarmed man wanted on misdemeanor charges. Prior to the riot, the local newspaper ran stories under the headlines "Officer

Shoots, Kills Suspect: Man Was Unarmed, Wanted on Misdemeanor Charges," and "Mom Asks: Why?" The main lessons of this case are that departments must devise some type of crisis communication plan that sets out timetables for release of information, who will release it (preferably a PIO), what kind of information can be disclosed, and the key publics to be addressed (including appropriate civic leaders). Furthermore, the use of the statement "no comment," generally viewed as a concession of guilt, should be avoided. It is suggested that different terminology be used to explain why the department is not able to disclose particular facts and information.

A more recent case study in Indianapolis (Chermak, McGarrell, and Gruenewald 2006) reported that several white off-duty officers of the police department were accused of being brutal and intoxicated, using racial and sexist slurs, repeatedly hitting two males (one African American and one white), and then arresting them. The police department attempted to portray the officers as simply doing their jobs to control rowdy behavior, while witnesses said the police were the aggressors. The news media made claims that the department was attempting to cover up what actually happened to minimize the responsibility of the officers. During the investigations, the chief of police resigned over the matter. The authors suggest that departments must be prepared to "make an effort to provide full accounts when crisis events occur" (Chermak, McGarrell, and Gruenewald 2006, 274) and that such events are likely to undermine public relations and community policing efforts if not handled correctly.

Summary

The managerial process is concerned with organizing, leading, planning, and controlling. The history of police management theory begins with the classical theorists, who stressed a bureaucratic, paramilitary approach to organizational design. Beginning in the early 1970s, behavioral theorists began attacking the classical approach, placing greater emphasis on worker participation, job satisfaction, more flexible designs, and recognition of the complex nature of the police role. The final theoretical development, contemporary police theory, emphasized police departments as open systems and the use of contingency theory. Private sector processes also became influential, particularly through the use of total quality management techniques. There has been much criticism of the traditional paramilitary design, which continues to be influential. Part of this influence includes increased use of PPUs, aggressive police methods, and the manner in which Compstat is utilized.

It is important to establish realistic and measurable police goals, including both quantitative and qualitative indicators. To properly evaluate a department's overall performance, both external (community) and internal (departmental), goals should be assessed. New dimensions of organization performance might include various "costs" of policing, including reporting how much money is spent and the use of force and authority. Unfortunately, attempts to change individual performance evaluation measures to include community policing criteria have been ineffective and, when attempted, have often simply increased reliance on promoting organization and internal processes. Because today's police departments are culturally diverse and vary widely with respect to skill levels, the managing of group behavior becomes important. From this perspective, both formal and informal groups (including police subcultures) are involved. Police unions, despite being controversial, have improved benefits and job conditions. It is important for management to develop a working relationship with union leaders Finally, if police are to improve police–media relations, they must become more transparent in dealing with the media, providing current and honest information with respect to both noncritical and crisis events.

Critical Thinking Questions

1. What aspects of classical and behavioral management theories have contributed the most to today's police organizations? What particular aspects should be discarded?

2. Provide an example of why police managers must be aware of both systems and contingency theory and how these theories may help them to develop appropriate operating policies for their organizations.

3. What influence does the paramilitary organization design have on present-day policing? Why is it so hard to change? Is it still necessary?

4. What impact has broken-windows theory had on policing? What about the future?

5. How would you use the Compstat process if you were a high-level police manager?

6. What is your opinion of Moore's proposal for measuring police performance? As a police chief, how would you attempt to implement these measures?

7. How would you, as a first-line supervisor, handle the difference between the manager's and street cop's culture?

8. As a midlevel manager, what steps would you take to implement new performance evaluation criteria for patrol officers?

References

Auten, J. H. 1981. "The Paramilitary Model of Police and Police Professionalism." *Police Studies* 4: 67–78.

Bercal, T. E. 1970. "Calls for Police Assistance." *American Behavioral Scientist* 13: 681–691.

Bittner, E. 1970. *The Function of the Police in Modern Society.* Washington, DC: U.S. Government Printing Office.

Bouza, A. V. 1985. "Police Unions: Paper Tigers or Roaring Lions?" In W. A. Geller (ed.), *Police Leadership in America: Crises and Opportunity,* pp. 241–280. New York: Praeger.

Boydstun, J. E. 1975. *San Diego Field Interrogation: Final Report.* Washington, DC: Police Foundation.

Bratton, W. 1996. "Remark: New Strategies for Combating Crime in New York City." *Fordham Urban Journal* 23: 781–785.

Bureau of Justice Statistics. 1997. *Implementing the National Incident-Based Reporting System: A Project Status Report.* Washington, DC: Department of Justice.

Cacioppe, R. L., and P. Mock. 1985. "The Relationship of Self-actualization, Stress and Quality of Work Experience in Senior Level Australian Police Officers." *Police Studies* 8: 173–186.

Chermak, S., McGarrell, E., and Gruenewald, J. 2006. "Media Coverage of Police Misconduct and Attitudes Toward Police." *Policing: An International Journal of Police Strategies & Management* 29: 261–281.

Chermak, S., and Weiss, A. 2006. "Community Policing in the News Media." *Police Quarterly* 9: 135–160.

Cordner, G. W. 1978. "Review of Work Motivation Theory and Research for the Police Manager." *Journal of Police Science and Administration* 6: 186–192.

Couper, D. C., and Lobitz, S. H. 1991. *Quality Policing: The Madison Experience.* Washington, DC: Police Executive Research Forum.

Cowper, T. J. 2000. "The Myth of the 'Military Model' of Leadership in Law Enforcement." *Police Quarterly* 3: 228–246.

Cumming, E., Cumming, I., and Edell, L. 1965. "Policeman as Philosopher, Guide and Friend." *Social Problems* 12: 276–286.

Doyle, M. A. 1980. "Police Culture: Open or Closed." In V. A. Leonard (ed.), *Fundamentals of Law Enforcement: Problems and Issues,* pp. 61–83. St. Paul, MN: West.

Engel, R. S. 2003. *How Police Supervisory Styles Influence Patrol Officer Behavior.* Washington, DC: National Institute of Justice.

Famega, C. N., Frank, J., and Mazerolle, L. 2005. "Managing Police Patrol Time: The Role of Supervisor Directives." *Justice Quarterly* 22: 540–559.

Federal Bureau of Investigation. n.d. *National Incident-Based Reporting System (NIBRS).* Washington, DC: FBI. Available online at http://www.fbi.gov/ucr/faqs.htm.

Franz, V., and Jones, D. M. 1987. "Perceptions of Organizational Performance in Suburban Police Departments: A Critique of the Military Model." *Journal of Police Science and Administration* 15: 153–161.

Gau, J. M., and Brunson, R. K. 2010. "Procedural Justice and Order Maintenance Policing: A Study of Inner-City Young Men's Perceptions of Police Legitimacy." *Justice Quarterly* 27: 255–279.

Gerth, H. H., and Mills, C. W. 1946. *From Max Weber: Essays in Sociology.* New York: Oxford University Press.

Goldstein, H. 1968. "Police Response to Urban Crisis." *Public Administration Review* 28: 417–418.

———. 1977. *Policing a Free Society.* Cambridge, MA: Ballinger.

———. 1987. "Toward Community-Oriented Policing: Potential, Basic Requirements, and Threshold Questions." *Crime & Delinquency* 33: 6–30.

———. 1990. *Problem-Oriented Policing.* Philadelphia: Temple University Press.

Gore, A. 1994. *Common Sense Government Works Better and Costs Less: Third Report of the National Performance Review.* Washington, DC: U.S. Government Printing Office.

Greene, J. A. 1999. "Zero Tolerance: A Case Study of Police Policies and Practices in New York City." *Crime & Delinquency* 45: 171–187.

Greene, J. R. 1989. "Police Officer Job Satisfaction and Community Perceptions: Implications for Community-Oriented Policing." *Journal of Research in Crime and Delinquency* 26: 168–183.

———. 2000. "Community Policing in America: Changing Nature, Structure and Function of the Police." In *Criminal Justice 2000, Volume 3: Policies, Processes, and Decisions for the Criminal Justice System,* pp. 299–370. Washington, DC: National Institute of Justice.

Griffin, G. R., Dunbar, R. L. M., and McGill, M. E. 1978. "Factors Associated with Job Satisfaction Among Police Personnel." *Journal of Police Science and Administration* 6: 77–85.

Harcourt, B. E. 2001. *Illusions of Order: The False Promise of Broken Windows Policing.* Cambridge, MA: Harvard University Press.

Hayeslip, P. W., and Cordner, G. W. 1987. "The Effects of Community-Oriented Patrol on Police Officer Attitudes." *American Journal of Police* 6: 95–119.

Herbert, S. 2001. "Policing the Contemporary City: Fixing Broken Windows or Shoring Up Neo-Liberalism?" *Theoretical Criminology* 5: 445–466.

Hornick, J. P., Burrows, B. A., and Phillips, D. M. 1989. "An Impact Evaluation of the Edmonton Neighborhood Foot Patrol Program," November. Paper presented at the Annual Meeting of the American Society of Criminology, Reno, NV.

Huberts, L. W. J. C., Kaptein, M., and Lasthuizen, K. 2007. "A Study of the Impact of Three Leadership Styles on Integrity Violations Committed by Police Officers." *Policing: An International Journal of Police Strategies & Management* 30: 587–607.

Kadleck, C. 2003. "Police Employee Organizations." *Policing: An International Journal of Police Strategies and Management* 26: 341–351.

Katz, C. M., Webb, V. J., and Schaefer, D. R. 2001. "An Assessment of the Impact of Quality-of-Life Policing on Crime and Disorder." *Justice Quarterly* 18: 825–876.

Kelling, G. L., and Bratton, W. 1998. "Crime Rates: Insiders' Views of the New York City Story." *Journal of Criminal Law and Criminology* 88: 1217–1231.

Kleismet, R. B. 1985. "The Chief and the Union: May the Force Be With You." In W. A. Geller (ed.), *Police Leadership in America: Crisis and Opportunity,* pp. 281–285. New York: Praeger.

Kraska, P. B., and Cubellis, L. J. 1997. "Militarizing Mayberry and Beyond: Making Sense of American Paramilitary Policing." *Justice Quarterly* 14: 607–629.

Kraska, P. B., and Kappeler, V. E. 1997. "Militarizing American Police: The Rise and Normalization of Paramilitary Units." *Social Problems* 44: 1–18.

Kraska, P. B., and Paulsen, D. J. 1997. "Grounded Research into U.S. Paramilitary Policing: Forging the Iron Fist Inside the Velvet Glove." *Policing and Society* 7: 253–270.

Lachlan, B., Blair, J. P., Skalski, P. D., Westerman, D. K., and Spence, P. 2007. *Police Forum* 16: 11–22.

Lefkowitz, J. 1973. "Attitudes of Police Toward Their Job." In J. R. Snibbe and H. M. Snibbe (eds.), *The Urban Policeman in Transition,* pp. 203–232. Springfield, IL: Charles C. Thomas.

———. 1974. "Job Attitudes of Police: Overall Description and Demographic Correlates." *Journal of Vocational Behavior* 5: 221–230.

Lind, E. A., and Tyler, T. R. (1988). *The Social Psychology of Procedural Justice.* New York: Plenum.

Maguire, E. R. 1997. "Structural Change in Large Municipal Police Organizations During the Community Policing Era." *Justice Quarterly* 14: 547–576.

Mastrofski, S. D. 1992. "What Does Community Policing Mean for Daily Police Work?" *National Institute of Justice Journal* August: 23–27.

McCluskey, J. D., Mastrofski, S. D., and Parks, R. B. 1999. "To Acquiesce or Rebel: Predicting Citizen Compliance with Police Requests." *Police Quarterly* 2: 389–416.

McElroy, J. E., Cosgrove, C. A., and Sadd, S. 1993. *Community Policing: The CPOP in New York.* Newbury Park, CA: Sage.

Moore, M. H. 2002. *Recognizing Value in Policing: The Challenge of Measuring Police Performance.* Washington, DC: Police Executive Research Forum.

Mottaz, C. 1983. "Alienation Among Police Officers." *Journal of Police Science and Administration* 11: 23–30

National Institute of Justice. 1997. *Measuring What Matters. Part Two: Developing Measures of What the Police Do.* Washington, DC: Department of Justice.

Novak, K., Hartman, J., Holsinger, A., and Turner, M. 1999. "The Effects of Aggressive Policing of Disorder on Serious Crime." *Policing* 22: 171–190.

Oettmeier, T. N., and Wycoff, M. A. 1997. *Personnel Performance Evaluations in the Community Policing Context.* Washington, DC: Community Policing Consortium.

Parnas, R. 1967. "The Police Response to the Domestic Disturbance." *Wisconsin Law Review* Fall: 914–960.

Reibstein, L. 1997. "NYPD Black and Blue." *Newsweek* June 2: 66, 68.

Reuss-Ianni, E. 1983. *Two Cultures of Policing: Street Cops and Management Cops.* New Brunswick, CT: Transaction Books.

Roberg, R. R. 1979. *Police Management and Organizational Behavior: A Contingency Approach.* St. Paul, MN: West.

Rosenbaum, D. P., Yeh, S., and Wilkinson, D. L. 1994. "Impact of Community Policing on Police Personnel: A Quasi-Experimental Test." *Crime & Delinquency* 40: 331–353.

Rosenfeld, R., Fornango, R., and Baumer, E. 2005. "Did Ceasefire, Compstat, and Exile Reduce Homicide?" *Criminology and Public Policy* 4: 419–450.

Sandler, G. B., and Mintz, E. 1974. "Police Organizations: Their Changing Internal and External Relationships." *Journal of Police Science and Administration* 2: 458–463.

Sampson, R. J., and Cohen, J. 1988. "Deterrent Effects of the Police on Crime: A Replication and Theoretical Extension." *Law and Society Review* 22: 163–189.

Sherman, L. W. 1997. "Policing for Crime Prevention." In L. W. Sherman, D. Gottfredson, D. MacKenzie, J. Eck, P. Reuter, and S. Bushway (eds.), *Preventing Crime: What Works, What Doesn't and What's Promising,* pp. 8/1–8/58. Washington, DC: Office of Justice Programs.

Skogan, W., and Frydl, K. 2004. *Fairness and Effectiveness in Policing: The Evidence*. Washington, DC: National Academies Press, National Research Council of the National Academies.

Skogan, W. G., and Hartnett, S. M. 1997. *Community Policing, Chicago Style*. New York: Oxford University Press.

Smith, B. 1940. *Police Systems in the United States*. New York: Harper & Row.

Spelman, W., and Eck, J. E. 1987. "Newport News Tests Problem-Oriented Policing." *NIJ Reports* January–February: 2–8.

Sunshine, J., and Tyler, T. R. (2003). "The Role of Procedural Justice and Legitimacy in Shaping Public Support for Policing." *Law & Society Review* 37: 513–547.

Walker, S. 1992. *The Police in America: An Introduction,* 2nd ed. New York: McGraw-Hill.

——— 2008. "The Neglect of Police Unions: Exploring One of the Most Important Areas of American Policing." *Police Practice & Research* 11: 95–112.

Watson, E. M., Stone, A. R., and DeLuca, S. T. 1998. *Strategies for Community Policing*. Upper Saddle River, NJ: Prentice Hall.

Weisburd, D., and McElroy, J. E. 1988. "Enacting the CPO Role: Findings from the New York City Pilot Program in Community Policing." In J. R. Greene and S. D. Mastrofski (eds.), *Community Policing: Rhetoric or Reality?,* pp. 89–102. New York: Praeger.

Weiss, A., and Freels, S. 1996. "The Effects of Aggressive Policing: The Dayton Traffic Enforcement Experiment." *American Journal of Police* 15: 45–64.

Whitaker, G. P. 1982. "What Is Patrol Work?" *Police Studies* 4: 13–22.

Wilson, D. G., and Bennett, S. F. 1994. "Officers' Response to Community Policing: Variations on a Theme." *Crime & Delinquency* 40: 354–370.

Wilson, J. Q. 1968. *Varieties of Police Behavior*. Cambridge, MA: Harvard University.

Wilson, J. Q., and Boland, B. 1978. "The Effect of Police on Crime." *Law and Society Review* 12: 367–390.

Wilson, J. Q., and Kelling, G. 1982. "Broken Windows: The Police and Neighborhood Safety." *Atlantic Monthly* March: 29–38.

Wilson, J. M. 2006. *Community Policing in America*. New York: Routledge.

Wilson, O. W. 1950. *Police Administration*. New York: McGraw-Hill.

Wilson, O. W., and McLaren, R. C. 1977. *Police Administration,* 4th ed. New York: McGraw-Hill.

Worral, J. L. 2002. *Does "Broken Windows" Law Enforcement Reduce Serious Crime?* Sacramento, CA: The California Institute for County Government.

Wycoff, M. A., and Skogan, W. G. 1993. *Community Policing in Madison: Quality from the Inside Out*. Washington, DC: National Institute of Justice.

Zhao, J. 1996. *Why Police Organizations Change: A Study of Community-Oriented Policing*. Washington, DC: Police Executive Research Forum.

CHAPTER 6

Organizational Change

CHAPTER OUTLINE

- The Change Process
    Resistance to Change
    Overcoming Resistance to Change
- The Madison Experience
    Laying the Foundation
    Key Elements to Change
    Results From Madison
- The Chicago Experience
    Laying the Foundation
    Key Elements to Change
    Results From Chicago
    Lessons Learned From Madison and Chicago
    A Final Lesson: Surviving Leadership Change
- Job Redesign and Community Policing
    Changing Officer Performance Measures

CHAPTER OUTLINE (continued)

- Innovation
    - Compstat as a Change Process
    - Police Departments as Learning Organizations
    - Organizational Learning
    - Police–Researcher Partnerships
    - Utilize Middle Managers
- Summary
- Discussion Questions
- References

KEY TERMS

- advisory committees
- balance of power
- beat meetings
- Chicago Alternative Policing Strategy (CAPS)
- change strategies
- experimental police district (EPD)
- external change
- group norms
- inertia
- innovation
- internal change
- job redesign
- learning organization
- MBWA
- organizational change
- quality leadership
- research and development (R&D)
- WHAM

AS DISCUSSED PREVIOUSLY, THE police have traditionally been organized and managed according to classical prescriptions. In other words, a department is structurally designed in a hierarchical, bureaucratic manner, where the leadership style is authoritarian and employees are tightly controlled. It is extremely difficult to make significant and sustained changes to such traditional, paramilitary departments. As past discussions have indicated, a less bureaucratic, decentralized orientation allows a department to more readily adapt to community needs and expectations. The purpose of this chapter is to describe how the change process and police strategies, especially toward community policing, can be applied in a constructive manner. Furthermore, the importance of developing a climate of innovation (and learning) will be discussed; without such a climate, the amount of effort required to implement new programs cannot be sustained.

The Change Process

Organizational change occurs when an organization adopts new ideas or behaviors (Pierce and Delbeq 1977). Usually, an innovative idea, such as a new patrol strategy or job design, is introduced and employee behavioral changes are supposed to follow. Consequently, the ultimate success of any organizational change effort depends on how well the organization can alter the behavioral patterns of its personnel—that is, change old behavior patterns to new behavioral patterns to "fit" the new strategy or method. Of course, the greater the degree of change required, the more significant will be the behavioral changes required. For instance, community policing requires a substantial change in the role and job design not only of police officers but also of their supervisors and managers. Thus, a transition toward community policing requires substantially greater behavioral change by personnel than would simply changing a patrol tactic or procedure. The corollary to this behavioral change process is that the greater the degree of planned change, the greater will be the resistance to it. A discussion follows of how resistance to change in policing develops.

Resistance to Change

Probably the most common characteristic of change is people's resistance to it. In general, people do not like to change their behavior. Adapting to a new environment or learning a new work method often results in feelings of stress and fear of the unknown (e.g., Will I like it? Will I be able to do it well?). The following is a discussion of the major reasons why resistance to change—using community policing as an example—is so common in police departments.

Inertia. A great deal of **inertia**, or "doing things as they have always been done," is strongly associated with paramilitary departments. People have what is known as "sunk costs" in their jobs and routines, including time, energy, and experience; these are powerful forces in resisting change. Individuals or groups with many such "investments" sunk into a particular department or job may not want changes, regardless of their merit. Community policing, for example, requires officers to do many of their old tasks in new ways and to take on new tasks with which they are not familiar. They may be "asked to identify and solve a broad range of problems; reach out to elements of the community that previously were outside their orbit; and put their careers at risk by taking on unfamiliar and challenging responsibilities" (Skogan and Hartnett 1997, 71). These expectations are often beyond the officers' capabilities and the traditional roles for which they were initially selected and trained (Lurigio and Rosenbaum 1994). There is little doubt that most officers would rather do what they believe they were hired for and what they perceive to be the "real" police role: crime fighting. Consequently, community policing is often dismissed as "social work," which takes important time away from their crime-fighting activities.

Management personnel will have the same inertia factor at work because they also have been selected and trained to do traditional policing. Although inertia occurs at all managerial levels, except possibly at the very top when a new police chief is brought in, the attitudes of sergeants are especially important. Because sergeants have the most direct influence over the day-to-day activities of street officers, it is crucial that they "buy into" the new program, promoting the department's new policies and procedures. To do so, sergeants must act as facilitators and trainers as well as supervisors.

Misunderstandings. Resistance to change is likely to occur when officers do not clearly understand the purpose, techniques, or consequences of a planned change because of inadequate or misunderstood communication. A major problem concerns the uncertainty about consequences of change. If employees are not told how they will be affected by change, rumors and speculation will follow, and resistance and even sabotage may be strong enough to severely limit the change effort. When change is imposed on officers, instead of occurring as a result of their participation, misunderstandings are more likely. For example, when police departments are attempting to move to community policing, they frequently make the mistake of not clearly articulating what new roles will be created and the effect of those new roles on all involved. In addition, departments often do not allow officers to participate in the planning and development of the new program to gain a sense of "ownership."

Group Norms. As discussed in the previous chapter, groups have an important impact on the behavior and attitudes of their members. **Group norms**, or expected behavior from group members, can be a powerful factor in resistance to change. If individual officers follow the norms strictly (e.g., that only law enforcement activities are important), they will not easily perceive the need for change. If significant departmental changes are to occur, police managers must consider group norms and influences and involve group consensus and decision making in planning for change. The major way to achieve such involvement is to allow for participatory management (discussed below).

Balance of power. Changes that are perceived to threaten the autonomy, authority, power, or status of a group or unit will most likely encounter resistance, regardless of their merit. For instance, such resistance was well documented in the team-policing experiments of the 1970s, when departments attempted to decentralize their operations into neighborhood teams (see Sherman, Milton, and Kelley 1973). Because this approach provided more control and autonomy for lower-level management (sergeants), middle management (lieutenants and captains) resisted the change (by subverting and, in some cases, sabotaging the plans) for fear that they would lose authority, power, and status. Because the failure of most team-policing efforts can be traced, at least in part, to the lack of support by midlevel managers, it is crucial that police executives plan for their role in the change process.

Inside Policing 6.1 provides a glimpse into the reasons for which officers resisted change in New York in that city's attempt to make a transition to community policing. Notice how virtually every reason overlaps, to some degree, with the major reasons for resistance discussed above. These reasons for resistance would be similar in most, if not all, traditional paramilitary police departments in the country.

Overcoming Resistance to Change

The research to date provides some important lessons to help police managers overcome resistance to organizational change in moving toward community policing. For instance, in a national survey of more than 1,600 agencies (Wycoff 1995), police chiefs and sheriffs were asked about the lessons they learned from their experiences with community policing. The most frequently mentioned lessons were (1) the need for preimplementation training of personnel, (2) the importance of taking a long view of the change process, (3) the need for support from elected officials and other city agencies, and (4) the importance of listening to and involving the community. In addition, 48 percent thought that implementation would require major changes in departmental policies or goals, 56 percent anticipated that rank-and-file employees would resist such changes, and 83 percent strongly supported the need for training in community policing and believed that existing training efforts were inadequate.

As suggested by the above discussions, a major factor in overcoming resistance to community policing is officer involvement and participation in the change process and program design. In a study of community policing implementation and officer attitudes in six small to midsize agencies in North Carolina (Adams, Roche, and Arcury 2002), a major finding was that those who perceive a *participatory management style* were more supportive of the change toward community policing. Importantly, the strongest support for a move toward community policing was found among officers in one city that allowed for the most involvement in designing the program and showed the clearest support for community policing by the command staff. In addition, it was found that, compared with traditional officers, community policing officers were significantly more satisfied with their jobs. Although it

INSIDE POLICING 6.1 Resistance to Organizational Change in New York

The following are examples of reasons why some police officers in the New York City Police Department resisted change toward a community policing philosophy. These examples are based on informal discussions with officers.

Failure to see the need for change

Some officers believe that community policing is merely a result of the commissioner (chief) wanting to try out his ideas in New York. They see this as a grand management experiment attempted at their expense.

Confusion over new roles and fear of the unknown

Many officers do not fully understand their new roles or what the department expects of them. Some officers perceive a conflict between their new role, where they are asked to "serve the public," and their traditional role, in which they exerted coercive control over the community.

Fear of loss of status, security, and power

Many officers in New York believe they are doing a credible job controlling crime and see themselves as having achieved a reasonable status in society; they have earned this status by being brave. Community policing, with its reduced emphasis on adventure and bravery and its enhanced focus on public service, has some officers fearing that their status will be diminished.

Lack of involvement with change

Some officers feel that they are simply being told this is the new philosophy and have no sense of participation in the decision. One superior officer stated after a training seminar, "Community policing is the new train—get on or get off." This attitude encourages the feeling that this program is being forced upon them.

Threat to existing social relationships

While foot patrol officers are getting acquainted with merchants and other citizens who live and work in their assigned communities, the radio car cops are busy responding to calls and, as they say, "busting their butts." They are beginning to resent the department's preferential attitude toward the beat cops and to resent the beat cops themselves, who they feel are not pulling their load and spend their time "schmoozing" with the public. One officer explained, "While I'm out here doing all the grunt work and risking my life, they're playing with the neighborhood kids or attending some community meeting."

Conflicting personal and organizational objectives

The police department is interested in getting officers to work with the citizens toward solving social problems, thereby improving the quality of life and making their streets safer. Some officers believe, however, that many of the problems brought forth by the public are not worthy of police attention and have little to do with crime. Although proponents of community policing believe that resolving such problems will create an environment less conducive to crime and thus lower the crime rate, to many officers this is a waste of their time. Some officers are also candid about their aversion to performing what they perceive as "social work."

SOURCE: Adapted from S. L. Pisani, "Dissecting Community Policing: Part 2." *Law Enforcement News,* May 31, 1992: 8, 10.

may be a less onerous task for management to allow for high levels of participation in small or midsize departments, the importance of participatory management in bringing about constructive change is strongly supported in the research and should be utilized by departments of all sizes.

A study by Lord and Friday (2008) regarding change efforts and officer attitudes toward COP found similar results as those discussed above. The study took place in the Concord (North Carolina) Police Department, where attitudinal measures of officers were taken both before (2002) and after (2005) COP was implemented. Concord made structural changes consistent with community policing, such as permanent assignment to areas, decentralization of authority, partnerships with citizens, and use of problem-solving methods. In 2002 the survey included 76 officers (of 123) and in 2005 it included 83 officers (of 148); two focus groups consisting of ranking officers and managers were also interviewed. In general, findings indicated that officer attitudes about their new job responsibilities were more positive toward COP before implementation than after, and officer attitudes about the effectiveness of COP did not change significantly over time. Four major managerial variables led to these results, including: (1) lack of feedback, (2) lack of job autonomy, (3) lack of preparedness (training), and (4) lack of adequate resources to take on new responsibilities.

What is important about these findings is that the major predictors in officer attitudes toward COP are all areas *under the control* of the police administration, meaning, of course, that police managers can significantly influence officer attitudes toward COP and its implementation. Specific policy implications gleaned from the focus groups included the following:

1. Supervisors should offer frequent feedback through performance evaluation of COP activities so that officers are aware of their level of performance;

2. Training in COP is paramount and should include information regarding policy, methods, history, and examples with hands-on opportunities and presentations;

3. Participatory management should be practiced, allowing officers to exchange ideas through informal meetings as well as by conducting surveys and interviews on a regular basis; and

4. Management should ensure that officers have adequate resources to engage in COP activities—this can be accomplished by building partnerships with outside agencies.

The Madison Experience

Possibly the earliest transition from traditional to community policing was in the Madison, Wisconsin, Police Department. The use of what was called quality leadership, including participation at all levels, smoothed the transition process and helped to overcome initial resistance to the new developments. The change process started in earnest within the department in the early 1980s, well before most of the present-day knowledge gained through research and evaluation was available. Thus, much of what the department accomplished in the way of change was groundbreaking. At the time, the department had approximately 280 commissioned personnel serving a community of approximately 175,000 (Couper and Lobitz 1991).

Laying the Foundation

In the early 1970s, with the appointment of a new chief, the Madison Police Department was operating on a high-control, central-authority model. This traditional style of police management continued through the early years of the chief's tenure but not without costs to the department and its members in terms of a high level of distrust, grievances, complaining, and confrontations. In 1981, after a 4-month leave of absence, the chief decided that something had to be done regarding the department's internal problems. After discussions with rank-and-file officers, it became clear that a "lack of communication" was a primary concern and a new management or leadership style was necessary. Consequently, the chief decided to let employees participate more in organizational decisions and to take on the role of facilitator for himself. This decision led to the establishment of the Officers' Advisory Council (OAC) to provide advice to the chief.

The development of the OAC was critical in clearing the way for a major change in leadership style. The council consisted of 12 peer-selected employees who served for a 2-year period. The OAC over time was given increased responsibility; it developed its ability to gather data and make recommendations using a problem-solving approach. The council learned that if it obtained data to support its recommendations, the recommendations would be put into practice; thus, it had significant input in departmental policies and procedures. The OAC's actions reflected the problem-solving and research orientation of the department's quality-improvement effort.

Key Elements to Change

Following development of the OAC, several key developments took place, including the formation of a committee on the future, a change in leadership style, the implementation of a new operating (experimental) district, and citizen involvement (Couper and Lobitz 1991; Wycoff and Skogan 1993). Each is described below.

1. *Committee on the Future.* In 1984, the Committee on the Future was formed to look at trends and how they might affect the police department in the coming years. The committee was composed of a diverse group of members who had at least 15 years of service remaining; the intent was to have members who had a vested interest in the future of the department. A member of the OAC was appointed to serve on this committee to link the two groups. After a year of meeting two to four times a month, the committee released a report of its findings listing three major recommendations:

1. Get closer to the people we serve.
2. Make better use of available technology.
3. Develop and improve health and wellness in the workplace.

This thinking about the future caused the department to reexamine its structure, internal practices, and the direction in which it was moving.

2. *Quality Leadership.* Early in 1985, almost parallel with the developments in the department, the mayor's office initiated a city-wide effort to improve the Quality/Productivity (QP)—now known as TQM—of the city's departments. A 4-day seminar conducted by W. Edwards Deming, the "father" of the quality movement in this country, was followed by a 15-day training seminar in QP principles and procedures for city employees. Five police

employees attended the sessions, which covered team building, group processes, facilitator skills, and the gathering and use of data.

Following the QP training, the department articulated the management philosophy of **quality leadership** to be used throughout the department, which included the following principles: teamwork for planning and goal setting, data-based problem solving, a customer orientation, employee input in decisions, policies to support productive employees, encouragement for risk taking and tolerance for mistakes, and the manager as facilitator rather than commander. Quality leadership, and its emphasis on employee input, became the means to the goal of a healthier workplace and a necessary prelude to community policing.

3. *Experimental Police District.* A decision was made to develop a prototype of the new design in one part of the department before attempting to redesign the entire organization; see Inside Policing 6.2 for discussion on the development and operation of the **experimental police district (EPD)**. The result was that the EPD was the first decentralized police facility in the department. Opened in 1988, the EPD housed approximately one sixth of the department's personnel and served approximately one sixth of Madison's population. The charge of the EPD was to promote innovation and experimentation in three areas:

1. Employee participation in decision making about the conditions of work and the delivery of police services;
2. Management and supervisory styles supportive of employee participation and of community-oriented and problem-oriented policing; and
3. The implementation of community-oriented and problem-oriented policing.

4. *Citizen Involvement.* To get citizens involved, eight community meetings were held in the project area, two in each alderman's (city counsel) district. The first set of meetings in each district was for people whom the department and alderman designated as community leaders. The second set of meetings was open to all concerned citizens. At the meetings, citizens were questioned about their knowledge of and satisfaction with police services, about neighborhood problems and concerns, and about how they felt police could work with them in responding to problems. The group process used at the meetings resulted in a listing of problems rated by priority.

Results From Madison

In their evaluation of the Madison Police Department's change process, Wycoff and Skogan (1994) found that "it is possible to change a traditional, control-oriented police organization into one in which employees become members of work teams and participants in decision making processes" (88–89). Further, some of the lessons learned in Madison for overcoming obstacles to change include the following:

1. It is possible to implement participatory management in a police department, and doing so is very likely to produce more satisfied workers. Many managers and employees in Madison believe that such an approach, which they call quality leadership, is a necessary condition for the implementation of community policing.

Development and Operation of the EPD

Planning

As a first step in the planning process, project team members identified departmental problems that they thought needed to be corrected, such as a lack of meaningful involvement with the community, lack of teamwork or team identity among officers, inflexible management styles and resulting loss of creativity, and lack of communications and information exchange among ranks. Project team members also conducted department-wide interviews in which team members met in small groups with all employees to find out what they thought needed to be corrected. The top preferences were voted on by the group and published in an EPD newsletter and sent to all employees. This was the first time that management had allowed employees to survey other employees on issues that heretofore were considered strictly management's concern.

Operation

The goal of the EPD managers was to become facilitators and coaches who allow and encourage creativity and risk taking among officers. They have given officers substantial latitude to decide their own schedules, their own work conditions, and how to address neighborhood problems. Managers also consider the input of officers before making decisions; they try to encourage problem solving by offering ideas, information, and scheduling alternatives. Although things moved slowly at the beginning, the managers began to see increased use of problem solving as a tool.

SOURCE: Adapted from D. C. Couper and S. H. Lobitz, *Quality Policing: The Madison Experience* (Washington, DC: Police Executive Research Forum, 1991), 36–37; and M. A. Wycoff and W. G. Skogan, *Community Policing From the Inside Out* (Washington, DC: National Institute of Justice, 1993) 26–27.

---

2. Decentralization contributed significantly to the creation of the new management style. It also contributed to the development of team spirit and processes, conditions that should facilitate community policing. Officers who work in the EPD believe the decentralized station improved relationships with the public; they report increased numbers of contacts with citizens in the community and an ever-increasing number of citizens who come to the station for assistance.

3. The managers of the Madison Police Department also thought that the best way to move toward decentralization and community policing was to change one part of the organization (i.e., the EPD) before proceeding with department-wide implementation.

4. During the long time frame for undergoing change and experimentation (over 2 decades), Madison continued to make efforts to recruit highly educated officers whose backgrounds, life experiences, and attitudes increased the likelihood that they would be supportive of change. (Adapted from Wycoff and Skogan 1994, 89–90)

Based on the research reviewed above, it appears that the bottom line with respect to the successful implementation of community policing can be tied directly to the amount of change made toward the following: (1) decentralized organization, (2) participatory management, (3) higher educational standards, (4) redefinition of the police role, and (5) involvement of a representative body of citizens.

The Chicago Experience

This section will take an inside look at the overall plan for change, as well as the **change strategies**, used by the Chicago Police Department in its attempt to move to community policing. Chicago's attempt at organizational change has been the largest scale effort to date (Skogan and Hartnett 1997). The experimental program consisted of 5 of the 25 police districts in the city, including 54 experimental beats; the experimental districts were referred to as "prototypes," since the program would eventually be expanded to include the 20 remaining traditional districts. The program was labeled the **Chicago Alternative Police Strategy** (CAPS), thus giving the department and city its own style of community policing. A total of 1,500 police personnel of all ranks went through orientation and skill-building sessions, and close to 700 beat meetings, attended by 15,000 people, were held during the first year and a half of the program.

Laying the Foundation

The department developed a mission statement and a 30-page supporting report describing the basic philosophy of community policing and identifying, step by step, many of the key components of change that were needed for the program to succeed. The report opened with a "rationale for change" that reviewed the limits of the traditional model of policing and argued for a "smarter" approach that would capitalize on the strengths of the city's neighborhoods. The report further argued that the department had to be "reinvented" to form a partnership with the community, one that stressed crime prevention, customer service, and honest and ethical conduct. The report was mailed to every departmental member; to help ensure that it would be read, it was included on the reading list from which questions would be drawn for the next promotional exam. It became the basis for planning the eventual city-wide implementation of CAPS.

Key Elements to Change

The organizational change process incorporated six key elements, briefly described below:

1. *The entire department and the city were to be involved.* Rather than forming special community policing units, the whole department would change. Thus, community policing roles were developed for all of the units, including the detective, tactical, gangs, and narcotics divisions, rather than just for uniformed officers. Only patrol would be utilized, however, until the program had proven to be effective. The commitment to city-wide involvement was reflected in the decision to use diverse districts spread throughout the city as prototypes for the program (several of which had high rates of crime), as well as existing personnel in the districts. As one executive put it, the department did not "stack the deck in favor of success."

2. *Officers were to have permanent beat assignments.* To develop partnerships with the community and to learn about the neighborhood, officers had to be assigned to one place long enough for residents to know them and learn to trust them. Additionally, officers had to have enough free time to allow them to engage in community work. In attempting to resolve the conflict between working with the public and responding promptly to calls for service, officers in each prototype district were divided into beat teams and rapid-response units. *Beat teams* (i.e., community policing focus) were to be dispatched less frequently to have time to work on community projects. The *rapid-response units* (i.e., traditional patrol focus) and other teams that worked throughout the district were to be assigned to other calls.

3. *The department was to have a strong commitment to training.* The department invested a significant effort in training officers and their supervisors in the skills required to identify and solve problems in working with the community. By emphasizing training, a message would be sent to the rank and file that community policing was real and upper management was committed to the program. A test would be administered at the end of the training program, which they had to pass; participants who did not pass would have to repeat the course. This appeared "to have a salutary effect on their attentiveness" (Skogan and Hartnett 1997, 101).

INSIDE POLICING 6.3   WHAM in Chicago

Management knew that there could be no real change without the support of rank-and-file members at the bottom of the organization. This became known as the "winning hearts and minds" (WHAM) component of organizational change. To win the hearts and minds of street officers, the following change strategies were used.

Changing the Job

Jobs were changed for the officers who served each prototype district by dividing them into beat teams and rapid-response teams. The department took this approach rather than forming what is known as a split-force of community policing officers and regular ("real") policing officers into separate units; such an approach has been shown to create tension between the two units and ultimately to undermine community policing. Using beat teams, a majority of officers' time could be spent within their assigned geographical area. This new beat integrity, including the freedom from responding to 911 calls, was accomplished by increasing the number of officers who served in the prototype districts by about 13 percent. In addition, a radio-dispatch plan was implemented that allocated selected calls to beat teams. Beat officers were to work with schools, businesses, and residents to identify and solve problems and to serve as coordinators for service requests to other city agencies. They attended various neighborhood meetings to work with existing community organizations, as well as regularly held public beat meetings, to increase communications between residents and beat officers. Over time, officers would alternate between beat work and rapid-response cars to ensure that community policing did not become confined to special units.

Changing Supervision

The role of sergeants was crucial to CAPS because prototype beat officers needed direction and mentoring in their new roles; sergeants were responsible for supervising rapid-response officers as well. Although the sergeants were given some initial CAPS training, it soon became apparent that their role was not clearly defined, and they often felt unsure about what was expected of them. The prototype sergeants were told that their job was to coach officers in their new community roles, but in reality they knew as little as the street officers about what that entailed. They soon became disgruntled and felt overworked. Additional training attempted to alleviate this role confusion; it was designed to encourage them to become teachers, coaches, and mentors. The additional training consisted of several skill-building sessions with respect to leadership styles, building partnerships, problem solving, and team building.

Avoiding the Social-Work Image

One of the lessons learned from other cities was that separate community policing units did not work. Members of these units inevitably were looked down on by their colleagues as "empty holsters" doing "wave-and-smiling" policing. The prototype districts that were selected joined the program as a unit, "warts and all"; they were not staffed by volunteers or specially selected officers, supervisors, or even district-level managers (two of whom—of five—never supported the program). Management also made a concerted effort to assure all sworn personnel that community policing was not a "soft-on-crime" approach. They stressed that officers would not become social workers, but rather referral specialists who could help solve problems (leading to crime) at the neighborhood level. In addition, it was emphasized that traditional police work would continue to be important and would be rewarded, with a strong emphasis on making arrests where appropriate.

SOURCE: Adapted from W. G. Skogan and S. M. Hartnett, *Community Policing, Chicago Style* (New York: Oxford University Press, 1997), 89–95.

4. *The community was to play a significant role in the program.* The foundation of CAPS was the formation of police–community partnerships, focused on identifying and solving problems at the neighborhood level. One of the major problem-solving roles for the police was to engage community resources by drawing other city agencies into identifying and responding to local concerns. This community involvement was developed in two ways. First, **beat meetings**, usually monthly, involved small groups of residents and beat officers. The meetings were held in church basements and park buildings throughout the city. Second, **advisory committees** were formed at the district level to meet with upper management and district staff; committees included community leaders, school council members, ministers, business operators, and other institutional representatives.

5. *Policing was to be linked to the delivery of city services.* Community policing inevitably involves the expansion of the police role to include a broad range of concerns that are outside the scope of traditional policing. Such expansion was considered necessary by management because they realized that although the police could put a lid on many crime-related problems, they could never eliminate them. They wanted to develop problem-solving systems that could keep the lid on even after they had moved on. In addition, the delivery of city services in the prototype districts was linked to the police department through the use of service-request forms. The requests for service generated by officers were closely tracked by city hall, which developed a system to prioritize and track each case.

6. *There was to be an emphasis on crime analysis.* The geographic analysis of crime was considered a key element of the program. Computer technology was to be used to speed up the collection and analysis of data, which would be used to identify crime problems in the beat area. A user-friendly crime-mapping system was developed for use on computers (see Chapter 8), with printouts to be distributed at beat meetings and made accessible to the public at each district station. Other planned analytic tools included "beat planners," which were beat officers' notebooks filled with local information. New roll-call procedures were also developed to encourage officers on various shifts to share information about their beats and community resources.

In addition to the six key elements developed in the organizational plan, Chicago also used a number of methods to help facilitate the organization-wide change process, especially with respect to **"winning the hearts and minds" (WHAM)** of rank-and-file members (see Inside Policing 6.3).

Results From Chicago

Findings reported below are from the 8- and 9-year evaluation (Chicago Community Policing Evaluation Consortium 2003) and the 10-year evaluation (Chicago Community Policing Evaluation Consortium 2004) of the CAPS program. It should be noted that the evaluations of CAPS was paid for by city funding (versus federal funding, which ebbs and flows), thus signaling the value the city had placed on evaluating the progress of this program.

Before CAPS was launched, public opinion of the police was not very positive but, for the most part, improved progressively through 2003. Three key trends in the quality of police service were measured by the consortium: (1) *demeanor* (i.e., questions relating to politeness, concern, helpfulness, and fairness); (2) *responsiveness* (i.e., questions relating to responsiveness, dealing with problems, and working with residents); and (3) *performance* (i.e., questions relating to helping victims of crime, preventing crime, and keeping order). Figure 6.1 illustrates trends in these measures from 1993 through 2003, that is, the percentage of citizens averaging a positive rating (the two best of four rating categories) on each index. Separate trends are recorded for whites, African Americans, and Latinos; no figures are given for Latinos in 1993 because that survey was conducted in English only. As can be seen, with a few exceptions, the trends across all three indexes for all races increased over the 10-year CAPS period. The only exception is with police demeanor and whites, who already had a very high rating to begin with. Only African Americans did not approach the 50th percentile with respect to police performance.

The lower right quadrant presents a summary index of all 10 individual survey questions relating to the three indexes. The *quality of service* index notes an improvement in white opinion by 13 percentage points. African American opinions grew by 15 percentage points between 1993 and 1999 before dropping off a few points by 2003. For Latinos, their positive view of police service grew by 17 percentage points between 1994 and 2003. Interestingly, the Commission points out that the "attitude changes ... could be much larger, because the data span a period of 11 years, and CAPS has become part of the ordinary business of the Police Department" (p. 43).

The primary concerns of the residents identified in beat meetings were not the types of serious crime problems traditionally associated with the police. For instance, the most commonly discussed problem, at 88 percent of the meetings, was *social disorder,* including a long list of minor offenses and conditions that frequently disturb neighborhood residents. These types of problems included prostitution, public drinking, panhandling, curfew or truancy violations, disturbances by teenagers, public exposure, gambling, trespassing, and landlords who lose control of their buildings. *Drug problems* (e.g., sales/use and drug houses) were discussed at 66 percent of the meetings, followed by *physical decay* (e.g., abandoned buildings and cars, graffiti) at 58 percent; *parking and traffic problems* (e.g., speeding/reckless driving) at 57 percent; *property crime problems* (e.g., burglary and theft) at 51 percent; *gang problems* (e.g., violence and intimidation) at 51 percent; *policing problems* (e.g., dissatisfaction to 911 call responses, criticism of CAPS implementation) at 47 percent; and *personal crime* (e.g., shootings and street crime) at 47 percent. In contrast, the primary problems identified by the police were *personal crime* followed by *property crime*; only about 30 percent of police identified problems associated with social disorder, which was *60 percent less* than identified by citizens (Skogan 2006).

In 2000, the Office of Management Accountability was created to develop and implement a new accountability process; in this process each district is responsible for defining

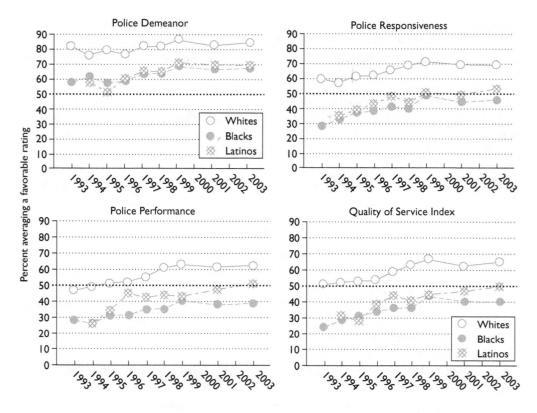

FIGURE 6.1 **Trends in Assessments of Police Service Quality, 1993–2003.**

Source: Chicago Community Policing Evaluation Consortium. 2004. *CAPS at Ten: Community Policing in Chicago.* January: 41.

problems and choosing strategies and, based on an analysis of its data, concentrating its resources on them. Because the accountability process is a departure for Chicago, it was introduced slowly. Some have described the process as a "kinder, gentler" version of New York's Compstat process. The accountability meetings—especially those at headquarters—were never intended to be a "gotcha" experience (Chicago Community Policing Evaluation Consortium 2003, 66–67). They were intended, however, to hold district commanders accountable for implementing various problem-solving strategies with respect to crime and community concerns.

In a recap of CAPS at 10 years, the Consortium (2004) emphasized the considerable task of making the many CAPS programs come together in a coordinated fashion, particularly since it requires the commitment of neighborhood residents, the police, and their many agency partners. Importantly, CAPS is not only a police department program, but also a city program, meaning that community policing is vested throughout the city and should therefore be less vulnerable than in most cities. The Chicago Police Department was also commended for its "unwavering cooperation and interest in the evaluation over the past decade" (Chicago Community Policing Evaluation Consortium 2004, 154). However, it was noted that CAPS continues to struggle with problem solving. Analysis of hundreds of beat-level plans found that efforts to solve local priority problems have not been effective; the same problems, in about the same locations, persist year after year. Beat meeting effectiveness in setting problem-solving agendas for the public has declined, and neither officers nor resident activists have had refresher training in problem solving. It was suggested that refocusing on problem solving could reengage the community in the active partnership promised by CAPS.

Lessons Learned From Madison and Chicago

Two of the most comprehensive organizational change efforts, from traditional policing to community policing, have taken place in Madison and Chicago. The change processes utilized had many similarities and some significant differences. While each relied on a report developed by departmental personnel to lay the foundation for change and to guide the change process, each attempted to improve communication with rank-and-file officers. Madison, however, spent significantly more time developing a true participatory (quality) leadership style. A comprehensive committee structure was developed and staffed with personnel throughout the department, whose recommendations were generally adopted. This level of employee participation in policing is unparalleled. It is also important to understand that both departments had strong support from their cities' top political leadership. In Madison, quality improvement was a city-wide movement, whereas in Chicago, the mayor used the CAPS program to shore up city hall's provision of services throughout the city. Both cities recognized the importance of, and relied heavily upon, the training of their personnel. Finally, both cities started with experimental programs, which, over time, were expanded throughout the department.

One significant difference was that Chicago used regular officers and supervisors ("warts and all") in its prototype districts, whereas Madison selected personnel who were "interested" in the program (effectively volunteers) for its experimental police district; EPD personnel could also decide their own schedules and work conditions. An important consideration regarding the use of regular officers, supervisors, and established beats is that the experimental or prototype programs will not be as likely to generate a "we-versus-they" mentality between experimental and regular officers. Such an approach can go a long way toward reducing the types of resistance to change discussed earlier and documented in Inside Policing 6.1.

One additional caveat should be noted. In Madison, a concerted effort had been made for approximately 2 decades to recruit highly educated officers who would be more likely to support change. If a true commitment to community policing is to take place, and if the police role is to be significantly broadened to carry it out, the level of higher education required for police may be an important factor. In Madison, it appears that the history of promoting higher education contributed significantly to establishing a more conducive atmosphere for large-scale organizational change.

Although both departments sought input from the community, the level of participation from each community differed significantly. Madison developed feedback mechanisms only (mainly surveys), whereas Chicago took the development of citizen communication and input to a new level for police departments. The involvement of beat officers who were geographically stable, and generally free from 911 response calls, allowed them to work closely with the community in problem solving. By conducting regularly scheduled, public beat meetings in a way that identified problems and made action plans, they could determine what residents considered the important problems in their areas and work to alleviate them. Trends in the assessment of police service quality through 2003, including performance, demeanor, and responsiveness, all have made solid gains since CAPS began.

It would appear that both departments have made significant progress toward implementing community policing, but they have done it in different ways. In Madison, *employee participation* in the change process was a strong point (**internal change**), whereas in Chicago, the development of *partnerships with the community* through beat teams was the strong suit (**external change**). Perhaps the most effective change approach to community policing would be to mix the internal practices from Madison with the external practices from Chicago while raising the educational standards for recruits.

A Final Lesson: Surviving Leadership Change

One of the problems in securing long-term change efforts and reforms in police departments relates directly to the tenure of the police chief and often the mayor as well. A transition in leadership at the top is frequently followed by changes from the new chief, dismantling, or to a lesser extent, discarding, key ingredients of the reforms and substituting his or her own agenda and policies. In policing, this change often means "backsliding" toward a re-centralized agency with a renewed emphasis on traditional "tough on crime" law enforcement programs. As noted by Roberg, Kuykendall, and Novak (2002), such a drift back to incident-based law enforcement actions (i.e., reactive versus preventive measures) provides the most immediate gratification and is more in keeping with the "dangerous and dramatic" self-image of many police officers, along with the expectations of many in the community (including politicians).

After 14 years of community policing under the CAPS program in Chicago, in late 2006, this is precisely what happened within the department after a new police chief was selected. Skogan (2008) reports that in 2003, the city's major newspaper created a crime scare during a period when the mayor was in the process of selecting a new chief. Politically, the most expedient response was to quickly appoint a candidate from the detective unit committed to tough enforcement. The new chief abruptly reorganized and refocused the department on "guns, gangs, and homicides." Shortly thereafter, the department's commitment to the community policing program deteriorated, as most districts lost their community policing managers who were subsequently put in charge of more traditional units. This conceptual switch further led officers to gravitate toward crackdown units as they became the focus of the new administration. Thus, the Chicago department, in short order, appears to have all but abandoned 14 years of CAPS development, returning to traditional policing roots and a "management structure driven by recorded crime."

Importantly, a shell of the program remains intact; it was not politically feasible to totally shut it down because the beat-oriented parts of community policing are "so deeply woven into the political organizational life of the city's neighborhoods." In the final analysis, this enduring commitment of the CAPS program into community life may allow the program to remain politically feasible, "perhaps to be resurrected when a crisis of legitimacy again haunts the police, and they have to rediscover community policing in order to rebuild again their credibility with the community" (Skogan 2008, 33).

Job Redesign and Community Policing

Just as police departments have been criticized for overreliance on traditional, paramilitary organization, so too has the traditional design of police jobs. Historically, many agencies have stressed a narrow perspective on the role of the police and the community and have consequently designed their jobs from a narrow, legalistic perspective. However, as the complexity of the police role has been recognized, the police have become better educated, and community policing has developed, it has become clear that traditional job designs are not meeting the needs of many police personnel, the department, or the community.

In attempting to enhance community livability through problem solving and crime-prevention efforts, community policing jobs are substantially redesigned by increasing the use of officer discretion and power, especially with respect to utilizing alternatives other than those available primarily through the criminal justice system. The enriched nature of a community police officer's day, in addition to regular patrol duties (including calls for service), might include the following (Mastrofski 1992):

- Operating neighborhood substations.
- Meeting with community groups.
- Analyzing and solving neighborhood problems.
- Working with citizens on crime-prevention programs.
- Conducting door-to-door surveys of residents.
- Talking with students in school.
- Meeting with local merchants.
- Making security checks of businesses.
- Dealing with disorderly people. (p. 24)

An observational study in Cincinnati by Frank, Brandl, and Watkins (1997) measured the average amount of time beat officers (traditional) and neighborhood officers (community policing) spent on their daily activities. Significant differences were found in seven of eight activity categories. For example, neighborhood officers spent a substantial amount of their time engaged in community-based service activities, especially meeting-related activities (11 percent), compared with beat officers (0 percent). Only routine patrol (22 percent) accounted for more of their time. In addition, service and problem-solving activities were performed to a much greater extent by neighborhood officers than by beat officers.

As expected, traditional police activities associated with patrol work made up a substantial majority of beat officer workloads (71 percent), including random patrol (33 percent), responding to noncrime calls (20 percent), and crime-related tasks, such as arrests, tickets/citations, and criminal reports (18 percent). These tasks were of much less significance for neighborhood officers; for example, only 5 percent of their time was spent on crime-related activities. This research shows that the content of community policing can be substantially different from the content of traditional policing. The authors suggest that police agencies now need to develop performance measures that are consistent with the activities performed by officers performing community policing duties, and, we might add, *recognizing and rewarding* them for such activities. The research on the impact of community policing activities on officer attitudes and performance is mixed. On the one hand, it appears that in programs with a high level of implementation, such activities can significantly increase levels of personal growth and job satisfaction, as well as improve attitudes toward the department, supervision, the community, and community policing (see Hayeslip and Cordner 1987; Hornick, Burrows, and Phillips 1989; Wycoff and Skogan 1993; Skogan and Hartnett 1997; Zhao, Thurman, and He 1999; Adams, Roche, and Arcury 2002). On the other hand, in programs that were either partially or poorly implemented, officers' attitudes and job satisfaction levels were not as positive, usually with no discernable differences between experimental and comparison groups (see Greene and Decker 1989; McElroy, Cosgrove, and

Sadd 1993; Rosenbaum, Yeh, and Wilkinson, 1994; Wilson and Bennett 1994; Weisburd and McElroy 1995).

In general, research results with respect to a high level of community policing implementation and **job redesign** are threefold: (1) officers who value *internal needs* for personal growth and have a service orientation (Cochran, Bromley, and Swando 2002) are more likely to benefit from a community policing–enriched job design; (2) more traditionally oriented officers or "careerists" (Greene 1989) who value *extrinsic rewards,* such as recognition and security, likely will not benefit from a job redesign; and (3) less clearly, in some departments with organization-wide community policing, all officers appeared to benefit from a job redesign. Interestingly, with respect to the third finding (that all officers appeared to benefit from a job redesign), a more recent study by Miller, Mire, and Kim (2009) of 235 sworn officers in a medium-size southern city discovered the job characteristics of *autonomy* and *feedback* were significant in predicting job satisfaction in four different models being measured. This meant that *all* of the officers highly valued their degree of independence on the job and the amount of feedback received regarding their performance; these are not common characteristics of traditional police job design, suggesting—at least in departments moving toward community policing—that they should be.

Changing Officer Performance Measures

For those police departments "moving" toward community policing, it is critical that they change traditional performance evaluation criteria to incorporate community policing values and practices. However, research to date indicates little progress has been made toward this transition. This is of concern since little in the way of community policing practices in the field will take place until they are recognized, evaluated, and rewarded. To obtain specific information on community policing officer evaluation, Lilley and Hinduja (2006) utilized the LEMAS national survey from 410 municipal and county agencies with at least 50 sworn officers. Three criteria from the survey were used as measures of community policing development: (1) whether a department had a formal written community policing plan, (2) whether officers were encouraged to engage in problem solving, or (3) whether officers had received at least 8 hours of community policing training. If departments met all three criteria, they were classified as community policing organizations ($n = 168$); if they met two criteria, they were classified as transitional ($n = 116$); all other organizations were classified as traditional departments ($n = 126$).

While the results indicated that there were incremental differences with respect to performance evaluation content regarding the different types of departments, overall the agencies were not statistically different with regard to evaluation focus, role, service expectation, innovation, and motivational approach. Furthermore, the vast majority of evaluation content (approximately 70 percent) was designed to benefit the police organization itself, bureaucratic processes, and conformity, rather than any external stakeholder such as the community or justice system. Interestingly, items pertaining to officer *grooming and appearance* were nearly equal in percentage of the evaluation as items regarding *aiding citizens.* Even evaluation systems that had been updated to incorporate community policing principles did not differ substantially in content or format. Some agencies simply tacked on a category labeled community policing to the end of the form with no clarification regarding the meaning. It appears that most agencies that have updated their formal evaluation process to include community policing concepts have simply modified traditional formats, which tend to focus on aiding the organization and internal processes. These findings suggest that relatively little movement has been made toward evaluating and rewarding community policing practices.

Innovation

If constructive and timely change is to take place in police departments, midlevel and top-level managers must develop an organizational climate that fosters and encourages innovation. **Innovation** refers to the development and use of new ideas and methods. Such a climate should be relatively open, trustworthy, and forward looking. In their study on police innovation in six American cities, Skolnick and Bayley (1986) made several recommendations for improving police effectiveness. As you read the recommendations, try to keep in mind how each does or does not apply to the experiences of Madison and Chicago.

First, and most important to successful innovation, is *effective and energetic leadership from the office of the chief.* Although executive leadership is vital to any enterprise, it is essential to traditional paramilitary police departments. Because such departments tend not to be democratically run, most members are aware of the chief's preferences, demands, and expectations. It is not enough, however, simply to espouse certain ideals and values; the chief must become an active, committed exponent of them.

The second requirement for successful innovation is that *the chief must be able to motivate* (and sometimes manipulate) *departmental personnel* into supporting the values that the chief espouses. Some resistance from the "old guard," who have strong ties to the status quo, is likely. Because these individuals may retain much influence, police executives often attempt to keep or enlist their support. As a result, chiefs may actually affirm conflicting norms, telling different audiences what each wants to hear. Consequently, nobody in the department knows what the chief stands for and everyone is confused. Preferably, a majority of the officers can be persuaded that the new values are superior. Persuasion is seldom easy, however, especially in departments that have associations and unions resistant to change. Nevertheless, innovatively inclined chiefs should be able to work with such associations and unions to gain the support of the rank and file.

Skolnick and Bayley (1986) noted that one of the ways of potentially lessening resistance from the old guard is to first implement change in one part of the department. In this way, the department can learn how best to change with the least amount of disruption, and those who are resistant have a chance to observe the potential benefits of the change. If the change is ultimately considered not beneficial for the entire department, it would not be implemented throughout the department.

A third requirement is that *integrity of innovation must be defended.* Once a new value system (one dedicated to the development of new concepts and methods) has been established, it will need to be protected from the pull to return to the status quo. Such protection is especially necessary in policing because police departments tend to be heavily tied to the traditional ways of doing things.

The fourth requirement for innovation is *public support.* Innovative crime prevention programs that are implemented with community input enjoy strong, often unexpected, support from the public. If properly introduced and explained to the community, police innovations will most likely be widely supported.

As Skolnick and Bayley (1986) pointed out, the need to sustain or defend innovation is critical, since the tendency to regress toward the traditional way of doing things is strong. What methods can police managers use to keep the department on the path toward innovation? Inside Policing 6.4 examines several types of management strategies that the Madison Police Department employed to gain momentum and sustain innovation in its organizational change process.

INSIDE POLICING 6.4   Sustaining Innovation in Madison

The major strategies used to sustain innovative changes in Madison are briefly described below.

Training

The management team completed 7 days of quality-productivity and quality-leadership training; during the last hour of each training day the chief appeared to answer questions and address concerns. Thus, he showed support for the new philosophy and served as a role model for the new leadership style. This training was followed by three similar 6-day sessions for sergeants. Quality-improvement training then began for all departmental employees, both civilian and commissioned.

Promotions

The first effort beyond training to start running the department in accord with the new philosophy involved implementing a new promotion policy. This was an important step because who is promoted sends a stronger message than any words from management. Consequently, the chief sent out a memorandum establishing the importance of the new promotion policy, which stated, in part,

> I strongly believe that if we are to "practice what we preach" in our Mission Statement to achieve excellence (i.e., teamwork, respect, problem solving, openness, sensitive and community-oriented policing)...we will have to alter the way in which we lead....The promotions I make from now on are going to people who have strong interpersonal and facilitative skills and who can adjust and adapt to the new needs and demands....In addition to being totally committed to the Mission of the organization [supervisors and managers] will have to be able to work in a team, become coaches, accept feedback, ask and listen to others in the team, and facilitate their employees' input and growth in the workplace.

Customer Surveys

To establish baseline data and to assess the quality and customer satisfaction of the department, a survey was developed. The survey asked citizens to rate police services from poor (1) to excellent (5) in seven areas: (1) concern, (2) helpfulness, (3) knowledge, (4) quality of service, (5) solving the problem, (6) putting citizens at ease, and (7) professional conduct. An open-ended question at the end asked: How can we improve? About 25 percent of the responses included feedback on this question.

Surveys were mailed each month (with a stamped, self-addressed return envelope) to all persons identified in every 50th case-numbered report, including victims, witnesses, complainants, and arrestees. The results are periodically published in the department's newsletter, in which both positive and negative comments regarding improvement are summarized.

Managing by Wandering Around

The department believes that leadership involves being seen and that leaders cannot be seen very well if they spend all their time behind a desk. Accordingly, the department has found that a very simple technique of **managing by walking around (MBWA)** is a powerful one. For most police managers, MBWA means getting out on the "street" (where the action is) and observing and asking or answering questions. In this way, managers learn what their employees need from them to do a quality job, as well as letting them know that managers care about quality work and are looking for ways to improve conditions and processes.

SOURCE: Adapted from D. C. Couper and S. H. Lobitz, *Quality Policing: The Madison Experience* (Washington, DC: Police Executive Research Forum, 1991), 59, 62–63, 66–67, 73–74, 80.

Compstat as a Change Process

As discussed previously, the allure of the Compstat process is that it allows for increased levels of managerial control, discretion, and accountability and therefore has the potential to significantly impact organizational change. This potential was evident in the CAPS accountability process described above, as a kinder, gentler version of New York's Compstat, where headquarter meetings were more constructive and never intended to be a "gotcha" experience. However, as developed in New York, Compstat meetings often turned into "browbeating" sessions where mid- and upper-level managers were essentially held accountable for crime rates in their jurisdictions. Such an approach would not only be dysfunctional to organizational change, but also, if enough pressure were applied, could potentially contribute to manipulations in crime reporting.

This is precisely what took place in New York, according to a survey of 491 retired NYPD captains who worked during the Compstat era (Messing, Celona, and Fanelli 2010). The captains stated they felt significant pressure from precinct commanders to downgrade major crimes (felonies) to misdemeanors so they would not be entered into the crime index (UCRs)—thus "lowering" the overall crime rate. Over one half of the respondents reported they were aware of reports being manipulated with an eye toward Compstat. The overall impression appeared to be that the captains felt far more pressure to downgrade index crimes and that the department demanded less integrity with respect to crime reporting than for the previous generation (prior to Compstat). NYPD spokespersons refuted this notion by pointing to a previous study and a crime-reporting audit by the state comptroller, indicating that the NYPDs crime statistics were accurate.

Interestingly, shortly after the above cited interview data were made public, the *Village Voice* released a set of secretly recorded tapes by an NYPD officer (Adrian Schoolcraft) who was concerned about how the public was being treated (Rayman 2010). The tapes of conversations—covering a 17-month period ending on October 17, 2009—with supervisors and officers at Bedford-Stuyvesant's 81st Precinct (including 117 roll calls) provides further evidence that Compstat in New York has led not only to tampering with crime reporting (i.e., underreporting crimes as described above), but also to overly aggressive zero-tolerance policing. Officers were instructed to arrest people for things like blocking the sidewalks, standing on certain street corners and building stoops (charges were usually dropped later). To attain the required quotas, the precinct's campaign led to a 900 percent increase in stop-and-frisks in the neighborhood. It should be noted that this is the same type of police behavior discussed in Chapter 5 that was occurring in the early to mid-1990s when the number of civilian complaints in New York, as reported to the Civilian Complaint Review Board (CCRB), increased by more than 60 percent, and the new police chief (who followed Bratton) implemented a policy directed at improving officer behavior known as "courtesy, professionalism, and respect."

Even with the types of problems surrounding the use and implementation of Compstat as originated in New York, the development of similar Compstat-type programs throughout the nation's police departments has been nothing short of phenomenal. A national survey of 445 large departments (over 100 sworn officers) and 85 small departments (50–99 sworn officers) by Weisburd, Mastrofski, Greenspan, and Willis (2004) found that approximately one third of large agencies had implemented a Compstat-like program, with an additional quarter planning such a program (see Table 6.1). The small agencies were much less likely to have implemented a Compstat model; with only 11 percent having done so. However, almost 30 percent were planning to implement such a program.

TABLE 6.1 PDs Who Have Implemented or Are Planning a Compstat-Like Program

DEPARTMENT SIZE	PERCENT YES	PERCENT NO, BUT PLANNING	PERCENT NO
Small (50–99 sworn)	11.0	29.3	59.8
Large (100+ sworn)	32.6	25.6	41.8

Because of rounding, rows do not add to 100.

Source: Adapted from D. Weisburd, S. Mastrofski, R. Greenspan, and J. Willis, *The Growth of Compstat in American Policing* (Washington, DC: Police Foundation, 2004).

Weisburd and his colleagues further examined the percentage of departments that claimed to have implemented specific features associated with Compstat-like programs. From these results, they found six key features associated with Compstat-like programs of large police agencies; these include the following, in order of their percentage of implementation:

1. Use data to assess progress toward objectives (30 percent).
2. Hold regularly scheduled meetings with district commanders to review progress toward objectives (26 percent).
3. Set specific objectives in terms that can be precisely measured (26 percent).
4. Develop, modify, or discard problem-solving strategies based on what the data show (25 percent).
5. Give middle managers control over more resources to accomplish objectives (23 percent).
6. Hold middle managers responsible for understanding crime patterns and initiating plans to deal with them (23 percent).

The researchers were also interested in understanding the motivations of departments that had recently adopted Compstat-like programs. The large department sample was separated into those agencies that said they had recently implemented a Compstat program ($n = 79$) and those that had not implemented such a program and were not planning to do so ($n = 178$). Those departments that had recently implemented Compstat ranked the *reduction of serious crime* and *increasing management control* over field operations substantially higher than departments not implementing/not planning to implement Compstat. Conversely, departments that had not implemented/were not planning to implement Compstat ranked substantially higher on *improving officer skill levels* and on *improving officer morale*; these goals are closely aligned with community policing programs. The authors conclude that the model of Compstat that has been touted in New York has had a strong influence on its adoption throughout the country. In addition, these findings suggest that Compstat may represent a movement in police efforts not only to develop more effective crime-control strategies and organization control, but also *away from community policing strategies* that rely on improved street officer skills and initiative.

An in-depth case study (Willis, Mastrofski, and Weisburd, 2004) of the Lowell (MA) Police Department's Compstat program, which had been implemented for 4 years at the time of the study, found similar results as those described in the national survey. The program was fairly successful in mission clarification (crime control/crime fighting) and internal accountability (holding midlevel managers more responsible, primarily for crime control). Both of these elements, however, further support the traditional paramilitary structure and role concept. On the other hand, those Compstat elements that did not easily fit within the existing bureaucratic structure were found to be undeveloped or underdeveloped. For example, the departments *did not shift* toward decentralized geographic command, flexibility, data-driven analysis, innovations in problem solving, or external accountability. In general, the *strengthening* of the command hierarchy under Compstat interferes with any attempt to streamline the agency toward innovation, experimentation, or risk taking.

A more recent ethnographic study of a Compstat program in a large southeastern police department (Dabney 2010), based on roughly 350 hours of ride-along observations and interviews, discovered that most of the rank-and-file officers either misunderstood or misinterpreted the core intent of the Compstat model. In general, because of the lack of a two-way flow of communication within the hierarchy, goals and strategies that were formulated at Compstat meetings were either diluted or diverted; beat officers and street-level supervisors tended to miss the concept that tactics should be comprehensive, flexible, and crime targeted in a geographic area. Instead of seeing the outcome as strategic in nature, the goal of officers became simply to produce arrests (of any kind), and the role of supervisors was to track officer-level efforts with weekly performance evaluations. Taking into account the findings from the national survey and the in-depth case studies, it appears, in general, that the manner in which Compstat is being implemented puts it at distinct odds with community policing. These findings strongly suggest that a New York–style Compstat program not only does not promote organizational change and innovation, but also actually strengthens the traditional bureaucratic, command hierarchy of the paramilitary structure. Accordingly, Compstat can best be used as a managerial process that allows for increased accountability with respect to utilizing data to assess community needs and crime patterns and, based on these assessments, to develop best practices patrol strategies and problem-solving methods to deal with the concerns.

Police Departments as Learning Organizations

The discussion of quality-management principles in the last chapter included the concept of continuous improvement. Continuous improvement cannot be accomplished without continuous learning, which is another way to sustain innovation in police departments. In other words, if management can develop an environment that promotes continuous learning, the department (and its members) would benefit from its own and others' experiences, including both success and failure. Such a learning environment leads to a **learning organization**, which is able to process what it has learned and adapt accordingly. According to Geller (1997), there are many structural and process ideas that would help police departments to become learning organizations. One idea is to create a **research and development (R&D)** unit that *actually does* research and development instead of only statistical descriptions of departmental inputs and outputs. Such a unit would be run by someone who understands R&D (suggesting a graduate degree) and be supported by a respectable budget (also not the norm). Such a unit might help foster an appreciation for the practical benefits of prior research in the field. It is virtually impossible to be a learning organization if the use of recent research findings is not part of departmental processes. See Voices From the Field for one chief's perspective on how his department's planning and research unit contributes to adaptation and change.

VOICES FROM THE FIELD

James Corwin
Chief of Police, Kansas City (MO) Police Department

Question: *What role does your planning and research unit serve in facilitating organizational change and adaptation?*

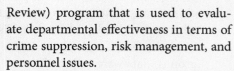

Answer: Implementing change, and the more difficult task of adapting to it, is challenging for any organization. Police agencies, by their nature, are generally more ordered and tradition-bound. The Kansas City, Missouri, Police Department's (KCPD) Research and Development Division is instrumental in facilitating and adapting to such change.

This division forecasts trends that could potentially affect the department, analyzes issues currently confronting the department, develops and recommends the implementation of programs that address these issues, and directs the formation of policies and procedures to help guide department members through the changes resulting from these programs. A variety of methods and research techniques are employed to accomplish these goals.

The division establishes and maintains relationships with peer city police departments across the nation that may have previously encountered or dealt with an issue currently facing KCPD. Such issues range from the challenge of collecting and interpreting data on biased-based policing (i.e., ìracial profilingî) to understanding the introduction and use of red-light photo enforcement. This technique allows us to adopt and modify proven strategies that increase the effectiveness and efficiency of our operations. For example, Research and Development Division personnel reviewed police performance measure and accountability models to help develop the KCPD CSTAR (Comprehensive Strategic Team Accountability

Review) program that is used to evaluate departmental effectiveness in terms of crime suppression, risk management, and personnel issues.

The Research and Development Division also develops and expounds on ideas using information obtained at seminars, symposia, and presentations. This method resulted in KCPD acquiring and implementing a paperless policy and acknowledgment system that allows KCPD personnel to review, sign, and refer to all departmental written directives electronically. The Research and Development Division's management of the system helped all personnel adapt to an electronic accountability system, which was a significant departure from its decades-old, paper-bound predecessor.

The Research and Development Division not only facilitates change, but also initiates change. When the KCPD was forced to contend with severe budget cuts, some alternative funding sources were sought. In response, the Research and Development Division submitted a plan to establish a Police Foundation designed to supplement the educational and equipment needs of the members of the department. The plan was eventually approved by executive command staff and implemented.

The Research and Development Division has been, and continues to be, an important contributor regarding KCPD's ability to embrace and adapt to future organizational change. Current projects include the implementation of a real-time crime center, a study of employing alternative fuels for department vehicles, the deployment of automated license plate recognition technology, and revising department personnel policies.

James Corwin started with the KCPD in 1979 and was appointed Chief in 2004. In February 2005, Corwin implemented the CSTAR program that is currently used to measure department effectiveness.

Organizational Learning

In a study on police organizational learning, Crank and Giacomazzi (2009) designed a strategy for an ongoing assessment of the implementation of four innovative areas of contemporary policing trends in the Ada (Idaho) County Sheriff's Office (ACSO). The authors noted that learning occurs in police agencies through its "conversations" with three parties in its environment: stakeholders (e.g., city council members, local business owners), the broad citizen base served by the department, and organizational personnel. To best determine to what extent the department was listening to its clientele and, in turn, adapting (learning) from the feedback, both quantitative (i.e., surveys) and qualitative (i.e., interviews, focus groups) data were collected.

The four policing innovations implemented by the sheriff's office, and how their level of effectiveness was evaluated, included the following: (1) citizens' perceptions of crime problems and satisfaction with police services (measured by citizen survey, resident/stakeholder focus groups, and deputy survey); (2) implemented the use of decentralized substations and long-term geographic assignment (measured by citizen survey, resident/stakeholder focus groups, and deputy survey); (3) implemented the use of problem-solving practices into routine patrol (measured by resident/stakeholder focus groups, deputy survey, and deputy focus groups); and (4) expanded the use of performance evaluations to include community policing/problem solving (measured by deputy survey and deputy focus groups).

The findings suggested that while all four areas studied were in need of substantial change, the ACSO was shifting its organizational priorities to match those found in its environment. These results suggested that a police department that is open to feedback from its constituencies can effectively adapt to changing environmental demands.

Police-Researcher Partnerships

A further idea that would help foster organizational learning would be to expand *police-researcher relationships*. Such partnerships allow the police department to get involved in a research project without all the necessary expertise or budget restraints, while learning something about itself; researchers, in turn, have increased impact on policy and practice and gain valuable access to the organization. While originally implemented in Australia (Bradley and Nixon 2009), one ongoing effort in the United States involves the Cincinnati Police Department (CPD) and faculty and graduate students from the University of Cincinnati's Policing Institute (UCPI), housed within the Division of Criminal Justice (Engel and Whalen 2010). The partnership is based on promoting evidence-based strategies necessary to facilitate best policies and practices. Graduate students from the UCPI are assigned to assist CPD personnel with the collection and analysis of new data, focusing on problem-solving efforts designed to reduce crime, violence, and disorder.

Utilize Middle Managers

One interesting structural suggestion to promote a learning organization is to use middle managers to facilitate critical thinking. Since middle managers in police departments (i.e., lieutenants and captains) are continually coming under fire in reorganization plans as being unproductive and even counterproductive, it may be constructive to give them something useful to do. Because they are between the policy makers above and the policy implementers below, why not charge them "with facilitating critical thinking about the efficacy of policies and implementation" (Geller 1997, 6). If departments were to do this; assuming proper development, training, and ability levels, the performance ratings of middle managers might reflect how well they enable their units and communities to constructively criticize and improve departmental operations.

Summary

The process of organizational change in policing requires the development of a culture that encourages innovation. The primary obstacles to change include inertia, misunderstandings, group norms, and the balance of power. Each of these obstacles makes the change process more difficult and requires a sustained effort by management if it is to be overcome. In general, ways to overcome obstacles to change in the direction of community policing include taking a long-term view of the change process, preliminary training of personnel, use of participatory practices, gaining support from elected officials and city agencies, and involving the community.

Two relatively successful examples of large-scale organizational change efforts are Madison and Chicago. Many of the reasons for the success of these departments overlap; for example, both improved communication with their personnel; both had political support; both relied on training; both started out with experimental or prototype districts; and both involved the community, especially in Chicago, where regularly scheduled beat meetings were held. Unique to Madison was its concentrated effort to recruit highly educated officers who were believed to be more supportive of change.

Job redesign is also an important consideration in changing a department toward community policing; it was suggested that individual differences must be considered when planning for job enrichment. In addition, it is critical that a department change its performance evaluation criteria and reward structure to reflect the needs of community policing. It was further noted that the use of a New York–style Compstat process not only does not support change and innovation, but also tends to increase support for the paramilitary, hierarchical command structure. However, the development of an organizational learning environment can be used to sustain change and innovation.

Critical Thinking Questions

1. Discuss four reasons why police officers tend to resist organizational change. Of the obstacles described regarding why officers may resist organizational change, which do you believe is the most serious? How would you attempt to overcome this obstacle?

2. Why do you think the change process in Madison was so successful?

3. What key strategies were used in Chicago's plan for organizational change? Which do you believe are the most crucial?

4. Discuss the major differences in the change processes used in Madison and Chicago. Which process do you believe will be more effective in the long run and why?

5. Regarding overcoming resistance to change toward community policing, what do you believe are the most important policies that police managers should use to help influence officer attitudes and to implement change?

6. Why is innovation important to the organizational change process? What management techniques would you use to sustain it? Does Compstat have a role to play in the change process?

7. What is meant by a learning organization? Discuss several ideas that would help police departments to become learning organizations.

8. With respect to police–researcher partnerships, would you, as a top-level administrator, establish relationships with academics and, if so, why?

References

Adams, R. E., Roche, W. M., and Arcury, T. A. 2002. "Implementing Community-Oriented Policing: Organizational Change and Street Officer Attitudes." *Crime & Delinquency* 48: 399–430.

Bradley, D., and Nixon, C. 2009. "Ending the 'Dialogue of the Deaf': Evidence and Policing Policies and Practices: An Australian Case Study." *Police Practice and Research* 10: 423–435.

Brody, D. C., DeMarco, C., and Lovrich, N. R. 2002. "Community Policing and Job Satisfaction: Suggestive Evidence of Positive Workforce Effects from a Multijurisdictional Comparison in Washington State." *Police Quarterly* 5: 181–205.

Chicago Community Policing Evaluation Consortium. 2000. *Community Policing in Chicago, Year Seven: An Interim Report.* Chicago: Illinois Criminal Justice Information Authority.

———. 2003. *Community Policing in Chicago, Years Eight and Nine.* Chicago: Illinois Criminal Justice Information Authority.

———. 2004. *CAPS at Ten: Community Policing in Chicago.* Chicago: Illinois Criminal Justice Information Authority.

Cochran, J. K., Bromley, M. L., and Swando, M. J. 2002. "Sheriff's Deputies' Receptivity to Organizational Change." *Policing: An International Journal of Police Strategies & Management* 25: 507–529.

"Community Policing Strategies." 1995. *Research Preview.* Washington, DC: National Institute of Justice.

Couper, D. C., and Lobitz, S. H. 1991. *Quality Policing: The Madison Experience.* Washington, DC: Police Executive Research Forum.

Crank, J. P., and Giacomazzi, A. 2009. "A Sheriff's Office as a Learning Organization." *Police Quarterly* 12: 351–369.

Dodenhoff, P. C. 1996. "LEN Salutes Its 1996 People of the Year, the NYPD and Its Compstat Process." *Law Enforcement News* December: 1, 4.

Engel, R. S., and Whalen, J. L. 2010. "Police–Academic Partnerships: Ending the Dialogue of the Deaf, the Cincinnati Experience." *Police Practice & Research* 11: 105–116.

Frank, J., Brandl, S. G., and Watkins, R. C. 1997. "The Content of Community Policing: A Comparison of the Daily Activities of Community and 'Beat' Officers." *Policing: An International Journal of Police Strategy and Management* 20: 716–728.

Franz, V., and Jones, D. M. 1987. "Perceptions of Organizational Performance in Suburban Police Departments: A Critique of the Military Model." *Journal of Police Science and Administration* 15: 153–161.

Geller, W. A. 1997. "Suppose We Were Really Serious About Police Departments Becoming 'Learning Organizations'?" *National Institute of Justice Journal,* December: 2–8.

Greene, J. R. 1989. "Police Officer Job Satisfaction and Community Perceptions: Implications for Community-Oriented Policing." *Journal of Research in Crime and Delinquency* 26: 168–183.

Greene, J. R., and Decker, S. H. 1989. "Policy and Community Perceptions of the Community Role in Policing: The Philadelphia Experience." *Howard Journal of Criminal Justice* 26: 168–183.

Hartnett, S. M., and Skogan, W. G. 1999. "Community Policing: Chicago's Experience." *National Institute of Justice Journal,* April: 3–11.

Hatry, H. P., and Greiner, J. M. 1986. *Improving the Use of Quality Circles in Police Departments.* Washington, DC: National Institute of Justice.

Hayeslip, P. W., and Cordner, G. W. 1987. "The Effects of Community-Oriented Patrol on Police Officer Attitudes." *American Journal of Police* 6: 95–119.

Hornick, J. P., Burrows, B. A., and Phillips, D. M. (1989). *An Impact Evaluation of the Edmonton Neighborhood Foot Patrol Program,* November. Paper presented at the annual meeting of the American Society of Criminology, Reno, NV.

Lilley, D., and Hinduja, S. 2006. "Organizational Values and Police Officer Evaluation: A Content Comparison Between Traditional and Community Policing Agencies." *Police Quarterly* 9: 486–513.

Lord, V. B., and Friday, P. C. 2008. "What Really Influences Officer Attitudes Toward COP: The Importance of Context." *Police Quarterly* 11: 220–238.

Lurigio, A. J., and Rosenbaum, D. P. 1994. "The Impact of Community Policing on Police Personnel: A Review of the Literature." In D. P. Rosenbaum (ed.), *The Challenge of Community Policing,* pp. 147–166. Thousand Oaks, CA: Sage.

Mastrofski, S. D. 1992. "What Does Community Policing Mean for Daily Police Work?" *National Institution of Justice Journal* 225: 23–27.

McElroy, J. E., Cosgrove, C. A., and Sadd, S. 1993. *Community Policing: The CPOP in New York.* Newbury Park, CA: Sage.

Messing, P, Celona, L., and Fanelli, J. 2010. *NYPD Stats Were Captain Cooked.*

Miller, H. A., Mire. S., and Kim, B. 2009. "Predictors of Job Satisfaction Among Police Officers: Does Personality Matter?" *Journal of Criminal Justice,* 37: 419–426.

Pierce, J. L., and Delbeq, A. L. 1977. "Organization Structure, Individual Attitudes and Innovation." *Academy of Management Review* 2: 27–37.

Pisani, S. L. 1992. "Dissecting Community Policing: Part 2." *Law Enforcement News,* May 31: 8, 10.

Rayman, G. 2010. *The NYPD Tapes: Inside Bed-Stuy's 81st Precinct.* Available online at http://www.village-voice.com/content/print/printVersion1797847.

Roberg, R. R., Kuykendall, J., and Novak, K. 2002. *Police Management,* 3rd ed. Los Angeles: Roxbury.

Rosenbaum, D. P., Yeh, S., and Wilkinson, D. L. 1994. "Impact of Community Policing on Police Personnel: A Quasi-Experimental Test." *Crime & Delinquency* 40: 331–353.

Sherman, L. W., Milton, C. W., and Kelley, T. V. 1973. *Team Policing: Seven Case Studies.* Washington, DC: Police Foundation.

Skogan, W. G. 2008. "Why Reforms Fail." *Policing & Society* 18: 23–34.

———. 2006. *Police and Community in Chicago: A Tale of Three Cities.* New York: Oxford University Press.

Skogan, W. G., and Hartnett, S. M. 1997. *Community Policing, Chicago Style.* New York: Oxford University Press.

Skolnick, J. H., and Bayley, D. H. 1986. *The New Blue Line: Police Innovation in Six American Cities.* New York: Free Press.

VanderVegt, G., Emans, B., and VandeVliet, E. 1998. "Motivating Effects of Task and Outcome Interdependence." *Group & Organization Management* 23: 124–143.

Weisburd, D., Mastrofski, S. D., Greenspan, R., and Willis, J. J. 2004. *The Growth of Compstat in American Policing.* Washington, DC: Police Foundation.

Weisburd, D., McElroy, J., and Hardyman, P. 1988. "Challenges to Supervision in Community Policing." *American Journal of Police* 7: 29–50.

Weisburd, D., and McElroy, J. E. 1995. "Enacting the CPO Role: Findings from New York City Pilot Program in Community Policing." In J. R. Greene and S. D. Mastrofski (eds.), *Community Policing: Rhetoric or Reality?,* pp. 89–102. New York: Praeger.

Willis, J. J., Mastrofski, S. D., and Weisburd, D. 2004. "Compstat and Bureaucracy: A Case Study of Challenges and Opportunities for Change." *Justice Quarterly* 21: 463–495.

Wilson, D. G., and Bennett, S. F. 1994. "Officers' Response to Community Policing: Variations on a Theme." *Crime & Delinquency* 40: 354–370.

Wycoff, M. A. 1995. *Community Policing Strategies.* Washington, DC: National Institute of Justice.

Wycoff, M. A., and Skogan, W. G. 1993. *Community Policing in Madison: Quality From the Inside Out.* Washington, DC: National Institute of Justice, December.

———. 1994. "Community Policing in Madison: An Analysis of Implementation and Impact." In D. P. Rosenbaum (ed.), *The Challenge of Community Policing: Testing the Promises,* pp. 75–91. Thousand Oaks, CA: Sage.

Zhao, J., Thurman, Q., and He, N. 1999. "Sources of Job Satisfaction Among Police Officers: A Test of Demographic and Work Environment Models." *Justice Quarterly* 16: 153–172.

CHAPTER 7

Selection and Development

CHAPTER OUTLINE

- Recruitment
    Recruitment Methods
    Targeting Females and Minorities
    Targeting the Service Oriented
    Cop Crunch
- Selection
    Preemployment Standards
    General Suitability
    Preemployment Testing
    Written Exams and Performance
    Too Smart for Policing?
- Development
    Recruit Training
    Community Policing Training
    Terrorism-Related Training
    Field Training
    Career Growth

- Summary
- Critical Thinking Questions
- Note
- References

KEY TERMS

- andragogy
- bona fide occupational qualification (BFOQ)
- career growth
- cognitive learning
- cop crunch
- deescalation of force
- disparate impact
- education

- field training officer (FTO)
- four-fifths rule
- in-service training
- job task analysis
- lateral entry
- Peace Officer Standards and Training (POST)
- pedagogy

- police training officer (PTO)
- problem-based learning training methods
- procedural justice
- screening in
- screening out
- specialized training
- training

A S NOTED IN THE previous chapters, the nature of policing and police departments is changing—becoming more complex and challenging—necessitating the importance of hiring and developing the highest-quality personnel available. Although the quality of police personnel has always been important, with the increased complexity of the police role and the movement toward community policing, the quality of personnel has perhaps become the key element in effective police operation.

The debate over the meaning of "quality," however, is not easy to resolve. For instance, does an individual need a certain level of intelligence, and how is that measured? Are certain physical characteristics a factor? Should higher education be required? What about ethical values? Considerations of quality also suggest that departments should select personnel, including women, who are representative of the communities they serve because they help provide a greater understanding of issues related to gender, race, and ethnicity. Diversity issues in policing are discussed in depth in Chapter 12.

Police selection and development are also influenced by a city or county civil service system. For instance, civil service requirements may have a significant impact on a department's criteria for selection, promotion, and discipline. Civil service provisions were enacted in 1883 with the passage of the Pendleton Civil Service Act, which tried to eliminate the spoils system, in which politicians could simply hire and fire police personnel based on their political affiliation or friendship. By establishing hiring standards that had to be met by all applicants, police departments gained considerable autonomy and freedom against political influence. But civil service also had a number of negative side effects. For instance, Wilson and McLaren, who were early critics of the civil service, believed that civil service rules provided too much security for "incompetent and untrustworthy" officers, who are virtually impossible to "weed out" (1977, 28). Today, although it is possible to terminate incompetent or dishonest police employees, as a result of civil service provisions, it is an onerous and time-consuming effort.

A police department makes essentially three selection decisions: *entry*, *reassignment*, and *promotion*. Decisions about police entrance are usually for the lowest level position (patrol), but supervisory and managerial-level entry are also possible. A few departments recruit for lower-level and middle-level managers (e.g., sergeants, lieutenants, and captains) from outside the department; this practice is known as lateral entry (discussed in the final section of this chapter). Some departments also select their chief of police from the outside. Because most sheriffs are elected, potential candidates may include persons outside the sheriff's department or even outside the law enforcement field.

All states have created state-wide standards for parts of the personnel process (e.g., selection, training, and promotion). For example, many states now have an organization called Peace Officer Standards and Training (POST). There is still considerable variation among states, however, and some departments do not adhere to the personnel standards that are established because they are not obligated by law to do so.

If high-quality police recruits are to be chosen, the selection process should be designed to screen in, rather than screen out, applicants. **Screening out** identifies applicants who are unqualified and removes them from consideration, while leaving all those who are minimally qualified still in the applicant pool. Recruits who may not be well qualified for police work are then selected from this pool. **Screening in** applicants, in contrast, identifies only the best qualified candidates for the applicant pool. The department will select its recruits from these applicants, thus ensuring a relatively high-quality candidate. Interestingly, many police departments still rely on screening out applicants, but the process has been under attack since at least 1973, when the National Advisory Commission on Criminal Justice Standards and Goals noted the following:

> The selection of police personnel should be approached positively; police agencies should seek to identify and employ the best candidates available rather than being content with disqualifying the unfit. The policy of merely *eliminating the least qualified results in mediocrity* because it allows marginal applicants to be employed along with the most qualified. (italics added, 1973)

Recruitment

The initial step in the selection process is recruiting *qualified candidates*. The relationship of the number of applicants to those who qualify (or meet standards) for positions is often a major factor in the quality of the personnel selected. Much information of the recruitment process can be gleaned from a national survey on recruitment and hiring for the Police Executive Research Forum (PERF) in 2002 (Taylor et al. 2005). The PERF study included 985 agencies (of 2,138 surveyed, a 46 percent return rate) representing all state police agencies and random samples of county and municipal agencies based on region of the country (northeast, south, midwest, and west), size of the populations served (less than 10,000, 10,001 to 49,999, and 50,000 or greater), and the number of sworn officers per department (from 1–20 to 500 and over). In addition, a more recent second study utilizing the same PERF dataset (Jordan et al. 2009) reported more detailed findings with respect to attracting females and minorities to law enforcement; the following sections discuss the findings of each of these studies.

Recruitment Methods

The most commonly reported recruitment methods in the PERF survey were (1) newspaper ads, (2) career fairs, and (3) the Internet. Approximately one half of the agencies utilized one of their own programs as a means to recruit young people, although larger agencies tended to use this approach more than smaller agencies. The most commonly used police programs for this purpose included (1) college internships, (2) explorer programs, and (3) school resource officers. The most commonly targeted groups for recruitment were those with previous police experience, followed by college graduates, racial and ethnic minorities, and women.

Targeting Females and Minorities

In attempting to recruit diverse groups of qualified applicants, it is important that departments recognize that different *recruitment strategies* may be necessary. One of the more effective strategies to attract diverse applicants is to specifically *target* them for recruit purposes. The PERF survey (1995) found that departments do use certain strategies to increase the number of female and minority applicants. For example, some promising practices targeting females included recruiting at events focusing on women, including women's trade shows, women's fairs, and women's fitness clubs. One department noted that they have a commitment to increasing opportunities for females so recruits can see women in positions of authority. Others use advisory committees to help determine effective ways to recruit women, while many use recruitment posters with females clearly present. For minorities, promising practices included the use of advisory groups or task forces to determine appropriate recruit strategies; one agency reported bringing different minorities onto the task force and using a person from each group to recruit fellow minorities (e.g., a Hispanic member would go into the Hispanic community to find places to advertise and recruit, an Asian member would do the same in the Asian community, and so on). Several agencies also noted partnering with minority organizations such as the NAACP to help recruit minorities. Posters with minority members prominently displayed were also used by many agencies.

The PERF results further indicated that significantly more black and Hispanic officers, and officers of other races, as well as females, are working in law enforcement and that the proportion of white officers has declined (by approximately 9 percent). These changes are likely the result of targeted recruitment strategies described above. Other highly targeted groups that may have increased because of recruitment strategies included 4-year college graduates and people with prior police service. College graduates appeared to increase as a proportion of officers (see "Education" below), and it appears that those with prior experience are being heavily recruited—but by other departments.

More specifically, the Jordan et al. (2009) research revealed at least five significant findings to our discussion on attracting and hiring female and minority candidates. First, it was discovered that only approximately 18 percent of agencies used a *targeted recruitment strategy* (some because of a court order or consent decree mandating diversifying officer makeup). A much larger percentage of state and large agencies targeted these populations compared with smaller agencies. For example, 90 percent of state agencies and 66 percent of the largest agencies (over 500 sworn personnel) target women; 88 percent of state agencies and 75 percent of large agencies target minorities. Conversely, of the smallest agencies (20 or fewer sworn personnel), only 11 percent target women and 8 percent target minorities. Overall, the results indicated that agencies that used special recruiting strategies did receive more applicants and hire more people from these groups; the number of minority hires increased by 3.2 times while female hires increased by 2.2 times.

A second finding, possibly associated with the first, was that a positive relationship was found between the annual *recruiting budget* and the number of applications from women and minorities and the number of women and minorities hired. In other words, the more resources put into the recruiting effort, the more successful the recruiting and hiring of women and minorities.

A third finding related to *special entry conditions*, where women and minorities may be allowed to have lower fitness standards and/or preferences on the waiting list; however, these conditions were actually used in less than 3 percent of agencies. Interestingly, even when such conditions were allowed, they did not affect the number of applications or hires from these groups. A fourth finding indicated that *starting pay* related to the number of both female and minority applicants, but had no impact on hiring of either group. On average, a $7,300 increase in starting pay resulted in an 89 percent increase in female applicants and a 145 percent increase in minority applicants.

Last, a fifth finding related to *higher education*, where a requirement of 2 years of college (i.e., 60 units) or a bachelor's degree did not impact the receipt of applications from or the hiring of women. For minorities, there was no impact on applications for either 2 years of college or a college degree. And, while there was no impact on hiring for a college degree requirement, there was a negative impact on the 2-year requirement. The authors speculated that possibly no negative impact was found for the college degree requirement on hiring because of the small number of agencies in the analysis requiring a bachelor's degree, thus limiting the ability to detect a relationship. An alternative explanation that no negative relationship was found between minority applicants with a college degree and hiring could be because these candidates simply scored higher on written and oral exams (see "Preemployment Testing" section later in the chapter). The impact of higher education on minority candidates, and policy implications, are discussed in detail in Chapter 14 on higher education.

In sum, as the authors noted, the above results indicated a pattern that supports a proactive and targeted approach to attracting qualified female and minority candidates to policing, as opposed to relying on more general recruiting strategies or providing preferential treatment.

Targeting the Service Oriented

Finally, an innovative recruitment strategy, focusing on the shift toward community policing, is being tried in several departments emphasizing a police image focusing on *service-oriented* individuals (i.e., working with the community to form crime-solving partnerships). This strategy, termed Hiring in the Spirit of Service (HSS), is a demonstration project funded by the Department of Justice and includes five departments representing both rural (Hillsborough County Sheriff's Office, Tampa Bay, FL; and King County Sheriff's Office, Seattle) and urban (Burlington, VT; Detroit; and Sacramento, CA) locations. For example, the Hillsborough Sheriff's Office aimed their marketing campaign at attracting people who are community service oriented and who have communication and people skills and leadership and organizational skills, not just traditional paramilitary skills traditionally associated with policing (Bowden 2004). A major marketing feature includes posters with photographs of 1 of 21 deputies, relating their personal rewards of serving the community in law enforcement. The poster contains bold-type headers with one of the following attributes: courage, integrity, commitment, or compassion. Under the header is a personal story on the deputy's background and sense of commitment. Inside Policing 7.1 provides an example of a poster (without the picture) of one of the female deputy's stories.

INSIDE POLICING 7.1 **Hillsborough County Sheriff Ad**

Courage: Do You Have What It Takes to Wear the Star?

When her mother was victimized in a home invasion, Stacie Woods decided to leave law school and become involved in the "hands-on" aspect of law enforcement. She became a Hillsborough County Sheriff's deputy.

"Every day is challenging and demanding in a different way." says Deputy Woods, who investigates street-level narcotics and handles complaints from citizens in high-crime areas. "It's typical for my unit to enter a neighborhood suffering from drug sales, vandalism, and basic decline. We join with that community, and through their support, we get the drug sellers arrested and work with Code Enforcement to improve the neighborhood's appearance. We sustain the relationship developed within the community so that future problems can be quickly identified and resolved." She adds, "Helping the whole community so the children there grow up in a safe environment is my real reason for doing what I do."

SOURCE: *Community Links* 2004. "The Art of Hiring for Service," August, p. 4.

One of the problems that historically has plagued police advertising has been the *police image* portrayed. Advertisements often present only the most favorable self-image of both the department and the police role, especially highlighting an ethnically and sexually diverse organization that continually performs adventurous and exciting work. Although this image, from a recruitment perspective, may be effective, it may also be deceitful, leading to employee disenchantment, frustration, and, possibly, resignation after hiring (see "Effectiveness of Recruit Training" later in the chapter). While departments must present an effective image for recruitment purposes, it is important that the image be accurate and realistic; in this way, the agency is more likely to attract the type of people it is targeting. Interestingly, with respect to the HSS project, the agencies involved not only developed a new marketing strategy emphasizing community service, but also worked on developing valid preemployment testing procedures, job task analyses, and performance measures relating to community policing and service-oriented practices (Scrivner 2006). The HSS project is an excellent example of an attempt to take police recruit and hiring practices into the twenty-first century and to correspond to a more sophisticated approach to policing. This project is also an example of the type of approach police departments would need to develop to be able to *actually implement* community policing—including problem-solving—practices and models at some future point in time.

Cop Crunch

Beginning in the 1990s and continuing into the early part of the twenty-first century, there has been a growing perception throughout the law enforcement community that a **cop crunch** was developing where departments would not be able to attract and hire sufficient numbers of qualified applicants to replace personnel who were leaving. It is believed that several factors contributed to this perceived "crunch," including an improved economy at the time and the lure of private-sector jobs that may offer better pay and benefits, the aging out of forces leading to increased levels of retirement, and competition from other departments. Utilizing the PERF data, Jordan et al. (2009) found that, in general, there is no lack of police personnel or of a strong pattern of decreasing staffing levels; thus, there is no support for an actual cop crunch throughout the nation. The mean level of staffing levels for sworn officers in 2002 was 96 percent, little changed from the 97 percent in 1999. However, there is a "troubled minority" of departments who did appear to have a significant concern with staffing levels. Approximately 10 percent of the responding agencies (89 of 843) reported having less than 90 percent of sworn officer positions filled in 2002. This problem was the most apparent in the smallest departments (1 to 20 officers) and the largest departments (over 500 officers) where 15 and 16 percent, respectively, had less than 90 percent of their positions filled.

The authors pointed out, however, the fact that a widespread cop crunch was not found with survey data that was collected in 2002 does not mean that a possible "shortage did not exist in 2008 or that a shortage will not exist in the future. Stakeholders need to monitor levels and prevent, if possible, significant hiring shortfalls" (Jordan et al. 2009, 340).

Selection

Following recruitment, the selection process attempts to determine which candidates are best suited to the needs of the department. The process must decide whether candidates have the requisite skills and abilities to perform effectively. To make such judgments, various selection criteria are used, including preemployment standards and preemployment testing, to establish a ranking system from which candidates are hired. It is crucial that these standards and tests be valid and reliable indicators of job performance. **Validity** is the degree to which a measure actually assesses the attribute it is designed to measure. For example, are the physical strength and agility criteria traditionally used for selection related to the ability to perform the job satisfactorily? If not, they are not valid criteria for selection. **Reliability** is a measure's ability to yield consistent results over time. In the physical strength and agility example, the measure would be reliable if a candidate taking the test on more than one occasion received the same or a similar score. Departments attempt to use criteria that are both valid and reliable; of course, it is possible to have selection criteria that are valid but not reliable or reliable but not valid. For instance, although a physical strength score may be reliable, it may not be a valid criterion if it cannot be shown to be job related.

In addition, validity is important because invalid criteria may have an adverse impact on groups that are protected by equal employment opportunity laws and regulations. The *Equal Employment Opportunity Act of 1972* extended to public agencies the "antidiscrimination in employment" provision of Title VII of the 1964 Civil Rights Act. Title VII prohibits any discrimination in the workplace based on race, color, religion, national origin, or gender. In *Griggs v. Duke Power Company* (1971) the Supreme Court held that an employer's requirement of a high school diploma and two standardized written tests for a position disqualified a higher percentage of blacks than whites and could not be shown to be related to job performance. Consequently, the standards had a **disparate impact** on *Griggs* specifically and on blacks in general. A selection method can be considered to have a legally disparate impact when the selection rate of a group is less than 80 percent of the most successful group; this is also known as the *four-fifths rule.* Prior to *Griggs* selection standards could be used as long they did not intentionally discriminate; after *Griggs,* standards could not be used that were intended to be impartial but in fact were discriminatory in practice.

In another important decision, *Albemarle Paper Company v. Moody* (1975), the Supreme Court found that selection and promotion tests or standards must be shown to be related to job performance; that is, the standard must be *job related.* This decision had far-reaching implications for police selection because all selection criteria must be shown to be related to on-the-job performance. It is important to note, however, that departments can require a standard, even though it may have a disparate impact, if the standard can be shown to be a valid predictor of job performance. For example, in *Davis v. City of Dallas* (1985), the Supreme Court upheld the Dallas Police Department's requirement of 45 hours of college credit, even though it discriminated against minorities, because of the professional and complex nature of police work. Legal precedent for higher educational requirements had previously been established by other professions. Such a job-related standard, known as a **bona fide occupational qualification (BFOQ),** is permissible under Title VII, even though it may exclude members of a protected group.

Police departments, of course, should attempt to use selection methods that not only are valid but also have no adverse impact. This means that departments must commit resources to validating their selection and testing methods, usually through a **job task analysis** that identifies the behaviors necessary for adequate job performance. Based on such identification, the *knowledge, skills, and abilities* required for on-the-job behaviors are formulated; procedures (e.g., tests and interviews) are then developed to identify candidates who meet these requirements. The procedures are then tested relative to their effectiveness in predicting job performance. For example, each of the five departments selected for the HSS project discussed in the previous section underwent an extensive job task analysis (including evaluating behavioral job dimensions and psychological screening dimensions) in attempting to characterize candidates who would best fit the service orientation in their move toward community policing.

Preemployment Standards

Candidates are measured against a department's view of what is required to become an effective police officer. A number of minimum standards are established that must be met prior to employment. These standards are usually quite rigid and establish certain finite qualifications, which, if not met, will most likely eliminate the candidate from further consideration. Such standards may include age, height and weight, vision, physical agility and strength, residency, education, background, psychological condition, and medical condition. Although not all departments have all of these requirements, they are common to many. The standards themselves, however, vary considerably.

Age. Traditionally, police departments have allowed applicants to be between the ages of 21 and 32–38, with some accepting applicants as young as 18. Many police experts and police managers believe that 18 to 21 year olds may not be mature enough to perform police work satisfactorily and, if hired, should only be assigned service duties. For this purpose some departments have police cadet or community service officer programs; when the person completes the educational requirement and/or meets the minimum age requirement, they apply to become a sworn officer. During the 1990s, agencies often increased their age requirements to attract more mature applicants. However, as the cop crunch hit some agencies at the turn of the century, they reduced their age requirements to attract more candidates. For instance, New York reduced the minimum age from 22 to 21 (Crime Control Digest 2001) and Chicago, after raising its minimum requirement from 21 to 23, relowered the requirement to 21 (Decker and Huckabee 2002).

Height and Weight. Stringent minimum and maximum height and weight requirements were standards for most departments in the past. As with age requirements, however, these requirements have been changing over the past several decades because of legal challenges. For instance, minimum height requirements have been challenged successfully as being discriminatory against both women and minority groups, especially Asians and Hispanics. For example, in *Vanguard Justice Society v. Hughes* (1979), the court noted that a 5-foot, 7-inch height requirement excluded 95 percent of the female population but only 32 percent of the male population and found this to be evidence of gender discrimination. Because of such rulings, the general standard has now become *weight in proportion to height*.

Vision. Vision requirements were also traditionally very stringent, ranging from 20/20 to 20/70 uncorrected in both eyes or 20/20 corrected with contacts or glasses. This standard too has been relaxed over the years, because such a requirement cannot be job validated and eliminates otherwise potentially strong candidates. Virtually all police departments, however, still maintain certain corrected and uncorrected vision requirements.

Physical Agility and Strength. Testing of physical agility and strength has been related to an assumed need for physical strength and endurance. For example, candidates would be required to drag a dummy, scale a wall, perform an agility run, or run a certain timed distance (a half mile to two miles); if they fell below a certain minimum, they would be eliminated. According to the national surveys by the Bureau of Justice Statistics (BJS) of nearly 3,000 state (49) and local police departments (1,947) and sheriff's offices (863), in local departments of all sizes, 50 percent use some form of physical agility testing; however, for departments serving more than 50,000 residents, more than 80% used physical agility tests. (Hickman and Reaves 2006a). For sheriff's offices of all sizes, 38 percent use a physical agility test; for agencies serving more than 100,000 residents, over 50 percent use this screening method; however, only the largest agencies (over 1,000,000 population) use physical agility testing over 80% of the time (Hickman and Reaves 2006b).

Since many of these standards cannot be shown to be *job related*, they tend to be discriminatory in nature, especially against women. For example, Lonsway (2003), in her national study of 62 police agencies (38 city, 21 county, and 3 state), found that although the vast majority (89 percent) use some form of physical agility testing, in agencies that did not use such a test, the representation of sworn woman officers was 45 percent higher (15.8 to 10.9 percent). In an attempt to improve the pass rate of otherwise capable applicants, some departments, such as San Antonio, offer physical fitness workshops that help prepare applicants for the physical agility test. The department also offers a workshop on the written exam (Taylor et al. 2005).

As Lonsway (2003) suggests, some of the less discriminatory alternatives include either no physical testing or health-based screening. No physical agility testing would eliminate the negative impact on female applicants of the selection process. Furthermore, there has been no evidence of an adverse impact on policing where this has been done. In Florida, for example, over one half of the local police agencies and sheriff's departments use no physical agility test, and no entry-level physical agility test is used by the FBI or the Bureau of Alcohol, Tobacco, and Firearms. When no physical testing is used, departments typically require a medical examination and do the physical training *in the academy*. With this approach, the physical performance of recruits is tested after they participate in a conditioning program as part of the training academy (i.e., postacademy testing), which not only mitigates the risk of discriminatory impact by allowing recruits to train for successful performance, but also may allow for better assessment of job-related tasks such as defense tactics (Gaines, Falkenberg, and Gambino 1993).

Residency. Whether a department has a residency requirement has a strong impact on those who may be recruited. There are essentially two types of requirements: (1) an applicant must reside within a geographic area (state, county, or city) for a specific period of time (1 year is common) prior to application (preemployment), or (2) an applicant must relocate after he or she is selected (postemployment). Proponents of such a requirement argue that it is important for individuals to have an understanding of the community in which they work and that those who live in the community have a greater stake in and concern for the community. While an assumption may exist that a postemployment residency requirement would increase citizens attitudes of the police because the officers are "more connected" to the community, there is no evidence supporting such an assumption. Opponents of residency requirements argue that they unnecessarily restrict the applicant pool because the best candidates may not live within the geographic limits; they can also have a negative impact on minority recruitment. It seems clear, however, that if departments wish to hire the best available personnel, then it makes little sense to establish policies that severely restrict the applicant pool.

Education. While there is a comprehensive discussion on higher education and policing in Chapter 14, we will briefly discuss higher education standards in this section. First, however, it should be recognized that only 1 percent of police agencies require a college degree for recruitment purposes, while about 9 percent require a 2-year college degree, and 8 percent require some college; over 80 percent require only a high school diploma (Hickman and Reaves 2006a). While there has been a trend of recruits entering the field with college degrees (up to one third in some departments; Taylor et al. 2005), because of the perceived cop crunch, many agencies are reducing their minimum educational requirements to increase applicant pools. For example, in Oregon, departments considered reducing the education requirement from 4 years to 2 years; another suggestion was to allow officers to finish their education within a certain number of years of hiring (Bernstein 2001). Another strategy used in many departments is to allow military experience to substitute for college credit. In New Jersey, for example, some agencies permit 2 years of military service to substitute for 4 years of college (Eisenberg and Scott 2004); more common, however, is for departments to substitute 2 years of military experience for 2 years of college (60 semester units).

General Suitability

Departments usually conduct an extensive investigation of an applicant's past experience, behavior, and work history in an attempt to assess his or her character and general suitability for police work. In general, this process is composed of a background investigation and a polygraph examination.

Background Investigation. A thorough background investigation, based on the extensive personal history provided by the candidate, is one of the most important aspects of the selection process. The investigator attempts to determine whether the person is honest and reliable and would make a contribution to the department. Family background, employment and credit history, personal references, friends and neighbors, education records, criminal and possibly juvenile records, drug use, and, when appropriate, military records are all checked to develop a general assessment of the person's lifestyle prior to applying for police work. In their landmark study of New York police applicants, Cohen and Chaiken (1972), found that applicants who were rated as excellent by the background investigators had the lowest incidence of misconduct (some 36 percent had personal complaints filed), whereas the applicants rated as poor had the highest incidence of misconduct (some 68 percent). Because these investigations are time-consuming and expensive, some police departments, especially smaller ones with limited resources, may not be very thorough. Snowden and Fuss (2000) found this to be true; that is, in larger departments more time was spent on training and background investigations, including greater use of secondary references and procedures. Because background investigations appear to be a good predictor of future police behavior, it is important that departments take no shortcuts at this stage.

Two important aspects of the background investigation relate to a candidate's *criminal record* and *history of drug use*. Generally, a criminal record does not automatically disqualify one from police service. With respect to misdemeanor convictions, departments vary widely, but the trend is to examine the type and extent of violations and make a determination based on the candidate's overall record. Several court cases have laid the foundation for what is a permissible drug use standard for police employment practices. For instance, a Dallas Police Department standard requiring police applicants not to have recent or excessive histories of marijuana use was upheld (*Davis v. City of Dallas* 1985). In *Shield Club v. City of Cleveland* (1986), the court upheld drug-testing requirements and the rejection of applicants who tested positive for narcotics, amphetamines, or hallucinogens. In both rulings, the courts indicated that such requirements were job related and therefore not discriminatory. It is also important to note that each of the departments utilized an objective testing system that prevented any form of individual discrimination.

The BJS survey (Hickman 2005) found that agencies today tend to be less strict with respect to criminal history and drug use. According to the survey, only about 33 percent of agencies required a "clean criminal record" compared with about 52 percent in 1989. Although the term "clean criminal record" may have been interpreted differently, the pattern is clear that screening standards relating to prior arrests, convictions, and drug use have been lowered in many departments (see Inside Policing 7.2).

Polygraph Examination. The polygraph, or lie detector, is used to check the accuracy of background information and to determine whether there has been any inappropriate behavior, past or present, on the applicant's part (e.g., criminal acts, illegal drug use). Although the polygraph has been touted by some as an effective tool in discovering problems with applicants, some research has suggested that it is not a reliable method to determine truth or falsehood of an individual's statements (see Hodes, Hunt, and Raskin 1985; Kleinmuntz and Szucko 1982; Rafky and Sussman 1985). One problem with the polygraph is the amount of stress it puts on a candidate and the resulting false positives that result (that is, when a candidate is falsely accused of lying). Therefore, some jurisdictions have made such testing illegal. Furthermore, some departments still ask questions about an applicant's lifestyle or sexual practices, which are private matters. If a polygraph examination is administered, all questions relating to the applicant's background should be job related. Finally, the polygraph should never be used as a substitute for the background investigation, but only as a supplement to it.

INSIDE POLICING 7.2 **Police Departments More Tolerant Regarding Past Drug Use**

Prior use of drugs by recruits has become more prevalent during the past 2 decades, and police agencies have had to wrestle with adopting more tolerant policies to attract candidates. This is also an interesting ethical debate, since it is possible that if officers who have used or abused drugs in the past are hired, they may need to arrest someone for acts they themselves have committed. Listed below are some departments that have recently changed their drug use policies.

- The Virginia State Police recently changed their guidelines to consider those who have tried (once) any Schedule I (heroin, mescaline, LSD) or Schedule II drug (cocaine, opium, barbiturates) more than 5 years before applying. Marijuana may have been used more than once, but not in the past 12 months. People convicted of DUI once, more than 5 years prior to applying, are also eligible.

- In Loveland, Colorado, it was difficult for the department to find anyone who had not experimented with pot. The department changed its policy to consider a recruit who had not used an illegal substance in the past 3 years (or more than 20 times) or sold or used any kind of illicit drug that is still a prosecutable offense. The department required its applicants to have some college; they believe there might be a correlation between attending college and admitting to using marijuana (this is an interesting dilemma for departments requiring higher education).

- In Seattle, Washington, applicants must not have used marijuana in the past 3 years, used no so-called "club drugs" within 5 years, no cocaine or methamphetamines within 10 years, and no manufacture or sale of drugs ever.

- The Metro-Dade Police Department in Florida allows for one-time use and some juvenile drug experimentation but bars outright all Schedule I and Schedule II drugs.

- The FBI, which until 2006 had one of the more stringent prior drug use standards, barring hard drugs for a period of 10 years prior to hiring and marijuana for up to 5 years, now has a policy that simply looks at whether an applicant is a current drug user and lied about it.

SOURCES: Adapted from K. Johnson, "Past Pot Use Won't Bar FBI Applicants," *Seattle Times* August 27, 2007: A5; J. Katz, "Prior Drug Use OK for Cops Nowadays," *San Francisco Examiner* June 18, 2000: A1; "Youthful Indiscretions," *Law Enforcement News*, March 15/31, 2002: 7.

Psychological Condition. Psychological screening to determine a candidate's suitability for police work has become more common over the past 2 decades; this screening may be written, oral, or both. The most commonly used written tests are the Minnesota Multiphasic Personality Inventory (MMPI), the California Personality Inventory (CPI), and the Inwald Personality Inventory (IPI), developed specifically for police screening (TELEMASP 1994). The MMPI was originally designed to test a mental patient's psychological state and thus has been widely criticized for inappropriate questions and for validity in assessing job performance. As a response to the criticisms, the measure has been revised and renamed the MMPI-2. The IPI seeks to evaluate the psychological fitness of the applicant by measuring various behavioral patterns and characteristics; it further attempts to identify deviant behaviors that could impact job performance. The CPI, in contrast to the other two tests, attempts to measure personality traits only in normal individuals, as well as characteristics important in everyday life.

According to the results of a meta-analytic study (a synthesis of 78 research studies) regarding psychological testing in law enforcement agencies, the CPI was found to be the strongest predictor of future job performance when measured against the various forms of the MMPI and the IPI (Varela et al. 2004). The authors concluded that the CPI was the strongest predictor of job performance since it measures normal personality traits in comparison with the MMPI and the IPI, which measure, at least in part, traits relating to psychopathology. A statewide survey conducted in Texas to determine the type and extent of psychological testing used in the initial hiring process (Lee 2006) found that of the 43 responding agencies (including municipal and county agencies and the Department of Public Safety), 70 percent relied on the MMPI or the MMPI-2 as their psychological screening test. These findings are not surprising, given the long tradition of MMPI use in law enforcement; however, undoubtedly the MMPI is the least valid and useful of the three tests reviewed here for initial selection purposes.

After the tests are administered, they are usually scored by a psychologist, who is looking for serious emotional problems that would disqualify a candidate or for a profile of a person who would make a "good" police officer. There is considerable controversy surrounding the use of psychological testing for police screening; for example, an earlier review of the research by Burbeck and Furnham (1985) suggested that such tests may be useful for screening out people suffering from some mental abnormality, but not for predicting job performance. Metchik (1999) also cautions that the "screening out" model has questionable validity and reliability, since it cannot differentiate individuals who will become mediocre officers from those who will become superior officers, and the potential for false positives (i.e., incorrectly eliminating good candidates) is high. The Texas survey described above also discovered that 95 percent of the agencies used psychological screening (through the MMPI/2) to select out unsuitable candidates, rather than to *"select in"* (or **screen in**) *the best available candidates*. Because this process also has a long tradition in policing, these findings are of considerable concern, since it is likely that the overwhelmingly majority of police departments use this same process. Importantly, this suggests, as Metchik (1999) notes above, not only are *mediocre candidates likely be selected, but also superior candidates* are likely to *be screened out*.

Medical Condition. Virtually all police departments have certain medical requirements that an individual must meet before being hired. A medical examination is given by a physician either designated by the department or chosen by the candidate. The exam attempts to determine the general health of the candidate and identify specific conditions, such as heart, back, or knee problems. In general, any "weaknesses" that may be aggravated by the requirements of police work will eliminate the candidate from further consideration—the costs of losing an officer to injury or illness, often with long-term disability compensation or a lawsuit, are too great. If a department requires some form of drug testing, it usually takes place during this phase of the process.

Preemployment Testing

The preemployment standards for police departments, and the legal justifications, change periodically. This is an area in which departments need specific, and the most current, information to select the best qualified candidates. Although preemployment standards are usually scored on a pass-fail basis and are used to eliminate candidates, preemployment tests are generally used to place candidates in order of rank. The two most commonly used tests are some form of written test and the oral interview. Some departments use the written test simply as a qualifier (i.e., on a pass–fail basis) and the oral interview as the only criterion for rank order.

Written Exam. Traditionally, departments have used some type of written civil service test, usually a standardized intelligence test or jurisdictionally specific knowledge test, to screen and rank order candidates. Few attempts, until recently, were made to determine whether these tests have any impact on the applicant's ability to perform successfully as a police officer. Although it is easy to argue that police officers should be intelligent and knowledgeable, it is difficult to determine what kind and level of intelligence or knowledge is being measured.

In addition, some research suggests that minorities tend to score lower on police entry exams (e.g., see Sproule 1984; Gaines, Costello, and Crabtree 1989). Thus, if a simple rank ordering of candidates is used, it will generally create an adverse impact. These problems have led to attempts to validate police written tests empirically since at least the late 1970s (e.g., see Crosby, Rosenfield, and Thornton 1979) and by departments to seek exams that are more objective and job related (Law Enforcement Assistance Administration 1973). Regarding validation, Gaines and Falkenberg (1998) reviewed the written exams of over 400 police applicants representing one jurisdiction; the authors found that while males and females did not score differently, blacks had significantly lower scores than whites. It was determined that exam scores were primarily a function of the *educational level* of the applicant and also unrelated to oral board scores. The exam had questionable validity in that it did not discriminate between highly qualified and less qualified applicants. Since the exam primarily measured educational level, the authors recommended simply adopting a minimum educational requirement. The authors argued that a more racially diverse pool of candidates would emerge using a 2-year college requirement in lieu of the exam. Alternatively, police departments could institute a written exam aimed at the level of a 2-year college student.

Written Exams and Performance

A study using data from the July 2003 training academy of over 1,500 police recruits from a major metropolitan police department (White 2008) indicated that the main predictor of superior academy performance was based on a *reading test* score. Academy performance was measured by calculating an overall average score of four exams taken over the entire 6-month academy, including a comprehensive final exam. The primary findings indicated that with respect to higher recruit exam scores, whites, Asians, and others scored higher than blacks and Hispanics; males scored higher than females; as age increased, exam scores decreased; and, as reading levels increased, exam scores increased. The most critical discovery appeared to be that of those who read at the *12th grade level or higher*, 34.4 percent posted an average of 90 percent or higher on the recruit exams, compared with 11.5 percent of those with lower reading levels. Conversely, college education, military experience, and residency had no significant impact on academy exam scores. It is surprising, even puzzling, that college education was not related to higher exam scores, since the academy is the one area of policing most like college, with respect to traditional college pedagogy and college-like exams (this subject is discussed in detail in chapter 14).

In one of the few studies relating civil service exam scores to measures of police performance on the street, Henson et al. (2010) collected data on 486 police recruits who entered the Cincinnati Police Department's academy program from 1996 to 2006. The authors looked at the relationships among civil service exam scores and training academy success (measured by quiz, spelling, midterm and final scores, and notebook and overall score) and active service performance (measured by three supervisory performance ratings, use of force complaints, and commendations). In general, the findings suggested a positive correlation between high civil service scores and academy performance scores, although results were mixed for performance evaluation ratings, that is, positive for an officers' second-year evaluation and 3-year evaluation average, but no relationship was found for the first-year evaluation. These findings along with those discussed above (White 2008) suggest that high civil service exam and/or reading scores are some of the best criteria on which police departments should base their hiring decisions.

In addition, no relationship was found between military experience and academy performance or active service performance; furthermore, a relationship was also found between military experience and increased citizen complaints. These findings suggest that prior military service should not be given any added weight to the application process, that is, to be substituted for other required criteria or given preferential weighting.

Finally, higher education did not have an impact on any of the measured criteria. However, as the authors pointed out, this finding was not unexpected in that only a simplistic measure of college education could be utilized because of lack of variation in the sample, that is, between those with some college and those with no college. In other words, no distinction was made among those with only a few units, an associate's degree, a college degree, or even a graduate degree.

Too Smart for Policing?

One interesting example of eliminating otherwise capable applicants—one who was thought to be *too smart*—occurred in New London, Connecticut. Robert Jordan, who scored a 33 on IQ tests that measure a person's ability to learn and solve problems, was denied an interview under a city policy where candidates who score above or below a range of 20–27 are generally not interviewed for positions. The national average for police officers is 21–22, the same as for bank tellers, salespeople, and office workers (*Law Enforcement News* 1997, 4). The authors of the IQ exams had established a set of low and high markers for specific occupations (in the case of policing 18–30), with the high marker eliminating people who would likely become bored with the job and soon resign (presumably leaving the city stuck with a high bill for training the officer). Jordan, who sued the city, lost the lawsuit in federal District Court (*Jordan v. City of New London* 2000) because the city was following the standards set up by the exam's authors (Hughes 2003).

In a sample of 65 midlevel managers (comprising mostly sergeants, lieutenants, and captains) representing 23 states, Hughes (2003) found little support for the contention by the court and the testing agency in the Jordan case, specifically, that intelligent recruits become bored with their jobs and subsequently leave them. While this was a small sample and needs to be replicated and enlarged, it nevertheless indicates the complicated issues with respect to testing intelligence and what level is appropriate to a specific field. In addition, the author suggests that this case (or others like it) could have some practical negative implications as well. First, it suggests to the public that the "best and brightest" are not present in the field of policing; second, the morale of officers around the country may well be negatively impacted as yet another slight against policing; and third, the future of police recruitment could be affected by the negative image generated by the Jordan case, driving away potential intelligent applicants interested in policing.

Oral Interview. Almost all police departments use some form of oral interview, usually at the end of the selection process. The interview allows police representatives (and sometimes community members) to observe the candidates directly with respect to their suitability for the department and to clear up any inconsistencies that may have developed in the earlier stages of the process. Candidates are measured on attributes that generally are not measured elsewhere, including motivation, verbal skills, confidence, potential for violence, decision-making skills, and overall demeanor. The interview is not usually substantive—that is, with specific questions about police policy or the department—but it can be. Typical questions might include the following: Why do you want to be a police officer? How have you prepared yourself for a career in law enforcement? What types of books or magazines do you read? Why do you want to work for this department? There will usually be a few questions about hypothetical situations and how the person would respond (i.e., make decisions) to them. For community policing departments, Campbelis (1999) proposes in-depth interviews designed to identify problem-solving skills and techniques that the candidate might possess. DeLong (1999) further recommends the use of problem-solving scenarios to enable the evaluator(s) to determine whether candidates have the needed attributes to adequately perform community policing activities.

Some departments use only the oral interview to rank order candidates. This method has been useful in helping departments to overcome potentially adverse impacts of other selection criteria and to increase the number of women and minority candidates. Although the interview is more flexible, it is also subjective, and there is no strong evidence that it is a useful predictor of future police performance (Burbeck and Furnham 1985). Other research indicates that the validity of the oral interview is also suspect and that the characteristics of the raters influence the ratings, and ultimately, the rankings of the candidates (Falkenberg, Gaines, and Cox 1990; Doerner 1997). Methods that help to improve the validity of the oral interview include using only those rating factors that are critical components of the job, training the raters so that they clearly understand the process and the way responses should be graded, and using set standards that raters can compare with candidate responses (Gaines and Kappeler 1992). Table 7.1 presents a summary of the general steps of the police selection process and the most important concerns at each step.

Table 7.2 represents the findings of the BJS national survey of local police department screening methods for new officer applicants in 2003 (Hickman and Reaves 2006a). As indicated in Table 7.2, nearly all used criminal record checks (99 percent), back investigations (98 percent), driving record checks (96 percent), and medical exams and personal interviews (over 90 percent). In addition, almost 9 in 10 officers were employed by departments that used psychological evaluations and drug testing. More than two thirds of officers worked in departments utilizing physical agility tests (80 percent), aptitude tests (74 percent), and credit checks (70 percent). Less than one half of departments conducted polygraph exams or personality inventories; although over 80 percent of the largest agencies use polygraph exams). Sheriff's offices, in comparison with local departments, required substantially fewer psychological evaluations, physical agility tests, written aptitude tests, and personality inventories; the remaining screening criteria were similar to local departments (Hickman and Reaves 2006b).

The selection of candidates for police departments is time-consuming and expensive. Given the costs, the steps of the process are normally arranged from the least costly and most likely to eliminate the most candidates to the most expensive. Accordingly, the written and physical agility tests are usually given at the beginning, followed by the medical exam,

TABLE 7.1 Process Summary of Police Selection

STEPS	RELATED ISSUES
Recruitment	Advertising, requests, and referrals
Selection criteria	Age, height, weight, vision, criminal record, and possible residency requirement
Written examination	General intelligence or job content
Physical examination	Agility and endurance
Oral interview	Communication skills, interpersonal style, and decision-making ability
Psychological testing and interview	Emotional stability and psychological profiles
Background investigation	Character, employment/credit history, education, references, and criminal record
Polygraph examination	Character and background information
Medical examination and drug testing	General health and specific problems

Source: Adapted from R. Roberg, J. Kuykendall, and K. Novak, *Police Management*, 3rd ed. (Los Angeles: Roxbury, 2002), 133.

TABLE 7.2 Local Police Officers Employed by Departments Using Various Recruit Screening Methods, 2003

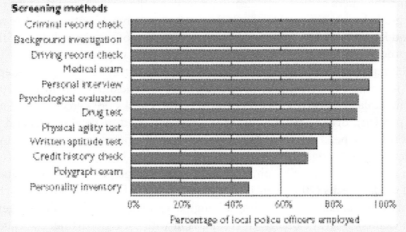

Source: Hickman, J. H., and Reaves, B. A. *Local Police Departments, 2003.* (Washington DC: Bureau of Justice Statistics, 2006), 8.

polygraph examination (if used), psychological testing (if used), background investigation, and finally the oral interview (if used).

Once candidates are selected, they are usually rank ordered and employed based on need. This ranking lasts for a given period—usually from 6 months to 2 years—before retesting is undertaken. Once selected, candidates start their developmental phase by attending a recruit training program.

Americans With Disabilities Act (ADA). The purpose of the ADA is to eliminate barriers to equal employment opportunity and to provide equal access to individuals with disabilities to the programs, services, and activities delivered by government entities (Rubin 1994). Thus, the ADA prohibits discrimination against qualified individuals with a disability; it does not mean that by having a disability, one is entitled to protection under the law, but if a person meets the selection criteria for a job and has a disability, he or she cannot be discriminated against for the job. Generally, blanket exclusions of individuals with a particular disability are not permissible. For instance, to exclude all persons with diabetes would ignore the varying degrees of severity and the ability to control the symptoms (Rubin 1994). Also, standards that tend to screen out individuals or groups of individuals on the basis of disability must be related to functions that are essential to the job. The ADA requires that applicants be given a conditional offer of employment prior to taking an exam or a test that may be disability related, including background investigations, psychological and medical exams, and polygraph tests. Although the full impact of the ADA on police selection is complicated and ongoing, departments will need to change some of their current procedures to ensure that selection criteria that screen out persons with disabilities are job related and that questions relating to disabilities (unless job related) are asked only after a conditional offer of employment has been made.

Development

Development of a police department's human resources for successful careers in police work begins with the training of the newly hired recruits, moves to a second phase of field training and evaluation, and continues into a third phase of long-term development or career growth.

Recruit Training

The initial training of the recruit is generally conducted through a police training academy, where the program content is determined by a state standards organization, often known as **Police Officers Standards and Training (POST)**. Although all police departments must meet minimum standards, some departments provide substantially more training than is minimally required. Larger departments often maintain their own academies, whereas smaller departments tend to send their recruits to regional or county academies.

Some states now require that people complete one of these basic training programs prior to being considered for employment. As a result, the department hires an already trained employee and does not have to pay for the cost of the training, including the recruit's salary while attending the academy. Another recent development in preemployment screening is testing for literacy. Because literacy skills in police applicants have been markedly declining and written civil service tests do not adequately screen for literacy, some states (e.g., Michigan and California) require all candidates to pass one of any number of tests designed to measure reading and writing skills before they begin the academy (Clark 1992). Since 1988, for example, the regional training center for Miami-area police departments has required participants in its preservice program to take a test to make sure that they can read at a 10th-grade level. The requirement was imposed because, according to the training center, earning a high school diploma does not guarantee that the graduate can read beyond the junior high school level (Clark 1992). Because the Miami example is undoubtedly reflective of a national concern, the arguments for moving toward requiring a college degree become even more evident.

Recruit training is influenced by program design and delivery. Some of the more important considerations in the design and delivery of a recruit training program include program orientation, philosophy and instructional methods, course content, and field training.

Program Orientation. One of the important issues in police training is whether the orientation should be stressful or nonstressful. *Stressful training* is like a military boot camp or basic training; *nonstressful training* has a more academic environment. Many recruit programs continue to have a stressful orientation, expecting recruits to be obedient and subjecting them to both intellectual and physical demands in a highly structured environment. Discipline and even harassment have been an integral part of many of these programs. A comprehensive national survey of recruit academy training programs by the BJS (Reaves, 2009) of 647 academies conducting basic law enforcement training—including state POST, state police, sheriff's office, county police, municipal police, college/university police, and multiagency police—found that over half (53 percent) described their training environment as following some type of stress model, while 47 percent described their training environment as following some type of nonstress model. Training environments tended to vary by type of academy. The highest percentage of academies utilizing some type of stress model was county police (89 percent), followed by state police (75 percent), sheriff's office (71 percent), and municipal police (66 percent). The highest percentage of academies utilizing some type of nonstress model was state POST at 64 percent followed by college/university (60 percent). In academies with a predominately stress-oriented training environment, 80 percent of recruits who started the training completed it; in comparison, in academies with primarily a nonstress-oriented training environment, 89 percent of recruits completed training.

Although stressful recruit training has a long tradition, no evidence exists that this approach is a valid way to train recruits (Berg 1990) or that it is any more or less effective than a nonstressful approach. Probably the most comprehensive study in this area (Earle 1973) indicated that nonstressful training produces officers who receive higher performance evaluations, like their work more, and get along better with the public. Given the trend toward community policing, problem solving, and higher educational requirements, a stress-oriented approach is likely to be counterproductive and should be eliminated from training programs, replaced by a more academic approach.

Philosophy and Instructional Methods. The philosophy of a program revolves around two primary approaches: training and education. **Training** can be defined as the process of instructing the individual *how* to do the job by providing relevant information about the job; **education** can be defined as the process of providing a general body of knowledge on which decisions can be based as to *why* something is being done while performing the job. Training deals with specific facts and procedures, whereas education is broader in scope and is concerned with theories, concepts, issues, and alternatives. Many police training programs are heavily oriented toward teaching facts and procedures to the exclusion of theories, concepts, and analytical reasoning. A strict reliance on this approach is problematic, because so much police work requires analysis and reasoning instead of application of specific procedures that supposedly fit all circumstances. Therefore, many academies are attempting to increase the percentage of time spent on an educational approach by employing professionals in the social sciences, especially criminal justice and criminology, psychology, and sociology, as instructors.

Another important aspect of program development is the type of instructional methods to be used. In large part, this is determined by what teaching philosophy is going to be emphasized; two contrasting teaching philosophies are pedagogy and andragogy (Knowles 1970). Pedagogy involves a one-way transfer of knowledge, usually in the form of facts and procedures, from the instructor to the student (recruit). The primary concern is to promote "absolute solutions" to particular situations. An alternative teaching philosophy, which promotes the mutual involvement of students and instructors in the learning process and stresses analytical and conceptual skills, is known as andragogy.

Knowles (1970) describes **pedagogy** as the art and science of teaching children and **andragogy** as the art and science of helping adults learn. While he does not suggest any fundamental differences between the way in which adults and children learn, he believes that significant differences emerge in the learning process as maturation takes place. Thus, where pedagogy involves *a one-way transfer of knowledge* between instructor and student through lectures, use of visual aids, student note taking, rote memorization, and taking factual tests, andragogy involves *a two-way transfer of knowledge* and active student participation through the use of problem analysis, role playing, group discussion and projects, independent student learning, and "acting out" to learn required skills in simulated situations. Thus, the instructor using androgogical teaching methods becomes a facilitator, helping to guide student learning through cognitive learning principles and critical thinking. At the same time, pedagogical teaching methods are also necessary, especially with respect to those activities that require memorization (e.g., laws and policies) and behavioral techniques (e.g., traffic stops and approaching a suspect).

Even though the relevance of an andragogical approach to police training has been recognized since at least the late 1970s (Roberg 1979), programs still tend to emphasize pedagogical methods emphasizing how to do a job rather than why or to develop critical thinking and decision making. Recruits would most likely benefit from such an approach with respect to topics that are relevant to community policing, including problem solving, cultural diversity, sexual harassment, conflict resolution, communication, and community organization skills (Birzer 1999, 2003). In addition, by becoming more actively involved in the learning process, officers may also become more self-directed, another important ingredient of community policing (Birzer and Tannehill 2001).

In a national survey of training academies, Bradford and Pynes (1999) analyzed course syllabi in an effort to determine the degree of cognitive versus task-oriented training. **Cognitive learning** can be defined as training that goes beyond learning a specific skill or task and instead focuses on the *process that establishes valid thinking patterns*. The authors found that less than 3 percent of basic training time listed in the curricula was spent in the cognitive and decision-making domain, with the remaining time spent in task-oriented activities. One exception to this finding was the Commonwealth of Massachusetts, where all subjects are taught in the cognitive domain, encompassing 90 percent of the curricula (720 of 800 hours). In 1997 the Massachusetts Criminal Justice Training Council realized that the goals of community policing required new teaching methods and strategies. A new training curriculum was designed with a greater cognitive focus. Task skills and methodology are still taught, but from a cognitive perspective. According to the Massachusetts Criminal Justice Training Council, the objective of cognitive training is getting the officer to "understand how to speak to, reason with, and listen to people and learn to use communication skills to manage a wide range of problematic situations. Physical tactics and tools, though readily available, are secondary to the *primary response of communication*" (Bradford and Pynes 1999, 289; emphasis added).

Problem-Based Learning. A relatively recent approach to recruit training, which incorporates a cognitive perspective, is known as **problem-based learning (PBL)**. PBL incorporates adult learning (andragogical) principles in attempting to help students develop problem-solving, critical thinking, and self-directed skills with respect to subject matter; PBL also typically occurs in a collaborative environment where communication skills are stressed (Barrows 2002). A study of a pilot program incorporating a portion of a PBL-based recruit curriculum was conducted in the Idaho POST academy in Meridian, Idaho (Werth 2009). In the program, recruits were divided into teams and were assigned to a PBL activity involving various aspects of a mock homicide investigation. The exercise was evaluated by staff members and lasted throughout the 10-week academy, culminating in week 10 with each team participating in 2 days of practical exercises revolving around the investigation. In the final part of the exercise, each team gave a presentation to the evaluators and classmates for an overall assessment of their case management.

Data were collected in the spring through fall of 2007 from the three separate recruit classes who had participated in the pilot program. Of the 147 recruits participating in the program, 122 completed surveys (83 percent) asking them questions relating to the extent they believed the PBL program helped them to develop skills necessary to be effective officers. The results were overwhelmingly positive and statistically significant in all areas, including developing new skills; relating class material to field work; useful in building problem-solving, decision-making, and collaboration skills (i.e., work in a group and with other groups).

These findings suggest that PBL methods can be introduced into training academies in stages, rather than attempting to change an entire academy curriculum and retrain an entire staff—both of which are expensive and time consuming. The pilot program described constituted approximately 70 of the 525-hour basic Idaho patrol officer academy; it was felt if the entire program was converted to PBL that recruits would become even more proficient at the skills attributed to this learning method. Further, the author pointed out that the Royal Canadian Mounted Police have changed their entire training academy to PBL and that both the Kentucky Criminal Justice Training Center and the Washington State Criminal Justice Training Commission are in the planning stages to convert their curriculums to PBL as well.

Curriculum Development and Content. Police training programs and curricula should be developed based on two criteria: first, the programs should incorporate the *mission statement* of the department and *ethical considerations,* and second, training should be based on what an officer *actually does* on a daily basis (Alpert and Smith 1990; Bayley and Bittner 1989). The subject matter should be based on a **job task analysis** if it is to be a valid indicator of the work performed by the recruits. The BJS survey (Reaves 2009) discovered that only 38 percent of academies use job task analyses to develop course content; the most common developmental methods used included input from academy staff (68 percent), state commissions (65 percent), and subject matter experts (46 percent).

As the complex nature of the police role has become more fully recognized (Roberg 1976), recruit training requirements, including the number of hours trained and the number of subjects covered, has increased significantly. The BJS study (Reaves 2009) found that the median number of hours of recruit training was 761 or about 19 weeks. As Table 7.3 indicates, county academies had the longest training programs (965 hours), followed by municipal police (883) and state police (881). State POST-run academies had the shortest programs, averaging 604 hours. In addition, a third (33 percent) of the training academies included mandatory field training in their programs. The highest percentage of agencies

TABLE 7.3 Duration of Basic Recruitment Training by Type of Academy, 2006

PRIMARY OPERATING AGENCY	CLASS	FIELD TRAINING	
	AVERAGE LENGTH	PERCENTAGE RECUIRING	AVERAGE LENGTH(H)
All types	761	33	453
State POST*	604	8	1678
State police	881	57	443
Sheriff's office	719	37	365
Country police	965	79	446
Municipal police	883	64	575
College/university	690	13	225
Multi-agency	751	31	312
Other types	657	36	335

* Peace Officer Standards and Training.

Source: Reaves, B.A. 2009. *State and Local Law Enforcement Training Academics, 2006.* Washington DC: Bureau of Justice Statistics, 6.

requiring field training in their requirements for recruits to finish basic training included county police (79 percent), municipal police (64 percent), and state police (57 percent). When not part of the recruit training program, field training was most typically administered by the agency employing the recruit.

The average length of a field training program associated with the academy was 453 hours; these ranged from a high of 1,678 hours at state POST programs to 225 hours at college and university programs.

Based on the BJS survey results, the diverse topics covered in basic recruit training can be seen in Table 7.4. In terms of instruction time devoted to various topics, firearms skills with a median instruction time of 60 hours was the longest training, followed by self-defense skills (51 hours), health and fitness (46 hours), and patrol, investigations, and emergency vehicle operations (40 hours each). Nearly all academies also provided basic first aid/CPR (24 hours), report writing (20 hours), and use of non-lethal weapons (12 hours).

Training in the legal areas of criminal law (36 hours) and constitutional law (12 hours) was provided in all academies. Nearly all academies included instruction on cultural diversity/human relations (11 hours), ethics and integrity (8 hours), basic community policing strategies (8 hours), and mediation skills/conflict management (8 hours). Nearly all academies also provided specialized training in domestic violence (14 hours), juveniles (8 hours), domestic preparedness (8 hours), and hate crimes (8 hours).

Community Policing Training

Table 7.5 compares community policing topics provided by training academies in the initial BJS survey in 2002 (Hickman 2005) with the results of the 2006 survey (Reaves 2009). As can be seen, with the exception of prioritizing crime problems (no change), there was a slight increase in each of the other community policing topics. During 2006 more than 80 percent of academies included training on identifying community problems (85 percent) and the history of community policing (83 percent). More than half of the academies

TABLE 7.4 Topics Included in Basic Training of State and Local Law Enforcement Training Academies, 2006

TOPICS	PERCENTAGE OF ACADEMIES WITH TRAINING	MEDIAN NUMBER OF HOURS OF INSTRUCTION
Operation		
Report writing	100	20
Patrol	99	40
Investigations	99	40
Basic first aid/CPR	99	24
Emergency vehicle operations	97	40
Computers/information systems	58	8
Weapons/self-defense		
Self-defense	99	51
Firearms skills	98	60
Non-lethal weapons	98	12
Legal		
Criminal law	100	36
Constitutional law	98	12
History of law enforcement	84	4
Self-improvement		
Ethics and integrity	100	8
Health and fitness	96	46
Stress prevention/management	87	5
Basic foreign language	36	16
Community policing		
Cultural diversity/human relations	98	11
Basic strategies	92	8
Mediation skills/conflict management	88	8
Special topics		
Domestic violence	99	14
Juveniles	99	8
Domestic preparedness	88	8
Hate crimes/bias crimes	87	4

Source: Reaves, B.A. 2009. *State and Local Law Enforcement Training Academics, 2006.* Washington, DC: Bureau of Justice Statistics, 6.

TABLE 7.5 Community Policing Topics in State and Local Law Enforcement Training Academies, 2002 and 2006

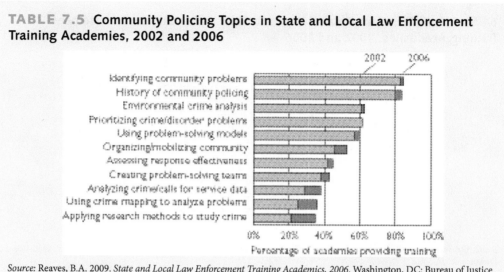

Source: Reaves, B.A. 2009. *State and Local Law Enforcement Training Academies, 2006.* Washington, DC: Bureau of Justice Statistics, 7.

included training on environmental causes of crime (62 percent), prioritizing crime problems (62 percent), using problem-solving models (60 percent), and organizing/mobilizing the community (54 percent).

Despite increases since 2002, less than half of academies included training in assessing effectiveness of problem-solving response effectiveness (45 percent), creating problem-solving teams (43 percent), analyzing crime/calls for service data (38 percent), using crime mapping to analyze community problems (36 percent), or applying research methods to study crime and disorder (35 percent). While important improvements in the last three topic areas are noteworthy, it is telling that less than half of the academies provide training in arguably the most critical aspects of community policing/problem solving; without this type of training community policing could not be effectively practiced at the street level.

Terrorism-Related Training

Overall, sizable increases in terrorism-related training between the 2002 and 2006 survey periods were found. Ninety percent of academies provided recruit training on terrorism-related topics in 2006, compared with 80 percent in 2002. In addition, training on the National Incident Management System/Incident Command System was included in 70 percent of academies in 2006—but was not included in the 2002 survey (Reaves 2009, 7). For topics included in both survey years, the number one topic presented (70 percent in 2006) was responding to the use of weapons of mass destruction (compared with 57 percent in 2002). As can be seen in Table 7.6, every additional terrorism-related recruit training topic increased in 2006 compared with 2002; the topics with over 50 percent of agencies providing training were understanding the nature of terrorism (62 percent vs. 48 percent) and an overview of relevant agencies (such as the Federal Emergency Management Agency and the FBI (57 percent vs. 44 percent).

Curriculum Updates. Departments must determine what subject matter is most important, because programs are constrained by time and resources. The amount of time devoted to any particular subject emphasizes to recruits the importance attached to that

TABLE 7.6 Terrorism-Related Topics in State and Local Law Enforcement Training Academies, 2002 and 2006

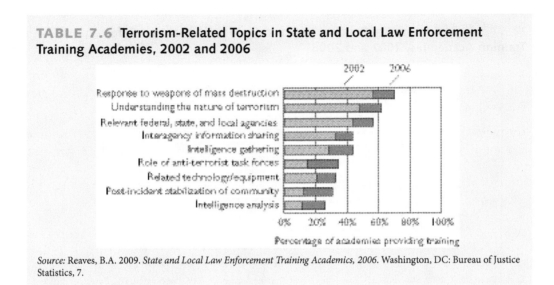

Source: Reaves, B.A. 2009. *State and Local Law Enforcement Training Academics, 2006.* Washington, DC: Bureau of Justice Statistics, 7.

subject by the department. Table 7.4 shows the varying amounts of hours devoted to certain topics, from a low of 4 hours to a high of 60 hours. It should be noted that in police training there will always be debate regarding what topics should be covered and for how much time. For example, given its importance to effective and just policing, should the area of ethics and integrity receive more time? Since the use of basic strategies is crucial to effective community policing, is 8 hours sufficient? And, as new developments occur in policing, what new or increased coverage of topics should be added to the curriculum? Some of these topic areas are addressed below.

Ethics and Integrity. Since ethics and integrity are at the heart of fair and just police practices, as well as democratic ideals, it is crucial that training academies not only devote the proper amount of time to this topic, but also, perhaps more importantly, incorporate it throughout the academy curriculum. In Inside Policing 7.3, an expert on police ethics discusses the need to integrate ethical training throughout the academy experience to define expectations and attempt to inculcate ethics into the organization culture.

Deescalation of Force. As Table 7.4 indicates, virtually all departments (99 percent) provide training in self-defense. While this topic most likely includes use of force issues, it may not include issues relating to the **deescalation of force** to reduce violence between police and citizens. Alpert and Moore (1993) suggest that *nonaggressive behavior that reduces violence* should be reinforced and *rewarded* by departments as the model for officers to copy. Importantly, this type of training would recognize and emphasize the use of nonaggressive behavior that, when appropriate, does not lead to an arrest. In other words, it needs to be recognized that many problems in the community can be solved without the need for an arrest or use of force.

Communication. One of the most important—if not the most important—training topics police can use to deescalate the use of force and to further procedural justice is the development and quality of *communication skills*. While the elaboration of communication skills is seldom addressed in training academies, it most likely should be taught as a stand-alone topic, as well as integrated with other topics where communication skills are especially important, for example, Domestic Violence; Human Relations; Mediation Skills/ Conflict Resolution found in Table 7.4 (also, see Juveniles below). Some contemporary research suggests if greater attention was paid to enhancing officer communication skills, police–citizen interactions (especially minority) could be substantially improved, thus lessening the extent to which physical force may be needed (e.g., see Dixon et al. 2008; Giles et al. 2006; Hajek et al. 2006).

Juveniles. While Table 7.4 indicates that nearly all departments (99 percent) include training on juveniles, it is likely that most of this training relates to differences between juvenile and adult law and procedures to be used when formally dealing with teens. In addition, it is important that a good portion of juvenile training relates to how interacting with teens may need to differ from interacting with adults.

One study, for example, of nearly 900 students from 18 different high schools in Chicago (Friedman et al. 2004) found that of the 58 percent of youth surveyed who were stopped at least once by the police (the majority were African American and Hispanic), about 60 percent believed they were disrespected by being yelled at, cursed at, called names, and having a gun pulled on them. In addition, they felt that the police had a condescending attitude toward them. Another study using responses from a written survey of 14- to 16-year-old

---

INSIDE POLICING 7.3 **Interview on Ethics With Edwin Delattre, Author of _Character & Cops_**

QUESTION: When it comes to training and ethics, what kind of program would you recommend? Do you think a special course in ethics is the way to go in police academy training?

DELATTRE: If such a course is expected to stand all by itself, it's doomed to failure because the newcomers get the impression that it has nothing really to do with the rest of their training and the responsibilities they'll have on a daily basis. There has to be a resonance between what you did in any course on ethics and what's done in all the other courses in programs of education. So, for example, when you explain to people that you're trying to make them competent with respect to policy and practice as it relates, say, to traffic chases, it's worth making the point that when you voluntarily accept responsibilities that affect the lives of others, you also accept the duty to become good at the fulfillment of those responsibilities. That kind of resonance is essential to affecting the culture of the institution and the expectations of the people who work in it in the right way.

QUESTION: What about the role of supervisory officers when it comes to making sure that the officers under them are kept at a pretty high level of ethics and integrity?

DELATTRE: It means forging a department in which the voice of recruitment, the voice of academy training, the voice of field training, the voice of supervision all the way to the top is one voice, and the ways of behaving are one way of behaving with respect to matters of character and integrity. This is how I do things here in the interest of justice and public service that can be trusted. You have to set an example that others will look to you and say "Yeah, this person really rings true when he says, 'We don't take, we don't beat up on suspects in custody, we don't falsify reports.' That's just exactly the way the person really is." There's no other way to achieve that I've ever heard of.

SOURCE: Adapted from: M. Simonetti Rosen, "A LEN Interview with Prof. Edwin J. Delattre of Boston University." _Law Enforcement News,_ May 15, 1997: 11–12.

high school students (Hinds 2007) found that the student's attitudes toward police legitimacy were positively linked to police use of *procedural justice*, that is, being treated in a fair and just manner. Perceived unfair treatment was significantly associated with the lowering of judgments with respect to police legitimacy. Other studies on juvenile attitudes toward the police and legitimacy have found similar results (e.g., see Geistman and Smith 2007; Sharp and Atherton 2007). These findings strongly indicate that the police need to review how they interact with juveniles not only to improve their relationships, but also to enhance legitimacy, which may ultimately affect how these youth cooperate with the police in their adult years. Inside Policing 7.4 takes a look at one department's attempt to improve relations with the city's youth.

Mentally Ill. Referring again to Table 7.4, we can see that while almost all departments have training on domestic violence (99 percent) and a large majority have a topic area on hate/bias crimes (87 percent), there is no training area on dealing with the mentally ill, which is becoming an important issue in many cities. One study (Vermette, Pinals, and Appelbaum 2005) of a sample of 126 police officers from throughout Massachusetts attending in-service mental health training asked the officers to rate the types of issues they consider the most important when dealing with the mentally ill. While all topics suggested were rated to be at least fairly important, the topics of dangerousness, suicide by cop, decreasing suicide risk, mental health law, and potential liability for bad outcomes received the highest ratings. The potential effectiveness of different types of training methods for working with the mentally ill were also evaluated. The highest ranked methods were videos and the use of small group discussion, while role playing was rated significantly lower.

Effectiveness of Recruit Training. How effective is the training provided to the recruits? What is the retention rate of recruits? One means of evaluation is to follow up on field performance to determine the areas in which recruits are having the most difficulty; methods used can include observation of recruits, the evaluation of recruit performance, and surveys of recruits, trainers, and supervisors. In general, the validity of the measurement will be greater if more than one of these methods is used. Once problems are identified, a determination can be made as to how to improve the program.

INSIDE POLICING 7.4   Teens to Help Write Section of Department's Manual

In what may be the first program of its kind in the state, Pleasanton, California, police have invited teens to help write a new section of the department's police training manual. The section will be "teen specific," and the new regulations will likely help guide officers on how teens should be approached differently on the street than adults. For example, teens may need more explanation than an adult of what law may have been violated.

Teens voiced concerns about their relationship with police at a "Youth Speak Out" event hosted by the Pleasanton Youth Commission. They said they often feel harassed and unfairly singled out by police. Teens say they want officers to be firm but not condescending, and they want explanations of what they did wrong and of the consequences. The police manual's new sections will be required training for new officers and will be part of the annual recertification training for current officers.

SOURCE: Adapted from M. Mendoza, "A New Program Calls on Teens to Help Write a Section of the Pleasanton Department's Manual in an Effort to Improve Relations," *Valley Times*, February 6, 2000: A3, A4.

One study has indicated just how important it is for police agencies to incorporate newly acquired skills and attitudes from the academy into the *organization culture*. For example, Haarr (2001), in a 16-month study, examined the attitudinal changes of recruits toward community policing, problem solving, and public relations through basic training, field training, and their first year of probation. The training curriculum of the Phoenix Regional Police Training Academy was revised to educate officers in the theories and practices of community policing and problem solving. The results indicated that the training academy had an initial positive impact on recruits' attitudes toward community policing and problem solving. However, over time, these positive attitudes dissipated as recruits returned to their respective departments for field training and were exposed to the work environment and organizational culture. In other words, field training processes and organizational environment factors (e.g., shifts, coworker attitudes, and whether the department requires officers to engage in community policing practices) were more powerful forces than basic training, suggesting that police agencies failed to reinforce the positive impacts that the training provided.

Haarr (2005) further explored why police recruits "drop out" of police work. Recruits were followed through the Phoenix Regional Police Basic Training Academy, to their respective police agencies, through field training, and the completion of a 1-year probationary period. The sample consisted of 113 dropouts from a total of 446 recruits, representing 25 cities.

Qualitative data from phone interviews indicated that recruits who resigned during *basic training* did so for several reasons, including attitudinal differences with classmates toward interactions with the public; appropriate and inappropriate work behaviors; the paramilitary, stress-oriented nature of the academy; and strict standards of physical fitness. Those recruits who resigned during the *field-training officer (FTO) phase* did so for reasons that related to the realities of police work and the organization, for example, conflict with their FTOs, conflict with their coworkers and how they interacted with the public, the phenomenon of running from call to call, the immense amount of paperwork, organizational policies and procedures, risks related to the job, and the possibility of being sued. In addition, several female recruits spoke of gender discrimination directed at them by their FTO(s) and supervisor(s). The recruits who resigned during the *1-year probationary period* indicated that they experienced continued conflict with the realization that their attitudes about police work and police–citizen interactions differed from that of their coworkers. In general, they realized that they would not be able to become involved in community policing activities as they had expected, and they felt conflicted over what they considered "heavy-handed" tactics used by coworkers, for instance, provoking subjects to fight and resist arrest, resulting in an escalation of the use of force.

These findings have significant policy implications relating to the police role, image, and ethics and integrity. It is necessary to portray the police role in an honest way; for example, is community policing really being practiced and rewarded? Furthermore, to hire quality, community-oriented officers with high ethical standards, it is mandatory that an organizational culture be developed that supports (including mandatory reporting of misconduct by peers or supervisors), rewards, and promotes people with these values. Otherwise, recruits with these values will continue to self-select out of the department and, perhaps, policing altogether. In addition, the costs to an agency for recruiting, selecting, and training highly qualified recruits are lost when they voluntarily resign from the selection process. And since the recruits who drop out must be replaced, the costs to the agency are essentially doubled.

Field Training

After successfully completing their work at the academy, recruits go through a final field-training program to prepare them for the reality of police work. As noted previously, however, approximately one third of all types of police agencies include field training as part of their recruit training process. This on-the-job, or apprentice, training has been an integral aspect of the recruit training process for some time, but it has become much more expansive since the mid-1970s. As the BJS national survey on training academies (Reaves 2009) indicates in Table 7.3, the average number of hours of field training, beyond recruit training, is 453.

FTO Program. The traditional method of new officers being broken in by experienced "old-timers" has given way to a highly structured FTO program, which for the first time used experienced officers trained to act as mentors to new recruits. The importance of FTOs cannot be overstated because they will have a significant impact not only on the training of the recruit but on imparting demeanor, values, and the department's culture as well. Up to this point, recruits have learned in the academy how to behave like police officers, but under the guidance of the FTO, the officer is exposed to the "real world" of policing. At this time, the FTO has the opportunity to subvert what has been taught by advising the rookie to "forget what you learned in the academy, I'll show you how we do it out here on the street."

Because of the importance of the position, one would think that police agencies would have a rigorous selection process with high standards. Unfortunately, this is not always the case. Much can be learned about the importance of maintaining high standards in the selection of FTOs from the Independent Commission on the Los Angeles Police Department (1991), known as the Christopher Commission Report in the wake of the Rodney King beating. Inside Policing 7.5 is an excerpt from the commission report, investigating the process then in use by the LAPD to select and train FTOs and the discovery of a "siege" mentality passed on to the trainees by many FTOs. As the commission notes, not only should rigorous selection standards be established, but also officers with an aptitude for and interest in training junior officers should be encouraged to apply.

With FTO programs, the probationary period is usually a highly structured experience in which new officers must demonstrate specific knowledge and skills. Frequent evaluations are made of the recruit's performance, usually by several FTOs, who supervise their work in different areas and different shifts. The original FTO training model developed by the San Jose Police Department (known as the San Jose model) in 1968 (McCampbell 1986) was innovative in its time and is still widely used throughout the field today. FTOs evaluate 30 relatively traditional aspects of a trainee's performance using a 1 to 7 "check-off" scale. The San Jose model, however, is not particularly flexible and has been difficult to adapt to community policing-type training.

One contemporary study of the San Jose model (Chappell 2007) of a police department (275 sworn officers), which had revamped its training academy to reflect a problem-solving, community policing approach, assessed whether community policing-type training was integrated into the field training. Analyzing the formal check-off evaluations (and narrative descriptions where required) of field activities spread over a 14-week training period, the findings indicated, with few exceptions, that community policing skills and tasks were not integrated into the field training experience. It appeared that while some of the daily observation tasks could have been modified to cover some community policing-type activities, FTOs overwhelmingly stuck to evaluating the skills related to traditional policing practices. The implications of these findings suggest that if a police organization wants to integrate community policing practices into its operations, it must first train FTOs in

---

INSIDE POLICING 7.5 LAPD: Selection and Training of FTOs

The commission's interviews of FTOs in four representative divisions revealed that many FTOs openly perpetuate the siege mentality that alienates patrol officers from the community and pass on to their trainees confrontational attitudes of hostility and disrespect for the public. This problem is in part the result of flaws in the way FTOs are selected and trained. The hiring of a very large number of new officers in 1989, which required the use of less experienced FTOs, greatly exacerbated the problem.

Any officer promoted to Police Officer III by passing a written examination covering departmental policies and procedures is eligible to serve as an FTO. At present there are no formal eligibility or disqualification criteria for the FTO position based on an applicant's disciplinary records. Fourteen of the FTOs in the four divisions the commission studied had been disciplined for use of excessive force or use of improper tactics. There also appears to be little emphasis on selecting FTOs who have an interest in training junior officers, and an FTO's training ability is given little weight in his or her evaluation.

The commission believes that, to become FTOs, officers should be required to pass written and oral tests designed to measure communication skills, teaching aptitude, and knowledge of departmental policies regarding appropriate use of force, cultural sensitivity, community relations, and nondiscrimination. Officers with an aptitude for and interest in training junior officers should be encouraged by effective incentives to apply for FTO positions. In addition, the training program for FTOs should be modified to place greater emphasis on communication skills and the appropriate use of force. Successful completion of FTO school should be required before an FTO begins teaching probationers.

SOURCE: Adapted from Independent Commission on the Los Angeles Police Department, *Report of the Independent Commission on the Los Angeles Police Department* (Los Angeles: California Public Management Institute, 1991), xvi–xvii.

---

problem-solving and community policing principles, and second, the field training evaluation form must be significantly revised to reflect the new philosophies and practices. Our attention now turns to one type of training program that has accomplished these changes.

PTO Program. A new type of field-training program has been developed by the Reno, Nevada, police department, known as the Reno model, for the purpose of initiating and training recruits with respect to the two main components of community policing: community partnerships and problem solving. This model, referred to as the **police training officer (PTO)** program, differs significantly from traditional models in that it emphasizes adult learning (androgogical) principles utilizing *PBL*, where trainees are presented with real-life problems that they must attempt to solve.

In the Reno model, PTOs assign "street" problems to trainees through which they learn about policing in the context of attempting to solve those problems. Trainees work through various responses with the help of their PTO. One of the tools used by the program is a learning matrix, shown in Table 7.7, which includes four "modes of policing" across the top and 15 "core competencies" down the side, representing 60 specific activities that police officers engage in while performing a given mode of policing. For example, Phase A refers to Nonemergency Incident Responses, and Cell A8 under Core Competencies for Community-Specific Problems refers to the following skills (not listed in the matrix): (1) Trainee will identify different community-specific problems; (2) Trainee will demonstrate proficiency in creating partnership and solving problems specific to the community or their geographic assignment (http://www.cityofreno.com/res/police/ptoprogram.php).

Jerry Hoover
Former Chief, Reno Police Department

Question: How has your department changed the FTO program to reflect community policing concepts?

Answer: We have designed and implemented a completely different model of field training at the Reno Police Department. The original training model, which was designed by the San Jose, California, Police Department in 1968, was the result of a changing police environment and numerous litigations regarding hiring and termination procedures. It was based on behavior modification and was a leading innovation in law enforcement training for decades. Since the advent of community-oriented policing and problem solving (COPPS), police administrators have expressed disappointment in their ability to imprint this philosophy on new officers using the San Jose Model.

I worked for five years trying to alter the San Jose Model so that it could be used to train under the COPPS philosophy, but with little success. After receiving a large grant from the Office of Community Oriented Policing Services (COPS), U.S. Department of Justice, the Reno Police Department created a partnership with the Police Executive Research Forum (PERF) to create a new model. The Reno model, as it has come to be called, is founded on adult-learning theory and practice. The model uses a problem-based learning method as the fundamental engine that drives the learning experience of the new officer.

Trainees are taught to solve problems, not just respond to calls for service. They become risk takers because a primary concept of the program allows them to learn from their mistakes. There are no checklists, nor numerical daily evaluations. Instead, the evaluation process is designed on principles of andragogy. The trainee and the police training officer (PTO) work together to create a positive learning environment. A learning matrix consisting of 60 topical areas is used to evaluate trainee performance. These evaluations are in the form of weekly coaching and training reports, problem-based learning exercises, neighborhood portfolio exercises, and prescriptive training plans (remedial training). These evaluation methods produce enough documentation to support decisions to either maintain or terminate a trainee's employment. The attrition rate of trainees in the Reno Model mirrors that of the San Jose Model: 10 to 15 percent generally fail the program.

We have had amazing success with this program in Reno and have received hundreds of requests for information from law enforcement agencies across the nation. Police administrators are very interested in the Reno model, not only for its adult-learning approach and emphasis on COPPS philosophy, but because we included leadership and ethics as founding principles in the design of the program. The outcome can be seen in new police officers who understand community policing and provide leadership to their communities at the beginning of their careers.

Jerry Hoover, former chief of police for Reno (NV), was instrumental in the development of the PTO program. As of 2009, over 150 police agencies had instituted PTO programs for post-academy officers.

The four modes and 15 core competencies were developed from a survey by the department of over 400 agencies who were asked to identify the important activities for a police officer working in a department where community policing and problem solving are practiced (Hoover, Pitts, and Ponte 2003).

TABLE 7.7 The Learning Matrix, Reno PTO Program

	PHASE A NON-EMERGENCY INCIDENT RESPONSE	PHASE B EMERGENCY INCIDENT RESPONSE	PHASE C PATROL ACTIVITIES	PHASE D CRIMINAL INVESTIGATION
Core Competencies				
Police vehicle operations	A1	B1	C1	D1
Conflict resolution	A2	B2	C2	D2
Use of force	A3	B3	C3	D3
Local procedures, policies, laws, philosophies	A4	B4	C4	D4
Report writing	A5	B5	C5	D5
Leadership	A6	B6	C6	D6
Problem-solving skills	A7	B7	C7	D7
Community-specific problems	A8	B8	C8	D8
Cultural diversity & special needs groups	A9	B9	C9	D9
Legal authority	A10	B10	C10	D10
Individual rights	A11	B11	C11	D11
Officer safety	A12	B12	C12	D12
Communications skills	A13	B13	C13	D13
Ethics	A14	B14	C14	D14
Lifestyle stressors/self-awareness/self-regulation	A15	B15	C15	D15
Learning activities	Introduction of neighborhood portfolio exercise	Continuation of neighborhood portfolio exercise	Continuation of neighborhood portfolio exercise	Final neighborhood portfolio presentation
	Problem-based learning exercise	Problem-based learning exercise	Problem-based learning exercise	Problem-based learning exercise
Evaluation activities	Weekly coaching and training reports	Weekly coaching and training reports	Weekly coaching and training reports	Weekly coaching and training reports

Source: http://www.cityofreno.com/res/police/ptoprogram.php.

The Reno PTO program is organized according to the four main phases listed in the learning matrix and divided over a 15-week cycle. Although the training team is responsible for answering calls for service, the training objective for each phase will be addressed. In addition, a unique feature of the program is how each trainee is evaluated throughout the program. To avoid confusion over the role of trainer and evaluator, the PTO program separates the two roles. All training officers attend a 40-hour course on how to be a PTO. They are then assigned to a trainee as a trainer or an evaluator; that is, a PTO may be a trainer for one trainee, but an evaluator for another. The evaluator reviews the training reports and interviews the trainer about the trainee's behavior and performance. After this review, the evaluator rides along with the trainee, comparing performance levels with the documented training reports and PTO interview, and then makes his or her independent assessment and recommendation. The recommendation is then forwarded to a Board of Evaluators (BOE) for final recommendation to the police chief.

The BOE is another unique feature of the PTO program. The board is made up of PTOs, training supervisors, and the training coordinator, who oversees the training process. The board's duties include reviewing performance of the trainees and PTOs, conducting evaluations of the program, and investigating training concerns. The board also reviews recommendations for termination submitted by training officers (evaluators) and, according to departmental needs, conducts exit interviews with trainees (Hoover, Pitts, and Ponte 2003). This is a well-thought-out program and should be given serious consideration by those agencies moving toward community policing concepts.

After the recruit has passed an FTO- or PTO-type program, he or she may become a permanent, sworn police officer or work for an additional period in the field on probationary status. During this time, officers are evaluated several more times, and if their performance is acceptable, they become permanent employees.

Career Growth

Once a person is recruited, selected, trained, and has completed probation in a police department, his or her career begins, and career growth becomes important. **Career growth** can involve individual development as well as a specific position within the department; it can involve training within or outside the department, and it attempts to match the needs of the individual with those of the department. Managers must not only be concerned with upgrading the knowledge and skills of officers in their current positions, but also must plan to incorporate officers' interests with *career paths* that involve position enhancement, new assignments, and promotion.

In addition to improving the officer's knowledge and skills in each area of assignment, there is a need to develop career-path programs that will financially reward officers for staying in patrol and performing well. In many departments, the only way to obtain a pay increase after 5 or 6 years of service (other than cost-of-living adjustments) is to be promoted or transferred to a specialized position. This is not an effective system because good performers, even though they may wish to stay in patrol, must be promoted or become specialists to receive increased compensation. Since the 1970s, the LAPD, for example, has had a career-path program that builds in several career-path levels below the rank of lieutenant, each with its own pay scale. This program allows officers to pursue police careers below the command level. All police departments should have *overlapping pay scales* in which patrol officers, if highly competent, could be paid at levels equal to those of management. Such a system would encourage many excellent officers to stay in patrol. This is the system in academe, for example, where the most highly regarded professors are often paid more than their managers (e.g., chairs and deans) and possibly even more than the college president.

In-service Training. The primary purpose of **in-service training** is the regular updating of all members of the department in a wide variety of subjects. It usually involves subject matter that all department members must know to function well. For example, officers must continually be aware of changing laws and ordinances, newly developed techniques, operating policies and procedures, and departmental changes and expectations. In general, in-service training courses last from 1 to 2 weeks and therefore tend to offer relatively limited coverage of their subject matter. An interesting development in Kentucky, which requires 40 hours of approved in-service training each year, allows a college-level course to fulfill the requirement under the following conditions: (1) the course is taken from a regionally accredited college or university; (2) a minimum of 3 semester credit hours is earned; (3) a grade of C or higher is received; (4) approval is granted from the head of the officer's agency; and (5) a college course can be used only once every 3 years. Such a development is an important step in recognizing the benefit of college courses and may have a side benefit of enticing officers to enroll in college or to continue their college educations.

The BJS national survey of local police departments (Hickman and Reaves 2006a) indicates that the average annual in-service training requirement for sworn officers in 2003 was 47 hours, including 24 state-mandated hours (see Table 7.8). It is interesting to note, however, that the larger agencies (serving populations over 250,000) require under 40 hours, whereas smaller to medium-size departments (serving under 250,000 population) require from 47 to 53 hours of in-service training (except for the smallest departments, serving under 2,500 citizens). Surprisingly, the largest agencies (serving over 1,000,000 population) required the least training at 30 hours, while the second smallest

TABLE 7.8 Annual In-service Training Requirements for Non-probationary Officers in Local Police Departments, by Size of Population Served, 2003

POPULATION SERVED	AVERAGE NUMBER OF HOURS REQUIRED	
	STATE-MANDATED	OTHER
All sizes	24	23
1,000,000 or more	23	7
500,000–999,999	20	18
250,000–499,999	20	14
100,000–249,999	24	23
50,000–99,999	18	32
25,000–49,999	21	28
10,000–24,999	20	31
2,500–9,999	28	25
Under–2,500	23	16

Source: M. J. Hickman and B. A. Reaves, *Local Police Departments, 2003.* (Washington, DC: Bureau of Justice Statistics, 2006), 9.

agencies (serving populations from 2,500 to below 10,000) required the most training at 53 hours. For sheriff's offices, the amount of hours provided for in-service training was about the same as for local police departments (Hickman and Reaves 2006b). Once again, it was found that the largest agencies (serving populations over 1,000,000) required the least amount of in-service training, while the smallest (serving populations under 10,000) required the most.

Specialized Training. **Specialized training** attempts to prepare officers for specific tasks (e.g., Special Weapons and Tactics SWAT or Hazardous Materials HAZMAT or for different jobs throughout the department (e.g., investigator, supervisor, or FTO)). Specialized training is essential if officers are to perform effectively outside the role of patrol officer.

Officers promoted to first-line supervisory positions (e.g., sergeant) should be provided with some form of *supervisory training*. Such training may be in-house or external and usually covers leadership behavior, specific job requirements, and policies and procedures. Once an officer is promoted to a managerial or executive-level position (e.g., lieutenant or higher), additional *management training* is necessary. The role of the police manager is even more complex than that of first-level supervisor and requires not only increased knowledge regarding management's role in the department but also long-range planning, policy development, and resource allocation. In California, for example, each of these types of training is required: police chiefs must complete an 80-hour executive-development course within 2 years of appointment; captains must complete an 80-hour management course within 12 months; lieutenants must complete an 80-hour management course (different in content from the captain's course) within 12 months; and sergeants must complete an 80-hour supervisory course within 12 months.

One of the most troublesome aspects of supervisory and management training for police is the evaluation procedure, or lack thereof. Although recruit training is often rigorously evaluated, training for experienced officers and managers rarely includes any meaningful evaluation. This lack of evaluation can be a serious problem because many of the participants may not take the training seriously and thus will not attain the skills and knowledge necessary to be effective. Consequently, departments should require all supervisory and managerial training programs to include meaningful performance evaluations, because only in this way can they be sure that their future supervisors and managers are effectively trained for their new roles.

Promotion and Assessment Centers. *Promotion* in police departments is usually based on one or more of several evaluative criteria, including an officer's (1) time on the job (seniority) or time in rank, (2) past performance, (3) written examination, (4) oral interview, and (5) college hours or degrees. In general, a percentage weight is assigned to each evaluative criterion used and an overall promotional score is assigned. As openings at the next level of rank occur, individuals are promoted according to their score. Which criteria are used and what weight is assigned varies by department, according to what the department or civil service commission regards as the most important. Often, police departments use only one or two criteria, even though the criteria may have little, if any, relationship to the supervisory or managerial position for which the candidate is applying. Such a process can lead to the selection of the wrong candidate for the position, which may have a long-term negative impact on the department and the officers being supervised.

In one of the few studies in this area Roberg and Laramy (1980) analyzed the promotional results of a large midwestern police department that used a written exam (70 percent), performance evaluation (11.25 percent), seniority (10 percent), and college credits (8.75 percent) as criteria for promotion to sergeant. In general, the results indicated that seniority (above the minimum requirement) should not be used as a criterion and that those with college hours scored higher on the written exam. The study concluded that the department needed to carefully *assess and validate the content of its promotional process* through analysis of the type of behavior required for effective job performance (e.g., supervisory ability). Because it is difficult to measure supervisory or managerial potential based only on the type of criteria used in the above study, many departments are now using an assessment center approach, which is perhaps the most promising method for selecting officers for promotion.

An *assessment center* is a process that attempts to measure a candidate's potential for a particular managerial position. It uses multiple assessment strategies, typically spread over a 2- or 3-day period, which include different types of job-related simulations and possibly the use of interviews and psychological tests. Common forms of job simulations include in-basket exercises (e.g., carrying out simulated supervisory or managerial assignments, such as writing memos or reports and responding to letters or personnel matters), simulations of interviews with subordinates, oral presentations, group discussions, and fact-finding exercises (Filer 1977). The candidate's behavior on all relevant criteria is evaluated by trained assessors, who reach a consensus on each participant. The primary advantage of this approach is that it evaluates all candidates in a simulated environment under standardized conditions, thus adding significantly to the validity and reliability of the selection process.

Lateral Entry. **Lateral entry** refers to the ability of a police officer, at the patrol or supervisory level, to transfer from one department to another, usually without losing seniority. This concept is viewed by many as an important step toward increased professionalism through the improvement of career growth. Lateral entry is not a new concept, having been strongly endorsed by the 1967 President's Commission Task Force on Police:

> To improve police service, competition for all advanced positions should be opened to qualified persons from both within and outside of the department. This would enable a department to obtain the best available talent for positions of leadership.... If candidates from within an agency are unable to meet the competition from other applicants, it should be recognized that the influx of more highly qualified personnel would greatly improve the quality of the services. *(1967, 142)*

Implicitly, this recommendation increases the competition for leadership positions; if those already within the department are not as well qualified, they will need to upgrade their skills and educational levels. Of course, this need is one of the primary obstacles to implementing lateral entry; older officers within the department feel that they, not "outsiders," should be provided the opportunity for advancement. Although this resistance can be a problem, probably of greater significance are the restrictions of civil service limitations, including retirement systems, which generally are not transferable. Because of these restrictions and lack of departmental support, lateral entry is still used sparingly today. Some legislative reforms that contribute to its implementation have been made; before lateral entry can become widely adopted, however, individual departments will need to openly, and perhaps aggressively, become its proponent. Undoubtedly, the expanded use of lateral entry would increase the quality of the applicant pool for most police departments, thus improving the selection of police supervisors and managers.

The next chapter will discuss the results of the selection and development process—namely, police field operations. These include primarily patrol and investigative work. Generally, recruits are assigned to patrol after leaving the training academy, whereas veteran officers, at some point in their careers, may choose to become detectives and specialize in investigations.

Summary

With the increasing complexity of the police role and the movement toward community policing, the quality of police personnel has become perhaps the key factor to the effective operation of police departments. Thus, screening in, as opposed to screening out, candidates should be used so only the best qualified are selected for the applicant pool. Candidates must meet a number of preemployment standards that attempt to depict a department's view of what is required to become an effective officer—for example, physical agility; educational, psychological, and background qualifications; and polygraph examinations. Preemployment selection tests are also used and usually include a written exam, oral interview, or both. Some departments, however, also require reading exams because the reading ability of applicants has declined in recent years.

In preparing recruits for the job, decisions must be made about program orientation, philosophy, instructional methods, course content, and program evaluation. Following academy training, recruits generally go through an on-the-job field-training program prior to job assignment; many departments use a FTO-type program or a more recently developed program related to community policing/problem solving, known as the PTO program. The career growth of officers is important because they must be prepared for changes not only in their current jobs, but also in job assignments and promotions. Departments should establish career paths that allow for employees at all levels to remain motivated throughout their careers. Finally, because promotions have long-term implications for the departments, administrators should carefully analyze the process and criteria used. Assessment centers may offer the greatest potential in this area.

Critical Thinking Questions

1. Describe the meaning of "quality" with respect to police personnel. Explain what you consider the most important criteria with respect to quality in police recruits.

2. Why is the process of "screening in" police applicants important? How might this process relate to the potential for community policing?

3. In screening for community policing officers, what type of written exam would you recommend, and what type of procedure would you use for the oral interview?

4. Should a college-degree requirement for recruit selection be defended as a bona fide occupational qualification? Why or why not?

5. Discuss whether you think that andragogical teaching and cognitive PBL can become an integral part of recruit training in the near future.

6. What percentage of the recruit academy curriculum do you think should be devoted to community policing/problem-solving training? Why?

7. Discuss what you believe to be the most important criteria in the selection of FTOs or PTOs. Discuss differences between FTO and PTO programs; which do you consider the most relevant to contemporary policing and why?

8. What types of in-service training programs or seminars would be most useful in your local or college police department?

Note

1. Personal correspondence with J. Hoover, September 24, 2003.

References

Albermarle Paper v. Moody. 1975. 10 FEP 1181.

Alpert, G. P., and Moore, M. H. 1993. "Measuring Police Performance in the New Paradigm of Policing." In *Performance Measures for the Criminal Justice System,* pp. 109–140. Washington, DC: Bureau of Justice Statistics.

Alpert, G., and Smith, W. 1990. "Defensibility of Law Enforcement Training." *Criminal Law Bulletin* 26: 452–458.

Barrows, H. (2002). "Is it Really Possible to Have Such a Thing as PBL?" *Distance Education* 23: 119–122.

Bayley, D., and Bittner, E. 1989. "Learning the Skills of Policing." In R. Dunham and G. Alpert (eds.), *Critical Issues in Policing: Contemporary Readings,* pp. 87–110. Prospect Heights, IL: Waveland Press.

Bayley, D., and Mendelsohn, H. 1969. *Minorities and the Police.* New York: Free Press.

Berg, B. L. 1990. "First Day at the Police Academy: Stress-Reaction Training as a Screening-out Technique." *Journal of Contemporary Criminal Justice* 6: 89–105.

Bernstein, M. 2001. "Police Rethink Requirements." *The Oregonian,* January 17.

Birzer, M. L. 1999. "Police Training in the 21st Century." *FBI Law Enforcement Bulletin* July: 16–19.

———. 2003. "The Theory of Andragogy Applied to Police Training." *Policing: An International Journal of Police Strategies & Management* 26: 29–42.

Birzer, M. L., and Tannehill, R. 2001. "A More Effective Training Approach for Contemporary Policing." *Police Quarterly* 4: 233–252.

Bowden, L. (2004). "Community Helps Devise Deputy Traits." *Community Links,* November: 10–11.

Bradford, D., and Pynes, J. E. 1999. "Police Academy Training: Why Hasn't It Kept Up With Practice?" *Police Quarterly* 2: 283–301.

Burbeck, E., and Furnham, A. 1985. "Police Officer Selection: A Critical Review of the Literature." *Journal of Police Science and Administration* 13: 58–69.

Campbelis, C. 1999. "Selecting a New Breed of Officer: The Customer-Oriented Cop." *Community Policing Exchange* 25: 1, 4–5.

Chang, J. 2003. "Police Learn About Sikhs." *San Jose Mercury News* June 7: 1B, 6B.

Clark, J. R. 1992. "Why Officer Johnny Can't Read." *Law Enforcement News* May 15: 1, 16–17.

Cohen, B., and Chaiken, J. M. 1972. *Police Background Characteristics and Performance.* New York: Rand Institute.

Commission on Peace Officer Standards and Training. 1995 (May 12). *Bulletin 95–9: Regular Basic Course Required Minimum Hours Increases From 560 to 664.* Sacramento, CA: POST.

Community Links. 2004. "The Art of Hiring for Service." August: 4.

Chappell, A. T. 2007. "Community Policing: Is Field Training the Missing Link?" *Policing: An International Journal of Police Strategies & Management* 30: 498–517.

Crime Control Digest. 2001. "Police Chiefs Try Many Strategies to Boost Applicant Pools." 5: 1–4.

Crosby, A., Rosenfield, M., and Thornton, R. F. 1979. "The Development of a Written Test for Police Applicant Selection." In C. D. Spielberger (ed.), *Police Selection and Evaluation*, pp. 143–153. New York: Praeger.

Davis v. City of Dallas. 1985. 777 F.2d 205 (5th Cir.).

Decker, L. K., and Huckabee, R. G. 2002. "Raising the Age and Education Requirements for Police Officers: Will Too Many Women and Minority Candidates be Excluded? *Policing: An International Journal of Police Strategies & Management,* 25: 789–802.

De Long, R. 1999. "Problem Solvers Wanted: How to Tailor Your Agency's Recruiting Approach." *Community Policing Exchange, Phase VI* 25, 2: 6.

Dixon, T. L., Schell, T. L., Giles, H., and Drogos, K. L. (2008). "The Influence of Race in Police–Citizen Interactions: A Content Analysis of Videotaped Interactions Taken During Cincinnati Police Traffic Stops." *Journal of Communication* 58: 530–549.

Doerner, W. G. 1997. "The Utility of the Oral Interview Board in Selecting Police Academy Admissions." *Policing: An International Journal of Police Strategies and Management* 20: 777–785.

Dowling, K. W. 1999. "Arresting the Arresting Response: Training Community Police Officers to be Problem-Solvers." *Community Policing Exchange* 25: 5.

Earle, H. H. 1973. *Police Recruit Training: Stress vs. Non-Stress.* Springfield, IL: Charles C. Thomas.

Eck, J. E. 2004. "Why Problems Don't Get Solved." In W. G. Skogan (ed.), *Community Policing: Can It Work?*, pp. 185–206. Belmont, CA.: Thomson/Wadsworth.

Eisenberg, T., and Scott, E. L. 2004. *Montgomery County Dep't of Police, Evaluation of Minority Recruiting Process, Final Report.* North Beach, MD: Personnel Performance.

Falkenberg, S., Gaines, L. K., and Cox, T. C. 1990. "The Oral Interview Board: What Does It Measure?" *Journal of Police Science and Administration* 17: 32–39.

Filer, R. J. 1977. "Assessment Centers in Police Selection." In C. D. Spielberger and H. C. Spaulding (eds.), *Proceedings of the National Working Conference on the Selection of Law Enforcement Officers.* Tampa: University of South Florida.

Friedman, W., Lurigio, A .J., Greenleaf, R., and Albertson, S. 2004. "Encounters Between Police Officers and Youths: The Social Costs of Disrespect." *Journal of Crime and Justice,* 27: 1–9.

Gaines, L. K., Costello, P., and Crabtree, A. 1989. "Police Selection Testing: Balancing Legal Requirements and Employer Needs." *American Journal of Police* 8: 137–152.

Gaines, L. K., Falkenberg, S., and Gambino, J. A. 1993. "Police Physical Activity Testing: An Historical and Legal Analysis." *American Journal of Police* 12: 47–66.

Gaines, L. K., and Falkenberg, S. 1998. "An Evaluation of the Written Selection Test: Effectiveness and Alternatives." *Journal of Criminal Justice* 26: 175–183.

Gaines, L. K., and Kappeler, V. E. 1992. "Selection and Testing." In G. W. Cordner and D. C. Hale (eds.), *What Works in Policing: Operations and Administration Examined,* pp. 107–123. Cincinnati, OH: Anderson.

Geistman, J., and Smith, B.W. 2007. "Juvenile Attitudes Toward Police: A National Study. *Journal of Crime & Justice* 30: 27–51.

"Getting the Inside Dope." 1996. *Law Enforcement News* October 31: 1, 14.

Griggs v. Duke Power Company. 1971. 401 U.S. 424.

Giles, H., Fortman, J., Daily, R., Barker, V., Hajek, C., Anderson, M. C. et al. 2006. "Communication Accommodation: Law Enforcement and the Public. In R. M. Dailey and B. A. Le Poire (eds.), *Applied Interpersonal Communication Matters: Family, Health and Community Relations,* pp. 241–269. New York: Peter Lang.

Haarr, R. 2001. "The Making of a Community Policing Officer: The Impact of Basic Training and Occupational Socialization on Police Recruits." *Police Quarterly* 4: 420–433.

———. 2005. "Factors Affecting the Decision of Police Recruits to 'Drop Out' of Police Work." *Police Quarterly* 8: 431–453.

Hajek, C., Barker, V., Giles, H., Louw, J., Peccioni, L., Makoni, S., et al. 2006. "Communication Dynamics of Police–Civilian Encounters: American and African Interethnic Data. *Journal of Intercultural Communication Research* 35: 161–182.

Henson, B., Reyns, B. W., Klahm, C. F., and Frank, J. 2010. "Do Good Recruits Make Good Cops? Problems Predicting and Measuring Academy and Street-Level Success." *Police Quarterly* 13: 5–26.

Hickman, M .J. 2005. *State and Local Law Enforcement Training Academies, 2002.* Washington, DC: Bureau of Justice Statistics

Hickman, M. J., and Reaves, B. A. 2006a. *Local Police Departments, 2003.* Washington, DC: Bureau of Justice Statistics.

———. 2006b. *Sheriffs' Offices, 2003.* Washington, DC: Bureau of Justice Statistics.

Hinds, L. 2007. "Building Police–Youth Relationships: The Importance of Procedural Justice." *Youth Justice* 7: 195–209.

Hodes, C. R., Hunt, R. L., and Raskin, D. C. 1985. "Effects of Physical Countermeasures on the Physiological Detection of Deception." *Journal of Applied Psychology* 70: 177–187.

Hoover, J., Pitts, S., and Ponte, D. 2003. *Executive Summary: The Reno Model of Post-Academy Police Training.* Reno, NV: Reno Police Department.

Hormann, J. S. 1995. "Virtual Reality: The Future of Law Enforcement Training." *Police Chief* July: 7–12.

Hughes, T. 2003. "Jordan v. The City of New London, Police Hiring and IQ." *Policing: An International Journal of Police Strategies & Management* 26: 298–312.

Independent Commission on the Los Angeles Police Department. 1991. *Report of the Independent Commission on the Los Angeles Police Department.* Los Angeles: California Public Management Institute.

International Association of Chiefs of Police. 1998. "Ethics Training in Law Enforcement." *Police Chief* January: 14–24.

International City Management Association. 1986. *Municipal Yearbook.* Washington, DC: International City Management Association.

Jordan, W.T., Fridell, L., Faggiani, D., and Kubu, B. (2009). "Attracting Females and Racial/Ethnic Minorities to Law Enforcement." *Journal of Criminal Justice* 37: 333–341.

Jordan v. City of New London. 2000. Unreported case retrieved. Available online at http://www.Tourolaw.edu/2nd Circuit/August/s99–9188.html.

Katz, J. 2000. "Prior Drug Use OK for Cops Nowadays." *San Francisco Examiner* June 18: A1; A18.

Kleinmuntz, B., and Szucko, J. J. 1982. "Is the Lie Detector Valid?" *Law and Society Review* 16: 105–122.

Knowles, M. S. 1970. *The Modern Practice of Adult Education: Andragogy Versus Pedagogy.* New York: Association Press.

Koper, C. S. 2004. *Hiring and Keeping Police Officers,* Research for Practice. August. Washington, DC: National Institute of Justice, Office of Justice Programs.

Law Enforcement Assistance Administration. 1973. *Equal Employment Opportunity Program Development Manual.* Washington, DC: U.S. Government Printing Office.

Law Enforcement News. 1997. "Dumb-da-dum-dum." *Law Enforcement News.* June 15: 4.

Lee, C. B. 2006. "Psychological Testing for Recruit Screening." *Texas Law Enforcement and Administrative Statistics Program Bulletin,* March/April.

Lonsway, K. A. 2003. "Tearing Down the Wall: Problems with Consistency, Validity, and Adverse Impact of Physical Agility Testing in Police Selection." *Police Quarterly* 6: 237–277.

Marion, N. 1998. "Police Academy Training: Are We Teaching Recruits What They Need to Know?" *Policing: An International Journal of Police Strategies & Management* 21: 54–79.

McCampbell, M. S. 1986. *Field Training for Police Officers: State of the Art.* Washington, DC: National Institute of Justice

McNamara, J. H. 1967. "Uncertainties in Police Work: The Relevance of Police Recruits' Background and Training." In D. J. Bordua (ed.), *The Police: Six Sociological Essays,* pp. 207–215. New York: Wiley.

Metchik, E. 1999. "An Analysis of the 'Screening Out' Model of Police Officer Selection." *Police Quarterly* 2: 327–342.

National Advisory Commission on Criminal Justice Standards and Goals. 1973. *Report on Police.* Washington, DC: U.S. Government Printing Office.

President's Commission on Law Enforcement and Administration of Justice. 1967. *Task Force Report: The Police.* Washington, DC: U.S. Government Printing Office.

Rafky, J., and Sussman, F. 1985. "An Evaluation of Field Techniques in Detection of Deception." *Psychophysiology* 12: 121–130.

Reaves, B. A. (2009). *State and Local Law Enforcement Training Academies, 2006.* Washington, DC: Bureau of Justice Statistics.

Roberg, R. R. (ed.). 1976. *The Changing Police Role: New Dimensions and New Perspectives.* San Jose, CA: Justice Systems Development.

———. 1979. "Police Training and Andragogy: A New Perspective." *Police Chief* 46: 32–34.

Roberg, R. R., and Laramy, J. E. 1980. "An Empirical Assessment of the Criteria Utilized for Promoting Police Personnel: A Secondary Analysis." *Journal of Police Science and Administration* 8: 183–187.

Roberg, R., Kuykendall, J., and Novak, K. (2002). *Police Management,* 3rd ed. Los Angeles: Roxbury.

Roberg, R., Novak, K., and Cordner, G. (2009). *Police & Society,* 4th ed. Los Angeles: Roxbury.

Romano, B., and Gonzales, S. 1991. "Police Striving for Cultural Sensitivity" *San Jose Mercury News,* November 10: B1, B2.

Rubin, P. N. 1994. *The Americans with Disabilities Act and Criminal Justice: Hiring New Employees.* Washington, DC: National Institute of Justice.

Sanders, B., Hughes, T., and Langworthy, R. 1995. "Police Officer Recruitment and Selection: A Survey of Major Departments in the U.S." *Police Forum.* Richmond, KY: Academy of Criminal Justice Sciences.

Schofield, D. L. 1989. "Establishing Health and Fitness Standards: Legal Considerations." *FBI Law Enforcement Bulletin,* June: 25–31.

Scrivner, E. (2006). *Innovation in Police Recruitment and Hiring: Hiring in the Spirit of Service.* Washington, DC: U.S. Department of Justice, Office of Community Orieted Policing Services.

Shield Club v. City of Cleveland, 1986. 647 R.Supp. 274 (N.D. Ohio).

Sharp, D. and Atherton, S. (2007). "To Serve and Protect? The Experiences of Policing in the Community of Young People from Black and Other Minority Groups." *British Journal of Criminology* 47: 746–763.

Shusta, R. M., Levine, D. R., Harris, P. R., and Wong, H. Z. 1995. *Multicultural Assessment: Strategies for Peacekeeping in a Diverse Society.* Englewood Cliffs, NJ: Prentice Hall.

Simonetti Rosen, M. 1997. "A LEN Interview with Professor Edwin J. Delattre of Boston University." *Law Enforcement News* May 15: 11–12.

"Solid Corps for Policing's Future." 1994. *Law Enforcement News,* April, 15: 4.

Snowden, L., and Fuss, T. 2000. "A Costly Mistake: Inadequate Police Background Investigations." *The Justice Professional* 13: 359–375.

Sproule, C. F. 1984. "Should Personnel Selection Tests be Used on a Pass–Fail, Grouping, or Ranking Basis?" *Public Personnel Management Journal* 13: 375–394.

Taylor, B., Kubu, B., Friedell, L., Rees, C., Jordan, T., and Cheney, J. 2005. *The Cop Crunch: Identifying Strategies for Dealing with the Recruiting and Hiring Crisis in Law Enforcement.* Washington, DC: PERF.

TELEMASP. 1994. "Background Investigation and Psychological Screening of New Officers: Effect of the Americans With Disabilities Act." *Texas Law Enforcement Management and Administrative Statistics Program Bulletin.* October.

Vanguard Justice Society v. Hughes. 1979. 471 F. Supp. 670.

Varela, J. G., Boccaccini, M. T., Scogin, F., Stump, J., and Caputo, A. 2004. "Personality Testing in Law Enforcement Employment Settings: A Meta-Analytic Review." *Criminal Justice and Behavior*, 31: 649–675.

Vermette, H. S., Pinals, D. A., and Applebaum. P. S. 2005. "Mental Health Training for Law Enforcement Professionals." *Journal of the American Academy of Psychiatry and the Law*, 33: 42–46.

Werth, E.P. (2009). "Student Perception of Learning Through a Problem-Based Learning Exercise: An Exploratory Study." *Policing: An International Journal of Police Strategies & Management*, 32: 21–37.

White, M. D. (2008). "Identifying Good Cops Early: Predicting Recruit Performance in the Academy." *Police Quarterly*, 11: 27–49

Wilson, O. W., and McLaren, R. C. 1977. *Police Administration*, 4th ed. New York: McGraw–Hill.

Winters, C. A. 1989. "Psychology Tests, Suits, and Minority Applicants." *Police Journal* 62: 22–30.

"Youthful Indiscretions: Doors Open Wider to Police Recruits with Prior Drug Use." (2002). *Law Enforcement News,* March 15/31: 7.

CHAPTER 8

Field Operations

CHAPTER OUTLINE

- The Patrol Function
    Historical Development
    Patrol Methods
    Use of Patrol Resources
- Selected Research on Patrol Operations
    Random Patrol
    Response Time
    Differential Response to Calls
- Focused Interventions
    Proactive Arrests and Crackdowns
    Guns and Gang Violence
    Policing Disorder: Zero-Tolerance and Quality-of-Life Policing
    Problem-Oriented Policing Focused on Disorder
    Juvenile Curfews
- Reactive Arrests and Intimate Partner Violence
- Police Pursuits
- The Investigative Function
    Historical Development

CHAPTER OUTLINE   (continued)

- Selected Research on Investigative Operations
    - Investigative Effectiveness
    - Career Criminal Programs
    - Bias Crime Programs
    - Detective–Patrol Relationships
    - Enticement and Entrapment
- Summary
- Critical Thinking Questions
- References

KEY TERMS

- bias crime
- computer-aided dispatch
- computerized crime mapping
- crackdowns
- crime suppression
- differential police response
- directed patrol
- dual arrest
- enticement

- entrapment
- event analysis
- field operations
- follow-up investigation
- general deterrence
- generalist
- hot spots
- intelligence-led policing
- law enforcement
- order maintenance
- proactive arrests

- preliminary investigation
- primary aggressor laws
- proactive
- quality-of-life policing
- random patrol
- reactive
- social services
- specialist
- specific deterrence
- target oriented

POLICE FIELD OPERATIONS CONSIST of two primary functions: patrol and investigations. Although most departments have other operational functions (e.g., traffic, vice, juvenile, crime prevention), a substantial majority of all police work involves either patrol or investigations. In local police departments, for example, about 65 percent of full-time officers perform patrol duties, while 16 percent primarily handle criminal investigations. In sheriff's departments, 41 percent of full-time deputies are assigned to patrol duty and 12 percent are assigned to investigative duties; in addition, because most sheriffs' offices operate jail facilities and have court-related functions, 24 percent are assigned to jail-related duties and 17 percent primarily perform court-related duties (Reaves and Hickman 2002). These two operational units deal with the greatest diversity of problems and have the most influence on the public's perception of the police. Accordingly, the focus of this chapter is on patrol work and secondarily on investigative or detective work.

In relatively small departments, patrol and investigations typically do not exist as separate units because the police are generalists. A **generalist** is an officer who performs a variety of activities—for example, conducting investigations that result from calls while on patrol that otherwise could be assigned to a **specialist**. In contrast, most medium or large departments tend to *specialize* their investigative activities. In these departments, once a patrol officer is dispatched to the scene of a crime, he or she may conduct a preliminary investigation and then call in the detectives for follow-up and further case development. In highly specialized departments, the patrol officer may call in the detectives as soon as it is ascertained that an investigation is necessary; once the detectives arrive, the officer returns to patrol duty.

The Patrol Function

Police patrol has been referred to as the "backbone of policing" (Wilson and McLaren 1977) because the vast majority of police officers are assigned to patrol and thus provide the greatest bulk of services to the community. Because patrol officers are also the most highly visible personnel in the department, the patrol unit forms the public's primary perception of any particular department. Thus, it is clear why patrol work is considered the backbone of policing.

In general, the *goals of patrol* include (1) crime prevention and deterrence, (2) apprehension of offenders, (3) creation of a sense of community security and satisfaction, (4) provision of non-crime-related services, and (5) traffic control. For departments practicing community policing, another important goal is (6) identifying and solving community problems with respect to crime and disorder. In attempting to achieve these goals, patrol officers perform essentially three functions: law enforcement, order maintenance, and social services. **Law enforcement** involves activities in which police make arrests, issue citations, conduct investigations, and in general attempt to prevent or deter criminal activity. **Order maintenance** may or may not involve a violation of the law (usually minor), during which officers tend to use alternatives to formal sanctions. Examples include loud parties, teenagers consuming alcohol, or minor neighborhood disputes. **Social services** involve taking reports and providing information and assistance to the public, everything from helping a stranded motorist to checking grandma's house to make sure she is all right. It is important to understand (as discussed in Chapter 1) that while police work is often viewed from a narrow, law enforcement perspective, research has continuously shown patrol work to be much broader in scope, and in practice it is more likely to involve order maintenance and social service activities (for discussion, see Roberg 1976).

Some of these activities may overlap functional areas. For example, traffic control can fall under any of the categories; although traffic enforcement would be a law enforcement function, directing traffic at the scene of an accident or providing medical assistance would be a service function. Interestingly, traffic control accounts for the most contacts with the public (Durose, Smith, and Langan 2007) and therefore has an important impact on how the public view the police. Attempting to solve community problems could also fall under different functions; for instance, planning with a citizen's group to establish a recreation center to keep at-risk juveniles off the street could be considered order maintenance, but may also relate to law enforcement through crime prevention activities. Based on one of the few observational analyses of patrol work, Inside Policing 8.1 provides an abbreviated description of the diverse and complex nature of a patrol officer's job.

Historical Development

Two critical developments of the 1930s helped change the nature of the patrol officer from a "neighborhood" cop who knew and who was known by the people on his beat: (1) the greatly increased use of the patrol car and (2) the development of *UCRs*. By adopting the UCR (i.e., Part I Crimes reported to the FBI) as their primary measurement of performance, the police began to stress the crime-fighting dimension of their role and became less interested in what they defined as non-crime-related activities.

INSIDE POLICING 8.1 Police Patrol: A Job Description

Based on extensive field observations, this behavioral analysis of a patrol officer's job describes the attributes required for successful performance in the field. Although completed almost 4 decades ago, the findings are still pertinent today, concluding that a patrol officer must do the following:

1. Endure long periods of monotony in routine patrol, yet react quickly and effectively to problem situations observed on the street or to orders issued by the dispatcher.

2. Exhibit initiative, problem-solving capacity, effective judgment, and imagination in coping with the numerous complex situations he or she is called upon to face (e.g. a family disturbance, a potential suicide, a robbery in progress, an accident, or a disaster).

3. Demonstrate mature judgment, as in deciding whether an arrest is warranted by the circumstances or a warning is sufficient or in a situation where the use of force may be needed.

4. Exhibit a number of complex psychomotor skills, such as driving a vehicle in emergency situations, firing a weapon accurately under varied conditions, and showing facility in self-defense and apprehension, as in taking a person into custody with a minimum of force.

5. Adequately perform the communication and record-keeping functions of the job, including oral reports, formal case reports, and departmental and court forms.

6. Endure verbal and physical abuse from citizens and offenders while using only necessary force in the performance of his or her function.

7. Exhibit a professional, self-assured presence and a self-confident manner in his or her conduct when dealing with offenders, the public, and the courts.

8. Be capable of restoring equilibrium to social groups (e.g., restoring order in a family fight, a disagreement between neighbors, or a clash between rival youth groups).

9. Tolerate stress in a multitude of forms, such as a high-speed chase, a weapon being fired, or a woman bearing a child.

10. Exhibit a high level of personal integrity and ethical conduct (e.g., refrain from accepting bribes or favors and provide impartial law enforcement).

SOURCE: Adapted from M. E. Baehr, J. E. Furcon, and E. C. Froemel, *Psychological Assessment of Patrolman Qualifications in Relation to Field Performance* (Washington, DC: Department of Justice, 1968), II-3–II-5.

These two developments, along with the influence of O. W. Wilson's bureaucratic or paramilitary approach to police management, led to the new professionalized police department. This increased level of "*professionalization*" was concerned with portraying a proper police image and running things by the book—literally—Wilson's influential *Police Administration* (1950). The image of the patrol officer was one of a nonpolitical, noncorruptible fighter of crime. It was believed that the increased use of the car would increase police efficiency through **crime suppression**, which had traditionally been regarded as the most important patrol function. In other words, because more area could be covered and response time would be shortened, crime could be better controlled or suppressed. According to Wilson and McLaren, patrol procedures should be designed to create the impression of a police "omnipresence," which would eliminate "the actual opportunity (or the belief that the opportunity exists) for successful misconduct" (1977, 320). The increased use of patrol cars, however, further isolated the officer from the community. Interestingly, some of the more professionalized departments took extra measures to *depersonalize* policing. For example, one strategy adopted to combat corruption was the frequent rotation of beat assignments.

The development of radio and the telephone also had a strong impact on the relationship between the police and the community. Being able to call police and dispatch them to help citizens changed patrol work. Instead of watching to prevent crime, police began waiting to respond to crime; that is, they went from a **proactive** (police-initiated) to a **reactive** (citizen-initiated) approach. As a result, citizens tended to request police assistance more often (the development of an emergency telephone number—911—has significantly contributed to this tendency), and this reinforced the all-purpose service orientation of the patrol function.

Poor people, in particular, began to use the police as lawyers, doctors, psychologists, and social workers. As Walker notes, "While the patrol car did isolate the police in some respects, the telephone brought about a more intimate form of contact between police and citizen by allowing the police officer to enter private residences and involving him in private disputes and problems" (1984, 88). What this meant was that the "professional" officer, who now knew less about the neighborhoods and people, was often ill equipped to perform non-crime-related functions and did not tend to like the order maintenance and public service aspects of police work (Sherman 1983).

Because police have often become deluged with 911 calls—many of which are not emergencies and do not necessarily require the response of an officer—some cities are developing and promoting the use of a *311 nonemergency number*. In the Baltimore, Maryland, Police Department, for example, the use of the 311 call system is credited with a 34 percent decrease in unnecessary calls to the 911 number, which represented a decrease of approximately 5,000 calls to 911 per week. Citizens had favorable views of the system, indicating that the 311 call system improved city services and police–community relations and reduced nonemergency calls to 911 (Mazerolle et al. 2002). A follow-up study of Baltimore's 311 system found that although the system appeared to free up time for patrol officers, most officers did not notice any increase in discretionary time (Mazerolle et al. 2005). The researchers thus recommended that 311 systems should also include a *dual-dispatching* policy, wherein patrol units would not be dispatched to 311 calls, but instead would follow-up with a community-oriented, problem-solving approach.

In some respects patrol work has come full circle and police departments are once again attempting to regain knowledge and awareness of the neighborhood context, although in a much more sophisticated fashion than in the past. As community policing continues to develop, patrol officers must become increasingly aware of the neighborhood context by working with citizens and community groups in the coproduction of public safety to identify and solve crime and disorder problems. Along with this change in role emphasis, it is further suggested (Stephens 1996) that attitudes must change concerning the amount of time police spend on calls, including taking the time to ask a different set of questions on each crime report: Have we been here before? What is causing this situation to occur or reoccur? How can it be prevented? What should the police do? The callers? The victims? The community? The government? In this way, the police change their emphasis from *incident oriented* to *problem oriented* and from *responding to problems* to *solving problems* that relate to or cause crime.

Terrorism and Patrol. In contemporary society, with a heightened awareness of potential terrorist acts, patrol work may need to change. De Guzman (2002), for instance, argues that patrol work will need to be more "target oriented," with greater emphasis placed on "event" analysis in addition to crime analysis. **Target oriented** is the concept used by officers to assess likely targets in their districts; that is, they should be watching over not only obvious places and persons who might be of danger but also where disruption in "safe places" might occur. This suggests that the police should be able to "deconstruct the obvious" (Crank 1999). In other words, they should attempt to determine the vulnerability of people and places and how they may become targets of terrorism. **Event analysis** suggests that the police should be aware of important celebrations, ideologies, and anniversaries of known activists, terrorists, or groups and attempt to determine whether these events may be connected to a possible terrorist act. Another change De Guzman believes may significantly impact terrorist acts is to intensify traffic enforcement. It is believed that "no-nonsense" (or even zero-tolerance) policies regarding traffic violations will limit the movement of terrorists. A number of Supreme Court decisions have expanded the use of traffic stops for the purpose of stopping, searching, and investigating. Thus, the previously unreliable "hunch" or "sixth sense" of the police is slowly being acknowledged by the courts as legitimate grounds for police intervention. Of course, while such an approach may, at least on the surface, appear better able to track and investigate certain people, there are important constitutional issues with respect to profiling and, perhaps just as important, police legitimacy (i.e., trust in the police). As discussed in Chapter 5, zero-tolerance policies have led to serious problems among minority groups, with a concomitant loss of police legitimacy.

Based on the above discussion, De Guzman (2002) suggests that these activities call for the police to return to, or "lean" toward, a legalistic style and begin "to apply their innate talent for sensing change" (89). While undoubtedly more emphasis will need to be placed on antiterrorist activities in the future, the police must be careful not to develop a "we versus they" attitude with respect to these activities. Thus, it seems more crucial than ever to promote a community policing approach, where vital information can be gained through improved relationships with the community. In this way, the public plays an important role in helping to combat not only traditional criminal activity but also potential terrorist acts. Additionally, this should also lead to gains in police legitimacy, which, in turn, will lead to additional help and information in preventing crime and terrorism.

Patrol Methods

The two most dominant methods of patrol are by automobile and by foot. As noted, the automobile had a revolutionary impact on policing—and today is the most dominant method of patrol. Because it offers the greatest coverage and most rapid response to calls, it is usually considered the most cost-effective method of patrol. Along with this increased coverage, however, came a trade-off in terms of isolation from the community. Suddenly, police officers lost contact with citizens in nonconflict and nonadversarial situations. The police, in the name of efficiency, essentially became "outsiders" in the communities they served. The urban riots of the early 1960s emphasized the problems that had developed in police–community relations. For instance, the President's Commission on Law Enforcement and Administration of Justice suggested that "the most significant weakness in American motor patrol operations today is the general lack of contact with citizens except when an officer has responded to a call" (1967, 53).

In recognition of the loss of contact with the community, there has been a resurgence of *foot patrol,* especially in downtown areas. The development of the portable radio vastly improved the capabilities of foot patrol officers, allowing constant communication with headquarters regarding conditions on their beat. Of course, foot patrol officers are severely limited in terms of mobility and response to calls. Consequently, they are sometimes paired with other forms of patrol, such as car, horse, or motor scooter. Some departments use a combination of foot and car or foot and motor scooter; that is, they allocate approximately one half of their time to walking their beat and the other half to motor patrol. Departments that utilize such a patrol method feel that they are getting the best of both forms of patrol—that is, a greater degree of citizen contact than provided by motor patrol alone and greater mobility than provided by foot patrol alone.

Two comprehensive evaluations of foot patrol revealed that although foot patrol may effect a slight reduction in crime, it primarily reduces citizens' fear of crime and changes the nature of police–citizen interactions—toward more positive and nonadversarial exchanges. The major studies were the Newark Foot Patrol Experiment, which included data on foot patrol in Newark and 28 additional cities in New Jersey (Police Foundation 1981), and the Neighborhood Foot Patrol Program, which was conducted in 14 neighborhoods of Flint, Michigan (Trojanowicz 1982). Later reports of the Flint study (Trojanowicz and Banas 1985) discovered a decrease in the disparity between black and white perceptions of crime and policing and an increased positive acceptance of the program and confidence in police services by black members of the community.

In general, it appears that for foot patrol to be successful, it must be implemented in areas where officers can see and frequently interact with citizens—shopping centers, neighborhoods, or areas with businesses or outside citizen activity. In addition, research indicates that the size of a foot patrol beat should be small enough that it can be covered at least once or twice per shift to improve police–community interactions and reduce the fear of crime (Greene 1987; Payne and Trojanowicz 1985; Sherman 1983; Trojanowicz and Banas 1985).

Departments may use numerous other patrol methods, depending on their particular needs and budgetary constraints. In general, *motorcycle patrol* is used for traffic control and enforcement in highly congested areas. One of the major problems with this form of patrol, however, is that it is extremely dangerous since just about any type of accident tends to cause harm to the rider. Wilson and McClaren stated that the hazard of motorcycle operation "is sufficient to condemn its use, and fairness to the officer and his family forbids it" (1977, 33). *Motor scooters* and *three-wheeled vehicles* are primarily used for traffic enforcement and in parks; they may also be used as part of "park-and-walk" programs, thus extending officers' mobility. *Bicycles* are often used in parks and beach areas and in conjunction with stakeouts; they offer good mobility and interaction with the public. Because of these assets, bicycle patrols have increased in departments implementing community policing. During the 1960s, *horse patrol* was used mainly for crowd control but today is being increasingly used in both downtown and park areas. *Planes* and *helicopters* are used primarily for traffic control, surveillance, and rescues; their mobility and observation capabilities are great, but so are their cost and noise levels. Helicopters are increasingly being used in both automobile and foot pursuits. Cities surrounded by large bodies of water use *boat patrol* for the enforcement of boating rules, emergency assistance, and other law enforcement activities, including surveillance and narcotics control. In deciding what form of patrol should be used, police managers must consider speed, access, density of population, visibility, cost, and community support.

Table 8.1 indicates different types of patrol methods and their utilization in large police departments. Table 8.1 also shows departments' diverse attempts to meet needs (e.g., parks, lakes, downtown areas, freeways) with different patrol staffing levels and types of patrol; for example, Detroit and Los Angeles staff over 60 percent of their patrol

TABLE 8.1 Patrol Allocation in Selected, Large Police Departments

| DEPARTMENT | DEPARTMENTS USING PATROL TYPE AND PERCENT OF ALL PATROL UNITS ACCOUNTED FOR | | | | | | PERCENT OF OFFICERS ON PATROL PER 24 HOURS | PERCENT OF UNITS WITH TWO OFFICERS |
	AUTO	MOTORCYCLE	FOOT	BICYCLE	HORSE	MARINE		
Atlanta	77	1	14	3	1	0	31	0
Baltimore	96	1	2	0	1	0	16	0
Chicago	82	1	15	1	0	0	26	52
Detroit	84	1	7	3	1	4	16	68
Houston	95	1	1	1	1	0	27	11
Los Angeles	64	6	5	15	0	0	19	63
New York City	54	1	39	5	1	0	19	57
Seattle	42	14	8	16	4	3	16	31

Source: Adapted from B. A. Reaves and A. L. Goldberg, *Law Enforcement Management and Administrative Statistics, 1997* (Washington, DC: Department of Justice, 1999), 71–80.

units with two officers, whereas Atlanta and Baltimore have no two-officer units. In addition, there are vast differences with respect to how departments use different types of patrol; for instance, while 50 percent of the departments assign 80 to 90 percent of their patrol resources to automobiles, Los Angeles, New York, and Seattle (with only 42 percent) assign 60 percent or less. Leaders in other types of patrol include motorcycle patrol (Seattle, 14 percent, and Los Angeles, 6 percent); foot patrol (New York, 39 percent, Chicago, 15 percent, and Atlanta, 14 percent); bicycle patrol (Seattle, 16 percent, and Los Angeles, 15 percent); horse patrol (Seattle, 4 percent); and marine patrol (Detroit, 4 percent, and Seattle, 3 percent).

Use of Patrol Resources

This section discusses how police resources are used, including patrol staffing (how many officers per car), resource determination (how many officers a department should have), resource allocation (how officers should be distributed), and computerized crime mapping (how to concentrate patrol activities).

Patrol Staffing. When automobiles first began to be used for patrol purposes, two or more officers were often assigned to a car. Since the 1940s, however, many departments have begun to use single-person cars. There has been considerable controversy surrounding this issue. Do *one-* or *two-officer cars* do more work? Which method is safer for the officer? Which is safer for the citizen? The most comprehensive study on this issue was undertaken in San Diego in the mid-1970s (Boydstun, Sherry, and Moelter 1977). The findings indicated that one-person units produced more arrests, filed more formal crime reports, received fewer citizen complaints, and were clearly less expensive. A second study replicating the San Diego analysis (Kessler 1985) found the same results and further indicated that two one-officer cars responded to the scene of an incident faster than one two-officer car. One-officer units also had a safety advantage. Even considering the danger of the area and shift assignment, one-officer units had fewer resisting-arrest problems and about an equal involvement in assaults on officers. A study of over 1,000 officers in three Australian state police forces (Wilson and Brewer 2001) indicated that in all 12 patrol activities measured, two-officer cars encountered more resistance from citizens than one-officer cars; this suggests that officers working together may handle interactions with the public in a qualitatively different—perhaps less cordial—manner than single officers.

Resource Determination. Probably the most frequently used method for resource determination is the *comparative approach,* which involves comparing one or more cities using a ratio of sworn officers per 10,000 population unit; if the comparison city(ies) has (have) a higher police–citizen ratio, it is assumed that an increase in personnel is justified, at least to the level of the comparison city. Table 8.2 indicates the significant differences in police–citizen ratios between selected major cities As can be seen, large northeast cities such as New York, Chicago, Baltimore, and Washington, DC, all have over 40 officers per 10,000 residents, while West Coast cites are all under 30 per 10,000, with some under 20. This is largely based on long-established staffing traditions. Although comparison is frequently used, it is not necessarily a valid indicator of needed strength, since individual cities are extremely diverse in their needs for police services, expectations, crime rates, and levels of violence. For example, the diversity of major cities in the same state can be observed by comparing San Jose with a police–citizen ratio of 14.6 to Los Angeles with a ratio of 25.3 or San Antonio with 15.9 to Houston with 22.6. The most likely need for police resources relates to a department's level of managerial effectiveness, use of technology, competency

TABLE 8.2 **Police–Population Ratios of Selected Major Cities**

CITY	SWORN OFFICERS PER 10,000 CITIZENS
District of Columbia	68.1
Chicago	47.2
Baltimore	47.3
Detroit	33.5
New York	42.9
Houston	22.6
Los Angeles	25.3
Seattle	22.0
San Antonio	15.9
San Jose, CA	14.6

Source: U.S. Department of Justice, Federal Bureau of Investigation. *Crime in the United States, 2008.* Washington, DC: U.S. Department of Justice, Federal Bureau of Investigation.

of officers, and policing styles. For example, because Washington, DC, has over three times the police protection of Seattle and more than four times as much as San Jose, one might assume that it would be the safest of the three cities, which is not the case.

It should be noted that the comparison method is perhaps most useful to a department and the community's political structure as a yearly gauge for its own needs and progress. In other words, compared with last year's (or that of several years ago) level of police services provided to the city, how does the department measure up? If, for example, it can be shown that a department significantly increased its services to the community, a strong case could be made to the mayor or city manager and the city council that the ratio, and thus the resources for the department, should be increased.

Another area of debate over police resources is whether adding *more police* has an impact on the crime rate. A review of 36 studies found little evidence that more police reduce crime (Marvell and Moody 1996). The same authors, however, provided their own 20-year analysis of 56 cities of over 250,000 population and of 49 states. Using complex statistical techniques, they found consistent results that, as the number of police in a jurisdiction increased, the level of crime was reduced the following year. Although its findings contradict an overwhelming majority of the research, this study is the most sophisticated to date and suggests that modest increases in police numbers may affect the crime rate (at least for the following year).

Additional experimental research on this topic is necessary, however, before too much emphasis is placed on the quick fix of simply adding more police to reduce crime, even though it may be politically expedient. Adding more police entails immense financial costs since police departments operate 7 days a week, 365 days a year. Indeed, Bayley (1994) noted that, on average, when accounting for sick time, vacations, and days off, a police department must hire approximately 10 additional police officers to be able to add 1 police officer to every patrol shift, 7 days a week, 365 days a year. Thus, a city would need to hire 100 police officers to get 10 additional officers on every patrol shift 7 days a week, 365 days a year. Despite the costs, research suggests police–citizen ratios have little, if any, direct impact on crime rates. As noted above, managerial effectiveness, competency of officers, policing methods, and technology all appear to be factors in how the police affect crime. Accordingly, how the police are used and what they do are probably more important than adding a limited number of new officers to a department.

Resource Allocation. Traditionally, police resources have been allocated equally over a 24-hour time period of three 8-hour shifts—for example, day shift: 8 AM to 4 PM; evening or "swing" shift: 4 PM to midnight; and "graveyard" shift: midnight to 8 am. During these shifts, officers patrol geographic areas of approximately equal size. Of course, such an allocation method does not take into account the fact that police calls vary by time of day, day of week, area of the community, and even time of year.

Because the workload distribution is not equal across time periods, days, or patrol areas, it is apparent that the equal allocation of police resources would mean that some officers were being overused (some would say overworked) while others were being underused. Such an arrangement presents operational problems, not only in attempting to respond to calls for service, but also in not being able to perform directed or preventive patrol duties. Underused officers are quite likely to become bored and unmotivated, whereas overworked officers are likely to become fatigued and stressed. Accordingly, allocation plans should be based on need rather than resource equalization.

In these plans, the two most important variables for determining allocation are *location* and *time*. Knowing the location of problems assists departments in dividing up a community into **beats** (sectors or districts), or geographic areas, of approximately equal workload. Time of occurrence is critical because it determines how officers will be grouped into working time periods, or **shifts.** As a general rule, the greater the number of problems or calls for service, the *smaller* the beat size should be. The time it takes to service a call is also important, since the resource being allocated is a skilled officer's time, which needs to be managed as effectively as possible. Once data on these variables have been collected and analyzed, beat boundaries, number of officers, and shift times are determined. Because of population shifts and changes in demand for service, it is important that departments continually reevaluate patrol beat boundaries and assignment of personnel.

Figure 8.1, showing the Kansas City, Missouri, Police Department's dispatched calls for service by time of day, indicates the evening shift has the greatest number of calls, with approximately 45 percent, followed by the day shift with approximately 35 percent, and the graveyard shift with approximately 20 percent. Figure 8.1 further depicts the wide variation of calls with respect to the time of day. For example, the evening shift has a range of calls from about 45 at 9 PM to 30 at midnight, while the graveyard shift ranges from about 30 calls at midnight to about 10 at 2 AM. Because of such wide variation of calls by time of day, departments often develop an "overlapping" shift to cover the increased workload; for instance, in Figure 8.1, such a shift might overlap the evening and graveyard shifts from approximately 2 PM to 10 PM when the workload for calls is the highest.

To overcome the inherent problems in the equal allocation of resources, many medium-size and large departments have adopted alternate scheduling, such as a 4–10 (or 12–4) plan; smaller departments generally do not have adequate personnel to utilize this schedule. With such a plan, officers work 4 days a week, 10 hours per day, with 3 days off in a row. Officers tend to like the 4–10 plan because it allows for increased leisure time, while the department gains increased coverage because of overlapping shifts, although there may be fatigue problems with such a compacted schedule.

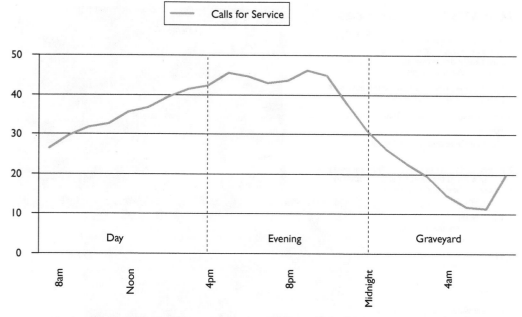

FIGURE 8.1 **Average Number of Dispatched Calls for Service by Time of Day.**

Source: Kansas City (Missouri) Police Department. *Annual Report 2002.*

Computerized Crime Mapping. One recent innovation with respect to resource utilization has been the development of **computerized crime mapping** to assist officers regarding where to concentrate their patrol activities. Data obtained through a department's **computer-aided dispatch** and records-management systems (which store and maintain calls for service, records of incidents, and arrests) are matched with addresses and other geographic information such as beats and districts; maps can then be computer generated for a geographic area to be overlaid with specific information (Rich 1996). The BJS national survey of nearly 3,000 state and local police departments in 2000 indicated that 15 percent of local departments, including over 80 percent of those serving 100,000 or more residents, utilized crime mapping (Hickman and Reaves 2003a). In sheriff's offices, 13 percent used crime mapping, including 44 percent of those serving 1 million or more residents (Hickman and Reaves 2003b).

In conjunction with the Chicago Police Department's development of its community policing strategy (see Chapter 6), where beat officers focus on problem solving, a crime-mapping system known as *ICAM* (information collection for automated mapping) was developed to help beat officers focus on problem solving. The system was developed to be user friendly so that all officers in the department could access the system and be provided with information to help them better understand the problems in their assigned areas. ICAM (depicted in Figure 8.2) can perform two main tasks: (1) it can produce a map of reported offenses of a particular type in an area, or (2) it can generate a list of the 10 most frequently reported offenses in a beat.

Officers also share the ICAM maps with residents through their beat meetings, thus giving them a chance to help the police cut down on crime through joint problem-solving efforts (Rich 1996). More recently, in Los Angeles, a new initiative from the LAPD allows

ICAM's Query Screens

From the ICAM Main Screen, the user can select the default setting to map the locations of all reported robberies occurring in the past 10 days in a district; the user simply has to:

1. Click on the primary offense scroll button to display the list of primary offenses.

2. From the list of primary offenses, click on "robbery."

3. Click on the button labeled "Do It!"

The user could choose to pose a different query to obtain a list of the most frequently reported offenses in a beat; in this instance, the user would:

1. Click on the "pick beat" scroll button to display the list of beats in the district.

2. From the list of beats, click on the desired beat.

3. Click on the button labeled "Do It!"

If the user wants to specify a different time and date range from the 10-day default period for the query, he or she moves to the following calendar screen and clicks on the time period desired.

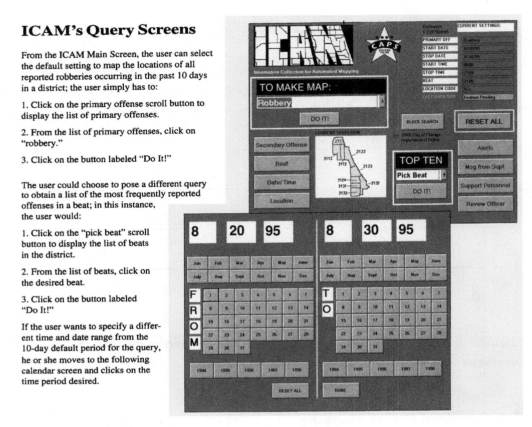

FIGURE 8.2 ICAM's Query Screens.

Source: T. F. Rich, *The Chicago Police Department's Information Collection for Automated Mapping (ICAM) Program* (Washington, DC: National Institute of Justice, 1996, 7).

residents to track crime patterns throughout the city, covering more than 470 square miles. Through the department's website (http://www.lapdonline.org), residents can access the date and location of specific crimes, including robbery, assault, rape, and homicide, up to 5 miles from a particular address (CJ Update 2006).

Selected Research on Patrol Operations

Prior to the 1960s, there was a limited amount of research about the patrol function. During the past several decades, however, a significant amount of research has been conducted on various aspects of patrol, much of it containing important policy implications. Except for team policing and community policing, covered in Chapter 4, some of the better controlled, more important studies are discussed in this section.

Random Patrol

Possibly the most influential early study on police operations, both for its breakthrough in initiating large-scale experimental research in police departments and for the general impact of its findings, was the Kansas City Preventive Patrol Experiment (Kelling et al. 1974).

Prior to this experiment, police departments had little interest in scientific observation or intellectual inquiry; many, in fact, were anti-research (Caiden 1977). The purpose of the

1-year experiment was to determine the effect of **random patrol** (i.e., officers patrolling "randomly" in their beats when not on assignment) on crime and citizens' feelings of security. For study purposes, one part of the city was divided into 15 areas, which were divided among three groups, each containing five beats. Each group was matched with respect to crime, population characteristics, and calls for service and assigned different levels of patrol as follows: *reactive beats* had no preventive patrol activities, *proactive beats* were assigned two to three times the normal number of patrol units (i.e., two to three cars per beat), and *control beats* maintained the normal level of patrol (i.e., one car per beat).

The results indicated that the three patrol conditions appeared not to affect (1) crime rates deemed suppressible by patrol (i.e., burglaries, auto thefts, larcenies involving auto accessories, robberies, and vandalism), (2) citizens' attitudes toward police, (3) feelings of security, or (4) rates of reported crime. Most police departments had routinely tried to ensure that a certain percentage of an officer's time was devoted to random patrol (normally 40 to 60 percent), yet this research raised important questions about the effectiveness of such an approach. The conclusions of the Kansas City study suggested that traditional preventive patrol was not as effective as most had believed and that this uncommitted time devoted to random patrol could be used more effectively.

Although there are several reasons why differing levels of patrol had no impact on either crime rates or citizens' attitudes (Feinberg, Kinley, and Reiss 1976; Larson 1975), the most likely reason is because normal patrol is spread so thin to begin with that simply adding another car or two to a relatively large area is unlikely to have any measurable impact. And because patrol strength cannot be increased to higher levels for any length of time, because of manpower and budgetary constraints, the Kansas City findings are as relevant today as they were in the 1970s. Much of the research reviewed below relates to how police can better manage their time or restructure their activities to reduce crime and provide better service to the community.

Response Time

Shortly after the preventive-patrol study, a follow-up investigation in the Kansas City Police Department raised serious questions about another common assumption of patrol: the effectiveness of *rapid response* times (Pate et al. 1976). Until this time, the assumption was that the faster the police responded to calls, the more satisfied citizens would be and the more likely that suspects would be apprehended. Based on these assumptions, police departments have spent considerable money attempting to reduce response times by introducing new technology (e.g., the 911 telephone number, vehicle-location console monitors, and computer-aided dispatchers) and sophisticated beat models (Caiden 1977). Overall, the research revealed that two primary factors limit the effectiveness of rapid police responses. First, the time between when a crime occurs and when a citizen discovers that the crime has occurred is an important factor. For example, it may be hours between when a burglary occurs and when the victim discovers the crime (Cordner, Greene, and Bynum 1983). Second, even when the crime directly involved the victim (e.g., violent crimes), the average citizen waits (approximately 6 minutes) to call the police—he or she often calls a friend or relative first. Thus, in many cases, there is virtually no chance to make an arrest at the crime scene, regardless of how quickly police respond (Spelman and Brown 1982). Furthermore, researchers discovered that *citizen satisfaction* with police departments depends less on a quick response than on knowing approximately *when* the officer will arrive. Other studies have confirmed these results (Sherman 1983; Spelman and Brown 1982).

The impact of this study was that police began to realize that they could respond differentially to calls; that is, because not all calls have the same level of importance, they can be assigned different priority levels. For example, noncritical calls can be responded to less quickly than critical calls. As long as citizens are informed of approximate arrival times, their satisfaction levels with the police remain high, even though they may not actually see an officer for an extended period of time or, in some cases, not at all. Of course, for critical calls (e.g., crimes in progress, injuries) it remains important for the police to respond as quickly as possible. One study from the United Kingdom (Coupe and Blake 2005) on in-progress burglary calls (i.e., when a burglary suspect is in the house) supports the need for police to respond quickly and with as many officers as possible. The researchers found that police were almost twice as likely to apprehend the suspect when they arrived in 4 minutes or less. Also, there was a higher success rate in apprehending burglars at the scene when at least six units responded. Thus, the workload of the department (higher workloads mean fewer cars available to respond) and whether a department uses one- or two-officer cars appear to be important factors when responding to *in-progress crime calls*.

Differential Response to Calls

The findings about response time led to investigations attempting to determine how the police can best manage demand for services. Essentially, managing demand requires categorizing requests for service and matching those requests with different police responses. Differential response programs classify calls according to their degree of seriousness, and the calls are subsequently responded to with (1) an immediate response by a sworn officer; (2) a delayed response by a sworn officer; or (3) no direct police response, but reports taken by telephone, mail, or having the citizen come to the police station (McEwen, Connors, and Cohen 1986). A substantial body of research on **differential police response (DPR)** indicates that alternative response strategies significantly reduced costs and improved effectiveness, did not affect citizens' levels of satisfaction, and did not increase crime (Cahn and Tien 1981; Cohen and McEwen 1984; McEwen, Connors, and Cohen 1986; Won-Jae 2002; Worden 1993).

It appears that citizens are comfortable with using alternative methods for reporting non-emergency crimes to the police. Kansas City, Missouri, residents indicated they were very willing to phone in criminal reports to the police, rather than wait for officers to respond. A smaller proportion of citizens also expressed willingness to report crime via the Internet or by going to police precincts. Some strategies, however, may not be available equally to everyone. For example, some lower-income and older residents may not have a computer with Internet access. Also, it appears non-white citizens are less supportive of crime reporting methods that do not involve face-to-face contact with an officer. Non-whites are significantly less likely to be comfortable with telephone, Internet, or mailed in reports, instead preferring to come directly to a station to report crime (Alarid and Novak 2008).

In a recent study of 20 Texas police departments using DPR (Won-Jae 2002), nearly 80 percent of all citizen calls were non-critical, and 15 percent of those calls were simply citizens requesting information. The remaining 20 percent of calls required immediate dispatch; the response time was approximately twice as fast (8 minutes) as delayed response time (17 minutes). The Texas departments drew the following benefits from DPR strategies: (1) a decrease in operating costs, (2) a decrease in the number of calls that needed immediate response, and (3) an increase in patrol officers' available time for community policing and crime prevention.

Focused Interventions

Directing what officers do rather than allowing uncommitted random patrol time became increasingly popular after the Kansas City experiment. The development of computerized crime analysis and, more recently, computerized mapping allows the police to more precisely identify patterns of crime and disorder. This increased precision allows patrols to be directed to primary crime areas at primary crime times.

As such, **directed patrol** is proactive, uses uncommitted time for a specified activity, and is based on crime and problem analysis. Of particular importance is the proactive dimension of the directed activity, be it making arrests, issuing citations, conducting field interrogations, or educating the public about crime. Proactivity produces more information, heightens citizen awareness of police, perhaps creates an impression of greater police watchfulness, and most certainly requires police to be more alert and active.

Targeting **hot spots** for crime developed out of research analyzing 911 calls in Minneapolis (Sherman, Gartin, and Buerger 1989), where researchers discovered that 5 percent of the addresses in the city accounted for 64 percent of all 911 calls. Thus a few locations, which were labeled hot spots, required a highly disproportionate amount of police time and resources. Following this research, the Minneapolis Hot Spots Patrol Experiment was designed to test the crime-prevention effects of extra patrol officers directed at hot spots for crime during *hot times* for crime over a 1-year period (Sherman and Weisburd 1995). Increased police presence was directed to a randomly selected 55 of the worst 110 hot spot street corners in the city. The remaining 55 received normal patrol coverage, primarily in response to citizen calls for service. Results indicated that increased police presence failed to reduce serious crime but did have a "modest" effect on disorder. Mere visibility seemed to have caused the modest effect on disorder because the officers' activities at the hot spots were unstructured and not very substantial.

Proactive Arrests and Crackdowns

Proactive arrests, which are initiated by the police, focus on a narrow set of high-risk targets. The theory is that a high certainty of arrest for a narrowly defined set of offenses or offenders will have a greater deterrent effect than will a low certainty of arrest for a broad range of targets (Sherman 1997). One of the most widespread developments in the use of proactive arrests in the mid-1980s was the use of police crackdowns. **Crackdowns** can be defined as an *intensive, short-term increase* in officer presence and arrests for specific types of offenses or for all offenses in specific areas. Drunk driving, public drug markets, streetwalking prostitutes, domestic violence, illegal parking, and even unsafe bicycle riding have all been targets for publicly announced crackdowns (Sherman 1990a). The theory behind this approach is that the use of such crackdowns makes the risks of apprehension far more uncertain than in any fixed level of police-patrol activity.

One of the early reviews of crackdowns covered 18 case studies of various target problems and attempted to analyze what is known to date regarding crackdowns (Sherman 1990b). The evidence appears to support the notion of an initial deterrent effect on some offenses, as well as support for the notion of *residual deterrence*; that is, some crime reduction continues even after the crackdown has ended. Interestingly, the case studies revealed that short-term crackdowns suffered less from *deterrence decay* (i.e., a lessening of the crime deterrent effect) than did longer-term crackdowns. This suggests that the use of crackdowns might be more effective if they are limited in duration and rotated across crime targets or target areas. With respect to deterrence decay, the cost-effectiveness of crackdown strategies should also be evaluated. For example, an experimental study of raids on crack houses (Sherman and Rogan 1995) found that although crime on the block dropped sharply after the raid, the deterrent effect decayed after only 7 days. Because of the labor-intensive nature of drug crackdowns, the strategy does not appear to be cost-effective in the long run.

Operation Safe Streets (Lawton, Taylor, and Luongo 2005) in Philadelphia stationed officers at 214 of the highest drug activity locations in the city 24 hours a day, 7 days a week. Crime data were compared for approximately 30 months prior to the intervention and 4 months after; the results revealed significant impacts on both violent and drug crimes within one tenth of a mile of the target sites. However, because of the increased costs for additional patrol coverage (up to a half million dollars a week in overtime), program tactics had to be shifted to a single officer patrolling multiple high crime areas (Moran 2002). The authors concluded that while crackdowns appear to be effective, because of high costs they are rarely sustainable and thus are not long-term solutions. The goal in the future would be "to engineer more cost-effective crackdowns, which can be sustained over time" (449).

Guns and Gang Violence

Several proactive arrest strategies have been used to reduce gun-related violence, often with a special focus on gang violence. The first major study in this area, known as the Kansas City Gun Experiment (Sherman, Shaw, and Rogan 1995), indicated that increased seizures of illegal guns in a high-crime area can reduce violent gun crimes. The experimental area contained extra gun-unit officers working overtime shifts who concentrated on detecting and seizing illegally possessed guns, while a control area had only regular levels of activity. Over a 29-week period, the number of gun crimes in the experimental area declined by 49 percent but by only 4 percent in the control area. There appeared to be little evidence of a displacement effect to neighboring beats. In addition, there was also a high degree of community support for the use of aggressive patrol tactics. This support was attributed to two important considerations: (1) police managers met with community leaders prior to implementation and secured their endorsement, and (2) police officers were told by their supervisors to treat citizens with respect and to explain the reasons for vehicle stops. This finding has important implications for virtually all strategies of police patrol. Unfortunately, as with other types of crackdowns, this program was extremely expensive and therefore not sustainable over the long term.

Using the Kansas City Gun Experiment as a model, McGarrell, Chermak, and Weiss (2001) evaluated a 90-day patrol project in Indianapolis that was intended to reduce violent crime involving firearms. The study compared two opposing police strategies: **specific deterrence**, where the goal was to focus on the seizure of illegal weapons from targeted offenders (i.e., suspicious-looking pedestrians and motorists), and **general deterrence**, where the goal was to maximize motor vehicle stops as a sign of increased police presence. A third comparison group area, where police activity was unchanged, was also evaluated. Significantly, gun-related crime declined by 29 percent compared with the prior year in the targeted offender-specific deterrence area, while increases occurred in the general deterrence and comparison areas. Further, there was little indication of displacement of violent crime to the five beats surrounding the targeted area.

Cohen and Ludwig (2003) evaluated the impact of Pittsburgh's Firearm Suppression Patrol (FSP) strategy. FSP was focused on specific target areas, where officers were relieved from responding to calls for service to focus on proactively seizing guns from citizens. Similar to Kansas City, police did this by engaging in traffic enforcement and pedestrian stops. The researchers found that FSP reduced shots fired by as much as 34 percent in the target areas and reduced gunshot-related injuries by 71 percent in these areas. This occurred despite a small number of gun seizures, suggesting the decreases were not the result of incapacitation but the result of the deterrent value of this type of patrol activity. A more recent program, known as *Project Exile,* targeting the use of guns in violent or drug crimes, shows initial promise. Implemented in Richmond, Virginia, the program involves sentence enhancements through the use of federal prosecutions, which generally provide longer sentences than those in state courts (as advertised extensively in print and electronic media, city buses, and business cards: "An illegal gun will get you five years in federal prison") (Rosenfeld, Fornango, and Baumer 2005). The evaluation found that Richmond's firearm homicide rate was significantly lower than the average rate among the nation's 95 largest cities after the implementation of Exile. In general, these findings support those of Kansas City with respect to the effectiveness of specific deterrence strategies over general deterrence strategies.

Growing out of these earlier hot spots gun projects, a series of multi-strategy, focused deterrence initiatives targeting violent-crime areas is showing promise. These projects focus on deterring the relatively small number of individuals involved in a disproportionate amount of gun violence, particularly gang members, while simultaneously providing services for anyone wanting to avoid violence.

The Boston Gun Project (Kennedy, Piehl, and Braga 1996) is an approach in which the police used a mix of strategies, known as "pulling levers," in an attempt to prevent gun violence, especially by gang members, many of whom were on probation. What became known as the *ceasefire strategy* was an attempt to reduce gang-related violence. This strategy emphasizes a team approach involving local and federal police and other justice system agencies, as well as private and community organizations. If gangs refrained from violent activity but committed other crimes, the normal approach of police, prosecutors, and the rest of the criminal justice system came into play. If the gangs hurt people, however, ceasefire members got involved (Kennedy 1998).

Ceasefire included criminal justice strategies such as joint patrols of police and probation officers (who teamed up to make sure convicted young adult offenders were not roaming the streets and were abiding by the law), federal and local prosecutors, school police and youth corrections, and joint ventures carried out with various federal agencies. Direct meetings between gang members and authorities also took place, with warnings of severe sanctions if violence continued.

Cease-fire also included community and private sector strategies, such as educational and employment opportunities. Community centers, the clergy, and gang-outreach workers also played a role in spreading the antiviolence message to young offenders and attempted to help them to enter mainstream society. The results were startling, with gang and gun-related homicides in the 24-and-under age category significantly reduced from 1990 to 1995; during one 28-month period there were *no* homicides in this age group (Clark 1997).

Loosely based on the Boston Gun Project is the Cincinnati Initiative to Reduce Violence (CIRV). Started in 2007, CIRV is based on the premise that conflict between street groups over issues of respect is responsible for a large portion of urban violence and that reaching out to these groups and their members with a specific deterrent message and offers of assistance to escape a violent lifestyle can reduce violence (University of Cincinnati Policing Institute 2009). Researchers working with law enforcement conduct detailed analyses of the individuals involved in violence, the groups they belong to, and the interrelationships among these groups. The individuals identified through this process are brought together with law enforcement, social service agencies, and community members at what are referred to as "call in" sessions where a specific deterrent message is conveyed. They are offered alternatives to their current lifestyle through social services, informed of the damage done to the community from their actions, encouraged to avoid violence, and warned of the consequences of violent acts; not only will the individuals involved in violence be pursued by law enforcement, but also the group or gang will be targeted for enforcement.

Early assessments are promising and show that gang-related violence in Cincinnati has declined, although the project is still relatively new, and more thorough research is still needed to determine whether the initiative is responsible for the entire decline (University of Cincinnati Policing Institute 2009). In Voices From the Field Dr. Robin Engel discusses her relationship with the Cincinnati Police and the importance of partnerships between researchers and police.

VOICES FROM THE FIELD

Dr. Robin Engel
University of Cincinnati

Question: *How would you describe your working relationship with the Cincinnati Police Department?*

Answer: In April 2001, the City of Cincinnati made international news when it erupted in race riots, sparked by the fatal shooting of a black suspect by a white Cincinnati Police Officer—it was the 15th fatal police shooting of a black suspect in six years. In October 2008, the Cincinnati Police Department received the International Association of Chiefs of Police (IACP)'s highest award in law enforcement—Motorola/Weber Seavey Award for Excellence in Law Enforcement—for its work with the Cincinnati Initiative to Reduce Violence (CIRV). Again in October 2009, I joined CPD commanders as they accepted the IACP/West Award for Excellence in Criminal Investigations. From race riots to international award winners in just seven short years, the CPD has traveled a long road of organizational change. I have been fortunate not just to witness the journey, but to become an integral part of the change process. There is no better opportunity or achievement for a researcher.

Police agencies have long been resistant—even hostile—to the work of academics. Traditionally, researchers sought to answer why police practices did not match the law on the books; to better document the gap between ideal and real. Police departments readily recognized the potential harm that academics could create and promptly closed their doors. For our part, academics fueled the fire with theories and evaluation research that often neglected to consider the realities of police work. Most academics were uninterested in the time and investment involved in assisting police agencies through the implementation process when academics are needed the most. This has changed significantly over the last decade, as police agencies around the world have embraced data-driven approaches and strategies based on research and evaluation. Academics and practitioners are finally recognizing the value in one another and productive partnerships are being formed.

This partnership is the result of hard work, patience, resilience, personality, and luck. The interesting thing about police organizational change is that it can be painfully slow and methodical, but simultaneously impacted immediately and significantly by single critical incidents. Plans for organizational change must include both short-term and long-term goals. To impact long-term change, academics must show their value in the short-term by changing their style and delivery of research. It needs to be quickly produced and meaningful for daily policing activities. Police agencies are placed at a disadvantage when they wait months or years for academic reports. As described by CPD Captain Daniel Gerard, "academics like theories, police like results." If you can demonstrate results, then you'll become a valued partner. Captain Gerard, incidentally, will learn a lot more about theories, as he is now enrolled in the University of Cincinnati's Criminal Justice Masters program where he will join Chief Thomas Streicher, Jr. and a host of other "CPD Chief's Scholars" as part of our partnership.

The personal and professional rewards for creating a valued police–academic partnership have been profound. I now split my time between the University and the police department, and so do the police. We value one another's expertise and work together on a variety of data-driven projects that are changing the quality of citizens' lives. Collaborative work on the CIRV Team has resulted in a 40 percent reduction in gang-member involved homicides. Clearly our investment in one another is paying off.

Dr. Robin Engel is the Director of the University of Cincinnati Policing Institute and an Associate Professor in the School of Criminal Justice.

The success of the Boston and Cincinnati programs likely rests on the specific deterrence effect of identifying and focusing on a particular problem and sustaining a cooperative team effort among criminal justice and public social-service agencies. Other police departments are adopting similar types of cease-fire deterrence strategies. For example, evaluations of ceasefire strategies in Minneapolis (McGarrell et al. 2006) and Lowell, Massachusetts (Braga, McDevitt, and Pierce 2006), also reported significant results in reducing homicides. However, a cease-fire strategy evaluated in Los Angeles (Tita et al. 2005), also patterned heavily after the Boston program, did not produce significant results with respect to gang violence. It is important to understand, however, that there are significant differences between the two cities. In Los Angeles, the government is not as centralized as in Boston; there are a variety of diverse, often conflicting, political structures that overlap one another. The gangs were also different in their makeup—larger, more entrenched, and mostly Latino in Los Angeles, and smaller, greater in number, and mostly African American in Boston. In addition, because of increased gang violence, the program was started before it could be properly organized and was never fully carried out as designed. The Los Angeles results provide an important policy lesson regarding the need to take differences between cities and departments into account when attempting to implement a program that has been successful elsewhere. Moreover, Weisburd and his colleagues (2010) stress that failure to fully plan and implement a program often results in weaker program effects.

Policing Disorder: Zero-Tolerance and Quality-of-Life Policing

As discussed in Chapter 5, the New York Police Department's use of Compstat-based zero-tolerance policies, aggressively targeting minor violations of traffic laws, ordinances, and misdemeanors in designated areas, has been credited by some with significant crime reductions (Bratton 1996; Kelling and Bratton 1998). Questions remain, however, with respect to how much of this reduction can be attributed to zero-tolerance arrests and whether the cost was worth it (citizen complaints of police abuse increased 60 percent). Upon closer scrutiny, the evidence strongly suggests that crime had been decreasing, sometimes as dramatically, but without the use of zero-tolerance tactics, in other major cities over the same time period (e.g., see Greene 1999; Harcourt 2001; Herbert 2001; Rosenfield, Fornango, and Baumer 2005; Witkin 1998).

Another strategy based on broken-windows theory, known as **quality-of-life policing**, targets the reduction of physical (e.g., graffiti) and social (e.g., prostitution) disorder to reduce serious crime. This tends to be a less aggressive strategy and assumes that as disorder is reduced, community members will work together to promote neighborhood safety, which, in turn, will help reduce crime. As with zero-tolerance policing, the better controlled research has not been supportive of narrow enforcement oriented quality-of-life strategies with respect to reducing serious crime. For instance, Novak et al. (1999) found that increased enforcement of joyriding and liquor laws had no effect on robbery and burglary rates. Katz, Webb, and Schaefer (2001) examined the effects of a quality-of-life initiative focused on social and physical disorder. They found a significant decline in calls for service regarding physical disorder and public morals (e.g., prostitution), but not for serious crime. Similarly, Worrall (2002), in his analysis of misdemeanor arrests relative to total arrests in 58 counties in California, found that felony property crime, but not felony violent crime, declined.

In a comprehensive observational analysis of social and physical disorder in 196 neighborhoods in Chicago, Sampson and Raudenbush (1999) found that, in general, serious crime (e.g., homicide, robbery, and burglary) was not correlated with public disorder. Robbery, however, had a low-level correlation with disorder, most likely because disorder increases the pool of potential victims with less recourse to police protection—especially those involved in prostitution and drug trafficking—who have cash on hand and thus are more vulnerable to robbery offenders. Thus, they concluded that there is no evidence that social or public disorder causes serious crime to increase, indicating that police targeting of low-level public offenses will have little, if any, impact on serious crime.

Problem-Oriented Policing Focused on Disorder

A multi-strategy and more focused approach than the zero-tolerance and quality-of-life approaches discussed above is the Beat Health Program of the Oakland, California, Police Department. This program emphasizes civil remedies to control drug and disorder problems by focusing on the physical decay and property management conditions of specific hot spot locations; thus, program staff interact primarily with non-offending third parties—landlords, business owners, and private property owners—responsible for the property. A special unit made up of Beat Health officers coordinates site visits by a group of city inspectors, known as *SMART (Specialized Multi-Agency Response Team)*. Depending on preliminary assessments made by Beat Health officers, representatives from agencies such as housing, fire, public works, and Pacific Gas and Electric are invited to inspect a problem location and to enforce local safety codes (see Inside Policing 8.2). An evaluation of the Beat Health program and SMART (Green Mazerolle and Roehl 1999) found during the 12-month post-evaluation period that the number of drug calls for service per square mile decreased by 16 percent in the Beat Health residential sites while increasing by about 5 percent in the control residential sites. The key component of this type of program is a combination of increased police activity and the cooperative working arrangement with other governmental agencies to enforce civil code violations.

Another multi-strategy hot spot study in Jersey City, New Jersey (Braga et al. 1999), evaluated the impact of using a *problem-oriented* approach in violent crime areas. The experiment included violent crime locations that made up 6 percent of the total of Jersey City but accounted for 24 percent of the assaults and 20 percent of the robberies. The violent crime locations were matched in pairs of treatment and control groups. The treatment areas were analyzed according to need and received a number of interventions that could be categorized as a "policing-disorder" strategy; almost all areas, however, received (1) a number of aggressive order-maintenance tactics, including repeat foot and radio car patrols, dispersing loiterers, issuing summonses for public drinking, and "stop-and-frisks" of suspicious persons, and (2) investigations into drug sales and drug enforcement. A little less than one half required storefront cleanups by owners and removal of trash on streets by the public works department; several areas also used increased lighting and housing-code enforcement.

The effects of the intervention were measured by analyzing six crime incident categories (robbery, nondomestic assault, property, disorder/vandalism, narcotics arrests, and total incidents) and six citizen-call categories (robbery, street fighting, property, disorder/nuisance, narcotics, and total calls). The findings indicated that the total number of both criminal incidents and calls for service was significantly reduced at the treatment areas relative to the control areas. The results of this experiment indicate that a problem-oriented approach, focusing on aggressive patrol and drug enforcement, may have a significant impact on reducing violent behavior.

A more recent experiment in Lowell, Massachusetts, modeled on the Jersey City program, also used a multi-strategy problem-oriented approach and focused on reducing disorder and calls for service in violent crime hot spots. Similar to the Jersey City program, the researchers matched 34 violent crime locations (encompassing 2.7 percent of Lowell but generating 23.5 percent of crime and disorder calls and 29.3 percent of violent crime calls) into 17 pairs of treatment and control groups. After a 1-year intervention involving strategies similar to those used in Jersey City, they discovered that the 17 treatment areas had a decrease in the number of calls for service and showed decreased signs of social and physical disorder compared with the control areas (Braga and Bond 2008).

These studies appear to have important implications for reducing drug problems and, concomitantly, for reducing violent and other crime and disorder problems using multiple patrol strategies and working with other government officials to enforce civil code violations.

The available research on broken-windows strategies suggests that with respect to serious, violent crimes, police should focus their available resources on directed and hot spot patrol activities, in particular multi-strategy problem-oriented approaches. However, they should avoid a narrow, zero-tolerance model focused mainly on social incivilities and misdemeanor arrests, which is not as promising and "may undermine relationships in low-income, urban minority communities where coproduction is most needed and distrust between the police and citizens is most profound" (Braga and Bond 2008, 600).

INSIDE POLICING 8.2   **Beat Health Program: A Case Study**

An anonymous caller to the Oakland Police Department drug hotline reported narcotics trafficking, abandoned vehicles, and trash at a single-family home in a nice area of the city. The
Beat Health team contacted the owner, who said the problems were probably caused by an
illegal tenant staying at the house with the permission of the legal tenant. Police records
revealed that the illegal tenant was on probation for drug charges.

An inspection of the property was conducted by the SMART team; each city agency inspector found violations—missing stair banisters, broken windows, possible electrical tampering,
overgrown weeds, trash, dog waste, abandoned vehicles, engine parts in the yard, and two
pit bulls. The Beat Health officer then arranged for the code-compliance officer to inspect the
inside of the residence, which resulted in the discovery of numerous citations for violations.
Within 3 months, the illegal tenant was evicted, the yard was cleared of abandoned vehicles
and trash, and code violations were fixed. The case was closed 6 months after it was opened
with the property being restored and no new calls or complaints received.

SOURCE: L. Green Mazerolle and J. Roehl, *Controlling Drug and Disorder Problems: Oakland's Beat Health Program*
(Washington, DC: National Institute of Justice, 1999), 3.

Juvenile Curfews

Juveniles contribute significantly to the overall crime rate; they account for approximately
23 percent of all index crime arrests and 26 percent of all property crime arrests (BJS 2008).
Accordingly, the use of curfew laws has increased dramatically over the past several decades
as a strategy to combat delinquency and serious crime. According to Reynolds, Seydlitz,
and Jenkins (2000), 80 percent of the 200 largest cities in the country (with populations of
100,000 or more) have juvenile curfew laws; such laws are also in effect in 75 percent of 60
moderate-size cities (with populations between 10,000 and 100,000). Because curfews are
becoming so prevalent, it is important to take a look at how effective they are at controlling
juvenile crime and delinquency. In addition, because juveniles often have a negative perception of their contacts with the police (see Chapter 7), it is likely that unless curfew laws
are *both* effective and implemented with care, they are likely to further undermine juvenile–
police interactions.

McDowall, Loftin, and Wiersema (2000) evaluated the impact of curfew laws on juvenile crimes from all 57 cities with a 1980 population of 250,000 or more. The researchers
used two measures of crime for persons age 17 and under: the UCR seven index crimes,
in addition to simple assault, vandalism, and weapon offenses (over a 12-year period), and
the homicide victims from the National Center for Health Statistics (over a 20-year period).
Most curfews began between 10:00 PM and midnight, and most ended between 4:00 and
6:00 AM; the majority of laws specified 17 as the upper age limit. The findings, depending
on the interpretation of arrest rates for different crimes, indicated either that curfew laws
had an impact on only 3 of the 10 crimes measured (burglary, larceny, and simple assault)
or had virtually no impact at all. The researchers concluded that any impact of curfew laws
was small, applied to only a few offenses, and if curfew laws do reduce juvenile offending,
their influence is not as large as generally thought.

Another juvenile curfew study (Reynolds, Seydlitz, and Jenkins 2000) in New Orleans
used a 1 year before–1 year after analysis of the most restrictive law in the country at
the time (1994). During the school year, the curfew began at 8:00 PM on weeknights and
at 11:00 PM on weekends; during the summer it began at 9:00 PM on weeknights and

at 11:00 PM on weekends. Official victim reports from the New Orleans Police Department were separated into four categories: property victimization for all ages, violent victimization for all ages, property victimization of juveniles (under age 17), and violent victimizations of juveniles. Official police records of nearly 20,000 juvenile arrests were also utilized. Findings indicated implementation of the curfew law had no impact because it did not significantly reduce victimizations (all ages), juvenile victimizations, or juvenile arrests during curfew hours. In addition, it was costly to maintain: the police department spent more than $600,000 in overtime funds for curfew enforcement during the year.

As with other types of crackdowns, curfew laws tend to be popular with the police and citizens for their intuitive appeal for crime reduction. However, the research clearly indicates that they do not significantly reduce crime and delinquency and they are prohibitively expensive for police departments to maintain. As Reynolds and his colleagues indicate, there is a need for "longer-term, more encompassing prevention and intervention strategies" (2000, 227).

Reactive Arrests and Intimate Partner Violence

Most **reactive arrests** are made in response to citizen complaints, are random, and are generally for minor offenses. Although little value is given to the general preventive nature of reactive arrests, one set of studies looked at the specific effects of arrest for misdemeanor intimate partner or domestic violence (i.e., assault on or battery of a domestic partner).

The traditional police response to intimate partner violence was to treat violence between intimate partners as a personal or family matter. Instead of arresting the offender, police officers were more likely to mediate or send the offender away from the home to "cool off." Some research even suggested that officers would delay responding to domestic violence calls in the hopes that it would be over by the time they arrived at the scene (Oppenlander 1982). As a result, in the 1970s and 1980s police made arrests in only about 7–15 percent of intimate partner violence cases (Hirschel 2009). Part of the reason for the failure to arrest was the belief that an arrest would have no influence on offenders.

The Minneapolis Domestic Violence Experiment (Sherman and Berk 1984) was the first study on the use of arrest in misdemeanor domestic violence, comparing arrest responses to non-arrest responses (either mediation or separation). The results indicated that suspects who were arrested were significantly less likely to become violent over the next 6 months. Subsequent replication studies, however, produced mixed, and often conflicting, results. For example, in Omaha, Charlotte, and Milwaukee, arrests appeared actually to increase domestic violence, but in Omaha, arrest warrants issued for offenders who fled the scene had a substantial deterrent effect. The results were mixed in two other cities, Colorado Springs and Miami. All four of the experiments that analyzed data by employment status of offenders found that arrests increased assaults among unemployed offenders, while reducing it among employed offenders.

In response to the Minneapolis study results and political pressure—especially from the women's movement at the time—police departments across the country implemented *mandatory arrest* policies (often dictated by their legislatures) in cases of misdemeanor domestic violence. The replication experiments indicate, however, that such a response was premature (ironically, in the past the police and legislators have not paid enough attention to important research findings; in this case, they may have paid too much, and on the basis of a single piece of research). A more recent and comprehensive study by Felson, Ackerman, and Gallagher (2005) based on National Crime Victimization Survey data for the years 1992 to

2002, including over 2,500 respondents who were victimized by their spouses, ex-spouses, or other intimate partners, appears to have important implications for policies regarding police intervention in intimate partner violence. The study focused on two main variables (arrest and reporting) and the social responses of three participants to the offender's violence: the victim, the police, and other third parties. The results indicated that offenders are not likely to reoffend as long as the incident *is reported*. When incidents were not reported, the likelihood of reoffending increased by 89 percent. Second, the results did not find arrest to be a deterrent for future occurrences. Third, there was no support for the hypothesis that offenders retaliate when victims (rather than third parties) call the police or sign complaints (even if they are eventually arrested).

Felson and his colleagues suggest some reasons why reporting partner violence may be such a strong deterrent, even if an arrest is not made: (1) a visit from the police may change the offenders' attitudes toward their behavior, (2) offenders may redefine their behavior as a criminal act, (3) the visit may change their perception of the costs of further violence (e.g., future arrests for reoffending), and (4) offenders may be deterred by the stigma associated with a police visit. Interestingly, the findings of Felson et al. may also apply to the Omaha study (Dunford, Huizinga, and Elliot 1990) noted above, where a substantial deterrent effect was found when arrest warrants were issued for fleeing offenders. The most important policy implication of this research is the need to *change citizens' reporting behavior*. As the authors note, one strategy would be to communicate to the public the substantial deterrent effect of reporting domestic violence by victims and third parties; another strategy would be to allow victims to seek police attention while maintaining their privacy, thus avoiding any perception of stigma attached to a visit by the police. Importantly, these results continue to question the deterrent value, and thus the use of mandatory arrest policies, for misdemeanor intimate partner violence.

Dual Arrest.   Research suggests that arrests in intimate partner violence cases have risen, with about 50 percent of cases in 2000 resulting in arrest (Hirschel 2009). One negative side effect arising from mandatory arrest laws, however, is that more victims are arrested along with offenders. This problem, known as **dual arrest**, occurs when police officers arrest both parties in intimate partner violence cases; officers simply arrest both people found at the scene without trying to determine who is the victim and who is the offender (Hirschel 2009).

In a study using official arrest data from 2,819 police departments in 19 states and a more in-depth analysis of an additional 25 police departments in 4 states, Hirschel and his colleagues (2007) found that states with mandatory or preferred arrest laws had higher intimate partner violence arrest rates. However, states with mandatory arrest laws, but not states with preferred arrest laws, also had higher rates of dual arrest. The overall dual arrest rate for intimate partner violence was 1.9 percent, with dual arrest more likely for same-sex couples than for heterosexual couples.

In response to the discovery that mandatory arrest laws have had the unintended consequence of increasing the arrest of victims, some states have enacted **primary aggressor laws**. These laws encourage officers to determine which of the parties in an intimate partner violence situation is truly the offender or primary aggressor (Hirschel et al. 2007).

Police Pursuits

A current controversy in police field operations is the issue of **police pursuits**. Police can chase suspects either on foot or by motor vehicle. A **police pursuit** is an event in which a suspect attempts to flee from police, typically to avoid arrest. Alpert and Fridell (1992) suggest that a vehicle pursuit is at least as dangerous to the public as the use of a firearm. Estimates on the number of police pursuits yearly run as high as 50,000, with the number of injuries they cause at approximately 20,000 (Charles, Falcone, and Wells 1992). A national survey of some 436 police departments (Alpert 1997), combined with case studies of approximately 1,250 pursuits in three departments (Metro-Dade, Miami; Omaha, Nebraska; and Aiken County, South Carolina), found that most pursuits are initiated for traffic violations: in Miami, 45 percent (448), in Omaha, 51 percent (112), and in Aiken County, 36 percent (5). A large percentage of pursuits, however, were also initiated for felonies: in Miami, 35 percent (344), in Omaha, 40 percent (89), and in Aiken County, 43 percent (6).

In addition, the survey indicated that 41 percent of the chases in Miami ended in personal injury (428) and 20 percent ended in property damage (213); in Omaha, 14 percent ended in personal injury (31) and 40 percent in property damage (91); in Aiken County, 12 percent ended in personal injury (2) and 24 percent in property damage (4). Arrests were made in 75 percent of the chases in Miami (784), 52 percent in Omaha (118), and 82 percent in Aiken County (14). Separate studies revealed that pursuits led to deaths of at least one person in 0.7 percent of all chases (a little less than 1 in 100 chases) in the Miami area (Alpert and Dunham 1988) and 0.2 percent in Minnesota (Alpert and Fridell 1992).

These are significant numbers and suggest that the police must pay careful attention to the development of proper policy, training, and enforcement of guidelines. In this regard, Alpert's (1997) survey revealed that while 91 percent of the responding departments had written policies governing pursuits (meaning nearly 10 percent did not), many of them were implemented in the 1970s. Forty-eight percent of the departments reported having modified their pursuit policy within the past 2 years, with most of those (87 percent) making the policies more restrictive. The strong effects of policy changes were evident in the findings from both the Metro-Dade and the Omaha departments.

In 1992 Metro-Dade adopted a *violent felony only* pursuit policy, and the number of pursuits decreased by 82 percent (from 279 to 51) the following year. In 1993 Omaha changed to a more permissive policy, allowing pursuits for offenses that were previously prohibited, and pursuits increased over 600 percent the following year (from 17 to 122). In a follow-up study analyzing 1,049 pursuit-driving reports over a 4-year period from the Metro-Dade Police Department, Alpert and Madden (1999) discovered that the more police cars that were involved, the more likely the pursuit was to result in a dangerous crash. Further, the odds of injury increased at higher speeds, at night, and in commercial rather than residential areas.

A BJS national survey found that nearly all (93 percent) local police departments had a written policy on pursuit-driving; 57 percent had a *restrictive policy* (i.e., based on criteria such as offense type or maximum speed); 27 percent had a *judgmental policy,* leaving the decision to the officer's discretion; and 5 percent *discouraged* all vehicle pursuits (Hickman and Reaves 2003a).

In addition, in Alpert's survey (1997), most departments reported that routine follow-ups to pursuits were mandated (89 percent). Most also indicated that they were either informal supervisory reviews (33 percent) or incident reports prepared by pursuing officers (47 percent). With respect to training, while 60 percent of the departments reported providing entry-level driver training at their academies, virtually all training focused on the mechanics of defensive and pursuit driving rather than on questions of when or why to pursue. Based on these findings Alpert (1997) suggests state and local police departments consider the following approaches:

1. Create and maintain systems to collect information on pursuit driving.
2. Review and update pursuit policies.
3. Evaluate the need for pursuit-specific training.
4. Support written policies with training and supervision.
5. Require that officers justify their actions or have a supervisor evaluate the pursuit (i.e., after-action reports and meaningful discipline for problem pursuits).

Alpert (1997) concluded that a balance must exist between the public's safety and the need to enforce the law and that an appropriate policy balancing these perspectives would *limit chases* to the pursuit of *violent felons*. In addition, Alpert believes that officers need more training and direction through policy to know when they can and cannot pursue. Finally, he suggests that pursuit policies should be similar to shooting policies, in which it has become reasonably clear when one can and cannot fire a weapon.

Until recently, foot pursuits of suspects have received very little attention; however, Dunham et al.'s (1998) study indicates approximately one third (30 percent) of the vehicle pursuits ended when the suspect stopped and either ran on foot or gave up. And, as an examination of assaults on officers (Pinizzotto, Davis, and Miller 1997) indicates, a significant number of officers assaulted during foot pursuits had no plan of action other than arresting the suspect. One department, in Collingswood, New Jersey, however, developed a foot pursuit policy as a result of an annual safety committee review indicating that several officers had been injured during foot chases (Bohrer, Davis, and Garrity 2000). Subsequently, the department established restrictions delineating when officers should not conduct foot pursuits, a review procedure for compliance with foot-pursuit policy, and twice-yearly foot pursuit training coinciding with use-of-force training and the firearms requalification process. Within 2 years after the new policies were established, significant changes in how officers handled foot pursuits were noted—especially with respect to improved communications and using a team concept to set up a perimeter area rather than simply chasing fleeing suspects—which has led to fewer injuries.

The Investigative Function

Investigators, or *detectives* (the terms can be used interchangeably), are specialists who respond to crimes serious enough to warrant an investigation. The primary goal of the criminal investigation is to increase the number of arrests for crimes that are prosecutable and will result in a conviction. As by-products of this goal, detectives recover stolen property and produce information that may be useful in solving other crimes, often through the development and manipulation of informants (Cawley, Miron, and Araujo 1977; Forst 1982; Waegel 1982; Wycoff 1982). As discussed previously, crime investigation responsibilities are usually specialized, especially in medium to large police departments. The most common specialization is to have separate detective units for crimes against persons (e.g., homicide, robbery and assault, sex crimes, vice, and narcotics) and crimes against property (e.g., arson, auto theft and burglary, and larceny; Greenwood and Petersilia 1975). Many departments today also have specialized detective units for juveniles, gangs, intelligence, arson, and computer and bias crimes.

Many departments allocate approximately 16 percent of their personnel to the detective and investigative function (Bayley 1994); the range in medium to large police departments is 8 percent to approximately 20 percent of sworn personnel. The criteria most often used to determine a department's needs for investigative personnel include whether detectives work in pairs or alone; the extent of patrol participation in investigations; level of training, experience, and competency of investigators; and the technological assistance available.

Patrol officers conduct the initial, or **preliminary investigation**, which is generally for the purpose of establishing that a crime has been committed and for protecting the scene of the crime from those not involved in the investigation. Once this has been done, detectives generally conduct **follow-up investigations** and develop the case. In some jurisdictions, the development phase involves working with the prosecuting attorney to prepare a case for trial. In others, this phase is the responsibility of investigators employed by the prosecuting attorney's office.

The basic responsibilities of the detective are to (1) determine whether a crime has been committed, (2) identify the perpetrator, (3) apprehend the perpetrator, and (4) provide evidence to support a conviction in court. Police consider a case *solved* if the first three objectives are successfully attained. Other outcomes, such as recovering stolen property, deterring criminal behavior, and satisfying crime victims, may also be part of the process (Brandl 2002). The disposal phase may or may not involve a prosecution or a conviction. Investigations can be terminated if the police determine that no crime has been committed, if they have insufficient evidence to proceed, or if there is no longer a suspect available (e.g., a murder–suicide).

Historical Development

Kuykendall (1986) analyzed the historical role of the police detective, who, in the mid-1850s to early 1900s, was more like a "secretive rogue" whose methods were as unscrupulous as those of the private detectives preceding them. Although some of their exploits were romanticized, the detectives were mostly inefficient and corrupt. They often had a close association with criminals, used and manipulated stool pigeons (i.e., snitches), and even had "deadlines" that established areas of a city in which detectives and criminals agreed that crime could be committed. Nineteenth- and early twentieth-century detectives believed that their work should be essentially clandestine. They were considered members of a "secret service" whose identity should remain unknown lest the criminal become wary and flee. Some detectives wore disguises, submitted court testimony in writing, and even used masks when looking at suspects. Although they did investigate crimes, detectives functioned primarily as a nonuniformed patrol force. They tended to go where persons congregated (e.g., beer gardens and steamboat docks) to look for pickpockets, gamblers, and troublemakers.

Just as police reformers of the early twentieth century hoped to replace the "neighbor" patrol officer with the "soldier" crime fighter, they also hoped to replace secretive rogues with scientific criminal investigators. The detective's relationships with criminals and snitches were criticized as corrupting and undesirable for a professional police officer. Furthermore, it was believed that the use of science would make such relationships unnecessary. The reformers stressed the importance of the detective as a perceptive, rational analyst, much like Sherlock Holmes. By the 1920s and 1930s, detectives were mostly investigating crimes after the fact rather than using clandestine tactics. Although many were ill prepared to utilize the newly developed scientific methods, this was less of a problem than it first appeared because the use of scientific evidence proved to be of value in only a few cases and rarely aided the police in identifying suspects. Consequently, the information that became most important in making arrests and ensuring successful prosecutions was derived from witnesses, informers, and suspects. As detectives stopped being secretive rogues, they gradually became inquisitors, who often coerced information from suspects to solve cases.

By the 1960s, important changes in criminal procedural laws (e.g., search and seizure, evidence, Miranda)—known as the *due process revolution*—and the continuing emphasis on efficiency in police departments had created a detective who was essentially a bureaucrat, or case processor. Although some detectives continued to work undercover, the majority were reactive and infrequently identified suspects who were not obvious. These detectives spent a greater proportion of their time processing information and coordinating with other criminal justice agencies than looking for suspects.

All the elements of the detective's role described above are present to some degree today. Some detectives are secretive, some are skillful in obtaining confessions without coercion, and all must invest considerable time in processing information. Whereas the emergence of the legalistic model of policing tended to produce a detective who was more bureaucrat than sleuth, subsequent approaches and models of policing (e.g., team and community) tend to have a broader view of the detective's role. As a result of crime-analysis techniques, the detective has continued to evolve, becoming somewhat less reactive (since the 1960s) and more proactive, with an emphasis on criminals rather than on crimes. Of course, this is not a new role for the detective, and thus far police departments have been able to make these changes without the extensive corruption problems historically associated with them (Kuykendall 1986).

Detectives today have multifaceted roles: they work undercover, they may operate sting programs, they may be involved in career-criminal programs, they may be involved in breaking up organized gang activity, and they may be involved in intelligence-gathering operations. Detectives involved in such activities, however, constitute a relatively small percentage of those involved in investigative work, with the substantial majority functioning more as bureaucrats than sleuths. To characterize the detective as a bureaucrat is not intended to demean the role, but rather to suggest the perspective from which most detectives should be viewed. Detectives spend a considerable amount of their time talking to witnesses, suspects, and victims and completing the necessary paperwork to prepare cases for prosecutors. They are primarily information processors, not the Sherlock Holmes or Dirty "Make My Day" Harry of fiction.

Terrorism and Investigation. Just as patrol work may need to change somewhat in response to the contemporary threat of terrorism, so too may investigative work. De Guzman (2002) suggests two potential areas of concern regarding investigation and terrorism. First, as noted above, police investigation has become primarily reactive in nature; it may need to again become more proactive. This means that evidence of a crime should not only be connected to a certain suspect, but also may have some connection to possible terrorist activity. This would be especially true if there were evidence that seemed not to fit with the nature of the crime committed; that is, could there be other motives attached to the offense under investigation? Second, for the most part, investigation remains highly individualized and disjointed from the rest of the department. Investigation units themselves tend to be highly fragmented. And, while community policing, along with its push for greater internal coordination, is being implemented in many departments, investigation remains, in general, untouched by the process. These conditions hamper the ability to solve cases and will be especially troublesome in cases involving terrorism. Consequently, it seems prudent for investigative units to integrate themselves with the rest of the department and redirect their functional focus, especially with respect to community policing practices.

Intelligence-Led Policing. A recent management innovation related to investigations is intelligence-led policing. This new approach to law enforcement, developed in the United Kingdom, involves intelligence analysis of data collected through improved data collection and sharing systems (Scheider, Chapman, and Schapiro 2009). It stresses collaboration, in particular the sharing of information, among federal, state, and local agencies, as well as within agencies. The shared information is systematically analyzed by trained intelligence analysts. The conclusions are then used to set priorities and prevent crime. Intelligence-led policing requires organizational changes to ensure the collection, analysis, and dissemination of information. The approach is only effective when based on sound information analyzed by trained intelligence analysts. Although initially developed in response to burglary and auto thefts, in the United States it is primarily focused on terrorism. Unfortunately, most small and medium police agencies in the United States lack the resources and specialized analysis training to effectively use intelligence-led policing to prevent terrorism, although some argue that it may be useful for responding to other serious crimes. For example, Scheider and his colleagues (2009) suggest that it may be useful as a form of problem solving if integrated into a community policing model and focused on all types of crimes. A more detailed discussion of intelligence-led policing is included in Chapter 15.

Selected Research on Investigative Operations

Several important investigative issues are discussed in this section, including investigative effectiveness and how investigative work can be improved, career criminal programs, bias crimes, detective–patrol relationships, and the twin issues of enticement and entrapment as applied to covert operations.

Investigative Effectiveness

In the mid-1970s, as a result of an in-depth study by Greenwood and Petersilia (1975), investigative units were criticized as ineffective and inefficient. In this study, operations in 25 detective units were observed and surveys were completed in 156 units. The major findings of this study indicated the following: (1) most serious crimes are solved through information obtained from victims rather than through leads developed by detectives; (2) in 75 percent of cases, the suspect's identity is known or easily determined at the time the crime is reported to the police; and (3) the major block of detective time is devoted to reviewing reports, documenting files, and attempting to locate and interview victims for cases that experience has shown are unlikely to be solved but are carried out to satisfy victims' expectations. William and Snortum (1984), who replicated the Greenwood and Petersilia study, reported similar findings, but came to a different conclusion, that is, that detectives make a valuable contribution to the investigative process through skilled interrogation and case-processing techniques.

In an extensive study of burglary and robbery investigations, Eck (1984) found that preliminary investigations by patrol officers and follow-up investigations by detectives are equally important for solving crimes. He further discovered that even in situations where the preliminary investigation by patrol officers did not develop any leads, detectives were able to identify a suspect in approximately 14 percent of the cases and make an arrest in 8 percent. Thus, Eck concluded that investigators do, in fact, make a meaningful contribution to the solution of criminal cases. To improve the effectiveness of investigations, he recommended that increased emphasis be placed on collecting physical evidence at the scene of a crime, identifying witnesses, using informants, and utilizing police records. It was further noted that successfully disposing of a case can be improved if: (1) patrol officers carefully gather evidence at the crime scene and communicate that information to the detectives on the case; (2) cases are more carefully screened for further development (i.e., deciding which cases can be ignored or given only minimal attention); (3) productivity measures are developed to ascertain whether individual detectives or detective units are meeting their goals; and (4) investigations are targeted (e.g., toward career criminals, who are known to have engaged in the behavior under investigation).

Finally, Farmer (1984) maintains that a broader approach to the study of the investigative function is needed. He notes that "the notion of case clearance as the sole objective of detective work is as inadequate as is the idea that the principal function of a detective is to solve crime" (49). In addition, there is proactive investigative work to be considered: "Investigators may pursue other equally important goals to aid citizens—including increasing citizen satisfaction, reducing fear, counseling victims, and deterring further crime" (50). In line with this reasoning, Eck suggests that criminal investigation can be improved by detectives focusing on justice and crime prevention: "If detective work were more than tracking down and arresting offenders, detectives would have to interact with communities...work more with other sections of the police force and other public and private groups to achieve their objectives" (1996, 181). Eck suggests four guiding principles to improve investigative effectiveness:

1. *Abandon crime control through apprehension as a principal goal* of investigations. There is little evidence that increased apprehensions by detectives make much of a difference in crime levels, except under special circumstances (see below).

2. Detectives should *focus on justice*. Offenders should be arrested because they violated the law. Detectives should find out who the offenders are and bring their evidence forward.

3. The special circumstances mentioned in item 1 are clear crime patterns. Obviously, arresting a repeat rapist or killer prevents crimes. As noted in point 4, *focusing on patterns* allows detectives to combine enforcement powers with many other techniques.

4. *Crime prevention through problem solving* should be emphasized. Detectives should look for patterns of crimes, determine why the patterns exist, and implement programs that stop the patterns (see Inside Policing 8.3).

INSIDE POLICING 8.3   Crime Prevention through Problem Solving

Although problem solving has generally been related to patrol officers, there have been many cases in which detectives have applied this approach. Because detectives are not tied to a radio and have more control over how their time is used, they may find it easier to address problems than would patrol officers. Two examples of how detectives have used problem solving are described below.

Domestic Homicides

In Newport News, Virginia, one of the homicide detectives felt that as satisfying as it was to solve murders, it would be more satisfying to prevent them from occurring. He noticed that half of the homicides the department had investigated in the previous year were related to domestic violence, and in half of these cases, the police had previously been to the address. This suggested the possibility of attempting early intervention with the couples involved.

The detective brought together representatives from many public and private organizations, including the prosecutor's office, women's advocates, hospitals, the local newspaper, the military, and others. In cooperation they developed a program that forced the couples involved in domestic violence into mandatory counseling. When certain conditions were present in an assault case (e.g., serious injury or presence of a gun), an arrest was mandatory. In such circumstances, it was decided that the prosecutor would not drop charges unless the abuser and the victim entered into counseling. If they completed counseling and if the victim agreed, the charges would then be dropped. Although no formal evaluation of this program has been conducted, the department reports that both domestic homicides and repeat domestic violence declined in the first year following implementation.

Gas Station Robberies

In Edmonton (Alberta, Canada), a robbery detective noted that one particular chain of gas stations had a very high robbery rate. Because of a high cigarette tax in Canada, there is a large black market for cigarettes, and cigarette theft can be lucrative. By reviewing crime reports, the detective noted that many of the robberies only involved the theft of cigarettes. He visited those stations and found that there was a single attendant in a small booth stocked with cigarettes, candy, and other small items. The detective worked with the managers of the gas station chain, and they identified a number of simple changes that could be made to the booth itself, to cigarette displays, and to various operating procedures. The gas station chain made the recommended changes. Since the changes were made, the police department reports a major decline in the robberies of this chain of gas stations.

SOURCE: Adapted from J. E. Eck, "Rethinking Detective Management." In L. T. Hoover, ed., *Quantifying Quality in Policing* (Washington, DC: Police Executive Research Forum, 1996), 178–180.

Advances in Physical Evidence: AFIS and DNA. Two relatively recent developments in physical evidence are likely to have a significant impact on investigative effectiveness. First is the *automated fingerprint identification system (AFIS)*, which allows for fingerprints recovered at a crime scene to be compared with thousands of other prints on file in a department's computer system. The computer will match fingerprints that are close to those found at the scene and a suspect can be identified. Modern AFIS programs search hundreds of thousands of scanned prints and identify possible matches in minutes (Brandl 2008). The flagged prints can then be checked by a fingerprint examiner to see whether they match. Unfortunately, many of these systems are local and often do not include prints from other jurisdictions. To overcome the limitations of local AFIS systems the FBI has developed an Integrated Automated Fingerprint Identification System (IAFIS). IAFIS contains fingerprints and criminal histories on over 55 million individuals (FBI website).

A more recent development, and one that may prove more influential than fingerprints, is the use of DNA evidence in criminal investigations. *DNA testing* allows for the comparison of human cell materials found at a crime scene (usually blood, semen, or hair) in an attempt to find a match between two samples. Since no two individuals, except for identical twins, have the same DNA makeup, it is essentially irrefutable evidence—that is, if properly collected, stored, and analyzed (serious mistakes in all of these areas have occurred). As with fingerprint identification, it used to be that the police first needed to identify a suspect to make a match; however, technology has allowed for the development of DNA banks through which comparison matches can be made, thus potentially saving the police enormous amounts of time in investigative follow-ups.

The FBI currently operates a DNA bank for the purpose of identifying suspects in cases. The Combined DNA Index System (CODIS) includes profiles on more than 8 million offenders (FBI website). Using databases, such as CODIS, DNA evidence may prove useful to police in investigations where no suspect has been identified and is not likely to be identified through traditional means—sometimes referred to as no-suspect cases. In a democracy it is important to keep in mind that while the development of fingerprint and DNA banks is a significant breakthrough, we must be careful not to interfere with individual rights (i.e., the Fourth and Fifth Amendments) when collecting samples for these banks.

Advances in forensic techniques have the potential to improve the ability of police to solve some crimes. However, unlike television portrayals, these techniques have not radically transformed the work of detectives. A recent study of homicide investigations between 1996 and 2003 in Manhattan revealed that DNA evidence was used in only 6.7 percent of prearrest homicide investigations. In fact, it was not collected in 54.5 percent of investigations and was collected and submitted but not available before the case was cleared in 38.8 percent of cases. According to Schroeder and White, "The results clearly suggest that DNA evidence was largely irrelevant to prearrest homicide investigations conducted by the NYPD during the study period" (2009, 326). However, they also noted that the collection of DNA from crimes increased between 1996 and 2003. Although it was still not used in most cases, the researchers suggested that the increased collection of DNA may eventually translate into greater use of the evidence to solve crimes.

A recent national survey of state and local law enforcement agencies revealed that in approximately 7.3 percent of unsolved rape cases and 5.6 percent of unsolved homicides, law enforcement agencies obtained DNA forensic evidence related to the crime but did not send it to a laboratory for testing (Strom and Hickman 2010). In an estimated 12,548 unsolved homicide and rape cases agencies had untested DNA evidence. The nation's largest police departments accounted for the majority of untested evidence in unsolved cases.

A number of barriers may limit the use of DNA in investigations. Police agencies may lack knowledge regarding the use and potential of DNA (Pratt et al. 2006; Schroeder and White 2009; Strom and Hickman 2010). Strom and Hickman (2010), for example, found that the most common reason for not submitting forensic evidence for analysis was the lack of a suspect. Yet, as noted above, forensic databases, such as CODIS, provide a means of checking samples against all DNA profiles in a database. Ideally, if a match is found, law enforcement will be provided information on the suspect (Beaver 2010). Another barrier involves the backlog at many crime laboratories. The time it takes for DNA results to be returned to police, in part because of case backlogs at many crime laboratories, may discourage police from sending DNA evidence for testing (Pratt et al. 2006; Schroeder and White 2009). In addition, some crime laboratories prioritize cases and place no-suspect cases lower on the priority list.

In addition to criminal justice system constraints, forensic evidence has inherent limitations as a method of solving crime. Many crimes involve no physical evidence of any kind, let alone DNA or fingerprints (Cole 2010). Even in cases where DNA or fingerprints are found, the perpetrators profile or fingerprints may not be in a database. In many cases, detectives may not need DNA evidence to make an arrest and clear a case. In fact, DNA evidence is sometimes collected and sent for testing while detectives, who may be under pressure to solve a case, continue with their investigation rather than wait on results, thus collecting DNA for prosecutors more so than their own investigations. Traditionally, physical evidence was used to confirm a known suspect rather than to identify an unknown person (Bayley 1994). It may take time for police agencies to view forensic evidence as a means of solving cases rather than as a means of confirming their work.

Research suggests that DNA evidence has not significantly changed detective work. As noted earlier, most crimes are solved through the identification of a suspect by witnesses or victims. Nonetheless, DNA may prove increasingly valuable in solving no-suspect cases, particularly as DNA databases become more extensive and police expand their use of DNA evidence. Recent research, however, suggests that many law enforcement agencies are unaware of the potential benefits of DNA testing or the testing resources available to them (Pratt et al. 2006). Indeed, Pratt and his colleagues concluded that law enforcement agencies view DNA as a tool useful to prosecutors but not detectives. Schroeder and White (2009, 338) suggest that "the value of DNA may be overestimated for police investigations but underestimated for later stages of the adjudication process." The future of DNA evidence in solving crimes may rest on issues related to funding, knowledge among police, agency policies, and the inherent limitations of physical evidence. Strom and Hickman (2010) suggest police need improved training to encourage the use of forensic testing for investigation, including in no-suspect cases.

Career Criminal Programs

Some police departments have begun implementing programs that attempt to arrest, prosecute, and convict repeat offenders (career criminals) at a significantly higher rate than normal police practices would allow. The theory behind such programs is that since a small proportion of criminals commit a disproportionate number of crimes (i.e., some research suggests that between 7 and 10 percent of individuals are responsible for committing 50 to 60 percent of crimes), if these offenders are convicted and subsequently incarcerated, there will be a significant reduction in the crime rate.

One of the most highly developed programs of this type is the *repeat offender project (ROP)* (known as "rope") of the Washington, DC, Police Department. The proactive ROP unit, consisting of approximately 60 officers, would target a small number of career criminals believed to be committing five or more index crimes a week. To arrest persons not wanted on a warrant, ROP officers had to develop evidence about specific crimes in which their targets had participated. This effort involved a number of activities, including "buy and bust" techniques, cultivating informants, investigating tips, and placing targets under surveillance.

Prior to program implementation, ROP's proposed procedures were evaluated by the local ACLU. The ACLU was concerned that ROP would be used as a "dragnet" operation that harassed and entrapped people. These concerns were alleviated when it was explained that ROP would use no formulas or "profiles" for target selection. Furthermore, the department made it clear that places where citizens have a right to privacy would be put under surveillance only with court permission (Epstein 1983). Target selection for ROP was based on informal understandings about what makes a "good" target. Common characteristics included the target's "catchability," deservedness, and longer-term yield (Martin and Sherman 1986).

A 2-year evaluation of the program concluded that by most measures used, the ROP unit achieved its goals of selecting, arresting, and contributing to the incarceration of repeat offenders. For example, targeted offenders were eight times more likely to be arrested, and while ROP officers made fewer arrests relative to other officers, the arrests were of high quality with respect to felony, drug, and weapons crimes. While the ROP program appears to have been successful, the authors of the study are cautious in their interpretations of the findings (Martin and Sherman 1986). They suggest that before other departments implement such programs they should recognize the potential side effects and dangers of "perpetrator-oriented proactive policing." For instance, the program is extremely costly in terms of time, resources, and expenses to equip the unit; thus, it may not be cost-effective in the long term. Additionally, ROP decreased its officers' arrest productivity and most likely other aspects of police service as well, especially with respect to reduced order maintenance activities. The unorthodox tactics used by ROP-type programs further create potential dangers to civil liberties. Although because of careful program planning and supervision, such problems appear to have been avoided by this particular ROP program, other departments would need to be just as cautious in their development of similar programs.

Bias Crime Programs

Although there is little accurate information regarding **bias crimes** (i.e., crimes that are racially or sexually motivated), they are a continuing concern for police. Blacks, Hispanics, Jews, homosexuals, and other minority groups that are targets of criminal activity because of their race, ethnicity, or sexual orientation are potential victims of bias crimes. Police departments need a mechanism to identify and record these crimes and develop specific responses. The training of officers about the possibility of such "hate" crimes is an important first step. When such crimes occur, the department must make a concerted response involving investigation, traditional patrol, and communication with the group that has been the target of the crime.

One study on bias crimes (Garofalo and Martin 1995) found that bias crime clearances were higher in departments where police responses to these crimes emphasized specialized investigations and arrest. It was further suggested that departments provide some type of motivation for inducing patrol officers to recognize and report bias crime when they encounter it. Concerning the manner in which bias crimes are handled, a study of 19 departments in the central United States by Walker and Katz (1995) found that four (25 percent) had separate bias crime units with written procedures for handling bias crimes. Six of the departments (37.5 percent) did not have a separate bias-crime unit, but either designated specific officers in an investigative unit to handle bias crimes or had special policies and procedures that all officers would follow. Six of the departments (37.5 percent) had neither a special unit nor special procedures. Of the 12 departments that did not have a special bias-crime unit, 8 provided no special training regarding hate crimes. Projecting the findings from this sample to the national level, it was estimated that special bias-crime units exist in only about 13 percent of municipal police departments. Clearly, more effort needs to be exerted in this area of law enforcement, especially with respect to developing specialized investigative units or personnel.

Detective–Patrol Relationships

The relationship in a police department between detectives and patrol officers is both extremely important and a source of potential conflict. This potential conflict must be addressed by the department because effective communication between the two is vital to the success of many investigations. It is crucial that investigators make an effort to develop and maintain a good rapport with patrol officers. This relationship should be based on frequent personal contacts, the acknowledgment of patrol officers' contribution to investigations, seeking out patrol officer advice when appropriate, and keeping officers informed as to the status of cases.

One of the major problems that continues to exist in many departments is related to the different status of detectives and patrol officers. Investigators tend to dress in civilian clothes, are often perceived to have more status in the department, and may even be of a higher rank or receive a higher salary. There are several ways to address this problem. One possible solution relates to the basic structure of the department—that is, using a community-policing model, in which detectives and patrol personnel work together as a team. Another solution is to create a personnel system that gives equal status and financial rewards to both patrol officers and investigators. Rotating personnel through various investigative slots, so that the position is not thought of as being "owned" by anyone, is also a constructive approach. As noted in Chapter 5 (see Inside Policing 5.2), the Cedar Rapids, Iowa, Police Department has eliminated the position of detective and instead selects qualified patrol officers to rotate into the investigative division as they would any other specialty. Police departments must also be alert to the manner in which detectives and patrol officers are treated. It is essential that patrol officers not be given the impression that, when compared to investigators, they are second-class citizens (Bloch and Weidman 1975).

Enticement and Entrapment

In the course of using covert or undercover investigations, the police must be extremely careful that they do not violate citizen rights and therefore harm police–community relations even though they increase arrest rates. Do certain investigative activities involve **enticement**? That is, by their existence do these activities encourage the commission of crimes? When does **entrapment** occur? That is, when are individuals provided by the police with both the opportunity and the intent to commit a crime? Whether the police play the role of victim or criminal, covert activities have the potential of enticing and entrapping. The differences between enticement and entrapment are subtle, but the implications for the citizen are profound. Creating opportunities for crime by the police is a legitimate police practice and assists the police in targeting offenses in a proactive manner. However, if the behavior of law enforcement officers causes an otherwise innocent person to commit a crime, then that person has a legitimate defense in court to have the charges dismissed.

In *sting operations,* undercover detectives set up their own fencing outlets and encourage thieves to sell them stolen merchandise; the transaction is generally videotaped for later use in court. Can such programs actually result in more victims? If criminals can easily sell stolen property for a competitive or higher price, will they steal more while the outlet is available? Does the cost-to-benefit ratio of such programs (e.g., more arrests, more useful information, or the development of informants) outweigh the potential hazards? What about a police officer playing an inebriated decoy on the street, waiting to be mugged? Can this practice cause an individual, who otherwise might not be inclined to steal, to take advantage of such an easy mark? Do career-criminal programs unfairly target certain individuals or groups for arrest? Does the random selection of targets for the undercover selling of drugs provide the intent to buy drugs? These are some of the questions that police departments face with respect to undercover operations. Extensive legal guidelines provide the framework for acceptable policies and procedures, but once again, the importance of community satisfaction should play an integral role in determining the extent and type of undercover activities a police department should use.

Summary

The primary activities of police field operations include patrol, the "backbone of policing," and investigative work. Recent research indicates that patrol activities related to law enforcement are more substantial than past research has shown, whereas detective work is primarily concerned with information processing rather than sleuthing. Patrol work is attempting to regain the neighborhood contextual knowledge that was lost in efforts to "professionalize" the police in the early 1960s and 1970s. Since the 1960s, as a result of crime-analysis techniques, investigative work has become more proactive, with an emphasis on criminals rather than on crimes. The majority of police officers are assigned to foot or automobile patrol. Resources for these activities are largely determined by intuition and comparison, although a new method of allocation is by computerized crime mapping.

Selected research on patrol and investigative operations emphasizes effectiveness relating to cost and crime reduction. Although research suggests that some patrol strategies are effective in reducing crime, they may also produce negative community relations. Thus, the more sensitive of these strategies should be carefully implemented, but not without community acceptance. For example, differential response, directed patrol, different types of proactive arrests, covert patrol, and career criminal programs must have strong community support if they are to be of mutual benefit to both the police and the public.

Critical Thinking Questions

1. Describe the three primary functions of patrol work and provide an example of each.

2. What is computerized crime mapping? How might such mapping improve patrol work?

3. Why was the Kansas City preventive patrol study important to policing at the time it was conducted? Are the implications still important today?

4. Describe Boston's cease-fire strategy and why it was so effective; discuss why a similar strategy in Los Angeles was not effective.

5. With respect to the research on the use of arrests in cases of intimate partner violence, what patrol policies would you formulate?

6. What major policies would you formulate for vehicle pursuits? For foot pursuits?

7. Discuss the general level of effectiveness of investigators. What policies would you implement to improve effectiveness?

8. How might advances in forensic analysis change detective work?

9. What are the benefits and drawbacks of DNA databases?

References

Alarid, L. F., and Novak, K. J. 2008. "Citizens' Views on Using Alternate Reporting Methods in Policing." *Criminal Justice Policy Review* 19: 25–39.

Alpert, G. P. 1997. *Police Pursuit: Policies and Training, May.* Washington, DC: National Institute of Justice.

Alpert, G. P., and Dunham, R. 1988. "Research on Police Pursuits: Applications for Law Enforcement." *American Journal of Police* 7: 123–131.

Alpert, G. P., and Fridell, L. 1992. *Police Vehicles and Firearms: Instruments of Deadly Force*. Prospect Heights, IL: Waveland Press.

Alpert, G. P., and Madden, T. J. 1999. "Toward the Development of a Pursuit Decision Calculus; Pursuit Benefits Versus Pursuit Costs." *Justice Research and Policy* 1: 23–41.

Baehr, M. E., Furcon, J. E., and Froemel, E. C. 1968. *Psychological Assessment of Patrolman Qualifications in Relation to Field Performance*. Washington, DC: Department of Justice.

Bayley, D. 1994. *Police for the Future*. New York: Oxford University Press.

Beaver, K. M. 2010. "The Promises and Pitfalls of Forensic Evidence in Unsolved Crimes." *Criminology & Public Policy*. 9: 405–410.

Bloch, P. B., and Weidman, D. R. 1975. *Managing Criminal Investigations*. Washington, DC: U.S. Government Printing Office.

Bohrer, S., Davis, E. F., and Garrity, T. J. 2000. "Establishing a Foot Pursuit Policy: Running into Danger." *FBI Law Enforcement Bulletin*. Washington, DC: Department of Justice.

Boydstun, J. E., Sherry, M. E., and Moelter, N. P. 1977. *Patrol Staffing in San Diego*. Washington, DC: Police Foundation.

Braga, A. A., and Bond, B. J. 2008. "Policing Crime and Disorder Hot Spots: A Randomized Controlled Trial." *Criminology* 46: 577–607.

Braga, A. A., McDevitt, J., and Pierce, G. L. 2006. "Understanding and Preventing Gang Violence: Problem Analysis and Response Development in Lowell, Massachusetts." *Police Quarterly* 9: 20–46.

Braga, A. A., Weisburd, D. L., Waring, E. J., Green Mazerolle, L., Spelman, W., and Gajewski, F. 1999. "Problem-Oriented Policing in Violent Crime Places: A Randomized Controlled Experiment." *Criminology* 37: 541–581.

Brandl, S. G. 2002. "Police: Criminal Investigations." In J. Dressler (ed.), *Encyclopedia of Crime & Justice*, pp. 1068–1073. New York: Thomson.

Brandl, S. G. 2008. *Criminal Investigation*, 2nd ed. Boston: Allyn & Bacon.

Bratton, W. 1996. "Remark: New Strategies for Combating Crime in New York City." *Fordham Urban Journal* 23: 781–785.

Bureau of Justice Statistics 2008. *Sourcebook of Criminal Justice Statistics—2008*. Washington, DC: U.S. Government Printing Office.

Cahn, M. F., and Tien, J. 1981. *An Alternative Approach in Police Response: Wilmington Management of Demand Program*. Cambridge, MA: Public Systems Evaluation, Inc.

Caiden, G. E. 1977. *Police Revitalization*. Lexington, MA: Lexington Books.

Cawley, D. F., Miron, H. J., and Araujo, W. J. 1977. *Managing Criminal Investigations: Trainer's Handbook*. Washington, DC: University Research Corporation.

Charles, M. T., Falcone, D. N., and Wells, E. 1992. *Police Pursuit in Pursuit of a Policy: The Pursuit Issue, Legal and Literature Review, and an Empirical Study*. Washington, DC: AAA Foundation for Traffic Safety.

CJ Update. 2006. "Online Crime Mapping Now Offered to Los Angeles Residents." *CJ Update*. Spring: 5.

Clark, J. R. 1997. "LEN Salutes Its 1997 People of the Year, the Boston Gun Project Working Group." *Law Enforcement News* December 31: 1, 4, and 5.

Cohen, J., and Ludwig, J. 2003. "Policing Crime Guns." In J. Ludwig and P. J. Cook (eds.), *Evaluating Gun Policy: Effects on Crime and Violence*. Washington, DC: Brookings Institution Press.

Cohen, M., and McEwen, J. T. 1984. "Handling Calls for Service: Alternatives to Traditional Policing." *NIJ Reports* September: 4–8.

Cole, S.A. 2010. "Forensic Identification Evidence: Utility Without Infallibility." *Criminology & Public Policy* 9: 375–379.

Cordner, G. W., Greene, J. R., and Bynum, T. S. 1983. "The Sooner the Better: Some Effects of Police Response Time." In R. R. Bennett (ed.), *Police at Work: Policy Issues and Analysis*, pp. 145–164. Beverly Hills, CA: Sage.

Coupe, R. T., and Blake, L. 2005. "The Effects of Patrol Workloads and Response Strength on Arrests at Burglary Emergencies." *Journal of Criminal Justice* 33: 239–255.

Crank, J. 1999. *Understanding Police Culture*. Cincinnati: Anderson.

De Guzman, M. C. 2002. "The Changing Roles and Strategies of the Police in Time of Terror." *ACJS Today* 22(3): 8–13. Greenbelt, MD: Academy of Criminal Justice Sciences.

Dunford, F. W., Huizinga, D., and Elliot, D.S. 1990. "The Role of Arrest in Domestic Assault: The Omaha Police Experiment." *Criminology* 28: 183–206.

Dunham, R. G., Alpert, G. P., Kenney, D. J., and Cromwell, P. 1998. "High-Speed Pursuit." *Criminal Justice and Behavior* 25: 30–45.

Durose, M. R., Smith, E. L., and Langan, P. A. 2007. *Contacts Between the Police and the Public, 2005.* Washington, DC: U.S. Department of Justice.

Eck, J. 1984. *Solving Crimes.* Washington, DC: Police Executive Research Forum.

———. 1996. "Rethinking Detective Management." In L. T. Hoover (ed.), *Quantifying Quality in Policing,* pp. 167–184. Washington, DC: Police Executive Research Forum.

Epstein, A. 1983. "Spurlock's Raiders." *Regardies* 3: 41–42.

Farmer, D. J. 1984. *Crime Control: The Use and Misuse of Police Resources.* New York: Plenum.

Federal Bureau of Investigation. 1991. *Uniform Crime Reports, Crime in the United States.* Washington, DC: Department of Justice.

Feinberg, S. E., Kinley, L., and Reiss, A. J. Jr. 1976. "Redesigning the Kansas City Preventive Patrol Experiment." *Evaluation* 3: 124–131.

Felson, R. B., Ackerman, J. M., and Gallagher, C. A. 2005. "Police Intervention and the Repeat of Domestic Assault." *Criminology* 43: 563–588.

Forst, B. 1982. *Arrest Convictability as a Measure of Police Performance.* Washington, DC: U.S. Government Printing Office.

Garofalo, J., and Martin, S. E. 1995. *Bias-Motivated Crimes: Their Characteristics and the Law Enforcement Response.* Carbondale, IL: Southern Illinois University.

Greene, J. 1999. "Zero Tolerance: A Case Study of Police Policies and Practices in New York City." *Crime and Delinquency* 45: 171–187.

Greene, J. R. 1987. "Foot Patrol and Community Policing: Past Practices and Future Prospects." *American Journal of Police* 6: 1–15.

Green Mazerolle, L., and Roehl, J. 1999. *Controlling Drug and Disorder Problems: Oakland's Beat Health Program.* Washington, DC: National Institute of Justice.

Greenwood, P., and Petersilia, J. 1975. *The Criminal Investigation Process.* Santa Monica, CA: Rand.

Harcourt, B. 2001. *Illusion of Order: The False Promise of Broken Windows Policing.* Cambridge, MA: Harvard University Press.

Herbert, S. 2001. "Policing the Contemporary City: Fixing Broken Windows or Shoring Up Neo-Liberalism?" *Theoretical Criminology* 5: 445–466.

Hickman, M. J., and Reaves, B. A. 2003a. *Local Police Departments, 2000.* Washington, DC: Bureau of Justice Statistics.

———. 2003b. *Sheriffs' Offices, 2000.* Washington, DC: Bureau of Justice Statistics.

Hirschel, D. 2009. "Making Arrests in Domestic Violence Cases: What Police Should Know." *In Short: Toward Criminal Justice Solutions.* Washington, D.C.: U.S. Department of Justice.

Hirschel, D., Buzawa, E., Pattavina, A., Faggiani, D., and Reuland M. 2007. "Explaining the Prevalence, Context, and Consequences of Dual Arrest in Intimate Partner Cases." Washington, DC: U.S. Department of Justice.

Kansas City Missouri Police Department. 2002. *Annual Report.* Kansas City, MO: Police Department.

Katz, C. M., Webb, V. J., and Schaefer, D. R. 2001. "An Assessment of the Impact of Quality-of-Life Policing on Crime and Disorder." *Justice Quarterly* 18: 825–876.

Kelling, G. L., and Bratton, W. 1998. "Declining Crime Rates: Insiders' Views of the New York City Story." *Journal of Criminal Law and Criminology* 88: 1217–1231.

Kelling, G. L., Pate, T., Dieckman, D., and Brown, C. E. 1974. *The Kansas City Preventive Patrol Experiment: A Summary Report.* Washington, DC: Police Foundation.

Kennedy, D. 1998. "Pulling Levers: Getting Deterrence Right." *NIJ Journal* July, pp. 2–8. Washington, DC: National Institute of Justice.

Kennedy, D., Piehl, A. M., and Braga, A. A. 1996. "Youth Gun Violence in Boston: Gun Markets, Serious Youth Offenders, and a Use Reduction Strategy." *Law and Contemporary Problems* 59: 147–196.

Kessler, D. A. 1985. "One- or Two-Officer Cars? A Perspective From Kansas City." *Journal of Criminal Justice* 13: 49–64.

Kuykendall, J. (1986). "The Municipal Police Detective: An Historical Analysis." *Criminology* 24: 175–201.

Larson, R. C. 1975. "What Happened to Patrol Operations in Kansas City? A Review of the Kansas City Preventive Patrol Experiment." *Journal of Criminal Justice* 3: 267–297.

Lawton, B. A., Taylor, R. B., and Luongo, A. J. 2005. "Police Officers on Drug Corners in Philadelphia, Drug Crime, and Violent Crime: Intended, Diffusion, and Displacement Impacts." *Justice Quarterly* 22: 427–451.

Martin, S. E., and Sherman, L. W. 1986. *Catching Career Criminals: The Washington, D.C. Repeat Offender Project.* Washington, DC: Police Foundation.

Marvell, T. B., and Moody, C. E. 1996. "Specification Problems, Police Levels and Crime Rates." *Criminology* 34: 609–646.

Mazerolle, L., Rogan, D., Frank, J., Famega, C., and Eck, J. E. 2002. "Managing Citizen Calls to the Police: The Impact of Baltimore's 3–1–1 Call System." *Criminology and Public Policy* 2: 97–124.

———. 2005. "Managing Calls to the Police With 911/311 Systems." *NIJ Research for Practice* February. Washington, DC: U.S. Department of Justice.

McDowall, D., Loftin, C., and Wiersma, B. 2000. "The Impact of Youth Curfew Laws on Juvenile Crime Rates." *Crime & Delinquency* 46: 76–91.

McEwen, J. T., Connors, E. F., and Cohen, M. I. 1986. *Evaluation of the Differential Response Field Test.* Washington, DC: U.S. Government Printing Office.

McGarrell, E. F., Chermak, S., and Weiss, A. 2001. "Reducing Firearms Violence Through Directed Police Patrol." *Criminology & Public Policy* 1: 119–148.

McGarrell, E. F., Chermak, S., Wilson, J. M., and Corsaro, N. 2006. "Reducing Homicide Through a 'Level Pulling' Strategy," *Justice Quarterly* 23: 214–231.

Moran, R. 2002. "City's Anti-drug Effort May Be Cut Back. Operation Safe Streets Cost Phila. Up to Half-Million Dollars a Week in Police Overtime." *The Philadelphia Inquirer,* June: A1.

Novak, K., Hartman, J. L., Holsinger, A. M., and Turner, M. G. 1999. "The Effects of Aggressive Policing of Disorder on Serious Crime." *Policing: An International Journal of Police Strategies and Management* 22: 171–190.

Oppenlander, N. 1982. "Coping or Copping Out." *Criminology* 20: 449–465.

Pate, T., Bowers, R. A., Ferrara, A., and Lorence, J. 1976. *Police Response Time: Its Determinants and Effects.* Washington, DC: Police Foundation.

Payne, D. M., and Trojanowicz, R. C. 1985. *Performance Profiles of Foot Versus Motor Officers.* East Lansing, MI: National Neighborhood Foot Patrol Center, Michigan State University.

Pinizzotto, A. J., Davis, E. F., and Miller, C. E. III 1997. *In the Line of Fire: A Study of Selected Felonious Assaults on Law Enforcement Officers.* Washington, DC: Department of Justice.

Police Foundation. 1981. *The Newark Foot Patrol Experiment.* Washington, DC: Police Foundation.

Pratt, T. C., Gaffney, M. J., Lovrich, N. P., and Johnson, C. L. 2006. "This Isn't CSI: Estimating the National Backlog of Forensic DNA Cases and the Barriers Associated with Case Processing." *Criminal Justice Policy Review* 17: 32–47.

President's Commission on Law Enforcement and Administration of Justice. 1967. *Task Report: The Police.* Washington, DC: U.S. Government Printing Office.

Reaves, B. A., and Goldberg, A. L. 1999. *Law Enforcement Management and Administrative Statistics, 1997: Data for Individual State and Local Agencies with 100 or More Officers.* Washington, DC: Department of Justice.

———. 2000. *Local Police Departments, 1997.* Washington, DC: Bureau of Justice Statistics.

Reaves, B. A., and Hickman, M. J. 2002. Census of State and Local Law Enforcement Agencies, 2000. Washington, DC: Department of Justice.

Reynolds, M. K., Seydlitz, R., and Jenkins, P. 2000. "Do Juvenile Curfew Laws Work? A Time-Series Analysis of the New Orleans Law." *Justice Quarterly* 17: 205–230.

Rich, T. F. 1996. *The Chicago Police Department's Information Collection for Automated Mapping (ICAM) Program.* Washington, DC: National Institute of Justice.

Roberg, R. R. 1976. *The Changing Police Role: New Dimensions and New Issues.* San Jose, CA: Justice Systems Development.

Rosenfeld, R., Fornango, R., and Baumer, E. 2005. "Did Ceasefire, Compstat, and Exile Reduce Homicide?" *Criminology and Public Policy* 4: 419–450.

Sampson, R. J., and Raudenbush, S. W. 1999. "Systematic Social Observation of Public Spaces: A New Look at Disorder in Urban Neighborhoods." *American Journal of Sociology* 103: 603–651.

Scheider, M. C., Chapman, R., and Schapiro, A. 2009. "Towards the Unification of Policing Innovations under Community Policing." *Policing* 32: 694–718.

Schroeder, D. A., and White, M. D. 2009. "Exploring the Use of DNA Evidence in Homicide Investigations." *Police Quarterly* 12: 319–342.

Sherman, L. W. 1983. "Patrol Strategies for Police." In J. Q. Wilson (ed.), *Crime and Public Policy,* pp. 145–163. San Francisco: Institute for Contemporary Studies Press.

———. 1990a. "Police Crackdowns." *NIJ Reports* March/April: 2–6. Washington, DC: National Institute of Justice.

———. 1990b. "Police Crackdowns: Initial and Residual Deterrence." In M. Tonry and N. Morris (eds.), *Crime and Justice: A Review of Research,* pp. 1–48. Chicago: University of Chicago Press.

———. 1997. "Policing for Crime Prevention." In L. W. Sherman, D. Gottfredson, D. MacKenzie, J. Eck, P. Reuter, and S. Bushway (eds.), *Preventing Crime: What Works, What Doesn't and What's Promising,* pp. 8/1–8/58. Washington, DC: Office of Justice Programs.

Sherman, L. W., and Berk, R. A. 1984. "The Specific Deterrent Effects of Arrest for Domestic Assault." *American Sociological Review* 49: 261–272.

Sherman, L. W., Gartin, P. R., and Buerger, M. E. 1989. "Hot Spots of Predatory Crime: Routine Activities and the Criminology of Place." *Criminology* 27: 27–55.

Sherman, L. W., and Rogan, D. P. 1995. "Deterrent Effects of Police Raids on Crack Houses: A Randomized, Controlled Experiment." *Justice Quarterly* 12: 755–781.

Sherman, L. W., Shaw, J. W., and Rogan D. P. 1995. *The Kansas City Gun Experiment.* Washington, DC: U.S. Government Printing Office.

Sherman, L. W., and Weisburd, D. A. 1995. "General Deterrence Effects of Police Patrol in Crime 'Hot Spots': A Randomized, Controlled Trial." *Justice Quarterly* 12: 625–648.

Spelman, W., and Brown D. K. 1982. *Calling the Police.* Washington, DC: Police Executive Research Forum.

Stephens, D. W. 1996. "Community Problem-Oriented Policing: Measuring Impacts." In L. T. Hoover (ed.), *Quantifying Quality in Policing,* pp. 95–129. Washington, DC: Police Executive Research Forum.

Strom, K. J., and Hickman, M. J. 2010. "Unanalyzed Evidence in Law-Enforcement Agencies: A National Examination of Forensic Processing in Police Departments." *Criminology & Public Policy* 9: 381–404.

Tita, G. E., Riley, K. J., Ridgeway, G., and Greenwood, P. W. 2005. "Reducing Gun Violence: Operation Ceasefire in Los Angeles." *NIJ Research Report* February. Washington, DC: U.S. Department of Justice.

Trojanowicz, R. C. 1982. *An Evaluation of the Neighborhood Foot Patrol Program in Flint, Michigan.* East Lansing, MI: National Neighborhood Foot Patrol Center, Michigan State University.

Trojanowicz, R. C., and Banas, D. W. 1985. *The Impact of Foot Patrol on Black and White Perceptions of Policing.* East Lansing, MI: National Neighborhood Foot Patrol Center, Michigan State University.

University of Cincinnati Policing Institute. 2009. *Implementation of the Cincinnati Initiative to Reduce Violence (CIRV): Year 2 Report.* Cincinnati: University of Cincinnati. Available online at http://www.cincinnati-oh.gov/police/downloads/police_pdf38580.pdf.

Waegel, W. B. 1982. "Patterns of Police Investigation of Urban Crimes." *Journal of Police Science and Administration* 10: 452–465.

Walker, S., 1984. "'Broken Windows' and Fractured History: The Use and Misuse of History in Recent Police Patrol Analysis." *Justice Quarterly* 1: 57–90.

Walker, S., and Katz, C. M. 1995. "Less Than Meets the Eye: Police Department Bias-Crime Units." *American Journal of Police* 16: 29–48.

Weisburd, D., Telep, C. W., Hinkle, J. C., and Eck, J. E. 2010. "Is Problem-Oriented Policing Effective in Reducing Crime and Disorder? Findings from a Campbell Systematic Review." *Criminology & Public Policy* 9: 139–172.

William, M., and Snortum, J. 1984. "Detective Work: The Criminal Investigation Process in a Medium-Size Police Department." *Criminal Justice Review* 9: 33–39.

Wilson, C., and Brewer, N. 2001. "Working in Teams: Negative Effects on Organizational Performance in Policing." *Policing: An International Journal of Police Strategies and Management* 24: 115–127.

Wilson, O. W. 1950. *Police Administration.* New York: McGraw–Hill.

Wilson, O. W., and McLaren, R. C. 1977. *Police Administration,* 3rd ed. New York: McGraw–Hill.

Witkin, G. 1998. "The Crime Bust." *U.S. News and World Report* May 25: 28–36.

Won-Jae, L. 2002. "Patrol Workload." *Texas Law Enforcement Management and Administrative Statistics Program,* March/April.

Worden, R. E. 1993. "Toward Equity and Efficiency in Law Enforcement: Differential Police Response." *American Journal of Police* 12: 1–32.

Worrall, J. L. 2002. *Does "Broken Windows" Law Enforcement Reduce Serious Crime?* Sacramento, CA: California Institute for County Government.

Wycoff, M. A. 1982. "Evaluating the Crime Effectiveness of Municipal Police." In J. R. Greene (ed.), *Managing Police Work,* pp. 15–36. Newbury Park, CA: Sage.

Part III

Police
Behavior

CHAPTER 9

Behavior and Misconduct

CHAPTER OUTLINE

- Perspectives of Police Behavior
  Universalistic Perspectives
  Particularistic Perspectives
  Socialization Versus Predisposition
- Classic Studies of Police Behavior
  Violence and the Police
  Justice Without Trial
  Varieties of Police Behavior
  City Police
  Working the Street: Police Discretion
- Decision Making and Police Discretion
  Organizational Variables
  Neighborhood Variables
  Situational Variables
  Individual (Officer) Variables
- Police Deviance
  Types of Deviance and Misconduct

CHAPTER OUTLINE   (continued)

The Prevalence of Police Deviance
The Trouble With Gratuities
Deviant Officers
The Persistence of Corruption
Police Sexual Misconduct
The Drug War and Police Deviance
■ Summary
■ Critical Thinking Questions
■ References

KEY TERMS

- abuse of authority
- discretion
- economic corruption
- grass eaters
- gratuity
- in-group solidarity
- legalistic style
- meat eaters
- noble-cause corruption
- occupational deviance

- particularist perspectives
- police corruption
- police culture
- police deviance
- police misconduct
- police violence
- predispositional theory
- racial profiling
- rotten-apple theory of corruption

- slippery-slope theory
- socialization theory
- subjugation of defendant's rights
- symbolic assailant
- systemic theory of corruption
- universalistic perspectives
- use corruption
- watchman style

THIS CHAPTER PROVIDES A discussion of police behavior. It considers many different perspectives of the conduct of the police, in terms of both the way police make decisions and the factors that motivate their decisions. It is concerned with a general discussion of both appropriate and inappropriate (deviant) police behavior. Two particular forms of deviance are considered in this chapter: the acceptance of gratuities and police corruption. Chapter 10 will address other forms of police deviance related to the exercise of police authority and the use of coercion. Issues and strategies for controlling police behavior will be discussed in Chapter 11.

Perspectives of Police Behavior

Police behavior may be described from universalistic or particularistic perspectives. **Universalistic perspectives** look at the ways officers are similar. They are widely used by police researchers because they provide ways to distinguish police work from other occupations. **Particularistic perspectives** emphasize how police officers differ one from another.

Universalistic Perspectives

A wide variety of research has sought to explain police behavior in universalistic terms. This research has been conducted from three perspectives: sociological, psychological, and organizational (Worden 1989).

Sociological Perspective. The sociological perspective emphasizes the social context in which police officers are hired and trained and in which police–citizen interactions occur.

Police officers, as a result of their training and work experience, tend to view situations in a certain manner and act accordingly. Most of the research in this area has attempted to identify external or contextual factors that influence an officer's discretion (Black 1980). Research on women in policing has discussed the absence of roles for female officers and the problems women have adapting to male expectations (Martin 1990).

Psychological Perspective. The psychological perspective is concerned with the nature of the "police personality." Officers may have a certain type of personality prior to employment, or their personality may change as a result of their police experience. One of the enduring issues in research on police behavior is whether the values and attitudes of police officers stem from their backgrounds and upbringing or are the result of the experience of police work. Between the 1970s and the 1990s, researchers considered experience in police work the most important determinant of the police personality. However, research has questioned this assumption, contending that predispositional factors (discussed later) may be more important than previously thought (Caldero 1997).

Organizational Perspective. The organizational perspective suggests that organizational (departmental) factors—formal, informal (cultural), and institutional—play an important role in police behavior. Research on the influence of formal factors looks at the ways the department structures police activity. For example, Greene and Klockars (1991) studied the caseloads of officers to assess the overall importance of law enforcement, order maintenance, and service activity in the daily work of the police. They discovered that police spend more time on law enforcement than had been previously thought. As discussed in Chapter 8, most of the research in the 1960s and 1970s discovered that law-enforcement activities accounted for only between 10 and 30 percent of an officer's workload. Greene and Klockars, however, found that police officers spend about 43 percent of their time on law enforcement, only 21 percent on maintaining order, and 8 percent on service. The second largest category, traffic, accounted for 24 percent of their time. Furthermore, recent research indicates that the amount of time spent on different core activities including law enforcement, problem solving, order maintenance, service, investigations, and patrol varies by assignment and that community policing officers have very different workloads from their traditional officer counterparts (Famega 2009; Smith, Novak, and Frank 2002).

Research on informal factors studies **police culture.** In some ways, policing is both a culture and a subculture. As a culture, police work is characterized by its own occupational beliefs and values that are shared by officers across the United States—for example, police everywhere value their assigned beats. Their territories and the way they deal with their territories define to a great extent their reputations in the department (Herbert 1997). Police organizations often have their own local cultures as well, variations of the broader occupational culture (Manning 1989, 1997). As a subculture, police work has many values imported from the broader society in which officers live. Subcultures often develop within police organizations among working groups of officers, where values and norms for behavior are set and enforced among subgroups (e.g., a particular police precinct or unit or officers on a particular shift). Research on institutional factors is concerned with how the department adapts to its environment. Institutional theory recognizes that concerns over efficiency and effectiveness are secondary to values carried by important actors such as a mayor or city council member. Crank and Langworthy (1991) discuss the ways in which various police practices reflect broader values and how the department acts on the values.

Particularistic Perspectives

Instead of emphasizing similarities among police, particularistic perspectives focus on decision-making differences among officers. Particularistic perspectives include typologies and other officer classification schemes, which are perspectives that identify different officer types or styles of policing.

Worden's (1989) research on police behavior suggests that officers, contrary to conventional wisdom, are not psychologically homogeneous—that is, they are not always intensely loyal to one another or preoccupied with order. Nor are they all suspicious, secretive, cynical, or authoritarian. The police socialization process does not necessarily result in officers having the same outlook.

Worden identified five ways in which police officers are different from one another. First is their view of human nature. Cynical police, for example, tend to be pessimistic, suspicious, and distrustful. The important issue here is the extent to which a person is cynical prior to employment, how that cynicism changes over time, and how it influences his or her behavior.

Second, officers have different role orientations. Some see themselves as crimefighters who deter crime by making arrests and issuing citations. Others believe that the police role involves not only fighting crime but also problem solving, crime prevention, and community service.

Third, officers have different attitudes toward legal and departmental restrictions. Some officers think that the ends justify the means in policing, often because they think that legal and policy guidelines are too restrictive, resulting in a criminal going free and thereby increasing crime and the suffering of victims. In addition, some officers believe that the criminal justice system is not punitive enough and it is up to them to guarantee punishment through "street justice."

Fourth, officers' clientele influences their beliefs and their behavior. Preferences of particular judges, for example, or pressure on patrol enforcement practices from Mothers Against Drunk Driving can influence patterns of police enforcement. The influence of particular groups can lead to selective enforcement of particular laws and alienate other groups with whom the police interact.

Fifth is the relationship between management and peer group support. Theoretically, police departments reward desired behavior and punish undesired behavior. Many observers, however, have noted that police departments are punishment oriented. They do not have many ways to reward good behavior, so they tend to control the behavior of line officers by setting up elaborate standard operating procedures and punishing officers for infractions. Consequently, officers often turn to their peer group members for aid—that is, to other officers of the same rank in the department. The peer group is very influential in policing. Officers depend on it for physical protection and emotional comfort. This dependency in turn can result in increased secrecy in the department.

Socialization Versus Predisposition

Policing is in the midst of broad change. The most visible changes are occurring under the umbrella of community policing, which emphasizes police discretion, problem solving, decentralization of authority, and community involvement. Departments are increasingly seeking personnel who have the attitudes, values, and skills for community policing.

Community policing concerns about hiring the "right" kind of officer have rekindled the debate about where officers' attitudes and values come from. If they come from the way officers adapt to their occupational environment, then commanders will have to change the department or the way it does its work. If they come from the background characteristics of officers, then administrators will have to change their hiring policies. These two ways of thinking about police officers' values and attitudes are called the socialization theory and the predispositional theory.

Socialization Theory. Beginning in the 1960s, as the body of knowledge about police behavior increased, social scientists suggested that police behavior was determined more by work experiences and peers than by preemployment values and attitudes. This was called the **socialization theory**—that is, individuals are socialized as a result of their occupational experiences. If a police officer becomes corrupt, it is because the police occupation contributes in some way to weaken values; in other words, corruption is learned within the department. This theory applies to any type of police behavior, good or bad.

Two socialization processes take place in police organizations. *Formal socialization* is the result of what transpires in the selection process, the training program, what is learned about policies and procedures, and what officers are told by supervisors and managers. *Informal socialization* takes place as new recruits interact with older, more experienced officers. One's peers play an important role in determining behavior, not only in the police occupation but also in other jobs. An understanding of informal socialization processes is important because what one learns on the job and from one's peers may contradict what is learned during the formal socialization process.

In many police departments the selection process attempts to eliminate individuals who may be prone to unnecessary violence or dishonest behavior. Therefore, police behavior—both good and bad—is seen as a consequence of behavior that is learned after employment. The police experience, and how individuals adjust to that experience, is the most important consideration in determining how "good" police behavior is to be achieved and how "bad" police behavior is to be avoided.

Van Maanen (1973) conducted participant-observation research within a small city police department in California, and he identified four stages of officer socialization, which are briefly described below.

Preentry Choice. Most individuals who choose a police career select it from among a variety of career choices. They tend to go into police work believing they are entering an elite occupation. Many already know someone or something about police work and already tend to identify with the goals and values of the police, at least as they understand them. Their motivation for entering police work is often related to doing something important in society.

Admittance: Introduction. The second stage is the police academy experience. All officers, after being hired, must take some form of academy training, where they learn the necessity of adhering to the rules and regulations of the department. The academy Van Maanen attended had a military atmosphere in which officers followed a rigid routine and were punished for deviating from it (e.g., being late). Officers spent much time studying the technical aspects of police work, and instructors elaborated on these aspects with police war stories. These stories provided important insights about the traditions and values of the department and what was considered "good" police work. Recruits learned that they must stick together and protect one another. Today, many academies are less stress oriented and more academically oriented, yet many of the lessons Van Maanen described are applicable today.

Change: Encounter. Once the police academy has been completed, new officers enter the third stage—going to work in the patrol division, each being assigned to a training officer.

Once they are in the field, they are taught what the work is really like. It is also during this phase that the new officers are "tested" by the older officers. Can they perform? Can they operate the equipment effectively? Do they have "common sense"? Are they willing to take risks? Officers are always tested about their willingness to "back up" other officers. Perhaps the most crucial "test" an officer must pass is related to his or her dependability in helping fellow officers when they are in trouble.

Continuance: Metamorphosis. In the final stage, new officers adjust to the reality of police work. In effect, this reality involves a large number of routine problems and bureaucratic tasks, with only an occasional exciting or adventurous activity. For some officers, however, the possibility of an exciting or adventurous "call" continues to be an important motivating factor. As they progress in police work, many officers learn that the public does not understand or support them. And they often decide that the police system—meaning managers and supervisors and how they enforce rules and regulations—is unfair. Perhaps the most common adjustment made by officers, at least in the city Van Maanen studied, was to "lie low and hang loose." That is, they did as little work as possible to avoid getting into trouble.

Predispositional Theory. In recent years there has been a renewal of interest in the predispositional theory, which suggests that the behavior of a police officer is primarily explained by the characteristics, values, and attitudes that the individual had before he or she was employed. If an officer is dishonest or honest, brutal or temperate in the use of force, he or she probably had those positive or negative traits before being hired. Predispositional theory focuses on the idea that the policing occupation attracts people with certain attitudes and beliefs; thus, socialization has less explanatory value.

The predispositional theory received early support from Rokeach, Miller, and Snyder (1971), who found that police held similar conservative political values. Individuals who wanted to become officers had a particular value focus: belief in the importance of authority together with a high emphasis on professional fulfillment.

Caldero and Larose (2003) extended Rokeach's research. Surprisingly, they found no differences between findings from 1971 and the views of respondents in their research in the early and mid-1990s. Their research consequently offers support for the predispositional theory and argues that "individual value systems are more important than occupational socialization" in understanding police behavior (Caldero and Larose 2003, 162). The central principles of these research efforts are as follows:

1. Police have distinctively different values from other groups in American society.
2. Police values are highly similar to the values of the groups they are recruited from.
3. Police values are also determined by particular characteristics of personality that set police officers apart from the groups from which they are recruited.
4. Police values are unaffected by occupational socialization.
5. The values carried by police officers are stable over time.
6. Regardless of racial or ethnic differences, police officers hold similar values.
7. Education has little impact on values held by police officers.
8. The police socialization process has little effect on the values of individual officers.

This research was discussed by Crank and Caldero (1999), who found that values consistent with police culture were already in place when police were hired. Moreover, after hiring, police values were little changed over an individual officer's career. Finally, screening processes ensured that police recruits held similar values, regardless of their ethnicity or gender. The perspectives developed by Crank and Caldero can be described as a "subcultural" theory of police attitudes and behavior, meaning that police values in general are not learned on the job, but are already learned when a recruit applies for police work. Police work selectively accents some of these values; for example, working-class values are reflected and intensified in the strong loyalties officers have for one another.

Classic Studies of Police Behavior

This section reviews important studies on police behavior. Many of these studies were written many years ago. Why then, you might wonder, if police work is changing so dramatically, are these old studies discussed here?

These studies are as important today as they were when they were written. In many ways, the fundamental issues facing the police, the problems they confront on their beats, and the people that they must work with have not changed a great deal. Indeed, one of the fundamental problems is that, despite truly staggering organizational changes that have occurred over the past half century, what officers do on the street has changed little. Assign an officer to walk a beat and he or she will view that work pretty much as officers did 100 years ago, spiced up only by technological gadgets. Keep in mind that it is not when the studies were written that is important; it is the currency of the ideas.

Violence and the Police

The first social science-oriented study of the police, *Violence and the Police* (1970), was conducted by Westley in Gary, Indiana, in 1949. Westley identified the importance of socialization as a significant factor in police behavior. He found that "old timers" indoctrinated recruits with the belief that if the recruits were to be good cops, they must take charge of situations in which they became involved. Being in charge of a situation meant that citizens, particularly those in the lower classes, had to show the officer respect. If a citizen failed to show respect or challenged an officer's authority, officers felt compelled to react. Officers believed that they could not back down when faced with challenges to their authority. To do so only encouraged citizens to challenge the police more often, thus making the police officer's job more difficult. Many of the officers in Gary stated that it would be appropriate to "punish" the citizen using some type of physical force.

Westley also found that the police in Gary believed that the public did not support them. They felt isolated from the public and did not believe that the public could be trusted. Consequently, many police officers were secretive about their daily routines. The police hated "stoolies"—police officers who took problems outside the department and "washed their dirty linen" in public. A concern for secrecy and protecting fellow officers was grounded in the fundamental belief that the public could not be trusted to fairly evaluate the appropriateness of police behavior. This research and analysis underscore the importance of in-group solidarity. **In-group solidarity**, or closeness and loyalty among officers, results from a perception that the public cannot be trusted. In-group solidarity and officer secrecy make it difficult to determine what police officers actually do. Solidarity is often accompanied by a code of silence in which officers will not discuss inappropriate police behavior or may lie about it to protect a brother officer, creating what has been called "the blue wall of silence."

Justice Without Trial

The important study *Justice Without Trial* (1966), by Skolnick, an analysis of two police departments, provided many important insights about the activities and behavior of police officers. One of these was related to the *production orientation* of a police department, meaning that police behavior was influenced by the goals or objectives that the department emphasized. For example, if a department was concerned about making arrests and issuing traffic citations, officers were likely to be aggressive in making arrests and issuing tickets.

Skolnick discussed the significance of danger in police work. He coined the phrase **symbolic assailant** to represent the person the police officer thinks is potentially dangerous or troublesome. Who is a dangerous person? Those "types" of people with whom the officer has had the most dangerous or troublesome experiences become, in effect, that officer's "symbolic assailant." From their experiences and from stories told by other officers, police develop a repertoire of **danger signifiers**, such as a person's actual behavior, language, dress, area, and, in some situations, age, sex, and ethnicity.

Such signifiers can be interpreted by the police as challenges to their authority. The person who is perceived to challenge their authority may be verbally or physically abused. Of course, such abuse confirms an officer's belief that a particular kind of person or a particular area is troublesome or potentially dangerous. Further, it convinces the person abused, and others who witness the abuse, that the police are repressive and brutal. Finally, the symbolic assailant has implications for the perception that racial minorities may be more dangerous or predisposed to trouble, which can contribute to our understanding of the modern phenomenon of racial profiling (Rice 2010).

Varieties of Police Behavior

Perhaps the most important study of police behavior conducted in the 1960s was Wilson's *Varieties of Police Behavior* (1968). Wilson studied eight police departments and reported that in many respects they were quite different. He discussed these differences in terms of three styles of policing. Since Wilson's study, there have been many other attempts to identify different styles of police behavior in terms of both departments and individuals. However, what makes Wilson's perspective unique is the fact that he was able to identify and create typologies of behaviors within different organizations. Thus, while individual street officers continued to enjoy a great deal of discretion, their discretionary decisions were influenced by the larger organizational culture of the police department. Organizational culture, in turn, was largely influenced by the political climate of the local city government.

Wilson found that there were two general categories of problems confronting police departments. *Law enforcement problems* were those behaviors considered serious enough to warrant a citation or arrest, such as serious traffic violations and most felonies and major misdemeanors. *Order maintenance problems* involved less serious violations of the law such as misdemeanors or problems that police usually handled without resorting to issuing citations or making arrests.

Wilson stated that differences in policing styles were found primarily in how order maintenance problems were handled. He identified three different organizational styles: watchman, service, and legalistic. To illustrate, assume that police discover a group of teenagers drinking beer in a public park, a problem in maintaining order.

In the **watchman style**, police officers are given a great deal of latitude as to how they handle such problems. Often there are no policies or procedures to guide them. Consequently, each officer is free to devise his or her own response or solution. The officers might take the beer and tell the teenagers to go home. They might even provide a lecture about excessive drinking, or they might do nothing at all. And if different officers observed the same problem, there would probably be several different responses to that problem.

In the **service style**, police see themselves as providing a product that the community wants. Such departments tend to be found in homogeneous communities with a common idea of public order. They train officers in what to do and how to do it. The police intervene frequently, but many do so informally, and an arrest is not an inevitable outcome. The officers might refer the beer-drinking teenagers to a department program involving teenage drinking or to a community program. Or they might call the parents to come and get their son or daughter. Of course, police in the service style do not do this with all order maintenance problems, but for those problems the community or the department considers important.

In the **legalistic style**, police try to enforce the law—write a citation or make an arrest—if possible. Police view themselves as law enforcers. They would probably arrest the teenage beer drinkers. Of course, police in the legalistic style do not always make arrests, but they tend to make more arrests and issue more citations than do police using the other two styles.

Later empirical replications of his theory have supported much of Wilson's observations (Langworthy 1985), although recent research questions whether a link exists between political culture and organizational behavior (Hassell, Zhao, and Maguire 2003; Liederbach and Travis 2008; Zhao and Hassell 2005).

City Police

Another important study of police behavior was conducted by Rubinstein (1973). Rubinstein, who worked as a patrol officer in Philadelphia, provided numerous important insights into police activity and behavior. His findings support Skolnick's contributions regarding the importance of the perception of danger in police behavior. Rubinstein suggested that a patrol officer's most important concern was physical control of those individuals with whom he or she interacted. Of course, officers do not perceive all persons as requiring physical control, but in general they tend to watch a suspect's hands, are always alert to the possibility of weapons, and may even stand close to suspects to limit their ability to lash out with a swing or a kick.

Whereas Wilson highlighted the importance of understanding organizational culture, Rubinstein's research emphasized the importance of an officer's working environment as a critical factor in police behavior. Officers learn on the job from other officers about what is important and what is not, the types of situations and people that are potentially dangerous, and how to respond to them. The police department can substantially influence how the officer responds, but much is left to the individual officer. Rubinstein's experience provides support for the socialization theory of police behavior.

Working the Street: Police Discretion

Brown's *Working the Street: Police Discretion* (1981) was a study of policing styles conducted in three southern California cities. Individual officer styles, Brown suggested, depended on a combination of their aggressiveness and selectivity of crime problems. Aggressiveness was the degree to which they actively seek out problems. Selectivity was the extent to which they were concerned only about serious crime problems.

Using these two variables, Brown identified four styles of police behavior: Old-style crime fighters are very aggressive and tend to be selective, concentrating primarily on felonies. These officers develop extensive knowledge of the area in which they work, use informants, and tend to be coercive. They are sometimes willing to act illegally to get "results." Clean-beat crime fighters believe in the importance of legal procedures. These officers are proactive and legalistic but do not tend to be selective. Almost all violations of the law are considered significant. Service-style officers do the minimum amount of work necessary to get by; that is, they are not aggressive but are selective. Only the most serious problems will result in their enforcing the law. Such officers tend to rely on informal solutions to problems rather than legalistic ones. Professional-style officers engage in limited self-initiated activity and are not selective. They are situationally oriented, although "tough" when necessary, and at other times they may be service minded. It should be apparent that the observations by Wilson, Rubinstein, and Brown contributed to distinct understandings of officer behavior. Each offered different levels of analysis when considering discretion (i.e., organizational factors, situational factors, and individual officer factors). Each perspective is incomplete because they forsake the other correlates of behavior. Thus a more complete model for understanding police behavior can be found by including each of these levels of analysis when attempting to understand street-level discretionary behavior.

Crank's *Understanding Police Culture* (1998) is included here because it integrates a great deal of writing about police work and shows present-day trends in thinking about the police. It is an effort to develop a "middle-range theory" about the police and to show how this theory can provide new insights into police work. Middle-range theory attempts to integrate findings from a broad body of research into a more general perspective.

Crank suggests that police culture emerges from the daily practice of police work. Culture, he argues, does not make the police different from the public. Rather, it humanizes the police by giving their work meaning. Rejecting the notion that police culture is a "dark force," he argues that culture is carried in police common sense, in the way in which everyday activities are celebrated, and in the way police deal with death and suffering. Consequently, to understand police culture, one must examine the physical setting in which police work occurs and the groups with which police interact, such as wrongdoers, the public, the courts, the press, and the department's administration. Because these groups tend to be similar everywhere, police culture tends to take on similar characteristics in different departments, and one can speak of a police culture generally.

Elements of police culture are organized around four central principles. The first and most central principle is *coercive territorial control*. The police are trained formally and socialized informally to view their work in terms of the use of force to control specific territories to which they are assigned. Police learn about the use of force, both in terms of a use-of-force continuum (see Chapter 10) and in terms of informal tactics that enable them to control the public in police-citizen encounters. The use of force is more than a set of skills, however. Force is acted out as a moral commitment to control their assigned territories. Herbert (1997) echoed the importance of territoriality. In his observations of Los Angeles officers, he found that the ability of the police to control behavior in an assigned geographic area was a central factor that influenced officer behavior.

The second principle is *the unknown*. Police activity routinely puts officers in circumstances that are unpredictable and may have outcomes beyond their control. Such unpredictability makes police work interesting. The common unpredictability of every-day encounters may mask significant danger. Police officers have a wide repertoire of skills to ensure that unknown situations do not deteriorate into dangerous life-threatening encounters.

The third principle is *solidarity,* or the intense bonding and sense of occupational unique-ness that officers feel for one another. It is produced by the dangers and unpredictability of their work and from the intense individualism that is part of the police ethos. Central to sol-idarity is conflict with other groups: police officers often feel alienated from the courts and the public and from outsiders and different ethnic groups. The greater the conflict with out-side groups, the greater the degree to which the police feel united in a sense of solidarity.

The fourth principle is *loose coupling*—the idea that police develop strategies and tactics to protect themselves when department goals and policies are perceived to undermine their ability to do their work. At the core of the police morality is the idea that they have to do something about "bad guys." Efforts by administrators to control police behavior, as well as by the courts to hold them accountable for due process, are often met with distrust by line officers when such efforts interfere with their sense of occupationally driven morality. Lying in court, keeping information from administrators, and circumventing due process are all ways in which some police officers carry out their work despite administrative rules limit-ing what they are permitted to do.

However, it is unclear whether a single police culture actually exists. Cochran and Bromley (2003) and Paoline (2003, 2004) argued that the reality of a single set of occupational atti-tudes, values, and norms for behavior might be overstated. Paoline identified several arenas where there may be variation in culture within the policing occupation, including variation between organizations, and officer styles. He also noted that there exists cultural variation between ranks within an organization. Specifically, upper management, middle manage-ment, and line officers may all adhere to different norms, attitudes, and values that shape their behavior. His assertions are supported by research that has identified different values between management and street officers (Reuss-Ianni 1983), as well as different supervisory styles among middle managers (Engel 2001). Finally, a "single police culture" might be less prevalent in the future as police departments continue to diversify. With the inclusion of more college-educated officers (see Chapter 14), more racial/ethnic minorities, and more women (see Chapter 12), considering police culture a monolithic entity may become less useful when describing police behavior.

Decision Making and Police Discretion

Police officers make decisions that affect the public in important ways. Yet scholarly knowl-edge about the way police make decisions is limited. When scholars talk about decision making, they generally mean decisions involving citizens and questionable behavior. When police see something that is "out of kilter," two important decisions must be made: (1) whether to intervene in a situation (this is not a choice if the officer is sent by the depart-ment) and (2) how to intervene (Wilson 1968). What kinds of decisions are available for an officer who makes a routine traffic stop? Bayley and Bittner (1989, 98) note that officers have 10 actions to select from at the initial stop (for example, order the driver out of the car), 7 strategies appropriate during the stop (for example, give a roadside sobriety test), and 11 exit strategies (for example, release the driver with a warning). From start to finish, this represents a total of 770 different combinations!

Decision making is different from the use of discretion. The circumstances above repre-sent decision making regarding when and how to intervene in situations. **Discretion** is more narrowly defined. The most commonly used definition is the decision not to invoke legal sanctions when circumstances are favorable for them (Goldstein 1998). Davis (1969, 4) described discretion as "whenever the effective limits on his power leave him free to make a choice among courses of action or inaction." In encounters with suspects, for example, police may be presented with a situation in which they have the legal basis for an arrest. They do not, however, always make an arrest. The decision not to make an arrest when it is legally justifiable is sometimes called non-enforcement discretion.

Discretionary decisions not to arrest occur often in police work. An officer may witness a person drinking beer in a park, which is a violation of local codes. This situation might be handled with a warning rather than a citation or an arrest. Why did the officer not make an arrest? The officer might feel sympathy for the suspect. Or the officer might be waiting to see how the suspect reacts, prepared to arrest him if the suspect resists or gets "smart-mouthed." The officer might view this situation as a problem that can be easily handled without going to the trouble of arresting the suspect. The officer might be about to go off duty and not want to spend time doing paperwork at the end of the shift. Or arrest might be inconsistent with either an officer's "style" (i.e., she or he simply does not arrest beer drinkers in parks) or the style of the police organization (i.e., officers in a watchman-style organization would be more apt to use non-application of the law). Many factors affect officers' decisions about whether they should intervene, what they should do after intervening, and whether they should make an arrest, even when legal circumstances are favorable.

There has been a considerable amount of research concerning variables that influence police decision making and discretion. Sherman (1985), Brooks (1989), Riksheim and Chermak (1993) and Skogan and Frydl (2004) have summarized research in this area. Their observations are grouped into four categories of variables: organizational, neighborhood (or community), situational, and officer (or individual). Figure 9.1 provides a visual depiction of how these factors simultaneously impact the discretion and decision making of street-level police officers.

Organizational Variables

There are several organizational (departmental) variables.

Bureaucratic Nature.   The bureaucratic nature of a police department is an important factor affecting police behavior, as discussed in Chapter 5. It should be emphasized that the purpose of bureaucratic procedure is to guide and direct police behavior (Alpert and Smith 1998; Auten 1988). And, as Wasserman (1992) observes, without written policy, departments relinquish policy decisions to the idiosyncratic judgments of street officers. Nevertheless, various researchers have questioned the effectiveness of the bureaucratic "control principle" (Alpert and Smith 1998). Cordner (1989) challenged the notion that written policy always contributes to the quality of police service. The discretionary demands of street activity may undermine bureaucratic efforts to control behavior (Adams 1990). Bureaucratic controls can backfire, contributing to police secrecy and undermining bureaucratic control. For these reasons, the effectiveness of bureaucracy as a way to stimulate some behaviors and dampen others is certainly limited. Highly bureaucratic departments also tend to be impersonal and may overemphasize punitive discipline in an attempt to control officers' behavior. This tendency may result in officers doing as little as possible in an effort to avoid getting into trouble.

Work Periods, Areas, and Assignments.   Another important organizational variable is the frequency with which officers change work periods (or shift or tour) and the

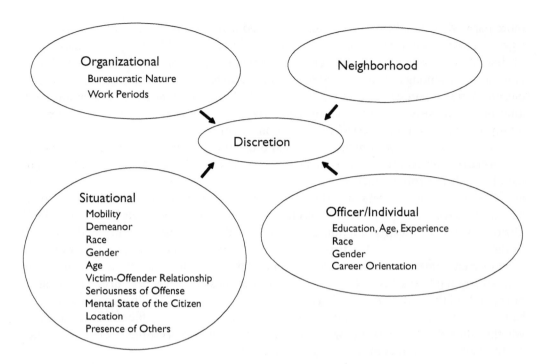

FIGURE 9.1 **Factors That Impact Police Discretion.**

areas (beat or district or sector) in which they work. The more frequent these types of changes, the more distant the relationship between citizen and officer. There may be less communication and less understanding about community problems. Also important is the size of the area in which the officer works; the smaller the area, the more likely that a service rather than an enforcement orientation will prevail (Mastrofski 1981). A small area with a high quantity of serious crime, however, is more likely to have a law enforcement style (Brooks 1989, 126–130).

There is also some indication that discretionary choices differ based on the assignment of the officer within the organization. Novak et al. (2002) compared the decision making of officers assigned to community policing tasks with that of officers assigned to traditional "911" duties. They found that while these officers used similar factors in their decision making, several important differences were observed. They found that community policing officers were more likely to use victim preference when making an arrest decision than their more traditional counterparts, indicating that community policing officers may be more responsive to citizens' demands. They also found that community policing officers were less likely to arrest hostile citizens and that traditional officers were much more likely to arrest intoxicated citizens. This appears to indicate officers assigned to community policing tasks may be more tolerant of non-conforming behavior than their counterparts.

Neighborhood Variables
To what extent do the characteristics of neighborhoods affect police performance? Clearly the kind of beats police patrol affect the work they do. As early as 1968, Wilson noted that in watchman-style departments, officers adapted their work to the kinds of problems that characterized their beats. This practice resulted in uneven delivery of service. Wilson and

Kelling (1982) extended this idea to argue that police should tailor their work to the kinds of problems they encounter, a theme expanded upon by Skolnick and Bayley (1986).

Characteristics of neighborhoods may also affect police behavior. One of the most interesting characteristics is racial composition. Research tends to support the view that the police write more reports, make more arrests, engage in more abusive behavior, and receive more citizen requests for police intervention in minority areas. As a result of this increased activity, police get to know the people in these areas better than in other areas. In addition, police tend to view minority areas as places where violent crimes are more likely to occur and where they are more likely to have their authority challenged. As a result, police are more suspicious and alert and more concerned for their own safety. Data consistently show that police arrest more individuals in minority areas than in other areas, although arrest rates are highly correlated with criminal activity (Sampson and Lauritsen 1997).

Another aspect of neighborhoods is their racial and ethnic heterogeneity. The greater the racial and ethnic diversity, the more likely the police will become involved in encounters with citizens whom they think are troublesome. Police tend to exercise a great deal of discretion in these areas, may tend to feel more insecure, are often more aggressive, and tend to make more arrests. They are much more likely to arrest and threaten use of force in racially mixed neighborhoods (Smith 1986).

Klinger (1997) outlines a theory to conceptualize the impact that neighborhood context has on officer behavior. He argues that officer decisions fall along a continuum of vigor (more formal actions or application of the law, like arrests) or leniency (less formal response) and that these responses vary by neighborhood. Officers who work together in particular patrol divisions develop in-group norms for behavior. Generally, officers react with greater vigor when the offense seriousness increases, however, this varies across space depending upon how much crime and deviance occurs within the area. In areas with lower levels of crime and lower levels of deviance, officers will respond with greater vigor for relatively less serious offenses. On the other hand, areas characterized by higher rates of crime and deviance will be met with officer leniency. This is because, among other reasons, crime and deviance are "normal" and to be anticipated in high crime areas; thus, any particular offense will have to be more serious to elicit a vigorous reaction by officers. Klinger (1997) argues that the workload norms developed by officers within patrol divisions may offer more explanation for officer behavior than community characteristics and expectations because communities exist within larger patrol divisions. Officers within patrol divisions create unique norms and expectations for each other.

Officers exercise higher levels of force during encounters with suspects in disadvantaged neighborhoods. Terrill and Reisig (2003) found that officers use higher levels of force in high-crime neighborhoods and neighborhoods with higher poverty rates, high unemployment, high rates of female-headed families, and high proportions of African Americans. At the same time they found that racial minorities experienced higher levels of force than whites. However, their analysis clearly revealed that neighborhood context was far more important than suspect race at explaining use of force by officers. They concluded that "race is confounded by neighborhood context: Minority suspects are more likely to be recipients of higher levels of police force because they are disproportionately encountered in disadvantaged and high-crime neighborhoods" (Terrill and Reisig 2003, 306).

Situational Variables

Many elements in a situation affect police behavior.

Mobilization. The manner in which the police are mobilized, or enter into a situation, is important in determining their conduct. In proactive, or police-initiated, encounters, officers are more likely to face antagonism from citizens. Proactive police behavior is more intrusive and less likely to be supported by victims and bystanders. As a result of the increased likelihood of a negative citizen response, police are more likely to make arrests and treat citizens harshly (Sherman 1985, 187). Consequently, proactive encounters are more likely to result in police–citizen antagonisms and conflict.

Demeanor and Attitude. The characteristics of both suspects and complainants are important variables in the discretion of police officers. Disrespectful, resistant, or uncooperative suspects are more likely to receive a more punitive officer response than those who are respectful, compliant, and cooperative. Disrespect toward an officer is a form of deviance itself that mobilizes officers to act more harshly, and officers' actions are compelled by the resistant citizens because this is viewed as a threat to the officer's legitimacy (Engel 2003) or their competency (Herbert 1997). However, Klinger (1994) contends that legal factors, specifically the criminal conduct of suspects after coming into contact with police, outweigh demeanor considerations.

The attitude of the complainant is another widely cited factor influencing police decisions to arrest, according to the research of Black (1980), Smith (1987), Worden (1989), Engel, Sobol, and Worden (2000), and others. Black, for example, observed that arrests were more likely to occur in both felony and misdemeanor situations when the complainant wanted the suspect to be arrested. But officers are less likely to do what the complainant wants if the complainant shows disrespect.

The demeanor of suspects and attitude of complainants may interact with individual officer styles. For example, a widely cited "test" that many police officers apply to suspects is called the attitude, or personality, test. Many officers believe that they cannot allow a citizen to challenge an officer's authority (Herbert 1997). The challenge can include a question about being stopped, too many questions in general, criticism of the officer, or failing to comply promptly to a police request for information. Of course, any physical resistance would also be included. Research suggests that citizens who flunk such tests are more likely to be verbally and physically abused or given a traffic citation or arrested (Van Maanen 1978). For example, a study by Lersch and Feagin (1996) that analyzed 130 newspaper reports of police brutality found that a citizen was equally likely to be assaulted for a "disrespectful" attitude toward the officer as for posing a serious bodily threat to the officer or another person; they also found that minority group citizens were involved in the vast majority of the incidents.

Race. Research on the importance of race in police behavior is mixed. A large body of research supports the contention that African Americans are treated more harshly than whites or are more likely to be arrested (Kappeler, Sluder, and Alpert 1994; Chambliss 1997; Maurer 1993). Some researchers contend that this situation is the result of the fact that African Americans, and possibly other minorities, may be more likely to resist police authority or display a "bad" attitude or outright hostility, from an officer's point of view. Others respond that hostility to the police derives from a history of police mistreatment.

Recently the issue of racial profiling has captured the attention of citizens and police administrators. **Racial profiling** refers to proactive police actions that rely on race or ethnicity rather than behavior that leads the police to identify a particular person as being, or having been, engaged in criminal activity (Ramirez, McDevitt, and Farrell 2000). The key component of this concept is that the encounter is police initiated and not part of some other source of information (such as a wanted person who fits the citizen's description). The second component is that police use race, rather than behavior, to initiate the encounter. Racial profiling might occur in the context of traffic stops, but can also be involved in other arenas (such as pedestrian checks).

There exists a belief among citizens that profiling is common among police agencies (Reitzel and Piquero 2006). The Gallup Organization conducted a survey of Americans that indicated that 59 percent felt racial profiling was widespread; among blacks, 77 percent felt it was widespread (Gallup Organization 1999). Further, 42 percent of blacks indicated that they have been stopped by the police because of their race or ethnicity. This corresponds with lower ratings of citizen satisfaction with police services among racial and ethnic minorities. In fact, in a survey by the BJS, fewer blacks and Hispanics reported that police used "legitimate" reasons for stopping them than whites (Durose and Langan 2007). At the same time there have been numerous examinations of police departments conducted

John R. Brown
Lt. Col., Pennsylvania State Police

Questions: Why is it important for police organizations to examine whether racial profiling exists? What should police departments be doing to respond to racially biased policing?

Answer: Racial profiling is an issue that is important to minority communities. Minority communities' trust in their organization will be negatively impacted if those citizens believe that their police department engages in racial profiling. It is important for leaders to examine the issue within their agency as a proactive initiative to prevent biased-based policing. Enforcement of the law should be based on the suspect's behavior and not race or ethnicity. Police departments that conduct studies and develop training and processes to prevent racial profiling enhance community trust within the diverse communities they service. Lack of community trust creates officer and citizen safety issues and hinders a department's ability to recruit diverse applicants for employment with the force. Lastly, it is important for law enforcement leaders to inform their diverse populations that the issue has been studied and proactive steps through training and accountability measures have been taken to ensure their policing is not influenced by bias. Building transparency into the process will enhance community trust and increase the agency's overall effectiveness in services, enforcement, and recruiting.

Police departments should create a Special Order or memo supporting a Zero-Tolerance Policy for biased-based policing. Once the policy is in place have all police personnel trained in cultural awareness/sensitivity and reinforce that enforcement has to be based on behavior not race or ethnicity. Departments should also begin to collect data and develop benchmarks that might identify a cause for review or concern. Reviews protect the department, the officer (s) or identify unacceptable behavior. If unacceptable behavior is identified ensure the appropriate level of accountability of administrative action is completed.

Lt. Col. Brown was appointed Deputy Commissioner of the Pennsylvania State Police (PSP) in 2004, where he commands the Administration and Professional Responsibility segments of the department.

across the nation to determine whether there is racial bias in police traffic enforcement patterns. These inquiries have often been conducted voluntarily by police departments, but they have also been conducted pursuant to lawsuits and mandated by state law (Tillyer, Engel, and Cherkauskas 2009).

Examinations into racial profiling tend to concentrate on whether racial/ethnic minorities are stopped more frequently than whites or whether post-stop outcomes differ across racial groups (e.g., arrests, citations, searches; Fridell 2004; Tillyer et al. 2009; Barnum and Perfetti 2010; Rice and White 2010). Results are far from consistent. And what remains largely unknown is exactly *why* racial and ethnic minority contacts with police vary in quantity and quality. One possible explanation is bigoted/racist police officers, which is consistent with the "rotten apple" theory discussed later in this chapter. Another rationale may be differential traffic offending by racial minorities, although upon closer inspection, this reason does not seem to hold up to empirical scrutiny. Perhaps it is cognitive stereotyping, in which officers believe minorities are more likely to possess guns and drugs than whites. It might also be differential officer deployment in predominantly minority communities in accordance with higher rates of crime and calls for police service (Withrow 2006). Thus it would logically follow that there will be disparity in police-minority contacts when examining city-wide traffic enforcement patterns. Further research is necessary to determine how widespread these disparities are and what causes them. Given the importance of identification of racial profiling in America, Voices From the Field discusses what police departments should be doing in response to bias in traffic enforcement.

Gender. The effects of gender on police behavior regarding arrests are relatively understudied. The masculine predispositions of police departments are widely cited (Martin 1980, 1990). Visher (1983) found that females were less likely to be arrested than males who engage in similar behavior, especially when females act in an appropriate, "ladylike" fashion. However, the opposite could be true as well. When females act outside of their gender role, they may be more likely to be sanctioned by the police because they are deemed more deserving of arrest. Further, the extent to which these predispositions affect police–citizen encounters is unclear. Kraska and Kappeler (1995) suggest that sexual violence by the police may be more widespread than previously thought. Opportunity, power, authority, and isolation increase the likelihood of sexual harassment of citizens (Sapp 1994). Attractive women are also more likely to be stopped by police officers for traffic violations, and the intent is not to issue a traffic citation but to make personal contact (see Kappeler, Sluder, and Alpert 1994).

Age. The age of the citizen encountering the police can influence police–citizen encounters in several ways, particularly when the citizen is a juvenile (or under 18 years old). Black (1976) stated that juveniles are less "respectable" than older people in that they hold a lower social standing in American society. Hence they pose a greater threat to officers and therefore are more likely to receive formal application of law, such as arrest (Brown 2005; Brown et al. 2009; Novak et al. 2002; Visher 1983). Brown et al. (2009) also reported environment influences officers' arrest decisions—all else being equal, juveniles encountered in economically and socially disadvantaged neighborhoods were significantly more likely to be arrested compared with adults encountered in these same locations. If indeed officers treat juveniles more harshly than adults, this observation may explain why juveniles often hold less favorable attitudes toward police than adults (Hurst and Frank 2000). However, the movement toward community policing may impact how officers interact with juveniles.

As Mastrofski, Worden, and Snipes (1995) noted, officers who expressed negative attitudes toward community policing were more likely to arrest juvenile offenders than their pro–community policing counterparts. Other researchers found that community policing officers may be more disposed to informal sanctioning when encountering juveniles, and the role of the community police officer may be as mentor and role model rather than law enforcer (Cordner 1995). In short, juveniles may hold a unique position in police–citizen encounters, and the true influence of suspect age may be unknown.

Suspect–Complainant Relationship. Another interesting situational variable is the relationship between the suspect and complainant. In general, if the relationship is close, the police may be reluctant to take official action (i.e., make an arrest) because they believe that it would be difficult to gain testimony from the victim in the courts. But the relationship has been, and remains, influential in the manner in which some police departments respond to calls about domestic violence or a family fight. In addition, when the relationship between the complainant and the suspect is close, the complainant may not wish the police to take official action. The preference of the complainant has a substantial influence on the officer's decisions. Although officers do not always do what complainants want, they are more likely to take official action, such as writing a report, if the complainant requests such action.

Seriousness of Offense. The type of offense also has an impact on police discretion—the more serious the crime, the greater the possibility of a formal response (Skogan and Frydl 2004). Violent crimes are more likely to result in an arrest for a simple reason—the victim is a witness to the crime. Consequently, about 50 percent of all violent crimes result in an arrest; only about 20 percent of property crimes do so. Police are more likely to arrest in felony encounters than in misdemeanor situations. This may seem like common sense, but in fact it is not (Friedrich 1980). As Black (1980) noted, the legal decision to arrest is based on probable cause, not the seriousness of the act. Because the legal standard of proof is probable cause, officers tend to make arrests during situations where there is greater and more probative evidence, regardless of the type of crime. Evidence sufficiency is often more likely to be present for serious offenses.

Mental State of the Citizen. Recently greater attention has been focused on the treatment of mentally disordered suspects by the police. Some have indicated that suspects who demonstrate symptoms of mental deficiency are treated more harshly by police, while observing a disproportionately higher number of mentally disordered people coming into contact with the criminal justice system. Teplin (1984) found the arrest rates for mentally disordered citizens to be 46.7 percent, compared with 27.9 percent for those not displaying such deficiencies, suggesting arrest was used with this special population to resolve conflict, rather than other discretionary choices available to officers. However, research conducted by Engel and Silver (2001) did not find support for this "criminalization hypothesis." They reported that factors such as seriousness of offense, seriousness of a weapon, and victim–offender relationship offered greater explanatory value than mental capacity of the citizen. In fact, they indicated that citizens with mental deficiencies were significantly less likely to be arrested than others—the opposite of what Teplin found. Novak and Engel (2005) conducted a similar inquiry using a different set of data, and they too found that officers were significantly less likely to arrest citizens who were believed to be mentally disordered. This was observed despite the fact that mentally disordered suspects were significantly more likely to be hostile and disrespectful during interactions with police. Recall earlier it was discussed that hostile demeanor typically increases the likelihood of arrest, but Novak and Engel (2005) reported that hostility and disrespect exercised by mentally disordered persons did not produce similar dispositions. They interpreted this by indicating that officers recognized that persons with mental disorders were likely less in control of their actions and less likely to appreciate the possible consequences of their hostility, leading officers to conclude arrest was an inappropriate outcome for this population. This appears to indicate that the relationship between mental deficiencies and police behavior deserves greater examination.

Location.   Police are also influenced by the location—public or private—of the call. Police are more likely to respond harshly in public settings than in private settings. This difference is the result of several factors: the type of crime (usually perceived as more serious crimes), the need to appear in control of the situation in public, the ambiguous role of the police in situations that occur in private places, and the fact that there are more police-initiated, or proactive, calls in public. As noted above, proactive police interventions with citizens are more likely to result in arrests and citizen resistance than are reactive police responses. Proactive interventions are usually the result of the police witnessing illegal behavior, usually at the misdemeanor level. Thus, as Black (1973) observed, police tend to be more proactive when a crime is not legally serious.

Presence of Others.   The presence of other police officers and bystanders has a slight influence on what police officers do (Parks 1982). If an officer thinks other police officers expect him or her to be harsh or punitive, or to write a report, or to make an arrest, then the officer is inclined to do so. Behaving in a manner that other officers believe to be appropriate is an important part of being accepted into the police subculture. Crank and Caldero (1999) suggest that officers who "wolf-pack" stops, that is, congregate in high numbers during routine stops, are more likely to create a variety of problems for managers. These problems include due process violations, violence, and increased levels of line-level secrecy.

Officers who work alone also tend to behave differently from officers who work in pairs. There is some support for the belief that officers working by themselves are more likely to make arrests because they are more concerned about taking control of a situation when working alone. Although two-person units may be less likely to make arrests, they are more likely to treat suspects harshly, possibly because each officer is concerned about what his or her partner will think, particularly if a suspect challenges police authority (e.g., asks questions, talks back, fails to follow police direction, or fights; Brooks 1989, 134–137; Sherman 1985, 189–192).

Discretionary decisions are difficult to bring under departmental control. The ability of the police to use discretion enables them to adapt their responsibilities to the characteristics of public-order problems on their beat (Sykes 1986) and efforts to control discretion have sometimes backfired, creating line-level resistance and secrecy (Crank 1998). Perhaps the best to be hoped for is stated by Guyot (1991, 96): "The challenge for departmental leadership is to reduce the vindictive decisions and increase the wise ones."

Individual (Officer) Variables
Many individual factors influence police behavior.

Education, Age, and Experience. Education is discussed at length in Chapter 14. It is difficult to separate age and experience because most individuals entering police work are young—typically in their twenties—and grow older as they are gaining experience. In general, younger officers may work harder and are more aggressive and more punitive than older officers. However, the quality of the older officers' work may be superior. While some older, more seasoned officers may do less work and become less punitive, others may actually become more punitive if they become excessively cynical.

Race. The race of the officer is also important to consider. The bulk of the research on race has been about African American officers. Some evidence indicates that they are more respected by the African American community, but they may also be stricter in dealing with African American citizens. When compared with white officers, African American officers tend to be more aggressive and to make more arrests in African American neighborhoods (Brooks 1989, 138–140). This, however, may be in part because of differential assignment of non-white officers to African American communities. Overall, the race of the officer has less explanatory power than many might assume, because when individuals don a police uniform they tend to become "blue" versus black or white, thus supporting the socialization process. However, the true impact of officer race on decision-making may be more complex than previously characterized, and recent research demonstrates that black and white officers may behave differently depending on (1) the type of behavior being considered, (2) characteristics of the environment, and (3) characteristics of whoever the officer is interacting with. For example, Sun and Payne (2004) examined racial differences in how officers engaged in coercive actions or supportive actions. They found black officers were more likely than their white counterparts to be coercive during encounters with the public. At the same time they also found black officers offered more support to citizens, but only in predominantly black communities. They further found the race of the citizen was unrelated to the exercise of coercion among black officers and that environmental factors had no impact on the level of coercion used by officers. Meanwhile, Brown and Frank (2006) also examined racial differences in the decision to arrest suspects. They reported that white officers were significantly more likely to arrest citizens in general than black officers. But interesting interactions were reported depending on the race of the officer and the race of the citizen. It appears that officers were more likely to arrest citizens when the encounter was intraracial (e.g., black officer–black citizen; white officer–white citizen). In fact, they reported the probability that a black officer would arrest a black citizen was 98 percent. If nothing else, a review of these two studies indicates that racial differences in officer behavior are complex and may vary across behavior, contexts, and racial characteristics of participants.

Gender. The gender of the officer is also presumed to be influential in the exercise of police discretion. There is some evidence to suggest that women are less aggressive. Early studies that support this observation, however, were conducted in the first decade of women's involvement in patrol work (see Martin 1989, 312–330, for a summary of these studies). Other recent research by Paoline and Terrill (2004) failed to find significant behavioral differences between males and females. Based on observations of police officers in two cities, they found that male and female officers exercise coercion in very similar ways. The only exception to this assertion is that male officers were significantly more likely to use coercion during encounters with male citizens. They hypothesize this lone difference as being a function of male officers viewing male suspects as more threatening than female suspects and thus employing more coercive strategies during these interactions. Further, they found that male and female officers apply verbal and physical coercion at parity. These results appear to indicate that there are few measurable differences between male and female officers in how or whether they use coercion. If women as a group tend to be less aggressive or use force less often than men, this finding may be either desirable or undesirable, depending on one's preference in policing styles. For the most part, however, the less aggressive (i.e., less forceful and abusive) the police, the more likely they are to have a positive relationship with the community.

Research examining the influence of officer gender in decision making is conflicting. DeJong (2004) reports that female officers are less likely to provide comfort to citizens during encounters. Rabe-Hemp (2008) and Schuck and Rabe-Hemp (2005) reported that females used fewer extreme controlling behaviors, while women were less likely to use supporting behaviors than male officers. While it may be intuitive to believe that female officers engage in different behaviors than male officers, Skogan and Frydl conclude that the body of research is "too small and the findings too variable to draw firm conclusions about the effects of officer sex on police practice" (2004, 151).

Career Orientation

There is also some indication that an officer's orientation toward community policing can influence behavior. Mastrofski, Worden, and Snipes (1995) examined officers' decisions to arrest citizens in Richmond, Virginia. They found that officers with more favorable attitudes toward community policing were more "selective" in making arrests compared with those officers with less favorable attitudes. They reported that arrest decisions for officers with less favorable views toward community policing were more strongly influenced by offense seriousness and evidence sufficiency compared with those with more positive views toward community policing. They argued that officers who support community policing tend to make different discretionary choices than traditional officers but were unable to thoroughly describe the arrest patterns for officers with positive views of community policing.

The degree to which all these variables influence individual officers varies, but in general the decisions officers make to stop someone, to behave in a certain way when interacting with citizens, and to select a way to solve a problem are determined by numerous factors besides the legality of a citizen's behavior. Yet, despite a great deal of research, scholars know little about the relative importance of extralegal factors. All that can be said for certain is that, in some circumstances, the police will make arrests based in part on factors other than whether the law is broken. Yet even the law is highly interpretive, and officers have wide discretion in the application of punishments for misdemeanors. The contribution of extralegal factors consequently continues to be a topic in need of thoughtful research.

Police Deviance

Unfortunately, not all police behavior is legal or proper. Sometimes police officers engage in acts that are inappropriate, and occasionally they do things that are illegal. Many people believe that police officers should be held to a higher standard than ordinary citizens. They hold the police as symbols of the moral fabric of society and their behavior as a standard for the public to emulate. Consequently, the police must display the image as well as the substance of propriety. They not only must be above reproach, but also must appear to be above reproach in both their professional and their personal lives.

Police deviance is behavior that does not conform to the standards or expectations. How are such standards determined? There are three major categories: ethical, organizational, and legal. Ethical standards are principles of appropriate conduct officers carry internally.

Ethical behavior is an expression of personal values. Organizational (departmental) standards can be both formal and informal; they are derived from policy, procedures, rules, and regulations of the department (formal) and from the expectations of one's peers (informal). Legal standards are represented by the laws officers are sworn to uphold and by due process, which establishes the means officers may use to achieve good ends.

Clearly, many of these standards carry the potential for conflict with others. Formal departmental policies may clash with informal cultural norms. The expectations surrounding the enforcement of the law may conflict with the principles of due process. And a police officer's personal values may be different from the ethical principles established by the department. In short, the standards expected of a police officer are extraordinarily complicated, and deviance, in one form or another, is almost impossible to avoid.

It is difficult to determine how frequently police engage in deviant behavior because officers are not always forthcoming about their own inappropriate behavior, partly because of the blue code of silence and partly because it is not always easy to distinguish between inappropriate and appropriate behavior. Given the many conflicting expectations facing police, it is likely that deviance is widespread; however, this is challenging to quantify empirically. Few police officers work even one shift without engaging in some form of behavior that is deviant by one standard or another. In fact, many police departments have so many rules and regulations that it is difficult not to violate some of them.

Types of Deviance and Misconduct

Identifying a commonly embraced definition of police deviance and misconduct is challenging; however, Kane and White (2009) provide a variety of different possible dimensions. Their categorization of misconduct comes from examining 21 years of information on officers in the NYPD who were involuntarily separated from the department. They recognize that officers may be disciplined for actions that occur while on duty as well as off duty. Unlike many occupations, police officers may be held accountable for behavior committed while off duty. An individual's occupational status of "police officer" can make a relatively ordinary crime (like drunk driving or intimate partner violence) suddenly newsworthy and create situations where police departments can discipline officers for off-duty misconduct or deviance.

Kane and White (2009, 745) classify misconduct as follows:

1. Profit-motivated crimes—non drug offense by on- or off-duty officers with the goal of generating profit;
2. Off-duty crimes against persons: assaults by off-duty officers (except for robberies);
3. Off-duty public order crimes: offenses against public order including drunk driving and disorderly conduct;
4. Drugs: drug possession or sale and failing or refusing to submit to department drug tests;
5. On-duty abuse: actions by officers in their line of work including excessive force, psychological abuse, or discrimination;
6. Obstruction of justice—attempts to subvert justice such as conspiracy, perjury, and official misconduct;
7. Administrative/failure to perform: actions in conflict with department policy related to attendance, performance, obedience, or reporting; and
8. Conduct-related probationary failures: terminations related to misconduct for those on probationary status.

These categories overlap with prior characterizations of deviance and misconduct. For example, Kappeler, Sluder, and Alpert (1994) identify police crime as the "officer's use of the official powers of his or her job to engage in criminal conduct" (21). In other words, an officer uses police authority to engage in violations of the criminal code. **Occupational deviance** is activity that does not conform to standards and is committed during the course of normal work activities or under the guise of the police officer's authority (22; see also Barker and Carter 1994, 6), **police corruption,** which involves the use of police power and authority for personal gain (see also Sherman 1978; Goldstein 1977), and **abuse of authority**. Finally, Kappeler and his colleagues observe that Carter's (1985, 22) definition of the term **abuse of authority** contains three different elements:

(a) Officers may physically abuse others through the use of excessive force.
(b) Officers may psychologically abuse citizens through the use of verbal assault, harassment, or ridicule.
(c) Officers may violate a citizen's constitutional, federal, or state rights. (Kappeler, Sluder, and Alpert 1994, 24)

The Prevalence of Police Deviance

It is incredibly difficult to gauge the extent of deviant behavior among the police. This is not surprising: People who commit illegal acts tend to keep them secret. In police departments, where peer support and loyalty are high, assessments of the extent of deviance will always be difficult and are likely to underestimate its true extent.

A few authors have assessed the prevalence of deviance in particular departments. Barker (1994) looked at five categories of deviance in what he called "South City." Using a questionnaire, he asked each officer to judge the extent to which individuals in the department engaged in, or had engaged in, each pattern while on duty. These activities included sleeping on duty (39.58 percent), brutality (39.19 percent), sex on duty (31.84 percent), perjury (22.95 percent), and drinking on duty (8.05 percent). A review of these data shows that deviance in some categories was quite high. Four of 10 officers were thought to be sleeping on duty by their fellow officers and the same number to be indulging in police brutality. Slightly over 1 in 5 were believed to engage in police perjury. It is not reasonable to assume that these numbers represent police everywhere: generalizing from one research setting to the entire population is bad science. Barker's findings, however, because they represent a seemingly normal department, are troubling. And there is evidence that other forms of deviance may be widespread.

Crank (1998) discussed two surveys to assess police deviance in one department in Illinois (Knowles 1996) and two in Ohio (Martin 1994). His overview presents two types of deviance not yet considered: racial and sexual harassment. Crank's discussion extends Sykes's (1996) analysis of these two surveys. Officers were asked in both surveys whether they had seen another officer harass a citizen based on race (see Inside Policing 9.1).

When these three surveys are considered together, they present a disturbing picture of police deviance. In all three departments, the findings suggested that deviance was widespread. In all three, there appeared to be strong peer support to cover up deviant activities. Finally, all three departments were typical—none had a particularly negative record of police corruption. These findings, when compared with findings presented in the previous discussion, suggest that police corruption may indeed be diverse in its types, widespread across departments, and hidden behind the secretive screen of department loyalties.

INSIDE POLICING 9.1 **Racial Harassment**

One of every four officers in the Illinois survey (26.2 percent) and one in six in the Ohio survey (14.9 percent) stated that they had witnessed racial harassment by their fellow officers. If one extrapolates these percentages back to the base populations from which they were drawn, one can appreciate the magnitude of the harassment and its potential for the alienation of minority citizens. According to the 1994 crime reports, Ohio has 18,721 sworn "local," or municipal, officers, and Illinois, outside the Chicago Police Department (which declined to participate in the Illinois survey), has 16,131. Certainly not all of these officers are active on the streets. One can allow a generous estimate that 50 percent of a police department is in administrative support. This reduces the street-officer populations to 9,360 in Ohio and 8,065 in Illinois. Calculating the population estimates from these reduced figures, one arrives at 2,113 instances of police harassment in Illinois and 1,395 in Ohio in a single year's time, excluding the largest department in either state. Thus, in the two typical states, dominated by smaller police departments but with a sprinkling of big-city departments as well, police racism is by any reasoning a pervasive phenomenon. Nor are these figures in some way inflated by groups that harbor ill will against the police: Keep in mind that these are numbers that the police are reporting about themselves.

SOURCE: Adapted from J. Crank, *Understanding Police Culture* (Cincinnati, OH: Anderson Publishing Co., 1998), 212.

TABLE 9.1 Charge Specifications Against Officers Terminated for Misconduct in the NYPD, 1975–1996

CHARGE SPECIFICATION	PERCENTAGE
Administrative/failure to perform	30.1
Drugs	19.0
Profit-motivated crime	15.7
Off-duty crime against persons	11.6
Obstruction of justice	10.8
Off-duty public order crimes	5.8
On-duty abuse	4.8
Conduct on probation	2.2

Adapted from Kane, R. J., and White, M. D. 2009. "Bad Cops: A Study of Career-Ending Misconduct Among New York City Police Officers." *Criminology and Public Policy* 8(4): 751.

Kane and White (2009) provide descriptive statistics of officers in the NYPD who have been terminated between 1975 and 1996, and these are represented in Table 9.1. While these data cannot provide adequate information regarding the prevalence of misconduct overall, they do provide good detail regarding the frequency of misconduct across their eight categories relative to each other.

The analysis provided by Kane and White (2009) reveals that 1,543 officers were terminated from the NYPD during the 21-year period. While this estimate appears high, they note that the NYPD employed around 78,000 different people during this period—officers terminated for misconduct only represent about 2 percent of the total. While it is challenging to estimate the prevalence of misconduct and deviance, these data suggest relatively few officers are ever terminated because of this behavior. Further, the most common form of misconduct is administrative in nature. Police crime (as defined by Kappeler et al. 1994) is far more rare.

The Trouble With Gratuities

One of the most perplexing areas of police deviance concerns gratuities. A **gratuity** is the acceptance of something of value, such as coffee, meals, discount-buying privileges, free admission to athletic or recreational events or movies, gifts, and small rewards. Most commonly it is coffee, beverages, or meals free or at reduced cost. Gratuities do not seem to be harmful, and they are often offered under the friendliest of circumstances. A beer "on the house" is, for many young people, an indication of their social worth, that they are valued by their friends and colleagues. Yet an officer who accepts gratuities may unknowingly undermine the legitimacy of his or her police department, endanger a future promotion, and possibly lose the job. Although acceptance of gratuities is a common practice in many police departments, it is considered unethical by the International Association of Chiefs of Police. Although many departments have an explicit policy that precludes accepting gratuities, these policies are frequently ignored by officers. Many police managers view violations of such policies to be a minor problem and may not enforce departmental regulations against them.

Although a police officer may enjoy gratuities at first, they have a way of unpleasantly complicating life. For example, in a survey of citizens in Reno, Nevada, a majority of citizens polled did not think police should accept any gratuities. Almost half of the respondents stated that if they provided a gratuity they would expect special consideration (e.g., extra patrol, warning instead of citation if stopped for traffic violation) by police officers (Sigler and Dees 1988).

Business owners may offer gratuities to encourage the police to spend more time at their establishment. Assume, for example, that an officer goes to the same restaurant every day to eat because a free meal is provided. The value of the meals, over a month's time, is equal to about $180. The restaurant owner likes having police officers around because she thinks it will decrease the likelihood of a robbery or unruly customers. However, if the owner offered to give the officer $180 in cash every month to spend the equivalent amount of time at the restaurant, the officer would probably not accept the money, and the police department would most certainly consider the acceptance of money a more serious problem than acceptance of the free meals. But there is no real difference in the two acts; both involve giving something of value for the express purpose of obtaining a private service—extra police protection or preferential treatment—from a public official.

DeLeon-Granados and Wells (1998) explored this gratuity exchange principle in a medium-size midwestern city. An outcome of the acceptance of gratuities is that the business offering the "perk" receives a disproportionate amount of police service compared with businesses that do not engage in such behavior. After all, to receive a free cup of coffee, the officer has to actually be at that location to receive it. Therefore, businesses that provide gratuities to police receive additional police presence, service, and safety compared with their counterparts. Their unique research found, perhaps not surprisingly, that officers were much more likely to be observed at establishments offering gratuities than at those that did not. This raises ethical issues regarding whether police presence should (in any part) be linked to whether the business provides "free stuff" to police officers.

Deviant Officers

Police officers vary in their vulnerability to corruption. Most do not become involved in corrupt activities. They are morally committed to their work and are not psychologically capable of illegal activity. Only a small percentage become "bent" to the extent that they commit illegal activity. What should society think about those who do?

One of the more important insights into police corruption was presented by the Knapp Commission, which conducted an investigation into the activities of the New York City Police Department in the late 1960s and early 1970s. Inside Policing 9.2 provides a summary of its findings, which remain comprehensive and influential.

Of particular importance in the inset is the description of grass eaters and meat eaters. **Grass eaters** are police officers who accept graft when it comes their way but do not actively solicit opportunities for graft. **Meat eaters** are officers who actively solicit opportunities for financial gain and are involved in more widespread and serious corruption (Knapp Commission on Police Corruption 1972).

A casual reader might think that meat eaters are a more serious problem than grass eaters because they certainly commit more serious crimes. Yet that is not so. The Knapp Commission found that the grass eaters were a more significant problem. They outnumbered meat eaters by a considerable margin, and even though they did not solicit illegal opportunities, they took advantage of them when opportunity provided. Their illegal involvement created a "wall of silence" behind which meat eaters could operate with impunity. The problem confronting efforts to clean up corruption, the commission found, was the **code of silence**, which they could not penetrate. The code of silence is the secrecy that line-level officers maintain about their activities, both from the public and from police administrators.

Barker (1996) expanded the Knapp Commission's typology of deviant officers, identifying five types. *White knights* are totally honest and may take an extreme stance in ethical issues. These officers are in the minority and are not deviant. *Straight-shooters* are honest but willing to overlook some of the indiscretions of other officers. They suffer in silence or seek out corruption-free assignments. *Grass eaters* engage in corrupt activities if the opportunity arises. *Meat eaters* actively seek out opportunities for corruption. Finally, *rogues,* at the far end of the scale, are considered an aberration even by meat eaters. They engage directly in criminal activities and in high-visibility shakedowns of citizens.

Research has provided some insight into the individual and community level correlates of misconduct and deviance. As presented previously, Kane and White (2009) examined the prevalence of misconduct in the NYPD that resulted in officer termination. They randomly selected officers from the same academy classes and collected data on both sets of officers to identify factors correlated with job-ending misconduct. They reported risk factors associated with misconduct, including officer minority race/ethnicity (black, Hispanic, and Asian)—minorities were significantly more likely to be terminated because of misconduct than their white counterparts. However, they suggest a caveat associated with this finding, namely, black officers became more represented within the NYPD and the rates of misconduct for blacks declined. They also note, perhaps not surprisingly, that officers with prior criminal histories or problems with previous employers were correlated with misconduct in their policing occupation. They suggest quality recruitment and screening tactics can

INSIDE POLICING 9.2 The Knapp Commission

The Knapp Commission was established in May 1970 by Mayor John V. Lindsay as a result of an article that appeared in the *New York Times* on April 25, which stated that there was widespread corruption in the New York City Police Department. The commission was given the task of determining the extent and nature of police corruption. Judge Whitman Knapp was appointed to head the investigation, which issued its final report in 1972.

The investigation found corruption to be widespread in the police department and many officers, both investigators and patrol officers, to be involved. Corruption was most extensive among investigators (what the commission called plainclothes officers) in the area of gambling. The plainclothes officers participated in what was known as a "pad." For example, each illegal gambling establishment in a precinct would contribute a certain amount of money (as much as $3,500 per establishment once or twice a month) to the officers. The total amount collected would be divided among the officers, each one receiving his "nut" (which was usually $300 to $400 per month, but at least one precinct had a "nut" of $1,200 per officer). Newly assigned officers had to wait 2 months before receiving a "nut," but all plainclothes officers who left the precinct were given 2 months' severance pay.

Corruption in the narcotics area was less organized but was also extensive. Many of the payments came from "shakedowns" of narcotics dealers. Such payments were known as "scores"; the highest payoff uncovered was $80,000. There was some evidence to suggest that such large payments to police officers were not uncommon. [Since the 1980s, corruption scandals in police departments have been primarily related to narcotics.]

Uniformed patrol officers did not receive the large sums of money that went to plainclothes officers, but many patrol officers were involved in corrupt activities. Some participated in small gambling "pads" and often collected money from construction sites, bars, grocery stores, parking lots, and other business establishments. They could also get money from traffic violators, tow trucks (for business given to the company), prostitutes, and defendants who wanted their court cases "fixed." These types of businesses were subject to a number of city laws, which, if violated, could result in a fine. To get around some of these laws, patrol officers were paid to "look the other way." Most often, the payoffs were $20 or less, but many officers were able to collect a large number of such payoffs in a month, adding substantially to their salary.

Ranking officers, sergeants, lieutenants, and even others above this level participated in corrupt activities, but the evidence was difficult to obtain above the level of lieutenant. This is because when ranking officers were involved they used a "bagman," usually a patrol officer, to collect the payoffs. He received a percentage of the payoff. If he was discovered, he had to be willing to take the fall.

Although the Knapp Commission was careful to point out that not all police officers in New York City were corrupt, those who were not corrupt were aware of the corruption problems and, for the most part, did nothing about them.

SOURCE: Adapted from Knapp Commission, *Report on Police Corruption* (New York: George Braziller, 1972), 1–11.

reduce the likelihood of hiring officers who will later engage in misconduct. They further report officers with higher levels of pre-employment education and who scored better in the academy were less likely to be terminated because of misconduct. This supports strategies to increase training quality and recruit individuals with higher levels of education into policing (an issue that will be discussed further in Chapter 14). Other research utilizing the same data suggests misconduct is more prevalent in communities characterized by structural disadvantage (i.e., high rates of poverty, female headed households, households receiving public assistance, unemployment, and low educational attainment) and population mobility (Kane 2002). This appears to suggest that certain environments are more suitable and provide more opportunities for officers to engage in misconduct.

The Persistence of Corruption

Corruption has been and continues to be one of the most frequent problems faced by police departments in the United States. Consider the New York City Police Department. It was found to have serious corruption problems in 1895 (by the Lexow Committee), in 1900 (by the Mazet Committee), in 1913 (as a result of the Curran investigations), in 1932 (by the Seabury Committee), in 1942 (as a result of the Amen investigation), and in 1952 (by the Brooklyn Grand Jury) (Caiden 1977, 159). The Knapp Commission followed with a new corruption exposé in the 1970s. In the mid-1980s, the department was rocked by the Buddy Boys scandal ("Drug Corruption" 1986, 1). In 1994 the Mollen Commission noted widespread drug extortion among members of the 75th Precinct. New York City has a large police department, with approximately 45,000 officers. It is unreasonable to assume, on the one hand, that all these officers will be honest or, on the other, that any particular incident indicates that the entire department is tainted. Yet the NYPD displays the persistence of corruption that characterizes many American police departments, large and small, and some of the most infamous corruption scandals in American police history originated in New York.

It is remarkable that many police departments have been as successful as they have at controlling corruption problems. As Walker (1984) observed, in the 1800s corruption was the business of many police departments. Today, although many have periodic scandals, they are usually less pervasive than in the past. Generally, present-day investigations tend to uncover only a small number of deviant police officers. They rarely uncover all the corrupt officers, nor do they reveal the officers who know what is taking place and say nothing.

Why does corruption continue to recur in police departments? There are essentially four reasons. First, police officers are very powerful and operate with autonomy and little direct supervision. By virtue of their authority they encounter widespread opportunities for corruption. They are constantly exposed to situations in which the decisions they make can have a positive or negative impact on a person's freedom and well-being. Citizens may try to influence this discretion by offering free coffee and meals, money, sex, property—any item of value that will result in a favorable decision. Sometimes an offer can be extraordinarily tempting. The Knapp Commission identified payoffs as high as $80,000 in drug cases, and that was in the late 1960s. Once officers begin to accept payoffs, they may become "addicted"—that is, they begin to depend on the extra income and spend accordingly.

Second, the community and political environment are influential in establishing attitudes toward corrupt activities. Corruption in other government agencies, among prominent politicians, and in the business world enables police officers to rationalize their own behavior. Murphy and Caplan make this point in the following statement:

> Operating in this larger environment, it is not surprising that police become cynical about their work and feel that "nothing is on the level." When they meet citizens from every walk of life who are willing to pay them to overlook the law…some officers come to see themselves as "operating in a world where [money is] constantly floating about,

[and they would be]...stupid and...fainthearted...not to allow some of [that money] to stick to their fingers." *(1991, 248)*

In police departments there are often many standards of behavior for officers to follow. In fact, there are so many standards that it is difficult to adhere to all of them. This multiplicity is also true of society in general. There are many laws, some of which are often violated by citizens, particularly traffic laws. Officers see instances of such behavior all around them, in both the public and the private sector, among both the poor and the rich. Many officers even come to believe that if they are to be good police officers (e.g., to help people, maintain order, keep citizens from being afraid, make arrests, ensure a successful prosecution), they have to violate some of the rules they are supposed to follow. Further, recall Kane's (2002) finding that communities characterized by structural disorganization have a higher incidence of misconduct, suggesting these areas may have decreased social capital and be more suitable environments for officer misconduct.

Third, there is widespread tolerance among citizens of some kinds of police deviance. Citizens encourage the police to violate due process and citizens' rights in order to arrest felons. Television regularly displays "good" policing as that which inflicts pain on suspected felons, even when their guilt or innocence is as yet undecided. Businesses encourage small corruptions by giving officers gratuities and other perks for preferential treatment. In sum, it is unclear whether citizens always want police to "play fair," thus encouraging their moral and economic corruption.

Fourth, patterns of deviance can themselves become standards of behavior. Officers may be introduced by their training officers, for example, to restaurants that provide meals discounted for police. When standards encompass deviant behavior, line officers become secretive. Enormous pressure is put on all officers not to discuss police behavior outside police ranks. Even non-deviant officers will not break the code of silence for fear of reprisal. This belief can carry over to the chief executive and managers in the department. In addition, executives and managers may be blamed and lose their jobs if the deviance is exposed, even if they are not involved. Caiden (1977, 165) has identified characteristics of departments that have had widespread corruption problems. He refers to such departments as being systematically corrupt. These characteristics are presented in Inside Policing 9.3.

Caiden argues that real progress in dealing with corruption was made in the 1950s and 1960s because the police began to understand that the basic problem was systemic, not just the result of a few "rotten apples" (169–171). The **systemic theory of corruption** is that corruption stems from the nature of police work, and if anticorruption protocols are inadequate, corruption will spread throughout a police department. The **rotten-apple theory of corruption** is that corruption is limited to a small number of officers who were probably dishonest prior to their employment. The term *rotten apple* stems from the metaphor that a few rotten apples will spoil the barrel; in other words, a few bad officers can spoil a department. It was the most prevalent theory of corruption prior to the 1960s and 1970s. This explanation is compatible with the predispositional theory of police behavior. A systemic theory of corruption tends to support the sociological perspective of police behavior.

Caiden may be too optimistic about the extent to which police corruption has been controlled. The drug "wars" begun in the 1960s have significantly increased the opportunities for corruption, with the possibility of financial payoffs that far exceed other forms of corruption. And there is some evidence that the rotten-apple theory is still influential. Dorschner's (1989) description of the Miami Police Department linked corruption to a rapid expansion in the number of personnel and an inadequate screening process. Yet, as he

---

INSIDE POLICING 9.3 Characteristics of Corrupt Police Departments

1. The department's professional code of ethics is contradicted in practice.

2. Police managers and officers encourage, aid, and hide illegal and unethical behavior.

3. Nonparticipants in corrupt activities are penalized because they do not receive any of the benefits of corruption, and they may have to endure the displeasure of corrupt officers.

4. When corrupt officers are investigated, they will be protected; or if they are found guilty of corrupt practices, they will not be punished severely.

5. Officers who do not like the corruption in the department have no one to assist them within the department, and if they complain to someone outside, they may not be believed.

6. Officers who consider exposing the corrupt practices of other officers may be intimidated, even terrorized, to "shut them up." In some cases, such officers may actually have to be protected from bodily harm.

7. The officers who are corrupt develop rationalizations for their behavior. These include the arguments that "everyone else is doing it," that others [attorneys and judges] are corrupt, that police officers deserve "something extra" because they risk their lives or because the public doesn't appreciate them and pay them enough.

8. Eventually corrupt officers accept their behavior as "normal," as a way of doing business in police work. If and when they are exposed, they may be genuinely surprised that their corrupt behavior is considered deviant. They may even argue that they are being unfairly singled out because such behavior is commonplace for many officers.

9. Those responsible for investigating corruption tend to suggest, in effect, that the corrupt officers are only a few "rotten apples."

10. Following a corruption scandal, efforts to reform the police department have only minimal influence in changing the attitudes of officers toward corruption, and the reforms are intended only to convince the public that something is being done to correct the problems.

SOURCE: Adapted from G. E. Caiden, *Police Revitalization* (Lexington, MA: D.C. Heath and Company, 1977).

---

notes, the police department had extensive problems with political corruption even prior to its rapid expansion. Its political atmosphere provided the environment for the development of systemic corruption.

Some research has found support for the rotten-apple theory. Lersch and Mieczkowski (1996) suggested that particular kinds of officers are more likely to be involved in questionable use-of-force incidents. They noted that 7 percent of sworn personnel in a large southeastern police department accounted for over one third of the use-of-force complaints from 1991 to 1994. These officers were younger than their peers and had less experience, and the incidents were more likely to result from proactive contacts with citizens.

Police Sexual Misconduct

Police sexual misconduct is defined as behavior by an officer who takes advantage of their authority and power to commit sexual violence or initiate a sexually motivated cue for the purpose of sexual gratification (Maher 2003). The research cited above provides insight into a poorly understood area of police behavior in sexual deviance. A similar view is provided by Kappeler (1993). In a review of litigation on police sexual misconduct, he found that the police lost 69 percent of the cases brought against them, a high number when one considers the average 10 percent for all other forms of civil litigation.

Many police have argued that much of this litigation stems from misunderstandings about police work. Many departments tended to justify sexual misconduct as a boys-will-be-boys attitude among their male personnel within the male-dominated workforce (see Sapp 1994). Maher (2008) indicates police sexual misconduct is related to a variety of factors inherent to the policing industry, including authority, power, unsupervised (low visibility) work environment, and secluded contact with citizens. The police culture that encourages solidarity and secrecy provides conditions suitable for deviant behavior.

Measuring the extent of police sexual misconduct is difficult because, similar to other forms of deviance, the behavior is rarely reported. However, McGurrin and Kappeler (2002) attempted to generate a greater understanding of the prevalence and characteristics of these incidents by examining newspaper articles over an 8-year period. They found 501 reported cases of police sexual misconduct. The majority of incidents involved rape/attempted rape or sexual assault/attempted sexual assault. Yet they found that over 8 percent of cases involved sexual abuse of a child. Officers tended to be male, on-duty, municipal line officers, with a modal age of 25. Numerous officers had been previously convicted of sex offenses. Over 40 percent of the incidents commenced with a traffic stop, and about half of these involved physical force. Of those that involved force, over half indicated that the officer's physical presence was sufficient to coerce the victim.

Maher (2003) attempted to estimate the prevalence of police sexual misconduct by providing 40 officers from 14 different jurisdictions self-administered surveys, supplemented with face-to-face interviews. Officers reported what appears to be an alarmingly high rate of sexual misconduct, by either firsthand or secondhand knowledge. Maher concluded that police sexual misconduct is common. For example, these 40 officers collectively recalled 213 incidents of nonsexual contacts (such as making a traffic stop to get a closer look at the occupant) within the previous year. They also reported 161 officer-initiated sexual contacts (e.g., an officer initiates consensual sexual contact with a citizen), 122 instances of voyeurism (e.g., officers seeking opportunities to see nude or partially clad citizens by looking in windows or parked cars where the occupants are engaged in sex), and 110 instances of citizen-initiated sexual contacts. Although far less frequent, officers also reported 27 instances of sexual contact with offenders (e.g., unnecessary searches, frisks, and pat-downs of a suspect for the purpose of sexual gratification). On average, officers reported firsthand knowledge of 16.77 sexual misconduct instances per year. Secondhand knowledge of sexual misconduct was far higher than what is discussed above. Maher also interviewed police chiefs regarding the extent of sexual misconduct. Chiefs believe sexual misconduct to be "common and very serious" (Maher 2008, 243) and that behavior like unwanted flirtation, consensual sex, and voyeurism is far more common than behavior that may be criminal (i.e., rape, sexual assault). Chiefs also indicated that in their view sexual misconduct is less prevalent in policing today because of the industry's commitment to professionalism, better officer selection strategies, and more education on sexual harassment.

The results reported by Maher (2003, 2008) differ from other research in that officers indicated that violent or "serious" misconduct was rare, and in fact officers he interviewed indicated that serious forms of misconduct should not be tolerated. Some of what he reported may appear to be consensual liaisons between officers and citizens. However, as both Maher (2003) and Kraska and Kappeler (1995) note, consensual sexual relationships are an illusion. The substantial power differential that police have in exchanges with the public results in an image of consensuality, when in fact sexual relations may stem from a citizen's fear of the consequences if she or he fails to submit to an officer's implied or direct demands.

Police departments attempting to deter this type of deviance should consider a number of different strategies. Police departments should proactively create policies prohibiting sexual misconduct, and personnel should receive formal and in-service training on what constitutes police sexual misconduct. While this appears to be a pretty basic response (and one that may not be overly effective), it is worth noting that in Maher's (2008) study only 30 percent of police chiefs indicated their officers receive any such training on sexual misconduct. Also, some chiefs he spoke to were reluctant to adopt such policies until they perceived it was a problem within their department. This is alarming given the fact that most police sexual misconduct goes unreported. Thus departments should make certain that citizens have opportunities to report sexual misconduct. This may include strategies such as complaints being filed with a non-government entity that addresses police misconduct in general or through other actors within their local government. Policies such as requiring citizens to file a misconduct complaint with the police department itself might discourage citizens from doing so. Maher (2008) suggests victims alleging police sexual misconduct should be able to make formal complaints in writing only, rather than being required to report misconduct in person. Departments must make efforts to encourage citizen complaints about misbehavior and take these complaints very seriously. Complaints should be fully investigated in the same manner and with the same vigor as any other crime, and departments should adopt a zero-tolerance approach when complaints are substantiated. Such misconduct, while perhaps rare, is positioned to erode the public trust that the police must have in a democratic society.

The Drug War and Police Deviance

Deviance is a persistent problem, and some forms of deviance may be intensifying. Drug corruption, in many different forms, appears to be on the increase among police. As a new century begins, the United States is deeply involved in a drug war, carried out by municipal police, federal police, and military troops, aimed at controlling the use and distribution of illegal narcotics. The authors are not going to debate the merits of drug legalization here—suffice it to say that there are persuasive arguments for both the legalization and the criminalization of illegal substances. Our concern is with the negative impact of the current drug interdiction on U.S. police.

Kappeler, Sluder, and Alpert (1994) identify four types of corruption:

1. **Use corruption** is when officers use drugs. Kraska and Kappeler (1988) found that about 20 percent of the officers they studied in a medium-size department admitted that they smoked marijuana.

2. **Economic corruption** occurs when officers seek personal gain. Officers might, for example, keep drug money confiscated from dealers.

3. **Police violence** is the use of force to extract confessions.

4. The **subjugation of a defendant's rights** to obtain a drug conviction includes police perjury and "flaking," or the planting of drugs on a suspect by a police officer to acquire evidence.

A relatively recent tool available to police in the war on drugs is *civil asset forfeiture*. Simply stated, assets may be forfeited to the government if they were used to facilitate a crime or if they are the fruits of criminal behavior. Regarding drug trafficking, assets often include homes, property, vehicles, boats, and aircraft. These assets, or the proceeds from their sale, are (in part) given back to the police to fund their enforcement activities. Additionally, since the legal proceedings are civil rather than criminal in nature, acquisition of assets is quite easy. Civil proceedings often do not afford the property owner the same due process protections as are found in criminal court, and property may be seized without notice or hearing. Further, the standard of proof for civil forfeiture is preponderance of evidence, which is significantly lower than proof beyond a reasonable doubt (Lersch 2002). In practice, assets are forfeited even when the property owner is not charged with a crime or when an agreement not to contest civil forfeiture is exchanged for dismissal of criminal charges.

This process presents a sticky situation for police organizations, particularly if they derive a significant proportion of their budget from civil asset forfeiture. Lersch (2002) indicates that the property (and not the criminal) may become the true target of investigation. Thus, even though individual officers may not derive direct compensation from these forfeitures, they may benefit from organizational rewards (such as promotion) for making the "big score." It is important to note that civil asset forfeiture is in no way indicative of deviant or corrupt behavior. However, it is important to note that this tool can provide fertile grounds and a legal rationale for engaging in drug-related corrupt behavior by street-level officers.

Use of violence and subjugation of rights have been described by Crank and Caldero (1999) as **noble-cause corruption**, which occurs when police abandon ethical and legal means to achieve so-called good ends (see also Delattre 1996, 190–214; Klockars 1983). Both violence and subjugation of rights may be used by police who are more concerned about the "noble cause"—getting bad guys off the street, protecting victims and children—than about the morality of "technically" legal behavior. Noble-cause corruption occurs when officers break the law to do something about the drug problem.

According to Crank and Caldero, noble-cause corruption and economic corruption may be inversely related. They argue that police departments during the twentieth century have been somewhat successful in combating economic corruption among the police. This success has been accomplished in large part by instilling police with a mission to do something about crime. The consequence is that, as police economic corruption decreases, noble-cause corruption seems to increase. Police today may be less likely to commit crime for personal gain, but they also may be more likely to commit crime to carry out ends-oriented justice.

Since the Knapp Commission proceedings, New York has experienced another cycle of corruption and scandal. This time, however, the problems were different from those cited in preceding scandals because of their linkages to drugs. The Mollen Commission, established in 1993, also sought to identify the presence of police corruption. Kappeler, Sluder, and Alpert (1994) summarize the commission's findings as follows:

> Witnesses told the commission of systematic corruption that was strikingly similar to the [mid-1980s] Buddy-Boys case. Michael Dowd, a former officer in the 75th precinct, bluntly described how he and his peers routinely robbed crime victims, drug dealers, and arrestees of money, drugs, and anything else of value. Dowd revealed that many officers were receiving substantial sums for protecting illegal drug operations; Dowd's share amounted to $4,000 each week. Dowd told of officers routinely using drugs and alcohol

while on duty, informing the commission that he regularly snorted lines of cocaine off the dashboard of his police cruiser. Other witnesses told of extensive use of excessive force culminating in the physical and psychological brutalization of many citizens *(Frankel and Stone 1993)*

Summary

Universalistic perspectives of police behavior are sociological, psychological, and organizational. Two particularistic theories are predisposition and socialization. The former explains police behavior in terms of the type of individual employed, while the latter is concerned with what happens after employment. Some of the more important studies of police behavior were made by Westley, Banton, Skolnick, Wilson, and Brown. These studies tend to support the importance of the socialization theory because the influential factors that they have identified are all related to the experiences of being a police officer. More recent research has suggested that predispositional factors are also important.

There have also been attempts to relate police behavior and discretion to a number of specific variables: organizational, neighborhood, situational, and officer. Legal factors tend to determine the decision to arrest, but extralegal factors also sometimes play a role. Despite a great deal of research on extralegal factors, their actual contribution to the use of police discretion is unclear.

Police deviance includes abuse of authority and deviant acts (contrary to standards) committed in the normal course of the job. The latter can be misconduct in terms of rules or corruption, such as accepting gratuities, which the authors consider inappropriate. Police corruption is marked by periodic scandals in some departments, and corruption involving drugs appears to be increasing.

Critical Thinking Questions

1. Do you believe the predispositional or socialization theories offer greater explanatory value in understanding police behavior? Why?

2. What contributions have Westley, Skolnick, Wilson, Brown, and Rubinstein made to understanding police behavior? How do the perspectives of these authors differ?

3. Explain Van Maanen's stages of socialization.

4. Discuss organizational (departmental) and neighborhood variables considered important in police behavior.

5. What are meat eaters and grass eaters? Which is the greater problem in controlling police corruption? Why?

6. What is a police gratuity? Is acceptance of gratuities a serious problem for American police? Why (not)?

7. What is meant by noble-cause corruption? Provide an example.

8. Why do you think certain police departments (e.g., the New York City Police Department) have a long legacy of corruption? Do you think some departments are "more corrupt" than others? If so, why do you believe this to be the case?

References

Adams, T. 1990. *Police Field Operations.* Englewood Cliffs, NJ: Prentice Hall.

Alpert, G., and Smith, W. 1998. "Developing Police Policy: An Evaluation of the Control Principle." In L. Gaines and G. Cordner (eds.), *Policing Perspectives: An Anthology,* pp. 353–362. Los Angeles: Roxbury Publishing Co.

Auten, J. 1988. "Preparing Written Guidelines." *F.B.I. Law Enforcement Bulletin* 57: 1–7.

Banton, M. 1965. *The Policeman in the Community.* New York: Basic Books.

Barker, T. 1994. "Police Deviance Other than Corruption." In T. Barker and D. Carter (eds.), *Police Deviance,* 3rd ed., pp. 123–138. Cincinnati, OH: Anderson Publishing.

———. 1996. *Police Ethics: Crisis in Law Enforcement.* Springfield, IL: Charles C. Thomas Publishers.

Barker, T., and Carter, D. 1994. "A Typology of Police Deviance." In T. Barker and D. Carter (eds.), *Police Deviance.* 3rd ed., pp. 3–12. Cincinnati, OH: Anderson Publishing.

Barnum, C., and Perfetti, R. L. 2010. "Race-Sensitive Choices by Police Officers in Traffic Stop Encounters." *Police Quarterly* 13: 180–208.

Bayley, D. H., and Bittner, E. 1989. "Learning the Skills of Policing." In R. G. Dunham and G. P. Alpert (eds.), *Critical Issues in Policing: Contemporary Readings,* pp. 87–110. Prospect Heights, IL: Waveland Press.

Black, D. 1973. "The Mobilization of Law." *Journal of Legal Studies, The University of Chicago Law School* 2: 125–144.

———. 1976. *The Behavior of Law.* New York: Academic Press.

———. 1980. *The Manners and Customs of the Police.* New York: Academic Press.

Brooks, L. W. 1989. "Police Discretionary Behavior: A Study of Style." In R. G. Dunham and G. P. Alpert (eds.), *Critical Issues in Policing: Contemporary Readings,* pp. 121–145. Prospect Heights, IL: Waveland Press.

Brown, M. K. 1981. *Working the Street: Police Discretion.* New York: Russell Sage Foundation.

Brown, R. A. 2005. "Black, White and Unequal: Examining Situational Determinants of Arrest Decisions from Police–Suspect Encounters." *Criminal Justice Studies* 18: 51–68.

Brown, R. A., and Frank, J. 2006. "Race and Officer Decision Making: Examining Difference in Arrest Outcomes Between Black and White Officers." *Justice Quarterly* 23: 96–126.

Brown, R. A., Novak, K. J., and Frank, J. 2009. "Identifying Variation in Police Officer Behavior Between Juveniles and Adults." *Journal of Criminal Justice* 38: 200–208.

Caiden, G. E. 1977. *Police Revitalization.* Lexington, MA: D. C. Heath.

Caldero, M. 1997. "Value Consistency Within the Police: The Lack of a Gap." Paper presented at the annual meeting of the Academy of Criminal Justice Sciences, Louisville, KY, March.

Caldero, M., and Larose, A. P. 2003. "Value Consistency Within the Police: The Lack of a Gap." *Policing: An International Journal of Police Strategies and Management* 24: 162–180.

Carter, D. 1985. "Police Brutality: A Model for Definition, Perspective, and Control." In A. S. Blumberg and E. Niederhoffer (eds.), *The Ambivalent Force,* pp. 321–330. New York: Holt, Rinehart and Winston.

Chambliss, W. 1997 "Policing the Ghetto Underclass: The Politics of Law and Law Enforcement." In B. Handcock and P. Sharp (eds.), *Public Policy: Crime and Criminal Justice,* pp. 146–165. Upper Saddle River, NJ: Prentice Hall.

Cochran, J. K., and Bromley, M. L. 2003. "The Myth(?) of the Police Sub-Culture." *Policing: An International Journal of Police Strategies and Management,* 26: 22–117.

Cordner, G. 1989. "Written Rules and Regulations: Are They Necessary?" *F.B.I. Law Enforcement Bulletin* July: 17–21.

———. 1995. "Community Policing: Elements and Effects." *Police Forum* 5: 1–8.

Crank, J. 1998. *Understanding Police Culture.* Cincinnati, OH: Anderson Publishing.

Crank, J., and Caldero, M. 1999. *Police Ethics: The Corruption of Noble Cause.* Cincinnati, OH: Anderson Publishing.

Crank, J., and Langworthy, R. 1991. "An Institutional Perspective of Policing." *Journal of Criminal Law and Criminology* 8: 338–363.

Davis, K. C. 1969. *Discretionary Justice.* Baton Rouge, LA: Louisiana State University Press.

DeJong, C. 2004. "Gender Differences in Officer Attitude and Behavior: Providing Comfort and Support." *Women and Criminal Justice* 15, 1–32.

Delattre, E. J. 1996. *Character and Cops: Ethics in Policing*, 3rd ed. Washington, DC: American Enterprise Institute.

DeLeon-Granados, W., and Wells, W. 1998. "'Do You Want Extra Police Coverage with Those Fries?' An Exploratory Analysis of the Relationship Between Patrol Practices and the Gratuity Exchange Principle." *Police Quarterly* 1: 71–85.

Dorschner, J. 1989. "The Dark Side of Force." In R. G. Dunham and G. P. Alpert (eds.), *Critical Issues in Policing: Contemporary Readings*, pp. 250–270. Prospect Heights, IL: Waveland Press.

"Drug Corruption—The Lure of Big Bucks." 1986. *Law Enforcement Journal* December 30: 1, 4.

Durose, M. R., and Langan, P. A. 2007. *Contacts between Police and the Public, 2005*. Washington, DC: Bureau of Justice Statistics.

Engel, R. S. 2001. "The Supervisory Styles of Patrol Sergeants and Lieutenants." *Journal of Criminal Justice* 29: 341–355.

Engel, R. S. 2003. "Explaining Suspects' Resistance and Disrespect Toward Police." *Journal of Criminal Justice* 31, 475–492.

Engel, R. S., and Silver, E. 2001. "Policing Mentally Disordered Suspects: A Reexamination of the Criminalization Hypothesis." *Criminology* 39: 225–252.

Engel, R. S., Klahm, C. F., and Tillyer, R. 2010. "Citizens' demeanor, race, and traffic stops." In Rice, S. K., and White, M. D. (eds.), *Race, Ethnicity and Policing: New and Essential Readings*, pp 287–308. New York: New York University Press.

Engel, R. S., Sobol, J., and Worden, R.E. 2000. "Further Exploration of the Demeanor Hypothesis: The Interaction Effects of Suspects' Characteristics and Demeanor on Police Behavior. *Justice Quarterly* 17, 235–258.

Famega, C. N. 2009. "Proactive Policing by Post and Community Officers." *Crime and Delinquency* 55: 78–104.

Fogelson, R. M. 1977. *Big-City Police*. Cambridge, MA: Harvard University Press.

Frankel, B. 1993. "Ex-NYC Officer Tells Stark Tale of Cops Gone Bad." *USA Today* September 28: A-3.

Frankel, B., and Stone, A. 1993. "You'll Be in the Fold by Breaking the Law." *USA Today* September 30: A1, A2.

Fridell, L.A. 2004. *By the Numbers: A Guide for Analyzing Race Data from Vehicle Stops*. Washington, DC: Police Executive Research Forum.

Friedrich, R. J. 1980. "Police Use of Force: Individuals, Situations, and Organizations." *Annals* 452: 82–97.

Gallup Organization. 1999. *Racial Profiling Seen as Widespread, Particularly Among Young Black Men*. Available online at http://www.gallup.com/poll/3421/racial-profiling-seen-widespread-particularly-among-young-black-men.aspx (accessed September 3, 2010).

Goldstein, H. 1977. *Policing a Free Society*. Cambridge, MA: Ballinger Books.

Goldstein, J. 1998. "Police Discretion Not to Invoke the Criminal Justice Process: Low Visibility Decisions in the Administration of Justice." In G. F. Cole and M. G. Gertz (eds.), *The Criminal Justice: Politics and Policies*, 7th ed., pp. 85–103. Belmont, CA: Wadsworth Publishing Co.

Greene, J. R., and Klockars, C. B. 1991. "What Police Do." In C. B. Klockars and S. Mastrofski (eds.), *Thinking About Police: Contemporary Readings*, pp. 273–285. New York: McGraw–Hill.

Guyot, D. 1991. *Policing as Though People Matter*. Philadelphia: Temple University Press.

Hassell, K. D., Zhao, J. S., and Maguire, E. R. 2003. "Structural Arrangements in Large Municipal Police Organizations: Revisiting Wilson's Theory of Local Political Culture." *Policing: An International Journal of Police Strategies and Management* 26, 231–250.

Herbert, S. 1997. *Policing Space: Territoriality and the Los Angeles Police Department*. Minneapolis: University of Minnesota Press.

Hoffman, P. B., and Hickey, E. R. 2005. "Use of Force by Female Police Officers." *Journal of Criminal Justice,* 33: 145–151.

Hopkins, E. J. 1931. *Our Lawless Police.* New York: Viking.

Hurst, Y. G., and Frank, J. 2000. "How Kids View Cops: The Nature of Juvenile Attitudes Toward the Police." *Journal of Criminal Justice* 28: 189–202.

Johnson, D. R. 1981. *American Law Enforcement.* St. Louis: Forum Press.

Kane, R. J. 2002. "Social Ecology of Police Misconduct." *Criminology* 40(4): 867–896.

Kane, R. J., and White, M. D. 2009. "Bad Cops: A Study of Career-Ending Misconduct Among New York City Police Officers." *Criminology and Public Policy* 8: 737–769.

Kania, R. 1972. "Police Corruption in New York City." In A. W. Cohn and E. C. Viano (eds.), *Police Community Relations: Images, Roles, Realities,* pp. 330–341. New York: J. B. Lippincott.

———. 1988. "Should We Tell the Police to Say 'Yes' to Gratuities?" *Criminal Justice Ethics* 7: 37–48.

Kappeler, V. E. 1993. *Critical Issues in Police Liability.* Prospect Heights. IL: Waveland Press.

Kappeler, V. E., Sluder, R. D., and Alpert, G. 1994. *Forces of Deviance: Understanding the Dark Side of Policing.* Prospect Heights, IL: Waveland Press.

Klinger, D. 1994. "Demeanor on Crime: Why 'Hostile' Citizens Are More Likely to Be Arrested." *Criminology* 32: 475–493.

Klinger, D. 1997. "Negotiating Order in Patrol Work: An Ecological Theory of Police Response to Deviance." *Criminology* 35: 277–306.

Klockars, C. 1983. "The Dirty Harry Problem." In C. Klockars (ed.), *Thinking About Police: Contemporary Readings,* pp. 428–438. New York: McGraw–Hill.

Knapp Commission on Police Corruption. 1972. *Report on Police Corruption.* New York: George Braziller.

Knowles, J. J. 1996. *The Ohio Police Behavior Study.* Columbus, OH: Office of Criminal Justice Services.

Kraska, P. B., and Kappeler, V. E. 1988. "Police On-duty Drug Use: A Theoretical and Descriptive Explanation." *American Journal of Police* 7 (1): 1–28.

———. 1995. "To Serve and Pursue: Exploring Police Sexual Violence Against Women." *Justice Quarterly* 12: 85–112.

———. 1999. "Exploring Police Sexual Violence Against Women." In L. K. Gaines and G. W. Cordner (eds.), *Police Perspectives: An Anthology,* pp. 324–341. Los Angeles: Roxbury Publishing.

Langworthy, R. H. 1985. "Wilson's Theory of Police Behavior: A Replication of the Constraint Theory." *Justice Quarterly* 3: 89–98.

Lersch, K. 2002. "All's Fair in Love and War." In K. Lersch (ed.), *Policing and Misconduct.* Upper Saddle River, NJ: Prentice Hall.

Lersch, K. M., and Feagin, J. R. 1996. "Violent Police–Citizen Encounters: An Analysis of Major Newspaper Accounts." *Critical Sociology* 22: 29–49.

Lersch, K., and Mieczkowski, T. 1996. "Who Are the Problem-Prone Officers? An Analysis of Citizen Complaints." *American Journal of Police* 15: 23–44.

Liederbach, J., and Travis, L. F. 2008. "Wilson Redux: Another Look at Varieties of Police Behavior." *Police Quarterly* 11: 447–467.

Maher, T. M. 2003. "Police Sexual Misconduct: Officers' Perceptions of its Extent and Causality." *Criminal Justice Review* 28: 355–381.

Maher, T. M. 2008. "Police Chiefs' Views on Police Sexual Misconduct." *Police Practice and Research* 9: 239–250.

Manning, P. 1980. *The Narc's Game.* Cambridge, MA: MIT Press.

———. 1989. "The Police Occupational Culture in Anglo-American Societies." In L. Hoover and J. Dowling (eds.), *Encyclopedia of Police Science.* New York: Garland Publishing.

———. 1997. *Police Work: The Social Organization of Policing,* 2nd ed. Prospect Heights, IL: Waveland Press.

Martin, C. 1994. *Illinois Municipal Officers' Perceptions of Police Ethics.* Chicago: Illinois Criminal Justice Information Authority, Statistical Analysis Center.

Martin, S. E. 1980. *Breaking and Entering: Policewomen on Patrol.* Berkeley: University of California Press.

———. 1989. "Female Officers on the Move?" In R. G. Dunham and G. P. Alpert (eds.), *Critical Issues in Policing: Contemporary Readings,* pp. 312–330. Prospect Heights, IL: Waveland Press.

———. 1990. *On the Move: The Status of Women in Policing.* Washington, DC: Police Foundation.

Mastrofski, S. 1981. "Policing the Beat: The Impact of Organizational Scale on Patrol Officer Behavior in Urban Residential Neighborhoods." *Journal of Criminal Justice* 4: 343–358.

Mastrofski, S. D., Worden, R. E., and Snipes, J. B. 1995. "Law Enforcement in a Time of Community Policing." *Criminology* 33: 539–563.

Maurer, M. 1993. *Young Black Men and the Criminal Justice System: A Growing National Problem.* Washington, DC: The Sentencing Project. U.S. Government Printing Office.

McGurrin, D., and Kappeler, V. E. 2002. "Media Accounts of Police Sexual Violence." In K. Lersch (ed.), *Policing and Misconduct.* Upper Saddle River, NJ: Prentice Hall.

Murphy, P. V., and Caplan, G. 1991. "Fostering Integrity." In W. A. Geller (ed.), *Local Government Police Management,* pp. 239–271. Washington, DC: International City Management Association.

Niederhoffer, A. 1967. *Behind the Shield.* New York: Doubleday and Co.

Novak, K. J., and Engel, R. S. 2005. "Disentangling the Influence of Suspects' Demeanor and Mental Disorder on Arrest." *Policing: An International Journal of Police Strategies and Management* 28: 493–512.

Novak, K. J., Frank, J., Smith, B. W., and Engel, R. S. 2002. "Revisiting the Decision to Arrest: Comparing Beat and Community Officers." *Crime and Delinquency* 48: 70–98.

Paoline, E. A. 2003. "Taking Stock: Toward a Richer Understanding of Police Culture." *Journal of Criminal Justice* 31: 199–214.

Paoline, E. A. 2004. "Shedding Light on Police Culture: An Examination of Officers' Occupational Attitudes." *Police Quarterly* 7: 205–236.

Paoline, E. A., and Terrill, W. 2004. "Women Police Officers and the Use of Coercion." *Women and Criminal Justice,* 15: 97–119.

Paoline, E. A., and Terrill, W. 2005. "The Impact of Culture on Police Traffic Stop Searches: An Analysis of Attitudes and Behavior." *Policing: An International Journal of Police Strategies and Management* 28: 455–472.

Parks, R. 1982. "Citizen Surveys for Police Performance Assessment: Some Issues in Their Use." *Urban Interest* 4: 17–26.

"Philadelphia Unveils Anti-corruption Plan." 1985. *Law Enforcement News* October 21: 1, 5.

Plitt, E. 1983. "Police Discipline Decisions." *Police Chief* March: 95–98.

Rabe-Hemp, C. E. 2008. "Female Officers and the Ethic of Care: Does Officer Gender Impact Police Behaviors? *Journal of Criminal Justice* 36, 426–434.

Ramirez, D., McDevitt, J., and Farrell, A. 2000. *A Resource Guide on Racial Profiling Data Collection Systems: Promising Practices and Lessons Learned.* Washington, DC: Bureau of Justice Assistance.

Reitzel, J. and Piquero, A. R. 2006. "Does it Exist? Studying Citizens' Attitudes of Racial Profiling." *Police Quarterly* 9; 161–183.

Reuss-Ianni, E. 1983. *Two Cultures of Policing.* New Brunswick, NJ: Transaction.

Rice, S. K. 2010. "Introduction to Part 1." In Rice, S. K., and White, M. D. (eds.), *Race, Ethnicity and Policing: New and Essential Readings,* pp. 11–14. New York: New York University Press.

Rice, S. K., and White, M. D. 2010. *Race, Ethnicity and Policing: New and Essential Readings* New York: New York University Press.

Riksheim, E. C., and Chermak, S. M. 1993. "Causes of Police Behavior Revisited." *Journal of Criminal Justice* 21: 353–382.

Rokeach, M., Miller, M., and Snyder, J. 1971. "The Value Gap Between Police and Policed." *Journal of Social Issues* 27–2: 155–171.

Rubinstein, J. 1973. *City Police.* New York: Farrar, Straus, and Giroux.

Sampson, R., and Lauritsen, J. 1997. "Racial and Ethnic Disparities in Crime and Criminal Justice in the United States." In M. Tonry (ed.), *Ethnicity, Crime, and Immigration: Comparative and Cross-National Perspectives,* pp. 311–374. Chicago: University of Chicago Press.

Sapp, A. D. 1994. "Sexual Misconduct by Police Officers." In T. Barker and D. Carter (eds.), *Police Deviance,* 3rd ed., pp. 187–200. Cincinnati, OH: Anderson Publishing.

Schuck, A. M., and Rabe-Hemp, C. 2005. "Women Police: The Use of Force by and Against Female Officers." *Women and Criminal Justice* 16, 91–117.

Sherman, L. W. 1978. *Scandal and Reform: Controlling Police Corruption.* Berkeley: University of California Press.

———. 1985. "Causes of Police Behavior: The Current State of Quantitative Research." In A. S. Blumberg and E. Niederhoffer (eds.), *The Ambivalent Force,* 3rd ed., pp. 183–195. New York: Holt, Rinehart and Wilson.

———. 1988. "Becoming Bent." In A. Elliston and M. Feldbert (eds.), *Moral Issues in Police Work,* pp. 253–265. Totowa, NJ: Rowan and Allanheld.

Sigler, R. T., and Dees, T. M. 1988. "Public Perception of Petty Corruption in Law Enforcement," *Journal of Police Science and Administration* 6: 14–19.

Skogan, W. and Frydl, K. 2004. *Fairness and Effectiveness in Policing; The Evidence.* Washington, DC: The National Academies Press, National Research Council of the National Academies.

Skolnick, J. H. 1966. *Justice Without Trial.* New York: John Wiley and Sons.

Skolnick, J., and Bayley, D. 1986. *The New Blue Line: Police Innovation in 6 American Cities.* New York: The Free Press.

Smith, B. W., Novak, K. J. and Frank, J. 2002. "Community Policing and the Work Routines of Street-Level Officers." *Criminal Justice Review* 26: 17–37.

Smith, D. 1986. "The Neighborhood Context of Police Behavior." In A. Reiss and M. Tonry (eds.), *Communities and Crime.* Chicago: University of Chicago Press.

———. 1987. "Police Response to Interpersonal Violence: Defining the Parameters of Legal Control." *Social Forces* 65: 767–782.

Sun, I. K., and Payne, B. K. 2004. "Racial Differences in Resolving Conflicts: A Comparison Between Black and White Police Officers." *Crime and Delinquency* 50: 516–541.

Sykes, G. 1986. "Street Justice: A Moral Defense of Order-Maintenance Policing." *Justice Quarterly* 3: 467–512.

———. 1996. "Police Misconduct: A Different Day and Different Challenges." *Subject to Debate: A Newsletter of the Police Executive Research Forum* March, April. 10–3: 1, 4–5.

Teplin, L. A. 1984. "Criminalizing Mental Disorder: The Comparative Arrest Rates of the Mentally Ill." *American Psychologist* 39: 794–803.

Terrill, W., and Reisig, M. D. 2003. "Neighborhood Context and Police Use of Force." *Journal of Research in Crime and Delinquency* 40: 291–323.

Tillyer, R., Engel, R. S., and Cherkauskas, J. C. 2009. "Best Practices in Vehicle Stop Data Collection and Analysis." *Policing: An International Journal of Police Strategies and Management* 33: 69–92.

Van Maanen, J. 1973. "Observations on the Making of Policeman." *Human Organization* 32, 407–418.

———. 1978. "The Asshole." In P. K. Manning and J. Van Maanen (eds.), *Policing: A View From the Streets,* pp. 221–238. Santa Monica, CA: Goodyear Publishing.

Visher, C. A. 1983. "Gender, Police Arrest Decisions, and Notions of Chivalry." *Criminology.*

Walker, S. 1984. "Broken Windows' and Fractured History: The Use and Misuse of History in Recent Patrol Analysis." *Justice Quarterly* 1: 57–90.

Wasserman, R. 1992. "Government Setting." In G. Garmire (ed.), *Local Government Police Management,* 2nd ed. Washington, DC: International City Management Association.

Westley, W. A. 1953. "Violence and the Police." *American Journal of Sociology* 59: 34–42.

———. 1970. *Violence and the Police.* Cambridge, MA: MIT Press.

Wilson, J. Q. 1968. *Varieties of Police Behavior.* Cambridge, MA: Harvard University Press.

Wilson, J. Q., and Kelling, G. 1982. "Broken Windows: The Police and Neighborhood Safety." *Atlantic Monthly* 127: 29–38.

Withrow, B. L. 2006. *Racial Profiling: From Rhetoric to Reason.* Upper Saddle River, NJ: Pearson Prentice Hall.

Worden, R. 1989. "Situational and Attitudinal Explanations of Police Behavior: A Theoretical Reappraisal and Empirical Assessment." *Law and Society Review* 23: 667–711.

Zhao, J., and Hassell, K. D. 2005. "Policing Styles and Organizational Priorities: Retesting Wilson's Theory of Local Political Culture." *Police Quarterly 8*, 411–430.

CHAPTER 10

Force and Coercion

CHAPTER OUTLINE

- Police–Citizen Interactions
    - Context of Force
    - National Estimates on Police Use of Force
- Learning to Use Force
    - Training
    - Areas of Training
    - Police Culture and the Use of Force
    - Controversy and the Use of Force
- Inappropriate Force
    - Brutality and Excessive Force
    - Physical and Psychological Force in Police
    - History
    - Frequency of Excessive Force and Brutality
    - Brutality in the Twenty-First Century
- Deadly Force
    - Individual and Situational Factors
    - Environmental and Departmental Variations
    - Racial Considerations
    - Legal and Policy Changes
- Summary
- Critical Thinking Questions
- References

- coercion
- command voice
- conducted energy devices (CED)
- continuum of force
- deadly force
- defense-of-life policy

- excessive force
- extra-legal police aggression
- fleeing-felon rule
- less lethal weapons
- mere presence
- officer survival

- physical force
- police brutality
- psychological force
- third degree
- use of force
- verbal force

THE **USE OF FORCE** is central to the police craft. Police carry the legal authority to maintain order, demand compliance, stop and detain people, and even kill if necessary. They are granted this authority to shield victims from dangerous felons; to control unruly, hostile, or physically abusive citizens; and to protect against immediate threats to human life.

Use of force is the most controversial aspect of the legal authority of the police. Yet its necessity is inescapable. It is a skill and a means to an end—the preservation of orderly social relations in accordance with societal laws and norms. Consequently, police use of force in the United States should be considered in the broader context of how it contributes to democratic relations among citizens.

Where does the right to use force come from? How can society reconcile the use of force with the democratic principles of freedom and equality? In 1970, Egon Bittner, briefly discussed in Chapter 1, provided important insights into the use of force. According to Bittner, the use of force can be justified in two ways. The first is self-defense: people can use force to defend themselves if they have a realistic belief that they are in danger. The second is based on the inherent police power to address matters of health, welfare, order, and safety; that is, the police are a "mechanism for the distribution of situationally justified force in society" (Bittner 1995, 129).

Why does society need a police mechanism for the distribution of force? Over its history, U.S. society has moved away from the use of force toward the use of democratic, rational processes for solving problems and disagreements among citizens. Yet it is impossible to abandon altogether the use of force in the pursuit of democratic justice. To preserve democratic processes, society grants to police an exclusive right that is not permitted to other citizens: the use of force to achieve democratic ends.

Many students of police behavior think that "force" refers only to violent behavior by the police. That is incorrect. Force, or **coercion**, occurs any time the police require citizens to act in a particular way. Force can be very mild, such as a simple request to see a driver's license. Even a request, however, is coercive because it carries with it the authority of the state to back up the request with greater force and the implicit recognition, by citizen and officer alike, that "no" is not an acceptable answer. Because the police carry the governmental authority to intervene in a citizen's activities, all police–citizen interactions carry elements of force or coercion, even when officers are not consciously trying to be forceful.

Police use of force and its justification are determined by two factors. The first is formal training based on state law, local departmental regulations, and due process constraints. The second factor is local police cultures, which represent understandings of police territorial responsibilities, danger, and the control of unpredictable situations.

This chapter examines how often police use force, police training on the use of force, and police culture before turning to the most difficult and controversial topics: excessive use of force and deadly force.

Police–Citizen Interactions

How often do encounters between police and citizens become situations in which force is used? Information is provided by a number of scholarly studies, including a recent series of surveys conducted by the BJS.

Context of Force

One of the most extensive and important studies of police–citizen encounters was conducted over 40 years ago by Reiss (1967). He reported on more than 5,000 observations of police–citizen interactions that took place in areas that were racially diverse and had different crime rates. About 86 percent of the encounters were reactive, resulting from citizen requests. About 14 percent of the encounters were proactive, initiated by police officers. Police were more likely to experience antagonism or injury in proactive encounters, primarily because, unlike in reactive situations, the person or persons they stopped did not request assistance from the police.

Reiss also found that approximately 60 percent of citizens behaved in either a detached or a civil manner toward police, about 30 percent were agitated (mildly upset), and about 10 percent were antagonistic. Almost all such antagonism came from suspects. Officers behaved in a businesslike or routine manner in about 74 percent of the encounters, were personal (jovial or humorous) in about 15 percent, and were hostile or derisive in about 11 percent. Reiss also noted that police behavior was closely related to citizen behavior; police were more likely to be hostile or derisive when citizens were agitated or antagonistic. The importance of a citizen's attitude in the exercise of police discretion was noted in Chapter 9.

During the 5,000-plus encounters, the police made only 225 arrests (less than 5 percent). About 50 percent of the persons arrested openly challenged police authority; the challenge, however, was more likely to be verbal than physical. Of those arrested, 98 (42 percent) were treated "firmly," while only 21 (9 percent) were handled with "gross" force. These figures mean that in all the police–citizen encounters observed, only about 2 percent involved any type of physical force. None involved the use of lethal, or deadly, force.

Reiss's research suggested that police–citizen encounters were most likely to result from citizen requests for help and that, in most cases, police treated citizens in a businesslike or routine manner. Most encounters were like those of any business providing a service to a client; they involved exchanges of information in a friendly or civil manner. Police were rarely antagonistic toward citizens, and when they were, it was typically in response to citizen-initiated hostilities. Overall, police officers infrequently made arrests, and when they did, they rarely used physical force.

Another important study of police–citizen encounters was conducted by Sykes and Brent (1983), who analyzed more than 3,000 police–citizen encounters. They identified three approaches to interacting with citizens, which he referred to as methods of regulation or supervision. The three methods of regulation are as follows:

1. *Definitional:* Officer asks questions or makes accusations. Serves to define the situation as an officer chooses by compelling citizens to focus on officer's question or accusation. Can also divert citizens' attention as a form of "cooling off."
2. *Imperative:* Officer gives order. Officer acts in a commanding way and "His force is in his grammatical form, his tone of voice, his emphasis." (Sykes and Brent 1983, 63)
3. *Coercive:* Officer threatens or uses force. For example, display of readiness, drawn weapon, holding someone back, or actual use of force.

Sykes and Brent found that the most common initial police response was definitional, occurring about 83 percent of the time. Police almost always spoke first when dealing with citizens; thus, they had the opportunity to direct the discussion with their questions. The second most common initial response was imperative, occurring in about 17 percent of encounters. Researchers did not find the coercive response to be used initially in any police–citizen encounter. It was eventually used, however, if citizens did not cooperate with the officers. Even then, the most common officer response was to repeat the initial approach one or more times to obtain cooperation.

From Sykes and Brent's research, it is clear that officers first try the definitional approach and, if a citizen does not cooperate, will frequently repeat it. If cooperation is not forthcoming or the citizen's behavior becomes threatening or too abusive, officers will become imperative and coercive. What is not clear, however, is how this sequence should proceed in a given situation. Should the department provide specific guidance, or should it be left to an officer's discretion? For instance, if one officer uses the definitional approach several times with an uncooperative citizen, is this officer "better" than one who uses it only once before making threats or using force? How can one judge which approach is better?

Bayley (1986) studied police interactions with citizens in Denver. He focused on two types of situations (domestic disturbances and traffic stops) in which officers made tactical choices about appropriate actions. This discussion will focus only on the traffic stops because of recent changes in the manner in which many police departments respond to domestic violence calls. Bayley divided police–citizen interactions into three stages: the *contact stage* describes tactical choices made when officers first approach citizens; the *processing stage* is concerned with decisions made during the interaction between contact and exit; the *exit stage* describes strategies used to end contact with the citizen.

Bayley identified several contact actions by police officers in traffic stops. In some situations, more than one action was used. These actions are listed in Table 10.1. Many are similar to the findings of Sykes and Brent.

Asking drivers or passengers questions or for documents (definitional approach) was the initial police action in a large majority of cases. Giving orders (imperative approach) was also sometimes used. Bayley's findings revealed the complicated nature of police–citizen transactions. In the three areas—contact, processing, and exit—officers used at least 28 different actions. By carefully reviewing the first actions, one can see how the use of coercion is part and parcel of police work, even when not directly used. The initial acts all involve various levels of coercion, from the relatively mild "asked passengers for documents," which

TABLE 10.1   Actions at a Traffic Stop

INITIAL ACTIONS OF POLICE OFFICERS AT TRAFFIC STOPS	
ACTION	**USE (%)**
1. Asked driver for documents	88.4
2. Explained reason for stop	28.0
3. Asked driver whether he knew reason for stop	25.6
4. Had driver leave the vehicle	20.1
5. Allowed driver to leave vehicle	16.5
6. Asked passengers for documents	15.9
7. Allowed or ordered passengers out of vehicle	9.2
8. Ordered driver and/or passengers to remain in vehicle	4.2
PROCESSING ACTIONS OF POLICE OFFICERS AT TRAFFIC STOPS	
ACTION	**USE (%)**
1. Checked whether vehicle and driver were wanted	59.1
2. Discussed nature of traffic violation	27.4
3. Searched vehicle from outside or inside	25.0
4. Gave roadside sobriety test	12.8
5. Body-searched driver and/or passenger	7.3
6. Questioned drivers and/or passengers	3.7
EXIT ACTIONS OF POLICE OFFICERS AT TRAFFIC STOPS	
ACTION	**USE (%)**
1. Issued traffic citation	43.3
2. Gave admonishment or warning only	20.7
3. Arrested driver (DUI or other offense)	15.8
4. Released without admonishment or warning	13.8
5. Issued citation and gave warning	12.8
6. Completed "contact" card (recorded information about driver)	9.8
7. Transported or arranged transportation for driver	2.4
8. Impounded vehicle	1.8
9. Insisted driver proceed on foot	1.8
10. Arrested passenger	1.8

Totals do not add up to 100% because more than one alternative was used in many traffic stops. In addition, some categories have been combined.

Source: D. H. Bayley, "The Tactical Choices of Police Patrol Officers." *Journal of Criminal Justice* (1986) 14: 329–348.

is not coercive, but carries the potential for a stronger response, to the more significant "ordered driver to remain in vehicle." Under processing actions, coercive behavior includes "body search." Exit actions range from the mildly coercive "gave admonishment" to the quite serious "arrested driver." Moreover, the original stop itself represents a seizure, an aggressive intervention of the state into the affairs of citizens.

This research provides an understanding of how practical applications of force are integral to police work. This realization may be uncomfortable for citizens. Yet, if we fail to see how force is intertwined with the daily routines of police work, we will not understand what the police are about.

Bayley and Garofalo (1989) studied 62 police officers in New York City to determine the extent to which they used some type of violence, including verbal aggression. They identified 467 potentially violent situations, of which 168 were proactive. Of these situations, although reports suggested possible violence, such as a fight or the reported presence of weapons, only 78 (17 percent) actually involved visible conflict when the police arrived. In 70 of these cases, the violence was not physical but involved only verbal threats or gestures. Police used physical force against citizens 37 times (8 percent), and citizens used it against the police 11 times. Police force was almost always limited to "grabbing and restraining." Police use of deadly force was not observed.

Most recently, Terrill (2001, 2003) studied police use of force in 3,544 police encounters with suspected offenders/disputants in Indianapolis and St. Petersburg. He found that police used verbal force in nearly 60 percent of encounters, patdowns and handcuffing in about 10 percent of encounters, and greater levels of force in about 5 percent of encounters. Only examining arrest cases, Terrill found that officers used force in about 19 percent of the arrest situations. About 12 percent of all police–suspect encounters involved some form of citizen resistance, although only 3 percent involved physical resistance on the part of citizens. Of those arrested, however, 29 percent displayed some form of resistance, with 12 percent engaging in physical resistance.

These studies indicate that, while police work rarely involves the use of significant levels of violence, the use or threat of force is ever present. The use of violence is one of the most important areas of study. The potential consequences to both the victim and the officer can be severe, including emotional trauma and the possibility of either physical injury or death, particularly when the police use deadly force.

National Estimates on Police Use of Force

The Police–Public Contact Survey (PPCS). In an attempt to assess overall use of force by the police during police–citizen contacts, the BJS developed a national questionnaire (Greenfeld, Langan, and Smith 1997). The PPCS, conducted every 3 years since 1995, surveys a nationally representative sample of residents age 16 or older, asking about their contacts with the police during the 12 months prior to the interview. In the 2005 survey (most recent available), a total of 63,943 individuals were interviewed (Durose, Smith, and Langan 2007). The survey asked about the prevalence of citizen contacts with the police, reasons for citizen contacts, and police actions during citizen contacts. Researchers estimated from the interviews that 43.5 million citizens had face-to-face contact with a police officer during the previous year. Traffic stops were the most likely reason for contact with police.

An estimated 707,520 people had force used or threatened against them during their most recent encounter with police. Although this number may seem large, it represents only 1.6 percent of the citizens police came into contact with. Of the contacts in which the police reportedly used force, over half (55 percent) involved some type of physical force (e.g., grab, kick or hit, pointing gun, chemical spray). The majority (83 percent) of citizens felt that the force used against them was excessive, although almost 17 percent of people who experienced police use of force reported provoking the officer to use force (e.g., threatening or resisting arrest). Additional survey findings from 2005 are presented in Table 10.2.

PPCS and the Survey of Inmates in Local Jails. While the PPCS is an important and useful step forward in collecting data on police use of force, Hickman and his colleagues (2008) argue that it likely underestimates the amount of force used by police. They point out that the PPCS does not survey individuals who recently had contact with police but who were incarcerated during the time of the survey, a high-risk use-of-force population. To overcome this limitation, Hickman and his colleagues combined the 2002 PPCS data

---

TABLE 10.2 Highlights From the 2005 Police–Public Contact Survey

INCIDENCE AND PREVALENCE OF CONTACT WITH POLICE

- An estimated 43.5 million U.S. residents age 16 or older (about 19 percent of all persons of this age) had at least one face-to-face contact with a police officer during 2005.

- Of the 43.5 million persons with police contact during 2005:

  - 71.5% had one contact.
  - 28.5% had two or more contacts.
  - The average number of face-to-face contacts per resident was 1.6.

REASONS FOR CONTACT WITH POLICE

- Sixty percent reported their latest (most recent) contact in 2005 was initiated by police. The remaining 40 percent of contacts were initiated by the resident or someone other than the police (such as a family member or acquaintance).

- The most common reason for police contact was being the driver of a motor vehicle that was pulled over by police, accounting for almost 18 million contacts.

- About 24 percent indicated the reason for the contact was to report a crime or other problem.

POLICE ACTIONS DURING CONTACTS

- In 2005 about 426,996 (2.4 percent) of the 17.79 million drivers stopped by police were arrested. Just over 57 percent of drivers stopped by police received a ticket.

- An estimated 307,063 (43.4 percent) force incidents involved the police pushing or grabbing the resident. An additional 8.6 percent of the force incidents involved the police kicking or hitting the resident.

- About half of the estimated 707,520 residents were shouted or cursed at, threatened with force, or had some other type of force used (e.g., chemical spray).

- Most (83 percent) of the people involved in a police-use-of-force incident thought the force used or threatened was excessive.

Source: Adapted from M. R. Durose, E. L. Smith, and P. A. Langan, *Contacts Between Police and the Public, 2005* (Washington, DC: Bureau of Justice Statistics, 2007). Available online at http://bjs.ojp.usdoj.gov/index.cfm?ty=pbdetail&iid=653.

with data from the 2002 Survey of Inmates in Local Jails (SILJ), which involved surveys of a nationally representative sample of 6,982 local jail inmates. Using the combined data, they found that 1.7 percent of the estimated 45.7 million police contacts involved force or the threat of force (beyond handcuffing) compared with an estimate of 1.5 percent for the 2002 PPCS alone. Overall, police used force in 20 percent of arrests compared with about 19 percent using the PPCS alone. In total, they estimated that police officers used force 760,000 times in 2002 compared with 664,458 times using the PPCS alone, an undercount of 95,542 uses of force. Despite the SILJ only accounting for 1 percent of all police contacts, they represented 13 percent of force incidents. Clearly, the PPCS alone underestimates the use of force by police officers.

These studies, covering different police departments over a 30-year period and including national estimates, show that police employ verbal force and the threat of physical force relatively often, but their use of actual physical force is much less common. In Voices From the Field, James Fyfe discusses his perspective on police use of force and use-of-force training. Dr. Fyfe, a former professor and retired NYPD lieutenant, was widely regarded as the nation's leading authority on police use of force during his long academic and professional career.

Learning to Use Force

The police learn about threats to their safety and the use of force both formally and informally. Formally, police are given direction by their department, including through training. Informally, police officers learn, from other officers on the job, the accepted methods and ways of thinking about their safety and the use of force. This section will look at these two different but related ways in which police departments provide direction in the use of force: formal training in levels of force and informal, cultural standards about the use of force in routine encounters.

Training

Officers are trained to use a **continuum of force**, from the least to the greatest, to match the intensity of a suspect's resistance (Terrill 2001). Ideally an officer employs the least force necessary to solve a problem, restrain a suspect, or control a situation. Skolnick and Fyfe's (1993) description of levels of force is adapted below. Table 10.3 presents the use-of-force continuum used by the New York City Police Department.

1. *Mere presence.* At the lowest level of force, the simple presence of an officer is usually enough to control most situations. **Mere presence** operates on the assumption that the visible authority of the state is sufficient to deter criminal wrongdoing. As a wide body of research has shown, however, the passive authority of the state alone is insufficient to deter all illegal behavior or gain compliance from everyone. As Wilson (1968) observed 30 years ago, officers have to get personally involved—they have to develop personal skills in the use of coercion to control some kinds of problems.

2. *Verbalization.* This stage is sometimes called **verbal force**. When officers speak, they are taught to do so persuasively. Officers verbalize their commands in "adult-to-adult" communications. That is, they communicate on the presumption that they are talking to adults who will understand and comply with their requests. *Example:* "Sir, would you please step out of the car."

3. *Command voice.* **Command voice** is more vibrant and is issued in the form of an order. Skolnick and Fyfe (1993) provide the following example: "Sir, I asked you for your vehicle papers once. Now I'm *telling* you to give them to me *now.*"

4. *Firm grips.* Physical grasps of the body direct a suspect when and where to move. They are intended to control a suspect's physical movements but not intended to cause pain. They can be restraining, holding, or lifting. *Example:* Two people are attempting to fight. An officer grabs one person to hold him back, or two or more officers working as a team may separate the two people or "swarm" one person.

5. *Pain compliance.* A suspect's compliance is gained by causing pain. Various techniques are taught that enable officers to cause pain without lasting injury. *Example:* A person the officer is attempting to handcuff pulls away, and the officer twists the suspect's arm to put on the cuffs.

6. *Impact techniques.* Impact techniques involve physical contact between the suspect and an officer's body or less lethal device. They are intended to knock down or incapacitate a dangerous suspect who has not responded to other techniques. Included among impact techniques are increasingly popular less lethal weapons, including beanbags shot from a shotgun, OC pepper spray, and the Taser. *Example:* A suspect under the influence of drugs resists the police so vigorously that she cannot be controlled. She is struck with a baton, or sprayed in the face, or stunned with an electrical weapon such as the Taser. More technologically advanced, **less lethal weapons** are currently being developed. For example, sticky foams may be fired from a large gun from 35 feet away. They act like contact cement, sticking the suspect to the floor or to whatever he or she touches. "Dazzler" light and laser weapons use brilliant pulses of light to distract, disorient, and control violent suspects and potentially violent crowds (Miller 1995, 485–486).

7. *Deadly force.* The highest level is force that is capable of killing a suspect. The purpose is usually to incapacitate a suspect who presents an immediate and potentially deadly threat to another person, not to kill the suspect. Death, however, is a frequent by-product. Skolnick and Fyfe (1993) describe three uses of **deadly force**: the carotid hold (or sleeper hold), which induces unconsciousness in a suspect and can be deadly in practice; the bar arm-control hold, in which the forearm is squeezed against the neck to cut off the flow of air; and the use of a firearm. *Example:* A suspect vigorously resists arrest, and the officer gets behind him and "chokes him out" to gain control of the suspect and place him in handcuffs.

As discussed earlier, there are often differences of opinion concerning what is and is not appropriate when police force is used. One important factor in determining appropriate use is the actual or perceived threat posed by the person resisting police authority (Terrill 2005). This threat potential is assessed not only in terms of the nature of the threat or actual resistance, but also by the physical size of the person in question and whether he or she is under the influence of drugs or alcohol or might have a weapon. In addition, any prior knowledge about the person and the potential for danger would be important. Also, if the police officer is biased or has had "dangerous" experiences with members of a minority group, then certain types of minority persons (e.g., young, black men) may be perceived by that officer to be potentially more dangerous than other people, an issue we will address shortly.

VOICES FROM THE FIELD

James J. Fyfe

Former Deputy Commissioner for Training, New York City Police Department

Question: What are some of the guiding principles of training officers in the use or force?

Answer: Training officers to use force should be based on the principle that, since the primary police responsibility is to protect life, they should use as little force as possible and should do everything reasonably possible to avoid using force at all.

This training should not be confused with the legal standard used by prosecutors in deciding whether to bring criminal charges against officers who have used force. The criminal law test typically is whether, at the instant they used force, officers reasonably feared for their safety. This standard distinguishes between use of force that is criminal and use of force that is not, but is an inadequate measure of acceptable police conduct. Like doctors, truck drivers, and professors, police officers can do many unprofessional and inappropriate things that do not reach the level of crime. In good police agencies, therefore, the test of whether police have used force reasonably involves examining whether, from the time they became aware that they were likely to encounter someone in an adversarial situation until they actually came face-to-face with the person, the officer tried to structure their meeting in ways that made use of force less likely. This is not as confusing as it sounds. In plainer English: a police shooting that occurs because an officer unnecessarily forced a confrontation and then had to shoot his way out of it is unacceptable even if it is not criminal.

Thus, training must emphasize tactics. We do this by encouraging officers to make certain that, before contacting potentially violent persons or groups, they have enough help on the scene to deter attacks on officers. Officers must also be trained to position themselves in ways that let adversaries know that they can't win any confrontation and that they have no choice but to submit to the police. For example, we train officers to respond to robbery calls by stopping their cars out of sight of the scene; by approaching covertly on foot; by taking cover behind parked cars or other objects; and by waiting to surprise suspects when they are totally exposed as they walk out of their victim's doors. When a shouted police command causes such bad guys suddenly to find that they are in the gunsights of officers they can hardly see, they virtually always surrender, so that no force is necessary to take them into custody.

This kind of bloodless intimidation is extremely effective with rational offenders who want to live another day. Not all the potentially violent people police contact are so rational, however. When dealing with the mentally ill or emotionally disturbed—something NYPD officers do once every 7.3 minutes—officers must try to avoid intimidation, because it is likely only to make things worse. Consequently, officers must be trained to avoid frightening emotionally disturbed persons. They must also be trained to avoid cultural taboos that may anger, or create confrontation with, members of some new immigrant groups.

Training must be precise and must also put flesh onto the vague phrases—like *reasonable and necessary*—found in most legal standards. In most cases, police departments do this by adopting some sort of scale of escalating force and matching levels of force to the provocation or condition involved. The one included in our NYPD training (see Table 10.3) tells officers that the only legitimate purpose of force is to stop the objectionable types of conduct listed in the scale's left column.

This scale does not mention police canines. This is so because virtually none of our patrol officers is accompanied by dogs. But NYPD's canine officers are trained that dogs—who are easily capable of causing serious injury every time they bite someone—rate only

(Continued)

slightly below deadly force on this scale. Our canines, therefore, are deployed only in extremely serious situations that might otherwise make it necessary to use firearms.

Force training must continue throughout officers' careers and, as I have suggested, should focus primarily on teaching officers to avoid force whenever possible. This is no easy task—it's very easy to teach officers to use their batons, sprays, and guns. But the well-trained, *really good street cops*—the role models for their colleagues—almost always can get the job done without having to use any of these devices or techniques. When the circumstances make this impossible, such officers training causes them instinctively to use no more than the appropriate degree of force from this scale.

Dr. James Fyfe was a professor at American University, Temple University, and John Jay College of Criminal Justice.

TABLE 10.3 The New York City Police Department Scale of Escalating Force

PROVOCATION OR CONDITION	APPROPRIATE FORCE RESPONSE
Imminent threat of death or serious physical injury	Deadly force: Usually the firearm
Threatened or potential lethal assault	Drawn and/or displayed firearm
Physical assault likely to cause physical injury	Impact techniques: Batons, fists, and feet
Threatened or potential physical assault likely to cause physical injury	Pepper spray
Minor physical resistance: grappling, going limp, pulling or pushing away, etc.	Compliance techniques: Wrestling holds and grips designed to physically overpower subjects and/or to inflict physical pain that ends when the technique is stopped and that causes no lasting injury
Verbal resistance: Failure to comply with directions, etc.	Firm grips on arms, shoulders, etc., that cause no pain, but are meant to guide people (e.g., away from a fight; toward a police car).
Refusal to comply with requests or attempts at persuasion (see below)	Command voice: Firmly given directions (e.g., "I asked for your license, registration, and proof of insurance, Sir. Now I am telling you that if you don't give them to me, I will have to arrest you."
Minor violations or disorderly conditions involving no apparent threats to officers or others	Verbal persuasion: Requests for compliance (e.g., "May I see your license, registration and proof of insurance, Sir?")
Orderly public places	Professional presence: The officer on post deters crime and disorder; the Highway Unit deters speeding

Areas of Training

The training regimen for the use of force is elaborate. Particular areas of training related to the use of force are discussed below.

Firearms. For most police trainees, the most popular training is in firearms (Marion 1998). It is frequently the highlight of the academy, although continuing (in-service) firearms training for veteran officers has been less systematic and probably less effective (Morrison 2003). Traditional firearms training is gradually giving way to situationally based training, which includes simulated firearms scenarios and the use of mobile targets. "Shoot–don't shoot" scenarios are used to teach officers to exercise restraint when using deadly force. Among the most popular of these are Firearms Training Systems and Professional Range Instruction Simulators, which present trainees with scenarios whose outcomes are manipulated by a specialist. Scenarios are presented whose outcomes are uncertain and typically call for the unholstering of a weapon. Many outcomes, however, do not call for the discharge of a weapon, and officers learn to react quickly so as *not* to shoot. When they shoot, a laser mounted on the weapon shows the number of target hits and locations of the hits.

OC Spray. Officers are required to train in the use of oleoresin (OC) spray. Some departments require that trainees submit to being sprayed; in others, being sprayed is voluntary. OC's location on the force continuum also varies. In the continuum presented in Table 10.3, it is located at level 6 as an impact technique. Some departments, however, consider it less powerful than a baton. The North Carolina Justice Academy, for example, locates OC spray just above mace and below hard hands, the PR-24 (baton), and swarming techniques (Lamb and Friday 1997). According to this perspective, officers are taught to use OC spray when they think a person is about to become belligerent to prevent the escalation of force (Trimmer 1993).

Taser. The so-called Taser fits in the category of **CEDs**, which are defined as weapons "primarily designed to disrupt a subject's central nervous system by means of deploying electrical energy sufficient to cause uncontrolled muscle contractions and override an individual's voluntary motor responses" (Police Executive Research Forum 2005). These weapons have become extremely popular in recent years and have largely superseded OC/pepper spray in many departments as the preferred option for dealing with belligerent and resisting subjects. Policies and practices vary, however, in regard to where the CED or Taser should be placed on the use-of-force continuum (Government Accountability Office 2005). The Police Executive Research Forum published 52 CED policy and training guidelines in 2005; several of the guidelines most pertinent to training are presented in Inside Policing 10.1.

Self-Defense. Officers are taught a variety of techniques for self-defense. Marion (1998) describes self-defense training as follows:

> Recruits may be taught some "come-along" or "hand holds" (Peak 1993) as well as pressure points. By the end of the University Academy, recruits learn the Infra-Orbital [under the base of the nose], the Mandibular Angle [behind the ear] and the Hypoglossal [under the jaw] pressure points (Faulkner 1994). They also learn take-downs and proper handcuffing techniques. The force continuum is stressed in self-defense training, where cadets are taught to use no more force than necessary to subdue a subject. But once again, officer safety is the primary concern of all the training. *(1998, 68)*

INSIDE POLICING 10.1 CED Training Guidelines

- CEDs should only be used against persons who are actively resisting or exhibiting active aggression or to prevent individuals from harming themselves or others. CEDs should not be used against a passive suspect.
- Agencies should create stand-alone policies and training curriculum for CEDs and all less lethal weapons and ensure that they are integrated with the department's overall use-of-force policy.
- Departments should not solely rely on training curriculum provided by a CED manufacturer. Agencies should ensure that manufacturers' training does not contradict their use-of-force policies and values. Agencies should ensure that their CED curriculum is integrated into their overall use-of-force systems.
- Training protocols should emphasize that multiple activations and continuous cycling of a CED appear to increase the risk of death or serious injury and should be avoided where practical.
- Training should include recognizing the limitations of CED activation and being prepared to transition to other force options as needed.
- Supervisors and command staff should receive CED awareness training so they can make educated decisions about the administrative investigations they review.
- Exposure to CED activation in training should be voluntary; all officers agreeing to be subjected to CED activation should be apprised of the risks associated with exposure to a CED activation.
- Audits should be conducted to ensure that all officers who carry CEDs have attended initial and recertification training.

SOURCE: Police Executive Research Forum, "PERF Conducted Energy Device Policy and Training Guidelines for Consideration," available on-line at http://www.policeforum.org/upload/PERF-CED-Guidelines-Updated-10–25-05%5B1%5D_715866088_1230200514040.pdf.

Officer Survival. Central to many training programs are classes on **officer survival**. Such classes deal with the major risks faced by police officers—officer stress, suicide, and threats. Officers are taught how to deal with the murder of a partner, about the police officers' memorial in Washington, DC, and about the federal pension their spouse will receive if they are killed. They are exposed to the bureaucratic paperwork associated with death. Extremely violent encounters, although rare in practice, are central to training. Officer survival is also a component of many other classes. Classes on police procedure instruct officers that concerns about safety provide a legal justification for a wide variety of actions, including patdowns. Finally, it is not unusual for officers to see training films emphasizing the hazards of police work.

Flashlights. A flashlight is infrequently thought of as a weapon, yet many officers use flashlights in just that way. For example, about two thirds of 365 impact weapon incidents in the Los Angeles County Sheriff's Department over a 5-year period involved flashlights rather than batons (Anderson 2003). As McEwen (1997) noted, policies on the use of flashlights are often ambiguous. Some departments provide policies forbidding the use of flashlights as weapons. When a flashlight is considered a weapon, it is regarded only as a backup.

The policy in one department McEwen assessed stated that "the department does not recognize the flashlight as a formal policy weapon." Recognizing that it may be needed in some circumstances, the policy further observed that "when a flashlight is utilized in an application of force, whether to restrain or to effect an arrest, or in defense against an attack, it will be considered a weapon and all requirements pertaining to the use of force and the reporting of such force will be applicable" (1997, 51). McEwen concludes that flashlights will be used as less lethal weapons and that policy needs to recognize this fact and bring flashlights under use-of-force policy.

Canines. An emerging area of interest in the use of force is the use of K-9 dog patrols. Many police departments use police canines for a number of purposes: to search for drugs, explosives, and individuals who might be trying to avoid or escape from the police and to control individuals and crowds (Golden and Walker 2002). Many officers also believe that the use of dogs to search for suspects who might be armed reduces the possibility that officers will be injured or killed. Although they are not trained to do so, some handlers permit their dogs to bite as a "reward."

The use of canines varies by department. Some departments do not recognize them as a level of force; others do. K-9's are listed by the North Carolina Justice Academy at a level just above swarm techniques and below deadly force (Lamb and Friday 1997). Campbell, Berk, and Fyfe (1998) argue that the widespread use of canines in some departments requires a revision in thinking about the use of force. In a study of the LAPD and the Los Angeles Sheriff's Department, they found that the use of canines was routine, and encounters often ended with bites, many serious. Inside Policing 10.2 describes the uses associated with canines.

Police Culture and the Use of Force

The use of force is also affected by informal standards of police culture. As noted in Chapter 1, police organizational culture refers to the assumptions police have developed in learning to cope with the problems they confront, including when and how to use force. These assumptions include accepted practices and rules of conduct under different situations as well as way of interpreting their work. Police culture provides officers with commonsense ways of thinking about activities (McNulty 1994). Reuss-Ianni refers to this as "precinct street cop culture," which carries the "values, and thus the ends, toward which officers individually and in task groups strive" (1983, 8). Although each department has its own culture, Crank (1998) has identified a wide variety of cultural themes, or building blocks of culture, that are so similar across departments that police officers generally can be described as participating in a police culture. Arguably the best illustration of how culture influences the use and interpretation of force is provided by the work of Jennifer Hunt.

Hunt (1985) described how police rely on informal, cultural standards in the use of force. By focusing too much on legal definitions of force, society tends to overlook the "understandings and standards police officers actively employ in the course of their work" (316). Hunt observed that police have *working notions of normal force,* which are standards of acceptable force learned on the street. They are different from what police learn in training; for example, that they should not hit a person on the head or neck because it could be lethal.

> On the street, in contrast, police conclude that they must hit wherever it causes the most damage in order to incapacitate the suspect before they themselves are harmed. New officers also learn that they will earn the respect of their veteran coworkers by not observing legal niceties in using force, but by being "aggressive" and using whatever force is necessary in a given situation. *(1985, 319)*

INSIDE POLICING 10.2 **Canines and Police Use of Force**

Should dogs be thought of as a kind of police use of force? Campbell, Berk, and Fyfe (1998) argue that they should. The use of dogs is common. Moreover, dog bites are frequently severe. Consider the following observations:

> The data show that using police dogs as a means of force has been common in the Los Angeles area. From the middle of 1990 through the middle of 1992, LAPD's (Los Angeles Police Department) police dogs (which varied in number between 13 and 15) bit 44 percent of the 539 suspects they helped to apprehend. A total of 37 percent ($n = 86$) were bitten badly enough that they were admitted to hospitals. As far as we have been able to determine, this was a greater number of hospitalizing injuries than was caused by all the noncanine officers in the department combined during the period. In 1990 alone, this bite-to-use ratio—the LAPD term for the percentage of persons bitten among those apprehended after canines had arrived at the scene—was 81 percent. For the LASD (Los Angeles Sheriffs Department), the bite-to-use ratio was 36 percent (119 bitten of 335 persons apprehended) over the slightly different period we studied. No deaths have resulted in Los Angeles, but some victims were permanently disfigured, whereas others have experienced persistent physiological and/or psychological problems. Indeed, survivors of police shootings in Los Angeles (and the vast majority do survive) typically have injuries less severe and less enduring than are suffered by the LAPD's canine bite victims. *(Campbell, Berk, and Fyfe 1998, 543)*

The study observes that the use of canines frequently lacks the rigor of policy that accompanies the use of other kinds of less lethal and lethal weaponry. When policies were in place, they were enforced in an incomplete and perfunctory way. Moreover, minority group members suffered a disproportionate number of dog bites, raising the specter that they might be used in a discriminatory way (see also Beers 1992).

The authors concluded that because of the hazardous and injurious consequence of dog bites, the implementation and review of department policy regarding canines should be conducted in a rigorous manner with other uses of force.

Force is normal, or acceptable, under two circumstances. First, it is normal because it is the natural outcome of strong, even uncontrollable, emotions normally arising from certain routine police activities. Second, it is justifiable if it establishes police authority in the face of a threat or is morally appropriate for the type of crime encountered by the officer. When officers use too much force, or when they do not use enough, they are the subject of reprimand, gossip, and avoidance. Hunt (1985) described how normal levels of force are learned in day-to-day practice and the psychological mechanisms that justify the use of force. By carefully considering the influence of culture, the reader can begin to understand how the difference between justified force and excessive force, so important in legal and administrative reviews of police behavior after an incident, is balanced by the ways street officers confront danger and gauge forceful responses.

Controversy and the Use of Force

On occasion, the use of force by police officers may conflict with community standards, legal factors, or departmental policy. These three types of conflicts are considered below.

Type 1: Conflicts With the Community. In Type I conflicts, the law and departmental policy may consider the police use of force appropriate, but a substantial segment of the community does not. Such conflict occurs most often in a minority neighborhood. The relationship between police and some minority citizens may be one of suspicion and distrust, so when the police, particularly officers who are not members of that minority group, use coercion, they have a substantial burden placed on them to prove that the use was appropriate. In these circumstances, incidents of force, even seemingly minor ones, feed into an accumulated reservoir of grievances in which any additional incident, however justified, can provoke community violence, rioting, and other antipolice activity.

An illustration of a case of Type 1 conflict occurred in New York City in 2006. About 4 am On November 25, 2006, the day of his wedding, Sean Bell, an African American, and two friends left a strip club in Queens, New York. They had an altercation with a man outside the club before heading to their car. An undercover police officer who had been working in the club that night overhead part of the argument and suspected that Mr. Bell and his friends were returning to their car to retrieve a gun. The detective followed Mr. Bell and his friends to their car. As the detective later testified, he approached Mr. Bell's car, wearing his police shield on his collar, and shouted police commands. Whatever Mr. Bell heard or saw, he pulled out of the parking spot, grazing the detective, then slammed into an unmarked police mini-van on the street. He backed up onto the sidewalk, hit a gate, and then drove forward, striking the mini-van again. The detective thought a passenger in the front seat was reaching for a gun and opened fire (Dwyer 2008). Four other police officers on the scene also opened fire. The officers fired a total of 50 bullets, striking the driver, Mr. Bell, 4 times, the front seat passenger 13 times, and the man in the back seat twice in the legs. Mr. Bell died in the car, while his two passengers both survived.

The incident generated outrage in the black community in New York, with protests and community leaders calling for an investigation. Two of the officers were charged with manslaughter and another was charged with reckless endangerment. After waiving their right to a jury trial, a State Supreme Court judge found all three officers not guilty. Hundreds protested the verdict and leaders called for a Federal investigation. Federal authorities, citing insufficient evidence, decided not to bring a civil rights case against the officers (Baker and Elgion 2010). A federal wrongful death civil suit is pending against the NYPD and the officers involved (Marzulli 2010). Seven police officers were charged with violating internal NYPD policy (Baker 2008), although a decision on whether to discipline the officers has also not yet been made (Marzulli 2010). As a result of the incident and the public response, the NYPD has been pressured to make policy changes and has already enacted some of the recommendations, including mandatory sobriety tests of officers involved in shootings (Phillips 2008).

Type 2: Conflicts Over Policy. A Type 2 conflict occurs when there are differences between law and departmental policy. For example, a department might decide to overlook illegal immigration because it thinks that enforcement will lead to loss of public support. Policy–law conflicts tend to involve the public. Some segments may favor the law, others the department. An area of considerable concern has to do with high-speed police chases (Alpert et al. 2000; Welch 2002). Consider a description of a chase incident in Tampa, Florida.

In 1994, over 11,000 cars were stolen in Tampa, Florida. In 1995, officers began to chase car thieves, and the number of auto thefts was cut in half. Further, the rate of overall crime dropped by 25 percent, and officers attributed this to the use of stolen cars by felons to commit other crimes. However, police involved in chases had been involved in several accidents. In one of these, officers careened into a utility pole. In another, they knocked a house off its foundation. More troubling, a car driven by a suspect crashed into another car and killed the two German tourists inside. This accident happened less than 3 weeks after a suspected car thief, followed by another sheriff's deputy, hit a car and killed two occupants (Navarro 1995, 18).

Since the 1980s, departments nationally are increasingly restricting high-speed pursuits. Chases require a police department to balance public safety with law enforcement. Unfortunately, these two goals move at cross-purposes sometimes, and increases in law enforcement sometimes threaten the public safety. Chases are dangerous; the suspect, police officers, and innocent bystanders are sometimes injured and killed. Police chases are the "most deadly force" (Alpert and Anderson 1986). Yet, many officers balk at the notion that they should withdraw from a chase and permit a suspected felon to escape. As Alpert (1989, 229) observes, "few would argue that police should not initiate a chase, but that is where the consensus disappears." Wide controversy exists regarding if and when a chase should be curtailed.

The consequences of a Type 2 conflict are usually twofold: Some segments of the community would be pleased by the pursuit policy; others would not. In Tampa, residents facing higher insurance costs and economic loss supported the policy restricting pursuits. Within the police department, however, many officers would probably be angry and upset. Brown (1983), in his study of two large police departments, found substantial differences among officers concerning the appropriate policy for the use of deadly force. In fact, in cities in which organizational policies concerning the use of force are more restrictive than state law, officer morale may become an important issue.

Type 3: Conflicts Between Norms. In a Type 3 conflict, an officer's behavior meets the expectations of some segments of the community but is inconsistent with both law and departmental policy. For example, assume that two police officers are working in a neighborhood that has extensive drug problems. They decide to harass and physically abuse individuals suspected of drug dealing. Such action is clearly illegal and in violation of departmental policy, but it may be applauded by many persons in the neighborhood. In such a situation, the police department might discipline the officers, perhaps even terminate them, and possibly recommend criminal prosecution. But the residents of the neighborhood might protest the action of the department, perhaps vigorously.

Type 3 conflict is most likely to occur when the police department and officers get too close to residents in a particular area and begin to enforce what they consider "neighborhood norms" rather than following the law. Community-oriented policing could result in this type of conflict if not carefully monitored. It remains to be seen whether the police can "resist" citizen pressure to "go outside the law to get the job done."

The examples provided in the three types of conflict illustrate important problems in determining the appropriateness of police behavior. Officers are sometimes required to make choices that will alienate part of their public. There are also many less dramatic examples concerning the exercise of police authority and the use of coercion. And there are many "gray areas." For example, a police officer might stop a citizen for a traffic ticket. If the citizen refuses to give the officer his or her driver's license, the officer must decide how to treat the citizen. At what point in this police–citizen encounter should the officer begin to use coercion? When should verbal threats be made? In many police departments the guidance provided to police officers in these areas is vague or nonexistent. Officers, police managers, and members of the community are likely to have opinions about appropriate behavior in these situations, and at times there will be conflicting expectations among these groups.

A contemporary example involves police use of Tasers. From the police perspective, Tasers contribute to officer safety and are very useful for controlling suspects who are resisting arrest or otherwise threatening officers or others. One recent study documented an 80 to 85 percent effectiveness rate for subduing suspects (White and Ready 2007). From the general public's perspective, Tasers similarly seem beneficial if police are able to use them in lieu of baton strikes or deadly force (firearms) to make arrests and control violent suspects. From this perspective, police are seen as more effective while resorting to lesser levels of force and coercion.

However, if police utilize Tasers preemptively and/or in place of lesser force (command voice, firm grips), it may lead to an increase in overall police use of force, an outcome that might not be regarded as favorable. Minority groups in particular may feel that police use Tasers too freely against them. Also, experience has shown that while Tasers are effective in controlling suspects, they do contribute to deaths in a very small percentage of cases involving suspects who are mentally ill, under the influence of drugs or alcohol, or suffering from heart or respiratory problems (Berenson 2004). It is easy to see how police, legal experts, community leaders, and others might have conflicting opinions about the appropriateness of police use of Tasers.

The recognition that some decisions will have no good outcome may be frustrating for young adults interested in a career in policing. Many individuals approach police work with a clear notion of "good guy versus bad guy" fixed in their minds. Unfortunately, policing is not like that, nor can it be. In a democratic society, as Wilson (1968) observed long ago, the use of force will always be controversial.

Inappropriate Force

In a democracy, police authority is constrained by democratic ideas of fair play. On the one hand, due-process laws provide the legalized means that police are permitted to use to pursue suspected criminals and to deal with citizens and suspects. Department policy provides the administrative means, such as the use-of-force continuum, that police are supposed to follow in their day-to-day activities (Terrill et al. 2003). On the other hand, many police officers are ends-oriented. They are more focused on the ends of criminal justice—arresting dangerous felons or acquiring information about criminal activity—than on following legally acceptable means to achieve those ends. Also, police culture seems to give more emphasis to "good" ends than to legal means, and it sometimes justifies questionable means in the pursuit of these good ends (Crank 1998; Klockars 1980).

The use of questionable and illegal force, as well as of unacceptably high levels of force and police brutality, has been a problem for the police throughout history (see, for example, Inside Policing 10.3). What is meant by inappropriate force? What constitutes brutality? Clearly, these questions must be at the center of any investigation into police misuse of force.

Brutality and Excessive Force

Police brutality is difficult to define. It means different things to different people. Two common approaches to defining brutality distinguish between brutality and excessive force. Kania and Mackey (1977, 28) define **excessive force** as violence "of a degree that is more than justified to effect a legitimate police function." According to Carter, **police brutality** is excessive force, but to a more extreme degree, and includes violence that does not support a legitimate police function (1994, 270). An officer who beats a suspect who has already been handcuffed, for example, is committing police brutality.

INSIDE POLICING 10.3 Use of Force, the Community, and Liability

According to an article in *Law Enforcement News* ("How Much Force Is Enough" 1998), in 1998 the Washington, DC, Metropolitan Police unveiled a new use-of-force policy. The policy was developed in response to an escalating number of shooting incidents in recent years. The Metropolitan Police had been involved in 640 shooting incidents during the 5-year period from 1992 to 1997. This is more shootings than in either the LAPD or the Chicago Police Department for the same period, both of which have double Washington's manpower. Moreover, 85 people had been shot and killed since 1990. Eight police officers had also been shot since 1993. In 1997, 3 officers were killed in a 3-month period.

The shootings had resulted in more than 300 civil suits against the District. One man, armed with a knife, was shot by SWAT team members 12 times and subsequently awarded $6.1 million dollars. Of particular concern was that police were shooting at a large number of cars. Since 1993, "54 cars have been shot at after officers said they had driven at them in 'vehicular attacks.' Nine people had been killed, all of them unarmed, and 19 wounded" ("How Much Force Is Enough" 1998, 1).

The following is an example of such an incident: A 16-year-old man, wanted for reckless driving and running red lights, was shot through his side window. In two other cases, one individual was shot while he sat at a roadblock. Another was shot while sitting in his vehicle during a traffic stop. Officers involved in these cases stated that they fired to stop a vehicular attack. However, all of these shootings were considered unjustified, and the city agreed to pay the families of the victims in out-of-court settlements.

In response to these problems, the police department revised its use-of-force policy, rewrote the continuum of force, and increased annual training requirements:

> Officers are trained to use certain measures to prevent an incident from escalating to brutal or deadly force. A suspect's body movement, for instance, will be met by a uniform presence. If a suspect is unresponsive, the officer may respond with verbal force. If threatening words or gestures are used, the officer assumes an escort position to lead the subject. To meet passive resistance, the officer may grab the suspect's wrists and pin his arms behind him. Responses to active resistance range from take-down techniques and pepper spray or other nonlethal weapons to the use of deadly force. *(10)*

Nightsticks and the use of arms across the front of a person's neck to render the person unconscious were banned. Officers were also prohibited from shooting through doors or windows unless someone was clearly visible and from firing on fleeing cars. Officers were told to get out of the way of cars being used as deadly weapons.

A survey of officers found that 75 percent of those who had used their firearms failed to meet department standards. Consequently, firearms instruction was increased from 8 to 16 hours yearly, and training was expanded to focus on defensive tactics and judgment. Officers were taught how to deescalate situations and reduce the need for deadly force. Finally, shooting review teams were to be sent to the scene of all shootings to thoroughly investigate them.

This definition, however, does not fully address some aspects of police behavior that are widely seen as brutal but are not violently forceful. As noted earlier, police use of force may range from verbal commands to physical force, and the majority of force incidents involve lesser forms of force, such as commands. While these actions may be taken legally to accomplish a legitimate police task, they may also be used inappropriately (e.g., racial slurs, threats, insults). Citizens tend to define brutality and excessive force broadly to include these lesser forms of aggression. Yet brutality and excessive force refer specifically to physical forms of force. The more general term, use of force, covers the range of behaviors from verbal to physical force but includes both legal and extra-legal force. Holmes and Smith, in dealing with this problem, focus on **extra-legal police aggression**, arguing that

> The concept *extra-legal police aggression* is preferable for several related reasons. First, there is broad agreement on the definition of aggression, which generally refers to "*any form of behavior that is intended to injure someone physically or psychologically*" (Berkowitz 1993: 3, emphasis in original). Second, excessive force and brutality are sometimes defined to include only willful actions on the part of police officers (e.g., Griffin and Bernard 2003), but aggression may or may not entail conscious deliberation on the actor's part...both unconscious and conscious mental processes may trigger extra-legal aggression by the police. Finally, the concept of aggression captures the critical point that these behaviors specifically aim to injure citizens.

Extra-legal police aggression occurs whenever a police officer engages in behavior that is intended to injure someone physically or psychologically, but serves no legitimate police function. Included within this definition are a wide variety of behaviors, such as physical violence (e.g., brutality), and lesser forms such as verbal threats and insults.

Physical and Psychological Force in Police History

Both physical and **psychological force** were commonplace well into the 1930s. Hopkins (1931, 212–215) reported on a study of the New York City Police Department in 1930 finding that in 166 cases (23.4 percent of the total cases studied) some type of **physical force** was employed. The most frequently used method was to strike the suspect one or more times with a fist (67 cases). Other methods included use of a rubber hose (19 cases) and a blackjack (12 cases). One suspect was "hung out the window, kicked and dragged by the hair" (1931, 215). Larson (1932, 95–100) also discussed some of the coercive methods commonly used by police during this period. These methods became associated with the term **third degree**. Various third-degree methods historically employed by the police are listed in Inside Policing 10.4.

Most police officers of this period tended to deny any use of physical force. However, Bruce Smith, a prominent police consultant of that era, commented about the third degree in this regard: "In every police station in this country about which I know anything, there is a room remote from the public parts of the building where prisoners are questioned" (Hopkins 1931, 195). The Wickersham Commission (National Commission on Law Observance and Enforcement 1931), discussed in Chapter 2, found that the police use of such methods was widespread.

INSIDE POLICING 10.4 Historical Methods of Psychological and Physical Force

Psychological Force

- Suspects are placed on "The Loop"—that is, moved from station to station to deny them access to family, friends, and attorneys.
- Suspects are placed in very small, completely dark cells. Rats are placed in women's cells to "exhaust their nervous energy." A prisoner in an adjoining cell is told to "moan" and "yell" during the night. A large stove is placed next to a cell, and the stove is filled with items (e.g., bones, vegetable matter, old tires) designed to give off a foul odor and increase the heat in the cell to unbearable levels (i.e., to create a "sweat box").
- Suspects are interrogated for long periods under bright lights and without food or water, and/or they are denied access to substances like tobacco to which they are addicted. Suspects are threatened with various weapons; for example, a gun with blank shells is fired at the subject.
- Murder suspects are required to touch or hold the hand of the murder victim.
- Police pretend to beat prisoners in an interrogation room adjoining that of the suspect. One police officer is "hard" and "tough" and threatens the suspect; the other officer is sympathetic and supportive and pretends to protect the suspect from harm in exchange for information or a confession (also known as "good cop, bad cop" and the Mutt and Jeff technique).
- Police officers make false promises about what will happen to the suspect.

Physical Force

- Suspects are beaten on all parts of their body (usually except for the head) with rubber hoses, clubs, blackjacks, fists, telephone books, straps, brass knuckles, pistol butts, and whips. Arms and legs are twisted. Testicles are kicked, twisted, squeezed, and used to lift suspects upward, and testicles are also burned with acid. Suspects are tortured with electric shocks, dental drills, and lighted cigars. Suspects are dragged or pulled by their hair.
- Suspects are drenched with cold water from a hose, their heads are held under water, water is forced into their noses, they are hung out the window, they are choked with neckties and ropes, and they are required to go without shoes until their feet are bleeding. Chemicals such as tear gas, scopolamine, and chloroform are employed.

SOURCES: Adapted from J. A. Larson, *Lying and Its Detection* (Chicago: University of Chicago Press, 1932), 95–121; E. J. Hopkins, *Our Lawless Police* (New York: Viking Press, 1931), 25, 128, 215.

Continued problems with coercive psychological techniques resulted in famous decisions of the Warren Court in the 1960s. In 1966 the *Miranda v. Arizona* Supreme Court decision observed that psychologically coercive techniques interfered with constitutional ideas of fair play. Consequently, the court issued its now famous requirement that suspects be advised of their right to an attorney and that the police's right to question suspects be restricted, except when that right has been waived or after an attorney has advised the suspect whether to talk to the police. As Vaughn (1992) has noted, other court rulings have expanded the rights of the police to use trickery and deception. By permitting open deception, however, several observers of the police have contended that the courts are encouraging the police to emphasize "good" ends over legal means (Skolnick and Fyfe 1993).

Police today continue to rely on deception, a form of psychological coercion, to secure information. The following are examples of contemporary uses of deception:

1. The person, or suspect, is not told the truth about why he or she is being questioned.
2. The suspect is not told that the person asking the questions is a police officer.
3. The suspect is told that he or she is being interviewed rather than interrogated and that he or she is free to leave at any time.
4. The police misrepresent the circumstances of the crime the suspect is alleged to have committed; for example, a suspect might be told there was an eyewitness or that there is other available evidence that "ties" the suspect to the crime.
5. The police may make the crime seem more serious (carrying a more severe punishment) than it is to induce the suspect to make a bargain to confess to a less serious crime.
6. The police provide a justification to the suspect for the act; for example, "the victim got what she deserved."
7. The police may make some type of promise that later can be denied or modified.

These examples illustrate that there are sometimes differences between what is legal and what is ethical. Generally, the police can *legally* use trickery and deception as long as their methods do not involve coercion or improper promises (the police cannot promise a light sentence, since that is the judge's prerogative, but they can promise to speak to the prosecutor on behalf of the suspect). While legal, however, is it right to lie? Is it right for an investigator to tell a suspect that his fingerprints have already been found at the scene of a crime if they have not? Is it right for a police officer to pretend to be a drug dealer and offer to sell drugs to a suspect? These are not clear-cut cases, of course. Such behavior by the police may seem unethical to some but merely clever to others. Some citizens would have their confidence in the police shaken if they thought the police did not use such methods. Others are shocked that they do.

The matter of police ethics, and the role of ethics in guiding and controlling police behavior, is discussed at greater length in Chapter 11.

Frequency of Excessive Force and Brutality

How widespread is extra-legal police violence and aggression? Barker (1986) studied the extent of police brutality, along with other types of police deviant behavior, in a city of moderate size in the southern United States. Based on questionnaire responses from 43 of 45 officers in that department, he found that about 40 percent used excessive force at times. Officers tended to believe that lying in court (committing perjury), sleeping on duty, and having sex or drinking on duty were more serious forms of deviant police behavior than the use of excessive force. This was particularly true when the excessive force was used against persons in custody. Almost half the officers said they would rarely, if ever, report another officer if he or she used excessive force.

In another study, Carter (1985) conducted a survey of 95 police officers in McAllen, Texas. He found that 23 percent believed that excessive force was sometimes necessary to demonstrate an officer's authority, and 62 percent believed that an officer had a right to use excessive force in retaliation against anyone who used force against the officer. In the areas of verbal abuse, slightly over one half of the officers believed that it was permissible to talk "rough" with citizens and that rough talk was the only way to communicate with some citizens.

Friederich (1980), in his comprehensive analysis of research on the use of force, found that police used force in only about 5 percent of encounters with offenders or suspects. In about two thirds of these encounters, the force was considered excessive. Because only a small percentage of all police–citizen encounters are with offenders or suspects and only about 5 percent of these types of encounters involve the use of force, his findings suggest that both the use of force and the use of excessive force are rare events in police work.

Official Complaints about Police Use of Force. As part of its continuing efforts to acquire data about the use of excessive force by law enforcement officers, the BJS expanded the 2003 LEMAS survey of police agencies to include questions on formal citizen complaints about use of force. The survey included questions about the number of citizen complaints regarding the use of force, the disposition of complaints, and information regarding policies and procedures relating to the processing of complaints (Hickman 2006). In 2002, local law enforcement agencies with 100 or more sworn officers received 26,556 citizen complaints about the use of force. Large agencies received the majority (84 percent) of complaints (22,238). In addition, the complaint rate was greater for larger agencies than for smaller agencies. For example, agencies with between 100 and 249 officers had 7.4 complaints per 100 officers responding to calls, whereas agencies with 1,000 or more officers had 19.1 complaints per 100 officers responding to calls.

Research on extra-legal police aggression, especially brutality, is extremely difficult to conduct. Police agencies are reluctant to study the issue or release data to researchers. Police officers engaged in these acts attempt to hide their actions from supervisors and the public. Moreover, offending officers believe that many, if not all, of the other officers (including supervisors and managers) who may be aware of this behavior will not report the brutality and will lie about the incident if it is investigated by the department or other individuals. As a result, the limited number of studies include a small number of jurisdictions, often rely on weak research designs, and use various, often imprecise, measures. Moreover, the evidence from the limited number of studies is not entirely consistent. Nonetheless, we are beginning to piece together a picture of the problem and, as discussed in the next chapter, devise approaches to deal with this important issue.

Perhaps the most infamous case of police brutality in modern history was the attack on Rodney King, which took place in Los Angeles in 1991. Inside Policing 10.5 describes this incident and some of the subsequent events connected with it. Interestingly, a comprehensive study of the Los Angeles police just prior to the King incident had indicated widespread officer support for the values and management of the police department (Felkenes 1991). Furthermore, widespread support was found among both white and minority and male and female officers. It was found that, overall, all patrol officers were very satisfied with their jobs and would recommend that their friends consider a job with the department. This research also found that Los Angeles police officers were likely to have a professional outlook concerning their role in society. The conflict between the shortcomings of the LAPD reported in the aftermath of the Rodney King incident and police officer support for the department reported in the Felkenes research vividly illustrates the differences that can exist between community and departmental expectations of the police role in society and the meaning of what is and is not police brutality.

Brutality in the Twenty-First Century

The police professionalism movement, discussed in Chapter 11, has placed powerful administrative and ethical controls on the behavior of line officers. Throughout the twentieth century, this and subsequent reform movements have tried to control violent and brutal police behavior. Looking back over the past 100 years, can one say that police brutality has decreased? What are the trends in brutality? Is it a problem that society needs to be concerned about?

This section looks at two opposing views on police violence and brutality. The first argues that brutality is a significant problem in major American cities and is not being dealt with successfully. The second contends that brutality should be considered against the backdrop of increasing levels of violence among the citizenry.

View 1: Brutality Is a Problem. In 1998 the Human Rights Watch published *Shielded From Justice,* an assessment of brutality in major American cities. It looked at brutality and accountability procedures in 14 large cities, selected to represent different regions and to provide an overall picture of police behavior across the United States. Its assessment of brutality and lax accountability was a harsh indictment of big-city policing:

> Police officers engage in unjustified shootings, severe beatings, fatal chokings, and unnecessarily rough physical treatment in cities throughout the United States, while their police superiors, city officials, and the justice department fail to act decisively to restrain or penalize such acts or even to record the full magnitude of the problem. Habitually brutal offenders—usually a small percentage of officers on a force—may be the subject of repeated complaints but are usually protected by their fellow officers and by the shoddiness of internal police investigations. A victim seeking redress faces obstacles at every point in the process, ranging from overt intimidation to the reluctance of local and federal prosecutors to take on brutality cases. Severe abuse persists because overwhelming barriers to accountability make it all too likely that officers who commit human rights violations escape due punishment to continue their abusive conduct. *(1998, 1)*

INSIDE POLICING 10.5 The Rodney King Incident

On March 3, 1991, Rodney G. King was stopped for a speeding violation and trying to evade the police. What ensued between King and police officers was videotaped by a "home-camera buff." King did not immediately cooperate with police and may have resisted the attempts of officers to arrest him. Several officers hit him with police batons and kicked him over 50 times. Before the incident was over, 27 police officers (2 of whom were black and 4 of whom were Latino), representing three different police agencies, were on the scene, and they stood by as King was brutally beaten and severely injured. The beating appeared to continue even after King had stopped making any meaningful effort to resist police authority. King received 11 skull fractures (including a shattered right cheek bone, shattered right eye socket, and fractured right sinus bones), a broken ankle, and numerous other injuries as a result of the beating. When the videotape was shown on local and national television, it created tremendous outrage across the United States. Other citizens came forward with examples of how they had also been mistreated by the police.

The reports of the officers involved in the incident indicate that they may not have been truthful in describing the events in question. For example, some officers reported that King drove his car in excess of 100 miles an hour to avoid the police. However, a tape recording of the conversations between pursuing officers and one police department never indicated a speed in excess of 65 miles an hour. Two of the officers involved were, in fact, charged with submitting a false report.

(Continued)

INSIDE POLICING 10.5 The Rodney King Incident
(Continued)

An independent commission, headed by Warren Christopher, former deputy attorney general and deputy secretary of state of the United States, was appointed to investigate the King incident and related incidents in the department. Information revealed in the investigation indicated that some of the officers involved did not take the King matter seriously and even made jokes about it. One officer said after the incident that he hadn't "beaten anyone this bad in a long time." At the hospital to which King was taken, one police officer reportedly told King that "we played a little hardball tonight and you lost."

The attitudes of some Los Angeles police officers concerning race, excessive force, and the shooting of suspects are illustrated in the police officer statements listed below. These statements were taken from records of computer communications between patrol cars and between patrol cars and police headquarters. These statements are an example of 1,450 similar remarks made in the 16 months preceding the King incident. The language is reported as given, including the spelling errors of the officers. Although the number of such remarks is less than one tenth of 1 percent of the total communication statements made during the period in question, the fact that such statements were made so openly indicates the possibility of both tolerance and support within the department for the values and beliefs represented by these remarks.

Statements Concerning Race

"Don't cry Buckwheat, or is it Willie Lunch Meat?"

"Sounds like monkey slapping time."

"Well... I'm back over here in the projects, pissing off the natives."

"If you encounter these Negroes shoot first and ask questions later."

"Just clear its [busy] out hear. This hole is picking up, I almost got me a Mexican last night but he dropped the dam gun to quick, lots of wit."

Statements Concerning Excessive Force

"I'm gonna bk my pursuit suspect... hope he gets ugly, so I can vent my hate."

"Capture him, beat him and treat him like dirt... Sounds like a job for the dynamic duo."

"After I beat him, what do I book him for and do I have to do a use of force [report]."

"Some of the suspects had big boot marks on their heads, once they were in custody."

"The last load went to a family of illegals living in the brush alongside the Pas frwy. I thought the woman was going to cry... so I hit her with my baton."

"I should shoot 'em huh, I missed another chance dammmmmmm. I am getting soft."

Some of the other findings of the Christopher Commission and of research conducted by newspaper reporters are listed below:

1. Supervisors in the department were aware of a "significant number" of officers who used excessive force repeatedly and who also lied in reports about what they had done. Sometimes these officers were even praised by supervisors.

2. The messages sent via the computer that indicated prejudice and a tendency toward violence on the part of some officers were ignored by police supervisors and managers.

3. It was rare for the department to find in favor of citizens who complained about the police use of excessive force. In over 2,000 citizen complaints filed between 1986 and 1990, only 42 were resolved in favor of the complainant. For the same period, the department brought excessive-force charges against officers in 80 cases, and in 53 of

these, officers were found guilty as a result of an internal affairs investigation. In some of these 53 cases, more than one officer was involved. In incidents involving several officers, all officers denied the allegations, and none of the officers who had been present at the incident reported another officer for the use of excessive force. The disciplinary action taken against officers for the use of excessive force varied. Some officers were suspended for more than 20 days, but some were treated more leniently than other officers, who had been disciplined for kissing a girlfriend while on duty, for the unauthorized use of the department's copying machines, and for sleeping on duty.

The commission stated, however, that it believed that only a small percentage of officers, perhaps 3 to 5 percent, was responsible for most of the racial and excessive-force problems (this figure means that at least several hundred Los Angeles police officers may have engaged in this type of behavior). The Christopher Commission also found serious problems with the police department's management and suggested that the chief of police retire when his term of office was over.

As a result of the King incident, four officers were charged with criminal assault, among other things, and placed on trial. Their defense was that prior to the events depicted on the videotape, King, whom they considered a large and potentially dangerous person, violently resisted their attempts to arrest him. They indicated that they believed King was under the influence of liquor or drugs and, from their training and experience, this would make him very difficult to control. When they were unable to control him physically, they used the Taser, but even after he was shocked with electricity, King continued to refuse police orders to lie down in a prone position with arms and legs spread; he even got up and "charged" one of the officers. Consequently, the officers began to use their batons and some kicks, as they were trained to do in such situations. The officers tended to perceive every movement by King, even when he was on the ground, as an indication that he continued to pose a threat. Therefore, they continued to beat him until he complied with police orders. Only one of the four officers in question believed that what they had done was excessive or that it constituted "police brutality."

The jury in the criminal trial found the four officers not guilty on all criminal charges except one, on which the jury was divided. Many citizens, who believed that the videotape of the beating was sufficient evidence to convict the officers, were outraged at what they considered an unjust verdict. There was widespread violence (more than 50 persons were killed), extensive property damage (numerous buildings were burned down), and looting in Los Angeles and several other cities. Many elected officials expressed their concern and demanded that additional steps be taken to hold the officers accountable for their actions.

Two of the officers were subsequently convicted in federal court for the violation of King's civil rights. Both were sent to federal prison. King also sued the city of Los Angeles and was awarded $3.6 million.

SOURCES: Adapted from "Inside View of L.A. Beating," 1991, *San Jose Mercury News*, March 19: 1A, 9A; "Doubt Shed on Cops Report in L.A. Beating," 1991, *San Jose Mercury News*, March 23: 1F, 4F; "L.A. Fires Only 1% of Officers," 1991, *San Jose Mercury News*, May 5: 4B; "Report Calls For Gates' Ouster," 1991, *San Jose Mercury News*, July 10: 1A, 6A. Used by permission.

Prosecution of cases has been infrequent and ineffective. Local prosecutors, the study argues, are frequently closely allied with police and are ineffective in efforts to prosecute police brutality. Indeed, most prosecutors examined by the Human Rights Watch did not keep a log of police brutality cases. The criminal section of the Civil Rights Division of the U.S. Department of Justice is responsible for prosecution of civil rights violations. This includes the excessive use of force and police brutality. Yet the record of prosecution has been bleak:

> In fiscal year 1997, the Civil Rights Division received a total of 10,891 complaints, with 31 grand juries and magistrates to consider law enforcement officers leading to 25 indictments and informations, involving 67 law enforcement agents; nine were convicted, 19 entered guilty pleas, and four were acquitted. *(Human Rights Watch 1998, 102)*

In other words, of over 10,000 complaints, only 28 resulted in convictions or pleas. This is a conviction rate of 2.6 per 1,000 cases. The data are clear: citizens hoping for criminal remedies at the federal level for police brutality are virtually certain to be frustrated.

Federal data also show an alarming rise in reports of police brutality over recent years. In 1989, a total of 8,953 cases were forwarded to the FBI. By 1996 the figure had risen to 11,721. Although the time interval is too short to make long-term inferences about trends, the data show an increase of 30 percent in reported cases over the 7-year period.

Human Rights Watch concluded that the most significant problem confronting big-city police departments was the lack of a system of effective accountability (discussed in Chapter 11). However, critics have countered that data collected by Human Rights Watch was derived primarily from high-profile cases. This is a selective bias that, outside of the FBI reports listed above, tells little about the ordinary cases encountered by police departments. Human Rights Watch responded to this concern by observing that it was difficult to obtain information from departments in instances that had not reached public attention and that prosecution for those cases was consequently even less common than the more visible cases that it discussed.

View 2: Brutality Is Not a Problem. Not all observers of the police believe that there is a brutality problem. Sulc (1995) argued that restraint, rather than brutality, is typical of police behavior toward citizens. He contended that police brutality is less prevalent than it was 20 years ago. Citing the news magazine *New Dimensions,* he observed that

> While the FBI's civil rights division reports 2,450 complaints involving law enforcement officers in 1989, during the same period, 62,712 law enforcement officers were victims of assaults. In 1990, there were more than 71,794 assaults against law enforcement officers nationwide, according to the Uniform Crime Reports. Sixty-five officers were killed. *(1995, 80)*

Sulc attributes the widespread perception of police violence to media attention:

> Police violence, although unquestionably a matter of serious import, isn't as bad as it appears. It is exacerbated by warped media treatment both in fiction (network shows) and in reporting (network news). The unusual stress of police work contributes to the overreaction of cops—the overreaction of media and public to the cops contributes to the stress. *(1995, 81)*

Tucker (1995) argues that the public tends to look at complaints against the police and fails to consider whether the complaints are justified:

> The truth, however, is that most complaints are either frivolous or unjustified. This is borne out by the experience of the old New York City board, which the Vera Institute of Justice, a nonpartisan organization, found to be prejudiced neither for nor against civilians or police officers. In 1990, the Board's annual report showed a total of 2,376 complaints for "excessive force," 1,140 for "abuse of authority," 1,618 for "discourtesy,"

and 420 for "ethnic slurs." Among the 2,376 complaints for excessive force (presumably the most serious charge), injuries were documented in 267 cases. These involved 71 bruises, 92 lacerations requiring stitches, 30 fractures, 22 swellings, and 41 "other." In the 2,286 cases that were pursued, 566 were dropped because the complainant became uncooperative, 234 were dropped because the complainant withdrew the charge, and 1,405 were closed with less than full investigation, usually because the complainants became unavailable. Only 81 cases resulted in a finding against the policeman. *(72)*

The "no-problem" perspective suffers from a tendency to blame police brutality on the behavior of their victims or on increases in crime, seeming to imply that police officers are not primarily responsible for their own behavior. Nor does the perspective acknowledge the very real problems victims of brutality face when they try to file reports—filing a report in a police department is frequently an intimidating experience, and full follow-up on reports that are filed is not common in many departments. This perspective nevertheless raises important points that should not be overlooked. The following six points summarize central policy issues confronting excessive force and police brutality.

1. The presence of brutality cannot be gleaned only from "official reports," which may be unsubstantiated. Individuals file brutality or excessive-force reports for a variety of reasons, and not all of the reports will accurately tap underlying instances of brutality. Also, scholars know from their studies of crime that official reports vary sharply from true levels, although that same argument suggests that brutality may well be higher than suggested by "official" reports.

2. Citizens may perceive behavior whose purpose is to ensure officer safety as acts of brutality. There is no question but that the experience of being arrested, searched, and cuffed is harsh and unpleasant. But it should not be dealt with in the same way as brutality, which is typically viewed by the public and police officials alike as inappropriate or illegal behavior.

3. The media are widely and correctly perceived to dramatize that which comes to their attention. This applies to the villainy of criminals, and it extends to the brutality of police as well. One should not assume that what is presented in the media is a thorough or accurate portrayal of the facts. Indeed, as Walker (1998, 30–32) has pointed out, what we receive from the media is the exceptional, not the normal, case. Unfortunately, bad officers are able to hide behind the protective veneer of police loyalty, and the media are frequently the only way that excessive force and brutality are brought to the attention of the public.

4. Police brutality emerges in the context of a police–citizen interaction, and it is unreasonable to believe that police can be wholly dispassionate in the conduct of criminal investigations and in dealing with rude individuals. Although dispassionate police work is a goal of police reformers, the ability to police without the expression of emotion, including anger, is improbable. It is important that police departments seek to control the angry or mean-spirited outbursts of officers against citizens, but it is also inconceivable that they will be wholly successful (Holmes and Smith 2008).

5. Research suggests that some officers exhibit single or rare instances of excessive force, and only a small percentage are rogues in their behavior, accounting for repeated violent acts. These two types of police officers should be dealt with in different ways—the rare or one-time offender subject to interdepartmental review and the repeat offender decertified and prosecuted.

6. The public, widely supportive of a "war on crime" and aggressive anticrime efforts, has created an environment in which police officers feel morally justified in the use of force. It is seemingly unfair to single out officers for the overuse of force when the message they frequently receive from powerful public, media, and political figures is to do just that.

Deadly Force

The term *deadly force* is defined as that force used with the intent to cause great bodily injury or death. Such deadly force is almost always limited to those situations when police use firearms in encounters with suspects. As noted, there are certainly other times when citizens may be seriously injured or killed as the result of the use of other types of force, but that is rarely, if ever, the intent of the police. Some police scholars have suggested, however, that choke holds be defined as deadly force because deaths do occur when such holds are employed (Fyfe 1983). When the police engage in a high-speed pursuit that results in an accident and someone dies, this may also be seen as use of force in which the outcome involved death. This fact does not mean that deaths resulting from these and other police activities are unimportant, but only that they are not included in the definition and therefore will not be considered.

Based on the definition above, there are three categories for which data are required if the extent of the use of deadly force is to be determined:

1. **Category 1: Death.** The police use a deadly weapon, and as a result, the person dies.
2. **Category 2: Injury.** The police use a deadly weapon, and the person is wounded but does not die.
3. **Category 3: Non-injury.** The police use a deadly weapon, but the person against whom it is directed is not injured.

A fourth possible category, but one that will not be addressed, relates to the total times the officer fires his or her weapon. A person who is shot at and killed, wounded, or missed may be fired at more than once. Research indicates that police officers miss with about 60 to 85 percent of the bullets they fire (Geller and Scott 1992). For example, on the one hand, an officer could shoot at a suspect five times and hit the suspect only once, causing either death or an injury. Or more than one bullet might strike the victim. On the other hand, an officer might shoot several times and not hit the intended person.

1. **Category 1: Death.** Sources of data for Category 1 use of deadly force can be found in three places: the National Center for Health Statistics (NCHS), FBI reports, and the study of individual cities. The NCHS data are found in the volumes on mortality that are published annually and based on reports from coroners and medical examiners. Under the "homicide" cause-of-death category, there has been a "police or legal" intervention subcategory since 1949. These data provide a very rough estimate of the number of people killed by police as the result of the use of deadly force. In the 42-year period from 1949 to 1990, police killed approximately 13,000 people, according to the NCHS.

However, the estimate of 13,000 may be low. An analysis of the records of 36 large police departments conducted by Sherman and Langworthy (1979) suggests that the center's statistics are approximately 25 to 50 percent too low because of reporting problems. This means that a more realistic estimate of citizen deaths from Category 1 use of deadly force is between 16,000 and 20,000 since 1949. Although there is no accurate way to determine the number of citizen deaths that have resulted from the use of deadly force since the 1840s when modern police departments were first established, it is not unreasonable to assume that 30,000 to 40,000 citizens, and possibly many more, have been killed by police officers in the United States.

The FBI collects data on the use of deadly force by police but does not publish the statistics. The data are based on what are called Supplemental Homicide Reports submitted to the FBI by police departments, and the submission of such reports is voluntary. Although the number of people reported killed by police may give an accurate picture of the use of deadly force in individual cities, the reports do not provide an accurate national overview.

One of the most comprehensive studies conducted in individual police departments was made by Matulia (1985), who studied citizens killed by the police in the 57 largest cities (250,000 population or higher) in the United States between 1975 and 1983. He found that the police had killed a total of 2,336 people, or an average of about 259 per year. He estimated that this figure represented about 70 percent of the total number of citizens killed by police each year in the United States. Using this estimate, the total number of citizens killed during this period would be about 370 per year. This estimate is consistent with NCHS data if Sherman and Langworthy's adjustment is taken into consideration, as well as with analyses by the BJS (Brown and Langan 2001; Fox and Zawitz 2007), which found annual fluctuations between about 300 and 450 (see Figure 10.1).

2. **Category 2: Injury.** Category 2 data (i.e., a person is shot and injured) are more difficult to acquire for the entire United States because there is no national reporting requirement. Fyfe (1988), however, provides some interesting insights into this category of data. He summarizes several studies conducted over varying time periods (2 to 9 years) from a total of 14 large cities in the United States. Although some variation exists among departments, these studies suggest that, in general, when the police shoot an individual, that person is approximately twice as likely to be wounded as killed. If this estimate is accurate for the entire United States, this means that for the period 1949 to 1990, police used deadly force that injured citizens between 32,000 and 40,000 times.

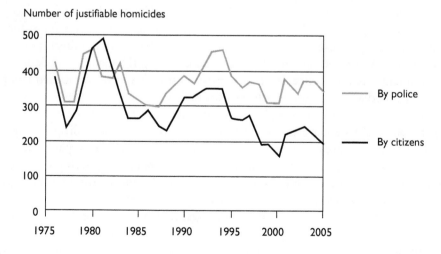

FIGURE 10.1 Number of Justifiable Homicides by Police and Citizens, 1976–2005.

Source: J. A. Fox and M. W. Zawitz, *Homicide Trends in the United States* (Washington, DC: Bureau of Justice Statistics, 2007). Available online at http://bjs.ojp.usdoj.gov/content/pub/pdf/htius.pdf.

3. **Category 3: Non-injury.** Data for Category 3 (i.e., a person is shot at but not injured) are even more difficult to obtain. However, there are some indications of the frequency of police actions in this area. In studies of four large cities, the frequency that officers shot and missed, as a percentage of total times they used their firearms, was 48.6 in Los Angeles during the period 1971 to 1975 (Fyfe 1978), 73.1 in Chicago for the period 1975 to 1977 (Geller and Karales 1981), 74.1 in Detroit for the period 1976 to 1981 (Horvath and Donahue 1982), and 51.0 in Philadelphia for the period 1987 to 1992 (White 2006). If these data are indicative of practices throughout the United States, it means that, depending on the city, police officers shoot at and miss two to four times as many people as they shoot at and either injure or kill.

The above discussion includes some very general projections about the use of deadly force in the United States. There is a need to determine how changes in training, departmental policy, programs (like community or problem-oriented policing), and new laws affect frequency of deadly force incidents. For example, as a result of changes in the policies concerning the use of Category 1 deadly force, there was an apparent decline in the number of citizens killed in the early 1980s (Fyfe 1988; "Big Decline in Killings" 1986). These policy and legal changes will be discussed later.

Van Raalte's (1986) research identifies as many as 30,000 officers killed in the line of duty in the twentieth century. However, he does not separate those killed in accidents from those killed by citizens. Historically, there is about a 1:4 or 1:5 ratio when comparing officers killed to citizens killed; that is, about one police officer is killed by a citizen for every four or five citizens killed by the police (Kuykendall 1981). Most recently, however, homicides of police officers have been decreasing at an even faster rate than homicides by officers, so the ratio in 1998 was about 1:6 (Brown and Langan 2001).

In recent years there has been substantial research concerning the circumstances in which police use deadly force. The research on police use of deadly force generally focuses on four important areas: (1) individual and situational factors, (2) environmental and departmental variations, (3) racial considerations, and (4) changes in law and policy.

Individual and Situational Factors

Researchers have explored a variety of individual-level characteristics related to police killings of citizens, including characteristics of officers, citizens, and the circumstances of shootings. For example, research reveals that those killed by police are disproportionately young, male, and African American. Research also finds that the majority of victims posed a real or eminent threat to police and that in many cases the victim was armed and police believed they posed a danger (see Smith 2004 for review).

The decision by an officer to use deadly force appears primarily to be the result of his or her perception of whether a threat exists and how frequently the officer is exposed to threats. As used here, "threat" could mean any situation in which the department permitted the use of deadly force. An officer's assignment appears to be a much more important predictor of the use of deadly force than age, intelligence, and educational background. Officers with more risky assignments are more likely to use deadly force.

Off-duty officers are involved in many shootings. As many as 15 to 20 percent of incidents of police use of deadly force involve an officer who is off duty. The more aggressive the off-duty officer is in intervening in potentially violent situations, whether or not encouraged to do so by the department, the higher the rates for the use of deadly force.

The race of the officer also appears to be important, largely because of the assignment and living practices of officers. For example, African American officers are more likely to use deadly force and to be the victims of its use than are other officers because they are more likely to live in, frequent, and be assigned to areas with high crime rates. Therefore, they are exposed to more situations in which they might have to use deadly force or become its victim (Fyfe 1988; Geller and Scott 1992).

Environmental and Departmental Variations

The frequency with which police use Category 1 deadly force varies considerably across the United States. Matulia found that the rates per 1,000 police officers varied from 0.44 in Sacramento, California (about 1 incident for every 2,000 police officers) to 7.17 in Jacksonville, Florida. Overall, the mean rate was 2.24 citizens killed for each 1,000 officers for the period 1975 to 1983. Of the 57 largest cities studied, 29 were below this rate and 27 were above.

Two categories of factors that may explain this variation in the frequency with which police use deadly force are environmental and organizational (departmental). Environmental factors—factors having to do with the community and neighborhood where the police do their work—include, among others, the level of poverty, the proportion of minority residents, the homicide rate, the overall arrest rate, violent-crime arrest rate, and gun density (i.e., ratio of gun ownership to total population). Generally, the police are more likely to shoot and kill citizens in cities with higher concentrations of impoverished minority residents and higher rates of violent crime, although these relationships may not be consistent across different size cities. For example, Smith (2004) found that police killings were related to the proportion of black residents and violent crime in medium size (100,000–249,000 residents) cities, but in our nation's largest cities with over 250,000 residents the violent crime rate was not significant and the proportion of black residents took on greater significance. Based on the findings, he suggested that

> Blacks in urban America are highly segregated and impoverished (Massey and Denton 1993). These large "threatening" populations concentrated in the nation's largest cities may produce much higher levels of antagonism between disadvantaged groups and the police. In smaller cities and large suburbs, on the other hand, ghetto communities are not as extensive or insular, and minorities may not be seen as a general threat. Thus a more generalized perception of threat may be less pervasive; rather, officers may respond to more specific threats from crime. *(Smith 2004, 158)*

In addition, in any area where there are higher poverty and divorce rates, often the police may be called on more to intervene in potentially dangerous situations (Fyfe 1980, 1988; Kania and Mackey 1977; Sherman and Langworthy 1979). These factors do not by themselves, however, explain all of the variation that may exist.

Departmental values, policies, and practices of political leaders and police managers also affect the frequency with which police use deadly force. Current research suggests that more restrictive shooting policies reduce the frequency with which deadly force is employed (discussed in more detail later). In addition, some evidence suggests that the leadership attitude in the city and department influences the frequency of use (Carmichael and Jacobs 2002). For example, the increase in the use of deadly force in Philadelphia in the 1970s appeared to be the result of the aggressive policing attitude of leaders in the city and the department. The training that officers receive may also be influential. Some departments may encourage officers to intervene aggressively in potentially dangerous situations rather than wait until adequate "backup support" is available. Officers, on their own initiative, may also engage in such behavior (Fyfe 1988).

What is not known about neighborhood and department variation is more striking than what is known. As difficult as it is to determine how often deadly force *fatalities* occur, it is even harder to know how many deadly force *incidents* occur (Blumberg 1997) involving injuries, misses, and mere threats. The proportion of deadly force incidents, rates of justifiable homicide, and firearms discharge rates varies dramatically across jurisdictions (Geller and Scott 1992) and departments (Fridell 1989). Blumberg has made the following observations:

> The inescapable conclusion one must draw from the available evidence is that nobody knows how many times each year law enforcement officers in the United States fire their weapons at citizens, how many citizens are wounded, or how many are killed as the result of police bullets. *(1997, 521)*

Racial Considerations

African American and Hispanic minorities are more likely to be shot by the police than are whites. One explanation for this disproportion is that such disparities in shooting incidents simply mirror ethnic and racial involvement in criminal activity. When compared with rates of police–citizen contacts, arrest rates, and resistance to or attacks upon the police, there is no apparent racial disparity in police use of deadly force. That is, in communities in which blacks are shot at a high rate from the percentage of contacts with police, their arrest rates and the likelihood that they will resist the police tend to be similarly high (Fyfe 1988; Geller and Scott 1992). Yet Fyfe, for example, found that police officers in Memphis were 15 times as likely to shoot at African American offenders who had committed property crimes as at white property-crime offenders.

Another explanation is that stereotypes portraying ethnic and racial minorities as dangerous may heighten officers' fear and influence shooting decisions (see Holmes and Smith 2008). Recent evidence suggests that part of the disproportion in shooting rates may be attributable to the influence of cultural stereotypes on our behavior. A number of recent experimental studies of weapon recognition (Payne 2001) and shoot/don't shoot decisions (Correll et al. 2002) demonstrate that stereotypes can influence our perceptions of and responses to people of different racial identities. In these studies, participants responded more quickly and made more mistakes (i.e., misperceived a weapon or shot unarmed persons) when the target was African American (compared with a white target), although none of the participants were trained police officers. In the most recent experimental study, the researchers included both citizens and police officers as participants. They found that the participants made video-game shoot/don't shoot decisions more rapidly for unarmed whites and armed blacks and more slowly for armed whites and unarmed blacks (Correll et al. 2007). This tendency was most pronounced among officers who worked in areas with large populations, high rates of violent crime, and greater concentrations of minorities. Police officers were not more likely to mistakenly "shoot" unarmed blacks, but the video game format did not entail the fatigue, stress, and real dangers of street-level work (Holmes and Smith 2008). Future studies may shed light on the interaction between stereotypes and fear in shoot/don't shoot decisions.

Because of the sensitivity of the racial issue in the use of deadly force, more restrictive policies have tended to reduce the number of African Americans who have been killed. Sherman and Cohn (1986) found that in the 15-year period between 1970 and 1984, the

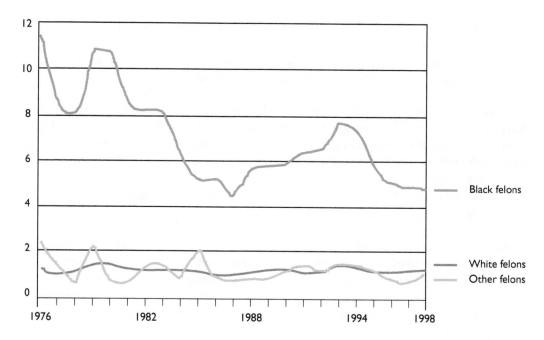

FIGURE 10.2 **Number of Justifiable Homicides by Police per 1 Million U.S. Population Age 13 or Older for Each Race.**

Source: J. M. Brown and P. A. Langan, *Policing and Homicide, 1976–1998: Justifiable Homicide by Police, Police Officers Murdered by Felons* (Washington, DC: Bureau of Justice Statistics, 2001), iii.

police use of deadly force declined substantially, largely because fewer African American citizens were killed by police. As Figure 10.2 indicates, this trend reversed itself during the period 1987–1993, probably because of the crack epidemic and the violence associated with it, but then resumed. The rate at which police used deadly force against African Americans in 1998 was about 50 percent lower than it had been in 1976, although it was still more than twice the rate for whites (Brown and Langan 2001). These trends suggest that prior to the adoption of more restrictive deadly force policies by many police departments, African Americans were more likely to be shot at in certain types of situations (e.g., running away from the scene of a crime) than were whites. Declines in racial disparities in deadly force incidents today are associated with departmental efforts to control discretion in the use of deadly force (Sparger and Giacopassi 1992).

Legal and Policy Changes

Blumberg identifies five changes in present-day laws and departmental policy regulating the use of deadly force:

1. Many states have modified the fleeing-felon rule and have tightened the legal basis for use of deadly force.

2. The shooting of unarmed, nonviolent suspects has been ruled by the Supreme Court to be a violation of the Fourth Amendment of the Constitution.

3. Almost all urban police departments have enacted restrictive administrative policies regarding the use of deadly force.

4. The courts have made it much easier for a citizen to file a lawsuit and collect civil damages as a result of a police action.

5. Social-science research has facilitated the understanding of the reasons for, and policy implications of, the use of deadly force. (1997, 507–508)

As late as 1967, few police departments had policies to guide officers in the use of deadly force. The state laws that existed at that time and that still exist in many states tended to broadly define occasions when officers could use deadly force. Perhaps the broadest of these legal guidelines was the **fleeing-felon rule**, which authorized the use of deadly force when attempting to apprehend individuals who were fleeing from a suspected serious crime. This rule dates from the early Middle Ages, when almost all crimes considered felonies were punishable by the death penalty; consequently, to kill those fleeing from suspected felonies did not seem inappropriate.

An alternative to the fleeing-felon rule was first developed and tested in New York. The New York Police Department, responding to concerns over the high number of officer and civilian shootings, formulated a restricted policy permitting the use of deadly force only under circumstances of immediate danger to an officer or the public. The policy resulted in a nearly 30 percent reduction in shootings of citizens by officers. No increase in the number of officers shot was observed (Fyfe 1979).

Changes in departmental policies have had more influence than changes in the law in determining when police officers use deadly force. Once police departments began to develop policies in this area, they often were more restrictive than state law. Initially, departments limited the number of situations in which police could use deadly force; for example, a policy might indicate that a person who was fleeing from a certain property crime could no longer be shot at.

By the 1980s, more and more police departments began to adopt what is often called a **defense-of-life** shooting policy. Generally, such policies restrict the use of deadly force situations to those in which the officer's life, or another person's, is in jeopardy or to prevent the escape of a person who is extremely dangerous. In some departments, even under these circumstances, deadly force can be employed only when other, less deadly, means seem inappropriate (Geller and Scott 1992).

Since the adoption of more restrictive deadly force policies, the number of citizens killed by police has declined. This decline is understandable when one considers that prior to the adoption of a defense-of-life policy, in some communities as many as 25 percent of the victims of police use of deadly force posed no threat to a police officer or another person when they were shot. Despite the fears of many officers, more restrictive guidelines have not resulted in an increased number of police injuries or deaths (Fyfe 1988). In addition, no evidence either confirms or refutes the belief of some police officers that more restrictive policies encourage suspects to try to run away from the police.

Summary

Force is central to the police role and, as such, an inherent part of police–citizen interactions. Yet its use is often controversial. Police are trained to act in terms of levels of force. However, local police cultural standards for the use of force often differ considerably from formal departmental policy and are more likely to support greater force than formal training and policy.

Most uses of force are legal, but some are questionable and even illegal. The public's definitions of excessive force and brutality often differ from those of the police. There are two views of police brutality. The first is that brutality is widespread because rogue police officers are permitted to hide behind lax accountability mechanisms. The second is that brutality is not a major problem and must be considered in the context of overall high levels of violent crime. While the frequency of illegal police violence or brutality is low, its importance should not be understated.

Police use of deadly force has been extensively studied, but its frequency is difficult to determine because of reporting problems. Research has examined the factors that contribute to the use of deadly force and attempted to explain why its frequency varies from community to community. In the past decade, policy guidelines for the use of deadly force have changed, and many police departments have adopted strict policies governing the use of such force. The result has been fewer citizens killed by the police.

Critical Thinking Questions

1. To what extent is police use of force and coercion inevitable? To what extent is police brutality inevitable?

2. Where should canines be placed on the use of force continuum? Pepper spray? Tasers?

3. How frequent is the police use of illegal violence? Why do police sometimes use illegal violence? Do you think it can ever be justified?

4. Why is it so difficult to measure the amount of force, including deadly force, the police use? What kind of a system could be developed to do a better job of measuring this important aspect of police behavior?

5. Many police departments have enacted deadly force policies that are more restrictive than the law in their states. Why do you think they have done this? Do you think it is proper for them to do this?

References

Alpert, G. P. 1989. "Questioning Police Pursuits in Urban Areas." In R. G. Dunham and G. P. Alpert (eds.), *Critical Issues in Policing: Contemporary Readings,* pp. 216–229. Prospect Heights, IL: Waveland.

Alpert, G. P., and Anderson, P. 1986. "The Most Deadly Force: Police Pursuits." *Justice Quarterly* 2: 1–14.

Alpert, G. P., Kenney, D. J., Dunham, R. G., and Smith, W. C. 2000. *Police Pursuits: What We Know.* Washington, DC: Police Executive Research Forum.

Anderson, D. C. 2003. "Managed Force," Ford Foundation Report. Available at http://www.parc.info/client_files/Articles/6%20-%20Ford%20Article.pdf.

Baker, A. 2008. "Officers Face Department Charges in Bell Killing." *The New York Times.* May 21. Available online at http://www.nytimes.com/2008/05/21/nyregion/21sean.html.

Baker, A., and Elgion, J. 2010. "Officers Won't Face Federal Charges in Sean Bell Killing." *The New York Times.* February 16. Available online at http://www.nytimes.com/2010/02/17/nyregion/17bell.html?scp=1&sq=officers%20won%27t%20face%20charges%20in%20sean%20bell%20killing&st=cse

Barker, T. 1986. "Peer Group Support for Police Occupational Deviance." In T. Barker and D. L. Carter (eds.), *Police Deviance,* pp. 9–21. Cincinnati, OH: Pilgrimage.

Bayley, D. H. 1986. "The Tactical Choices of Police Patrol Officers." *Journal of Criminal Justice* 14: 329–348.

Bayley, D. H., and Garofalo, J. 1989. "The Management of Violence by Police Patrol Officers." *Criminology* 27: 1–12.

Beers, D. 1992. "A Biting Controversy." *Los Angeles Times Magazine,* February 9: 23–26, 43–44.

Berenson, A. 2004. "Claims Over Tasers' Safety Are Challenged." *New York Times*, November 26. Available online at http://www.nytimes.com/2004/11/26/business/26taser.html.

Berkowitz, L. 1993. *Aggression: Its Causes, Consequence, and Control.* Philadelphia, PA: Temple University Press.

"Big Decline in Killings of Citizens by Police." 1986. *San Francisco Chronicle*, October 20: 23.

Bittner, E. 1995. "The Capacity to Use Force as the Core of the Police Role." In V. Kappeler (ed.), *The Police and Society: Touchstone Readings*, pp. 127–137. Prospect Heights, IL: Waveland. Reprinted from *The Functions of Police in Modern Society.* Washington, DC: National Institute of Mental Health.

Blumberg, M. 1997. *Controlling Police Use of Deadly Force: Assessing Two Decades of Progress.* In R. G. Dunham and G. P. Alpert (eds.), *Critical Issues in Policing*, 3rd ed., pp. 507–530. Prospect Heights, IL: Waveland.

Brown, J. M., and Langan, P. A. 2001. *Policing and Homicide, 1976–1998: Justifiable Homicide by Police, Police Officers Murdered by Felons.* Washington, DC: Bureau of Justice Statistics.

Brown, M. F. 1983. "Shooting Policies: What Patrolmen Think." *Police Chief* 50: 35–37.

Campbell, A., Berk, R., and Fyfe, J. 1998. "Deployment of Violence: The Los Angeles Police Department's Use of Dogs." *Policing* 22: 535–561.

Carmichael, J. T., and Jacobs, D. 2002. "Violence by and Against the Police." In R. G. Burns and C. E. Crawford (eds.), *Policing and Violence*, pp. 25–51. Upper Saddle River, NJ: Prentice Hall.

Carter, D. L. 1985. "Police Brutality: A Model for Definition, Perspective, and Control." In A. S. Blumberg and E. Niederhoffer (eds.), *The Ambivalent Force: Perspective on the Police*, pp. 321–330. New York: Holt, Rinehart & Winston.

———. 1994. "Theoretical Dimensions on the Abuse of Authority by Police Officers." In T. Barker and D. Carter (eds.), *Police Deviance*, 3rd ed., pp. 269–290. Cincinnati, OH: Anderson.

Correll, J. Park, B., Judd, C. M., and Wittenbrenk, B. 2002. "The Police Officer's Dilemma: Using Ethnicity to Disambiguate Potentially Threatening Individuals." *Journal of Personality and Social Psychology* 83: 1314–1029.

Correll, J. Park, B., Judd, C. M., Wittenbrenk, B, Sadler, M. S., and Keesee, T. 2007. "Across the Thin Blue Line: Police Officers and Racial Bias in the Decision to Shoot." *Journal of Personality and Social Psychology* 92: 1006–1023.

Crank, J. P. 1998. *Understanding Police Culture.* Cincinnati, OH: Anderson.

"Doubt Shed on Cops' Report in L.A. Beating." 1991. *San Jose Mercury News,* March 23: 1F, 4F.

Durose, M. R., Smith, E. L., and Langan, P. A. 2007. *Contacts Between Police and the Public, 2005.* Washington, DC: Bureau of Justice Statistics.

Dwyer, J. 2008. "Three Men Who Had No Reason to Run." *The New York Times*. April 5. Available at http://www.nytimes.com/2008/04/05/nyregion/05about.html.

Faulkner, S. 1994. "A Ralph Nadar Approach to Law Enforcement Training." *Police Studies* 17: 21–32.

Felkenes, G. T. 1991. "Affirmative Action in the Los Angeles Police Department." *Criminal Justice Research Bulletin* 6: 1–9.

Fox, J. A., and M. Zawitz. 2007. *Homicide Trends in the United States.* Washington, DC: Bureau of Justice Statistics. Available online at http://bjs.ojp.usdoj.gov/content/pub/pdf/htius.pdf.

Fridell, L. 1989. "Justifiable Use of Measures in Research on Deadly Force." *Journal of Criminal Justice* 17: 157–165.

Friederich, R. J. 1980. "Police Use of Force: Individuals, Situations, and Organizations." *Annals of the American Academy of Political and Social Sciences* 452: 82–97.

Fyfe, J. J. 1978. "Shots Fired: An Examination of New York City Police Firearms Discharges." Ph.D. dissertation, University of New York at Albany.

———. 1979. "Administrative Interventions on Police Shooting Discretion." *Journal of Criminal Justice* 7: 309–323.

———. 1980. "Geographic Correlates of Police Shooting." *Journal of Research in Crime and Delinquency* 17: 101–113.

———. 1983. "Enforcement Workshop: The Los Angeles Chokehold Controversy." *Criminal Law Bulletin* 1961–1967.

———. 1988. "Police Use of Deadly Force: Research and Reform." *Justice Quarterly* 5: 165–205.

Geller, W. A., and Karales, K. J. 1981. *Split-Second Decisions: Shootings of and by Chicago Police.* Chicago: Chicago Law Enforcement Study Group.

Geller, W., and Scott, M. 1992. *Deadly Force: What We Know.* Washington, DC: Police Executive Research Forum.

Golden, J. W., and Walker, J. T. 2002. "That Dog Will Hunt: Canine-Assisted Search and Seizure." In J. T. Walker (ed.), *Policing and the Law,* pp. 71–89. Upper Saddle River, NJ: Prentice Hall.

Government Accountability Office. 2005. *TASER Weapons: Use of Tasers by Selected Law Enforcement Agencies.* Washington, DC: author. Available online at http://www.gao.gov/new.items/d05464.pdf.

Greenfeld, L., Langan, P., and Smith, S. 1997. *Police Use of Force: Collection of Statistical Data.* Washington, DC: Bureau of Justice Statistics.

Griffin, S. P. and Bernard, T. J. 2003. "Angry Aggression among Police Officers." *Police Quarterly* 6:3–21.

Hickman, M. J. 2006. *Citizen Complaints about Police Use of Force.* Washington, DC: Bureau of Justice Statistics.

Hickman, M. J., Piquero, A. R., and Garner, J. H. 2008. "Toward a National Estimate of Police Use of Nonlethal Force." *Criminology & Public Policy* 7: 563–604.

Holmes, M. D. and Smith, B. W. 2008. *Race and Police Brutality: Roots of an Urban Dilemma.* Albany: State University of New York Press.

Holmes, M. D., and Smith, B. W. Unpublished manuscript. "Intergroup Dynamics of Extra-Legal Police Aggression: A Theory of Race and Place."

Hopkins, E. J. 1931. *Our Lawless Police.* New York: Viking.

Horvath, F., and Donahue, M. 1982. *Deadly Force: An Analysis of Shootings by Police in Michigan, 1976–1981.* East Lansing: Michigan State University.

"How Much Force Is Enough." 1998. *Law Enforcement News,* November 30: 1, 10.

Human Rights Watch. 1998. *Shielded From Justice: Police Brutality and Accountability in the United States.* New York: Human Rights Watch.

Hunt, J. 1985. "Police Accounts of Normal Force." *Urban Life* 13: 315–341.

"Inside View of L.A. Beating." 1991. *San Jose Mercury News,* March 19: 1A, 9A.

Kania, R. R. E., and Mackey, W. C. 1977. "Police Violence as a Function of Community Characteristics." *Criminology* 15: 27–48.

Klockars, C. 1980. "The Dirty Harry Problem." *Annals* 452: 33–47.

Kuykendall, J. 1981. "Trends in the Use of Deadly Force by Police." *Journal of Criminal Justice* 9: 359–366.

"L.A. Fires Only 1 Percent of Officers." 1991. *San Jose Mercury News,* May 5: 4B.

Lamb, R., and Friday, P. 1997. "Impact of Pepper Spray Availability on Police Officer Use-of-Force Decisions." *Policing* 20: 136–148.

Larson, J. A. 1932. *Lying and Its Detection.* Chicago: University of Chicago Press.

Marion, Nancy. 1998. "Police Academy Training: Are We Teaching Recruits What They Need to Know?" *Policing* 21: 54–79.

Marzulli, J. 2010. "Sean Bell Case: Judge Rejects City Bid to Delay Civil Suit Against NYPD Cops Involved in Shooting." *New York Daily News.* March 10. Available online at http://www.nydailynews.com/news/ny_crime/2010/03/10/2010-03-10_sean_bell_case_judge_rejects_city_bid_to_delay_civil_suit_against_nypd_cops_invo.html.

Massey, D. S. and Denton, N. A. 1993. *American Apartheid: Segregation and the Making of the Underclass.* Cambridge, MA: Harvard University Press.

Matulia, K. R. 1985. *A Balance of Forces,* 2nd ed. Gaithersburg, MD: International Association of Chiefs of Police.

McEwen, T. 1997. "Policies on Less-Than-Lethal Force in Law Enforcement Agencies." *Policing* 20: 39–59.

McNulty, E. 1994. "Generating Common-Sense Knowledge Among Police Officers." *Symbolic Interaction* 17: 281–294.

Miller, M. R. 1995. *Police Patrol Operations.* Placerville, CA: Copperhouse Publishing Company.

Miranda v. Arizona. 384 U.S., 436,466 (1966).

Morrison, G. B. 2003. "Police and Correctional Department Firearm Training Frameworks in Washington State." *Police Quarterly* 6: 192–221.

National Commission on Law Observance and Enforcement. 1931. *Report on Lawlessness in Law Enforcement,* no. 11. Washington, DC: U.S. Government Printing Office (also known as the Wickersham Commission).

Navarro, M. 1995. "The Debate Over High-Speed Police Chases." *New York Times National,* Dec. 17: 18.

Payne, B. K. 2001. "Prejudice and Perception: The Role of Automatic and Controlled Processes in Misperceiving a Weapon." *Journal of Personality and Social Psychology* 81: 181–192

Peak, K. 1993. *Policing America: Methods, Issues, Challenges.* Englewood Cliffs, NJ: Prentice Hall.

Phillips, A. 2008. "NYPD Changes Sought in Wake of Sean Bell Shooting." *The New York Sun.* June, 9.

Police Executive Research Forum. 2005. "Conducted Energy Device (CED) Glossary of Terms." Available online at http://www.policeforum.org/upload/PERF-CED-Guidelines-Updated-10–25-05%5B1%5D_715866088_1230200514040.pdf.

President's Commission on Law Enforcement and the Administration of Justice. 1967. *Task Force Report: The Police.* Washington, DC: U.S. Government Printing Office.

Reiss, A. J., Jr. 1967. *The Police and the Public.* New Haven, CT: Yale University Press.

"Report Calls for Gates' Ouster." 1991. *San Jose Mercury News,* July 10: 1A, 6A.

Reuss-Ianni, E. 1983. *The Two Cultures of Policing: Street Cops and Management Cops.* New Brunswick, NJ: Transaction.

Sherman, L. W., and Cohn, E. G. 1986. *Citizens Killed by Big-City Police: 1974–1984.* Washington, DC: Crime Control Institute.

Sherman, L., and Langworthy, R. 1979. "Measuring Homicide by Police Officers." *Journal of Criminal Law and Criminology* 9: 317–331.

Skolnick, J., and Fyfe, J. 1993. *Above the Law: Police and the Excessive Use of Force.* New York: Free Press.

Smith, B. W. 2004. "The Impact of Police Officer Diversity on Police-Caused Homicides." *The Policy Studies Journal* 31: 147–162.

Sparger, J., and Giacopassi, D. 1992. "Memphis Revisited: A Reexamination of Police Shootings After the Garner Decision." *Justice Quarterly* 9: 211–225.

"Stun-Gun Charges Shake NYPD to the Rafters." 1985. *Law Enforcement News* May: 6, 13.

Sulc, L. B. 1995. "Police Brutality Is Not a Widespread Problem." In P. Winters (ed.), *Policing the Police,* pp. 79–85. San Diego: Greenhaven.

Sykes, R. E., and Brent, E. E. 1983. *Policing: A Social Behaviorist Perspective.* New Brunswick, NJ: Rutgers University Press.

Terrill, W. 2001. *Police Coercion: Application of the Force Continuum.* New York: LFB Scholarly Publishing.

———. 2003. "Police Use of Force and Suspect Resistance: The Micro-process of the Police-Suspect Encounter." *Police Quarterly* 6: 51–83.

———. 2005. "Police Use of Force: A Transactional Approach." *Justice Quarterly* 22: 107–138.

Terrill, W., Alpert, G. P., Dunham, R. G., and Smith, M. R. 2003. "A Management Tool for Evaluating Police Use of Force: An Application of the Force Factor." *Police Quarterly* 6: 150–171.

Trimmer, R. 1993. "Pepper Spray After Concord: Legal Issues for Policy Makers." *North Carolina Justice Academy,* July.

Tucker, W. 1995. "Inner-City Crime is a Worse Problem than Police Brutality." In P. Winters (ed.), *Policing the Police,* pp. 69–78. San Diego: Greenhaven.

Van Raalte, R. 1986. Interview. *Law Enforcement News* March: 9–12.

Vaughn, M. 1992. "The Parameters of Trickery as an Acceptable Police Practice." *American Journal of Police* 11: 71–95.

Walker, S. 1998. *Sense and Nonsense About Drugs and Crime: A Policy Guide,* 4th ed. Belmont, CA: West/Wadsworth.

Welch, M. 2002. "Police Pursuits: Just One Form of Police Violence." In R.G. Burns and C. E. Crawford (eds.), *Policing and Violence,* pp. 147–166. Upper Saddle River, NJ: Prentice Hall.

White, M. D. 2006. "Hitting the Target (or not): Comparing Characteristics of Fatal, Injurious, and Noninjurious Police Shootings." *Police Quarterly* 9: 303–330.

White, M. D., and Ready, J. 2007. "The TASER as a Less Lethal Force Alternative: Findings on Use and Effectiveness in a Large Metropolitan Police Agency." *Police Quarterly* 10: 170–191.

Wilson, J. Q. 1968. *Varieties of Police Behavior: The Management of Law and Order in Eight Communities.* Cambridge, MA: Harvard University Press.

CHAPTER 11

Accountability and Ethics

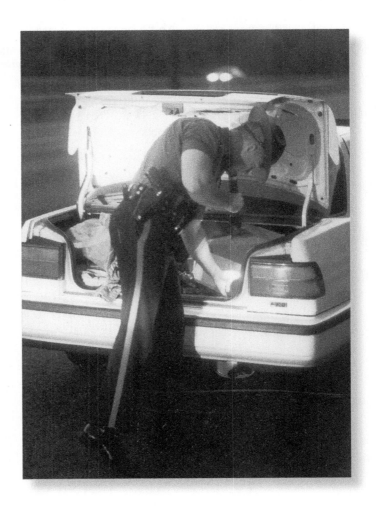

CHAPTER OUTLINE

- Internal Accountability Mechanisms
    Bureaucratic Organization and Management
    Internal Investigation
    Issues in Internal Investigations
    Early Warning/Early Identification Systems
    Effectiveness of Internal Investigations

CHAPTER OUTLINE (continued)

- External Accountability Mechanisms
    - Civilian Review
    - Police Auditor Systems
    - Legal Control
- The Limits of Oversight Mechanisms
- Professional Standards
    - The Police Professionalization Movement
    - Criteria of Police Professionalization
- Ethical Standards
    - Ethical Perspectives
    - Ethical Dilemmas
- The Limits of Professional and Ethical Standards
- Summary
- Critical Thinking Questions
- References

KEY TERMS

- accreditation
- Commission on Accreditation for Law Enforcement Agencies (CALEA)
- certification
- civilian review board
- civil liability
- decertification
- early warning/early identification system
- ethical formalism
- ethical relativism
- ethical utilitarianism
- exclusionary rule
- exoneration
- false complaints
- Garrity interview
- grievance arbitration
- internal affairs
- police-auditor systems
- professionalism
- reliability
- sustained complaints
- unfounded complaints
- unsubstantiated complaints
- validity

THE POLICE ARE THE most visible representatives of the criminal justice system in the United States. Yet, in important ways, the police stand apart from society. Their special dispensation is the use of force so that citizens can live together in peace. Nevertheless, by virtue of the authority granted to them to use force, they have the potential to undermine due processes of law (Skolnick 1994). This potential may be infrequently utilized, yet citizens are concerned about police abuse of authority.

The police are respected and feared at the same time. They are respected by many citizens who highly regard the commitment police make to their work, but they are also feared because of the enormous life-and-death authority that they carry. The accountability of the police to democratic processes continues to be one of the central issues confronting the police throughout modern times (McMullan 1998).

To whom are the police accountable? One might be tempted to answer that they are accountable to elected and appointed officials, the general public, people who receive police service (e.g., victims, suspects), and other parts of the criminal justice system (e.g., prosecuting attorneys, judges). Yet this answer overlooks important issues of accountability. Do citizens understand police work well enough to judge the behavior of the police? Should police be responsible for assessing the behavior of their own officers? And what happens when the public encourages the police to break the law to do something about law-breaking people? In short, the issues of accountability are complicated, and there is little agreement on who has the authority to hold the police accountable, the means by which they should be held accountable, or for what they should be held accountable (Geller 1985).

The control of police behavior occurs in two fundamentally different ways. The first is through mechanisms of oversight. These are based on the idea that if a police officer's behavior can be tracked, then illegal or inappropriate behavior can be identified and corrected or punished. Oversight mechanisms are both internal and external to a police department. Internally, oversight is through departmental investigation, early warning systems, and the restraints of bureaucratic organization and management. Externally, oversight occurs through citizen review, external auditing, and legal remedies for police misconduct.

The second way is through standards, which will be considered in the second half of this chapter. According to this view, officers can be hired with, or trained in, standards of conduct by which they can gauge their behavior. Both professional and ethical standards of "right behavior" fortify them with an appropriate way of thinking about their work and thereby control their behavior.

Internal Accountability Mechanisms

Three oversight mechanisms within police departments will be considered here: standard managerial processes, early warning systems, and internal complaint reviews.

Bureaucratic Organization and Management

The most important day-to-day source of accountability for police officers is in the way their department is organized and managed (Walker 2005). Accountability is carried out through the design and operation of principles of bureaucratic organization, as extensively discussed in Chapter 5. This idea will be reviewed here primarily in terms of management–employee relations.

Written Directives. In police departments, bureaucratic standards are omnipresent. As Alpert and Smith observe, "law enforcement is a paradigm of operational control. Virtually every aspect of policing is subject to some combination of either policy, guideline, directive, rule, or general order" (1999, 353). The organization of rules and regulations takes on a specific language in a bureaucracy. Principal terms are listed below. These terms provide the statements that guide the behavior of the department and indicate the responsibility of officers within it.

1. *Departmental policies* are not, as often thought, rules but rather statements of guiding principles that should be followed. A policy should be thought of as a guide to thinking rather than a fixed outcome. A policy is a general statement that gives guidance to police officers as to the proper course of action (e.g., a use-of-force policy).

2. A *goal* is a general statement of purpose that is useful in identifying the role and mission of the police (e.g., to apprehend criminals).

3. An *objective* is a more specific and measurable statement of purpose that is related to a goal (e.g., make arrests in 25 percent of burglary cases).

4. A *procedure* identifies a method or series of steps to be taken when performing a task or attempting to solve a problem (e.g., how to investigate a traffic accident).

5. Finally, a *rule,* or *regulation,* is a specific statement that identifies required or prohibited behavior by officers (e.g., all officers must dress in a certain manner). The terms *rule* and *regulation* are often used interchangeably.

Administrative guidance focuses on a wide variety of topics. Under principles of departmental supervision, managers' responsibilities aim at ensuring that officers' behaviors are consistent with bureaucratic policies and standards. Written directives (policies, procedures, rules, regulations), as Carter and Barker (1994, 22–23) have observed, are important for the following reasons:

1. They inform officers of expected standards of behavior.
2. They inform the community of the departmental mission, goals, values, policies, procedures, and expected standards of officer behavior.
3. They establish a common foundation for the execution of the police process to enhance operational consistency, equal protection, and due process.
4. They provide grounds for disciplining and counseling errant officers.
5. They provide standards for officer supervision.
6. They give direction for officer training.

Within a bureaucratic environment, standards are expressed in written terms as departmental policy and guidelines. Yet, in a police department, managers may not follow policies and standards to the letter. In practice, managers may react in a variety of ways when officers deviate from those written standards. They may (1) ignore it, (2) act formally or informally, or (3) protect the officer.

A manager's formal responses to improper behavior may include counseling or training (advising or teaching the person how to improve) or some type of disciplinary action (reprimand, suspension, demotion, or termination). The more public criticism there is of certain types of police behavior, the more likely managers are to use some form of punitive discipline. Some managers like to make an example of an employee to send a signal to other officers that certain types of behavior will not be tolerated. Employees, however, may consider this type of managerial response politically motivated and unfair. From the employees' point of view, they are being made a scapegoat to satisfy political interests.

If a manager believes a deviation exists but has insufficient evidence to act formally, he or she might respond informally, perhaps by transferring the employee to a new work area or assignment. Certain types of assignments can be used so often in a department that they become known as punitive assignments (e.g., the jail or foot patrol during the winter). Sometimes, for instance, if the problem is related to the behavior of the officer when interacting with the public, the officer may be assigned to a job with minimal public contact. In addition, the manager may hope that this type of informal, punitive control will result in a resignation or retirement.

The effectiveness of written standards rests, in part, on the willingness of supervisors to hold officers accountable. Given that supervisors are recruited from the ranks of patrol officers, it seems likely that they will sometimes choose not to punish subordinates (Holmes and Smith 2008). A manager may be aware of a deviation but elect to protect the officer for at least five reasons. The manager may (1) approve of the "deviant" activity or behavior, (2) believe that the most likely official departmental response would be too punitive, (3) be influenced by the so-called code-of-silence in policing, (4) believe that acknowledging the deviation would result in criticism of his/her management ability, or (5) simply want to avoid dealing with the problem by denying that it exists.

Limitations of written directives. Policies, procedures, rules, regulations, and objectives are written standards against which an officer's behavior is judged by supervisors. Officers are expected to conform to these standards. In many police departments, standards number in the hundreds and are printed in very thick manuals. Standards tend to accumulate over time as police departments are faced with a wide variety of situations. It is not uncommon for police officers to be unfamiliar with many of these standards because some are rarely used.

Why do police departments have so many policies? Part of the reason lies in the unpredictable nature of the police function. Police work is highly varied and carried out in a diversity of circumstances. Policies attempt to provide direction in unclear situations. Auten notes that the absence of policy leaves officers "in the dark in the expectation that they will intuitively divine the right course of action in the performance of their duties" (1988, 1–2).

Policies, while providing a standard for behavior, suffer from significant limitations. In practice, they are sometimes rule oriented and tell officers what not to do rather than suggest a possible course of action. This can have an alienating effect on individual officers. Some researchers contend that the rigid bureaucracy characteristic of many police departments is principally responsible for the alienation of line officers and the intensification of more secretive elements of police culture. Consider the following statement Manning recorded during an interview:

> . . . 140 years of fuck-ups. Every time something goes wrong, they make a rule about it. All the directions in the force flow from someone's mistake. You can't go eight hours on the job without breaking the disciplinary code . . . the job goes wild on trivialities.
> *(1978, 79)*

A related issue is that police work, by its nature, requires officers to make quick discretionary decisions in varied, unpredictable situations. It has proven difficult, if not impossible, for police managers to formulate written guidelines that effectively cover all the varied situations that police officers encounter on the street. Consequently, policing continues to require officers to act based on "an intuitive grasp of situational exigencies" (Bittner 1970). Officers learn much of what they need to know to make good decisions and do good police work on the job, by apprenticeship and trial and error, rather than by referring to the manual of policies, procedures, rules, and regulations. In this context, written guidelines can seem irrelevant at best and, at worst, an impediment to effective policing (Cordner 1989).

Internal Investigation

All police departments have some way of responding to citizen complaints or internal concerns about police behavior. In many small and moderate-size departments, this response may be the part-time responsibility of only one officer, probably a supervisor or manager. In larger departments, it has been the practice to establish a unit, often called **internal affairs**, to respond to complaints.

Police officer misconduct may come to the attention of police administrators and/or internal affairs units in a number of ways. Citizens may file a complaint about a particular police officer (an issue we will explore later in the chapter). Fellow police officers may file a formal complaint or provide an anonymous tip to supervisors or an internal affairs unit. Police supervisors or internal affairs units may uncover misconduct through proactive means (e.g., early warning systems). Finally, a police agency may be alerted to misconduct from other external agencies (e.g., other police departments).

The Investigative Process. When police officers are being investigated as suspects in a crime, they have the same legal procedural rights as any other suspect. But what rights should they have when they are being investigated administratively by supervisors, managers, or internal affairs units? States vary in the rights afforded police officers facing discipline. California has enacted into law what is, in effect, a police officer's bill of rights. Inside Policing 11.1 provides a summary of these rights.

The process for investigating complaints against officers tends to be similar to other types of investigations. The steps used by many police departments are briefly summarized below (D'Arcy et al. 1990):

1. Review the complainant's allegation to determine what departmental standard(s) was violated.

INSIDE POLICING 11.1 **Police Officer's Bill of Rights**

When any police officer is under investigation and subjected to interrogation that could lead to punitive action, the interrogation shall be conducted under the following conditions. These rights do not apply to an interrogation in the normal course of duty, which might involve counseling, instruction, or informal verbal admonishments.

1. The interrogation shall be conducted at a reasonable hour, preferably when the police officer is on duty, or during normal waking hours, unless the seriousness of the investigation requires otherwise. If the interrogation takes place during off-duty time, the officer shall be compensated in accordance with regular departmental procedures.

2. The persons to be present at the interrogation must be identified in advance, and the officer will not be interrogated by more than two investigators at one time.

3. The police officer will be informed of the charges against him or her prior to any interrogation.

4. The interrogation will be for a reasonable period of time.

5. The police officer shall not be subjected to any offensive language or threats of punitive action, except that an officer refusing to respond to questions or submit to interrogation shall be informed that failure to answer questions that are directly related to the investigation may result in punitive action. There will be no promise or reward offered as an inducement to answer any question.

6. The interrogation may be recorded by either the persons conducting the interrogation or the officer under investigation or both. The officer in question is entitled to written or recorded copies of the interrogation if additional action is contemplated by the department or if there is to be a continuing investigation.

7. If prior to, or during, the interrogation it is decided that the officer may be charged with a criminal offense, the officer will immediately be informed of his or her constitutional rights.

8. If a formal written statement of charges is filed against a police officer by the department, the officer has a right to request that a representative of his or her choice be present during any interrogation.

SOURCE: Adapted from the *California Government Code*, Section 3303.

2. Contact and interview all witnesses and reinterview the complainant if necessary.

3. Collect all other evidence, such as photographs, medical reports, police reports, and so on.

4. Obtain background information on the complainant (e.g., criminal history and any prior allegations against officers).

5. Obtain background data concerning the officer (e.g., prior complaints, personnel evaluations, prior disciplinary actions by the department).

6. Interview all departmental members who may be involved.

Although internal investigations and criminal investigations are similar, there are important differences. Carter (1994) identifies several pertinent differences in internal investigations:

1. The Fourth Amendment guarantees apply to police officers at home and off duty, as they do to any citizen.

2. Lockers at the police station, a police car, and other elements of on-duty performance are unlikely to be protected by the Fourth Amendment.

3. If an unlawful search occurs, the fruits of that search may be used during a disciplinary hearing but not in a legal proceeding. This may not apply to departments that have elaborate policies on the internal investigation process.

4. Under *Garrity v. New Jersey* (1967), statements compelled during an internal investigation cannot be used later in a court of law. Such compelled testimony for internal investigations is routine practice and is not protected by the Fifth Amendment from use within administrative processes and hearings, but it cannot be used in a criminal prosecution for the very reason that it was compelled, not voluntary. This type of compelled testimony is frequently referred to as a **Garrity interview**.

Complaint Outcomes. Investigations into citizen complaints are typically classified in one of four possible ways: **Sustained complaints** are ones that, as the result of an investigation, are determined to be justified. **Unsubstantiated complaints** are ones that, in the opinion of those making the decision, have no supporting evidence and so cannot be considered either true or false. The majority of citizen complaints against officers are classified in this manner because it is often difficult to determine with reasonable certainty that the complainant's allegation is true. **Unfounded complaints** are those that the investigation determines did not occur as alleged by the complainant. **Exoneration** of an officer occurs when the investigation results in a finding that the alleged complaint is essentially true but the officer's behavior is considered justified, legal, and within organizational policy (Perez 1994).

If an officer is found guilty of the complaint, she or he can appeal the outcome. Avenues of appeal typically include the parent government's civil service system and the courts. If the complaint is sustained, the officer will receive some sort of punishment. Carter (1994) identifies several kinds of punishments:

1. *Termination of employment.* This is complete severance, including loss of salary and benefits.

2. *Demotion/loss of rank.* Loss of rank is a significant action because it represents loss of salary and liability in career growth. It may not include "grades," which are salary increments within ranks.

3. *Punitive suspension.* An officer is barred from work and denied salary for a designated period, usually not exceeding four weeks. In many jurisdictions the officer cannot even work off-duty in positions that require police authority.

4. *Punitive probation.* An officer stays on duty with full salary and benefits. A subsequent sustained misconduct allegation may result in dismissal.

5. *Reassignment.* This is often used in conjunction with some other kind of punishment. An officer may be taken out of a specialized position or moved to another shift or location.

6. *Mandatory training.* An officer may receive training on the issue related to the misconduct.

7. *Reprimand.* An officer is officially admonished for his or her behavior. It is in written form, usually from a division commander, with a copy placed in the personnel file.

8. *Supervisory counseling.* This is a discussion with the officer concerning a problem usually related to some performance factor or procedure. It is intended to be both instructive and corrective. It does not typically become a part of the employee's personnel file. *(367–368)*

Research concerning the number, types, and dispositions of complaints against police is limited. Several studies, however, provide useful insights. A summary (Independent Commission 1991; Dugan and Breda 1991; Petterson 1991; Walker 1998; Wallace 1990; "Younger NYC Cops" 1989) is presented below:

1. Although less than 1 percent of citizens complain about police methods and behavior, as many as 10 to 15 percent may think that they have something to complain about—either what officers did or failed to do.

2. The rate of complaints varies among police departments, from about 6 to 81 complaints per 100 officers per year.

3. The percentage of sustained complaints also varies among police departments, from about 0 to 50.

4. Complaints concerning the excessive use of police force are usually sustained less often than other types of complaints.

5. It appears that a small number of police officers account for a disproportionate number of complaints. Although the research varies, a reasonable estimate is that approximately 10 percent of the officers in a police department receive at least 25 or 30 percent of the complaints by citizens.

6. It also appears that a disproportionate number of complaints are filed against younger, less experienced officers. As many as two thirds or more of all complaints in some departments may involve officers who are 30 years of age or younger and who have 5 or less years of experience.

Table 11.1 presents data on citizen complaints about excessive force in the nation's 10 largest cities and reveals widespread differences between rates of complaints per 100 officers and the percentage of sustained complaints. The frequency of complaints varies sharply from city to city. To understand these differences, several factors must be considered.

The number and types of complaints against the police, in general, are the result of actual differences in police behavior, the perceived receptivity of a police department to accepting and acting upon complaints, and a political climate that either discourages or encourages

TABLE 11.1 Citizen Complaints About Police Use of Force in 2002

CITY	NUMBER OF COMPLAINTS	COMPLAINTS PER 100 OFFICERS	% SUSTAINED
New York City	4,450	12.37	3.98
Los Angeles	419	4.50	0.48
Chicago	2,890	21.46	4.84
Miami–Dade	75	2.36	8.00
Houston	230	4.30	0.43
Philadelphia	442	6.45	4.07
Phoenix	17	0.62	5.88
San Antonio	133	6.47	3.76
Dallas	131	4.45	9.16
Detroit	1,172	30.54	14.93

Source: U.S. Department of Justice, Bureau of Justice Statistics. *Law Enforcement Management and Administrative Statistics: 2003 Sample Survey of Law Enforcement Agencies.* Washington, DC: U.S. Department of Commerce, Bureau of the Census.

citizens to complain. In some communities, citizens do not complain about the police because they do not think it will do any good or because they are afraid the police will retaliate. Some departments make it difficult for citizens to complain by creating a cumbersome complaint process and by the negative (e.g., unfriendly, rude, curt, discouraging) behavior of officers when citizens attempt to complain.

The political climate in a community may be particularly important in encouraging or discouraging complaints against the police. On the one hand, a new mayor or other elected official who calls for an aggressive "crackdown" on crime or who talks about the police as the "thin blue line" between citizens and criminals may be indicating to citizens that their concerns about police excesses will not be taken seriously. On the other hand, a new mayor or chief of police might encourage citizens to come forward with complaints about the police. Such encouragement, however, may result in an increase in frivolous as well as serious complaints.

The reasons for variations in sustained complaints are also related to the degree to which departments have well-defined standards for police behavior, take those standards seriously, and conduct thorough investigations into complaints. Low rates of sustained complaints may result from a departmental culture that implicitly encourages officers to engage in aggressive police work and fails to thoroughly investigate accusations of misconduct.

Issues in Internal Investigations

There are several controversies concerning the internal investigation of police officers. These include the physical location of the internal affairs unit, the personnel assigned to work in internal affairs, whether complaints should be encouraged, whether internal affairs units should be proactive or reactive, what should be done about false complaints, the type and severity of discipline for officers who have sustained complaints, and whether the police can effectively police themselves.

Location and Personnel. Does the location of internal affairs units influence the number of citizen complaints? It is possible that a citizen who believes he or she has been abused by the police will be reluctant to go to the police department to file a complaint. As Perez observes,

> The uniforms, badges, guns, and paramilitary carriage of police officers at a station house might be too much to confront for more passive complaints. A system that requires complaints cannot be made exclusively for those citizens having the audacity to confront the government. *(1994, 103)*

As a result of this possibility, some police departments have placed the internal affairs unit in another location away from police headquarters. This change of location may also have a positive impact on the public perception of the police, because citizens may believe that the police are taking their complaints seriously.

Most often the personnel who conduct internal investigations are sworn police officers, but some departments also use civilians for investigations on the assumption that some citizens who want to complain will be more comfortable with a civilian than a police investigator. Also, the use of civilians creates the public perception that complaints will be taken more seriously and be more thoroughly investigated. In addition, because a substantial number of complaints are made by minority citizens, internal affairs units may also be staffed with minority members. This use of civilian (nonsworn) minorities may even be necessary if the police department has no minority officers who can be assigned to the internal affairs unit.

Assignment to internal affairs is often controversial. Internal affairs investigators are rarely popular with other officers. The term "headhunter," or some other uncomplimentary nickname, is sometimes used by officers to describe internal affairs investigators. As a result, some police chiefs and sheriffs have made it clear that assignment to, and effective performance in, an internal affairs unit is a "fast track" to advancement/promotion within the agency.

Orientation of Internal Affairs Units. Should citizen complaints against the police be encouraged? Encouraging citizens to come forward—either openly or anonymously—has several possible consequences. On the one hand, it may increase the trust between police and citizens and provide managers with valuable information about officer behavior (Walker and Graham 1998). On the other hand, it may also result in more complaints, justified or otherwise. Unfortunately, in departments that encourage complaints, a morale problem may develop as an increasing number of officers have to endure investigations into complaints. Whether or not complaints are sustained, internal affairs investigations are often stressful for the officers involved and unpleasant for officers throughout the department.

Should internal affairs units be reactive or proactive? A reactive unit investigates only those complaints that are brought to its attention. A proactive unit seeks out officers involved in deviant behavior. For example, an internal affairs investigator might purposely commit traffic violations and, when stopped by an officer, offer a bribe to avoid a citation. If the officer takes the money, he or she is usually terminated and may be criminally prosecuted. Such a proactive approach may be strongly resented by officers because it creates a climate of mistrust between them and managers. Although some authorities recommend that internal affairs units be proactive (Murphy and Caplan 1991, 261–263), managers must be aware of the possible adverse consequences of such action.

Although it is not clear how often it occurs, citizens make **false complaints** about police officers. How should the police respond? In some jurisdictions, persons suspected of filing a false report can be criminally prosecuted. Police officers can also sue the person for defamation if he or she falsely accuses an officer of criminal conduct, misconduct, or incompetence.

While it is the officer involved who decides whether to file a civil suit against a citizen who made a false complaint, the police department decides whether to file criminal charges. Should they have that right? Although filing criminal charges may act as a deterrent against false complaints, it may also have a chilling effect on citizens with legitimate grievances, making this a most difficult question to resolve.

Responding to Sustained Complaints. When complaints against officers are sustained, what should be done? The alternatives include counseling, retraining, verbal reprimands, written reprimands, demotions, suspension without pay, and termination. Unfortunately, there is no standard to follow. Generally, of course, the more serious the behavior of the officer, the more severe the punishment.

After their examination of 171 sustained complaints involving excessive force or improper police tactics in the LAPD, the Christopher Commission (Independent Commission 1991) concluded that the type of disciplinary measures taken against the officers were too lenient. Only about 12 percent of the officers were terminated, resigned, or retired. Approximately 58 percent were suspended without pay for a period of time, and the remainder received some type of reprimand.

Officers do not have to accept the recommended disciplinary action if they believe it is inappropriate. Many police departments have an appeals process that allows the officer in question to challenge the type of discipline recommended. Officers can challenge in court what they perceive to be extreme forms of discipline. In unionized agencies, another option for officers may be to file for **grievance arbitration**. One recent study found that grievance arbitration typically reduces the amount of discipline that is ultimately imposed by 50 percent (Iris 2002). Consequently, disciplinary actions by managers may be based, at least in part, on an assessment of whether the officer will appeal or file a grievance. The authors of this book are aware of instances in which police managers knew of inappropriate behavior but took no action because they believed that the appeals process would undermine any effort to punish the officer.

Another factor affecting the complaint process is the likelihood of civil litigation (discussed in Chapter 3) if the complaint is sustained. Some departments may be reluctant to discipline officers for fear that it will be interpreted as an admission of negligence on the part of the department. In some instances, citizen complaints cannot be investigated because the complainant will not cooperate until the civil suit is resolved. Consequently, the investigation of a citizen complaint may not be completed for a long time, possibly a year or more.

Early Warning/Early Identification Systems

A modern approach to police officer accountability that combines the bureaucratic and internal investigation methods is the use of an **early warning system** (EWS), also called an **early identification system** (Walker 2003c). These systems track specific types of officer behaviors and then alert management when individual officers exceed the threshold for such behavior. For example, Alpert and Walker (2000) found that 73 percent of agencies responding to a survey reported that they identified officers for intervention who had three or more use-of-force reports in 1 year. These data-based management systems provide a centralized means of tracking supposed risk indicators, such as citizen complaints against officers, internal rule violations, use-of-force reports, charging of suspects with resisting arrest, sick days, and accidents. These systems are based on the premise, noted above, that a small percentage of officers are responsible for a large percentage of improper behavior. For instance, Lersch and Mieczkowski (1996), in their study of a large police department in the Southeast, found that 2.9 percent of the officers in their study accounted for about 25 percent of the complaints. Brandl and his colleagues (2001) found that 10 percent of the officers in a large midwestern police department accounted for 25 percent of citizen complaints of excessive force. Similarly, an analysis of excessive force complaints in the LAPD revealed that 10 percent of officers accounted for 27.5 percent of complaints (Christopher Commission 1991; also knows as the Independent Commission of the LAPD 1991).

EWSs attempt to identify such officers quickly so discipline or other corrective action can be taken sooner rather than later. Walker (2005) argues that EWSs can also help to alter the behavior of line-level supervisors who may wish to ignore the misbehavior of their subordinates. By providing information that cannot be ignored, since it can also be reviewed by higher-level supervisors, line-level supervisors may be forced to address the misbehavior of officers identified by the system.

These systems suffer from a number of limitations (see Holmes and Smith 2008 for a discussion of their limitations). They are dependent on official records of behavior that officers may actively hide from supervisors. In addition, since citizen complaints are often a primary indicator in these systems, they are dependent on effective citizen complaint mechanisms (Walker 2005). As such, agencies that discourage citizen complaints will be unable to operate effective EWSs. Most importantly, the indicators used in these systems are based largely on assumptions rather than research. While the indicators make intuitive sense, we must await research before we know whether they will live up to the promises.

It goes without saying that an EWS must be used with due regard for the rights of officers as well as citizens. An officer might come to the attention of the EWS because they are highly productive (i.e., make a large number of arrests) or because they work a particularly tough assignment (Lersch, Bazley, and Mieczkowski 2006). In fact, proponents of EWSs encourage agencies to use a variety of indicators and consider the productivity of officers. All the EWS does is identify officers who might be engaging in a pattern of improper conduct. Investigation and judgment are still required to determine whether there really is a problem and whether corrective action is needed. Also, if intervention is needed, the initial response is often counseling or retraining unless the improper conduct has been very serious (see Table 11.2).

TABLE 11.2 Early Intervention Alternatives

- Referral to department employee-assistance program
- Referral to professional family-counseling service
- Referral to credit-counseling services
- Retraining on traffic stop tactics
- Verbal judo training

Source: Samuel Walker, *Early Intervention Systems for Law Enforcement Agencies: A Planning and Management Guide* (Washington, DC: Office of Community Oriented Policing Services, 2003), 38.

Effectiveness of Internal Investigations

Can the police effectively regulate the behavior of their own? Historically, there has been a recurring debate on this question.

Proponents of internal (departmental) review argue that the police can conduct fair investigations of other officers, that internal review is necessary to maintain police morale, that external review interferes with the authority of the chief executive, and that other methods (e.g., elected and appointed officials, the courts) are available to citizens if they are not satisfied. In addition, many police officers do not believe that external review of police conduct is likely to be impartial. They believe that such reviews and recommendations for discipline will often be politically motivated.

External review proponents argue that internal investigations of police complaints are the actions of a system closed to outsiders and favorably predisposed toward police officers. As such, they argue that citizen input will result in more thorough and fair investigations of complaints that result in more sustained complaints and more discipline for guilty officers, which will better deter misconduct than internal mechanisms (Walker 2001). Furthermore, proponents argue that external mechanisms are more likely to be perceived as independent and fair, resulting in greater satisfaction for those who complain and improved perceptions of the police generally (Walker 2001). If the public perceives that the police are unresponsive and unfair in their investigation of complaints, public confidence in the police will be eroded. Consequently, involving citizens in the complaints process has the capacity to restore trust and confidence in police–citizen relations (West 1988).

External Accountability Mechanisms

The second set of oversight mechanisms are those outside the police department. They have emerged primarily in response to concerns that police departments do not hold their members sufficiently accountable. Three external oversight mechanisms—civilian review, police auditors, and legal remedies—are considered here.

Civilian Review

A **civilian review board** is an effort to control police behavior by establishing an external form of review for allegations of police misconduct. It should be noted, however, that even in those communities that have some type of external review, the police department usually continues to conduct its own investigations of complaints.

Research indicates that about 80 percent of the 50 largest cities in the United States have some type of external review of citizen complaints against the police and that more than 100 external oversight agencies are now in existence (Walker 2001, 2003a; Walker and Bumphus 1991). The creation of an external review board is usually related to a political perception that the police are out of control and typically follows in the wake of a police scandal.

A Brief History of Civilian Review. Citizen participation in the review of complaints against the police can be traced to the Progressive Era (1890–1913), when reformers wanted to reduce the influence of corrupt politicians (Caiden 1977). Yet throughout the first half of the twentieth century, there was little progress in establishing citizen review. In its 1967 report, the President's Commission on Law Enforcement and Administration of Justice noted the problems faced by citizens when they tried to complain about police brutality. Such citizens might be arrested, or the police might file criminal charges against them for making a false report. Many police departments had no formal internal investigations unit or procedure. The commission found that less than 10 percent of citizen complaints were substantiated, and even when they were, officers were infrequently or too lightly punished.

Both the National Advisory Commission on Civil Disorders (1968) and the National Commission on the Causes and Prevention of Violence (1969) reached similar conclusions. These studies found that police departments had inadequate investigative procedures and resisted efforts to make complaint procedures more meaningful.

Terrill (1991; see also Walker 2001) divides the discussion about civilian review into three time periods, which he calls "climates of opinion." The first era was the late 1950s and 1960s, during which various forms of civilian review boards were first suggested. These early proposals, considered politically controversial, were vigorously resisted by the police. Several cities, such as Chicago and New York, struggled to establish some form of civilian review; only Philadelphia established a review process that lasted for several years, but it too was eventually abandoned, in part for political and legal reasons, but also in large measure because the police department's internal affairs unit processed many more cases and meted out much harsher punishments than did the civilian review board (Caiden 1977; Terrill 1991).

The second era, the 1970s, was distinguished by increases in public concern about the criminal justice system. Urban riots, the civil rights movement, the President's Commission on Law Enforcement and Administration of Justice (1967), and the National Advisory Commission on Civil Disorders (1968) all called attention to troubling behavior on the part of the police. This period was marked by increased public support for civilian review.

Several communities (e.g., Detroit and Miami–Dade County, Florida) established some type of civilian oversight of the police. However, these civilian review processes were not without problems and resistance. The city of Detroit, over the opposition of the Detroit Police department, established a five-person Board of Police Commissioners, which continues today. Its role includes the development of policies and procedures in consultation with the chief of police and approval of the police budget. The board also created the Office of Chief Investigator, who was given a staff of both civilian and police investigators. The chief investigator is responsible for coordinating the investigation of complaints and disciplinary matters in the police department. The board has the authority not only to receive complaints but also to review the investigation of complaints undertaken by the police department and either to affirm or to change any disciplinary action taken against officers.

During the third era, the 1980s and 1990s, several major cities established review processes, including the San Francisco Office of Citizen Complaints, the San Diego Police Review Commission, and the Dallas Citizens' Police Review Board. Police opposition to civilian review did not change, however, nor did their principal arguments. Although the police no longer considered civilian review part of a communist plot to overthrow the government, as they had in the 1960s, police executives, departments, and unions continued to argue that it undermined managerial authority and the professionalism of the police. To strengthen their argument, many departments worked hard to improve their internal investigations of citizen complaints.

Petterson's survey (1991) of 19 communities with some type of civilian review board indicated the diversity of approaches in this area. One of the boards was established in the 1960s, 4 in the 1970s, and 14 in the 1980s. Fourteen of the boards conducted their own investigations, whereas the others relied on investigations by the police department. Only 1 of the boards, however, was actually authorized to determine the discipline to be imposed on officers. The others could only recommend disciplinary measures that the police department may or may not use.

Today, civilian review boards encompass many different types of organizational designs and purposes. Walker and Kreisel (1996) identified five dimensions along which civilian review boards vary. They are discussed in Inside Policing 11.2.

INSIDE POLICING 11.2 Organizational Features of Citizen Review

The Nature of Citizen Input

How are citizens involved in the review process? There are three ways:

1. Citizens conduct the initial fact-finding investigation.
2. Citizens have input into the review of complaints but do not conduct the investigation.
3. Citizens monitor the process but do not review individual complaints.

The Complaint-Review Process

Review boards may have two purposes:

1. They review individual complaints. Virtually all boards do this.
2. They review department policies and make recommendations for changes. About 66 percent of the boards also do this.

Jurisdiction

Do boards monitor police officers only, or are they also responsible for other public employees? Seventeen percent of the boards studied also set up other boards with the authority to monitor other public employees.

Organizational Structure

1. The majority (85 percent) had a multi-member board. Boards ranged in size from 3 to 24 members. Twenty-seven percent of these boards included sworn police officers. This structure deals with one of the most important questions affecting civilian review: Who has representation on the civilian review board? Many minority group members, while seeking advocacy, are concerned with the issue of tokenism.
2. The remainder (15 percent) are administrative boards with a single administrative director. These boards presume that administrative procedure, rather than representation, is the best way to conduct a review of police behavior.

Operating Policies

There are four different policies, each of which has direct implications for police accountability:

1. Independent investigative powers are held by about 33 percent of all review boards.
2. Subpoena power is held by 38 percent.
3. Public hearings are conducted by about half (46.2 percent).
4. About 32 percent provide legal representation for the officer, for the citizen, or both. Each of these four policies may be described as a different element of a "criminal trial" model. Only 11 percent of the boards studied had all four elements. Two of the review boards had none.

SOURCE: Adapted from S. Walker and B. W. Kreisel, "Varieties of Citizen Review," *American Journal of Police* (1996): 15: 65–88.

The Limits of Civilian Review. The decision by a community to establish some form of civilian review of police behavior is usually based on the assumption that it will be more effective and fair than an internal investigation by the police. The limited research in this area, however, tends not to support this assumption. Caiden (1977) concluded that attempts to institute civilian review in the 1970s failed because the police resisted such attempts and used both political and legal means to limit their potential effectiveness.

West (1988) found that complaint procedures (internal or external) were not related to the number of complaints filed or the seriousness of those complaints. But when complaints were encouraged by either the police or civilian review boards, they were less likely to be sustained. It appeared that frivolous and minor complaints occurred more frequently when complaints were encouraged.

Perez (1994) has identified several problems associated with civilian review. First, civilian review boards do not tend to find problems occurring any more frequently than internal affairs units do. He observes that

> No fair system will find the police guilty of misconduct very often because, in a legalistic sense, the police are not guilty of misconduct very often.
>
> One must also consider a sociological reality. Most civilian review board members develop an appreciation for the police and for police work. Over time, they are less and less prone to be tough on officers, and they actually begin to find fault with complainants. *(1994, 146)*

Consequently, civilian review is unlikely to change the efficiency or effectiveness of police review. Finally,

> Members of civilian review boards…seem to have a sort of "boys will be boys" attitude toward truthfulness….When a lie is discovered by civilian systems, it is considered to be a part of the "playing of the game," a natural product of a system designed to investigate misconduct…. Thus, while chiefs take lying very seriously, civilian review boards largely do not. *(1994, 147)*

Perez notes three additional limitations of civilian review. First, it is too far removed from the day-to-day existence of the line officer to understand and respond to the dynamics of illegal behavior. Second, civilian review can take away opportunities for the immediate supervisor to deal creatively with problems. Inadvertently, civilian review undermines the ability of the police department to "generate genuine humility and acceptance of error on the part of young, developing police officers" (161). Finally, civilian review tends to discourage the use of internal socialization processes. Perez believes that the role of peers and their contribution to the socialization of recruits is an inevitable and essential part of police work. It should be encouraged, not discouraged.

Police Auditor Systems

Police auditor systems have developed more recently than civilian review board systems. The most important difference is that police auditors do not usually investigate or even monitor individual citizen complaints—that is left to the internal processes of the police department. Instead, the auditor model focuses on the police organization and its policies and practices. In the fashion of the Government Accounting Office, police auditors examine different aspects of the ongoing operation of the police department to ensure that legal requirements are being met and that the most efficient and effective practices are being followed. As noted by Walker (2003a), the auditor model

> [s]eeks to identify problems in the complaint process or other police policies and recommend corrective action to the chief executive.... The underlying assumption is that these recommendations will have a preventive effect, reducing the likelihood of certain forms of misconduct occurring in the future. *(6–7)*

Jurisdictions with well-established police auditors include the San Jose Police Department (Nurre 2008) and the Los Angeles County Sheriff's Department (Bobb 2007). Others include Austin, Boise, Omaha, Philadelphia, Portland, Reno, Sacramento, Seattle, and Tucson. Among the principles that seem to make this model most effective are independence from the law enforcement agency, free access to internal police data and documents, public reporting of findings and recommendations (see Table 11.3), and direct access to the chief/sheriff (Walker 2003b).

Legal Control

Criminal, civil, and administrative laws are important tools in the control of police. Like all citizens, the police are required to obey substantive criminal laws. In addition, some states impose criminal penalties for officers who misuse the authority and license given them by standards commissions. Such officers can be decertified. Procedural laws, called criminal procedure or due process, provide legal guidelines for the police when enforcing substantive laws. They govern the process of investigating crimes and apprehending suspects.

TABLE 11.3 Police Auditor Recommendations and Results in San Jose, California

| YEAR | AUDITOR RECOMMENDATIONS | | |
	ADOPTED	NOT ADOPTED	PENDING
1996	9	1	0
1997	4	0	0
1998	1	0	0
1999	7	1	0
2000	10	2	1
2001	12	2	3
2002	5	2	0
2003	7	0	0
2004	2	0	0
2005	4	0	0
2006	1	1	2
2007	1	0	2
2008	0	0	1
Total	87	10	4

Source: Shivan Nurre, *2008 Year-End Report* (San Jose, CA: Office of the Independent Police Auditor, 2008), 78–83. Available online at http://www.sanjoseca.gov/ipa/reports/08ye.pdf.

Police officers and departments may also be sued civilly if they fail to act in a responsible manner.

Legal issues affecting police work are examined in depth in Chapter 3. The focus here is specifically on the role played by the law in controlling police behavior as another means of establishing external accountability.

Exclusionary Rule. One method of legal control over police behavior is the **exclusionary rule**. This is a rule imposed by the U.S. Supreme Court that requires that any evidence gathered by the police through improper searches or seizures (including interrogations) must be excluded from trial. The purpose of the exclusionary rule is to take away any incentive that the police might have to "bend the rules" and thereby to encourage them to respect peoples' constitutional rights more closely. This legal principle was explained in more detail in Chapter 3.

Decertification. Another method of legal control involves the possible **decertification** of individual officers. Over three fourths of the states have some form of decertification (Goldman and Puro 1987). In Florida, for example, the Criminal Justice Standards and Training Commission is authorized to "decertify" (or suspend or put on probation) officers for (1) violating the legal rights of individuals; (2) "negligent deprivations of liberty or property"; (3) failing to maintain the required qualifications for the job; (4) falsifying or misrepresenting information during the application process; and (5) "gross insubordination, gross immorality, habitual drunkenness, willful neglect of duty, incompetence, or gross misconduct." A national decertification index is operated by the International Association of Directors of Law Enforcement Standards and Training to help with the problem caused when officers lose their certification in one state and attempt to obtain police employment in another state. This index currently has 11,456 records from 29 participating states.

Civil Liability. One of the most common legal methods to control police behavior is a civil liability suit. This means that a police officer, his or her supervisor, the chief, and the police department (or at least the governmental unit—i.e., the city of which the department is a part) can be sued for monetary damages for negligent behavior. Civil liability has become a firmly established fact of life for police officers and police departments in recent decades. The threat of being sued is often mentioned by police officers as one of their constant worries (Scogin and Brodsky 1991). Presumably, this threat has the desired effect of discouraging officers from misusing their authority. Civil liability is discussed in much greater detail in Chapter 3.

Criminal Liability. When police officers violate a criminal law, they can be held for criminal prosecution in both state and federal courts. Criminal law prosecution sometimes occurs when excessive use of force is alleged, for example. In these kinds of cases, officers might be charged with assault or, in the case of deadly force, manslaughter or murder. Police officers caught in corruption investigations often face charges of theft, fraud, extortion, or some type of misuse of official authority. As noted, criminal prosecution might take place in a state or federal court. It is not uncommon for federal prosecution to be initiated if state prosecution is declined or unsuccessful, since federal law enforcement agencies and the U.S. Department of Justice bear some responsibility for helping control police abuses at the state and local levels.

Criminal Violations of Civil Rights. Police officers, like anyone else, can also be charged with criminal violations of civil rights, as defined in Title 242, Section 18, of the

U.S. Code. It is difficult to prove beyond a reasonable doubt that a police officer committed a crime—either state or federal—as a result of the possible use of excessive or deadly force. To do this, it is usually necessary to establish that the officer had criminal intent to engage in the behavior. The prosecution must establish that the officer knew and understood the nature and consequences of his or her action—that the officer knew that what he or she was doing was a crime and did it anyway. For this reason, officers who are accused of using excessive force are often prosecuted federally for having violated the civil rights of the victim. This approach has proven successful—in many cases police officers have been found not guilty in a state court of assault or murder but have subsequently been found guilty of civil rights violations in a federal court (e.g., the officers in the Rodney King incident).

Pattern or Practice Litigation. Another method of external oversight that uses federal law is civil litigation against an entire agency alleging a pattern or practice of violating citizens' rights (Walker 2005). Using this approach, the U.S. Department of Justice can sue (or threaten to sue) a state or local law enforcement agency in federal court, leading to consent decrees, memoranda of understanding, or other court findings or settlements through which the agency agrees to make changes. This method of oversight is very powerful—the mere threat of a federal civil rights lawsuit is often enough to motivate a local or state agency to implement significant improvements in policies, training, and complaint investigation.

The Limits of Oversight Mechanisms

Oversight of police in a democracy is clearly necessary. Many proponents of vigorous police oversight have argued that police agencies can create a culture of rule following. Walker (2005) argues that a combination of proper rules, reporting procedures for officers, citizen complaint mechanisms, and early intervention systems can make the formal and informal culture of police organizations more accountable. Proper supervision and external oversight, vigorous investigations, and appropriate interventions (e.g., training or punishment) may influence officer behavior to some degree. Yet the discretion and autonomy officers have in their work allows them to disregard rules and avoid reporting requirements. Moreover, the low visibility of police work and the self-protective aspects of police culture make supervision of officers and investigation of misbehavior inherently difficult (Holmes and Smith 2008). Indeed, oversight mechanisms, especially those focused on punishment, are in many ways responsible for the development of the more secretive elements of police culture.

Chapter 1 defined the organization culture as "the pattern of basic assumptions that a given group has invented, discovered, or developed in learning to cope with its problems of external adaptation and internal integration, [and] that have worked well enough to be considered valid" (Schein 1985, 9). The culture is made up of values that guide the behavior of police officers. Sparrow, Moore, and Kennedy (1990) have listed what they consider some of the most influential values of police officers. These values are summarized in Inside Policing 11.3.

The values that undergird police culture are derived substantially from daily work experiences. The most important elements of police culture reflect how officers adapt to their environment. Culture is the process of adaptation shared, discussed, and finally formed into habits. Cultural values are the meanings associated with those habits.

It is the type and frequency of problems confronted by the police—not the hopes of police reformers or administrators—that determine the way police do their work and what

> ### INSIDE POLICING 11.3   Building Blocks of Police Culture
>
> 1. The public wants the police to be crime fighters, and that is what the police think of themselves as being, the primary crime-fighting organization in government.
> 2. No one other than another police officer understands the "real" nature of police work and what is necessary to get the job done.
> 3. Police have to stick together; loyalty to one another is more important than anything else because everyone else, including the public, politicians, and police managers, seems to try to make the job of police officers more difficult. And these individuals are often unfair in their evaluations of the police.
> 4. Police cannot "win the war" on crime without violating legal, organizational, and ethical standards.
> 5. The public does not support or appreciate the police, and they expect too much of police officers.
>
> SOURCE: Adapted from M. Sparrow, M. Moore, and D. Kennedy, *Beyond 911: A New Era for Policing* (New York: Basic Books, 1990), 51.

is important to them. Externally imposed control systems, often failing to understand this simple truth, backfire by intensifying resentment and secrecy. Police will not change unless their working environment is in some way changed, but they will become more secretive. As reformers and administrators intensify their efforts to hold the police accountable for an impossible mandate—to police a democracy—the strength of the secretive elements of police culture may also increase (Manning 1998).

The next section looks at moral/ethical standards, as distinct from legal standards, which control behavior by providing officers with an internal gauge for their work. These standards are preventive because officers are expected to anticipate outcomes of their behavior before they act. They can be divided into professional standards and ethical standards.

Professional Standards

The concept of **professionalism** in policing is associated with the recurring attempts of reformers to ensure that police officers are honest, efficient, and effective. More specifically, an occupation, to be considered a profession, must adopt certain criteria. Recognition that such adoption is a prolonged process is called a process-criterion approach. As an occupation becomes a profession, one criterion is the learning of a systematic process that uses the scientific method (Cullen 1978; Geison 1983). Inside Policing 11.4 provides a list of the criteria the authors believe indicate that an occupation has reached professional status.

The Police Professionalization Movement

Occupations that adopt the criteria presented in Inside Policing 11.4 are professionalized and are recognized as such by the public and other professional organizations. Their members believe in these criteria and are accorded the status of professionals (Hall 1968). As professionals, they are granted wide latitude to decide how to conduct their work. Even when they work in bureaucratic organizations, they have the autonomy to define problems in their area of expertise, to respond to those problems, and to gauge the success of their work. In a word, they are largely left alone by managers. Members of professions, such as doctors and lawyers, operate on these principles.

INSIDE POLICING 11.4 Professional Criteria

1. Professionals are represented by professional associations, which serve the purpose of transmitting knowledge of the field.

2. Professionals are provided autonomy to perform their work. Even in organizations characterized by a bureaucracy, professionals are granted the opportunity to do their work with only limited control by supervisors.

3. A profession encompasses a unique body of knowledge, associated with research, which must be constantly updated.

4. Professionals require lengthy and formal training.

5. Professionals require certification of quality and competence.

6. Professionals have a commitment to service on behalf of a clientele.

SOURCES: J. B. Cullen, *The Structure of Professionalism* (Princeton, NJ: Princeton University Press, 1978); G. L. Geison, ed. *Professions and Professional Ideology in America* (Chapel Hill: University of North Carolina Press, 1983); R. Hall, "Professionalization and Bureaucratization," *America Sociological Review* (1968) 33: 92–104.

These conditions have not been true of the police. The police professionalization movement, begun in 1893 by the International Association of Chiefs of Police and central to efforts to reform the police ever since, sought to bureaucratize the police through specialization of function and intense control of line officers (Fogelson 1977). Rather than fostering independent decision making in line officers, the movement sought centralization of command under the authority of the chief. Individual officers were not admitted to the ranks of professionals, but instead were controlled with ever-tighter accountability (Fogelson 1977). Police departments, not police officers, became professionalized (Regoli et al. 1988).

As the police professionalization movement unfolded, officers were considered the product of a management system controlled by police executives. Police executives blended bureaucratic management and chain-of-command control to attempt to force line officers to go along with the reforms the executives wanted (Kuykendall and Roberg 1990). Consequently, police officers below the executive level were (and continue to be) rarely considered professional colleagues, but only a group of individuals that had to be "managed." These police officers were left out of the professionalization process. One consequence of this trend was the development of sharply antagonistic relationships between line personnel and management (Reuss-Ianni 1983). Such antagonisms continue to be a critical issue in the twenty-first century.

As subordinates, police officers have been told what not to do more often than what to do, and they have been laden with rules and policies seeking to control their behavior rather than to expand and sharpen their discretionary skills (Alpert and Smith 1999). Therefore, the professionalization movement itself, except for commitment to service (discussed later), did not contribute toward professionalization of policing. True professionalism did not begin until the community policing movement—with its emphasis on the decentralization of authority and empowerment of line officers—began to gain ground.

Criteria of Police Professionalization

Characteristics of policing as a true profession are described below.

Autonomy. The development of professional autonomy is a central criterion in the process of professionalization. Autonomy provides professionals with the discretion to carry out their work, and its presence shows that society acknowledges their professional status.

Police departments, as previously noted, have historically sought to control the behavior of line officers. The community policing movement, however, emphasizes increased autonomy and with it the decentralization of authority and the use of creative techniques in solving problems. Each of these items expands the autonomy of police officers and thus represents movement toward professionalism.

Decentralization of authority occurs in two ways. One is the transfer of authority to make tactical decisions down the chain of command. For example, patrol officers may be given the authority to decide what kinds of crime problems to focus on. Line officers are expected to make tactical decisions traditionally reserved for sergeants and lieutenants. The second way is geographic decentralization, meaning that officers are assigned to specific areas and take increased responsibility in solving the problems confronted in those areas.

Increased decision making is a relaxation of traditional constraints on the use of police discretion. Wilson and Kelling (1982) argued that officers should be provided with broad latitude in controlling common public-order problems on their beat. Such problems, if unaddressed, lead to neighborhood degradation and the onset of serious crime. By allowing officers wider latitude to deal with these problems, more effective long-term solutions to crime can be developed.

"Creative, customized police work," according to Skolnick and Bayley (1986), is important in finding creative solutions to recurring public-order problems. Goldstein (1998) suggests that officers engaged in problem-solving analysis redefine problems in non-criminal terms. Tailor-made responses, he contends, are a critical ingredient in finding effective solutions.

A Unique Body of Knowledge. Another criterion of professionalism is that a profession has an area of unique expertise that only its practitioners are qualified to assess. Such expertise can be gained in three ways.

The first way, common especially before the 1960s, is to study the work of experts. These are well-educated, experienced practitioners, usually executives such as O. W. Wilson and August Vollmer, who lectured and wrote journal articles and books. Wilson's famous *Police Administration* (1950) contains many useful ideas about how to manage police departments. Many of his ideas were the result of his extensive experience, but some were taken from writers about general management principles. Many police today continue to depend almost exclusively on the knowledge of experts as a basis for their actions.

The second way to gain expertise is by consulting/modeling. In this method, the management and practices of a police department are analyzed by an expert or consultant who then compares the results to a model of what he or she considers desirable—for example, an effective way to select and train officers.

Models come from several sources. One source is the creativity and imagination of the expert or consultant. Another might be a police department that the consultant likes or considers progressive. If the consultant has been a police manager, the model might be his or her former department. Or models may come from books written by other experts in the field.

The third way to acquire expertise is by scientific research. Scientific research is empirical—that is, based on what can be observed. Two conditions apply to scientific observations. The first is that the observation has **validity**, meaning that what the observer sees is what is actually going on. The second is that it has **reliability**, meaning that if other observers conducted the research again in the same setting, they would be likely to come to similar (if not precisely the same) conclusions.

Research conducted by Sherman and his colleagues (1997, 1999) and by Skogan and Frydl (2004), for example, shows how scientific research has had powerful effects on police knowledge. It has dramatically expanded knowledge about what works in policing. It has enabled scholars systematically to compare a wide variety of research on policing. And it has provided a benchmark for thinking about the quality of police research.

Education and Training. A further criterion of professionalism is formal preparation. Professionals typically undergo extensive training and education, followed by certification.

Chapter 7 identified the types and extent of police training. Higher education is becoming increasingly important in all aspects of policing, as discussed in Chapter 14. Over the past 3 decades, the numbers of educated officers and the quantity of education that they possess have increased dramatically. Nevertheless, it does not yet approach the level expected in other professions.

Certification and Accreditation. Professionalism also requires **certification** as a criterion of its members to ensure quality and competence. Usually state-level organizations give licenses or certifications. The legal profession, for example, has state bar associations, and all lawyers must pass the bar examinations in their state to practice law there.

State standards organizations fulfill this function for the police. They set standards for the selection, training, and certification of police officers. Currently, nearly all states have such organizations—the titles of which vary. For example, in Arizona the state organization is called the Law Enforcement Officer Advisory Council; in Kentucky it is called the Kentucky Law Enforcement Council. The central function is training, defined by Berg (1994) as learning the techniques for particular processes or procedures through example and instruction.

The first standards organization, established in California in 1959, was the POST. Its purpose is "to raise the level of competence of local law enforcement officers, to help improve the administration, management, and operation of local law enforcement agencies" (Commission on POST 1990, 4). In attempting to accomplish this mission, the commission does the following:

1. Develops minimum selection standards and minimum required knowledge and skill standards for the training of all levels of police officers (i.e., entry, supervisor, technical, managerial, and executive).
2. Develops and approves training programs that meet POST standards.
3. Provides management and research assistance and services to local law enforcement agencies.
4. Provides financial reimbursement to local agencies for officers who attend some POST-approved training courses. *(4)*

Today POST commissions exist in nearly every state. They provide a wide diversity of training that focuses on skills, knowledge, cultural diversity, attitudes, and ethics.

An important aspect of licensing is **accreditation**. Professional organizations frequently provide for means of accreditation of member associations. Universities, for example, are periodically reviewed and accredited by regional accreditation boards. The purpose of accreditation for the police is to determine whether a department meets general standards of policy and training. This determination is accomplished through self-assessment and external review in an attempt to match national standards set up by the Commission on Accreditation for Law Enforcement Agencies (**CALEA**). If a department is deemed to meet these standards, it is accredited by CALEA for a 3-year period, which is renewable on reassessment if the department remains in compliance with the standards.

Proponents of accreditation believe that self-assessment helps to identify departmental strengths and weaknesses and may reduce the exposure to liability. Departments in several states have been offered reduced insurance rates for completing the process (Williams 1989). Accreditation may help departments to address administrative issues and policies and, perhaps by tightening up in these areas, to become more professional and less exposed to liability (McAllister 1987). Nearly all of the accreditation standards, however, require only that a formal policy or procedure be established or that records be maintained. The process used to determine the extent that CALEA-revised policies and procedures are actually implemented and followed is largely an honor system.

The standards set by CALEA are extensive, and if all are applied, it is likely that a department would become more, not less, formalized and bureaucratic. Also, most of the standards that apply to patrol work focus on law enforcement rather than order maintenance and service (Mastrofski 1990). This situation is not entirely consistent with community policing. According to Cordner and Williams (1995, 1996, 1999), an examination of these standards regarding their applicability to community policing indicated, for the most part, that the standards are either silent or neutral on the subject. It is possible that such standards could constrain departments that are attempting to implement community policing, especially in the areas of officers' participation, encouraging risk taking in applications of discretion and removing organizational barriers to creativity (Cordner and Williams 1996, 256). Cordner and Williams suggested that CALEA and its sponsoring organizations (including the International Association of Chiefs of Police, the National Sheriffs Association, the National Organization of Black Law Enforcement Executives, and the Police Executive Research Forum) address the following concerns in the future:

1. Improve its research and development capacity and establish a more proactive posture toward contemporary changes in policing.
2. Play a more active role in big-picture issues affecting policing.
3. Pay more attention to accreditation issues and participate more actively in CALEA's direction and focus. *(1996, 378–379)*

Some observers have suggested that, in relatively well-developed departments committed to community policing, accreditation could impede managers' efforts to promote change (Oettmeier 1993; Sykes 1994). This conclusion would hold until the accreditation process places more significant emphasis on problem solving, innovation, and community input, instead of focusing on bureaucratic rules and regulations. On the other hand, in less well-developed departments that have inadequate policies and procedures, accreditation may be very beneficial.

Commitment to Service. One of the most important criteria of a professional is a "commitment to service." Service means a formal obligation to act on behalf of the professional's clientele to render service as needed (Rhoades 1991). This is one area in which the police professionalism movement has contributed to the professionalism of individual officers.

One of the principal objectives of the movement was to instill a sense of calling in police officers. Early twentieth-century reformers, concerned about the lax standards many recruits brought to police work, sought to instill in officers a commitment to law enforcement.

To them, this meant a commitment to a belief in the contribution of police to society. The movement was successful in instilling this sense of commitment in police recruits. Chapters 4 and 5 discussed the service activities of police officers. Indeed, in many departments today, police work is mandated as a 24-hour obligation. In a reversal of direction, some reformers today are concerned about the overcommitment of police to their work, believing that police officers are overzealous in their pursuit of "bad guys" (Chapter 9).

Ethical Standards

The most effective method for controlling a person's behavior is for that person to believe in the standards of conduct he or she is supposed to follow. Ethical standards identify right and wrong behavior in any endeavor in life. Individual ethical standards about integrity, responsible behavior, use of coercion, and compassion provide officers with internal guides for their conduct. If officers do not have an internalized standard of ethics, they are more likely to engage in some form of deviant behavior (e.g., corruption or brutality). Inside Policing 11.5 gives the code of ethics for police officers for the state of California. Part of this code was adopted from the International Association of Chiefs of Police's code of ethics, which is utilized by many states.

INSIDE POLICING 11.5 Law Enforcement Code of Ethics

The purpose of the police code of ethics is to ensure that all peace officers are fully aware of their individual responsibility to maintain their own integrity and that of their department. Every peace officer, during basic training or at the time of appointment, must swear to abide by the following code of ethics. The officer is also expected to abide by certain canons (rules) that embody those ethics.

Code

As a law enforcement officer, my fundamental duty is to serve humanity; to safeguard lives and property; to protect the innocent against deception, the weak against oppression or intimidation, and the peaceful against violence or disorder; and to respect the constitutional rights of all people to liberty, equality, and justice.

I will keep my private life unsullied as an example to all; maintain courageous calm in the face of danger, scorn, or ridicule; develop self-restraint; and be constantly mindful of the welfare of others. Honest in thought and deed in both my personal and official life, I will be exemplary in obeying the laws of the land and the regulations of my department. Whatever I see or hear of a confidential nature or that is confided to me in my official capacity will be kept ever secret unless revelation is necessary in the performance of my duty. I will never act officiously or permit personal feelings, prejudices, animosities, or friendships to influence my decisions. With no compromise for crime and with relentless prosecution of criminals, I will enforce the law courteously and appropriately without fear or favor, malice or ill will, never employing unnecessary force or violence and never accepting gratuities.

I recognize the badge of my office as a symbol of public faith, and I accept it as a public trust to be held so long as I am true to the ethics of the police service. I will constantly strive to achieve these objectives and ideals, dedicating myself to my chosen profession—law enforcement.

Canons

1. The primary responsibility of police officers and departments is the protection of citizens by upholding the law and respecting the legally expressed will of the whole community, not that of a particular political party or clique.

2. Police officers should be aware of the legal limits on their authority and the "genius of the American system," which limits the power of individuals, groups, and institutions.

3. Police officers are responsible for being familiar with the law and not only their responsibilities, but also those of other public officials.

4. Police officers should be mindful of the importance of utilizing the proper means to gain proper ends. Officers should not employ illegal means, nor should they disregard public safety or property to accomplish a goal.

5. Police officers will cooperate with other public officials in carrying out their duties. However, the officer shall be careful not to use his or her position in an improper or illegal manner when cooperating with other officials.

6. In their private lives, police officers will behave in such a manner that the public will "regard [the officer] as an example of stability, fidelity, and morality." It is necessary that police officers conduct themselves in a "decent and honorable" manner.

7. In their behavior toward members of the public, officers will provide service when possible, require compliance with the law, respond in a manner that inspires confidence and trust, and will be neither overbearing nor subservient.

8. When dealing with violators or making arrests, officers will follow the law; officers have no right to persecute individuals or punish them. Officers should behave in such a manner so that the likelihood of the use of force is minimized.

9. Officers should refuse to accept any gifts, favors, or gratuities that, from a public perspective, could influence the manner in which they discharge their duties.

10. Officers will present evidence in criminal cases impartially because the officer should be equally concerned with the prosecution of criminals and the defense of innocent persons.

SOURCES: Adapted from California Commission on Peace Officers Standards and Training, *Administrative Manual* (1990); c-5; J. M. Pollock-Byrne, *Ethics in Crime and Justice* (Pacific Grove, CA: Brooks/Cole, 1989).

Ethical Perspectives

Attempts to identify appropriate ethical standards for the police have proven difficult. Different schools of thought concerning what is and is not ethical show the difficulty encountered by reformers concerned with police behavior.

Ethical Formalism. The school of **ethical formalism** places moral worth on "doing one's duty." An officer who believes that police should "go by the book" is an ethical formalist. Legalistic policing is a kind of ethical formalism. An element of legalistic policing, as noted earlier, was that officers strive for the full enforcement of the law. Police legalism does not provide for fine distinctions in police discretion. On the contrary, legalistic departments justify their presence in terms of their capacity to enforce the law fairly among all groups.

Ethical Utilitarianism. According to the school of **ethical utilitarianism**, it is the results of one's actions that determine what is moral or good. Behavior is judged not by the goodness of the acts, but by the consequences that they bring. For example, if an officer thought an illegal search was necessary to arrest a serious criminal, a utilitarian argument could be used to justify that search. An officer who says that she or he would sooner be "judged by 12 than carried by 6" is taking a utilitarian point of view—it is wiser to use deadly force in an ambiguous although perilous encounter and take a chance of being convicted of illegal behavior by a jury than to hesitate and possibly be killed by the suspect.

Ethical Relativism. Perhaps the most complicated ethical position of all is **ethical relativism**. Relativism means that which is considered good varies with the particular values of groups and individuals. This perspective can be used to justify enforcing certain laws in some neighborhoods but ignoring them in others (Pollock-Byrne 1998, 12–30). Police might object strenuously that they are not relative in their ethics. Yet, the idea of "full enforcement" of the law is neither realistic nor possible (Goldstein 1998). The discretionary nature of police work is widely cited. Consequently, an ethically relativistic approach to policing is probably a more realistic description of day-to-day police ethics than any other.

Inside Policing 11.6, adapted from Pollock (1997), displays in summary form several schools of ethics.

Elements of community policing are consistent with ethical relativism. One of the tenets of community policing is that community values should determine what is "good" in police work. But what a particular neighborhood considers "good" police work may result in the police tolerating certain types of illegal behavior or in officers engaging in illegal tactics

---

INSIDE POLICING 11.6 Schools of Ethics

Religion

  What is good is that which conforms to God's will.
  How do we know God's will?
  Bible or other religious document.
  Religious authorities.
  Faith.

Ethical Formalism (Deontological Ethics)

  What is good is that which conforms to doing one's duty and the categorical imperative.
  What is the categorical imperative?
  Act in such a way that one would will it to be a universal law.
  Treat each person as an end and not as a means.

Utilitarianism

  What is good is that which results in the greatest benefit for the greatest number.
  Act utilitarianism "weighs" the benefits of an act for just those people and just that incident.
  Rule utilitarianism "weighs" the benefits after determining the consequences of making that behavior a rule for the future.

Egoism

  What is good is that which results in the greatest benefit for me.
  Enlightened egoism, however, may allow one to reciprocate favors and may be practiced by a "good" person (because it benefits the self to be nice to others).

  SOURCE: Adapted from J. Pollock, "Ethics and Law Enforcement." In R. G. Dunham and G. P. Alpert (eds.), *Critical Issues in Policing*, 3rd ed. (Prospect Heights, IL: Waveland Press, 1997), 348.

to solve problems (e.g., conducting illegal searches of suspected drug dealers). Inside Policing 11.7 describes an incident in one western city in which ethical relativism resulted in police officers tolerating illegal behavior.

Ethical Dilemmas

Police confront profound ethical dilemmas. To fail to recognize this fact is to fail to understand the nature of policing. An ethical dilemma central to the craft of policing is the conflict between means and ends.

In their day-to-day practice, police confront what is widely called the "Dirty Harry" problem, that is, a conflict between means and ends. The end is so obviously good that they feel compelled to pursue it. Yet there are not legal means to do so. Should the officer use illegal or "dirty" means to pursue an unquestionably good end? Klockars notes that police will tend to justify dirty means if "what must be known and, importantly, known before the act is committed, is that it will result in the achievement of the good end" (1991, 414).

INSIDE POLICING 11.7 **Ethical Relativism and the Law in Police Work**

In Santa Ana, California, in the early 1980s, most of the people who frequented the downtown part of the city at night were "overwhelmingly Mexican." This area, in effect, became a *corso,* a customary part of Spanish life in which mariachi bands play and sing in cafes and bars and then come out onto the street, creating a festive atmosphere. Some of the persons participating in the *corso* were illegal aliens, but police officers made no attempt to determine the status of those individuals who frequented the area. In addition, officers did not usually provide assistance to agents of the Immigration and Naturalization Service (INS), whom many city residents called the "green gestapo" (referring to the green card that legal residents are supposed to have). In fact, the police department had a history of not cooperating with the INS because the police chief did not agree with the methods used by INS agents to identify and arrest illegal aliens (many of whom were otherwise law abiding). Known prostitutes also frequented the downtown area at night. One prostitute, Sugar, was a drug addict who had four children. Sugar openly solicited young men to have sex. In one incident, Sugar met a young man on the street, then engaged him in a short conversation, and then walked together with him around the corner of a building to a more private area. When the young man returned, a foot patrol officer called out in Spanish, "How was it?" The bystanders, who apparently knew what was going on, laughed at the young man's obvious embarrassment. The officer in question said: "We don't arrest these people [because] they are young men...who work hard [to] save up money to bring their families from Mexico.... They're gonna have sex. There just isn't any point in arresting people for having sex."

Notice that in this example, the community, meaning those individuals who frequented the downtown area at night, openly tolerated the practice of prostitution by drug addicts; consequently, the police ignored this illegal behavior as long as prostitutes did not appear to be under the influence of drugs at the time of the sexual activity. In addition, some officers undoubtedly thought it would be pointless to enforce laws against prostitution in such circumstances. This example also illustrates how community values can be in conflict with laws enforced by other government agencies such as the INS.

SOURCE: Adapted from J. H. Skolnick and D. H. Bayley, *The New Blue Line* (New York: Free Press, 1986), 40–43.

Klockars presented a compelling argument that the Dirty Harry problem is at the core of the police role. Police tend to think that they are dealing with people who are factually, if not legally, guilty. Consequently, an officer's belief in the certainty of guilt is not always determined by factual accuracy but by police cultural standards: "Dirty Harry problems," Klockars observes, "can arise wherever restrictions are placed on police methods and are particularly likely to do so when police themselves perceive that those restrictions are undesirable, unreasonable, or unfair" (1991, 414). In other words, Dirty Harry problems are probably more widespread, and less certain in the likelihood of factual guilt, than the police think that they are.

The particular ways that means versus ends conflicts affect police work are expanded by Crank and Caldero (1991). The core of police work, they argue, is the "noble cause" (see Chapter 9). This is the belief in the absolute rightness of doing something about criminals. It is a compelling commitment to "get bad guys off the street." Police, they note, not only dislike lawbreakers and troublemakers, but also identify intensely with victims of crime and feel a moral responsibility for their assignments. The "noble cause" is corrupted when police consider it justifiable to break the law to apprehend or punish suspected wrongdoers. Noble-cause corruption means that officers are willing to violate legal means to achieve a noble end (Delattre 1996). Officers, Crank and Caldero (1991) contend, are hired into policing already morally committed to the idea of the noble cause. They are frequently hostile to due-process ideas at the time they are hired, and police culture reinforces this hostility. Only later in their career, as they move up the departmental ladder and gain broader perspective, do some officers begin to understand how the police are part of a broader system of competing moral values.

Noble-cause corruption takes many different forms. It includes testifying wrongly or testimonial deception (Barker 1996), fluffing up evidence (Barker and Carter 1999), and in more extreme cases, drug corruption (Manning and Redlinger 1977). It encompasses all situations in which police bend the rules to sustain an arrest or get a conviction.

The Limits of Professional and Ethical Standards

The idea that codes of conduct can prevent misconduct seems reasonable. Yet prevention has proven to be difficult. First, although professional and ethical standards provide a good model for police work, they may have limited impact on its reality. They tend to be in written form, presented to satisfy external audiences, with little impact on day-to-day police behavior.

Second, the need for controls is driven to a certain extent by the people-based, unpredictable nature of police work. This same unpredictability, however, limits the effectiveness of those controls. And unpredictability cannot be removed from police–citizen interactions (Harmon 1995).

Third, the study of ethics can result in the development of arguments to justify deviating from established ethical or professional standards. Officers who subscribe to different ethical schools of thought may use those schools to justify their behavior. It is not hard to review the research on police ethics, for example, to find adequate justification for breaking the law to get bad guys off the street, if that is what a police officer believes in.

Fourth, the manner in which officers carry out their day-to-day activities is affected as much by informal group ethics—the "ethics of the street"—as by any of the ethical schools discussed. The exercise of discretion, whether or not officers follow departmental standards

Sylvester Daughtry, Jr.

Executive Director Commission on Accreditation for Law Enforcement Agencies, Inc.

Question: *What are the most effective methods for promoting accountability in policing?*

Answer: Growing up in a rural setting with ten siblings in a three bedroom home significantly affected my understanding of accountability. In fact, it colored my understanding of responsibility, loyalty, dependability, and the importance of maintaining trusting relationships. Sharing a bedroom with three brothers fostered a reality that each of us had duties that directly affected the others. Although we had different perspectives and priorities, we kept family first to ensure our safety, nourishment, and good reputation within the community. In many ways, the concept of accountability within the profession of public safety is similar to my family experience, and in reflection many of my leadership attributes were the product of these early years.

I have always believed that what gets measured gets done. Law enforcement organizations have so many operational, administrative, public relations, and contractual areas to manage, it is vitally important they develop strong systems to ensure accountability. These systems should always incorporate an independent review that provides substantive feedback for continuous organization improvement. Nearly every organization failure is predictable with the right information. Therefore, it is important to have strong reviews of every component of public safety agencies on a continuing basis. If properly employed, these reviews provide the information necessary for good decision making, the prevention of corrupt behavior, the development of meaningful solutions, internal confidence among staff, and trust

within the community. Accreditation is an example of a system that creates accountability within public safety agencies and it works to ensure best practices permeate the organization. Its impartial independent review provides assurance that the agency is doing the right things in the right way. And because the public deserves the best service, accreditation provides a framework for not only breadth of service considerations, but also quality of service reviews.

Accreditation itself is not the panacea for ensuring internal and external accountability, but rather is a tool used by "accountable" leaders to promote professionalism. It serves as a form of checks and balances to ensure critical tasks are conducted, fair reviews occur, the agency and its personnel are prepared to provide service, cooperative agreements and partnerships are instituted, and appropriate policies are applied. All of these things are prerequisites to developing and maintaining the public's trust. In short, voluntarily submitting to an external review builds trust. Trust contributes to an organization culture of accountability.

Just like the relationship between my siblings who shared a bedroom with me, accountability for public safety agencies is a concept that must be developed as a core value. It is the framework which serves to support organizations during difficult times and it is the principle that assures citizens that public safety officials will be there during times of crisis. And when they arrive they will understand their relationship and responsibility to the community. The badge itself has always been an outward sign of public trust, and the oath of office taken before receiving the badge is a promise to always remain accountable.

Sylvester Daughtry, Jr., was appointed the Executive Director of CALEA in 1999.

or the law, use force, lie, accept gratuities, or engage in other corrupt practices, may be affected as much by peer group processes as formal ethical and professional standards.

In Voices From the Field, Sylvester Daughtry, Jr., the Executive Director of CALEA, presents his view on police accountability.

Price (1996, 87) sums up the challenge confronting the police in her essay on the quest for professionalism:

> Eradicating the excessive use of force and the scourge of police corruption are the most critical internal issues police face if they are to continue the long and arduous course toward professionalism. There have been many successes of late for law enforcement, especially in communications technology, forensics, information systems, interagency cooperation, and the development of a commitment to their peers, if not to professional conduct. But until attitudes of the police towards those they serve can be changed, they will continue to make their own jobs more difficult and more dangerous—and professionalism for the police will not come to pass. *(1996, 87)*

Summary

Police accountability is concerned with controlling line-officer behavior. Two kinds of accountability mechanisms are oversight (internal and external) and standards (professional and ethical). Internal oversight mechanisms include bureaucratic procedure, internal investigation, and early warning/early identification systems. The primary external mechanisms of accountability are citizen review boards, police auditors, and legal controls. Officers are controlled primarily through the administrative procedure. Internal investigations are usually associated with internal affairs units; external review is usually associated with civilian review boards. The legal methods to control the police include criminal prosecution in both state and federal courts, the exclusionary rule, decertification, and civil suits.

Two primary sources of standards for police officers are professional and ethical training. The police professionalization movement has historically represented efforts to make the police occupation a profession. However, because of its preoccupation with the image of the department, it focused on controlling the behavior of line officers. Other trends in policing are consistent with ideas of professionalism at the individual level. These include community policing, efforts to expand and refine police discretion, and advances in functional research. The expansion of police professional organizations, state standards organizations, and accreditation all indicate increasing levels of police professionalism.

By considering different ethical schools of thought, one can see how officers facing the same problem might come to quite different solutions. The "Dirty Harry" dilemma, for example, is commonly confronted by police officers and has no easy solution.

Critical Thinking Questions

1. Which is more effective for controlling police behavior: an internal affairs unit or a civilian review board? Why?

2. Should internal affairs be reactive or proactive? Which would be more effective? Why?

3. Which is a more effective method of external oversight of the police: a civilian review board or a police auditor? Why?

4. How would each of the three ethical perspectives assess the "Dirty Harry" problem? As a citizen, how do you want the police to respond in "Dirty Harry" situations?

5. How would you (as an officer or a citizen) respond to witnessing an instance of police misconduct?

6. As a citizen, would you feel comfortable going to your local police precinct to file a complaint?

References

Alpert, G., and Smith, W. 1999. "Developing Police Policy: An Evaluation of the Control Principle." In L. K. Gaines and G. W. Cordner (eds.), *Policing Perspectives: An Anthology*, pp. 353–362. Los Angeles: Roxbury Publishing.

Alpert, G., and Walker, S. 2000. "Police Accountability and Early Warning Systems: Developing Policies and Programs." *Justice Research and Policy* 2: 59–72.

Auten, J. 1988. "Preparing Written Guidelines." *FBI Law Enforcement Bulletin* 57: 1–7.

Barker, T. 1996. *Police Ethics: Crisis in Law Enforcement*. Springfield, IL: Charles C. Thomas Publishers.

Barker, T., and Carter, D. 1999. "Fluffing Up Evidence and Covering Your Ass: Some Conceptual Notes on Police Lying." In L. K. Gaines and G. W. Cordner (eds.), *Policing Perspectives: An Anthology*, pp. 342–350. Los Angeles: Roxbury Publishing.

Berg, B. 1994. "Education v. Training." In A. Roberts (ed.), *Critical Issues in Crime and Justice*, pp. 93–109. Thousand Oaks, CA: Sage Publications.

Bittner, E. 1970. *The Functions of Police in Modern Society*. Boston: Northeastern University Press.

Bobb, M. 2007. *Los Angeles County Sheriff's Department: 23rd Semi-Annual Report*. Los Angeles, CA: Police Assessment Resource Center. Available online at http://www.parc.info/client_files/LASD/%20 23rd%20Semiannual%20report.pdf.

Brandl, S. G., Stroshine, M. S., and Frank, J. 2001. "Who are the Complaint-Prone Officers? An Examination of the Relationship between Police Officers' Attributes, Arrest Activity, Assignment, and Citizens' Complaints about Excessive Force." *Journal of Criminal Justice* 29: 521–529.

Caiden, G. E. 1977. *Police Revitalization*. Lexington, MA: D. C. Heath.

Carter, D. 1994. "Police Disciplinary Procedures: A Review of Selected Police Departments." In T. Barker and D. Carter (eds.), *Police Deviance*, 3rd ed., pp. 355–376. Cincinnati, OH: Anderson.

Carter, D., and Barker, T. 1994. "Administrative Guidance and the Control of Police Officer Behavior: Policies, Procedures, and Rules." In T. Barker and D. Carter (eds.), *Police Deviance*, 3rd ed., pp. 13–28. Cincinnati, OH: Anderson.

Commission on Accreditation for Law Enforcement Agencies. 2006. *Standards Manual*, 5th ed. Fairfax, VA.

Commission on Peace Officer Standards and Training. 1990. *POST Administrative Manual*. State of California: POST.

Cordner, G. W. 1989. "Written Rules and Regulations: Are They Necessary?" *FBI Law Enforcement Bulletin* 58, 7: 17–21.

Cordner, G. W., and Williams, G. L. 1995. "The CALEA Standards: What Is the Fit With Community Policing?" *National Institute of Justice Journal* August: 39–49.

———. 1996. "Community Policing and Accreditation: A Content Analysis of CALEA Standards." In L. T. Hoover (ed.), *Quantifying Quality in Policing*, pp. 243–261. Washington, DC: Police Executive Research Forum.

———. 1999. "Community Policing and Police Agency Accreditation." In L. Gaines and G. W. Cordner (eds.), *Policing Perspectives: An Anthology*, pp. 372–379. Los Angeles: Roxbury Publishing.

Crank, J. P. 1998. *Understanding Police Culture*. Cincinnati, OH: Anderson.

Crank, J. P., and Caldero, M. A. 1991. "The Production of Occupational Stress Among Line Officers." *Journal of Criminal Justice* 19: 339–350.

Cullen, J. B. 1978. *The Structure of Professionalism*. Princeton, NJ: Princeton University Press.

D'Arcy, S., et. al. 1990. "Internal Affairs Unit Guidelines." San Jose, CA: San Jose Police Department.

Delattre, E. J. 1996. *Character and Cops: Ethics in Policing,* 3rd ed. Washington, DC: American Enterprise Institute.

Dugan, J. R., and Breda, D. R. 1991. "Complaints About Police Officers: A Comparison Among Types and Agencies," *Journal of Criminal Justice* 19: 165–171.

Fogelson, R. 1977. *Big-City Police.* Cambridge, MA: Harvard University Press.

Garrity v. New Jersey. 385 U.S. 483 (1967).

Geison, G. L. (ed.). 1983. *Professions and Professional Ideologies in America.* Chapel Hill: University of North Carolina Press.

Geller, W. A. (ed.) 1985. *Police Leadership in America: Crisis and Opportunity.* New York: Praeger.

Goldman, R., and Puro, S. 1987. "Decertification of Police: An Alternative to Traditional Remedies for Police Misconduct." *Hastings Constitutional Law Quarterly* 15: 50–80.

Goldstein, J. 1998. "Police Discretion Not to Invoke the Criminal Justice Process: Low Visibility Decisions in the Administration of Justice." In G. F. Cole and M. G. Gertz (eds.), *The Criminal Justice: Politics and Policies,* 7th ed., pp. 85–103. Belmont, CA: Wadsworth.

Hall, R. 1968. "Professionalization and Bureaucratization." *American Sociological Review* 33: 92–104.

Harmon, M. M. 1995. *Responsibility as Paradox: A Critique of Rational Discourse on Government.* Thousand Oaks, CA: Sage Publications.

Holmes, M. D., and Smith, B. W. 2008. *Race and Police Brutality: Roots of an Urban Dilemma.* Albany: State University of New York Press.

Independent Commission on the Los Angeles Police Department. 1991. *Report.* Los Angeles: California Public Management Institute. (Also known as the Christopher Commission.)

Iris, M. 2002. "Police Discipline in Houston: The Arbitration Experience." *Police Quarterly* 5: 132–151.

Klockars, C. 1991. "The Dirty Harry Problem." In C. Klockars and S. D. Mastrofski (eds.), *Thinking About Police: Contemporary Readings,* pp. 428–438. New York: McGraw-Hill.

Kuykendall, J., and Roberg, R. R. 1990. "Police Professionalism: The Organizational Attribute." *Journal of Contemporary Criminal Justice* 6: 49–59.

Lersch, K., Bazley, T., and Mieczkowski, T. 2006. "Early Intervention Programs: An Effective Police Accountability Tool, or Punishment of the Productive?" *Policing: An International Journal of Police Strategies and Management* 29: 58–76.

Lersch, K., and Mieczkowski, T. 1996. "Who Are the Problem-Prone Officers? An Analysis of Citizen Complaints." *American Journal of Police* 15: 23–44.

Manning, P. K. 1978. "Rules, Colleagues, and Situationally Justified Actions." In P. K. Manning and J. Van Maanen (eds.), *Policing: A View From the Street,* pp. 71–89. Santa Monica, CA: Goodyear.

———. 1998. *Police Work: The Social Organization of Policing,* 2nd ed. Prospect Heights, IL: Waveland.

Manning, P. K., and Redlinger, L. 1977. "Invitational Edges of Corruption: Some Consequences of Narcotic Law Enforcement." In P. Rock (ed.), *Drugs and Politics,* pp. 279–310. New Brunswick, NJ: Society/Transaction Books.

Mastrofski, S. 1990. "The Prospects of Change in Police Patrol: A Decade in Review." *American Journal of Police* 9: 1–79.

McAllister, B. 1987. "Spurred by Dramatic Rise in Lawsuits, Police Agencies Warm to Accreditation." *Washington Post* March 17: A7.

McMullan, J. 1998. "Social Surveillance and the Rise of the Police Machine." *Theoretical Criminology* 2: 93–117.

Murphy, P. V., and Caplan, G. 1991. "Fostering Integrity." In W. A. Geller (ed.), *Local Government Police Management,* pp. 239–271. Washington, DC: International City Management Association.

National Advisory Commission on Civil Disorders. 1968. *Report.* Washington, DC: U.S. Government Printing Office.

National Commission on the Causes and Prevention of Violence. 1969. *To Establish Justice, to Ensure Domestic Tranquility.* Washington, DC: U.S. Government Printing Office.

Nurre, S. 2008. *Year-End Report.* San Jose, CA: Office of the Independent Police Auditor.

Oettmeier, T. N. 1993. "Can Accreditation Survive the '90s?" In J. W. Bizzack (ed.), *New Perspectives on Policing.* Lexington, KY: Autumn House Publishing.

Perez, D. 1994. *Common Sense About Police Review.* Philadelphia: Temple University Press.

Petterson, W. E. 1991. "Police Accountability and Civilian Oversight of Policing: An American Perspective." In A. J. Goldsmith (ed.), *Complaints Against the Police: The Trend to External Review,* pp. 259–289. Avon, England: Bookcraft Limited.

Pollock, J. M. 1997. "Ethics and Law Enforcement." In R. G. Dunham and Alpert, G. P. (eds.), *Critical Issues in Policing,* 3rd ed., pp. 337–354. Prospect Heights, IL: Waveland.

Pollock-Byrne, J. M. 1998. *Ethics in Crime and Justice: Dilemmas and Decisions,* 3rd ed. Belmont, CA: West/Wadsworth.

President's Commission on Law Enforcement and Administration of Justice. 1967. *Task Force Report: The Police.* Washington, DC: U.S. Government Printing Office.

Price, B. R. 1996. "Police and the Quest for Professionalism." In J. Sullivan and J. Victor (eds.), *Criminal Justice: Annual Editions 96/97,* pp. 86–87. Guilford, CT: Brown and Benchmark.

Regoli, R., Crank, J. P., Culbertson, R., and Poole, E. 1988. "Linkages Between Professionalization and Professionalism Among Police Chiefs." *Journal of Criminal Justice* 16: 89–98.

Reuss-Ianni, E. 1983. *Two Cultures of Policing: Street Cops and Management Cops.* New Brunswick, NJ: Transaction Books.

Rhoades, P. W. 1991. "Political Obligation: Connecting Police Ethics and Democratic Values," *American Journal of Police* 10: 1–22.

Schein, E. H. 1985. *Organization Culture and Leadership.* San Francisco: Jossey–Bass.

Scogin, F., and Brodsky, S. L. 1991. "Fear of Litigation Among Law Enforcement Officers." *American Journal of Police* 10: 41–45.

Sherman, L. W. 1999. "Policing for Crime Prevention." In C. Eskridge (ed.), *Criminal Justice: Concepts and Issues,* 3rd ed., pp. 131–148. Los Angeles, CA: Roxbury Publishing.

Sherman, L., Gottfredson, D., MacKensie, D., Eck, J., Reuter, P., and Bushway, S. 1997. *Preventing Crime: What Works, What Doesn't, and What's Promising.* Washington, DC: U.S. Department of Justice.

Skogan, W., and Frydl, K. (eds.). 2004. *Fairness and Effectiveness in Policing: The Evidence.* Washington, DC: National Research Council.

Skolnick, J. 1994. *Justice Without Trial: Law Enforcement in Democratic Society,* 3rd ed. New York: John Wiley and Sons.

Skolnick, J., and Bayley, D. 1986. *The New Blue Line. Police Innovation in Six American Cities.* New York: Free Press.

Sparrow, M., Moore, M., and Kennedy, D. 1990. *Beyond 911: A New Era for Policing.* New York: Basic Books.

Sykes, G. W. 1994. "Accreditation and Community Policing: Passing Fads or Basic Reforms?" *Journal of Contemporary Criminal Justice* 10: 1–16.

Terrill, R. J. 1991. "Civilian Oversight of the Police Complaints Process in the United States." In A. J. Goldsmith (ed.), *Complaints Against the Police: The Trend to External Review,* pp. 291–322. Avon, England: Bookcraft.

Walker, S. 1998. *Sense and Nonsense About Crime and Drugs: A Policy Guide,* 4th ed. Pacific Grove, CA: Brooks/Cole.

———. 2001. *Police Accountability: The Role of Citizen Oversight.* Belmont, CA: Wadsworth.

———. 2003a. "Citizen Oversight, 2003: Developments and Prospects," *New York State Government, Law and Policy Journal* 5: 5–10.

Walker, S. 2003b. "Core Principles for an Effective Police Auditor's Office." Report of the First National Police Auditors Conference. Omaha, NE: University of Nebraska at Omaha, Department of Criminal Justice. Mimeo.

Walker, S. 2003c. *Early Intervention Systems for Law Enforcement Agencies: A Planning and Management Guide.* Washington, DC: Office of Community Oriented Policing Services.

———. 2005. *The New World of Police Accountability.* Thousand Oaks, CA: Sage Publications.

Walker, S., and Bumphus, V. W. 1991. *Civilian Review of the Police: A National Review of the 50 Largest Cities.* Omaha, NE: University of Nebraska.

Walker, S., and Graham, N. 1998. "Citizen Complaints in Response to Police Misconduct: The Results of a Victimization Survey," *Police Quarterly* 1: 65–89.

Walker, S., and Kreisel, B. W. 1996. "Varieties of Citizen Review: The Implications of Organizational Features of Complaint Review Procedures for Accountability of the Police." *American Journal of Police* 15: 65–88.

Wallace, B. 1990. "S. F. Watchdog Upholds Few Charges." *San Francisco Chronicle.* May 29: 1: 4–6.

West, P. 1988. "Investigation of Complaints Against the Police." *American Journal of Police* 8: 101–121.

Williams, G. L. 1989. *Making the Grade: The Benefits of Law Enforcement Accreditation.* Washington, DC: Police Executive Research Forum.

Wilson, O. W. 1950. *Police Administration.* New York: McGraw–Hill.

Wilson, J. Q., and Kelling, G. 1982. "Broken Windows: The Police and Neighborhood Safety." *Atlantic Monthly* March: 29–38.

"Younger NYC Cops Comprise Bulk of Arrests for Misconduct." 1989. *Law Enforcement News* August 5: 1.

Part IV

Contemporary Issues

CHAPTER 12

Diversity

CHAPTER OUTLINE

- Racial Minorities in Policing
    - Unequal Treatment
    - Performance of African American Police
- Women in Policing
    - Unequal Treatment
    - Performance of Women Officers
- Affirmative Action
- Equal Employment Opportunity
- Reverse Discrimination
- Increasing Diversity in Police Departments
    - Promotional Opportunities
- Integration of Minorities and Women Into Policing
    - Police Culture
    - Structural Characteristics
    - Pregnancy and Maternity
    - Sexual Harassment
- Future Prospects
- Summary
- Critical Thinking Questions
- References

- affirmative action plan
- civil service, or merit, system
- diversity
- defeminization
- double marginality

- empirical evidence
- hostile work-environment harassment
- police culture
- police*woman*
- *police*woman

- quid pro quo harassment
- reverse discrimination
- sexual harassment
- structural characteristics
- testimonial evidence

POLICING IN AMERICA REMAINS a white male–dominated industry, even after decades of calls from reformers to diversify policing in terms of race, ethnicity, and gender. Indeed, representation of females and racial/ethnic minorities has increased dramatically during the past 20 years; however, these groups remain underrepresented in most police organizations, particularly in smaller and rural police departments, which make up the overwhelming majority of departments in United States. As America continues to become more diverse, **diversity** of police departments has again become important for both political and performance reasons. Although it is clear that diversity has widespread political support in many communities, the actual difference that diversification makes in police effectiveness is less clear.

In general, it is believed that a diverse police department is more effective than one that is not. Diversity has become so important that it is often considered a significant strategy to reform departments with performance problems, particularly as they relate to use of force and community fear and distrust. The evidence regarding the impact of diversity on police effectiveness can be categorized as either testimonial or empirical. **Testimonial evidence** is based on the opinions of individuals who have strong political beliefs about the importance of diversity or whose experience (e.g., as citizens or police officers) has led them to believe that a diverse department is either more or less effective. In general, testimonial evidence about the effectiveness of diversity is usually favorable. **Empirical evidence** regarding the effectiveness of diversity based on data is derived from systematic study of one or more effectiveness criteria (e.g., crime rates, arrest rates, and citizen trust of police or fewer complaints, civil suits, and confrontations). It is not clear whether diversity makes a measurable, sustained difference in the effectiveness of the police. There is some evidence, however, that diversity can make a difference in some areas of police effectiveness in the short term. For example, Weitzer (2000) analyzed surveys of three Washington, DC, communities, where each community possessed different racial and class characteristics and found that citizens in middle-class communities reported that black and white officers act similarly in their communities; however, citizens in lower-class communities were more likely to report perceived variations in officer behavior. However, when asked whether they would prefer to have mostly white or mostly black officers working in their neighborhood, black and white teams, or no preference, the majority of citizens indicated they would prefer racially mixed policing teams or indicated "no preference." This was true regardless of community racial characteristics or economic characteristics. Also, citizens in New York who came into contact with female officers (when they were first put on patrol) had a higher regard for the police department than they had before (Sichel et al. 1978). Having a diverse police department may also improve its effectiveness and efficiency. The police rely heavily on the active participation of citizens to achieve their goals, and police departments who lack diversity may be more challenged to accomplish this. This issue is explored by Chief Castor in the Voices from the Field section of this chapter.

Given all the possible factors that can influence the relationship between police and citizens, it is unlikely that a police department that is a perfect cultural match for a community will necessarily be more effective for that reason alone. In the long term, the integrity, competence, and style of the officer and the philosophy, strategies, and methods of the department have the greatest impact on effectiveness. However, diversity continues to have substantial political support because many persons believe that it is equitable to employ minorities and women, given the discrimination they have experienced in the past.

VOICES FROM THE FIELD

Jane E. Castor
Chief of Police, Tampa Police Department

Question: Is it important for police organizations to have gender, racial, and ethnic diversity? Why?

Answer: The men and women of the Tampa Police Department have successfully reduced crime and improved the quality of life in our community over the past 7 years. Part I crime has dropped 56 percent. While there are a myriad of factors that played into this dramatic reduction, one of the driving forces is the very positive partnership we have built with the community. In order to achieve successful buy-in from the community, a law enforcement agency must develop a foundation of mutual trust. The best way to do that is to mirror the community that we serve.

Diversity should be a core element of any law enforcement organization, from the executive staff that develops the policy and procedures to the street level officers who carry out those policies in our community. The importance cannot be underscored. In order to feel a part of a community, individuals must sense that their cultural value system, beliefs and customs are represented in the most visible arm of the government. And in law enforcement we are all aware that is it less often an issue of right and wrong, than the perception of right and wrong. Perception is individual reality.

Officers must be able to relate to every segment of the community that they serve. Just as importantly, the organizational staff must allow the diversity of experience, ethnicity and race to weigh in on those decisions that ultimately affect the entire community.

In 2009, Jane Castor was named Law Enforcement Executive of the Year (by the National Association of Women Law Enforcement Executives) and became Tampa's first female police chief.

Historically, police departments have systematically discriminated against minorities and women in employment, assignments, promotions, and social acceptance. In addition, many white men have not, and do not, consider minorities and women their equals in terms of either capabilities or competencies. Beginning in the 1960s, governmental intervention was required to eliminate discrimination in employment and promotion. Legally, and in terms of government policy, this intervention became known as affirmative action (discussed in a later section).

During the early to mid-1960s there occurred inner-city riots and campus demonstrations that were often "sparked" by police actions. These events raised questions that went to the very core of the police role and operations in a democratic society: Are the police isolated from the community? How important is it to have community representation in police departments? How important to the community are the non-enforcement aspects of the police role? What type of individuals should be recruited as police officers? As has been discussed, several national commission reports, addressing these and other fundamental questions about the police, cited the need to increase especially minority but also female representation throughout the police field. The following is a brief discussion of the history of minorities and women in policing.

Racial Minorities in Policing

Very little has been written about the early development of racial minority police officers in this country. Virtually all the literature that is available concerns African Americans and makes it clear that blacks and other minority members, until recently, have had very little access to policing. For example, even though there were black police officers in Washington, DC, as early as 1861 (Johnson 1947), by 1940 they represented less than 1 percent of the police population (Kuykendall and Burns 1980). Since World War II, however, there has been a steady increase in the proportions of black officers, as well as other minorities, in policing. In general, although the proportions of blacks and other minorities reflect the available workforce in some communities, most departments do not have minority personnel equal to their numbers in the available workforce (see "Increasing Diversity in Police Departments").

Minority representation of police grew in many cities only as a result of pressure from the black community. In Chicago, for instance, black citizens complained frequently of the "stupidity, prejudice and brutality" of white officers (Gosnell 1935, 245). After 1940, use of black police increased as a result of the emerging political participation of blacks. Liberal whites (Rudwick 1962) often supported organized movements. Often a church or civic group would become concerned about crime rates, law enforcement in black areas, or race relations because of either racial tension or a desire for integration. Believing that using black officers to patrol black areas would substantially reduce black hostility toward the police, community leaders would usually agree to make a few experimental appointments (Johnson 1947).

Unequal Treatment

Even though African Americans were increasingly being hired into policing, they were not treated equally in the areas of powers of arrest, work assignments, evaluations, and promotions. Frequently, black officers were allowed to patrol only in black areas and to arrest only other black citizens. If a white person committed a crime in a black neighborhood, a black officer would have to call a white officer to make the arrest. In a 1959 survey of 130 cities and counties in the South, 69 required black officers to call white officers in arresting white suspects, and 107 cities indicated that black officers patrolled only in black neighborhoods

(Rudwick 1962). Elysee Scott, associated with the National Organization for Black Law Enforcement Executives, who grew up in a small Louisiana town in the 1950s, remembers that the black police officers rode in cars marked "Colored Police" and were allowed to arrest only "colored" people (Sullivan 1989).

Black officers were frequently restricted in type and location of assignments, and superior officers negatively manipulated performance ratings. Dismissal because of race was also a possibility. In addition, black and white officers rarely worked together (Gosnell 1935); even as late as 1966, squad cars were not totally integrated in the Chicago Police Department (National Center on Police and Community Relations 1967). Promotions were rare for black officers. Leinen (1984) reported that in the mid-1960s, only 22 police departments had promoted blacks above the rank of patrol officer. Even when promotions did occur, blacks were not congratulated by whites or given duties involving active command. In at least one instance, black lieutenants were assigned to walk a beat as patrol officers (Gosnell 1935). However, Hickman and his colleagues (2001) found no direct effects of officer race on outcomes of internal department disciplinary procedures in their examination of Philadelphia police officers. This may suggest that the kinds of discrimination that did exist in the past are less common today.

Performance of African American Police

As noted above, the riots of the mid-1960s were a major reason that increased emphasis was placed on the role of minorities in policing. Because a large number of these riots were triggered by incidents involving white officers patrolling black areas, many people thought that community relations would be improved if there were African American officers in these areas. Several national reports came to the same conclusion. For instance, the President's Commission on Law Enforcement and Administration of Justice stated,

> Police officers have testified to the special competence of Negro officers in Negro neighborhoods. The reasons given include: they get along better and receive more respect from the Negro residents; they receive less trouble … they can get more information; and they understand Negro citizens better. *(1967, 162)*

Historically, evidence to support the belief that black officers would perform more satisfactorily in black areas has been mixed. On the one hand, many black citizens wanted black officers because it would provide an opportunity for more public jobs, more understanding, less white police brutality, and more effective supervision of black criminals (Landrum 1947; Myrdal 1944). On the other hand, Rudwick (1960) has argued that blacks from lower socioeconomic classes preferred white to black officers. He found that poorer, uneducated blacks frequently asked for white officers when in need of help and were more likely to plead guilty to a charge made by a white officer (Rudwick 1962).

Some evidence indicates that black officers are actually more punitive on black citizens than white officers. In a study in Philadelphia in the 1950s, Kephart (1957) found that the majority of black officers believed it was necessary to be "stricter" with their "own" people than they were with nonblacks. Alex (1976) found that black officers were actually challenged more by young blacks and may have viewed themselves as protectors of the black community. In contrast, black officers needed to prove to the white officers that they were not biased and therefore treated black suspects the same as they treated white suspects or even more harshly. More contemporary research on this issue draws similar conclusions. Brown and Frank (2006) reported black officers were significantly more likely to arrest black citizens than white officers.

In his influential book *Black in Blue* (1969), Alex termed this dilemma "double marginality." This **double marginality** was evident by the mid-1960s, when the apparent desire of many black citizens for black police began to lose appeal. Studies conducted in San Diego and Philadelphia, for example, found that some black citizens felt that blacks who chose to become police officers were "selling them out." Of course, given the tenor of the times—police officers in general were viewed as enemies in minority communities—such a finding is hardly surprising. It is also interesting to note that while many still take the view that predominantly minority neighborhoods need minority patrol officers, others view such an approach as a form of segregation. It is ironic that many of those same people who, during the riots of the 1960s, demanded that black officers be sent into black areas later condemned the same practice as racist (Sullivan 1989, 342). Also, there is some evidence to suggest that the racial and ethnic composition of the police organization can influence behavior, but not in the manner that may be expected. Part of the rationale for diversifying police organizations was that minority officers may "police" minority communities differently. Historically, the white-male dominated police were viewed as treating minorities more punitively, and presumably this disparity would be less prevalent if minorities were more adequately represented within policing. Recent research has examined this from the perspective of race and traffic stops, specifically, determining whether the racial composition of police patrol divisions impacted the proportion of minorities stopped within that area. Even after taking racial composition of the neighborhood into account, Wilkins and Williams (2008) found that increased representation of black officers within a patrol division resulted in higher proportions of blacks stopped. This was true also for ethnicity: patrol divisions with higher proportions of Hispanic officers had correspondingly higher proportions of Hispanics stopped (Wilkins and Williams, 2009). This may be because of the impact of officer socialization—minority officers may be more likely to identify with other officers than minority citizens, and racial/ethnic differences in police organizations alone may have little influence on reducing disparity in behavior.

Weitzer (2000, 320) indicated that having racially mixed policing teams could have several benefits. First, the teams can have a moderating effect on officers of each race. This means that officers could "check and balance" or compensate for the behavior of their partners. Second, racially mixed teams can lead to socializing each officer in ways to interact with citizens of different races. Third, racially mixed teams provide a symbolic benefit for the police department, indicating unity and cohesion between officers of different races. Based on these results, there appears to be very little benefit from adhering to the old style of assigning officers to communities based on the race of the officer or makeup of the community (e.g., black officers in predominantly black communities, white officers in predominantly white communities).

Today, as African American officers become more self-assured and less likely to accept discriminatory practices, double marginality is less of a problem. On the one hand, in one study conducted in the aftermath of the Miami riots of the early 1980s, Berg, True, and Gertz (1984) found that black police officers were far less detached and alienated from the local community than were white or Hispanic officers. On the other hand, some police officials believe that black officers have trouble relating to the community because they tend to identify with their white colleagues, who often have a limited understanding of cultural differences (Felkenes 1990; Georges-Abeyie 1984). It is difficult to know how large an issue double marginality remains for minority officers, but one thing seems clear: as long as there is tension between minority communities and police departments, minority officers will be caught in the middle. It is anticipated that as the degree of discrimination lessens, both within and outside police departments, the problem of double marginality will lessen accordingly.

INSIDE POLICING 12.1 **Dallas Police Department Reports Minority Officers Reflect City Makeup**

Long a target of protests over its racial makeup, the Dallas Police Department is making progress in its efforts to make the ranks of its sworn employees reflect the increasingly diverse population it serves. For the first time, the number of black employees at the officer rank is virtually proportional to the city's black population, according to statistics kept by the departments. In the near future, the share of Hispanic officers also will be proportional to the city's Hispanic population.

As of early 1998, 29 percent of the department's 1,145 officers were black and 18.8 percent were Hispanic. The 1990 census, which the city uses to set hiring goals, showed that Dallas had 29.5 percent black residents and 18.8 percent Hispanics. Asian Americans make up less than 1 percent of officers and senior corporals. The department, however, has a ways to go before minorities are proportionately represented in its upper ranks. Whites, who make up 55.3 percent of the city's population, account for about 75 percent of the 1,697 senior corporals, sergeants, lieutenants, captains, and chiefs. While the department acknowledges the imbalance, it continues to make headway in improving promotional opportunities for all officers.

The figures on the number of minority officers are heartening in light of the tenuous, nearly incendiary police–minority relations that were the norm less than 10 years ago, a period in which the racial dynamics of the department were a major issue. To remedy the scant numbers of minorities on the force, the City Council adopted an affirmative action plan in 1988. Revised in 1993, the plan stipulated that each new class of police recruits should be one third black, one third Hispanic, and one third female. It also set promotional goals for women and minorities in each rank.

In 1992, protesters massed outside the department, charging that the effort was moving too slowly in hiring and advancing minorities. Two years later, an internal audit concluded that in the early 1990s the department had fired dozens of officers with questionable credentials. Critics of the affirmative action plan, including the Dallas Police Association (DPA), charged that standards had been lowered, leading to the firing of unqualified applicants. The DPA still opposes affirmative action, particularly the practice of "skip promotions" allowing minorities who score lower on tests to rank higher on promotion lists than whites with better scores. The apparent progress made by the department shows that the time is near to dismantle the controversial practice, said the DPA's president, Glenn White: "If you continue to hire minorities and get them in, having an affirmative action program with skip promotions is not necessary. They'll make it on their own."

Other observers cautioned that progress does not mean police now can become complacent on the issue of minority representation in the upper ranks. "If we can reach the representation goal at the police officer level, why not at the senior corporal, sergeant, and lieutenant and above?" said Thomas Glover, president of the Texas Peace Officers' Association, a predominantly black organization.

SOURCE: Adapted from "Dallas PD Says Black Officers Mirror City Makeup," *Law Enforcement News*, March 7, 1998. Reprinted with permission from *Law Enforcement News*, John Jay College of Criminal Justice, New York City.

Women in Policing

Women remain significantly underrepresented in policing. This might be in part because the crime-fighter image that is often portrayed in policing does not coincide with social perceptions of acceptable female behavior. Policing often involves male-attributed activities, such as aggression, and physical competence. Common characteristics associated with women (e.g., compassion, empathy, and nurturing) are seen as less needed, if not undesired, in police work (DeJong 2004; Garcia 2003; Milton 1972; Parsons and Jesilow 2001). Regardless of the reasons why women remain underrepresented in policing, it is often indicated that healthy and effective police organizations would benefit from a more integrated force.

Females officers at the beginning of the twentieth century were to aid male officers by performing duties deemed to be "unmasculine" or "not true police work," such as supervising juveniles in custody and clerical work. But contemporary policing operates with male and female officers enjoying equal police powers and responsibilities (Garcia 2003; Miller 1999; Miller and Hodge 2004). The first woman to hold full police powers was Lola Baldwin in Portland, Oregon, who in 1905 was hired in a social-work capacity with the responsibility of protecting young girls and women. Such a crime-prevention role was viewed as separate from the traditional police role; as Walker notes, "Once the police began to think in terms of preventing juvenile delinquency, they responded to the traditional argument that women had a special capacity for child care" (1977, 85). Between 1905 and 1915, several police departments across the country copied Portland's example.

The policewoman idea achieved the status of an organized movement in 1910 with the appointment of Alice Stebbins-Wells to the LAPD. Like Baldwin, Stebbins-Wells had a background in social work and was assigned to care for young women in trouble with the law and to prevent delinquency among juveniles of both sexes (Walker 1977). Stebbins-Wells became the national leader for the policewomen's movement, which lasted into the 1920s. Her appointment led to the appointment of women to similar positions (as police social workers) in police departments in at least 16 cities by 1916 (Walker 1977). By 1925, 210 cities had women working in police positions—417 as police social workers and 355 as jail matrons (Owings 1925).

Between 1925 and 1965, both the numbers and the functions of policewomen increased, but only minimally. For example, a 1967 survey of police departments in the nation's largest cities indicated that there were only 1,792 women with police powers (Berkeley 1969). When they were represented on the force, policewomen typically comprised less than 2 percent of the personnel (Eisenberg, Kent, and Wall 1973; Melchionne 1967) and were excluded from patrol duties. During this period, most police departments had policies that not only discouraged the hiring of women, but often included quotas as well, usually 1 percent or less (Simpson 1977).

Unequal Treatment

Prior to the 1950s, the role of women in policing was restricted primarily to social-welfare assignments, including dealing with juvenile and family problems; being prison matrons; detecting purse snatchers, pickpockets, and shoplifters; investigating sexual assault; and clerical work (Eisenberg, Kent, and Wall 1973). During the 1950s, their role was expanded to cover narcotics and vice investigations (Garmire 1978). In this period, it is ironic that the advocates for women in policing tended to argue that because of their "unique" contributions, including their skills with women and children, defusing domestic violence, and doing undercover work, they should be allowed to join the law enforcement profession (Melchionne 1967). Of course, such an argument most likely added to the prevailing view that women could handle specialist activities in "their areas" but were not suited for general police work. As Balkin notes, "It is an interesting if unanswered question why there was reluctance to demand simple equality for women in police work" (1988, 30). Undoubtedly, a large part of the answer lies in the strong tradition placed on the law enforcement, as opposed to social service, nature of the job. In addition, Wilson and McLaren, in their highly influential text, *Police Administration* (see Chapter 4), were firmly against the equal employment of women. They argued that while women could be of some value in specialized activities and units, they were not qualified to head such units. Men, they noted, were more effective administrators and "were less likely to become irritable and overly critical under emotional stress" (1963, 334).

Although these stereotypical images of women and police work were soon to be challenged, the major breakthrough for the equal treatment of policewomen on the job was the passage of the 1972 amendments to the Civil Rights Act of 1964. After this date, police departments were required, often under the threat of a court order, to eliminate such discriminatory practices of hiring and job assignment. The changes that followed were drastic. For example, in 1971 there were fewer than 12 policewomen on patrol in the United States; by 1974, this number was approaching 1,000 (Garmire 1978).

In 1968, the first women were assigned to patrol work in the Indianapolis Police Department (Milton 1972). Within 5 years, many of the nation's largest police forces, including those of New York, Philadelphia, Miami, Washington, and St. Louis, had women working in patrol (Sherman 1973). By 1979, the percentage of policewomen assigned to patrol was approximately 87 in city departments serving populations over 50,000 (Sulton and Townsey 1981). In a comprehensive survey for the Police Foundation (1990) of municipal departments serving populations ranging from 50,000 to over a million, it was shown that the integration of women into all police assignments has continued to grow at a steady pace. The data indicated that by 1986, 98 percent of the responding departments assigned women to patrol, and women were being assigned to field-operations units (including patrol, special operations, and traffic assignments) in slightly greater proportion than their overall representation in policing (Martin 1989). Today, policewomen are assigned to virtually all police functions.

Performance of Women Officers

Early critics of gender diversity in policing argued that women could not handle the "physically demanding" job of patrol that had barred them from patrol work. The influence of officer gender on behavior is inconsistent and mixed, making it difficult to make firm statements or broad conclusions. There is conjecture that gender diversity will change policing because females are presumed to be less aggressive and coercive and more nurturing and supportive than males. However, there is insufficient empirical evidence to support this stereotype (Skogan and Frydl 2004), and the evidence that does exist is often conflicting or highly contingent on the nature of the behavior being examined and the context of the situation. For example, early evaluations of the first generation of women patrol officers found that they performed in a highly satisfactory manner. The first study of women on patrol was conducted in Washington, DC, in 1973 (Bloch and Anderson 1974). A matched pair of 86 newly trained policewomen and policemen were placed on patrol and evaluated for 1 year. The results indicated that men and women performed in a generally similar manner.

Women responded to similar calls and had similar results in handling violent citizens. Some interesting differences were also found: women made fewer arrests but appeared to be more effective than men in defusing potentially violent situations. Additionally, women had a less aggressive style of policing and were less likely to be charged with improper conduct. The unmistakable conclusion drawn from these results was that female officers can perform effectively on patrol.

Two additional major studies closely followed the Washington study, both with similar conclusions. In 1975, Sherman conducted an evaluation of policewomen on patrol in the St. Louis County Police Department; the first 16 women put on patrol in the county were compared with a group of 16 men who had been trained with the women officers. The results indicated that the women were equally as effective as the men in performing patrol work. Once again, some interesting differences were noted: women were less aggressive, made fewer arrests, and engaged in fewer "preventive" activities, such as car and pedestrian stops. Citizen surveys indicated that women were more sensitive and responsive to their needs and handled service calls, especially domestic disturbances, better than men.

The second study, conducted in New York City in 1976 by Sichel et al. (1978), was comparable to the Washington study in methodological rigor and sophistication. Once again, comparison groups of 41 women and men officers with similar background characteristics were evaluated. Based on 3,625 hours of observation on patrol and some 2,400 police–citizen encounters, the results indicated that both groups of officers performed in a similar manner. Again, however, women officers were judged by citizens to be more respectful, pleasant, and competent; furthermore, citizens who came into contact with women officers tended to have a higher regard for the police department. Similar findings on the effectiveness of policewomen on patrol have been reported throughout the 1970s in departments of widely divergent sizes and geographical locations.

A review of these studies by Morash and Greene (1986) pointed out that despite the generally favorable evaluations, gender biases were inherent in the study designs. For example, there was an emphasis on traits stereotypically associated with "maleness" and policing, and approximately two thirds of the policing situations observed were related to direct or potential violence, even though such incidents are not frequently encountered. Also important, although the studies found differences in men's and women's behavior, they did not consider the possibility that the women's policing style in resolving conflicts and disputes, rather than escalating incidents into unnecessary arrests, might have had a beneficial rather than a negative effect. Public policing may indeed benefit from police styles that play down the values of coercive authority, conflict, and interpersonal violence (Morash and Greene 1986).

Contemporary research presents mixed results on the influence of gender and behavior. Specifically, much of the extant research indicates that male and female officers make similar arrest decisions during encounters with suspects (Feder 1997; Robinson 2000). Examinations of behavior beyond law enforcement draw similar conflicting conclusions. Research by Rabe-Hemp (2008) examined whether female officers engaged in different levels of social control during encounters with citizens. She categorized this controlling behavior as either lower level (e.g., verbal commands or advising citizens to leave the scene or cease engaging in disorderly behavior or wrongdoing) or extreme levels (threatening, searching, interrogating, restraining or arresting citizens). Further, she examined gender difference in supporting behaviors, such as telling the citizen to seek assistance from family or friends, use the legal process, or file a complaint. She found that female officers were less likely to engage in extreme controlling behaviors than male officers. However, this cannot be interpreted as a criticism of female officers or otherwise suggest they are unable, unwilling, or incapable of engaging in such behavior—it is more plausible that female officers are able to deescalate potentially physical confrontations with citizens. Meanwhile, she also reported lower level controlling behavior or the propensity to provide citizens with support did not vary across officer gender. Female officers were as likely to engage in verbal social control strategies as males, and male officers were as supportive as females. Rabe-Hemp (2008, 431) concludes that "assuming female officers manifest stereotypically feminine traits in policing tasks is clearly an overly simplistic conceptualization of the meaning and impact of gender in policing."

Other studies also indicate that female officers use force and coercion at parity with their male counterparts. Paoline and Terrill (2004) found little difference in the use of coercion by officers between genders. Similarly, Hoffman and Hickey (2005) found that female officers used unarmed physical force during arrests at approximately the same rate as male officers. This represents a significant departure from the stereotypical belief that female officers, because of their gender, are less capable or willing to engage in this behavior. However, they also noted that female officers exercised force with a weapon (i.e., firearms, flashlights, batons, OC spray) at a lower rate than male officers. Thus suspects were significantly less likely to endure injuries during encounters with female officers, because female officers were less likely to use weapons during these encounters. Bazley, Lersch, and Mieczkowski (2007, 190) found that while male and female officers employ force similarly, they also find that females "applied force levels within a narrower range of justifiable options than their male counterparts," suggesting that female officers respond differently to the level of resistance they encounter.

Finally, Parsons and Jesilow (2001) argue that the attitudes and behavior of female police officers differ very little from that of their male counterparts. They attribute these similarities to a number of factors, including self-selection, department screening, and socialization. They posit that many women who are drawn to policing possess a propensity for the stereotypically masculine characteristics outlined previously (i.e., aggression, physical competence, logic, and stable emotions). Typically, police departments continue to select and train officers according to the traditional law enforcement orientation. They further find that occupational socialization contributes to similarities in values, beliefs, and behaviors for both men and women (although women often find this process more difficult and isolating than male officers). This has separated male and female officers alike from the general population. The result is a collection of male and female officers who are more similar than many might believe.

Affirmative Action

The National Advisory Commission's *Report on Police* stated that "when a substantial ethnic minority population resides within the jurisdiction, the police agency should take affirmative action to achieve a ratio of minority group employees in approximate proportion to the makeup of the population" (1973, 329). The National Advisory Commission on Civil Disorders (1968, 316) suggested that police departments should not only intensify their efforts on minority recruitment but also increase the numbers of minorities in supervisory positions. Attempts to remedy past discriminatory employment and promotional practices are reflected in an **affirmative action plan**. In other words, the department tries to make an affirmative, or positive, effort to redress past practices and ensure equal employment opportunity. Such plans have been developed voluntarily, although often with political pressure or by court order following legal action.

In one study of the nation's 50 largest cities, Walker (1989) found that affirmative action plans appeared to play an important role in police employment trends. Nearly two thirds (64 percent) of the departments reported operating under an affirmative action plan at some point during the 5-year period. Interestingly, 23 of the affirmative action plans were court ordered, and only 7 were voluntary. McCrary (2007) examined whether court-ordered affirmative action litigation impacted the racial composition of police departments or city crime rates. A caution of affirmative action is that police departments may hire less-qualified, less desirable individuals to meet court-imposed quotas and this would compromise public safety. He compared 314 cities across more than 30 years and concluded that the litigation resulted in a 14 percent increase in hiring of black officers. He also found little support that litigation impacted crime—affirmative action did not appear adversely impact public safety. Much of the growth of minorities in policing over the past several decades can be attributed to affirmative action plans and policies (see Inside Policing 12.1).

The impact of affirmative action plans on recruiting females is less clear. Zhao, He, and Lovrich (2006) examined hiring practices of a representative sample of police departments serving over 25,000 residents to determine what factors impacted female recruitment between 1993 and 2000. They found that the proportion of female officers increased from 9.03 percent to 10.59 percent, with significant increases in white females (6.72 percent to 7.39 percent) and Hispanic females (0.50 percent to 0.80 percent). However, the proportion of black female officers in police departments did not change significantly. However, the proportion of black female officers in police departments did not change significantly. Zhao and colleagues went on went on to examine what factors did explain these changes. They found that while informal affirmative action plans increased the proportion of females overall and white females in particular, informal affirmative action plans were unrelated to the proportion of black and Hispanic females. Furthermore, police departments with court-imposed affirmative action plans were not correlated to the proportion of female officers overall or across any racial or ethnic categories. In other words, "a formal affirmative action program does not have a significant effect on hiring of female police officers" (Zhao, He, and Lovrich 2006, 480). Factors that increased the proportion of black and Hispanic females were largely external to the department—the size of the black and Hispanic population of the city was related to increasing diversity in black and Hispanic female officers, respectively. This research calls into question the effectiveness of court-ordered affirmative action plans at increasing gender diversity and also notes that while informal plans may increase the proportion of female officers overall, they have no impact on increasing black or Hispanic female representation in police departments.

Equal Employment Opportunity

In general, the legal challenges to discrimination in employment are brought under either (1) the "equal protection of the laws" clause of the Fourteenth Amendment (which protects citizens of all states) or (2) the Equal Employment Opportunity Act of 1972 (which extended to public agencies the "anti-discrimination in employment" provisions of Title VII of the 1964 Civil Rights Act). Title VII prohibits any discrimination in the workplace based on race, color, religion, national origin, or sex. The Equal Employment Opportunity Commission was established in 1964 to investigate possible violations of the act.

Moran (1988, 274) suggests that much of the resistance to affirmative action litigation rests on the belief by many police executives that the **Civil Service**, or **merit system**, is a fair and effective means of producing a professional force. This system generally involves selecting in rank order those individuals who obtained the highest combined score on an objective, multiple-choice, written exam (many of which have been shown to be culturally biased and not job related) and an oral interview. Additionally, candidates must meet several physical, medical, and personal requirements to qualify for appointment to the department. The problem with this "fair" and "effective" system is that it has excluded women, except in some specialized positions, and many minorities from police work.

The federal courts began to recognize that many selection standards that appeared to be neutral in form and intent in fact operated to exclude minorities and women. In general, the courts have indicated (Moran 1988, 275–276) that a police department must: (1) establish that a selection procedure can be scientifically linked to job performance (i.e., "job validated") or (2) restructure the selection process in a manner that does not discriminate against qualified minorities. The outcome of the affirmative action litigation has been that, from a scientific perspective, there was very little "merit" in the police-selection process. In fact, such standards as height, weight, age, and gender have not been correlated to job performance.

In the landmark decision in this area, *Griggs v. Duke Power Co.* (1971), the U.S. Supreme Court held that the use of a professionally developed examination (for intelligence) could not be used if it had a discriminatory effect. The Court pointed out that Title VII prohibited tests that are neutral in form but discriminatory in operation; that is, if a selection practice excludes minorities or women (even though not intended to do so) and cannot be shown to be job validated, it is prohibited. Griggs further found that once discrimination has been established, the burden of proof in establishing the validity of the practice shifts to the defendant (i.e., employer). In other words, once a police department has been judged to engage in a discriminatory practice, the department must indicate to the court that the practice (or requirement) is job related (Moran 1988).

In contrast, if a selection standard or requirement does not have a discriminatory impact, there is no need for validation. Furthermore, if a requirement can be shown to be a valid requirement for the job, even if it may have a discriminatory impact, it may be allowed to remain as a requirement. Chapter 14, for example, discusses how higher education may be shown to be a bona fide occupational qualification for policing and thus allowed as a requirement for initial selection.

Reverse Discrimination

Increasing the proportional representation of ethnic minorities and women in policing is an extremely complex undertaking that has important social, ethical, and legal implications. Although there is undoubtedly a need for an increase, the question is how to do so fairly. When affirmative action plans for selection and promotion (which may include the use of quotas, separate lists, and "skip" promotions, although often temporary; see Inside Policing 12.1) are put into practice, individuals who are not part of that plan—usually white men—often feel they have been discriminated against. This situation has become known as **reverse discrimination**. As with affirmative action policies, there has been much litigation in this area.

Haarr (1997) described the resentment and bitterness white officers held toward many black supervisors because of perceived inequities associated with affirmative action and dual promotion lists. During her observations and interviews with officers in one city, white officers (both male and female) indicated that they believed that less qualified black officers were promoted over more highly qualified whites. Two thirds of officers felt blacks had an unfair advantage in the promotional process. Conversely, blacks appeared to support the process as a mechanism for leveling the playing field because of culturally biased exams and the firmly entrenched "old-boy network" of promoting white men. Regardless of whether the dual-list strategy in this department was fair, just, or achieved its designed goals, one fact is clear: The process contributed significantly to alienation and animosity between races within the department. Further, Haarr reported that social patterns of interaction were largely intraracial, and this might, in part, be the result of these perceived inequities in the promotional process.

The litigation in this area is as complicated as the issue itself. In 1974, for example, the Detroit Police Department voluntarily adopted a policy of promoting one black officer to sergeant for each white officer promoted. The Detroit Police Officers Association filed suit against the department, claiming that the policy discriminated against white males. In *Detroit Police Officers' Association v. Young* (1978), the Sixth Circuit court ruled that preferential treatment had been granted to blacks solely on the basis of race and that the policy therefore discriminated against all others. In a similar suit, *U.S. v. Paradise* (1987), the U.S. Supreme Court upheld racial quotas as a means of reversing past discrimination. The Alabama Department of Public Safety was ordered to promote one black officer to corporal for each white officer promoted to rectify "blatant and continuous patterns of racial discrimination" (the department had only 4 of 66 black corporals and no blacks at the sergeant level or above). The Court justified the ruling, saying that it did not impose an unacceptable burden on innocent third parties since the "one-for-one" requirement was temporary and would only postpone the promotion of qualified whites. Additionally, the promotion quota advanced blacks only to the level of corporal (not higher ranks) and did not require layoffs or dismissals of white officers. More recently, the Court considered a matter related to promotional examinations, and while this case involved firefighters, the holding is relevant because both firefighters and police officers are civil service employees and promotional examinations are often similar in format. The city of New Haven, Connecticut, administered examinations for those seeing promotion to the ranks of lieutenant and captain. White candidates outperformed minorities on the exam, creating a liability catch-22 for the city. Certification of the exam would create a disparate racial impact on minority candidates; however, if they throw out the exam, then they could face liability from white candidates. They opted to not certify the exam, and white and Hispanic candidates argued their rights were violated until Title VII, which prohibits (among other things) intentional employment discrimination based on race. The Court agreed that the Civil Service Board violated Title VII by not certifying the exam (*Ricci v. DeStefano* 2009). But in doing so the Court provided a roadmap for cities to reject exam results like in New Haven in the future. Cities must demonstrate a strong basis of evidence that they would have been subjected to liability. New Haven failed to meet that burden in the current case, but it may be the case that similar situations could arise within policing in the future.

As the above court interpretations indicate, rulings in this area are subject to changes by the judges who try the cases. Based on *Paradise*, however, it appears that the Supreme Court, in its attempt to balance equal employment opportunities, is equally concerned about blatant racial discrimination as well as unacceptable injuries to innocent third parties.

Increasing Diversity in Police Departments

The number of women and minorities in police departments has increased consistently since the 1960s, even though the increase has been uneven. Walker (1989) reported that of the nation's 50 largest cities, between 1983 and 1988, nearly half (45 percent) made significant progress in the employment of black officers; however, 17 percent reported a decline in their percentage of African Americans. Sklansky (2006) indicated that the percentage of minority officers in major police departments has increased dramatically between the 1960s and 2000 and that at least two cities (Detroit and Washington, DC) are over 50 percent minority. Three police departments (Los Angeles, San Francisco, and Washington, DC) have a higher proportion of black officers than black residents. Forty-two percent of the departments reported significant increases in the percentage of Hispanic officers employed, while approximately 11 percent indicated a decline, and 17 percent reported no change. Latino representation in police departments is more likely within cities that experience rapid growth in Latino populations (Perez McCluskey and McClusky 2004).

A survey of municipal police departments serving cities of 50,000 or more (Martin 1989) indicated that in 1978 women made up 4.2 percent of sworn personnel, and by 1986 they made up 8.8 percent. In local departments with 100 or more officers, about 99 percent have women officers, but fewer than 1 percent have 20 percent or more female representation. Furthermore, most of these departments are sheriffs' departments, where many women officers work in the jails (Carter, Sapp, and Stephens 1989). The BJS conducts regular surveys on the cultural changes taking place in policing. The increasing percentages of women and minorities can be readily observed in Figure 12.1. Women comprised 11.3 percent of all full-time local police officers in 2003 compared with 10.6 percent in 2000, 10 percent in 1997, 8.8 percent in 1993, 8.1 percent in 1990, and 7.6 percent in 1987. Black officers accounted for 11.7 percent of the total in 2000 (unchanged since 1997) compared with 11.3 percent in 1993, 10.5 percent in 1990, and 9.3 percent in 1987. Hispanic officers made up 9.1 percent of the total in 2003 compared with 8.3 percent in 2000, 7.8 percent in 1997, 6.2 percent in 1993, 5.2 percent in 1990, and 4.5 percent in 1987. All minorities made up about 23.6 percent of the total in 2003. This is a steady increase of minority representation compared with 1987, when minorities made up 14.6 percent of police personnel (Reaves and Goldberg 2000; Hickman and Reaves 2006).

The uneven increase in both women and minority officers in departments of varying size is shown in Table 12.1. Although women comprised 11.3 percent of all local police officers in 2003, their percentages were highest in large jurisdictions, with 17.3 percent of officers in jurisdictions of 1 million or more in population and 15.6 percent in jurisdictions with at least 500,000 residents but fewer than 1 million (see Table 12.1). In contrast, females comprise only 5.7 percent of officers in jurisdictions with fewer than 2,500 people.

Minority officers, who made up approximately 11.7 percent of the total, also had the highest percentages in large jurisdictions, with black officers making up approximately 19 to 25 percent in jurisdictions over 250,000 residents; Hispanic officers were the most represented in jurisdictions with populations over 250,000, making up 11.3 percent. Each of these groups had the highest percentage of officers in jurisdictions with over 1 million population. Other minorities, including Asians, Pacific Islanders, American Indians, and Alaska Natives, represented 2.8 percent of the total (see Table 12.1). This is important to note because the typical municipal police department is small, and relatively few police organizations serve jurisdictions greater than 250,000. Females and racial/ethnic minorities are even more likely to be underrepresented in these departments.

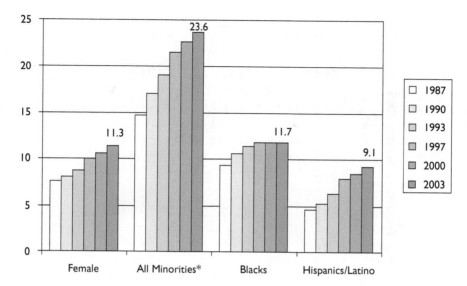

FIGURE 12.1 **Percentage of Women and Minority Local Police Officers, 1987–2003.**

Source: B. A. Reaves and A. L. Goldberg, *Local Police Departments, 1997* (Washington, DC: Bureau of Justice Statistics, 2000), 4; M. J. Hickman and B. A. Reaves, *Local Police Departments, 2003* (Washington, DC: Bureau of Justice Statistics, 2006), iii.

Three recent surveys of women in policing further point out their uneven development and continued gender-specific problems. The first survey of 800 police executives by the International Association of Chiefs of Police (IACP) reported that women make up 12 percent of the police officers but are not represented at all in nearly 20 percent of the departments ("Plenty of Talk" 1999). Furthermore, the IACP found that 91 percent of the departments had no women in policy-making roles, and 10 percent reported that gender bias was one of the reasons women were not promoted. It was also found that women had filed more than one third of the lawsuits against departments charged with gender bias and sexual harassment. Based on the findings, the IACP recommended that police departments should implement fairer screening procedures, institute more rigorous policies against sexual harassment, and increase recruiting drives designed to attract and retain more women in policing. The Albuquerque Police Department has been identified by police executives as a possible model for other departments regarding policewomen. In the past 3 years, women in the academy class have increased from just 8 percent to 25 percent. In the January 1999 class, the department reports, one third of the recruits were women. Several years ago, however, despite participation in job fairs and a competitive salary, the department was still having problems recruiting female candidates. But significant changes seem to have turned the situation around. Those changes included (1) hiring a trainer to help women candidates pass the physical conditioning tests, (2) switching to weapons that were better suited to women's smaller hands, and (3) finding a body-armor manufacturer that was willing to construct bulletproof vests that accommodated female bodies ("Plenty of Talk" 1999). Another program in Vermont focuses on gender-specific issues designed to encourage females to consider policing and to provide necessary skills designed to enhance professional development. This program is described further in Inside Policing 12.2.

TABLE 12.1 Race and Ethnicity of Full-Time Officers in Local Police Departments, by Size of Population Served, 2003

POPULATION SERVED	PERCENTAGE OF FULL-TIME SWORN EMPLOYEES WHO WERE						PERCENTAGE OF FULL-TIME SWORN EMPLOYEES WHO WERE								
	TOTAL			WHITE			BLACK/AFRICAN AMERICAN			HISPANIC/LATINO			OTHER*		
	TOTAL	MALE	FEMALE	TOTAL	MALE	FEMALE	TOTAL	MALE	FEMALE	TOTAL	MALE	FEMALE	TOTAL	MALE	FEMALE
All sizes	100	88.7	11.3	76.4	69.4	7.0	11.7	9.0	2.7	9.1	7.8	1.3	2.8	2.5	0.3
1,000,000 or more	100	82.7	17.3	61.1	53.2	7.9	16.7	11.3	5.4	19.3	15.7	3.6	2.8	2.6	0.2
500,000–999,999	100	84.4	15.6	61.9	54.1	7.8	24.4	18.0	6.4	7.8	6.8	1.0	6.0	5.4	0.6
250,000–499,999	100	85.4	14.6	66.6	57.7	8.9	19.4	15.3	4.1	11.3	10.0	1.3	2.7	2.4	0.3
100,000–249,999	100	89.0	11.0	76.0	68.2	7.8	11.9	9.8	2.1	9.1	8.2	0.9	3.0	2.8	0.2
50,000–99,999	100	91.2	8.8	83.3	76.6	6.7	7.4	6.3	1.1	7.0	6.2	0.8	2.3	2.2	0.1
25,000–49,999	100	91.8	8.2	87.5	80.8	6.7	5.8	4.9	0.9	5.5	5.0	0.5	1.2	1.0	0.2
10,000–24,999	100	93.3	6.7	90.4	84.6	5.8	4.4	4.0	0.4	3.0	2.8	0.2	2.1	1.9	0.2
2,500–9,999	100	93.8	6.2	89.8	84.5	5.3	4.2	3.7	0.5	3.4	3.2	0.2	2.6	2.3	0.3
Under 2,500	100	94.3	5.7	88.5	83.8	4.7	5.7	5.1	0.6	3.4	3.2	0.2	2.5	2.2	0.3

Note: Details may not add to total because of rounding.

*Includes Asians, Native Hawaiians or other Pacific Islanders, American Indians, Alaska Natives, and any other race.

Source: M. J. Hickman and B. A. Reaves, *Local Police Departments, 2003* (Washington, DC: Bureau of Justice Statistics, 2006) p. 7.

INSIDE POLICING 12.2 Recruiting Women into Law Enforcement

Recognizing the fact that females remain underrepresented in policing and citing research identifying the advantages of having gender diversity in the workforce, staff at the Vermont Works for Women (a nonprofit organization that has a track record of recruiting and preparing women to work in nontraditional occupations) created Step Up to Law Enforcement. This program, established in 2004, is a nine-week, pre-academy, gender-specific training course designed to provide training and a real world introduction to working in policing and corrections.

The program emphasizes key components including physical conditioning (designed to prepare applicants for pre-employment physical fitness tests and the physical rigors of the academy), women's resources (career planning designed for female officers) and classroom instruction on topics related to policing and corrections. The program also addressed other aspects of applying for and working in the police industry, including recruitment examination training, topics related to criminal justice, workshops on issues related to policing, introducing firearms skills, and other personal development skills (including self-esteem building, communication, goal setting, and problem solving). The program also has a post-program mentoring component with policing and correctional professionals.

The program creates camaraderie and support networks for females seeking employment in male-dominated industries. It provides opportunities to expose participants to policing and career opportunities that they may otherwise not have considered. It also demystifies policing and exposes females to the realities of policing to encourage them to make informed choices regarding whether to pursue these career paths.

After 4 years, over half of the program participants had secured employment in either police departments or correctional facilities.

SOURCE: Tuomey, L. M., and Jolly, R. 2009. "Step Up to Law Enforcement: A Successful Strategy for Recruiting Women into the Law Enforcement Profession." *The Police Chief*. Available online at http://policechiefmagazine.org/magazine/index.cfm?fuseaction=display_arch&article_id=1820&issue_id=62009.

The second survey of some 700 state and local police departments with 100 or more full-time sworn officers by the BJS (Reaves and Goldberg 1999) found that sheriffs' departments employed the highest percentage of female officers (15 percent)—although many of those worked in the jails rather than on patrol—followed by county departments (11 percent), municipal departments (9 percent), and state agencies (5 percent). The third survey, by the National Center for Women and Policing (2002), found that women held 12.7 percent of all sworn positions in 2001.

With respect to ethnicity and policewomen, Table 12.1 indicates that the proportion of minority women was related to city size—that is, as the size of the city increased, so, too, did the proportion of minority female representation. For example, black women constituted 5.1 percent of female officers in jurisdictions over 1 million and 6.5 percent in jurisdictions over 500,000. Furthermore, minority women made up a disproportionately large share of women in policing—approximately 35 percent in 2000. It has been suggested that this large proportion of minority female officers—who are mostly black (2.2 of the 3.0 percent)—may be related to several factors (Martin 1989). First, black women may view policing as an attractive occupational choice because they have a narrower range of options to choose from because of racial differences in education and job discrimination. Second, black women have historically worked in occupations involving physical labor and therefore may be less likely to be bothered by this aspect of the work than white women. Third, municipal departments may be disproportionately recruiting and hiring minority women to simultaneously meet affirmative action goals related to racial and sexual integration.

The data indicate that many police departments are culturally diverse and becoming more so all the time. Even though this trend is uneven throughout the country, it is probable that within the next several decades, half or more of local police officers will be women and minorities. Such growth, however, assumes a continued emphasis on affirmative action and equal employment opportunity programs, which may be subsiding in some departments (see Chapter 14).

Promotional Opportunities

A comparison study of 290 police departments of female police supervisors (Martin 1989a) shows that women represented 2.2 percent of all municipal supervisory levels in 1978 and 7.6 percent in 1986 (including 3.7 percent at the sergeant level; 2.5 percent at the lieutenant level; and 1.4 percent above the lieutenant level).

Another study of departments with 100 or more sworn personnel by the National Center for Women and Policing ("Equality Denied" 2001) found higher percentages of women supervisors. The center evaluated the number of females in supervisory positions among large police departments as well as smaller and rural police departments. They found that for women, while underrepresented in police departments, the disparity is more pronounced at higher levels of the organizational chart. Women made up 9.6 percent of supervisory positions (lieutenant and sergeant) in large agencies and 4.6 percent in smaller/rural agencies. Among top command positions (captain or above), women were represented at the rate of 7.3 and 3.4 percent. In sum, while the proportion of women in American police departments continues to experience modest increases, the proportion of females in positions of power and policy making in these organizations remains alarmingly low (see Figure 12.2).

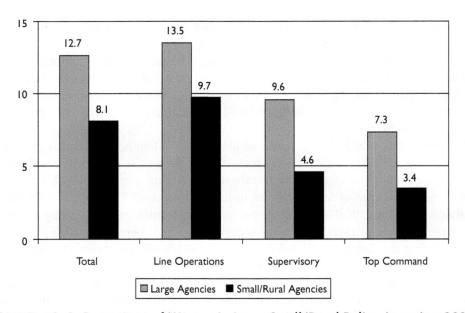

FIGURE 12.2 Percentage of Women in Large Small/Rural Police Agencies, 2001.

Source: Equality Denied: The Status of Women in Policing (National Center for Women & Policing, 2001) 7, 12, and 13.

Data on minority promotions are more limited than data on women. According to officials in African American and Hispanic national organizations, there is no agency that routinely and systematically gathers information about the promotion of minorities. Despite the lack of data, many affirmative action specialists claim that most minority officers are not promoted equally with white officers and remain essentially at the entry level (Sullivan 1989). As with female officers, however, it is also true that because minority members have not been well integrated into policing, until recently they have not had a sufficient amount of time in which to be promoted. The type of progress being made in Dallas (see Inside Policing 12.1) may be indicative of departments adopting affirmative action plans; approximately 48 percent of the department's officers are minority, and about 25 percent account for supervisory or command positions.

Wide variation exists in promotion practices among police departments. In general, it appears as though the departments with the best records of promoting minority officers are those in cities that have large minority populations and minority leadership in the mayor's office or at the top levels in the police department. Thus, as Sullivan (1989) has noted, promotions tend to be more likely for black officers in Chicago and Atlanta (or Detroit) or for Hispanic officers in Miami (or Los Angeles) than for their colleagues in cities with larger white populations and power bases. Walker and Turner (1993) reported the percentage of black and Hispanic officers in eight nationally representative large police departments and the percentage holding supervisory ranks is considerably lower than minority representation among officers. Sklansky (2006), highlighting the LAPD, reported the proportion of non-white officers was around 60 percent; however, minority (particularly Hispanic) representation decreased at higher levels of the hierarchy. In 2000, nearly 70 percent of the top command in the LAPD was white.

The Supreme Court's ruling in *Paradise* also appears to set the direction in attempting to balance the need to rectify past discriminatory practices while protecting innocent third parties from discrimination. Rulings such as *Paradise*, along with continued emphasis on minority recruitment and affirmative action plans, should contribute substantially toward a higher percentage of minority personnel in supervisory positions in the near future. One interesting dilemma has developed, however, with respect to minority promotions at the local level—namely, "federal raiders," who recruit away top minority candidates (Sullivan 1989). Because federal agencies usually require some law enforcement experience prior to employment, federal agents often recruit their personnel from local police departments. Furthermore, because federal agencies tend to be viewed as more prestigious and may pay more, it is easy to understand why they are often successful in recruiting the best qualified personnel (especially minorities and women) local departments have to offer. Such "raiding" results in the loss by local departments of the minority officers with the greatest potential for promotion.

There are several examples of underrepresented groups within the highest position of police chief in major cities. In 1982 there were 50 black police chiefs, and in 1988 there were 130—an increase of 160 percent. At one point in the 1990s, 6 of the 10 largest cities in the country, including cities in the South, had a black chief. For example, Lee P. Brown, founding member of the National Organization of Black Law Enforcement Executives, served as chief in Houston and New York City prior to his retirement and was appointed the nation's "drug czar." Beverly Harvard served as the nation's first African American female chief of a major U.S. police department in Atlanta. Such appointments are important because these chiefs serve as role models and will be sensitive to the recruitment and promotion of minority officers.

Officer's motivation to seek promotion appears to vary by race and gender, and suggesting that police organizations simply "encourage" underrepresented groups to seek promotion may be ineffective or even counterproductive. Whetstone (2001) explained personal, professional, and organizational reasons influenced whether officers sought promotion. White officers were significantly more likely to indicate promotion was a personal goal, where minorities were significantly more likely to seek promotion to achieve a leadership role. Whetstone further noted that whites were *less* likely to be encouraged to seek promotion than minorities. Similarly, Archbold and Schultz (2008) and Archbold and Hassell (2009) found female officers reported being consistently encouraged by supervisors to seek promotion. However, they indicated female officers felt they were being encouraged because of their gender, rather than being highly qualified or being effective leaders. This created an unanticipated negative effect—females were actually less likely to pursue promotion in part because they were encouraged to do so under what they interpreted as illegitimate reasons.

Whetstone went on to comment that male officers were much more likely to not seek promotion because doing so would result in a loss of pay. While promotion almost universally includes an increase in base salary, a sergeant's earning potential can decrease because they may not be able to engage in lucrative off-duty assignments (or "side jobs"). Female officers, on the other hand, were significantly more likely to cite child care concerns for opting out of the promotional process (see also Archbold and Hassell 2009). Shifts are often assigned based on seniority, with new sergeants given the least desirable shifts (e.g., midnights). Because overnight child care options are scarce, a promotion to sergeant could be viewed as an unnecessary hardship for officers, particularly female officers.

It is important for police organizations to encourage and promote diversity at all levels of the hierarchy, and minorities and females appear particularly underrepresented in supervisory positions. But addressing the issue of disparity at supervisory levels appears to be quite complicated and should be approached delicately. Simply "encouraging" minorities and females to be promoted can cause some to feel slighted and marginalized, resulting in otherwise qualified individuals choosing not to seek promotion. Additionally, there appear to be a variety of factors that influence the decision to pursue (or not pursue) promotion, and some of these decisions vary across race and gender. Responsible organizations will need to take these into consideration while creating a culture that provides qualified officers with the opportunity to seek promotion.

Integration of Minorities and Women Into Policing

From the preceding discussion, it is apparent that an increasing percentage and number of both minorities and women are entering the law enforcement field. Much of this increase, however, is caused by the passage of the 1972 amendments to the Civil Rights Act of 1964. These amendments, and subsequent court decisions based on them, forced police departments to alter, rather radically in some instances, their selection and promotional practices. Hence, the question remains: How well are these "non-traditional" officers being treated once inside the department? This section looks at how well women and minorities appear to be integrating into the police work environment, as well as prospects for the future.

Because many male officers have been opposed to women in policing in general and women on patrol in particular (see Bloch and Anderson 1974; Sherman 1975; Martin 1980; Charles 1981; Linden 1983), it is not surprising that women have had a particularly difficult time breaking into policing. Even though many departments are moving toward community policing, for the most part they remain tradition-bound and masculine. As Linden

(1983) points out, men tend to object to women on patrol because they fear that women will not be able to cope with physical violence and that the image of the police will suffer. For example, a survey of police departments in the Northwest (Brown 1994) indicated that only one third of male patrol officers actually accepted a woman on patrol and that more than half did not think that women can handle the physical requirements of the job as well as men. Martin (1980) further notes that women threaten to disrupt the division of labor, the work norms, the work group's solidarity, the insecure occupational image, and the sexist ideology that is contrary to the men's definition of the work as "men's work" and their identity as masculine men.

Police Culture

The major underlying dilemma confronting women in policing is the **police culture**, which has as its foundation a sexist and macho perception of the role of police. As Martin has noted,

> The use of women on patrol implies either that the men's unique asset, their physical superiority, is irrelevant (as it is, on most assignments) or that the man with a female partner will be at a disadvantage in a physical confrontation that he would not face with a male partner. *(1989, 11)*

The nature of police work creates a peer culture between officers that makes it difficult for women to assimilate. Franklin (2005) summarizes elements of police culture to include machismo/adventure, coercive power and control, heterosexism, solidarity and group loyalty, sexism, physical conflict resolution, glorification of violence, desire for action, and excitement and danger. She concludes that these elements "form the social systems that serve to keep women from fully participating in policing" (2005, 7). According to this research, women continue to be seen as outsiders and inappropriate for policing by many within the policing industry.

As emphasized previously, in general, the police role is not physically demanding and requires a much stronger mental than physical capacity. In addition, no research has ever indicated that strength is related to police functioning, nor has there been any research to suggest that physical strength is related to an individual's ability to successfully manage a dangerous situation (Charles 1981).

As the earlier review of the research on the performance of policewomen indicated, women not only perform satisfactorily on patrol, but also tend to be exemplary in the less aggressive, nontraditional aspects of the role (e.g., interacting with citizens, handling domestic disturbances). This suggests that in many respects, women may actually be better suited for police work than men. McDowell (1992) reports that the Christopher Commission (investigating the LAPD after the Rodney King beating) found that the 120 officers with the most use-of-force reports were all men and that civilian complaints against women were consistently lower. Policewomen, by contrast, tended to meet the public better, handled domestic violence better, and dealt with rape victims better.

Women face other hurdles in attempting to be accepted into the policing profession. For instance, the use of sexist language, sexual harassment, sexual jokes, tokenism, and sex-role stereotyping all contribute to severe adjustment problems for women (Martin 1989; Martin and Jurik 1996). Men frequently use language to keep women officers in their "place" by referring to them as "ladies" or "girls," suggesting that they need to be protected. Women who do not conform to sex-role stereotypes and are "tough" enough to gain respect as officers may be labeled as "bitches" or "lesbians" in an attempt to neutralize their threat to male dominance (Berg and Budnick 1986; Prokos and Padavic 2002), a process referred to as **defeminization**. Men's cursing can also create problems for women, since men may feel inhibited—and resentful—about swearing in front of women, and yet men may lose their "respect" for women who swear.

Possibly because of the hurdles women face on entering policing, some research (Martin 1979) has suggested that two separate identities may develop: the **police woman** and the **police woman**. The former attempts to gain her male colleagues' approval by adhering to traditional police values and norms, with law enforcement her primary orientation; the latter attempts to perform her duties in a "traditionally feminine manner" by making few arrests, infrequently using physical activity, and placing strong emphasis on "being a lady." While Martin's research included only 32 female officers, 7 of whom were classified as police*women* and 8 as *police*women—with the rest in between—it is important that police departments promote policies and practices that allow female officers to be "themselves" and to utilize the particular strengths that many bring to the job. In fact, Rabe-Hemp (2009) suggests this may actually be the case. She found through interviews with officers that females tend to negotiate between the *police*women and police*women* ends of the spectrum. Female officers she interviewed rated themselves higher than their male counterparts across "feminized forms of police work" (Rabe-Hemp 2009, 124) including dealing with victims, children and juveniles, and community policing. However, female officers were critical of female peers who appeared to proscribe to a dominate end of the *police*women and police*women* continuum.

In general, research on policewomen suggests that they are still struggling for acceptance, believe that they do not receive equal credit for their work, and are often sexually harassed by their coworkers (Daum and Johns 1994). One study of over 500 women officers from nine western states revealed that open sexual discrimination and sexual harassment were far more common today than expected, especially by supervisors and commanders, who not only tolerate such practices by others but frequently engage in such practices themselves (Timmins and Hainsworth 1989). The survey also indicated that duty assignments were often based on gender. Martin (1989a) further notes that frequent sexual jokes and informal harassment cause many women to avoid interaction with men that might be viewed as having a sexual connotation. To maintain their moral reputation, they may sacrifice the opportunity to build close interpersonal relationships that are so necessary for gaining sponsors and mentors (i.e., an influential person who provides guidance and assistance). Without backing from the informal political network within the department, women are likely to have a more difficult time being promoted or gaining specialized job assignments.

This lack of access to the informal political network within a department also applies to minority officers. Although there are many reasons why minorities may not be assigned to specialized jobs or promoted equally with whites, some of which were discussed earlier, Sullivan (1989) believes that the major reason is that minority networks usually do not reach the upper echelons of power and the existing white network. He suggests this is a "catch 22" situation—that is, minority promotions will increase only when more minority officers are promoted. Once again, it is important to recognize how important equal promotional opportunities are for both minority and female officers.

Structural Characteristics

Women also face problems relating to the **structural characteristics** or features of police departments (Martin 1989). For example, most training academies place a strong emphasis on physical fitness. Once a certain level of fitness and performance has been achieved, however, it generally need not be maintained; that is, few departments require any testing of physical performance beyond that of the academy. Such an emphasis tends to magnify the importance of physical differences between the sexes, which, of course, tends to perpetuate the sex-role stereotype. This is not to suggest that police officers should not be physically fit, but that fitness should be within the parameters of job-related standards. Furthermore, if physical standards are job related, then they certainly should be maintained throughout an officer's career, at least in those jobs where such a requirement is necessary.

Training academies also often fail to place the proper amount of importance on the development of *interpersonal skills* that are essential to effective police work. Such skills are usually more highly developed in women than men, and their absence from the training curriculum deprives women of excelling in an important job-relevant area. Consequently, as Martin has observed: "New women recruits enter male turf on male terms with little recognition of their own problems or strengths" (1989, 12). Associated with the problem of not recognizing the importance of interpersonal skills is the performance-evaluation process itself. Despite the favorable response to the effectiveness of women on patrol, internal performance-evaluation criteria tend to have a gender bias favorable toward males. Some research (Morash and Greene 1986) has discovered that such criteria tend to emphasize traits that are primarily associated with a male stereotype (e.g., forcefulness and dominance). Additionally, Lonsway (2003) reviewed research related to women's lack of physical prowess making them unsuitable for police work. She noted that while there are times when physical strength is advantageous for officers, these situations are relatively rare in everyday policing. Further, she notes that police departments have been unable to create valid tests that can predict successful performance of physical activities.

Pregnancy and Maternity

An important policy area concerning women officers is that of pregnancy and maternity or disability leave. As more women enter policing and become pregnant, their treatment becomes important not only to the officer and her family, but also to the department and the community. Title VII of the Civil Rights Act was amended in 1978 to add the Pregnancy Discrimination Act, which outlaws discrimination on the basis of pregnancy, childbirth, or any medical condition they might cause. Employers are thus required to treat pregnancy as they would any other temporary disability (Rubin 1995a). The Family and Medical Leave Act (FMLA) of 1993 also provide employees to take up to 3 months leave for medical conditions that include pregnancy.

While over time police departments have continued to integrate the Pregnancy Discrimination Act and the FMLA into their personnel policies, the practice of how police organizations address pregnancy varies considerably. Also, as Kruger (2007) notes, the FMLA has limitations for policing and departments can identify exceptions to accommodating pregnant officers. Recognizing that it is unfair to force females to choose between professional goals and family choices, Kruger provides a series of recommendations for policing:

1. Light duty assignments: Typically these assignments involve tasks where the officer is not on the street. Police departments should identify temporary light duty positions for officers on disability, and if such assignments already exist then pregnant officers must be afforded the opportunity to be assigned to them.

2. Fetal protection policies: Certain type of police functions may be hazardous to fetuses. For example, firearm training involves discharging lead dust into the air that,

if breathed by a pregnant woman, can create health issues. Pregnant officers should be advised of any such risks and given the option to make up any missed training to avoid falling behind non-pregnant peers.

3. Maternity uniforms and equipment: Police uniforms and equipment should be modified to accommodate changes in body structure.

4. Maternity leave: While leave is protected by FMLA policies, police organizations vary in regard to whether leave is paid and whether officers have adequate sick leave accrued. Typically employees return to work 6 to 8 weeks after childbirth but given the unique physical exertions of policing, this time may need to be more flexible.

5. Job sharing and flex time: Some employers accommodate family situations by having two employees share jobs or modify work schedules. Given that policing is a 24-hour, 7-day-a-week industry, police organizations may be able to accommodate these requests. But existing organizational and human resource policies may not currently be suited to consider job sharing and will have to be more fully examined. *(Kruger 2007, 81–86)*

She goes on to recognize employees also share some of the responsibility in managing pregnancy and family planning professionally. Certain stages in an officer's career may be particularly unsuited for maternity (e.g., academy training, FTO or probationary periods) and officers may choose to defer pregnancy until later. Recognizing this, planned child care may be part of the employee's responsibility (Kruger 2007). An issue not raised is related to organizational size—larger police departments may be more structurally equipped to provide the accommodations discussed above. Smaller, rural police departments may challenged to provide opportunities such as job sharing (because there may not be a second officer with whom to share the job). Pregnancy and maternity will impact large and small departments differently, and policies will need to be tailored for each organization.

Sexual Harassment

The discussion on police culture above established that policewomen still face sexual harassment by their coworkers. If women officers are to gain equal treatment and status in police departments, sexual harassment must be taken seriously by the department and eliminated. Title VII of the Civil Rights Act prohibits sex discrimination. Sexual harassment is simply another form of sex discrimination. **Sexual harassment** in the workplace has been defined as follows:

Unwelcome sexual advances, requests for sexual favors, and other verbal or physical conduct that enters into employment decisions and/or conduct that unreasonably interferes with an individual's work performance or creates an intimidating, hostile, or offensive working environment. *(Rubin 1995b, 1–2)*

Sexual harassment applies to men as well as women and to same-sex harassment as well. In general, there are two forms of sexual misconduct:

1. **Quid pro quo harassment** requires the employee to choose between the job and the sexual demands. Once equal access to employment opportunities are blocked for refusing the demands, Title VII has been violated (Rubin 1995a). This type of harassment usually occurs between a supervisor and subordinate (Rubin 1995b).

2. **Hostile work-environment harassment** occurs when unwelcome conduct is so severe or pervasive that it interferes with a person's job. Unlike quid pro quo harassment,

which usually occurs as an isolated incident or single offending act, a hostile work environment usually includes repeated incidents or a series of events (Rubin 1995a).

Some research confirms that sexual harassment continues to exist in American police organizations. Somvadee and Morash (2008) utilized a Sexual Experience Questionnaire (developed by Fitzgerald et al. 1988) to categorize harassment in policing across several dimensions: gender harassment (suggestive, crude, sexist remarks), unwanted sexual attention, and sexual coercion. In interviews with 117 female officers across a number of different agencies, they found gender harassment to be quite common. The most common form of harassment was suggestive stories or offensive jokes—83.7 percent of officers indicated experiencing this behavior at least once over the previous 2-year period. Other common forms of harassment included being treated differently because of sex (69.2 percent), crude sexual remarks (68.3 percent), putdowns because of sex (53.8 percent), and sexist remarks (51.2 percent). Unwanted sexual attention was less common; however, 45.2 percent of officers reported discussion of sexual or personal matters at work. Other unwanted sexual attention included unwelcome touching (36.7 percent). Other more perverse harassment was rare, relatively speaking, although quite alarming. A total of 5.1 percent of female officers experience subtle sexual bribery over the previous 2-year period, and 5.9 percent reported being treated badly for sexual noncooperation.

This harassment has negative impacts on female officers. Haarr (1997) conducted interviews with and observations of officers in a Midwestern police department. Every female participant in her study reported experiencing some degree of sexual harassment. Often this was done to marginalize women in the police department, indicating that policing is not a legitimate occupation for women. Further, Morash and Haarr (1995) indicated that sexual harassment was a significant contributor to female officer workplace stress. Any sexual harassment, no matter how seemingly benign or harmless to the perpetrator, can have significant impacts on women with regard to stress, socialization, and patterns of interaction within the organization.

Collins (2004) examined sexual harassment cases that were filed with the Florida Criminal Justice Standards and Training Commission between 1993 and 1997. Female officers alleged that male officers exposed them to crude or offensive remarks in 73 percent of the cases, and 33 percent of the cases alleged "frequent sexist remarks." Twenty-four percent of the cases alleged sexual coercion, namely, job-related considerations would be traded for sexual favors. Thirty-six percent of these cases ended in punitive discipline for the harasser, such as probation, remedial training, suspension, or some combination thereof. Termination resulted in only 16.7 percent of the cases. While this research provides a good overview of the nature and outcome of sexual harassment cases, it is unclear whether it is descriptive of sexual harassment in general because so few cases are officially reported.

It is crucial that police departments have a policy that defines and prohibits sexual harassment, because failure to have such a policy may be construed as *deliberate indifference,* exposing the department to claims of liability. Employees who claim sexual harassment will not have to prove economic or psychological injury to win a claim. Even when such a policy exists, the department may still be held liable. Departments can also be held liable even if they did not know of the offending behavior if a court determines that they should have known of it. Departments are also generally liable for the acts of their supervisory personnel (Rubin 1995a). Accordingly, every complaint of sexual harassment should be taken seriously and acted upon immediately with a follow-up investigation. Confidentiality should be maintained, and every step of the investigation should be documented. Whenever harassment is found, swift remedial action—including warnings, reprimands, suspension, or dismissal—should be taken (Rubin 1995a). This action not only sends a message that sexual harassment will not be tolerated, but also indicates (to the courts) that the department is seriously attempting to control it.

Future Prospects

Over the past 3 decades, substantial progress has been made in the recruitment and hiring of minorities and women in policing. However, although some departments have accomplished this voluntarily, others have been reluctant and were forced by the courts. This situation, combined with the traditional police culture, has created some serious problems for minorities and women with respect to integration and equal treatment within the field.

It is apparent that police departments will continue to struggle with the complex problems associated with minority hiring and promotion. If they are to increase or, in some instances, maintain their minority representation, they should pay particular attention to several areas (Sullivan 1989). First, agencies must continue to actively recruit among minorities while attempting to improve community relations and eliminating the reasons many minorities have had to distrust the police. Second, because studies have indicated that many of the entry-level paper-and-pencil tests are not job validated, it may be necessary to design a new series of tests that can more accurately measure potential police performance while ensuring that they do not discriminate against racial or ethnic groups. Finally, because minority members may have been at a disadvantage prior to their police service, departments may need to initiate special programs to help these officers develop needed skills and knowledge in order to perform effectively on the job. This final suggestion applies equally to female candidates, especially with respect to the physical requirements of the hiring process.

To improve the recruitment and retention of women in policing, departments must attempt to accelerate change in the traditional, militaristic, male-dominated, sexist police culture. Although some important strides have been made with respect to deemphasizing the highly militaristic and masculine approach to police organization and management, especially by those departments moving toward community policing, such traditions are firmly entrenched and difficult to overcome. Of course, as more women enter the field and move into supervisory positions where they can have an impact on policy, change is likely to occur more quickly. As with minority personnel, police departments must continue to eliminate those aspects of the selection process that are discriminatory toward women and that cannot be job validated.

It is important for departments to implement policies and practices that are not discriminatory. It is crucial that minority and women personnel become fully integrated into police work. Only then can these officers become true role models and not merely tokens within their departments. Quite possibly the best recruitment device at a police department's disposal is its own personnel, who can act as sponsors and mentors for others who wish to enter the field.

Over the next decade, one important influence on minority and women recruitment is making police work attractive to them. Since these groups are recruited vigorously by other public-sector (including federal police departments) and private-sector agencies, the pool of qualified applicants may actually be shrinking. Accordingly, it may be even more difficult in the future to recruit qualified candidates. At least one study (Hochstedler and Conley

1986) has indicated that one major reason blacks tend to be underrepresented in municipal police departments is that they simply choose not to pursue a career in policing. One thing is clear: if departments are to remain competitive for minorities and women in the future, they must have an active and innovative recruitment strategy, promote a police culture that treats all employees equally and with respect, and, if necessary, have an equitable plan regarding selection, duty assignment, and promotional opportunity.

Summary

The development of diversity in policing was traced in this chapter. Included in this analysis was a look at how minorities and women, once they enter the profession, are treated unequally, even though their performance is, in general, satisfactory. There has been litigation regarding the impact of equal employment opportunity legislation and the use of the Civil Service, or merit, system. Reliance on the use of a non-job-validated merit system for both selection and promotion in policing has led to the belief by many police traditionalists that a form of reverse discrimination and lowering of standards is taking place. Although implementing affirmative action plans in policing is complex, such plans have played an important role in police employment trends, in some cases significantly increasing the number and percentage of minorities and women. Once inside the department, however, these "nontraditional" officers have not always been well received—in large part because of the traditional police culture. As more minority and women officers enter policing and are promoted to higher ranks, their integration and acceptance into the field should become easier. Whether police departments can continue to attract qualified minority and women personnel depends on the public's interest in the police occupation, an active recruitment strategy, a departmental culture that treats members equally and with respect, and possibly a well-developed affirmative action plan.

Critical Thinking Questions

1. Is diversity important in policing? Explain why or why not.

2. Briefly discuss the types of unequal treatment received by minority and female officers when they first entered policing. Were their experiences essentially the same, or did they differ in significant ways?

3. What is the Civil Service system? Is it discriminatory? Why or why not?

4. Discuss the importance of the Griggs and Paradise decisions by the U.S. Supreme Court regarding affirmative action plans.

5. In the push to diversify American police departments, some suggest the unintended consequence of reverse discrimination may occur. Discuss whether this perspective merits concern.

6. Briefly discuss the growth of diversity in police departments over the past several decades. What is the significance of this growth?

7. Briefly describe several problems confronting women and minorities in attempting to integrate into the police work environment. What are the prospects for the future?

References

Alex, N. 1969. *Black in Blue.* Englewood Cliffs, NJ: Prentice Hall.

———. 1976. *New York Cops Talk Back.* New York: Wiley.

Archbold, C. A., and Hassell, K. D. 2009. "Paying the Marriage Tax: An Examination of the Barriers to the Promotion of Female Officers." *Policing: An International Journal of Police Strategies and Management* 32: 56–74.

Archbold, C. A., and Schulz, D. M. 2008. "Making Rank: The Lingering Effects of Tokenism on Female Police Officers' Promotion Aspirations." *Police Quarterly* 11: 50–73.

Balkin, J. 1988. "Why Policemen Don't Like Policewomen." *Journal of Police Science and Administration* 16:29–38.

Barker, A. M., and Heckeroth, S. E. 1997. "Deterring Sex-Harassment Liability: It Takes Proactive Policy and Commitment." *Law Enforcement News* April 15:14–15, 18.

Bazley, T. D., Lersch, K. M., and Mieczkowski, T. 2007. "Officer Force Versus Suspect Resistance: A Gendered Analysis of Patrol Officers in an Urban Police Department." *Journal of Criminal Justice* 35: 183–192.

Berg, B., and Budnick, K. 1986. "Defeminization of Women in Law Enforcement: A New Twist in the Traditional Police Personality." *Journal of Police Science and Administration* 14:314–319.

Berg, B., True, E., and Gertz, M. 1984. "Police, Riots, and Alienation." *Journal of Police Science and Administration* 12:186–190.

Berkeley, G. E. 1969. *The Democratic Policeman.* Boston: Beacon.

Bloch, P., and Anderson, D. 1974. *Policewomen on Patrol: Final Report.* Washington, DC: Police Foundation.

Brown, M. 1994. "The Plight of Female Police: A Survey of NW Patrolmen." *The Police Chief* 61:50–53.

Brown, R. A., and Frank, J. 2006. "Race and Officer Decision Making: Examining Difference in Arrest Outcomes Between Black and White Officers." *Justice Quarterly* 23: 96–126.

Carter, D. L., Sapp, A. D., and Stephens, D. W. 1989. *The State of Police Education: Policy Direction for the 21st Century.* Washington, DC: Police Executive Research Forum.

Charles, M. T. 1981. "Performance and Socialization of Female Recruits in the Michigan State Police Training Academy." *Journal of Police Science and Administration* 9:209–223.

Collins, S. C. 2004. "Sexual Harassment and Police Discipline: Who's Policing the Police?" *Policing: An International Journal of Police Strategies and Management,* 27: 512–538.

Daum, J., and Johns, C. 1994. "Police Work From a Woman's Perspective." *The Police Chief* 61:46–69.

DeJong, C. 2004. "Gender Differences in Officer Attitude and Behavior: Providing Comfort and Support." *Women and Criminal Justice* 15: 1–32.

Detroit Police Officers Association v. Young, 446 F. Supp. 979 (1978).

Eisenberg, T., Kent, D. A., and Wall, C. R. 1973. *Police Personnel Practices in State and Local Government.* Washington, DC: Police Foundation.

Feder, L. 1997. "Domestic Violence and Police Response in a Pro-Arrest Jurisdiction." *Women and Criminal Justice* 8: 79–98.

Felkenes, G. T. 1990. "Affirmative Action in the Los Angeles Police Department." *Criminal Justice Research Bulletin* 6:1–9.

Fitzgerald, L., Shullman, S. L., Bailey, N., Richards, M., Swecker, J., Gold, Y., Ormerod, M., and Weitzman, L. 1988. "The Incidence and Dimensions of Sexual Harassment in Academia and the Workplace." *Journal of Vocational Behavior* 32: 152–175.

Franklin, C. A. 2005. "Male Peer Support and the Police Culture: Understanding the Resistance and Opposition of Women in Policing." *Women and Criminal Justice,* 16(3): 1–25.

Garcia, V. 2003. "Difference in the Police Department." *Journal of Contemporary Criminal Justice* 19:330–344.

Garmire, B. L. (ed.). 1978. *Local Government, Police Management.* Washington, DC: International City Management Association.

Georges-Abeyie, D. 1984. "Black Police Officers: An Interview with Alfred W. Dean, Director of Public Safety, Harrisburg, Pennsylvania." In D. Georges-Abeyie (ed.), *The Criminal Justice System and Blacks,* pp. 161–165. Beverly Hills, CA: Sage.

Gosnell, H. F. 1935. *Negro Politicians: The Rise of Negro Politics in Chicago.* Chicago: University of Chicago Press.

Griggs v. Duke Power Co, 401 U.S. 432 (1971).

Haarr, R. N. 1997. "Patterns of Interaction in a Police Patrol Bureau: Race and Gender Barriers to Integration." *Justice Quarterly* 14:53–85.

Hickman, M. J., Lawton, B. A., Piquero, A. R., and Greene, J. R. 2001. "Does Race Influence Police Disciplinary Process?" *Justice Research and Policy* 3:97–113.

Hickman, M. J., and Reaves, B. A. 2006. *Local Police Departments, 2003.* Washington, DC: Bureau of Justice Statistics.

Hochstedler, E., and Conley, J. A. 1986. "Explaining Underrepresentation of Black Officers in City Police Agencies." *Journal of Criminal Justice* 14:319–328.

Hoffman, P. B. & Hickey, E. R. 2005. "Use of force by female police officers", *Journal of Criminal Justice* 33:145–151.

Johnson, C. S. 1947. *Into the Mainstream: A Survey of Best Practices in Race Relations in the South.* Chapel Hill: University of North Carolina Press.

Kephart, W. M. 1957. *Racial Factors and Urban Law Enforcement.* Philadelphia: University of Pennsylvania Press.

Kruger, K. J. 2007. "Pregnancy and Policing: Are They Compatible? Pushing the Legal Limits on Behalf of Equal Employment Opportunities." *Wisconsin Women's Law Journal* 61: 61–89.

Kuykendall, J. L., and Burns, D. E. 1980. "The Black Police Officer: An Historical Perspective." *Journal of Contemporary Criminal Justice* 4:4–12.

Landrum, L. W. 1947. "The Case of Negro Police." *New South* 11:5–6.

Leinen, S. 1984. *Black Police, White Society.* New York: New York University Press.

Linden, R. 1983. "Women in Policing—A Study of Lower Mainland Royal Canadian Mounted Police Detachments." *Canadian Police College Journal* 7:217–229.

Lonsway, K. A. 2003. "Tearing Down the Wall: Problems With Consistency, Validity, and Adverse Impact of Physical Agility Testing in Police Selection." *Police Quarterly* 6: 237–277.

Lonsway, K., Carrington, S., Aguire, P., Wood, M., Moore, M., Harrington, P., Smeal, E., and Spillar, K. 2002. *Equality Denied: The Status of Women in Policing: 2001.* Beverly Hills, CA: National Center for Women and Policing.

Martin, S. E. 1979. "Policewomen and Policewomen: Occupational Role Dilemmas and Choices of Female Officers." *Journal of Police Science and Administration* 7:314–323.

———. 1980. *Breaking and Entering: Policewomen on Patrol.* Berkeley: University of California Press.

———. 1989. "Women in Policing: The Eighties and Beyond." In D. J. Kenney (ed.), *Police and Policing: Contemporary Issues,* pp. 3–16. New York: Praeger.

Martin, S. E., and Jurik, N. C. 1996. *Doing Justice, Doing Gender: Women in Law and Criminal Justice Occupations.* Thousand Oaks, CA: Sage.

McCrary, J. 2007. "The Effect of Court-Ordered Hiring Quotas on the Composition and Quality of Police." *The American Economic Review* 97: 318–353.

McDowell, J. 1992. "Are Women Better Cops?" *Time* 132:70–72.

Melchionne, T. M. 1967. "Current Status and Problems of Women Police." *Journal of Criminal Law, Criminology and Police Science* 58:257–260.

Miller, S. L. 1999. *Gender and Community Policing: Walking the Talk.* Boston: Northeastern University Press.

Miller, S. L., and Hodge, J. P. 2004. "Rethinking Gender and Community Policing: Cultural Obstacles and Policy Issues." *Law Enforcement Executive Forum* 4:39–49.

Milton, C. 1972. *Women in Policing.* Washington, DC: Police Foundation.

Moran, T. K. 1988. "Pathways Toward a Nondiscriminatory Recruitment Policy." *Journal of Police Science and Administration* 16:274–287.

Morash, M., and Greene, J. R. 1986. "Evaluating Women on Patrol: A Critique of Contemporary Wisdom." *Evaluation Review* 10:231–255.

Morash, M., and Haarr, R. N. 1995. "Gender, Workplace Problems and Stress in Policing." *Justice Quarterly* 12: 113–140.

Myrdal, G. 1944. *An American Dilemma: The Negro Problem and Modern Democracy.* New York: Harper & Brothers.

National Advisory Commission on Civil Disorders. 1968. *Report of the National Advisory Commission on Civil Disorders.* Washington, DC: U.S. Government Printing Office.

National Advisory Commission on Criminal Justice Standards and Goals. 1973. *Report on Police.* Washington, DC: U.S. Government Printing Office.

National Center on Police and Community Relations. 1967. *A National Survey of Police and Community Relations, Field Survey V.* Washington, DC: U.S. Government Printing Office.

National Center for Women and Policing. 2002. *Equality denied: The status of women in policing: 2001.* http://www.womenandpolicing.org/PDF/2002_Status_Report.pdf, retrieved August 31, 2009.

Owings, C. 1925. *Women Police.* New York: F. H. Hichcock.

Paoline, E. A., and Terrill, W. 2004. "Women Police Officers and the Use of Coercion." *Women and Criminal Justice,* 15(3/4): 97–119.

Parsons, D., and Jesilow, P. 2001. *In the Same Voice: Women and Men in Law Enforcement.* Santa Ana, CA: Seven Locks Press.

Perez McClusky, C., and McClusky, J. 2004. "Diversity in Policing: Latino Representation in Law Enforcement." *Journal of Ethnicity in Criminal Justice* 2: 67–81.

"Plenty of Talk, Not Much Action: IACP Survey Says PDs Fall Short on Recruiting, Retaining Women." 1999. *Law Enforcement News* January 15/31:1, 14.

Police Foundation. 1990. *Community Policing: A Binding Thread Through the Fabric of Our Society.* Washington, DC: Police Foundation.

Prokos, A., and Padavic, I. 2002. "'There Oughta be a Law Against Bitches': Masculinity Lessons in Police Academy Training." *Gender, Work and Organization* 9, 439–459.

President's Commission on Law Enforcement and Administration of Justice. 1967. *Task Force Report: The Police.* Washington, DC: U.S. Government Printing Office.

Rabe-Hemp, C. E. 2008. "Female Officers and the Ethic of Care: Does Officer Gender Impact Police Behaviors?" *Journal of Criminal Justice* 36: 426–434.

———. 2009. "POLICEwomen or PoliceWOMEN? Doing Gender in Police Work." *Feminist Criminology* 4: 114–129.

Reaves, B. A. 1996. *Local Police Departments, 1993.* Washington, DC: Bureau of Justice Statistics.

Reaves, B. A., and Goldberg, A. L. 1999. *Law Enforcement Management and Administrative Statistics, 1997: Data for Individual State and Local Agencies With 100 or More Officers.* Washington, DC: Bureau of Justice Statistics.

———. 2000. *Local Police Departments, 1997.* Washington, DC: Bureau of Justice Statistics.

Reaves, B. A., and Smith, P. Z. 1995. *Law Enforcement Management and Administrative Statistics, 1993. Data for Individual State and Local Agencies With 100 or More Officers.* Washington, DC: Bureau of Justice Statistics.

Ricci v. DeStefano, 557 U.S. ___ (2009).

Robinson, A. L. 2000. "Effect of a Domestic Violence Policy Change on Police Officers' Schemata." *Criminal Justice and Behavior* 27: 600–624.

Rubin, P. N. 1995a. "Civil Rights and Criminal Justice: Employment Discrimination Overview." *Research in Action.* Washington, DC: National Institute of Justice.

———. 1995b. "Civil Rights and Criminal Justice: Primer on Sexual Harassment." *Research in Action.* Washington, DC: National Institute of Justice.

Rudwick, E. 1960. "The Negro Policeman in the South." *Journal of Criminal Law, Criminology and Police Science* 11: 273–276.

———. 1962. *The Unequal Badge: Negro Policemen in the South, Report of the Southern Regional Council.* Atlanta: Southern Regional Council.

Sherman, L. J. 1973. "A Psychological View of Women in Policing." *Journal of Police Science and Administration* 1: 383–394.

———. 1975. "Evaluation of Policewomen on Patrol in a Suburban Police Department." *Journal of Police Science and Administration* 3: 434–438.

Sichel, J. L., Friedman, L. N., Quint, J. C., and Smith, M. E. 1978. *Women on Patrol—A Pilot Study of Police Performance in New York City.* New York: Vera Institute of Justice.

Simpson, A. E. 1977. "The Changing Role of Women in Policing." In D. E. J. MacNamara (ed.), *Readings in Criminal Justice,* pp. 71–74. Guilford, CT: Dushkin.

Sklansky, D. A. 2006. "Not Your Father's Police Department: Making Sense of the New Demographics of Law Enforcement." *The Journal of Criminal Law & Criminology* 96:1209–1244.

Skogan, W., and Frydl, K. 2004. *Fairness and Effectiveness in Policing; The Evidence.* Washington, DC: The National Academies Press, National Research Council of the National Academies.

Somvadee, C., and Morash, M. 2008. "Dynamics of Sexual Harassment for Policewomen Working Alongside Men." *Policing: An International Journal of Police Strategies and Management* 31: 485–498.

Sullivan, P. S. 1989. "Minority Officers: Current Issues." In R. G. Dunham and G. P. Alpert (eds.), *Critical Issues in Policing: Contemporary Readings,* pp. 331–345. Prospect Heights, IL: Waveland.

Sulton, C., and Townsey, R. A. 1981. *Progress Report on Women in Policing.* Washington, DC: Police Foundation.

Timmins, W. M., and Hainsworth, B. E. 1989. "Attracting and Retaining Females in Law Enforcement." *International Journal of Offender Therapy and Comparative Criminology* 33: 197–205.

Tuomey, L. M., and Jolly, R. 2009. "Step Up to Law Enforcement: A Successful Strategy for Recruiting Women into the Law Enforcement Profession." Available online at http://policechiefmagazine.org/magazine/index.cfm?fuseaction=display_arch&article_id=1820&issue_id=62009.

U.S. v. Paradise, 107 U.S. 1053 (1987).

Walker, S. 1977. *A Critical History of Police Reform.* Lexington, MA: Lexington Books.

———. 1989. *Employment of Black and Hispanic Police Officers, 1983–1988: A Follow-Up Study.* Omaha, NE: Center for Applied Urban Research, University of Nebraska at Omaha.

Walker, S., and Turner, K. B. 1993. *A Decade of Modest Progress: Employment of Black and Hispanic Police Officers, 1983–1992.* Mimeo. Omaha: University of Nebraska at Omaha.

Weitzer, R. 2000. "White, Black, or Blue Cops? Race and Citizen Assessments of Police Officers," *Journal of Criminal Justice* 28: 313–324.

Whetstone, T. S. 2001. "Copping Out: Why Police Officers Decline to Participate in the Sergeant's Promotional Process." *American Journal of Criminal Justice* 25: 147–159.

Wilkins, V. M., and Williams. B. N. 2008. "Black or Blue: Racial Profiling and Representative Bureaucracy." *Public Administration Review* 68: 652–662.

———. 2009. "Representing Blue: Representative Bureaucracy and Racial Profiling in the Latino Community." *Administration and Society* 40: 775–798.

Wilson, O. W., and McLaren, R. C. 1963. *Police Administration,* 3rd. ed. New York: McGraw–Hill.

Zhao, J., He, N., and Lovrich, N. P. 2006. "Pursuing Gender Diversity in Police Organizations in the 1990s: A Longitudinal Analysis of Factors Associated with the Hiring of Female Officers." *Police Quarterly* 9: 463–485.

CHAPTER 13

Stress and Officer Safety

CHAPTER OUTLINE

- The Concept of Stress
- Occupational Stress
- Overview of Stressors
    - Police Stressors
    - Emerging Sources of Stress
- Line-of-Duty and Crisis Situations
    - Posttraumatic Stress Disorder
    - Shift Work
    - Social Supports and Police Stress
- Consequences of Stress
    - Alcohol Abuse
    - Drug Abuse
    - Suicide
    - Marital and Family Problems
    - Policies and Programs

CHAPTER OUTLINE   (continued)

- Officer Safety
    Danger and Police Work
    Safety and the Mentally Ill
    Improving Safety and Reducing Fatalities
- Summary
- Critical Thinking Questions
- References

KEY TERMS

- actual danger
- acute stress
- chronic stress
- critical-incident debriefing
- crisis intervention team
- distress
- eustress
- peer-counseling program
- perceived danger
- person-initiated danger
- physiological stress
- police stressors
- posttraumatic stress disorder (PTSD)
- potential danger
- psychological stress
- sensitization training
- situational danger
- social-supports model
- stressor-outcome model
- suicide prevention training

Although negative effects of stress on society in general have been well documented by both the medical and the social science professions, certain occupations induce more stress than others. Police work entails unique stressors (sources of stress) that are non-existent or less prevalent in many other occupations. Some of these include departmental practices, shift work, danger, public apathy, boredom, and exposure to human misery. In addition, officers are expected to be in control at all times, yet they encounter people at their very worst, often on a daily basis. This demand of ongoing restraint, coupled with a set of unique job stressors, may lead to high levels of stress and, concomitantly, poor performance or dysfunctional behavior. This chapter will look at the concept of stress and stressors unique to police work, stress and emotional problems, policies and programs to help cope with stress, and officer safety.

The Concept of Stress

Stress is a highly complex concept because of the overlap of both physiological and psychological processes. **Physiological stress** deals with the biological effects on the individual, including such factors as increased heart disease, high blood pressure, and ulcers (Violanti 2005). **Psychological stress** is much less clear and more difficult to evaluate. According to Farmer (1990), most psychologists prefer to use the term *stress* to refer to the physiological changes that can be determined and the term *anxiety* to capture the psychological effects. This book will use the more popular conception of stress, which includes anxiety within its scope.

Although stress is difficult to define, one of the more accepted interpretations comes from the pioneering work of Selye, who suggests that "the body's nonspecific response to any demand placed on it" can cause stress (1974, 60). A person can be considered under stress when he or she is required to adapt to a particular situation.

Selye further identifies two main types of stress: **eustress**, which is positive, and **distress**, which is negative. Some stress, then, is considered positive or pleasurable—for example, the stress produced by a challenging sporting activity. Police stress, by contrast, relates to those aspects of police work that lead to negative feelings and consequences.

Two forms of distress may affect police behavior (Farmer 1990). The first of these is **acute stress**, which represents high-order emergency or sudden stress, such as shootings or high-speed chases. The second type is **chronic stress**, low-level, gradual stress that includes the day-to-day routine of the job. Each type of stress is important to police work, but acute stressors require large amounts of physical and psychological adaptation; chronic stressors do not. In studying the possible effects of stress, there are several key concerns:

1. *Stress, like beauty, is in the eye of the beholder.* One person's experience of stress may have little or nothing in common with another person's.
2. *Stress is cumulative.* Minor stresses may pile up to produce major stress that leads to a heart attack or actual physical or mental breakdown.
3. *Prolonged emotional stress.* Stress that is a part of the everyday work environment can produce wear and tear on the body, with effects that may prove irreversible if not treated in time.
4. *When it comes to stress, there are no supermen or superwomen.* Stress tolerance levels may vary from person to person, but everyone is susceptible to the ravages of stress. *(Territo and Vetter 1981, 7)*

Occupational Stress

How stressful is police work? In general, there has been a tendency to give an alarmist answer, which is interesting in that existing research does not unanimously support this conclusion (Terry 1981, 1985). Terry has suggested that the reason for the push to support policing as a high-stress occupation may lie in an attempt to develop professional recognition and create a professional self-image. He says,

> The concept of stress . . . provides a tidy symbolic representation of the crime control and order maintenance functions of police work as well as providing a ready link to other professional occupations that bear responsibility for other people's lives. *(1985, 509)*

This perspective is interesting, especially in light of the fact that some of the earlier research does not support this view. Pendleton et al. (1989) compared the stress and strain levels of police officers, firefighters, and government employees and found that government workers experienced the greatest stress and firefighters the least, with police falling in the middle. Thus, they concluded that, contrary to popular belief, the police as a work group do not experience more health and social problems than all other occupations. The study urged caution, however, in that the research could not control for the possibility that police work could actually be more stressful but those officers selected for the job might simply be better able to manage stress and avoid strain. In a study of more than 500 officers in an Australian police department, Hart, Wearing, and Headey (1995) discovered that, compared with other groups, police display relatively high levels of psychological well-being and concluded that, collectively, their findings indicate that policing is not highly stressful. This more recent research suggests that policing may not be as stressful as previously believed.

Some research suggests that levels of stress vary by job assignments. Specifically, Wallace, Roberg, and Allen (1985), in a study of five police departments, found that narcotics investigators had significantly higher job burnout rates than either former narcotics investigators or patrol officers. In another comparative study of job burnout and officer assignment, Roberg, Hayhurst, and Allen (1988) discovered that although narcotics investigators had the highest levels of burnout, civilian dispatch personnel exhibited significantly higher levels of occupational stress than did either former narcotics investigators or patrol officers. The conclusion is that although patrol work may be stressful, other job assignments (including civilian dispatchers) may actually be more stressful. Accordingly, while appropriate actions to prevent or reduce stress for patrol officers are certainly warranted, it should be recognized that all police personnel should be afforded appropriate stress-reduction programs.

Overview of Stressors

Loo (2005) summarizes **police stressors** into five distinct categories: stressors related to (1) police work itself, (2) the police organization, (3) the criminal justice system, (4) the public or community, and (5) personal life and family. He elaborates as follows:

> Police work itself is the source of many stressors due to work overload, shift work, exposure to violent and life-threatening situations, and frustrations in trying to solve cases. The police organization is another source of stressors because of departmental politics, inadequate resources to do the job, lack of support and recognition from management, and autocratic leadership styles, among other factors. The criminal justice system is a common source of stress because of the demands of court appearances, being challenged in court, and the perception that the justice system is slow and too lenient on criminals. Relations with the public and community can be major sources of stress when police believe that their efforts are not appreciated by the community they serve and that the public is apathetic about supporting the police. Complaints and assaults against police only reinforce the belief that they stand alone. Finally, but importantly, policing affects the family in substantial ways. Shift work, temporary assignments, and postings disrupt family life as well as the officersí social life and, likely, physical and mental health. Because police want to protect their families from violence, crimes, and nastiness that they experience on the job, spouses and children may view police as uncommunicative and distant, thus leading to marital problems and marital breakdown. *(Loo 2005, 103, 104)*

Police Stressors

Violanti and Aron (1995) ranked 60 police work stressors for 103 officers in a large police department in New York State. The top 15 stressors are ranked by their mean scores in Table 13.1. The top two stressors were "killing someone in the line of duty" and "fellow officer killed." Although these incidents occur infrequently, they have a significant psychological impact on the individuals involved. It is further interesting to note that 8 of the top 15 (i.e., killing someone, officer killed, physical attack, chases, use of force, auto accidents, aggressive crowds, and felony in progress) are stressors related to potentially dangerous aspects of the work. Shift work was also reported as a major stressor because sleep patterns, as well as eating habits and family relationships, may be affected by rotating shifts. "Inadequate department support" (by supervisors) was another high-ranking stressor because of the paramilitary structure of the department that minimizes interpersonal relationships between supervisors and subordinates. Other findings indicated that officers with work experience of 6 to 10 years had higher mean stressor scores than those with work experience of 1 to 5 years. This may be because newer officers with less work

TABLE 13.1 Police Stressors Ranked by Mean Scores

STRESSOR	MEAN SCORE
Killing someone in the line of duty	79.4
Fellow officer killed	76.7
Physical attack	71.0
Battered child	69.2
High-speed chases	63.7
Shift work	61.2
Use of force	61.0
Inadequate department support	61.0
Incompatible partner	60.4
Accident in patrol car	59.9
Insufficient personnel	58.9
Aggressive crowds	56.7
Felony in progress	55.3
Excessive discipline	53.3
Plea bargaining	52.8

Overall mean score of 60 ranked stressors = 44.8.

Source: Adapted from J. M. Violanti and F. Aron, "Police Stressors: Variations in Percent Among Police Personnel," *Journal of Criminal Justice* (1995) 23: 290.

experience may remain challenged and still cling to idealism, whereas the more experienced officers may be less enchanted with police work and thereby find it more stressful and frustrating.

The most significant early study attempting to identify police stressors was that of Kroes, Margolis, and Hurrell (1974), whose research design was similar to that of the Violanti and Aron (1995) study. These researchers interviewed 100 male officers and asked them what they considered the most "bothersome" aspects about their job (it was assumed that "bothersome" and "stressful" were synonymous terms). Table 13.2 indicates the 12 categories into which the responses fell and the frequency of the responses.

Court leniency with criminals and the scheduling of court appearances on "off days" were the highest stressors. The second highest stressors were administrative policies regarding work assignments, procedures, personal conduct, and lack of administrative support. The third most significant stressor was the inadequacy and poor state of repair of equipment. The fourth stressor was poor community relations, including apathy and negative responses exhibited by the public toward officers.

The most striking difference between the 1974 and 1995 studies is the dangerous stressors of the job listed in the 1995 study but not listed in the earlier study. Although society and the police may be more concerned about violent crime today, it is important to note that one of the reasons for these differences may be the ways the surveys were completed. The 1995 study used a 60-item check-off list (listing potential dangerous stressors); the 1974 study asked officers to list those aspects of policing that were "bothersome" to them.

TABLE 13.2 Bothersome Aspects of Police Work

CATEGORY	DEFINITION	NUMBER OF RESPONSES
Courts	Court rulings and procedures	56
Administration	Administrative policies/ procedures; administrative support of officers	51
Equipment	Adequacy/state of repair of equipment	39
Community relations	Public apathy/negative reaction to and lack of support of policemen	38
Changing work shifts	28-day rotating shift schedule	18
Relations with supervisor	Difficulties in getting along with supervisor	16
Non-police work	Tasks required of officer that are not considered police responsibility	14
Other policemen	Fellow officers not performing their job	8
Bad assignment	Work assignment that the officer disliked	6
Other	Stresses that did not readily fit into the above categories	5
Isolation/boredom	Periods of inactivity and separation from social contacts	3
Pay	Adequacy or equity of salary	2

Note: Because officers may mention more than one stressor, the overall total can exceed 100.

Source: Adapted from W. H. Kroes, B. L. Margolis, and J. L. Hurrell, Jr., "Job Stress in Policemen," *Journal of Police Science and Administration* (1974) 2: 145. Reprinted by permission.

In this 1974 study, crisis situations that might affect officer health and safety were categorized under "Other" because so few officers mentioned them. Kroes, Margolis, and Hurrell (1974) suggest there may have been two reasons for such a surprising finding. First, officers may not think of such situations as merely bothersome so much as threatening and dangerous. Second, officers may not consciously think about physical dangers at work so as to maintain their psychological well-being.

A similar finding was reported in the Crank and Caldero (1991) study discussed below, where concerns over occupational danger were among the least frequently cited stressors. As one officer commented, "The stress caused by work on the street is nothing compared to the stress caused by the administration in this department" (1991, 336). In addition it is likely that larger, urban police departments contend with higher crime rates, and thus the perception of danger is most likely higher than in medium or small departments.

The survey conducted by Crank and Caldero (1991) studied 167 line officers in eight medium-size municipal departments in Illinois. Responses were categorized into five areas: organization, task environment, judiciary, personal or family concerns, and city government. More than two thirds of those responding (68 percent) identified the department as their principal source of stress, especially problems relating to management and supervisors (42 percent), followed by shift changes (17 percent). The second most frequently cited source of stress (16 percent) was the task environment, with citizen contact as the primary source in this category (29 percent) and concerns regarding potential danger the second source (21 percent). The judiciary was the third ranked source (7 percent); the primary concern was related to the court's failure to prosecute criminals adequately. Personal or family concerns were ranked fourth (4 percent), while city government was ranked fifth (3 percent).

The findings of this 1991 study are similar to those of the 1974 and 1995 studies regarding stress relating to inadequate department support and shift work. The difference in the dangerousness of the work is most likely caused by the size of the department; larger departments tend to be forced to contend with higher levels of crime. Interestingly, with respect to the courts or judiciary, both of the 1990s findings had relatively low rankings (third of five in 1991, and 30 of 60 in 1995) compared with the 1974 findings (first). It is likely that in the years since the study by Kroes, Margolis, and Hurrell (1974), officers have learned more about and adapted to court decisions with which they may not agree. It is also likely that departments have improved courtroom training to ensure that officers meet certain requisites when testifying in court. Such training should emphasize the importance of thorough reports and documentation, evidence, courtroom behavioral tactics, interface with the prosecution, case review, and prior mental rehearsal. And it is likely that improved courtroom demeanor and presentation by police officers can help to curtail "unfavorable" court decisions.

Emerging Sources of Stress

In their interviews with approximately 100 people, including law enforcement administrators, union and association officials, mental-health practitioners, and 50 line officers and family members from large and small departments, Finn and Tomz (1997) discovered that today's police are encountering new emerging sources of stress. As an example, although community policing has produced increased job satisfaction among many officers, others have found the transition to be stressful. Lord (1996, 2005), in her studies of the Charlotte–Mecklenburg Police Department, which was attempting to move to community policing, also found increased levels of stress among officers and sergeants, particularly with respect to role conflict and role ambiguity. Some officers felt that the higher expectations of solving community crime problems enhanced job pressure and burnout. Further, certain officers experienced reactions of disdain from those not involved in community policing. Community policing requires attributes that some officers may not possess and were not screened for: interpersonal, verbal, and problem-solving skills. Therefore, the transition to community policing may be difficult and require training and communication to circumvent this emerging form of stress.

Many respondents thought that there had been a rise in violent crime and that they no longer had the upper hand; heavily armed criminals and increased incidents involving excessive violence and irrational behavior created added tension. Additionally, they thought that the violent crime issue had been exacerbated because many departments had not increased the number of officers and in some instances had downsized. Thus, police employment had not increased commensurate to respective rises in the population and crime rates in some locations. With respect to violent crime, these findings would appear to be consistent with the Violanti and Aron study (1995), where "killing someone in the line of duty," "fellow officer killed," "physical attack," "use of force," and "insufficient personnel" were ranked relatively high.

A newer source of stress involves what officers perceive as negative media coverage, public scrutiny, and prospective litigation. Many officers felt stressed by negative publicity such as that surrounding the Rodney King incident, the Abner Louima incident, the Amadou Diallo shooting in New York, police corruption scandals, allegations of police abuse in post-Katrina New Orleans, and other dubious police incidents. Generally, the media focus attention on offenders' rights as opposed to victims' rights or officers' rights, which was resented by officers. More important, respondents demonstrated an increased fear of lawsuits, both civil and criminal, and consistently worried about the use of force endangering their lives.

Finally, it has been recognized that stress may vary across gender and racial lines. As discussed in the previous chapter, women and racial/ethnic minorities often experience harassment, discrimination, and bias within the policing occupation. It follows that these experiences (coupled with the typical sources of stress) can result in higher levels of stress among females and people of color. He, Zhao, and Archbold (2002) reported that female officers had significantly higher levels of depression and somatization (e.g., physical reactions to stress such as headaches, nausea, and stomach pains) than their male counterparts. Morash and Haarr (1995) reported similar results in which women reported higher levels of stress than men. This difference was even greater for black female officers, possibly as a reaction to double stigmatization. They went on to note that women reported different sources of stress, specifically difficulties related to their outsider status in policing. Women reported stressors that included bias, language and sexual harassment, and stigma resulting from appearance. Minorities reported feeling invisible within the organization as a source of stress and significantly higher levels of stress from lack of advancement opportunity as well as stigma resulting from appearance (see also Morash, Kwak, and Haarr 2006). Piquero (2005) examined strain and stress among police officers in Baltimore and found that female officers reported higher levels of depression. The sources of stress also appeared to vary across gender—male officers reported elevated levels of stress from job-related tasks and the media, while females identified gender-specific stressors such as discrimination.

However, recent research by He, Zhao, and Ren (2005) complicates this area of study. Consistent with earlier research, they found that female officers had higher levels of stress than male officers. But their research also indicated that white males experienced higher levels of stress than black male officers, whereas stress levels did not vary between white and black female officers.

Eisenberg (1975) pointed out that minority officers face the additional stresses of rejection and skepticism by members of their own race and may not be accepted into the "police family," a source of support, camaraderie, and occupational identity. In support of Eisenberg, Haarr and Morash (1999) found in their national survey of over 1,000 officers in 24 departments that African American officers were significantly more likely than Caucasians to use bonding with officers with whom they shared a racial bond as a strategy for coping with stress.

Line-of-Duty and Crisis Situations

The continual potential for crisis situations in the line of duty is what tends to differentiate police work from most other occupations. On the one hand, the level of "routine" patrol activities can be extremely busy, emotionally draining, and potentially dangerous. On the other hand, the routine can become extremely boring and uneventful. The reason this situation may be so stressful is the idea of the "startle" response—that is, when the police officer must respond rapidly, at any point in time, to any number of extreme situations. The amount and type of activity on any particular patrol depends on many factors, including the type of city, beat, and shift. In some departments, especially in larger cities, officers are becoming more and more immersed in a continuous round of serious calls dealing with violence, drugs, and gang warfare. In such patrol areas there can be little doubt that the high workload, combined with intense emotional demands and potential physical harm, is conducive to high levels of stress and strain.

Anderson, Litzenberger, and Plecas (2002) conducted a research project in which they monitored the heart rates of individuals while on patrol. They noted that a particular indicator of physical stress is an elevated heart rate. Thus, their research attempted to monitor and categorize activities that produced the highest elevation in heart rates among police officers. They learned that heart rates begin to elevate prior to commencement of the shift. Officers, once in uniform, experienced anticipatory stress, resulting in a 23 percent increase in heart rates. In fact, they found that an officer's heart rate was 17 percent higher than at rest during the entire shift. This indicates that officers are experiencing physical reactions to policing, even absent critical incidents.

Critical incidents resulted in even higher elevations in heart rates. Some critical incidents increase heart rates because they are physically demanding (e.g., tussling with suspects, wrestling, fighting, and handcuffing). However, they also found that heart rates are impacted by activities such as vehicle pursuits, being dispatched to calls for service, and talking to suspects. Further, heart rates remained high even after the critical incident was terminated. For most critical incidents, officer heart rates remained above average even 30 to 60 minutes *after* the incident occurred. This appears to indicate that even routine shift work has a significant physical impact on officers. The authors conclude by suggesting that debriefing officers after critical incidents and at the end of a shift can assist them in coping with the stress that is inherent to police work.

Posttraumatic Stress Disorder

The psychological stress caused by frequent or prolonged exposure to crises or trauma can lead to a condition known as **posttraumatic stress disorder (PTSD)**. Although officers may not suffer physical injury, the emotional trauma may be catastrophic and could result in PTSD. While some officers recover within a few weeks, others may experience permanent trauma, which could adversely affect both the department and their personal lives. This disorder has been found in many Vietnam veterans who had been exposed to the stresses and violence of the war experience.

Martin, McKean, and Veltkamp (1986) conducted a study of a group of 53 officers and discovered that 26 percent suffered from posttraumatic stress. Stressors leading to PTSD included shooting someone; being shot; working with child abuse, spouse abuse, and rape cases; being threatened or having family threatened; and observing death through homicide (including colleagues being killed), suicide, or natural disaster. Another study of 100 suburban officers found a correlation between duty-related stress and symptoms of PTSD (Robinson, Sigman, and Wilson 1997). Thirteen percent of the sample met the criteria for PTSD; the best predictors for the diagnosis were associated with a critical event related to the job and exposure to a death-and-life threat. Sixty-three percent of the respondents stated that a **critical-incident debriefing** (i.e., counseling) would be beneficial following an extremely stressful crisis event.

Stephens and Miller (1998) examined the prevalence of PTSD among 527 police officers in New Zealand and further examined whether PTSD was related to on-the-job traumatic experiences or those experienced off the job. They found that the presence of PTSD among police officers was similar to that in the civilian population who have experienced traumatic events. They also reported that as the number of traumatic events experienced by the individual officer increases, so, too, do the likelihood and frequency of PTSD symptoms. Traumatic events experienced on duty were more strongly related to PTSD. Among the most traumatic events were knowing of a police officer's death, a robbery/mugging or hold-up encounter, and chronic distress.

Loo (1986) found that officers experienced the most stress reactions within 3 days after a critical incident. The majority reported a preoccupation with the traumatic incident (39 percent) and anger (25 percent). Other reported symptoms of PTSD were sleep disturbances, flashbacks, feelings of guilt, wishing it had not happened, and depression (see Table 13.3). Many of the officers continued to report increased anger and lowered work interest 1 month after the incident. The course of recovery varied, but the average time for a return to "feeling normal" was 20 weeks after the critical incident.

Martin and his colleagues (1986) concluded from their study that **sensitization training** regarding officers' work with victims, as well as their own victimization, should be conducted early in their careers. Such training may help to increase their empathy for crime victims and cope with their own reactions to the stress caused by dealing with such situations. Kureczka (1996) believes that officers will not ask for help for fear of being stigmatized. In

TABLE 13.3 Common Reactions to Stress in Policing

PHYSICAL REACTIONS	EMOTIONAL REACTIONS	COGNITIVE REACTIONS	BEHAVIOR/COPING REACTIONS
• Headaches • Muscle aches • Sleep disturbances • Changes in appetite • Decreased interest in sexual activity • Heart disease • Ulcers • High blood pressure	• Anxiety • Fear • Guilt • Sadness • Anger • Irritability • Feeling lost or unappreciated • Withdrawal	• Flashbacks • Nightmares • Slowed thinking • Difficulty making decisions and problem solving • Disorientation • Lack of concentration • Memory lapses • Posttraumatic stress disorder	• Reduced motivation • Reduced job satisfaction • Lack of job involvement • Absenteeism • Premature retirement • Poor relationships with non-police friends • Divorce • Substance abuse • Suicide

Sources: Adapted from A. W., Kureczka, "Critical Incident Stress in Law Enforcement," *FBI Law Enforcement Bulletin* (Feb./March 1996): 15.; V. B. Lord, "An Impact of Community Policing: Reported Stressors, Social Support, and Strain Among Police Officers in a Changing Police Department," *Journal of Criminal Justice* (1996) 24(6): 503–522; V. B. Lord, D. O. Gray, and S. B. Pond, 1991. "The Police Stress Inventory: Does it Measure Stress?" *Journal of Criminal Justice* (1991) 19:139–150; Violanti, J. M. "Dying for the Job: Psychological Stress, Disease, and Mortality in Police Work." In H. Copes (ed.) *Policing and Stress*, pp 87–102. Upper Saddle River, NJ: Pearson Prentice Hall.

other words, in an effort to preserve their "macho" image, officers remain reluctant to discuss their emotional responses to critical incidents.

PTSD can also have a financial impact on the department. It has been estimated, for example, that 70 percent of police officers involved in deadly force incidents leave the department within 5 years (Vaughn 1991). According to Kureczka, replacing a 5-year veteran costs about $100,000, including retraining, benefits, testing for replacements, and overtime. In contrast, prompt treatment costs approximately $8,300, and delayed treatment costs about $46,000. Consequently, quick treatment for officers is not only professional but also the most cost-effective option.

As a routine practice, department policy should mandate that officers visit a mental health professional for evaluation and further treatment, as needed, subsequent to any critical incident. Stress-management programs should be provided to all recruits, and ongoing stress-education programs should be provided for all officers. As an added precaution, Kureczka advocates the use of officers who are specially trained to recognize problems and make referrals as deemed necessary. Such a **peer-counseling program** has been established in the Fort Worth Police Department, under the supervision of the Psychological Services Unit (Greenstone, Dunn, and Leviton 1995). Peer counselors are available 24 hours a day, 7 days a week, and serve voluntarily and without compensation in addition to their regular police duties. The counselors receive basic training in crisis intervention and critical-incident debriefing.

Finally, counseling services or some type of stress-management program should also be made available to family members. In turn, family members might be able to understand and provide further nurturing and support (see social supports discussion below) to the officer involved. More important, intervention and treatment may circumvent suicide, the worst possible outcome of work-related stress.

Although little is actually known about the amount or effect of PTSD among police officers, it has been suggested that such a disorder might lead to increased brutality by the police. Kellogg and Harrison (1991), for instance, contend that much police brutality can be attributed to PTSD. Although they present no empirical evidence to support their claims, it seems likely that some officers suffering from posttraumatic stress could vent their anger and frustration on citizens through violence. Consequently, this is an important area for future study. It is important that scholars attempt to determine how widespread PTSD may be among the nation's police as well as its potential impact on police behavior.

Shift Work

Shift work not only adversely affects an officers' performance, but puts an added burden on family and friends. While the rest of society orchestrates their leisure activities around a "day" schedule, officers reserve their activities for days off because on work days many find it difficult to do anything other than eat, sleep, and go to work. According to O'Neill and Cushing (1991), relationships with family and friends are disrupted, and many officers experience sleep alterations (consisting of subjective self-ratings of poor sleep quality, difficulty in falling asleep, frequent awakenings, and insomnia), persistent fatigue (which does not disappear after sleep, weekends, or vacations, thus differing from physiological fatigue caused by physical and/or mental effort), behavioral changes (such as irritability, tantrums, malaise, and inadequate performance), and digestive troubles (including dyspepsia to epigastric pain and peptic ulcers). Charles and colleagues (2007) reported that working night shifts was correlated with sleep-related problems. In their sample of Buffalo Police officers, those assigned to night shifts slept in shorter durations and were more likely to snore (which is often associated with fatigue and other sleep-related issues). To combat fatigue that appears inherent to working this shift they advocate for worksite exercise programs to improve officers' sleep quality and avoid work-related problems and safety issues.

Some evidence indicates that many of the problems associated with shift changes, including sleep problems and fatigue, use of alcohol and sleeping pills, increased sick time, and accidents, can be substantially reduced if schedules are designed to accommodate the body's natural circadian rhythm, which controls sleep–wake cycles. For example, in Philadelphia, three major changes were made in officers' schedules in an attempt to reduce such problems:

- Shifts were changed every 18 days rather than every 8 days, allowing more time to adjust to the change.

- The rotation shifted forward from day to evening to graveyard, rather than backward, as had been the previous practice. Because the typical circadian clock runs on about a 25-hour day, the natural tendency is to shift to a later (rather than an earlier) hour.

- Consecutive work days were reduced from 6 to 4, allowing officers to catch up on lost sleep and avoiding the cumulative sleep deprivation that night-shift workers often experience. (Bain 1988)

After 11 months on the new schedule, officers reported significant declines in sleep problems and fatigue on the job. Automobile accidents while at work declined by 40 percent, sleeping pill and alcohol usage dropped by 50 percent, and sick time declined by 23 percent (Bain 1988).

There is little doubt that many departments could improve officers' job performance by redesigning traditional shift schedules to coincide more accurately with natural sleep patterns. In Voices From the Field, Bryan Vila, who directs crime control and prevention research for the Department of Justice, discusses the impact that fatigue can have on police officers.

Other innovations in shift work might include allowing officers to determine the frequency of their shift rotation with an option to modify it at least annually or semi-annually according to seniority. Further, permanent or semi-permanent shifts as opposed to rotating shifts might be more desirable. The Michigan State Police, for instance, have instituted such modifications and have allowed individual work sites to make their own choices through majority vote (Finn and Tomz 1997). O'Neill and Cushing (1991) recommend that a minimum number of officers should work the early morning shifts (i.e., shifts that fall between 2:00 and 6:00 AM), with callbacks assigned to the day shift so that nonessential tasks are completed during the day. Additionally, they suggest that officers be allowed to bid for another shift at least twice a year and that midnight shifts be limited to 4-day weeks. Although shift work cannot be eliminated, different and innovative approaches such as these above may mitigate its damaging impact on officers and their families.

Social Supports and Police Stress

Almost all research on police stress has been based on a **stressor-outcome model**, meaning that a stressful circumstance or stressor leads directly to a negative outcome, such as psychological stress or a physical ailment. Another perspective to the study of stress, however, the **social-supports model**, suggests that an individual may be more or less insulated against the effects of stressors depending on whether he or she has a social-support network—friends, coworkers, and family members—in place. In other words, social supports

VOICES FROM THE FIELD

Bryan Vila, Ph.D.
Professor, Washington State University–Spokane

Question: *What impact does officer fatigue have on stress and safety?*

Answer: Police departments long have ignored one of the greatest threats to police officers' health, safety, and ability to perform their jobs—fatigue. More than 100 years of research on the effects of fatigue in the work place have made it clear that excess tiredness arising from sleep loss, disruption of the body's natural rhythms (awake during the day, asleep at night), and working too many hours tends to decrease alertness, impair performance, and worsen mood. Yet most police departments routinely continue to allow officers to work more hours in a day, week, or month than would be legal for interstate truck drivers, pilots, train engineers, or several other occupational groups. The most extreme examples I have found during the past decade include officers in several states who worked more than 3,000 hours of overtime on the job in a single year. This is roughly the equivalent of working 14 hours per day, 365 days in a row.

How fit can officers be when they work long hours? Two recent research studies found that being awake for 17 straight hours impaired hand–eye coordination, decision making, and cognition as much as having a 0.05 percent blood-alcohol level. Being awake 24 straight hours was equivalent to a 0.10 percent blood alcohol—substantially higher than the level required in most U.S. states for DUI. Worse still, as NASA advised Congress in 1999, fatigue cannot "be willed away or overcome through motivation or discipline" because it is rooted in basic biology. It doesn't matter whether you're an Olympic athlete, a special operations commando, or a cop on the beat—if you don't get enough good quality sleep, you will be less able to deal with people tactfully or drive a vehicle safely. Nor will you be as able to analyze to what's happening in the world around you and choose the best, and safest, course of action.

The long-term consequences of repeatedly failing to get sufficient sleep are brutal. Too-tired officers are more likely to be injured, become ill, lose their tempers, and make bad decisions. They also are less able to handle stress constructively. It's easy to see how this set of problems can create a vicious cycle where worsening health or foul-ups on the job cause more stress, more problems and stress make it harder to sleep well, and less sleep causes more health, safety, and performance problems.

Fortunately, law enforcement agencies in the United States and Canada finally are starting to recognize fatigue as a serious threat. In the best departments, police executives and employee organizations are working together to assure that officers are alert and fit for duty. These fatigue management programs limit work hours and outside employment and minimize shift changes that disrupt officers' sleep schedules and family lives. They also educate officers about the dangers of fatigue and how to get enough sleep and stay healthy despite the challenges of overtime assignments, shift work, off-duty court appearances, and the emotional and physical demands of the job.

Dr. Bryan Vila is a professor at Washington State University. Prior to academia, Vila directed the Division of Crime Control and Prevention Research at the U.S. Department of Justice's National Institute of Justice and was a police officer for 17 years.

The opinions presented here are the author's and do not necessarily represent those of the U.S. Department of Justice or the NIJ.

may help people cope with stressful circumstances and thus lessen the potential negative effects. From this perspective, Cullen et al. (1985) studied police stress in five suburban police departments in a large midwestern city.

The researchers classified police stress along two different dimensions: that involving work and that affecting the officer's personal life. Work-related stressors were chosen that were not infrequent situations but ongoing parts of the police officer's job, such as role problems, court problems, potential danger, and shift changes. Social support measures included two work-related sources—peer support and supervisory support—and two non-work sources—family support and community support. It was discovered that work stress was most significantly influenced by perceived danger, which could be counteracted by supervisory support. Life stress was influenced not only by perceived danger, but also by court problems and shift changes. It was further found that family support counteracted stress in personal life.

Danger was the only stressor significantly related to both dimensions of stress. Although the respondents worked in communities with relatively low rates of serious crime and 86 percent disagreed with the statement, "A lot of people I work with get physically injured in the line of duty," the vast majority of the sample also felt that they had a "chance of getting hurt in my job." In other words, they perceived the *potential* for physical injury as ever-present and inherent in their work. Thus, even though policing may not be very dangerous in low-crime communities, the threat of injury is constant and may have stress-related consequences. Another interesting finding was that both court problems and shift changes were significantly related to stress in an officer's personal life, but not to work stress. This finding is important in that it "sensitizes us to the possibility that officers may adjust to the more strenuous features of their occupation while at work but nevertheless suffer deleterious effects on their general psychological health" (Cullen et al. 1985, 514).

In more recent research, Patterson (2003) reported that seeking social support reduced the impact of work stressors and emotional distress. However, he concluded that stress management programs should be expanded to consider a range of stressful life events, including off-duty stressors.

It was clear that supervisory support mitigated work stress, while family support was helpful in lessening personal-life stress. These findings suggest that departments should establish programs and provide training adequate to deal with stress in both work and personal life, while taking into account various social supports.

Consequences of Stress

There has been a limited amount of research on the relation between stress and emotional problems experienced by police officers. The research that has been done has been primarily concerned with alcohol and drug abuse, suicide, and marital and family-related problems, including divorce.

Alcohol Abuse

Hurrell and Kroes (1975) have suggested that police work may be especially conducive to alcoholism because officers frequently work in an environment in which social drinking is commonplace. "The nature of their work and the environment in which it is performed provides the stress stimulus" (241). They further contend that some police administrators have reported informally that as many as 25 percent of the officers in their departments have serious alcohol-abuse problems. It should also be noted, however, that other police administrators believe that alcohol-related problems are substantially lower.

In their survey of 852 police officers in metropolitan Sydney (Australia), Richmond et al. (1998) reported relatively high rates of unhealthy lifestyles. They found that almost half of the respondents reported excessive consumption of alcohol and that younger officers were particularly likely to consume. In fact, they reported that about two fifths of male officers and about one third of female officers reported binge drinking. They warned that excessive consumption of alcohol could have detrimental effects on officer performance, including slower reaction time, impaired performance, absenteeism, and liver problems. They reported that other research found alcoholic liver disease deaths among officers (1.2 percent) to be twice as high as in the general public (0.6 percent). They also noted a high level of other unhealthy behavior, including smoking, being overweight, and absence of exercise. Davey, Obst, and Sheehan (2000) found the frequency at which officers consumed alcohol was similar to the national averages; however, they did report that officers were more likely to engage in binge drinking. In their sample of 4,193 officers, 30 percent were classified as at risk for harmful levels of consumption, while 3 percent were classified as alcohol-dependent. Consumption and substance abuse may not be limited to off-duty behavior. Perhaps most startling was the fact that 25 percent of their sample reported drinking alcohol while on duty.

There is some evidence suggesting a relationship between strain and alcohol use among officers. Swatt, Gibson and Piquero (2007) found support for Agnew's General Strain Theory as a way to conceptualize alcohol use as a coping mechanism. Specifically, officers with higher levels of strain (stress) reported correspondingly higher levels of anxiety/depression and anger. They went on to report that anxiety/depression was positively related to problematic alcohol intake, although no relationship was observed for anger and alcohol. This provides partial support for the assertion that officers use alcohol as a mechanism to cope with anxiety and depression that is brought on by job-related stress.

Police departments have traditionally used the "character flaw" theory to deal with alcohol abuse. This theory calls for the denunciation and dismissal of officers with an alcohol problem because they will reflect badly on the department's reputation. What is not recognized is that "alcoholism may result from the extraordinary stresses of the job and that eliminating the officer does not do away with the sources of stress" (Hurrell and Kroes 1975, 241). Today, however, many departments are attempting to deal with alcoholic employees through in-house educational programs and admittance to outpatient programs designed to deal with such problems.

The following benefits are expected to accrue to those departments that develop procedures to help problem drinkers or alcoholics recover from their illness:

1. Retention of the majority of officers who had suffered from alcoholism.
2. Solution of a set of complex and difficult personnel problems.
3. Realistic and practical extension of the department's program into the entire city government structure.
4. Improved public and community attitudes caused by the degree of concern for the officer and his or her family and by eliminating the dangerous antisocial behavior of officers.
5. Full cooperation with rehabilitation efforts from the police associations and unions that may represent officers.
6. The preventive influence on moderate drinkers against the development of dangerous drinking habits that may lead to alcoholism. In addition, an in-house program will motivate some officers to undertake remedial action on their own, outside the scope of the department program. *(Dishlacoff 1976, 39)*

Drug Abuse

Although there is little direct evidence about the amount of drug abuse among police officers, there is little doubt that, along with the general population, the problem is rising.

The principal category of illegal drugs is narcotics. In an attempt to reduce this problem, departments utilize drug testing to screen out police applicants who may have a drug-abuse problem (see later discussion). In addition, police administrators are increasingly testing officers on the job for illegal drug use. Because drug use is illegal and officers are required to enforce laws against it, the usual result of a positive testing is dismissal from the force. Kraska and Kappeler (1988) examined on- and off-duty drug use by police officers in one police department. They reported that 20 percent of officers had used marijuana while on duty. Use was actually higher among middle management (27.3 percent) than among line officers (21.9 percent). Further, the overall performance ratings of officers who used drugs on duty were actually higher than that of officers who did not report on-duty drug use. While this study was largely exploratory and consisted of a relatively small sample of 49 officers from one jurisdiction, the results are reason for serious concern regarding the extent of illegal drug use by police officers.

Another area of growing concern is the abuse of anabolic steroids, which can lead to severe physical and psychological problems. This may become an increasingly important issue for police administrators, given that the culture of physical fitness and weight-lifting often coexists with policing (*Law Enforcement News* 2000). Some of the potential adverse effects of these drugs include increased aggression or mania (known as "roid rage"), increased risk of heart disease, acne, liver damage, heart disease, and psychological dependence (resulting from improved strength, athletic ability, and physique). In men, sterility, impotence, and an enlarged prostate gland are also likely to develop from steroid abuse; in women, abuse may lead to menstrual and other irregularities, including increased body and facial hair, baldness, and a deepening voice. Like other drugs, users can experience psychological effects of withdrawal (Humphrey et al. 2008).

Beside the potential for violent and unusual police behavior, additional problems relating to steroid abuse include increased officer-to-officer conflicts and officer complaints about the department, its policies and procedures, or working conditions (Swanson, Gaines, and Gore 1991). Because of the potential harm that may accrue from abnormal behavior associated with steroid abuse, several police departments have implemented drug testing for steroids (*Law Enforcement News* 2000, Humphrey et al. 2008). Police departments must not only educate their officers about the use of steroids, but also develop effective policies and programs to eliminate the illegal use of steroids before it becomes a problem.

Suicide

Suicide has become the most dreaded consequence of a police officer under stress. Although it is difficult to obtain accurate data regarding whether police suicides are higher than those of the general population, it appears to be true, at least in some departments. Most of the early research suggests that the prevalence of suicide among police officers is higher than in the general population. In a comparison of police with 130 other occupations, Guralnick (1963) estimated the police suicide rate to be 1.8 times that of the general population. Guralnick also found that police were more likely to commit suicide than be killed in a homicide. Richard and Fell (1975) ranked police as the third highest group in suicide among 130 occupations, and Violanti, Vena, and Marshall (1986) reported that police were three times as likely to commit suicide compared with other municipal workers.

Data from a 40-year (1950–1990) study of 2,611 Buffalo police officers suggest that the frequency of suicides has increased in the past decade from an average of one suicide every 1.75 years to one every 1.42 years (Violanti and Vena 1995). This same study found that police were eight times more likely to commit suicide than to be killed in a homicide and three times more likely to commit suicide than to die in job-related accidents. The researchers looked at 138 deaths, all white males, including 39 police officers and 99 other municipal workers. Of the 39 police officer deaths, 29 were suicides (74 percent), 3 were homicides, 6 were accidental, and 1 was undetermined. Of the 99 municipal worker deaths, 14 were suicides (14 percent), 4 were homicides, 77 were accidents, and 4 were undetermined. According to these numbers, police officers were approximately five times more likely to commit suicide than city workers (74 percent of all deaths compared with 14 percent), a staggering difference and one that needs an explanation.

The results of the Buffalo study indicated that police are at a higher risk for committing suicide for a variety of reasons, including access to firearms (95 percent of the suicides were by firearm), continuous exposure to human misery, shift work, social strain and marital difficulties, drinking problems, physical illness, impending retirement (i.e., separation from police peers and subculture), and lack of control over their jobs and personal lives ("What's Killing America's Cops?" 1996). Other research supports the general tenor of these findings. For example, Ivanoff (1994) found that 94 percent of police suicides in New York involved a firearm and that 57 percent were believed to be precipitated by relationship difficulties; Cronin (1982) and Wagner and Brzeczek (1983) found that the majority of police officers committing suicide abused alcohol; Loo (1986) found that 15 percent of police suicides in the Royal Canadian Mounted Police had been exposed to a traumatic work incident; and Gaska (1982) found a 10-fold risk of suicide among police retirees. Interestingly, other findings (Ivanoff 1994) also found in New York that officers tend to kill themselves because of personal problems, substance abuse, and depression, not job-related stress. These are continuing life problems that people do not know how to solve. Ivanhoff's study, issued by the New York City Police Foundation, based its findings on surveys of 18,000 patrol officers between 1990 and 1993 and on studies of 57 suicides of officers from 1985 to 1994. These findings are noteworthy because they suggest that police suicides may not result from job stress, which, in turn, may suggest that different types of intervention strategies are necessary. It is clear that more research is needed to better understand the causes and effects of police suicides and prevention programs.

However, the relationship between suicide and policing is far from consistent. For example, Stack and Kelley (1999) observed inconsistencies in the empirical research and noted that most research on police suicide was limited to samples drawn from a few local police departments. To combat this apparent shortcoming, their analysis used the 1985 National Mortality Detail File and included data from 12,000 local police departments, 3,000 sheriff's offices, 49 state police agencies, and various federal law enforcement agencies. Suicide rates for police officers were compared with those for other males in the population. Their analysis indicated that suicide rates for police officers (25.6 per 100,000) were only slightly higher than the suicide rate for non-police (23.8 per 100,000). Further, after controlling for socioeconomic status and other variables, *being a police officer was not significantly related with the odds of death by suicide.* This appears to indicate that while the policing occupation may be inherently stressful, occupational stress may not truly be related to suicide.

One of the primary problems of attempting to prevent police suicide is that, traditionally, officers refrain from asking for help. Often they do not want to appear weak in front of their peers and they see themselves as problem solvers, not persons with problems. In addition, officers fear the possible negative effects on their career if they come forward with a problem. Officers should receive training to help them recognize and avoid psychological factors leading to suicide. It is important to understand that suicide generally results not from a single crisis but from the accumulation of apparently minor life events. Training should begin at the academy before new officers are exposed to the police socialization process. Ivanhoff suggests that **suicide prevention training** include the recognition of psychological depression, communication skills, conflict resolution, and maintenance of intimate relationships. Loo (2005) outlines a variety of suicide prevention measures that police departments should consider:

1. Recruitment selection criteria: police departments conduct thorough screenings of officer applicants, and often factors related to suicide predisposition or precipitating factors can be identified. While screening out applicants demonstrating these factors may be challenging, certainly departments should closely monitor these officers to determine whether indicators of suicide risk develop.

2. Stress management and inoculation training: police departments should provide ongoing training on how officers can self-manage chronic stress and stress associated with critical incidents.

3. Supervisor training: police administrators and those responsible for supervising officers should be trained to identify EWS for suicide. This appears particularly important for sergeants who interact with street-level officers on a regular basis and can best identify changes in behavior.

4. Psychological assessments for special duties: special attention should be focused on officers in particularly high-stress inducing assignments, such as SWAT or undercover officers.

5. Critical incidents: crisis intervention teams should be in place to conduct debriefings and assessments after traumatic incidents. The team could consist of specially trained police personnel as well as non-police like clergy and health care professionals.

6. Psychological services: contracting with external health care providers to provide ongoing psychological services for officers.

7. Programs to promote healthy lifestyles.

8. Suicide hotlines.

9. Peer and spousal support programs.

10. Preretirement counseling and postretirement networks: retirement can often be particularly challenging for officers for a variety of reasons. New retirees experience a loss of camaraderie that they have grown accustomed to and many police departments have mandatory retirement after specific years of service (Barker 1999). Relatively young retirees may need additional assistance managing finances in retirement. Retirement networks can provide opportunities for retirees to serve as peer counselors within departments or mentor young officers. *(119–122)*

Marital and Family Problems

Maintaining healthy social support networks can insulate officers from the negative consequences associated with police-related stress. However, often the occupation contributes to officer divorce and the breakup of these important support networks. In addition to all of the other factors that contribute to divorce, certain job characteristics appear to contribute to marital breakup and family problems. Officers are required to work rotating or odd shifts, including weekends and holidays, which make it more challenging to maintain a healthy family routine. Quality time with spouses, children, and non-police friends is less predictable, creating stress and often resentment. Police officers routinely view trauma and human suffering, which results in a hardening of emotions, which officers bring home with them. Police work can also create opportunities for infidelity that may not be present in other occupations (Kappeler and Potter 2005, Miller 2007, Kroes, Margolis, and Hurrell 1974). The occupation appears to provide an environment that would be risky for police marriages.

Alexander and Walker (1996) found that police work also had an adverse impact on officers' lives, especially their social lives. The major problems were identified as long hours, shift work, and canceled leave. Surprisingly, dangerous duties and working with the opposite sex did not usually adversely affect officer spouses. And Roberts and Levenson (2001) reported that male officers are prone to take job-acquired stress home to their spouses. Both officers and spouses reported adverse reactions to the officers' on-the-job stress, and they concluded that stress and exhaustion probably have a negative impact on the family unit.

In view of these types of family problems, it has been assumed, as with alcoholism and suicide rates, that divorce rates for police officers are far higher than normal for the rest of the population. Some research has supported this view, but the preponderance of the empirical research has indicated that divorce rates for police are no higher than for many other occupations (the divorce rate for the general population is approximately 50 percent). Davidson and Veno (1978), in their review of the literature, cite several weaknesses in the studies that support high divorce rates for police, including the failure to consider a number of factors that strongly influence divorce rates, such as age at marriage and number of children. McCoy and Aamodt (2010) examined 449 different occupations and reported divorce and separation rates for police officers to be lower than the national average.

Whether police divorce rates are higher than those of the rest of the population is not really the issue: Healthy organizations should be mindful of the well-being of their members and ideally would provide mechanisms or services to counteract any job-related issues that could lead to family problems. Because marital and family problems can have such a devastating impact on job performance, many police departments are developing programs aimed at helping family members understand and cope with the stressors inherent in police work. The Los Angeles County Sheriff's Department, for example, offers an 8-week spouses' training program, which includes an overview of departmental operations and the duties of law enforcement personnel (Stratton 1976). In Minnesota, the Couple Communications program (Maynard and Maynard 1980) helps officers and their spouses identify issues in their marriage that might produce additional on-the-job stress. In Indiana, the state police initiated an employee-assistance program (Lambuth 1984) designed to help employees and their families deal with emotional problems by referral to proper treatment agencies. Such programs should, in the long run, lead to improved job performance.

Policies and Programs

Based on the literature reviewed, there are a number of policies and programs that could be implemented by police management to help control the stressors encountered by police personnel. Of course, not every department can, or should, attempt to implement all of the recommendations. Each department has different needs and budgetary constraints and therefore must decide what type of policies and programs best fit its particular needs. The following recommendations, however, provide a proper foundation for controlling police stress in both working and non-working environments:

1. Establish quality-of-worklife activities designed to improve communication and increase participation in decision making throughout the department.

2. Address workplace environmental issues, including quality of equipment, work space, compensation packages, and related aspects.

3. Develop training programs in stress awareness. Police should consider stress management as simply another skill to be learned, like criminal law or police procedure.

4. Establish specific stress programs. These can be part of a larger departmental psychological services, a health program, or a general employee-assistance program.

5. Establish operational policies that reduce stress. Consider the effects of shift assignments and scheduling, report writing, and so forth.

6. Improve management skills overall, especially in people-oriented aspects of supervision and management; include stress management skills in supervisory practice.

7. Utilize peer-counseling programs. Because peers may have already experienced many of the same problems, they can be of invaluable help to fellow officers.

8. Develop support groups by taking advantage of the natural groups that already exist informally and formally within the department.

9. Establish physical fitness programs that can strengthen the individual to withstand occupational stress. Such programs should also address stress-related dietary issues.

10. Encourage family activities as an important source of assistance to the officer. In particular, as spouses know more about police work and its stresses, they are in a better position to provide support. *(Adapted from Farmer 1990, 214–215)*

Research by Dowler (2005) offers empirical support for several of the above policy recommendations and found that officers reported lower levels of occupational burnout and lower levels of depression related to their jobs when their were stress debriefing programs available. Social support from family and friends also decreased feelings of burnout and depression, and officers felt less depressed if there was support from police administration. Individual officers can also engage in positive coping strategies to reduce stress, many of which are consistent with activities engaged among non–police officers. These activities can include the following:

1. Developing a system of social support.

2. Ventilating feelings properly.

3. Regular exercise programs.

4. Proper diet that excludes high-fat foods.

5. Development of other recreation activities.

6. Regular vacations.

7. Muscle relaxation exercises.

8. Meditation.

9. Biofeedback.

10. Participation in self-help groups. *(adapted from Waters, Irons and Finkle 1982: 25)*

Officer Safety

Each year the FBI compiles information on officer safety across several broad categories—officers feloniously killed, officers accidentally killed, and officers assaulted. These reports provide useful descriptive information on officer safety and permit observation of longitudinal trends. Before proceeding, it is necessary to provide a few words of caution when interpreting these data. Estimating officer safety is challenging because the FBI are reliant on local police agencies to voluntarily provide them with accurate information. Some have questioned the validity of data contained in the FBI reports. Uchida and King (2002, 7) examined longitudinal trends in police reporting and reported that it is difficult to completely trust the accuracy of these data. They observed what appeared to be alarming and counter-intuitive discrepancies between number of assaults, number of officers, and population served. They concluded these data "should be viewed carefully" and called for external benchmarks to assess their validity. These data may be prone to under-reporting that is inherent with other data collected by the FBI (for instance, the UCRs), but unfortunately these are the only data available that provide national estimates of officer safety in felonious non-lethal encounters (but see also National Law Enforcement Officers Memorial Fund 2009). We agree with Uchida and King and recommend these data be viewed carefully.

Between 1999 and 2008, 530 police officers were feloniously killed on duty and another 746 were killed in duty-related accidents, for a total of 1,276. In addition, 586,915 officers were assaulted over the same 10-year period (FBI 2009). The data in Figure 13.1 cover over 35 years of felonious police killings and show that a measurable drop occurred between 1976 and 1986. Since that time, the number of officers feloniously killed has leveled off. Notable dips in the number of officers feloniously killed occurred in 1991 (42 deaths) and 2008. In 2008 a total of 41 officers were feloniously killed in the line of duty, and this represents the fewest fatalities over the past 30 years. Figure 13.1 also indicates that the most frequently used method to kill officers was firearms. Over 69 percent of officer deaths occurred with a handgun.

Figure 13.2 depicts the various circumstances at the scene of the incident at which police officers were feloniously killed or assaulted. For officers killed, the primary circumstance was an arrest situation (e.g., during robberies or burglaries or pursuing suspects, drug-

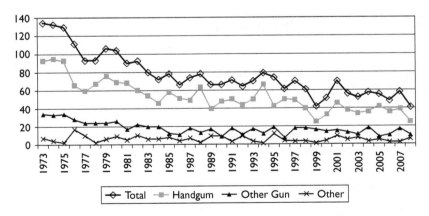

FIGURE 13.1 Police Officers Feloniously Killed in the Line of Duty, 1973–2008.*

*2001 excludes 72 officers killed on September 11.
Source: FBI, *Law Enforcement Officers Killed and Assaulted, 1973–2008*.

related matters, and other arrests); the second leading circumstance involved ambushes; the third circumstance was traffic pursuits and stops. The fourth circumstance involved answering disturbance calls (e.g., bar fights, man with gun, family quarrels). It is interesting to note the similarities as well as the differences between felonious assaults and killings. Certain circumstances appear highly correlated with assault and fatalities (e.g., disturbance calls, arrests situations). Ambushes that resulted in a fatality were 50 times more likely than ambushes resulting in assault. This suggests that when officers are surprised in an ambush, death is far more likely.

Another set of data reviewed involves police officers who are accidentally killed and the circumstances at the scene of the incident. As Figure 13.3 shows, 746 officers were

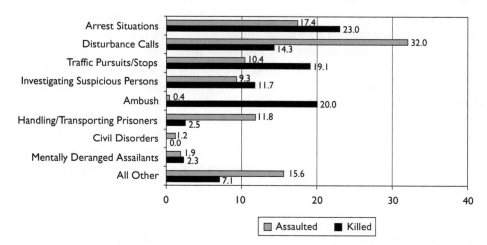

FIGURE 13.2 Law Enforcement Officers Feloniously Killed and Assaulted: Circumstances at Scene.

Source: Federal Bureau of Investigation, 2009. Law Enforcement Officers Killed and Assaulted, 2008. Available online at http://www.fbi.gov/ucr/killed/2008/.

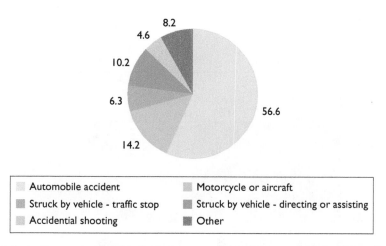

FIGURE 13.3 Percentage of Law Enforcement Officers Accidentally Killed (n = 746): Circumstances at Scene, 1999–2008.

Source: Federal Bureau of Investigation, 2009. Law Enforcement Officers Killed and Assaulted, 2008. Available online at http://www.fbi.gov/ucr/killed/2008/.

accidentally killed while on duty between 1999 and 2008. The leading circumstance of accidental death was automobile accidents, which accounted for slightly over 56.6 percent. A similar category includes motorcycle and aircraft deaths (14.2 percent) A total of 10.2 percent of officers were killed when struck by a vehicle directing traffic or assisting motorists, and 6.3 percent were killed during traffic stops. A small but noteworthy proportion of accidental deaths were attributed to accidental shootings (4.6 percent). All other types of on-duty accidental deaths comprised 8.2 percent of the total. These data reinforce the fact that officers are most likely to be accidentally killed in events related to operating a police vehicle and engaging traffic enforcement.

In 2008, 11.3 officers per 100 were assaulted. Figure 13.4 provides information on the rate of officer assaults. The rate of officers assaulted has declined modestly, but steadily, since 2000 when 12.7 officers per 100 were assaulted. Geographically, the southern states had the highest assault rate at 12.4 per 100 officers, followed by midwestern states with 11.5 per 100, western states with 10.7 per 100, and northeastern states with 9.4 per 100. By population grouping, assault rates ranged from 17.2 per 100 officers in cities of over 250,000 inhabitants to 6.7 assaults per 100 officers in cities under 10,000 inhabitants. Clearly, there is a significant difference in assault rates depending on what part of the country and on the size of the city or county department in which the officer works (FBI 2009).

Inside Policing 13.1 provides details of selected high-profile felonious killings of officers that occurred in 2009. In 2009, the National Law Enforcement Officers Memorial Fund reported that despite overall declines in officer fatalities, there was a 26 percent increase in firearms-related deaths from 2008. A large number of deaths were during disturbance calls or ambushes, which is consistent with data provided from the FBI. The National Law Enforcement Officers Memorial Fund reported that multiple officer shootings accounted for almost one third of firearms-related fatalities—an increase from previous years.

Danger and Police Work

How dangerous is police work? Danger can be considered from three perspectives: perceived, potential, and actual. **Perceived danger** relates to the individual's or public's belief

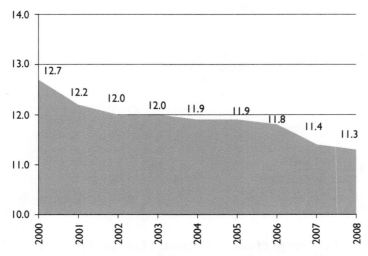

FIGURE 13.4 **Law Enforcement Officers Assaulted per 100 officers, 2000–2008.**

Source: Federal Bureau of Investigation, Law Enforcement Officers Killed and Assaulted, 2000-2008. Retrieved March 11, 2010 at http://www.fbi.gov/

INSIDE POLICING 13.1   Multiple Officers Feloniously Killed, 2009

On April 4, 2009, three officers of the Pittsburgh Police Department were killed and two others were wounded after responding to a domestic disturbance. The 22-year-old accused gunman, allegedly wearing a bulletproof vest, opened fire on Officer Paul Sciullo (2-year veteran) as the officer entered the house. Officer Stephen Mayhle (2-year veteran) was shot backing him up. Officer Eric Kelley (14-year veteran) was also shot attempting to assist the officers. The officers were shot with an assault rifle at 7:05 AM. The suspect surrendered after a 4-hour standoff with the police.

On November 29, 2009, four Lakewood, Washington, police officers were shot and killed in an apparent ambush. Officers Ronald Owens (12-year veteran), Tina Griswold (14-year veteran), Greg Richards (8-year veteran), and Sergeant Mark Renninger (13-year veteran) were seated in a coffee shop working on laptop computers around 8:15 AM when a man, later identified as Maurice Clemmons, entered the shop and brandished a handgun to the clerk. Clemmons approached the officers and fired point-blank at them. Despite wearing bulletproof vests, all officers died at the scene. Two days later, another officer stopped to assist a stranded motorist whose plates were traced to a stolen vehicle. The officer was approached by a man who he recognized as Clemmons. The officer shot Clemmons when he reached for a gun that he had taken from one of the officers in the coffee shop shooting.

SOURCES: Adapted from http://www.thepittsburghchannel.com/download/2009/0406/19108441.pdf, http://www. thepittsburghchannel.com/news/19096134/detail.html, http://www.post-gazette.com/pg/09094/960660–100.stm, http:// www.komonews.com/news/local/78101617.html, and http://www.msnbc.msn.com/id/34194122/ns/us_news-crime_ and_courts/.

---

about danger in police work. It is influenced by a variety of factors, including media coverage, television, movies, books, and the actual experiences of officers. In general, many people, including police officers, believe that police work is a very dangerous job. **Potential danger** relates to those situations that could become dangerous for an officer, for example, a felony car stop or investigating a suspicious circumstance. Potentially dangerous encounters are often characterized by a suspect's behavior that adds to the officer's concern (e.g., threats, shouting, challenges to police authority, and name calling). **Actual danger** involves the actual number and rates of injuries and deaths that result from accidents and attacks from citizens.

Another useful way to analyze danger in police work is to categorize it in terms of how it is precipitated; that is, is it initiated by a person or is it a function of the situation? Few occupations include both the possibility and the reality of **person-initiated danger**, that is, an attack by another person. **Situational danger** is a function of a particular problem, for example, a high-speed chase in policing, a taxi driver's risk of a traffic accident, the use of certain equipment, or the height at which a person has to work.

One of the more telling aspects of danger to police is that officers initiate a substantial number of the encounters in which they are injured or killed, and they often know that these situations are potentially dangerous. In one study on officer fatalities, Konstantin (1984) discovered that, contrary to popular belief, most police are not killed in citizen-initiated contacts; rather, approximately 75 percent of incidents resulting in officer deaths were initiated by the officers themselves. In addition, most officers are killed in the types of situations that they know are the most dangerous; the top three incidents were attempting arrests, situations involving robbery, and general car stops. Other situations, in order of occurrence, were assaults on officers, investigating suspicious persons, car stops of known offenders, responding to domestic disturbances, handling mentally deranged persons, and handling prisoners. Even with this knowledge, officers may fail to follow the training and procedures that would reduce the likelihood of injury or death.

The general conclusions that can be reached from this study are important if officer fatalities are to be reduced. First, most fatalities occur in situations that the police know are dangerous; second, most of the incidents (approximately three quarters) that lead to killings are *initiated* by the officers themselves. Such conclusions suggest that the police are often not prepared to handle these potentially dangerous situations. It appears obvious that more thorough preparation and training in these areas could help officers to make better decisions about whether to intervene and, once the decision is made, how to handle the situation from the safest perspective. As Konstantin points out,

> Police training emphasis on the great majority of routine encounters that are citizen-initiated is well-meaning but insufficient. Such emphasis should not come at the expense of training officers to approach carefully situations where they themselves make decisions to intervene. *(1984, 42)*

However, the issue of proactive police behavior and dangerousness is a matter of debate. Police culture has supported the notion that traffic enforcement is extremely dangerous, in part because of the fear of the unknown. As such, the Supreme Court has over time relaxed civil liberties during traffic stops, in part based on considerations of officer safety (see Chapter 3). But how dangerous, really, is traffic enforcement? Lichtenberg and Smith (2001) used the aforementioned FBI data to determine the "danger ratio" associated with traffic enforcement. They defined danger ratio as the number of harmful encounters (i.e., death or assault) divided by the total number of activities (i.e., traffic stops). They conclude that, in fact, traffic encounters are really not all that dangerous. Examining data over a 10-year period, they found that officers are killed in about one in every 9.2 million traffic stops. Further, officers are assaulted at the rate of about 1 in every 20,512 traffic stops. Whether these estimates are alarmingly high or very low might be in part interpreted through the lens of the consumer, but the authors suggested that the Supreme Court overestimated the dangerousness of these encounters when determining legal precedent.

As discussed previously, 23.0 percent of officers who are killed are killed during arrest situations. These situations also result in 17.4 percent of all officer assaults. However, it is prudent to question under what circumstances suspects are most likely to resist or be combative during arrest encounters. Kavanagh (1997) examined arrests made over a 1-year period in New York. He found that circumstances that increased the likelihood of force being used by either police or citizens included seriousness of the crime, suspect intoxication, whether other arrestees were present, and suspect disrespect. Like Konstantin, he found that officer-initiated arrests increased the likelihood of violence. Interestingly, he found that arrests that occurred during the daytime also had an increased likelihood of violence. Factors unrelated to violence included officer race, officer education, citizen race, and citizen gender. Hence, it appears that it is possible to determine situational factors in advance that increase the chances of violence during arrest encounters. Understanding these factors, with focused training on how to recognize and diffuse these encounters, can assist the police in reducing the number of assaults that occur during arrest situations.

Under what circumstances are officers injured during assaults? Kaminski and Sorensen (1995) examined 1,550 nonlethal police assaults in Baltimore County over a 2-year period.

They found that the odds an officer was injured during an assault increased when certain situational characteristics were present. Officers were more likely to be injured during an assault when (1) more than one officer was assaulted, (2) suspects used bodily force rather than a weapon, (3) there was a single assailant, (4) suspects were under arrest, attempting to escape, or fighting upon arrival (rather than approaching or conversing with the officer), (5) the assailant was not intoxicated, and (6) officers were responding to disturbances or other legal situations (rather than domestic disputes).

The authors suggested that these final two findings may be because officers perceive encounters with intoxicated citizens and domestic disputes to be dangerous and thus exercise greater caution when encountering these citizens. They found that officers were more likely to be injured during encounters with non-white suspects, indicating these encounters were characterized by greater hostility. They also reported that characteristics of the officers themselves were related to injury. For example, short and tall officers were more likely to sustain injury when compared with "medium"-size officers, and younger officers and officers without a college education were more likely to be injured than seasoned veterans or officers with a college education. Finally, they found that some individual officers sustained injuries on multiple occasions. Based on their findings, they outline several policies police managers could initiate to reduce officer injuries:

1. Encourage greater proficiency with unarmed defensive tactics.
2. Provide additional in-service training for officers with less than 5 or 6 years of service.
3. Teach tailor-made defensive tactics for officers who are either short or tall.
4. Identify officers who are at risk for multiple injuries and work with these officers to reduce the number of use-of-force encounters.
5. Train to assist officers in identification of high-risk assailants (e.g., hostile suspects who attempt to escape during arrest situations).
6. Offer community relations and awareness programs to reduce tension and hostility between police and non-white suspects.
7. Continue to hire officers with higher education levels.
8. Encourage greater caution when responding to non–domestic disturbance calls.

Are officers more likely to experience assaults in specific communities? Kaminski, Jefferis, and Gu (2003) researched the spatial distribution of aggravated assaults on Boston police officers over a 7-year period. Among other things, they found that officers are more likely to be assaulted in areas characterized by economic distress and family disruption. They also reported that areas with high arrest rates had correspondingly higher rates of officer assaults. They remarked that high arrest areas present a greater risk level for officer-focused violence. This factor was the most important variable in their analysis of officer assaults.

How dangerous is policing compared with other occupations? McLeod (1990) looked at the mortality rate of 56 occupations for males between the ages of 16 and 64 and compared it with the normal death rate for all working men. This database considers the causes of death regardless of whether the deaths occurred on or off the job; thus, people in high-mortality occupations tend to die not only more often on the job but also from physical or mental ailments (e.g., hypertension, stroke, cirrhosis, or suicide) that may cause death off the job.

Of the 56 occupations listed, deckhands and tankermen (on ships) had the highest mortality rating of 3.93 (i.e., a deckhand's death rate is 3.93 times the normal rate for all working men). The next highest mortality rates, in rank order, were as follows: (2) structural metal workers (3.17); (3) roofers (2.29); (4) industrial helpers (2.22); (5) foresters (2.19); (6) miners and drillers (2.17); (7) operating engineers (2.17); and (8) construction workers (2.13). Police officers and firefighters were ranked 31st, with a 1.07 mortality rating. In a separate study of police mortality, Hill and Clawson (1988) found that police officers' average age at death appears to be only slightly lower (by 7 months) than that of individuals employed in 194 other occupations. Thus, it appears that police work is only moderately dangerous compared with other occupations.

Much of the current discussion has focused on safety issues related to assaults and officer deaths. But no conversation on police safety would be complete without discussing the propensity for officers to be injured in accidents unrelated to the act of controlling or arresting a criminal suspect. However, data on officer injuries are less available than information on deaths and injuries related to assaults. Brandl and Stroshine (2003) examined accident reports completed by city employees within a large urban city. They found that of all the injuries sustained by officers, over half (50.4 percent) were to the result of on-the-job accidents. The remaining injuries were related to subjects who were resisting (39.2 percent) or assaultive (10.4 percent). This implies that if discussions of officer safety only included those injuries sustained during law enforcementñrelated incidents with suspects, then more than half of the true injuries would be counted. Of officers who were injured as a result of an accident, 24.7 percent reported having contact with infectious diseases. Their research indicated that officers were somewhat less likely to seek medical attention for injuries than for those involved with assaults/resistant suspects. But 13.8 percent of accidents involved time off from work, where officers injured during assaults (7.5 percent) and resisting arrest encounters (11.8 percent) experienced less time off from work. Thus, the outcomes of accident-related injuries were at least as serious as those sustained during interactions with resistant/combative suspects.

Safety and the Mentally Ill

In recent years, requests for police assistance in handling people who are mentally ill have increased substantially. This may be a result of a variety of factors, including deinstitutionalization of state and psychiatric hospitals, criminalization of mental illness, overuse of medication (and inability for people with mental illness to consistently self-medicate), and privatization (Cordner 2006). LaGrange (2000) indicated that 89 percent of officers in one city had contact with a mentally disordered citizen during the previous year. Interacting with these special populations often increased the actual or perceived risk to officer safety, as many officers believe they are not adequately trained or prepared to intervene with citizens suffering from mental illness (Finn and Sullivan 1987). As a result, police often rely on the use of force or make arrests during encounters with these citizens. Teplin (1984) indicated that police make arrests in 46.7 percent of encounters with mentally ill citizens compared with 27.9 percent of other citizens. Recently Engel and Silver (2001) and Novak and Engel (2005) found that mentally ill citizens are no more likely to be arrested by the police after taking into consideration other important situational factors; however, mentally ill persons were more likely to be hostile, which can create officer safety issues. Interactions with mentally ill persons can be stress inducing and present unique safety risks for untrained officers.

In response to this problem many jurisdictions have implemented programs to share responsibility by creating formal networks between law enforcement and social-service agencies. A National Institute of Justice study of such network arrangements indicated that benefits accrue not only to the agencies involved, but also to individuals who need help (Finn and Sullivan 1988). Networks that focus on the mentally ill have special units, on call 24 hours a day, that screen individuals for the most advisable disposition, identify the most appropriate facility to refer them to, and provide on-the-scene emergency assistance when necessary. These units consist either of specially trained police officers or of social workers hired by the department to perform these functions; in addition, some networks utilize social service agencies to provide the special unit.

One successful **crisis intervention team** can be found in Memphis. Following a police shooting of a mentally ill citizen, a crisis intervention team was created that consisted of police officers (with special crisis intervention training), emergency medical/psychiatric services, hospitals, and families of people with mental illness. These partners are more effective in determining non-confrontational outcomes of encounters with the mentally ill and more effective in determining whether evaluation of citizens taken into custody is necessary. For example, if citizens are identified as displaying mental illness, they may be taken to the hospital for evaluation, rather than being taken to jail and placed in the general population there. This program has had beneficial results, including reduced use of deadly force, fewer injuries to both officers and citizens, lower arrest rates, and reduced stigma and perception of danger attached to mental illness (Vickers 2000). Other programs have experienced similar success in New Orleans (Wellborn 1999) and Albuquerque (Bower and Pettit 2001). Research also indicates that officer-reported crisis intervention training can improve awareness of support programs and improved attitudes toward citizens with schizophrenia, which can improve and sensitize the manner in which officers interact with these special populations (Compton et al. 2006). Crisis intervention teams and additional officer training can improve interactions with the mentally ill and reduce the likelihood of injury for both citizens and officers (Skeem and Bibeau 2008). But intervention programs are not one-size-fits-all, and police departments will need to identify approaches that best fit their environment to improve the effectiveness of public safety initiatives (Cordner 2006; Reuland, Draper, and Norton 2010) and reduce the likelihood of officer injury.

With respect to the homeless and public inebriates, most networks have made arrangements directly between the police department and one or more detoxification facilities or homeless shelters. The parties involved have typically agreed to strict referral and admission procedures (Finn and Sullivan 1988).

Improving Safety and Reducing Fatalities

From the research presented here, it is clear that more training and new or clearer policies are needed in several key areas of police officer safety. There appears to be a need for continual retraining in safety procedures as well. For instance, arrest situations, traffic stops, investigation of suspicious persons or situations, and disturbance calls all need more attention. Since approximately half of all police killings are accidental, departments should review the circumstances in which they occur and review the level of training and policies they provide in these areas. One study of police killings in drug situations (Sherman et al. 1989), for instance, advised that rehearsing each drug raid could substantially reduce the danger to police.

The FBI, in its in-depth studies of officers killed in the line of duty (1992) and officers who survived a serious assault (1997), has also made a number of training and policy recommendations. The researchers found that in a significant number of incidents, officers made tactical errors, such as improperly approaching a vehicle or suspect, or failed to conduct a thorough search of a suspect. Increased training was recommended in those areas as well as in the handling of traffic stops, weapons retention, handcuff use, and waiting for backup. With respect to traffic stops, department regulations should include sections on officer safety, including the proper selection of a safe stop location, dispatcher notification, and wearing of soft body armor. Body armor, or bulletproof vests, has been credited with saving more than 2,000 officer lives since 1980; FBI statistics indicate that about 42 percent of police officers killed with guns since 1980 could have been saved if they had been wearing vests ("Congress OK's $75M Body-Armor Fund" 1998). In addition, the FBI recommends that citizens be advised of the proper response when stopped by a marked police unit (i.e., they should remain in the vehicle, keep hands in plain view, and wait for further directions from the officer). Finally, since a large number of officers are killed while off duty (approximately one of every seven), departments should provide a well-defined policy for off-duty performance (e.g., carrying or not carrying firearms and how to act when observing an offense).

Another strategy that deserves continued evaluation is adoption and use of less lethal weapons. Although use of force is described in greater detail in Chapter 10, commentary on officer safety is deserved here. For decades the police had few options when facing aggressive and hostile suspects, and often officers relied on open-hand techniques, impact weapons (such as nightsticks, batons, or PR-24s), and of course firearms. However, technological developments have provided officers with additional midlevel options, including OC spray or CEDs, or Tasers. These options have been met with welcome arms in the policing community primarily because they can be deployed when officers and suspects are at a distance. The General Accountability Office (2005) indicated that Tasers can be discharged from 25 feet. These devices provide officers an intermediate use of force option that can reduce the likelihood of officer (and suspect) injury. The same report estimates that over 7,000 police departments use Tasers. However, at the same time there is some controversy surrounding CEDs. Amnesty International (2008) noted an unacceptable frequency of in-custody deaths during CED applications and called for police departments to discontinue their use or significantly limit when they can be used. While Smith et al. (2007) indicate a lack of consensus in the research community regarding the causal relationship between CEDs and unintended fatalities, they also point out that relatively little is known regarding officer and suspect injuries.

An emerging body of literature suggests that the use of CEDs and OC spray reduces officer injury. In their research of Richland County and Miami–Dade, overall Smith et al. (2007) conclude that use of these devices reduce the incidence of injury as well as reduce the nature of injuries. MacDonald, Kaminski, and Smith (2009), in analyzing data from 12 separate agencies, found CED or OC use was associated with decreased risk of suspect injury. When examining the introduction of CEDs in Orlando they found that the incidence of suspect injury decreased 53 percent and officer injury decreased 62 percent. In Austin, Texas, suspect injury decreased 30 percent and officer injury declined 25 percent after the police departments introduced CEDs into their use-of-force repertoire. They concluded that "law enforcement agencies should encourage the use of OC spray or CEDs in place of impact weapons and should consider authorizing their use as a replacement for hands-on force tactics against physically resistant suspects" (MacDonald, Kaminski, and Smith 2009, 2,273). Defining appropriate use of these less lethal weapons should continue to engender public debate; it is encouraging to note that these devices can be associated with improved officer safety.

Police managers, especially first-line supervisors and midlevel managers (i.e., sergeants and lieutenants), can also contribute to the reduction of the number of injuries and deaths (Roberg, Kuykendall, and Novak 2002). They must be ever-vigilant to make sure that officers follow departmental safety and response guidelines. In addition, all incidents involving the use of force and citizen resistance should be reported and used by a department not only to assess the officer's style and discretion but also as a basis for improving future police responses. Any time a police officer or citizen is injured or killed, the department should undertake an immediate and comprehensive reassessment of all related programs, policies, and personnel. This type of response is necessary because police managers need to reduce the fear level of officers if they hope to modify some of the behavior resulting from irrational fear, including verbal abuse of citizens, overreliance on the use of force, unnecessary and excessive force, and brutality. Police managers must convince officers that officer safety, next to integrity, is the most important priority in the department (Roberg et al. 2002, 332).

Roberg and colleagues (2002) further suggest that departments undertake an extensive community education program to instruct citizens how to behave when interacting with officers; this goes beyond the FBI's recommendation about citizens' behavior in traffic stops. Essentially, citizens need to understand that they must cooperate with the police and follow police orders and that citizen grievances should not and cannot be resolved "in the streets," but rather, if necessary, in the courts or through some other formal mechanism. Unfortunately, some people believe that it is their right to challenge police authority at the very moment that authority is being exercised. The police will have problems with such individuals until there is a change in citizen attitudes. Just as the police must modify their behavior in some situations to secure public respect and cooperation, citizens must also modify their behavior to reduce officers' fear.

Summary

Stress and danger confront the police, but there are methods to reduce both. There are two major categories of police stressors: departmental practices and the inherent nature of police work. The first may include authoritarian structure, lack of administrative support, or minimal participation in decision making; the second may include rotating shift work, boredom, danger, public apathy, and exposure to human misery, including death or injury to fellow officers. In addition, some new forms of stress include efforts toward community policing, especially role conflict and role ambiguity, increased levels of violence with which the police must deal, perceived negative news media coverage, fear of air- and blood-borne diseases, and, for some white officers, cultural diversity and political correctness. In addition, the psychological stress caused by frequent or prolonged exposure to crises or trauma can lead to posttraumatic stress disorder, which can have serious adverse affects, including increased levels of brutality.

Police stress can also lead to alcohol and drug abuse, suicide, and various family problems. Social support systems (e.g., supervisory and family support) can mitigate work stress and general life stress. There are numerous policies and programs designed to reduce police stress. Finally, although police fatalities have lessened over the past 2 decades, policing is a potentially dangerous occupation. Most officer fatalities occur in situations that the police know to be dangerous, and the officer typically initiates them. Research has demonstrated that situational and community-level factors are significantly related to the likelihood that an officer will sustain injury from an assault. More and better training is needed about managing dangerous situations, particularly related to the use of OC spray and CEDs. Policy review, management's insistence on adhering to departmental safety and response guidelines, and community education can all play roles in reducing danger to the police.

Critical Thinking Questions

1. Briefly define the concept of stress; differentiate between the two forms of stress that may affect police behavior.

2. Describe the two major categories of police occupational stressors and provide several examples of each.

3. Discuss at least three types of new sources of stress for today's police. Will police work become more or less stressful in the future? Discuss.

4. What is posttraumatic stress disorder and how does it apply to the police?

5. Describe the social supports for the study of stress and their implications for policing.

6. Discuss the common methods officers use to cope with occupational stress (e.g., alcohol abuse, drug abuse, suicide). Are officers more prone to these coping mechanisms than other occupations? What can police organizations do about this?

7. Discuss at least three aspects of police stress that influence the quality of family life. What are some programs that attempt to deal with such problems?

8. Is policing a dangerous occupation? What factors are commonly associated with officer assaults and injuries? Discuss why this is the case.

References

Alexander, D. A., and Walker, L. G. 1996. "The Perceived Impact of Police Work on Police Officers' Spouses and Families." *Stress Medicine* 12: 239–246.

Amnesty International. 2008. "'Less than Lethal'? The Use of Stun Weapons in US Law Enforcement." London: Amnesty International Publications.

Anderson, G. S., Litzenberger, R., and Plecas, D. 2002. "Physical Evidence of Police Officer Stress." *Policing: An International Journal of Police Strategies and Management* 25: 399–420.

Bain, L. J. 1988. "Night Beat." *Psychology Today* June: 10–11.

Barker, J. C. 1999. *Danger, Duty and Disillusion: The Worldview of Los Angeles Police Officers.* Prospect Heights, IL: Waveland.

Bower, D. L., and Pettit, W. G. 2001. "Albuquerque Police Department's Crisis Intervention Team: A Report Card." *FBI Law Enforcement Bulletin* 70: 1–6.

Brandl, S. G., and Stroshine, M. S. 2003. "Toward an Understanding of the Physical Hazards of Police Work." *Police Quarterly,* 6: 172–191.

Charles, L. E., Burchfeil, C. M., Fekedulegn, D., Vila, B., Hartleyu, R. A., Slaven, J., Mnatsakanova, A., and Violanti, J. M. 2007. "Shift Work and Sleep: The Buffalo Police Health Study." *Policing: An International Journal of Police Strategies and Management* 30: 215–227.

Compton, M. R., Esterberg, M. L., McGee, R., Kotwicki, R. J., and Oliva, J. R. 2006. "Crisis Intervention Team Training: Changes in Knowledge, Attitudes and Stigma Related to Schizophrenia." *Psychiatric Services* 57: 1199–1202.

"Congress OK's $75M Body-Armor Fund." 1998. *Law Enforcement Journal* May 15: 1.

Cordner, G. 2006. *People with Mental Illness: Problem-Oriented Guides for Police, Problem-Specific Guides Series No. 40.* Washington, DC: U.S. Department of Justice.

Crank, J. P., and Caldero, M. 1991. "The Production of Occupational Stress in Medium-Sized Police Agencies: A Survey of Line Officers in Eight Municipal Departments." *Journal of Criminal Justice* 19: 339–349.

Cronin, T. J. 1982. "Police Suicides: A Comprehensive Study of the Chicago Police Department." Master's Thesis, Lewis University.

Cullen, F. T., Lemming, T., Link, B. G., and Wozniak, J. F. 1985. "The Impact of Social Supports on Police Stress." *Criminology* 23: 503–522.

Davey, J. D., Obst, P. L., and Sheehan, M. C. 2000. "Developing a Profile of Alcohol Consumption Patterns of Police Officers in a Large Scale Sample of an Australian Police Service." *European Addiction Studies.* 6: 205–212.

Davidson, M. J., and Veno, A. 1978. "Police Stress: A Multicultural, Interdisciplinary Review and Perspective, Part I." *Abstracts on Police Science* July/August: 190–191.

Dishlacoff, L. 1976. "The Drinking Cop." *Police Chief* 43: 34–36, 39.

Dowler, K. 2005. "Job Satisfaction, Burnout, and Perception of Unfair Treatment: The Relationship Between Race and Police Work." *Police Quarterly,* 8(4): 476–489.

"Drug Use by Cops Seen as Growing Problem." 1985. *Law Enforcement News,* September 1, 12.

Eisenberg, T. 1975. "Job Stress and the Police Officer: Identifying Stress Reduction Techniques," In W. H. Kroes and J. J. Hurrell, Jr. (eds.), *Job Stress and the Police Officer: Identifying Stress Reduction Techniques,* pp. 26–34. Washington, DC: Department of Health, Education, and Welfare.

Engel, R. S., and Silver, E. 2001. "Policing Mentally Disordered Suspects: A Reexamination of the Criminalization Hypothesis." *Criminology* 39: 225–252.

Farmer, R. E. 1998. "Law Enforcement Line-of-Duty Deaths and Assaults." *Law Enforcement Bulletin.* September: 5.

———. 1990. "Clinical and Managerial Implications of Stress Research on the Police." *Journal of Police Science and Administration* 17: 205–218.

———. 2006. *Law Enforcement Officers Killed and Assaulted, 2005.* Washington, DC: Department of Justice.

Federal Bureau of Investigation. 1992. *Killed in the Line of Duty: A Study of Selected Felonious Killings of Law Enforcement Officers.* Washington, DC: Department of Justice.

———. 1997. *Law Enforcement Officers Killed and Assaulted, 1996.* Washington, DC: Department of Justice.

———. 2004. *Law Enforcement Officers Killed and Assaulted, 2003.* Washington, DC: Department of Justice.

———. 2009. *Law Enforcement Officers Killed and Assaulted, 2008.* Washington, DC: Department of Justice.

Finn, P., and Sullivan, M. 1987. "Police Handling of the Mentally Ill: Sharing Responsibility With the Mental Health System." *Journal of Criminal Justice* 17: 1–14.

———. 1988. "Law Enforcement and the Social Service System: Handling the Mental Ill." *Research in Action,* Washington, DC: National Institute of Justice.

Finn, P., and Tomz, J. E. 1997. *Developing a Law Enforcement Stress Program for Officers and Their Families.* Washington, DC: National Institute of Justice.

French, J. R. P. 1975. "A Comparative Look at Stress and Strain in Policemen." In W. H. Kroes and J. J. Hurrell (eds.), *Job Stress and the Police Officer,* pp. 60–72. Washington, DC: Department of Health, Education, and Welfare.

Gaska, C. W. 1982. "The Rate of Suicide, Potential for Suicide, and Recommendations for Prevention Among Retired Police Officers." Ph.D. dissertation, Wayne State University.

General Accountability Office. 2005. *Taser Weapons: Use of Tasers by Selected Law Enforcement Agencies.* Washington, DC.

Greenstone, J. L., Dunn, J. M., and Leviton, S. C. 1995. "Police Peer Counseling and Crisis Intervention Services Into the 21st Century." *Crisis Intervention and Time-Limited Treatment* 2: 167–187.

Grencik, J. M. 1975. "Toward an Understanding of Stress." In W. H. Kroes and J. J. Hurrell, Jr. (eds.), *Job Stress and the Police Officer: Identifying Stress Reduction Techniques,* pp. 163–181. Washington, DC: Department of Health, Education, and Welfare.

Guralnick, L. 1963. "Mortality by Occupation and Cause of Death Among Men 20–64 Years of Age." *Vital Statistics Special Reports* 53. Bethesda, MD: Department of Health, Education, and Welfare.

Haarr, R. N., and Morash, M. 1999. "Gender, Race, and Strategies of Coping With Occupational Stress in Policing." *Justice Quarterly* 16: 303–336.

Hart, P. M., Wearing, A. J., and Headey, B. 1995. "Police Stress and Well-Being: Integrating Personality, Coping and Daily Work Experience." *Journal of Occupational and Organizational Psychology* 68: 133–156.

He, N., Zhao, J., and Archbold, C. A. 2002. "Gender and Police Stress: The Convergent and Divergent Impact of Work Environment, Work–Family Conflict, and Stress Coping Mechanisms of Female and Male Police Officers." *Policing: An International Journal of Police Strategies and Management* 25: 687–708.

He, N., Zhao, J., and Ren, L. 2005. "Do Race and Gender Matter in Police Stress? A Preliminary Assessment of the Interactive Effects." *Journal of Criminal Justice* 33: 535–547.

Hill. K. Q., and Clawson, M. 1988. "The Health Hazards of 'Street Level' Bureaucracy: Morality Among the Police." *Journal of Police Science and Administration* 16: 243–248.

Humphrey, K. R., Decker, K. P., Goldberg, L., Pope, H. G., Gutman, J., and Green, G. 2008. "Anabolic Steroid Use and Abuse by Police Officers: Policy and Prevention." *The Police Chief* 75: 66–70, 72, 74.

Hurrell, J. J., Jr., and Kroes W. H. 1975. "Stress Awareness," In W. H. Kroes and J. J. Hurrell, Jr. (eds.), *Job Stress and the Police Officer: Identifying Stress Reduction Techniques,* pp. 234–246. Washington, DC: Department of Health, Education, and Welfare.

Ivanoff, A. 1994. *The New York City Police Suicide Training Project.* New York: Police Foundation.

Kaminski, R. J., Jefferis, E., and Gu, J. 2003. "Community Correlates of Serious Assaults on Police" *Police Quarterly* 6: 119–149.

Kaminski, R. J., and Sorensen, D. W. M. 1995. "A Multivariate Analysis of Individual, Situational and Environmental Factors Associated with Police Assault Injuries." *American Journal of Police* 14: 3–48.

Kappeler, V. E., and Potter, G. W. 2005. T*he Mythology of Crime and Criminal Justice*, 4th ed. Long Grove, IL: Waveland.

Kavanagh, J. 1997. "The Occurrence of Resisting Arrest in Arrest Encounters: A Study of Police–Citizen Violence." *Criminal Justice Review* 22: 16–33.

Kellogg, T., and Harrison, M. 1991. "Post-traumatic Stress Plays a Part in Police Brutality." *Law Enforcement News* April 30: 12, 16.

Konstantin, D. N. 1984. "Homicides of American Law Enforcement Officers, 1978–1980." *Justice Quarterly* 1: 29–45.

Kraska, P. B., and Kappeler, V. W. 1988. "Police On-Duty Drug Use: A Theoretical and Descriptive Examination." *American Journal of Police* 7: 1–28.

Kroes, W. H., Margolis, B. L., and Hurell, J. L, Jr. 1974. "Job Stress in Policemen." *Journal of Police Science and Administration* 2: 145–155.

Kureczka, A. W. 1996. "Critical Incident Stress in Law Enforcement." *FBI Law Enforcement Bulletin* 65: 10–16.

LaGrange, T. 2000. "Distinguishing Between the Criminal and the 'Crazy': Decisions to Arrest in Police Encounters with Mentally Disordered." Paper presented at the annual meeting of the American Society of Criminology, San Francisco, CA.

Lambuth, L. 1984. "An Employee Assistance Program That Works." *Police Chief* 51: 36–38.

Law Enforcement News. 2000. "The Strong Arm of the Law: Steroid-Using Cops—A Problem for Policing?" 26(527): 1, 6.

Lichtenberg, I. D., and Smith, A. 2001. "How Dangerous Are Routine Police–Citizen Traffic Stops? A Research Note." *Journal of Criminal Justice* 29: 419–428.

Loo, R. 1986. "Suicide Among Police in a Federal Force." *Suicide and Life-Threatening Behavior* 16: 379–388.

———. 2005. "A Psychosocial Process Model of Police Suicide." In H. Copes (ed.) *Policing and Stress*, pp 103–125. Upper Saddle River, NJ: Pearson Prentice Hall.

Lord, V. B. 1996. "An Impact of Community Policing: Reported Stressors, Social Support, and Strain Among Police Officers in a Changing Police Department." *Journal of Criminal Justice* 24: 503–522.

———. 2005. "The Stress of Change: The Impact of Changing a Traditional Police Department to a Community-Oriented, Problem-Solving Department." In H. Copes (ed.) *Policing and Stress*, pp 55–72. Upper Saddle River, NJ: Pearson Prentice Hall.

Lord, V. B., Gray, D. O., and Pond, S. B. 1991. "The Police Stress Inventory: Does it Measure Stress?" *Journal of Criminal Justice* 19: 139–150.

MacDonald, J. M., Kaminski, R. J., and Smith, M. R. 2009. "The Effect of Less-Lethal Weapons on Injuries in Police Use-of-Force Events." *American Journal of Public Health* 99: 2268–2274.

Martin, C. A., McKean, H. E., and Veltkamp, L. J. 1986. "Post-Traumatic Stress Disorder in Police and Working with Victims: A Pilot Study." *Journal of Police Science and Administration* 14: 98–101.

Maynard, P. E., and Maynard, N. W. 1980. "Preventing Police Stress Through Couples Communication Training." *Police Chief* 47: 30, 31, 66.

McCoy, S. P., and Aamodt, M. G. 2010. "A Comparison of Law Enforcement Divorce Rates With Those of Other Occupations." *Journal of Police and Criminal Psychology* 25" 1–16.

McEwen, J. T. 1995. "National Assessment Program: 1994 Survey Results." *Research in Action*. Washington, DC: National Institute of Justice.

McLeod, R. G. 1990. "Who Has California's Deadliest Jobs?" *San Francisco Chronicle,* January 22.

Miller, L. 2007. "Police Families: Stresses, Syndromes, and Solutions." *The American Journal of Family Therapy* 35: 21–40.

Morash, M., and Haarr, R. 1995. "Gender, Workplace Problems, and Stress in Policing." *Justice Quarterly* 12: 113–140.

Morash, M., Kwak, D-H., and Haarr, R. 2006. "Gender Differences in the Predictors of Police Stress." *Policing: An International Journal of Police Strategies and Management* 29: 541–563.

National Law Enforcement Officers Memorial Fund. 2009. *Law Enforcement Officers Deaths: Preliminary 2009*. Washington, DC: NLEOMF.

Novak, K. J., and Engel, R. S. 2005. "Disentangling the Influence of Suspects' Demeanor and Mental Disorder on Arrest." *Policing: An International Journal of Police Strategies and Management* 28(3): 493–512.

O'Neill, J. L., and Cushing, M. A. 1991. *The Impact of Shift Work on Police Officers*. Washington, DC: Police Executive Research Forum.

Patterson, G. T. 2003. "Examining the Effects of Coping and Social Support on Work and Life Stress Among Police Officers." *Journal of Criminal Justice* 31: 215–226.

Pendleton, M., Stotland, E., Spiers, P., and Kirsch, E. 1989. "Stress and Strain Among Police, Firefighters, and Government Workers: A Comparative Analysis." *Criminal Justice and Behavior* 16: 196–210.

Piquero, N. L. 2005. "Understanding Police Stress and Coping Resources Across Gender: A Look Toward General Strain Theory." In H. Copes (ed.) *Policing and Stress*, pp 126–139. Upper Saddle River, NJ: Pearson Prentice Hall.

Reuland, M., Draper, L., and Norton, B. 2010. *Improving Responses to People With Mental Illness: Tailoring Law Enforcement Initiatives to Individual Jurisdictions*. New York: Council of State Governments Justice Center.

Richard, W., and Fell, R. 1975. "Health Factors in Police Job Stress." In W. W. Kroes and J. J. Hurrell (eds.), *Job Stress and the Police Officer*, pp. 73–84. Washington, DC: U.S. Government Printing Office.

Richmond, R. L., Wodak, A., Kehoe, L., and Heather, N. 1998. "How Healthy Are the Police? A Survey of Life-Style Factors." *Addiction* 93: 1729–1737.

Robinson, H. M., Sigman, M. R., and Wilson, J. R. 1997. "Duty-Related Stressors and PTSD Symptoms in Suburban Police Officers." *Psychological Reports* 81: 835–845.

Roberg, R. R., Kuykendall, J., and Novak, K. 2002. *Police Management,* 3rd ed. Los Angeles: Roxbury Publishing Co.

Roberg, R. R., Hayhurst, D. L., and Allen, H. E. 1988. "Job Burnout in Law Enforcement Dispatchers: A Comparative Analysis." *Journal of Criminal Justice* 16: 385–393.

Roberts, M. D. 1975. "Job Stress in Law Enforcement: A Treatment and Prevention Program." In W. H. Kroes and J. J. Hurrell, Jr. (eds.), *Job Stress and the Police Officer: Identifying Stress Reduction Techniques.* pp. 226–233. Washington, DC: Department of Health, Education, and Welfare.

Roberts, N. A., and Levenson, R. W. 2001. "The Remains of the Workday: Impact of Job Stress and Exhaustion on Marital Interaction in Police Couples," *Journal of Marriage and Family* 63: 1052–1067.

Robinson, H. M., Sigman, M. R., and Wilson, J. R. 1997. "Duty-Related Stressors and PTSD Symptoms in Suburban Police Officers." *Psychological Reports* 81: 835–845.

Selye, H. 1974. *Stress Without Distress.* Philadelphia: Lippincott.

Sherman, L. W., DeRiso, D., Gaines, D., Rogan, D., and Cohn, E. 1989. *Police Murdered in Drug-Related Situations, 1972–1988.* Washington, DC: Crime Control Institute.

Skeem, J., and Bibeau, L. 2008. "How Does Violence Potential Relate to Crisis Intervention Team Responses to Emergencies?" *Psychiatric Services* 59: 201–204.

Smith, M. R., Kaminski, R. J., Rojek, J., Alpert, G. P., and Mathis, J. 2007. "The Impact of Conducted Energy Devices and Other Types of Force and Resistance on Officer and Suspect Injuries." *Policing: An International Journal of Police Strategies and Management* 30: 423–446.

Stack, S., and Kelley, T. 1999. "Police Suicide." In D. J. Kenney and R. P. McNamara (eds.), *Police and Policing: Contemporary Issues,* 2nd ed., pp. 94–107. Westport, CT: Praeger.

Stephens, C., and Miller, I. 1998. "Traumatic Experiences and Post-Traumatic Stress Disorder in the New Zealand Police." *Policing: An International Journal of Police Strategies and Management* 21: 178–191.

Storch, J. E., and Panzarella, R. 1996. "Police Stress: State–Trait Anxiety in Relation to Occupational and Personal Stressors." *Journal of Criminal Justice* 24: 99–107.

Stratton, J. G. 1976. "The Law Enforcement Family: Programs for Spouses." *Law Enforcement Bulletin* March: 16–22.

Swanson, C., Gaines, L., and Gore, B. 1991. "Abuse of Anabolic Steroids. " *FBI Law Enforcement Bulletin* August: 19–23.

Swatt, M. L., Gibson, C. L., and Piquero, N. L. 2007. "Exploritng the Utility of General Strain Theory in Explaining Problematic Alcohol Consumption by Police Officers." *Journal of Criminal Justice* 35: 596–611.

Teplin, L. A. 1984. "Criminalizing Mental Disorder: The Comparative Arrest Rates of the Mentally Ill." *American Psychologist* 39: 794–803.

Territo, L., and Vetter, H. J. (eds.) 1981. *Stress and Police Personnel.* Boston: Allyn & Bacon.

Terry, W. C. 1981. "Police Stress: The Empirical Evidence." *Police Science and Administration* 9: 61–75.

———. 1985. "Police Stress as a Professional Self-Image." *Journal of Criminal Justice* 13: 501–512.

Uchida, C. D., and King, W. R. 2002. "Police Employee Data: Elements and Validity." *Justice Research and Policy* 4: 1–9.

Vaughn, J. 1991. "Critical Incidents for Law Enforcement Officers." In J. Reese, J. Horn, and C. Dunning (eds.), *Critical Incidents in Policing,* p. 148. Washington, DC: U.S. Government Printing Office.

Vickers, B. 2000. "Memphis, Tennessee, Police Department's Crisis Intervention Team." *Bulletin From the Field.* Washington, DC: Department of Justice, Office of Justice Programs.

Violanti, J. M. 1995. "The Mystery Within: Understanding Police Suicide." *FBI Law Enforcement Bulletin* 64: 19–23.

———. 1996. "Police Suicide: An Overview." *Police Studies* 19: 77–89.

———. 1997. "Suicide and the Police Role: A Psychosocial Model." *Policing: An International Journal of Police Strategies & Management* 20: 698–715.

———. 2005. "Dying for the Job: Psychological Stress, Disease, and Mortality in Police Work." In H. Copes (ed.) *Policing and Stress*, pp 87–102. Upper Saddle River, NJ: Pearson Prentice Hall.

Violanti, J. M., and Aron, F. 1995. "Police Stressors: Variations in Perception Among Police Personnel." *Journal of Criminal Justice* 23: 287–294.

Violanti, J. M., and Vena, J. E. 1995. "Epidemiology of Police Suicide." *Research in Progress*, NIMH Grant MH47091–02.

Violanti, J. M., Vena, J. E., and Marshall, J. R. 1986. "Disease Risk and Mortality Among Police Officers." *Journal of Police Science and Administration* 14: 17–23.

Wagner, M., and Brzeczek, R. J. 1983. "Alcoholism and Suicide: A Fatal Connection." *FBI Law Enforcement Bulletin* 52: 8–15.

Wallace, P. A., Roberg, R. R., and Allen, H. E. 1985. "Job Burnout Among Narcotics Investigators: An Exploratory Study." *Journal of Criminal Justice* 13: 549–559.

Waters, J., Irons, N., and Finkle, E. 1982. "The Police Stress Inventory: A Comparison of Events Affecting Officers and Supervisors in Rural and Urban Areas." *Police Stress* 5: 18–25.

Wellborn, J. 1999. "Responding to Individuals with Mental Illness." *FBI Law Enforcement Bulletin* 68: 6–8.

"What's Killing America's Cops? Mostly Themselves, According to New Study." 1996. *Law Enforcement News* November 15: 1.

CHAPTER 14

Higher Education

CHAPTER OUTLINE

- The Development of Higher Education Programs for Police
    - Federal Programs and Support for Higher Education
    - Quality of Higher Education Programs
    - Higher Education Requirements for Police
    - Police Chiefs, Promotion, and Higher Education
- The Impact of Higher Education on Policing
    - Higher Education and Attitudes
    - Higher Education and Performance
    - Use of Force and Liability
    - Leadership and Promotion
    - Other Significant Findings
    - Summary of Higher Education Findings and Directions for Future Research
    - Higher Education and Job Satisfaction
    - Higher Education, Community Policing, and Terrorism
    - Police Executives' Views on Higher Education
    - Chief's Scholar Program

CHAPTER OUTLINE   (continued)

- Validating Higher Education for Police
    Higher Education as a Bona Fide Occupational Qualification
    Higher Education and Discrimination
- Higher Education Incentive Programs
- Higher Education Requirements and Policy Implications
- Summary
- Critical Thinking Questions
- References

KEY TERMS

- *Arnold v. Ballard*
- Bona fide occupational qualification (BFOQ)
- *Castro v. Beecher*
- *Chief's Scholar Program*
- Crime Control Act
- *Davis v. City of Dallas*
- *Griggs v. Duke Power Co.*
- Law Enforcement Assistance Administration (LEAA)
- Law Enforcement Education Program (LEEP)
- National Advisory Commission on Higher Education for Police
- National Advisory Commission on Criminal Justice Standards and Goals
- Omnibus Crime Control and Safe Streets Act
- Police Executive Research Forum (PERF)
- President's Commission on Law Enforcement and Administration of Justice
- *The Challenge of Crime in a Free Society*

THERE HAS BEEN A long-standing debate over whether a college education for police officers is necessary or even desirable. In present-day society, with the ever-expanding complexity of the police role and the transition toward community policing, this question is more significant than ever. Interestingly, the initial requirement of a high school diploma to enter the field of policing occurred at a time when most of the nation's population did not finish high school. Thus, a requirement of a high school education actually identified individuals with an above-average level of education. Statistics from the Department of Health, Education and Welfare, for instance, indicates that immediately after World War II, less than half of the 17-year-old population had earned a high school diploma in 1946 (National Advisory Commission 1973). Although it is difficult to determine precisely when the high school diploma, or its equivalent, the general education diploma, became a standard requirement for a majority of the country's police departments, it was a well-established trend after World War II.

Today, the high school diploma has essentially been replaced by a college degree as the above-average level of educational attainment in the United States. In fact, 24 percent of Americans age 25 and over have a 4-year college degree or higher (U.S. Census Bureau 2000). Consequently, those police departments that have not raised their educational requirements for entry have failed to keep pace with their tradition of employing people with an above-average education. Additionally, police forces at different governmental levels have traditionally required different levels of education for employment. For example, most federal agencies have required at least a college degree for quite some time, but only a minimal number of city and state police and sheriff's departments require one. Many others require a minimum 2-year degree or its equivalent in college units. Baro and Burlingame (1999) noted that an increasing number of officers are completing college units even without a formal degree requirement. However, they argue that this could represent "degree inflation" because an associates' degree (2-year) today may only be the equivalent of a high school diploma in the 1960s (Baro and Burlingame 1999, 60).

The debate over higher education, however, is much more complicated than determining whether police requirements are above or below national population norms. The development of higher education programs and the ensuing debate is the focus of this chapter.

The Development of Higher Education Programs for Police

The debate over higher educational requirements for police officers is not new. Starting in the early 1900s, Berkeley, California, Police Chief August Vollmer called for the recruitment of officers who were not only trained in the "technology of policing," but also understood "the prevention of crime or confrontation through [their] appreciation of the psychology and sociology of crime" (Carte 1973, 275). Contrary to traditional practices of the time, Vollmer felt that such skills must not only be learned through on-the-job experience, but also first be taught in the classroom.

Calling for the "very best manhood in the nation" to join the police profession (Carte 1973, 277), Vollmer campaigned strongly for police courses in higher education and the need for college-educated personnel throughout the police ranks. He was primarily responsible, along with the faculty, for the establishment of the first police school in higher education at the University of California, Berkeley, which he joined part time in 1916 and full-time in 1932 after his retirement from the Berkeley Police Department (Caiden 1977). For his efforts to reform and professionalize the police, Vollmer eventually gained a reputation as the father of modern American policing.

Following Berkeley's lead, other programs emphasizing police education were developed at major universities. Between the early 1920s and mid-1930s, a number of schools established programs of study for criminal justice professionals, primarily the police. Although the majority of these programs lasted only a few years, several continue to this day, including those at the University of Chicago, Indiana University, Michigan State University, San José State University, and Wichita State University.

These early programs laid the foundation for higher education in criminal justice, which was typically labeled police science, police administration, or law enforcement. Such curricula were developed in selected 4-year institutions and many community colleges through the mid-1960s. The focus of these programs was usually on administration and supervision issues in policing, as well as on the practical applications of the "science" of policing, including such topics as patrol procedures, traffic enforcement, criminalistics, criminal investigation, and report writing. It is interesting to note that during these years, most police departments had no formalized training programs; many of these programs were designed to fill this "training gap."

Two significant and interrelated events took place in the mid to late 1960s that required the country to take a hard look at the level of professionalism and quality of U.S. police forces as well as the rest of the criminal justice system. These two events played a major role in ushering in the "golden age" of higher education for the police (Pope 1987).

The first event was the enormous increase in the crime rate that began in the early 1960s, leveled off in the early 1980s, and started moving upward again in the mid-1980s. In 1968, for the first time in 3 decades of opinion sampling, the Gallup poll found crime ranked as the most serious national issue (ahead of civil rights, the cost of living, and poverty), as well as the most important local issue (ahead of schools, transportation, and taxes). Furthermore, Gallup found that 3 persons in 10, and 4 in 10 for both women and residents of larger cities, admitted that they were afraid to go out alone at night in their own neighborhoods (Saunders 1970).

The second event was the inner-city riots, which occurred in the mid-1960s. The burning, looting, and general turmoil in many of the nation's major cities was the catalyst that spurred the public and the government into action. At this juncture, the "war on crime" began (Pope 1987).

"Crime in the streets" thus became a national issue in the 1964 presidential campaign. The following year, Congress passed the Law Enforcement Assistance Act of 1965, a modest grant program that expressed a national concern about the adequacy of local police departments. Two years later, the **President's Commission on Law Enforcement and Administration of Justice** issued a comprehensive report titled *The Challenge of Crime in a Free Society* (1967) documenting the serious impact of crime on U.S. society. Although the report issued over 200 specific proposals for action involving all levels of government and society, a majority of the recommendations—either directly or indirectly—dealt with the police as the "front line" of the criminal justice system.

Serious and continuing problems between the police and the community, especially minority group members, were a major concern of the commission. It was thought that without respect for the police or community participation in crime prevention (both major foundations of community policing), there could be little impact on the crime rate. Because much of this problem was associated with the low quality of police personnel, many of the commission's recommendations dealt with the need for "widespread improvement in the strength and caliber of police manpower ... for achieving more effective and fairer law enforcement" (President's Commission 1967, 294). The commission thought that one of the most important ways to upgrade the quality of police personnel would be through higher education. Consequently, one of their most significant, and controversial, recommendations was that the "ultimate aim of *all* police departments should be that *all* personnel with general enforcement powers have baccalaureate degrees" (109, emphasis added). Perhaps just as important, the commission further recommended that police departments should "take *immediate* steps to establish a minimum requirement of a baccalaureate degree for all supervisory and executive level positions" (110, emphasis added).

Federal Programs and Support for Higher Education

Shortly thereafter, Congress passed the *Omnibus Crime Control and Safe Streets Act* of 1968, which created the **Law Enforcement Assistance Administration (LEAA)**. Through LEAA, the federal government poured literally billions of dollars into the criminal justice system—focusing on the police—in an attempt to improve their effectiveness and reduce crime. This money was initially earmarked for the research and development of "innovative" programs in policing, but was instead used primarily to purchase additional hardware (e.g., cars and communications equipment, weapons) that departments could not afford on their own and secondarily for training. The result was that most police departments, rather than introducing new programs, instead operated from a perspective of "more of the same."

Under LEAA an educational-incentive program, known as the **Law Enforcement Education Program (LEEP),** was established in the late 1960s. It provided financial assistance to police personnel, as well as to others who wished to enter police service, to pursue a college education. The impact of LEEP on the growth of law enforcement programs in both 2-year and 4-year schools was nothing short of phenomenal. For example, it has been reported that in 1954 there were a total of 22 such programs in the country (Deutsch 1955), but by 1975 the numbers had increased to more than 700 in community colleges and nearly 400 in 4-year schools (Korbetz 1975).

In 1973, a highly influential *Report on Police* (1973) by the **National Advisory Commission on Criminal Justice Standards and Goals** further advanced the higher-education recommendations made by the president's commission. The report included a *graduated timetable* that would require all police officers, at the time of initial employment, to have completed at least *2 years of education* (60 semester units) at an accredited college or university *by 1975, 3 years* (90 semester units) by *1978*, and a *baccalaureate degree* by *1982*. In the same year, the American Bar Association issued another influential report, *Standards Relating to the Urban Police Function,* which recognized the demanding and complex nature of the police role in a democracy. The American Bar Association further elaborated on the need for advanced education to meet the professional skills required by such a role:

> Police agencies need personnel in their ranks who have the characteristics which a college education seeks to foster: intellectual curiosity, analytical ability, articulateness, and a capacity to relate the events of the day to the social, political, and historical context in which they occur. (212)

The *Violent Crime Control and Law Enforcement Act of 1994,* known as the **Crime Control Act,** became the most comprehensive federal crime legislation since the Omnibus Crime Control and Safe Streets Act of 1968. The Crime Control Act allocates approximately $30 billion to various criminal justice agencies, with almost $11 billion for state and local law enforcement, including almost $9 billion to hire an additional 100,000 police officers under the COPS program (U.S. Department of Justice 1994). These new officers were to be used by local departments to help further their community policing efforts. In addition, the legislation provides for federal funds to be used to establish a police corps and a scholarship and recruitment program for local police departments. This is the largest federal investment in education for law enforcement personnel since the creation of the Law Enforcement Education Program ("Dissecting the Crime Bill" 1994).

Quality of Higher Education Programs

The meteoric, unregulated rise of programs in police science or law enforcement led to serious questions about their academic rigor and viability. The increase coincided with the infusion of federal moneys distributed through LEEP. To capture their fair share of the federal funds, many schools hurriedly spliced together programs to study the police. Because of a lack of qualified faculty, many part-time instructors, frequently selected from the local police or sheriff's departments, were employed to teach classes. Because instructors generally lacked proper academic qualifications, little attempt was made to introduce current research or critical analysis of contemporary issues and practices. Instead, instructors focused on training, using readily available models from their own experience. They concentrated on their department's operating policies and procedures and offered "war stories" from their street experiences as examples of the "way things are." The students taking these courses were overwhelmingly in-service, that is, full-time police or criminal justice employees returning to school through the provision of LEEP funds. Because they are narrowly focused, training-oriented programs are not traditionally found in a university setting, so it is not surprising that they encountered stiff opposition from the well-established, academic disciplines. For example, the picture of police science majors wearing uniforms enhances the image of a training environment rather than an academic one (Fig. 14.1).

In the late 1960s and early 1970s, many programs began to broaden their focus, emphasizing criminal-justice–related topics rather than technical police training. The titles of the programs began to change to reflect this broader approach; common new titles were Departments of Criminal Justice, Criminology, or Administration of Justice. Reflecting on these changes, Pope comments,

> Curriculums became much less practice oriented (at least in the four-year institutions) and more academically based. Some criminal justice programs even took a more critical stance toward the criminal justice system, adding courses based on a radical perspective. Many programs eliminated courses on patrol, traffic and the like, or at least expanded offerings to include race, gender, victims and related issues. It was a period when criminal justice attempted to gain academic respectability and institutional support. *(1987, 4)*

Following a decade of tremendous growth, accompanied by severe criticism of police programs in higher education, the Police Foundation put together a commission of noted educators, police administrators, and public officials to evaluate the quality of these programs. Known as the **National Advisory Commission on Higher Education for Police Officers,** the commission spent 2 years conducting a national survey and documenting the problems of police education (Sherman and the National Advisory Commission 1978). The report was extremely critical of the state of the art of police education at the time. It

FIGURE 14.1 San José State University Police Science students collecting evidence in the early 1960s. Notice that the students wore uniforms.

recommended significant changes in virtually all phases of police higher education, including institutional, curriculum, and faculty. Among the more crucial recommendations, the commission proposed the following:

1. The majority of federal funds for police higher education should go to programs with broad curriculums and well-educated faculty rather than to narrow technical programs.

2. No college credit should be granted for attending police department training programs.

3. Community colleges should phase out their terminal 2-year degree programs in police education.

4. Colleges should employ primarily full-time police-education teaching staffs, seeking faculty members with Ph.D. degrees in arts and sciences.

5. Prior employment in criminal justice should be neither a requirement nor a handicap in faculty selection.

6. Government policies at all levels should encourage educating police officers before they begin their careers.

These recommendations struck at the heart of many police programs throughout the country and consequently were not well received by many. However, as discussed above, improvements had already begun.

The commission's call for eliminating terminal 2-year degree programs in police education further emphasized the importance it attached to a broad-based education, enhanced by a campus setting where "greater student interaction with diverse kinds of people" could take place (Sherman and National Advisory Commission 1978, 115). The changing nature of the criminal justice student was also significant because the commission recommended that police should be educated *prior* to employment; this argument attacked the very basis of the LEEP program, which provided an overwhelming amount of its funds to in-service personnel only. This recommendation started a serious debate on whether police departments should place more emphasis on "recruiting the educated" or on "educating the recruited." The commission thought that the "occupational perspective" of full-time police work "probably reduces the impact of college on students" (Sherman and National Advisory Commission 1978, 13).

As the LEEP program was eventually phased out, so too were many of the weaker police programs in higher education. The stronger programs continued to recruit Ph.D.s trained in criminal justice and other social sciences for their faculties, thus establishing a more scholarly approach toward teaching and research. The emphasis on a broader-based curriculum became firmly established, and the students became less vocationally and in-service oriented.

These changes in higher education in criminal justice, including faculty quality, student body makeup, and curricular content, have allowed the field to mature quite rapidly. However, there continue to be widespread differences with respect to academic rigor and course content across criminal justice programs. As such, many of these programs are still not widely accepted by traditional academic disciplines. To address this, some programs are attempting to become broader based and more theoretically oriented by expanding their curriculums beyond traditional criminal justice system issues. These departments may also change their titles to reflect this broader perspective, for example, to "Law, Society, and Justice" or "Justice Studies." In general, on college campuses where degree programs have become firmly established, program quality and student interest continue to increase.

Higher Education Requirements for Police

Advances in raising educational requirements for police have been slow and sporadic. Until the 1980s, in many police departments, an officer with a college degree was often viewed with contempt or resentment; it was not understood why anyone with a degree would want to enter policing. Indeed, a college degree requirement is still virtually nonexistent. A national study conducted by the BJS (Hickman and Reaves 2006) of approximately 3,000 state and local law enforcement agencies, serving communities of all sizes, indicates that only 1 percent of departments required a college degree for employment in 2003 (see Table 14.1).

Table 14.1 also indicates that in some jurisdictions the figure is considerably higher than 1 percent; for example, it is 5 percent for departments in cities serving more than 500,000 residents but fewer than 1,000,000. Only 1 percent of departments serving more than 1,000,000 residents require a 4-year degree. However, 18 percent of departments serving more than 1,000,000 residents do require some college, while 9 percent of all departments required a 2-year degree. For sheriffs' offices, the BJS survey (Hickman and Reaves, 2003) reports that 12 percent of offices serving more than 1,000,000 residents require some college and that 6 percent of all offices required a 2-year degree. Fewer than 1 percent require a degree.

The BJS survey (Hickman and Reaves 2006) further reported that the percentage of officers employed by a state or local department with some type of college requirement for new officers in 2003 was 33 percent, or about three times that of 1990 (10 percent). For sheriffs'

TABLE 14.1 Minimum Educational Requirement for New Officers in Local Police Departments by Size of Population Served, 2003

Population Served	PERCENTAGE OF AGENCIES REQUIRING A MINIMUM OF:				
	Total With Requirement	High school diploma	Some college[a]	2-Year college degree	4-Year college degree
All sizes	98	81	8	9	1
1,000,000 or more	98	72	18	7	1
500,000–999,999	99	72	13	9	5
250,000–499,999	99	84	8	4	3
100,000–249,999	98	81	13	3	2
50,000–99,999	100	76	17	6	1
25,000–49,999	99	77	10	11	1
10,000–24,999	99	82	7	9	1
2,500–9,999	99	83	7	9	—
Under 2,500	97	82	6	9	0

Note: Detail may not add to total because of rounding.
[a]Nondegree requirements.
—, less than 0.5%.

Source: M. J. Hickman, and B. A. Reaves, *Local Police Departments, 2003*. (Washington, DC, Bureau of Justice Statistics, 2006).

offices (Hickman and Reaves 2003), the percentage of officers with some type of college requirement also increased about three times, from 4 percent in 1990 to 13 percent in 2000. Additionally, from 1990 to 2000 the percentage of officers employed by a state or local department with a degree requirement increased from 3 to 9 percent; for sheriffs' offices, the percentage with a degree requirement increased from 3 to 5 percent. These trends are encouraging, but there is clearly room for improvement.

Even though the development of *formal* educational requirements has been slow, some research suggests that up to one third of officers in the field have a baccalaureate degree, most likely because of the increased number of colleges and universities offering criminal justice/criminology degrees. For instance, a national survey for the **Police Executive Research Forum (PERF)** in 2002 (Taylor et al. 2005) of 985 municipal, county, and state police found that approximately one third of officers nationwide had a college degree. Possibly of greater significance, however, is the PERF finding that only 0.5 percent (one half of 1 percent) of agencies required more than 2 years of post-secondary education. In addition, many agencies are reducing minimum educational requirements to increase applicant pools. As discussed in Chapter 7, because of a "cop crunch" in some areas, departments are not only reducing minimum educational requirements, but also substituting military experience for college credit. These findings suggest that while a modest trend of college graduates entering the field is developing, agencies themselves are doing little to increase the rate of college graduates in their ranks and, in some cases, are implementing policies that lessen the importance of a college degree. Such findings do not bode well for continued progress toward community policing or professionalism of the field. Note: PERF is a key term and must be in bold,

Police Chiefs, Promotion, and Higher Education

Just as the percentage of police officers holding college degrees has increased, so too has the number of police chiefs holding degrees. A study conducted by PERF ("Survey Says Big-City Chiefs Are Better-Educated Outsiders" 1998) of 358 city and county police chiefs in jurisdictions of 50,000 or more residents discovered that 87 percent held bachelor's degrees, almost 47 percent had master's degrees, and nearly 5 percent had law or doctoral degrees. This is an important finding because it suggests that with highly educated police chief executives as role models, higher education may now be emerging as an important part of the police culture. It is likely that these chiefs will begin to emphasize, and even require, higher education as part of their overall strategy to improve their departments, including promotional and hiring practices.

The continuing increase in college-educated officers suggests it will become increasingly difficult to earn a promotion without a college education in the years to come. One study, for example, of 51 sheriffs' departments and municipal police agencies in Colorado indicated that 22 percent had a written policy requiring a college degree for promotion (Nees 2003). The PERF survey by Carter and Sapp (1992) found a growing trend for departments to tie educational requirements to promotion. Some 20 percent of those responding indicated that they had either a formal or an informal policy requiring some level of advanced education for promotion; only 5 percent required a college degree. In addition, a notable number of police chiefs said they believed a graduate degree should be required for officers in command ranks.

The Arlington, Texas, Police Department is an example of what the relationship between promotion and higher education requirements may look like in the future. Arlington, with

TABLE 14.2 **Development of Higher Education Requirements in the Arlington, Texas, Police Department**

> **FOR ENTRY**
>
> - 1986: Bachelor's degree required for new recruits with no prior police experience. Associate's degree required for recruits with a minimum of 2 years experience.
>
> - 1999: Bachelor's degree required of all new recruits, regardless of experience.
>
> **FOR PROMOTION**
>
> - 1991: Bachelor's degree required for deputy chiefs.
>
> - 1995: Bachelor's degree required for lieutenants.
>
> - 1999: Master's degree required for assistant chiefs.
>
> - 2000: Bachelor's degree required of officers seeking promotion.

Source: T. Bowman, "Educate to Elevate," *Community Links*, August 2002, 11.

approximately 600 sworn and 180 non-sworn personnel, began phasing in college degree requirements in 1986; currently, about 75 percent of Arlington officers hold a bachelor's degree (Bowman 2002). Table 14.2 chronicles the development of the Arlington Police Department's emphasis on higher education.

As Table 14.2 indicates that, by 1999, all new recruits in Arlington were required to hold a bachelor's degree. With respect to promotion, by 1991 a bachelor's degree was required for deputy chiefs and in 1995 for lieutenants. A master's degree requirement was instituted in 1999 for assistant chiefs; and in 2000 at least a 4-year degree was required of officers seeking promotion. In Voices From the Field, Arlington's Police Chief Theron Bowman, who holds a Ph.D. degree, discusses the advantages he sees in requiring a college degree for all officers in his department.

The Impact of Higher Education on Policing

If college is going to become a requirement for policing, it will be necessary to indicate to the courts the relevance of such a requirement to on-the-job performance. Over the past 4 decades, research on higher education and police officer behavior has focused on two major areas: the relationship between education and police attitudes and the relationship between education and police performance. Although the quality of the research and the consistency of the findings have varied tremendously, it appears that some important general trends and conclusions can be drawn.

Higher Education and Attitudes

Much of the early research on higher education and the police centered on exploring the relationship between higher education and police attitudes, generally, by comparing levels of authoritarianism (i.e., open/closed belief system) of college-educated police to police with little or no college. While much of this early research was less sophisticated in design than contemporary research (especially with respect to small sample sizes and lack of relevant control variables), the findings were virtually unanimous in their support for higher education and police who were more open minded. For instance, it was shown that police with some college (Smith, Locke, and Walker 1968) and those with college degrees (Smith,

VOICES FROM THE FIELD

Theron Bowman
Chief of Police, Arlington, Texas, Police Department

Question: What impact on performance have you noticed since raising the department's educational standards to a college degree for new recruits and for promotion?

Answer: Since the Arlington Police Department raised educational standards to a college degree, we have noticed that officers more readily and more routinely make very good decisions in difficult situations independent of supervisory oversight and direction. Our officers have a broader understanding of society and an improved ability to communicate. The ability to connect with residents while understanding big-picture sociological problems leads to innovative solutions to crime-related problems. This allows supervisors the opportunity to focus on the department's mission rather than micro-managing officers' response to calls for service. The overall effect is enhanced problem-solving skills, which leads to a higher level of service to citizens.

As indicated by numerous studies since the 1970s, suggesting that college education enhances law enforcement, we also enjoy other benefits of higher education in our ranks. These benefits include fewer citizen complaints, greater acceptance of diversity, better behavioral and performance characteristics, and fewer disciplinary actions from serious crashes, use-of-force charges, or other heinous allegations.

A four-year degree is required of any officer seeking to promote; assistant chiefs must hold a master's degree. We have found that these requirements are viewed favorably by aspiring promotees. They enjoy the recognition of the importance of their education or, for those who were "grandfathered" in, look forward to embarking on an academic challenge that they expect will enhance their experience as supervisors. Our supervisors are expected to analyze trends using precise research methods and to submit requests for changes in policies or procedures with thorough documentation. Supervisors are expected to take a global approach in their perspective by involving or seeking input from other city departments (such as code enforcement, fire, and building inspectors), from state and federal agencies, and any other stakeholders they can identify.

It's important to note that the degree sought is not as crucial as the experience acquired in a college setting, both academic and social. We want officers who have proven that they can learn not only from books, but from the real-life experience obtained in a college environment. Achieving a college degree indicates a sense of determination, a desire to succeed, and a commitment to quality. The successful completion of the rigorous demands of a college experience is an indication of a candidate's and promoting officer's abilities and tenacity.

Dr. Theron Bowman has served as Chief of the Arlington Police Department since 1999. He earned his doctorate (Ph.D.) from the University of Texas at Arlington.

Locke, and Fenster 1970) were significantly less authoritarian than their non–college-educated colleagues. Guller (1972) and Roberg (1978) found that police officers who were college seniors showed lower levels of authoritarianism than officers who were college freshmen and of similar age and work experience; this indicated that the higher the level of education, the more flexible or open one's belief system may be. Dalley (1975) further discovered that authoritarian attitudes correspond with a lack of a college education and increased work experience; he suggested that a more liberal attitude is more conducive to the discretionary nature of law enforcement.

In addition, early research indicated that college-educated officers were thought to be more understanding of human behavior, to be more sensitive to community relations, and to hold a higher, more professional, service standard (Miller and Fry 1976; Regoli 1976). Further, some evidence indicated that college-educated officers were not only more aware of social and ethnic problems in their community, but also had a greater acceptance of minorities (Weiner 1976).

With respect to the study by Roberg (1978) cited above, the relationships among higher education, belief systems (attitudes), and on-the-job performance (supervisory ratings) of 118 patrol officers of the Lincoln, Nebraska, Police Department were analyzed. It should be noted that this was a highly educated department for the time period, at least partially attributable to their 2.5 percent pay increase for every 30 semester hours of college credit earned, culminating in a 10 percent increase for completing a college degree. Of the patrol officer study participants, 27 percent had a college degree; 24 percent were upper class (junior–senior standing), 43 percent were lower class (freshman–sophomore standing), and 13 percent had completed high school, but with no college credits.

The findings were consistent across all educational levels in that "officers with higher levels of education had more open belief systems (were less authoritarian) and performed in a more satisfactory manner on the job than those patrol officers with less education"; and, patrol officers with "college degrees had the most open belief systems and the highest levels of job performance, indicating that college-educated officers were better able to adapt to the complex nature of the police role" (Roberg 1978, 344). In addition, control variables included age, seniority, student status (preservice, in-service, and continuing), and college major (by highest percentage of participants: criminal justice, education, business, sociology, and psychology); no control variable had an impact on the results. The overall findings suggested that the university experience led to more open belief systems, which, in turn, led to improved performance. Furthermore, all college graduates in the study were from a major land-grant state university (University of Nebraska–Lincoln) that could be considered to have high-quality academic programs. This suggests that the overall quality of the educational experience is likely to be an important factor in determining the impact of higher education on police.

Higher Education and Performance

Because police departments are so diverse, it is difficult to define performance measures; that is, what is considered "good" or "poor" performance may vary from department to department. The criteria used to measure police performance, then, are not clear-cut and are often controversial. Accordingly, research findings on police performance will usually be more useful if they are based on a wide variety of performance indicators. The research described next, on the relationship between higher education and police performance, is based on a number of different indicators, or measures, of performance. Another issue today, as noted in Chapters 5 and 6, is that while many departments state they are "doing" community policing, they have not changed their performance evaluation criteria to reflect "non-traditional" activities required of community policing, such as citizen interactions and communication, organizing and running community meetings, problem solving, and the deescalation of force in solving conflicts, to name but a few. Thus, the exact type of activities in which college educated officers may excel frequently are not even measured or rewarded.

Researchers over nearly 4 decades have found college to have a positive effect on numerous individual performance indicators. For example, several researchers have found college-educated officers to have fewer citizen complaints filed against them (Cascio 1977; Cohen and Chaiken 1972; Wilson 1999; Lersch and Kunzman 2001; Johnston and Cheurprakobkit 2002). Additional research has indicated that college officers tend to have fewer disciplinary actions taken against them by the department, have lower rates of absenteeism, receive fewer injuries on the job, are involved in fewer traffic accidents (Cohen and Chaiken 1972; Cascio 1977), and are better decision makers (Worden 1990; Johnston and Cheurprakaobkit 2002).

In a study on decision making, LaGrange (2003) interviewed 156 officers in Cleveland, Ohio, and, based on their perceptions of events, found that college education played a significant role in handling difficult situations involving mentally ill persons. Officers with college degrees reported making psychiatric referrals much more frequently (over 80 percent) compared with those with some college or a high school education (about 50 percent), while making far fewer arrests (2 percent) compared with officers with some college (12 percent) or high school only (19 percent). The author concluded that college-educated officers are more likely to use a set of "interpretive tools" to deal more appropriately with complex situations.

It is worth noting that at least one study has found a relationship between higher education and experience with respect to performance. Smith and Aamodt (1997) in a study of 299 officers from 12 municipal departments in Virginia found that the benefits of a college education did not become apparent until the officers gained some experience. This finding suggests that the overall impact of higher education may not become readily apparent until a certain level of on-the-job experience has been attained, which, in a field as complex and demanding as policing, is not surprising.

Use of Force and Liability

Several contemporary studies on the use of force indicate that citizen encounters involving inexperienced and less educated officers resulted in increased levels of police force (Terrill and Mastrofski 2002). Another study conducted in the state of Florida ("For Florida Police" 2002) reported that police officers with just a high school diploma made up slightly more than 50 percent of all sworn law enforcement personnel between 1997 and 2002, yet they accounted for nearly 75 percent of all disciplinary actions issued by the state. A study on deadly force by McElvain and Kposowa (2008), using data from 186 officer-involved shootings in southern California, found that college educated officers were 41 percent less likely to discharge their firearms than were officers with a high school diploma or some college only.

A large observational study by Paoline and Terrill (2007) of over 3,300 police–citizen encounters in the Indianapolis and St. Petersburg police departments analyzed the influence of an officer's level of education and years of experience on use of force on suspects, as measured by both verbal and physical coercion. The data were collected as part of the Project on Policing Neighborhoods by means of both observations and interviews. Findings indicated that officers with some college education or a 4-year degree were significantly less likely to use verbal (coercive) force during encounters with suspects. However, only encounters involving officers with a 4-year degree resulted in significantly less use of physical force. It was further found that encounters involving officers with greater levels of on-the-job experience also resulted in less verbal and physical force. This research, when viewed in total, indicates that college-educated police officers engage the public differently than officers with lower levels of education and greater levels of experience further add to the deescalation of use of force. These findings add to the validity of the Smith and Aamodt (1997) study described above, which suggested that experience greatly adds to the value of higher education.

Another study by Rydberg and Terrill (2010) utilizing the same two Project on Policing Neighborhoods data sets of over 3,300 officers described above (Paoline and Terrill, 2007) analyzed the effect of higher education on arrests, searches, and use of force; force was defined as acts that threaten or inflict physical harm on citizens. Findings indicated no relation between higher education and the probability of an arrest or search occurring in a police–suspect encounter. However, officers with some college or a college degree were significantly less likely to use force in an encounter. With respect to explicating these findings, the authors suggest that unlike arrests and searches, the use of force is not inherently an end product to a police–citizen encounter, but may be used throughout an encounter to control the behavior of a suspect. Thus, there is great discretion in the application of force, and therefore it is likely that "as opposed to the decision to arrest or search, there is more room for officer education to have an impact on discretion with respect to force" (Rydberg and Terrill 2010, 111). This finding is critical in that it suggests that officers are performing their enforcement job without the need to resort to the use of force; this approach can go a long way toward improving citizen perceptions of procedural justice and police legitimacy (see Chapter 5 for further discussion).

There is also some evidence that college-educated officers become involved in cases of "individual liability significantly less frequently than non-college officers" (Carter and Sapp 1989, 163) and that college-educated officers tend to have a broader understanding of civil rights issues from legal, social, historical, and political perspectives (Carter and Sapp 1990). This appears to complement the research cited above indicating college-educated officers use lower levels of force during encounters with the public because high proportions of civil suits are based on excessive use of force. Because lawsuits claiming negligence on behalf of police departments are on the increase, as well as the amount of damages being awarded—often between $1 million and $2 million per case), this is another important area for future research. If a correlation between higher education and reduced liability of risk can be established, the availability and cost of risk insurance to police departments could be substantially affected.

Leadership and Promotion

Some interesting findings with respect to the future development of police departments indicate that college-educated officers are more likely to attain promotions (Cohen and Chaiken 1972; Roberg and Laramy 1980; Whetstone 2000; Polk and Armstrong 2001), and are more likely to take leadership roles in the department and to rate themselves higher on performance measures (Cohen and Chaiken 1972;; Krimmel 1996). Truxillo, Bennett, and Collins (1998) studied a cohort of 84 officers in a southern metropolitan police department over a 10-year period and found that college education was significantly correlated with promotions as well as with supervisory ratings of job knowledge. Kakar (1998) indicates that those officers with higher education rated themselves higher in leadership, responsibility, problem solving, and initiative-taking skills in comparison with less educated officers.

Other Significant Findings

Of course, not all of the research findings on higher education and policing are positive or provide significant findings. For example, in one large-scale reanalysis of survey findings in a 1977 study, Worden (1990) found that the effects of higher education on attitudes and performance were so small that, in general, they were not statistically significant. Interestingly, however, *he did discover* that supervisors found educated officers to be more reliable employees and better report writers, and citizens found them to be exceptional in their use of good judgment and problem-solving abilities.

As discussed in Chapter 7, one surprising finding with respect to higher education was White's (2008) study of police recruit academy performance. He found that the main predictor of what was termed superior academy performance (based on an average score on four written exams) was a reading test score at the 12th grade level or higher and higher education had no effect on the results. These findings are troubling, especially with respect to a college degree, since to get through college one must master—at least to some degree—test taking in a variety of formats; it is difficult to imagine that college graduates read at no higher level than those with a high school degree. A few pertinent questions come to mind with respect to this finding. It was found that designated "high" performers scored a 90 percent or better average on four exams; however, this included over 25 percent of the recruit class; which appears to be a rather large number of "high" performers. It would be interesting to know whether a college degree had any impact on the "very top" performers, which included only 3.9 percent of the recruit class. It would further be of interest, from a quality perspective, to know what type of institutions of higher learning the recruits attended as well as their academic majors.

Summary of Higher Education Findings and Directions for Future Research

While some of the research is not as methodologically strong as we might like and the findings are not always consistent (Skogan and Frydl 2004), the preponderance of available research supports, *in general,* that a *college degree* (not some college or a 2-year degree) has a significant impact on police attitudes and behavior. Essentially, the research reviewed indicates that a college education is related to less authoritarian beliefs, greater tolerance toward others, a greater acceptance of minority groups and understanding of civil rights issues, and more professional attitudes. Additionally, the research suggests that college-educated officers tend to make better decisions than their non–college-educated colleagues, are less likely to use force or be involved in civil liability complaints, and are more likely to take leadership roles and be promoted.

It is worth noting that the above results are in accord with other major research efforts measuring the effect of higher education on student belief systems. For example, in the mid-1960s, Feldman and Newcomb (1969) reviewed hundreds of research reports over a 40-year period, often conducting their own analyses, and found freshman-to-senior differences with respect to "declining authoritarianism, dogmatism, and prejudice, together with decreasingly conservative attitudes toward public issues and growing sensitivity to aesthetic experiences" (326). More recently, Pascarella and Terezini (1991, 2005), in an extensive review of the literature over a 30-year period, found that the impact of college education on students was related to improvements in communication skills, reflective judgment, and critical thinking.

Research should continue to explicate the impact of higher education on those with a 4-year degree versus those with a 2-year (associate's) degree or those who have only some college credits. Another important measure relates to whether an individual has attended a college for all 4 years or transferred from a junior college after 2 years, where class experiences and rigor are usually quite different; if an associate's degree is earned, the student will only complete 2 years at a 4-year institution, primarily taking courses in their major field of study—often criminal justice.

It would further be of interest to compare the impact of college on preservice students (those who complete their degrees prior to employment), in-service students (those who are employed while pursuing their degree), and continuing students (those who take courses both prior to and after entering police work). This area of research would provide empirical evidence with respect to the concept of "recruiting the educated" versus "educating the recruited," a primary recommendation put forth in 1978 by Sherman and the National Advisory Commission (1978).

As noted above regarding quality of education, it is pertinent to determine the type of educational institution attended, as well as the specific major, to determine whether there are any significant differences. Regarding academic major, Carlan (2007) examined the perceptions of 1,114 officers from 16 departments across Alabama with respect to the benefits of a degree in criminal justice compared with more traditional majors. Since criminal justice majors often remain devalued by traditional academic disciplines as being too narrow in scope and professional in nature, this is an important research question.

In the sample, there were 299 officers possessing a criminal justice degree (including associate's, bachelor's, or master's) and 230 possessing a degree in a non-criminal justice discipline (which were not identified). The findings indicated that officers perceived the criminal justice degree greatly enhanced understanding of the law and of the criminal justice system. In four additional areas pertinent to liberal arts disciplines—human relations skills, communication skills, administrative skills, and critical thinking skills—there were no significant differences found in comparison with other majors. These findings support not only the value of a criminal justice major to policing, but also many of the core values emphasized in a liberal arts education. However, officers did not perceive their programs to be as highly committed to social problems or human behavior. The author suggests this finding—at least in Alabama—leads to the possibility that criminal justice programs may not be supporting the major goal of conceptual development; thus, they are likely oriented somewhere in the middle of a continuum ranging from liberal arts to vocational/professional.

As noted at the beginning of this section, even though many police departments state they are performing community policing, they have yet to change their performance criteria (i.e., formal evaluations) to capture the more complex activities required—precisely those types of activities in which college graduates would most likely excel. Consequently, research should be devoted to seeking out departments that have adapted their performance evaluations to match community policing performance criteria and measure whether college graduates perform these types of activities in a more satisfactory manner than non–college graduates

Future research should also investigate the impact of on-the-job experience (length of service or seniority) and higher education to help determine the effects of experience independently and co-dependently with education. Clearly, there is much exciting research to be conducted regarding the impact of higher education on policing. We believe, however, that the overwhelming majority of significant research findings on higher education and the police will continue to be found at the baccalaureate level, especially for those who have attended a 4-year institution full time and graduated prior to becoming employed.

Higher Education and Job Satisfaction

Does higher education lead to increased job satisfaction for officers? The number of job satisfaction studies related to policing is surprisingly small. Early research in this area suggested that officers with a college education would be more frustrated and less satisfied because of unmet expectations for promotion (Niederhoffer 1967). There is some evidence that highly educated officers are more likely to terminate their careers in policing (Levy 1967; Cohen and Chaiken 1972; Stoddard 1973; Weirman 1978) and to hold differing and more negative views of job satisfaction (Griffin, Dunbar, and McGill 1978; Mottaz 1983). It is possible, and even likely, however, that such results may be related to the traditional bureaucratic nature, and macho culture, of police departments. Since it appears that higher education affects authoritarian attitudes, it would follow that college-educated police would be less willing to work in, and be less satisfied with, authoritarian departments and managerial practices. For example, Kakar (1998) indicates that with respect to job satisfaction, college-educated officers self-reported lower scores, coupled with higher scores of levels of frustration as a result of not feeling rewarded and/or feeling understimulated by the duties of traditional patrol work. In addition, officers with higher levels of education felt unrewarded and expressed frustration because of their inability to use their professional knowledge. Although this may appear to be a negative finding, it most likely simply indicates that college-educated officers prefer more challenging and stimulating jobs. Dantzker (1998) also reported findings of lower levels of job satisfaction with higher education.

Sherwood (2000) suggested that all officers—regardless of education level—are interested in job satisfaction, and departments that are more advanced in instituting community policing may hold an advantage over more traditional departments in providing it to their personnel. He further states that job satisfaction may be linked to the "use of a variety of skills, the ability to follow the task through to a conclusion, freedom to make decisions, and knowledge of the effectiveness of one's efforts" (Sherwood 2000, 210). Similarly, Griffin, Dunbar, and McGill (1978) recommended that structural changes (i.e., decentralization) be implemented in police departments to allow for more control among lower-level officers. Significantly, this is consistent with the less hierarchical structure and more autonomous style of community policing that, logically, should be most appealing to officers with higher education. As noted by Baro and Burlingame (1999, 64), "the community-policing movement indicates that police organizations and the police role could change in ways that require more education."

Higher Education, Community Policing, and Terrorism

As we have discussed throughout the text, there is a movement toward community policing, although stifled after the events of 9/11, by many police departments throughout the country. While some departments simply play "lip service" to a community policing paradigm, others continue to make significant strides toward the development of such a program. In brief, the heart of a community policing program revolves around the development and implementation of a problem-solving capacity. As noted by Goldstein (1979, 236), a problem-oriented approach suggests that the police develop "a more systematic process for examining and addressing the problems that the public expects them to handle."

In Chapter 8 we discussed some of the implications resulting from the events of 9/11 and the impact of terrorism on patrol work. One writer (DeGuzman 2002) suggests that greater attention will need to be to be placed on "event analysis" in addition to crime analysis. This means that greater emphasis will need to be placed on analyzing and assessing likely targets and events that may be connected to possible terrorist activities. One such analytic method, discussed previously (see Chapter 3), that could be used for this purpose is the SARA process (scanning, analysis, response, and assessment). Many of the topics described above must be used to effectively utilize this process. In addition to the need to be proficient in analytic and evaluation processes regarding potential terrorist acts, officers will need to develop strong ties with different cultures throughout their communities. In this way, important information can be gained from the public, who can then play a role in helping to combat not only traditional criminal activity but also potential terrorist threats.

From the above discussion, it appears that the challenges posed by the threat of terrorism will require officers who are both analytically and socially aware. Being well versed in the latest crime fighting technology will not be enough—it must also be accompanied by an awareness of social context. According to Roberg and Bonn (2004), the analytical skills provided by higher education will prepare officers for the complex challenges of terrorism, while exposure to the humanities and social sciences will produce a more sophisticated, "socially conscious" and culturally aware officer. Undoubtedly, the real threat of terrorist acts further complicates the police role in the twenty-first century, which, in turn, requires a more sophisticated police officer and organization. A valid community policing (including problem-solving) approach appears capable of fulfilling these needs.

Police Executives' Views on Higher Education

In Table 14.3, the advantages and disadvantages of college-educated officers, as reported by police executives throughout the country, are summarized. The findings of the PERF study (Carter, Sapp, and Stephens 1989), in which nearly 500 police executives were surveyed

TABLE 14.3 Police Executives' Opinions: Advantages and Disadvantages of Police Officers With Higher Education

ADVANTAGES	DISADVANTAGES
COLLEGE-EDUCATED OFFICERS ARE MORE LIKELY TO:	COLLEGE-EDUCATED OFFICERS ARE MORE LIKELY TO:
Communicate better with the public	Leave policing
Write better reports	Question orders
Perform more effectively	Request reassignment
Receive fewer citizen complaints	
Show more initiative in work performance	
Be more professional	
Use discretion more wisely	
Be promoted	
Make better decisions	
Show more sensitivity to racial or ethnic groups	
Have fewer disciplinary problems	

Source: Adapted from D. L. Carter, A. D. Sapp, and D. W. Stephens, *The State of Police Education Policy Directions for the 21st Century* (Washington, DC: PERF, 1989), xxii–xxiii. Used by permission.

with respect to their opinions on higher education and policing, are consistent with most of the research findings discussed thus far. Citing the study, a resolution was passed by the members of PERF (college-educated police chief executives) calling for all police applicants to possess 30 semester units from an accredited college or university. This requirement was to be increased in increments of 15 units until the minimum requirement for employment in policing was the baccalaureate degree (Police Executive Research Forum 1989).

Reflecting on the advantages of higher education described above, the police chief of Tulsa, Oklahoma, pushed through a policy requiring all police recruits to have a college degree. Inside Policing 14.1 describes the reasoning behind Tulsa's degree requirement.

Chief's Scholar Program

In Chapter 6 we described the nature of police–researcher relationships between the University of Cincinnati's Policing Institute UCPI, housed within the Division of Criminal Justice, and the Cincinnati Police Department CPD (Engel and Whalen, 2010). In this relationship, UC graduate students become embedded within the CPD to help with data collection and analysis. Conversely, an innovate graduate program, know as the **Chief's Scholar Program**, selects highly qualified CPD police officers to become full-time (on-duty status) master's degree students in the Criminal Justice department at the university. Officers are selected based on the assumption that they will become future leaders within the CPD; the Division of Criminal Justice at UC absorbs the officers' instructional costs. The officers take regular graduate classes but are on a 1-year fast-track program; each must write a thesis

---

INSIDE POLICING 14.1 No BS: Tulsa PD Rookies Required to Have 4-Year Degree

Beginning with the January 1998 class, recruits entering the Tulsa, Oklahoma, police academy are required to have a 4-year college degree after the City Council unanimously endorsed a proposal by Police Chief Ron Palmer to increase the police department's college requirement from the current 108 credit hours. The department is used to being on the cutting edge of higher education for police, having required 108 credit hours since 1981. "It wasn't a quantum leap for us, but it's certainly something that's unusual for a city of our size, and it's unique among major cities," observed Palmer, who has a master's degree.

Chief Palmer believes that college-educated officers are better grounded to meet the demands of the job and are less likely to be the subjects of citizen complaints or engage in misconduct. He also believes that officers with college degrees "come to you a bit more mature, they're a little more aware of diversity issues, and they're more prone to use their minds to problem-solve than one that doesn't have that type of background." Currently, about 73 percent of the department's 794 officers have college degrees, while an additional 20 percent have 60 hours or more of college credit. More than 40 sworn members have master's degrees, and the department has 1 member with a Ph.D. and 3 officials with law degrees.

At the same time, he points out, the requirement has not hampered the department's efforts to attract more minority recruits, as some thought might happen. "That doesn't appear to be the case," said Palmer. "We've hired [minorities] at the same level for the past 2 or 3 years, which was the result of a multicultural recruiting task force that partnered with the community. Coupled with this, we do a fairly strong recruiting effort not only in Tulsa, but outside the state, to get the numbers we feel will satisfy our goals."

SOURCE: Adapted from "Men and Women of Letters: No BS: Tulsa PD Rookies to Need Four-Year Degrees." *Law Enforcement News*, November 30, 1997: 1.

based on their current work assignments, priorities of the agency, and personal interests. At the conclusion of the program, each of the Chief's scholars has a research-based thesis that is presented to the administration for their consideration and implementation within the agency.

This is the type of program the author's suggest is a "win–win–win" relationship for academe, police, and Cincinnati residents. The authors further note, however, that it is incumbent on the leadership of both organizations to ensure that the partnership becomes institutionalized and therefore isolated from personnel changes. We would add that a Chief's Scholars Program has such potential advantages for all three parties (academe, police, and citizens) that it would be worth exploring the possibility for city, county, or state administrations to share funds to help cover the costs (along with local universities) of similar types of Scholars programs throughout a state; future programs could even develop into a regional Scholars program, where several police agencies would "share" a centrally located university.

Validating Higher Education for Police

Given the increasing number of college-educated officers in the field, such slow progress in developing higher-education standards is perplexing, especially considering the evidence that, in general, college education has a positive effect on officer attitudes, performance, and behavior. With such support for higher education, why have standards not been significantly raised by most police departments? Carter, Sapp, and Stephens (1989) identified two common reasons: (1) fear of being sued because a college requirement could not be quantitatively validated to show job relatedness and (2) fear that college requirements would be discriminatory against minorities. Each of these important issues warrants discussion.

Higher Education as a Bona Fide Occupational Qualification

As the PERF study of police executives reported (Carter, Sapp, and Stephens 1989), one of the primary reasons departments had not embraced higher education requirements more vigorously was the dilemma of not being able to validate such a requirement for the job, thus opening the department to a court challenge. Establishing higher education requirements as a **bona fide occupational qualification (BFOQ)**for police work could be an important step in facilitating the use of advanced education as a minimum entry-level selection criterion. A brief discussion of higher education as a bona fide occupational qualification for police work follows.

Interestingly, the courts in this country have continuously upheld higher education requirements in policing to be *job-related*. In *Castro v. Beecher* (1972), the requirement of a high school education by the Boston Police Department was affirmed, citing the recommendations of the President's Commission on Law Enforcement and Administration of Justice (1967) and the National Advisory Commission on Civil Disorders (1968). *Arnold v. Ballard* (1975) supported the notion that an educational requirement can be quantitatively job validated in stating that such requirements "indicate a measure of accomplishment and ability which... is essential for ... performance as a police officer" (738). And in *Davis v. City of Dallas* (1985), the court upheld a challenge to the Dallas Police Department's requirement of 45 semester units (equivalent to one and a half years of college) with a minimum of a C average from an accredited university.

In *Davis,* the court's decision was based partially on the complex nature of the police role and the public risk and responsibility that are unique to it. Such a decision indicates that higher standards of qualification can be applied to the job because police decision making requires an added dimension of judgment. This logic has been applied by the courts to other occupations, such as airline pilots and health-related professions. Thus, the *Davis* decision can be viewed as the next logical step in increasing police professionalism and may provide further support for police executives to require higher education (Carter, Sapp, and Stephens 1988).

To validate the need for higher education requirements, possibly the best approach, one that has withstood the scrutiny of the courts, is to use national studies and commission reports (e.g., National Advisory Commission on Criminal Justice 1973, President's Commission on Law Enforcement 1967, and others cited in this chapter) and the opinion of experts (including both police scholars and police executives). The PERF study recommended a preventive approach for a department that is going to require higher education for employment. This can be accomplished by having an expert prepare a *policy support paper* citing the "benefits and need of college-educated officers" (Carter, Sapp, and Stephens 1988, 16). The study further suggested that, although general studies and reports should be used, the policy support document should be specific to the individual department. The probability of litigation should be substantially lessened with such a document, and the educational program can also be based on the policies developed in the document; Inside Policing 14.2 provides an example for the framework of such a policy.

Higher Education and Discrimination

A second area of concern reported to PERF by police executives was the potential impact the higher education requirement might have on the employment of minorities. If minority group members do not have equal access to higher education, such a requirement could be held to be discriminatory by the courts. Not only that, but there are also obvious ethical and social issues raised. Any educational requirements for policing, then, must not only be job-related but also nondiscriminatory.

In the *Davis* case, the suit contended that higher education requirements were discriminatory in the selection of police officers. According to Title VII of the Civil Rights Act, there cannot be employment barriers (or practices) that discriminate against minorities, even if they are not intended to do so. However, in *Griggs v. Duke Power Co.* (1971), the U.S. Supreme Court held that if an employment practice is job related (or a "business necessity"), it may be allowed as a requirement, even though it *has* discriminatory overtones. Thus, courts must base decisions on the balance between requirements necessary for job performance and avoiding discriminatory practices. In *Davis,* the city of Dallas conceded that the college requirements did have a "significant disparate impact on blacks" (1985, 207). As noted above, the court held that the complex requirements of police work (e.g., public risk and responsibility, amount of discretion) mitigated against the discriminatory effects of a higher education requirement.

In other words, if certain requirements for the job can be justified, even though they may discriminate against certain groups, the benefits of such requirements may be judged to outweigh the discriminatory effects. Following this line of reasoning, if higher education requirements can be shown to be a bona fide occupational qualification, such a requirement would be considered a business necessity and thus a legitimate requirement for successful job performance.

Some data suggest, however, that requiring a bachelor's degree may have an impact on race. For example, Decker and Huckabee (2002) explored the effect of raising educational requirements to a bachelor's degree by analyzing recruit information from the Indianapolis Police Department over 4 years. They concluded that almost two thirds (65 percent) of successful candidates overall would have been ineligible, and 77 percent (30 of 39) of African

Developing a Higher Education Policy for Police Departments

Each department should have a written policy defining college education as a bona fide occupational qualification as it uniquely relates to the department, regardless of the requirements adopted. The department can then be fully prepared for any questions concerning the validity of any new educational requirements.

Policy development should include input from all levels of the department, particularly the local collective-bargaining organizations. This provision will lead to a common understanding of the rationale for the policy, enhance its acceptance, and expedite its implementation.

Promotional Requirements

If the entry-level educational requirements are raised, then the educational requirements for promotion should also be reviewed. As more highly educated officers enter policing, more highly educated supervisors, managers, and police executives will be needed.

Policy Standards

Educational policies should specify standards, especially that college credit and degrees be awarded from an accredited college or university. Acceptable credit should be based on a minimum grade average of C, or 2.0 on a 4.0 scale. Other standards could include the requirement that college credits earned be directly in pursuit of a degree. This rule ensures that the student has a liberal arts background in addition to courses in a major area.

Women and Minority Candidates

Attracting qualified women and minority candidates continues to be a concern for police departments. It is increasingly evident, however, that there is no need to limit entry or promotional educational requirements for these groups so long as innovative and aggressive recruiting programs are in place.

SOURCE: Adapted from D. L. Carter and A. D. Sapp, 1992. "College Education and Policing: Coming of Age," *FBI Law Enforcement Bulletin*, January 1992: 12.

American applicants did not have degrees. While the research did not discuss whether any recruitment efforts were made to increase the pool of college-educated minority applicants, it is worth noting that 9 of the 39 African American applicants did possess baccalaureate degrees. Of course, since a college degree was not a requirement for the job, one cannot be sure how such a requirement would have impacted the applicant pool. Even though in this instance a college degree requirement had an impact on race and on the overall applicant pool, this is likely to occur when departments are attempting to improve the quality of their personnel by raising standards. There is little doubt that departments that raise their educational requirements will also need to significantly enhance their recruitment efforts, as other professional organizations have done (Inside Policing 14.1 describes the Tulsa PDs efforts in this area). It appears that if strong recruitment efforts are made to attract college-educated minorities, a college degree requirement should not seriously impact minority hiring. Importantly, as discussed in Chapter 7, a college degree requirement may actually increase the total number of both minority and female applicants.

Higher Education Incentive Programs

For those departments recruiting college-educated officers, it is important that supporting programs and policies be established. One of the most important strategies for college recruitment is the use of incentives relating to higher education levels. For example, the national PERF study found that most of the departments had developed one or more educational incentive programs to encourage officers to continue their education beyond that required for initial employment. As Table 14.4 indicates, some of these include tuition assistance or reimbursement, incentive pay, shift or day-off adjustments, and permission to attend classes during work hours.

A more contemporary study (Stewart 2006) of 47 Texas police departments, diverse in size (e.g., Houston Police Department with 5,732 sworn officers and Greenville Police Department with 46 sworn officers) and organization structure, found that approximately 90 percent offer at least one type of educational policy. The most common type of policy was for pay incentive (n = 30; 64 percent), followed by full tuition reimbursement (n = 19; 40 percent), partial tuition reimbursement (n = 15; 32 percent), and adjustments to shift/ days off schedule (n = 5; 11 percent). Table 14.5 depicts the various types of educational pay incentives available.

TABLE 14.4 Higher Education Incentive Policies for Sworn Officers

COLLEGE INCENTIVE POLICY	NUMBER[a]	PERCENTAGE
Tuition assistance or reimbursement	302	62.1
Educational-pay incentive	261	53.7
Adjustments of shifts or days off	207	42.6
Permission for class attendance while on duty	115	23.7
Other programs or policies[b]	57	11.7
No educational incentives	43	8.8

[a]Based on sample of 486 departments.
[b]Includes tuition for POST-approved course only, leaves of absence for college, fellowship and scholarship programs, and in-service training programs for college credit. Most agencies have more than one incentive.

Source: Adapted from D. L. Carter and A. D. Sapp, "College Education and Policing: Coming of Age," *FBI Law Enforcement Bulletin*, January 1992: 13.

TABLE 14.5 Education Pay Incentive Programs

	NUMBER	%	AVERAGE DOLLAR AMOUNT (MONTHLY)	MOST COMMONLY REPORTED AMOUNT	RANGE
Bachelor's degree	27	57.4	$119	$100 ($n$ = 11)	$40–280
Associate's degree	24	51.1	$ 59	$ 50 (n = 10)	$20–100
Master's degree	18	38.3	$170	$150 ($n$ = 4)	$65–480
Doctorate degree	2	4.3	$480	—	$280–680

Source: Adapted from D. M. Stewart, *College Educational Standards* (Huntsville, TX: Texas Law Enforcement Management and Administrative Statistics Program, 2006), May/June: 7.

As Table 14.5 indicates, nearly 60 percent of agencies provide an additional average monthly pay increase of $119 to officers with bachelor's degrees, and approximately 50 percent raise officer monthly pay on average by $59 for obtaining an associate's degree. However, substantially fewer agencies award educational accomplishment exceeding an undergraduate degree. Only about 38 percent reward officers with master's degrees ($170 monthly average), and only two agencies (4.3 percent) provide money for those obtaining a doctorate degree ($480 monthly average).

With respect to promotional incentives for the Texas agencies; a little over 30 percent ($n = 16$) have at least one type of formal or informal policy requiring college education for promotion. The most common policies were written policies mandating a college degree ($n = 10$; 21 percent) or a certain number of college credits ($n = 7$; 14 percent) for promotion. Table 14.6 depicts departmental policies requiring education requirements for promotion to a particular rank or bonus points awarded on promotion exams for completing a certain amount of college credits. Approximately 40 percent of the agencies ($n = 18$) have at least one such policy; more specifically, 14 agencies (30 percent) require a college degree or college credits for promotion (to sergeant, lieutenant, or captain), and 4 agencies (8.5 percent) award bonus points for a degree or credits on promotion exams.

In conclusion, almost 90 percent ($n = 42$) of the departments have at least one educational incentive policy, and approximately 57 percent ($n = 27$) allocate higher salaries to sworn officers with bachelor's degrees. In addition, approximately 40 percent ($n = 18$) of the departments require at least some level of college for promotion or award bonus points for a certain amount of college credits on promotion exams.

Higher Education Requirements and Policy Implications

As discussed above, if college education is ever to become an entry-level requirement for policing, it is important that supporting policies also be established. Additionally, of course,

TABLE 14.6 College Education Required and Bonus Points Awarded for Promotion

	NUMBER	%
Agencies that require at least some college education for promotion or award bonus points for college education on promotion exams	18	38.3
Agencies that require a college degree or college credits for promotion	14	29.8
Agencies that require a college degree or college credits for promotion to the following ranks:		
Sergeant	8	17.0
Lieutenant	12	25.5
Captain	13	27.7
Agencies that award bonus points on promotion exams for having completed a particular amount of college education	4	8.5

Source: D. M. Stewart, 2006. *College Education Standards* (Huntsville, TX: Law Enforcement Management and Administrative Statistics Program) May/June: 6.

it is helpful to have a competitive salary scale, good employment benefits, and high-quality working conditions. It is important to point out that over the past decade, many medium and large police departments have implemented highly competitive salary structures, in line with, and often substantially above, the starting salaries for college graduates in most public- and many private-sector jobs. In addition, health benefits and retirement packages are generally very good. In the long term, however, it appears that the implementation of a community policing paradigm (or something similar) will likely be necessary to significantly enhance police working environments, creating a professional atmosphere where college graduates will feel comfortable and can flourish. As one former Baltimore City police officer has observed (Moskos, 2003),

> But too many potentially good police won't join an organization filled with Marine haircuts, snappy salutes and a six-month boot camp. Too few people with four-year degrees and liberal upbringing want a job in a conservative organization with archaic grooming codes....What other civilian profession hides behind a conservative faux-military facade? What other occupation demands that you stand at attention every time a boss enters the room? If police departments treated their employees more like professionals, more professionals would join the police. *(8)*

In the final analysis, it appears as though enough evidence (both empirical and experiential) has been established to support a strong argument for a college-degree requirement for entry-level police officers:

1. The benefits provided by a higher education, combined with social and technological changes, the threat of terrorism (along with civil rights issues), and the increasing complexity of police work, suggest that a college degree should be a requirement for initial police employment (see Inside Policing 14.3 for further discussion on changes supporting a college degree requirement).
2. The types of significant changes described above further call for the development of the police field to move away from the status of a vocational craft toward a bona fide profession, which not only understands the importance of research, but also relies on valid and reliable research to guide their policy decisions.
3. If educational and recruitment policies are appropriately developed, a higher education requirement should not adversely affect minority recruitment or retention.

Recognizing that there are diverse types of police departments throughout the country, with differing styles of operation, levels of performance, and community needs, it is apparent that some can adapt to a college-degree requirement more readily than others. Consequently, perhaps some type of *graduated timetable* for college requirements—similar to those found in the National Advisory Commission's *Report on Police* (1973)—would be appropriate (the commission recommended that all officers be required to have a baccalaureate degree by 1982). A graduated timetable could again be set up for phasing in, first, a 2-year degree requirement and, second, a baccalaureate degree for initial selection purposes. At the same time, requirements could be established for supervisory and executive personnel, first at the baccalaureate level and then, at least for executives, at the master's level.

These requirements could also be adjusted to account for different types of agencies; for example, larger agencies serving larger and more diverse populations could have the requirements phased in earlier. The bottom line, however, would ultimately require any

---

Support for College Education Requirement for Entry-Level Police Officers

At least three significant changes support a college degree requirement for initial selection of police.

Organizational Changes

Today's police departments are very different from those that existed when LEAA and LEEP were begun in the 1970s. Many more police officers and managers have college degrees (and advanced degrees), and the police cultural bias against "college cops" has significantly declined. The challenges of community policing require officers to use more discretion in problem solving and decision making. At the same time, officers must be aware of cultural differences in, and sensitivity to the needs of, the community. Research has suggested that successful community policing is dependent on the quality of educated police officers.

Societal Changes

Today's police officers need to be culturally sensitive and willing to value ethnic differences. Most college degree programs offer courses in such areas as cultural diversity, ethics, and cross-cultural comparisons, and some even require a foreign language. In addition, courses in sociology, psychology, and other human-behavior courses (including criminal justice and criminology) all contribute to a better understanding of the complex society in which we live. Research has demonstrated that officers who are exposed to such an educational experience deal better with diverse community groups.

Police departments must also recognize that as members of the community are becoming more educated, their expectations of police service will also increase. Thus, police departments must raise their educational requirements to represent the populations they serve.

Technological Changes

Today's police officer is faced with more modern technology than ever before. The field notebook has been replaced by the laptop computer. The Internet, World Wide Web, and e-mail have greatly expanded resources and data-collection techniques, and the emphasis on solution-oriented policing has placed greater demands on crime analysis, problem solving, and computer sophistication.

As innovative programs are developed to address crime and disorder, departments must have officers who can evaluate their impact with methodologically sound techniques. Most college-degree programs require coursework (e.g., computer science, research methods, and math and statistics) that is beneficial in today's technologically sophisticated environment.

SOURCE: Adapted from R. Garner, "Community Policing and Education: The College Connection," *Texas Law Enforcement Management and Administrative Statistics Program*, January 1998: 7–9.

---

officer with general enforcement powers to have a degree, regardless of location or type of agency. Those departments or cities that feel they could not comply with such a requirement could contract with a nearby agency that can meet the requirements. Such an arrangement is not without precedent because many small and/or rural cities that feel they cannot afford to support their own police department contract for local police services through larger municipal or county agencies.

It is likely, however, that for higher education to become entrenched throughout the field, a serious push will be needed from the federal government, perhaps along the lines of the Justice Department's COPS program, which provided funds nationally to promote community policing (but with stronger requirements and oversight attached). Initially, federal funding could be provided to departments for achieving measurable standards, including broad-based recruiting efforts (including universities), developing educational incentive programs, elimination of policies that restrict applicant searches (including residency requirements), and the development of a written policy defining college education as a bona fide occupational qualification as it relates to departmental needs (Roberg and Bonn, 2004).

Summary

Berkeley Police Chief August Vollmer began a campaign for higher education for police that has continued to the present. Major universities developed programs for police education, despite the resistance of many street officers. Research has indicated that higher education can be job validated for police entry and that such a requirement should not have an adverse impact on minority recruitment or retention if appropriate recruitment policies and efforts are developed. To this end, police departments would be wise to develop a written policy defining college education as a bona fide occupational qualification as it relates to the department.

In general, college education for entry-level police officers can be supported based on ongoing changes, including organizational, societal, and technological changes. In the final analysis, enough evidence has been established to support the requirement of a college degree for policing. A graduated timetable for development and federal funding for support will most likely be necessary for national recognition and implementation.

Critical Thinking Questions

1. Why were the President's Commission on Law Enforcement and Administration of Justice and the National Advisory Commission on Criminal Justice Standards and Goals important to higher education for police?

2. In your opinion, was LEAA successful? Why or why not?

3. Briefly describe what impact you believe the Violent Crime Control and Law Enforcement Act of 1994 has had on policing.

4. Briefly describe what you believe to be the important empirical research on the impact of higher education on policing. What areas are in need of further research?

5. In your opinion, can higher education be supported as a bona fide occupational qualification in policing? Why or why not?

6. Do you think that the field of policing can ever be regarded as a "profession" if higher education requirements are not ultimately adopted? Give several specific reasons why or why not.

7. If you were a police chief, would you attempt to require higher education requirements first for entry-level positions or for promotions? Discuss your reasons.

8. As an upper level police manager, how might you go about developing some form of a Chief's Scholar Program?

References

American Bar Association. 1973. *Standards Relating to the Urban Police Function.* New York: author.

Arnold v. Ballard, 390 F. Supp. (N.D. Ohio 1975).

Baro, A. L., and Burlingame, D. (1999). "Law Enforcement and Higher Education: Is There an Impasse?" *Journal of Criminal Justice Education* 10(1): 57–73.

Bowman, T. 2002. "Educate to Elevate." *Community Links,* August, 11–13.

Caiden, G. E. 1977. *Police Revitalization.* Lexington, MA: D. C. Heath.

Carlan, P. E. 2007. "The Criminal Justice Degree and Policing: Conceptual Development or Occupational Primer?" *Policing: An International Journal of Police Strategies and Management* 30: 608–619.

Carte, G. E. 1973. "August Vollmer and the Origins of Police Professionalism." *Journal of Police Science and Administration* 1: 274–281.

Carter, D. L., and Sapp, A. D. 1989. "The Effect of Higher Education on Police Liability: Implications for Police Personnel Policy." *American Journal of Police* 8: 153–166.

———. 1990. "Higher Education as a Policy Alternative to Reduce Police Liability." *Police Liability Review* 2: 1–3.

———. 1992. "College Education and Policing: Coming of Age." *FBI Law Enforcement Bulletin,* January: 8–14.

Carter, D. L., Sapp, A. D., and Stephens, D. W. 1988. "Higher Education as a Bona Fide Occupational Qualification (BFOQ) for Police: A Blueprint." *American Journal of Police* 7: 1–27.

———. 1989. *The State of Police Education: Policy Direction for the 21st Century.* Washington, DC: Police Executive Research Forum.

Cascio, W. F. 1977. "Formal Education and Police Officer Performance." *Journal of Police Science and Administration* 5: 89–96.

Castro v. Beecher, 459 F.2d 725 (lst Cir. 1972).

Cohen, B., and Chaiken, J. M. 1972. *Police Background Characteristics and Performance.* New York: Rand Institute.

Dalley, A. F. 1975. "University and Nonuniversity Graduated Policemen: A Study of Police Attitudes." *Journal of Police Science and Administration* 3: 458–468. **NOTE**: This is a DIRECT title (i.e, NonUniversity) from the Journal.

Davis v. City of Dallas, 777 F.2d 205 (5th Cir. 1985).

Dantzker, M. L. 1998. "Police Education and Job Satisfaction: Educational Incentives and Recruit Educational Requirements." *Police Forum* 8 (3): 1–4.

Decker, L. K., and Huckabee, R. G. 2002. "Raising the Age and Education Requirements for Police Officers: Will Too Many Women and Minority Candidates Be Excluded?" *Policing* 25: 789–801.

Deutsch, A. 1955. *The Trouble With Cops.* New York: Crown Publishers.

DeGuzman, M. C. 2002. "The Changing Roles and Strategies of the Police in Time of Terror." *Academy of Criminal Justice Sciences Today* 12: 8–13.

"Dissecting the Crime Bill: New Era for Law Enforcement and Higher Education." 1994. *Law Enforcement News* October 15: 1, 7.

Engel, R. S., and Whalen, J. L. 2010. "Police–Academic Partnerships: Ending the Dialogue of the Deaf, the Cincinnati Experience." *Police Practice & Research* 11: 105–116.

Feldman, K. A., and Newcomb, T. M. 1969. *The Impact of College on Students.* San Francisco: Jossey–Bass.

"For Florida Police, Higher Education Means Lower Risk of Disciplinary Action." 2002. *Law Enforcement News* October 31: 1, 10.

Goldstein, H. 1979. "Improving policing: A Problem-Oriented Approach." *Crime and Delinquency* 25: 236–258.

Griffin, G. R., Dunbar, R. L. M., and McGill, M. E. 1978. "Factors Associated With Job Satisfaction Among Police Personnel." *Journal of Police Science and Administration* 6: 77–85.

Griggs v. Duke Power Co., 401 U.S. 432. 1971.

Guller, I. B. 1972. "Higher Education and Policemen: Attitudinal Differences Between Freshman and Senior Police College Students." *Journal of Criminal Law, Criminology, and Police Science* 63: 396–401.

Hickman, M. J., and Reaves, B. A. 2006. *Local Police Departments, 2003.* Washington, DC: Bureau of Justice Statistics.

Hickman, M. J., and Reaves, B.A. 2003. *Sheriffs' Offices, 2000.* Washington, DC: Bureau of Justice Statistics.

Johnston, W., and Cheurprakobkit, S. 2002. "Educating Our Police: Perceptions of Police Administrators Regarding the Utility of a College Education, Police Academy Training and Preferences in Courses for Officers." *International Journal of Police Science and Management* 4: 182–197.

Kakar, S. 1998. "Self-Evaluation of Police Performance: An Analysis of the Relationship Between Police Officers' Education Level and Job Performance." *Policing: An International Journal of Police Strategies and Management* 21: 632–647.

Korbetz, R. W. 1975. *Law Enforcement and Criminal Justice Education Directory, 1975–1976.* Gaithersburg, MD: International Association of Chiefs of Police.

Krimmel, J. T. 1996. "The Performance of College-Educated Police: A Study of Self-Rated Police Performance Measures." *American Journal of Police* 15: 85–96.

LaGrange, T. C. 2003. The Role of Police Education in Handling Cases of Mental Disorder." *Criminal Justice Review* 28:88–113.

Levy, R. J. 1967. "Predicting Police Failures." *Journal of Criminal Law, Criminology, and Police Science* 58: 265–276.

Lersch, K. M., and Kunzman, L. L. 2001. "Misconduct Allegations and Higher Education in a Southern Sheriff's Department." *American Journal of Criminal Justice* 25: 161–172.

McElvain, J. P., and Kposowa, A. J. 2008. "Police Officer Characteristics and the Likelihood of Using Deadly Force." *Criminal Justice and Behavior* 35: 505–525.

Meese, E. 1993. "Community Policing and the Police Officer." *Perspectives on Policing* 15, Washington, DC: National Institute of Justice and Harvard University.

"Men and Women of Letters: No BS: Tulsa PD Rookies to Need Four-Year Degrees." 1997. *Law Enforcement News* November 30: 1.

Miller, J., and Fry, L. 1976. "Reexamining Assumptions About Education and Professionalism in Law Enforcement." *Journal of Police Science and Administration* 4: 187–196.

Moskos, P. 2003. "Old-School Cops in a New-School World." *Law Enforcement News* Oct. 15/31: 8.

Mottaz, C. 1983. "Alienation Among Police Officers." *Journal of Police Science and Administration* 11: 23–30.National Advisory Commission on Civil Disorders (1968). *Report.* Washington, DC: U.S. Government Printing Office.

National Advisory Commission on Criminal Justice Standards and Goals (1973). *Report on Police.* Washington, DC: U.S. Government Printing Office.

Nees, H. 2003. "Education and Criminal Justice Employees in Colorado." *Police Forum* 1: 5–9.

Niederhoffer, A. 1967. *Behind the Shield: The Police in Urban Society.* Garden City, NY: Doubleday.

Paoline, E. A., and Terrill, W. 2007. "Police Education, Experience, and the Use of Force." *Criminal Justice and Behavior* 34: 179–196.

Pascarella, E. T., and Terenzini, P. T. 1991. *How College Affects Students: Insights From Twenty years of Research.* San Francisco: Jossey–Bass.

———. 2005. *How College Affects Students (Vol. II): A Third Decade of Research.* San Francisco: Jossey–Bass.

Police Executive Research Forum. 1989. *A Resolution of the Membership of the Police Executive Research Forum.* Washington, DC: PERF.

Polk, E., and Armstrong, D. A. 2001. "Higher Education and Law Enforcement Career Paths: Is the Road to Success Paved by Degree?" *Journal of Criminal Justice Education* 12: 77–99.

Pope, C. E. 1987. "Criminal Justice Education: Academic and Professional Orientations." In R. Muraskin (ed.), *The Future of Criminal Justice Education,* Brookeville, NY: Long Island University.

President's Commission on Law Enforcement and Administration of Justice. 1967. *The Challenge of Crime in a Free Society.* Washington, DC: U.S. Government Printing Office.

Regoli, R. M. 1976. "The Effects of College Education on the Maintenance of Police Cynicism." *Journal of Police Science and Administration* 4: 340–345.

Roberg, R. R. 1978. "An Analysis of the Relationships Among Higher Education, Belief Systems, and Job Performance of Patrol Officers." *Journal of Police Science and Administration* 6: 336–344.

Roberg, R., and Bonn, S. 2004. Higher Education and Policing: Where Are We Now?" *Policing: An International Journal of Police Strategies & Management.* 27: 469–486.

Roberg, R. R., and Laramy, J. E. 1980. "An Empirical Assessment of the Criteria Utilized for Promoting Police Personnel: A Secondary Analysis." *Journal of Police Science and Administration* 8: 183–187.

Rydberg, J., and Terrill, W. 2010. "The Effect of Higher Education on Police Behavior." *Police Quarterly* 13: 92–120.

Saunders, C. B. 1970. *Upgrading the American Police.* Washington, DC: The Brookings Institution.

Sherman, L. W., and the National Advisory Commission on Higher Education for Police Officers. 1978. *The Quality of Police Education.* San Francisco: Jossey–Bass.

Sherwood, C. W. 2000. "Job Design, Community Policing, and Higher Education: A Tale of Two Cities." *Police Quarterly,* 3 (2), 191–212.

Skogan, W., and Frydl, K. 2004. *Fairness and Effectiveness in Policing: The Evidence.* Washington, DC: The National Academies Press, National Research Council of the National Academies.

Smith, A. B., Locke, B., and Fenster, A. 1970. "Authoritarianism in Policemen Who Are College Graduates and Noncollege Graduates." *Journal of Criminal Law, Criminology, and Police Science* 61: 313–315.

Smith, A. B., Locke, B., and Walker, W. F. 1968. "Authoritarianism in Police College Students and Nonpolice College Students." *Journal of Criminal Law, Criminology, and Police Science* 59: 440–443.

Smith, S. M., and Aamodt, M. G. 1997. "The Relationship Between Education, Experience, and Police Performance." *Journal of Police and Criminal Psychology* 12: 7–14.

Stewart, D. M. 2006. *Collegiate Educational Standards.* Huntsville, TX: Texas Law Enforcement Management and Administrative Statistics Program, May/June.

Stoddard, K. B. 1973. "Characteristics of Policemen of a County Sheriff's Office." In J. R. Snibbe and H. M. Snibbe (eds.), *The Urban Policemen in Transition,* pp. 281–297. Springfield, IL: Charles C. Thomas.

"Surprise! The Police Corps Is Back—Not That It Ever Left." 1997. *Law Enforcement News* January 31: 1, 10.

"Survey Says Big-City Chiefs are Better-Educated Outsiders." 1998. *Law Enforcement News* April 30: 7.

Taylor, B., Kubu, B., Friedell, L., Rees, C., Jordan, T., and Cheney, J. 2005. *The Cop Crunch: Identifying Strategies for Dealing with the Recruiting and Hiring Crisis in Law Enforcement.* Washington, DC: PERF.

Terrill, W., and Mastrofski, S. D. 2002. "Situational and Officer-Based Determinants of Police Coercion." *Justice Quarterly* 19(2): 215–248. Truxillo, D. M., Bennett, S. R., and Collins, M. L. 1998. "College Education and Police Job Performance: A Ten-Year Study." *Public Personnel Management* 27(2): 269–280.

U.S. Census Bureau. 2000. "Profile of Selected Social Characteristics: 2000, DP-2." Available online at http://www.factfinder.census.gov.

U.S. Department of Justice. 1994. *The Violent Crime Control and Law Enforcement Act of 1994.* Washington, DC: U.S. Government Printing Office.

Weiner, N. L. 1976. "The Educated Policeman." *Journal of Police Science and Administration* 4: 450–457.

Whetstone, T. S. 2000. "Getting Stripes: Educational Achievement and Study Strategy Used by Sergeant Promotional Candidates." *American Journal of Criminal Justice* 24: 247–257.

White, M. D. 2008. "Identifying Good Cops Early: Predicting Recruit Performance in the Academy." *Police Quarterly* 11: 27–49.

Wilson, H. 1999. "Post-Secondary Education of the Police Officer and Its Effect on the Frequency of Citizen Complaints." *Journal of California Law Enforcement* 33: 3–10.

Worden, R. E. 1990. "A Badge and a Baccalaurcate: Policies, Hypotheses, and Further Evidence." *Justice Quarterly* 7: 565–592.

CHAPTER 15

Emerging Issues

CHAPTER OUTLINE

■ Changes in American Society
    The Aging Population
    Diversity
    Economics
    Immigration and Migration
■ Modern Problems
    Racial Profiling
    Immigration Enforcement

Eyewitness Identification
Persons With Mental Illness
Cyber Crime
- Modern Technology
Suspect Control and Officer Safety
Crime Detection and Crime Solving
Information Technology
Communications and Interoperability
Social Media
- Long-Term Trends
Collaboration
Privatization
Federalization
Militarization
Globalization
- Competing Police Strategies
- Terrorism and Homeland Security
- Compstat and Performance Management
- COP, POP, and ILP
- Summary
- Critical Thinking Questions
- References

KEY TERMS

- cyber crime
- deinstitutionalization
- eyewitness identification
- federalization
- geographic information systems (GIS)
- globalization
- global positioning systems (GPS)
- information technology
- intelligence-led policing (ILP)
- interoperability
- militarization
- privatization
- racial profiling
- USA Patriot Act

P REDICTING THE FUTURE IS very tricky. One might think it would be sufficient to extrapolate current trends in policing, but the importance of often uncontrollable external (environmental) influences cannot be overestimated. Something unexpected always occurs to undermine even the most reasonable forecasts, reminding us that the future will be predictable in the same way as the past—in retrospect.

Thoughtful observers have noted that police in the United States are in the midst of profound changes. Within police departments, shifts in role, function, technology, and philosophy are important trends. Outside the police system itself, changes in the character of those being policed, along with changes in government, the academic world, the criminal world, and technology, may lead to changes even more fundamental and far-reaching than those seen in the past 25 years. There are so many things going on affecting the American police that trying to make sense of its "present" is already difficult; delineating its "future" is nearly impossible. Nevertheless, this chapter will try to identify trends in present-day society and policing that indicate directions policing might take in the future.

Police departments are *institutionalized organizations*—that is, they are responsible for acting on behalf of the values a society holds dear. Unlike economic organizations (businesses), which prosper through their own technical efficiency, police organizations prosper by successfully supporting and reproducing society's sense of right and wrong. To do this, they must look beyond themselves to the groups that make up society.

Who are these groups? Police departments must deal with criminals and provide assistance to citizens. They also must address the concerns of mayors, city councils, organizations such as Mothers Against Drunk Driving, business groups, and police unions. They must deal with prosecutors and the courts, and they must always be sensitive to changes in the law. They must deal with hostile relations between different ethnic groups. They must contend with rebellious youth and youth gangs. They always must keep an eye on the media, which can support or embarrass the police with printed or televised news. Increasingly, they are linking with the military to deal with such problems as drug smuggling and international terrorism. In short, the police must deal with an environment of great complexity. The police have the ethical responsibility to help all these groups get along, to help solve their problems, and to intervene when citizens get into conflicts or hurt one another.

In addition, the police must respond to technological changes. Consider the ways in which technology has changed the police over the past century. Installing a two-way radio in a police car in the first third of the twentieth century profoundly changed the delivery of police service. The linkage of these two technologies (cars and radios) with the telephone made it possible for citizens to call the police station and for the station to dispatch a police car to respond to the citizen's needs. This style of policing, based on motorized preventive patrol and rapid response, still constitutes the dominant style of policing in most communities today. It would have been an unlikely prediction 100 years ago.

Changes in American Society

One set of factors that is likely to influence the future of policing involves changes in society. This section reviews some ongoing demographic, economic, and geographic changes in American society that seem likely to affect policing (see also Table 15.1 for a summary of demographic changes in the United States during the twentieth century) in the coming decades.

The Aging Population

The United States has a growing and graying population. The total population passed 300 million in 2007 and is expected to reach 400 million in 2043 (U.S. Census Bureau 2007b). The twentieth century saw the average life span greatly increase, from under 50 years in 1900 to 77.7 years as of 2006 (Centers for Disease Control 2009a). In 1900, those over 65 years old—considered elderly—constituted 4 percent of the population; today this group accounts for 13 percent of the population and by 2040 will account for 20 percent of all Americans (Administration on Aging 2009; U.S. Census Bureau 2010a). The over-65 group numbered less than 5 million in 1900, but will grow to about 80 million in 2050 (see Figure 15.1).

The new elderly pose unique dilemmas for criminal justice. First, among those over 85, three fourths of the men are still married, but fewer than 4 of 10 women are (Roberts 1994). Why? Women live, on average, 5 years longer than men (Centers for Disease Control 2009b). Men die younger, leaving many widows. This longevity does not mean that the quality of life for surviving women is high. On the contrary, they are one of the populations most highly vulnerable to victimization. Also, 1 in 5 of those over 85 (both genders) are

TABLE 15.1 Demographic Changes in the United States During the Twentieth Century

- The U.S. population more than tripled from 76 million people in 1900 to 281 million people in 2000. The growth of 32.7 million people in the 1990s represented the largest numerical increase of any decade in U.S. history.

- The U.S. population grew increasingly metropolitan each decade, from 28 percent in 1910 to 80 percent in 2000. Suburbs rather than centralized cities accounted for most of the metropolitan growth. By 2000, half of the U.S. population lived in suburban areas.

- The population of the West grew faster than the population in each of the other three regions of the country in every decade of the twentieth century.

- The Northeast was the most densely populated region and had the highest percentage of its population living in metropolitan areas throughout the century.

- At the beginning of the century, half of the U.S. population was less than 22.9 years old. At the century's end, half of the population was more than 35.3 years old, the country's highest median age ever.

- Children under age 5 represented the largest 5-year age group in 1900 and again in 1950. By 2000, the largest 5-year age groups were people ages to 39 and 40 to 44, large segments of the baby-boom generation.

- The United States' gender composition shifted from a majority male population to a majority female population around midcentury.

- From 1980 to 2000, the Hispanic population more than doubled.

- By the end of the century, three states—California, Hawaii, and New Mexico—and the District of Columbia—had majority "minority populations" (including Hispanics).

- Prior to 1950, over half of all occupied housing units were rented. By 1950, home ownership became more prevalent than renting.

- In 1900, the most common household contained seven or more people; from 1940 to 2000, it contained two people.

- In 1900, nearly half of the U.S. population lived in households of six or more people; by 2000, more than half lived in households of one, two, or three people.

- Between 1950 and 2000, married couple households declined from more than three fourths of all households (78 percent) to just over one half (52 percent)

Source: U.S. Census Bureau, *Demographic Trends in the 20th Century* (Washington, DC: U.S. Government Printing Office, 2002a), Special Reports, Series CENSR–4. Available online at http://www.census.gov/prod/2002pubs/censr-4.pdf.

institutionalized. As this institutionalized population dramatically increases over the coming decades, there are likely to be sharp increases in white-collar crime in the health care industry against the elderly.

Second, the elderly, usually dependent on fixed budgets, tend to mobilize to vote against tax increases to support social infrastructure. They particularly tend to oppose property tax increases needed to support school budgets. The growing elderly population will likely strain the Social Security System and Medicaid as well as the resources of their adult-

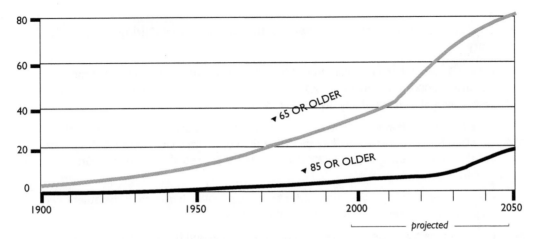

FIGURE 15.1 Total Number of Persons Age 65 or Older, by Age Group, 1900–2050, in Millions.

SOURCE: U.S. Census Bureau, *Decennial Census Data and Population Projections.* Available online at http://www.aoa.gov/agingstatsdotnet/Main_Site/Data/Data_2008.aspx.

age children. The grandchildren of these elderly, then, may encounter poorer schools and recreational opportunities, as well as overburdened parents. If these conditions materialize, one might anticipate increases in juvenile crime to accompany the growing elderly population.

The post–World War II period has been characterized as the *baby boom* for the large numbers of children born to returning veterans. Yet this population's growth has not continued, but instead reversed. Baby boomers were the first population in U.S. history not to replace itself in population numbers. This phenomenon has been called the *baby bust*. The slowed growth in the numbers of young people in the 1990s was a symptom of the baby bust; since the 1970s the U.S. birth rate has been flat (Centers for Disease Control 2009b) while average life spans have lengthened. The numbers of young, unlike the numbers of elderly, are not expected to increase over the coming decades.

The most crime-prone population is widely regarded by criminologists to be those between the ages of 18 and 24. Judging by population forecasts, this population will not increase at high rates for many years. The number of Americans in the 18- to 24-year age group is not expected to exceed the 1980 level for at least 50 years (Roberts 1994). Another consequence of this imbalance between older and younger Americans may be more difficult police recruiting challenges, since police departments traditionally focus on 21 to 25 year olds when looking for new employees.

Diversity

The United States is in the midst of a dramatic population transformation. Immigration from abroad, large-scale internal migration, and the way in which these migration patterns are distributed across the landscape will profoundly change the face of the U.S. population.

Consider the changing pattern of foreign migration into the country. In the 1980s, half as many people emigrated from Europe to the United States as in the 1960s; more than five times as many came from Asia, twice as many from Mexico, the Caribbean, and Central America, and nearly four times as many from Africa. Even these groupings mask important regional and local differences. The 1990 Census counted 179 ancestry groupings for the

Latino category alone. In the 1990s, the number of Asians more than doubled. Legal immigration slowed after 2001 for national security reasons, but illegal immigration across the Mexican border for economic reasons increased. The long-term implications are clear. By the middle of the twenty-first century, no racial or ethnic group will constitute a majority in the United States (Roberts 1994).

Growth and change involve the relocation of many kinds of people. People tend to think of migration in terms of foreign immigration. Yet this is a proportionally small aspect of overall migration. Blue-collar workers in search of jobs tend to migrate at a much higher rate than their white-collar counterparts. City dwellers in search of a better lifestyle move to the rural hinterland or to the *exurbs,* the semi-rural areas just beyond a city's suburbs. This region is increasingly popular to well-off members of the middle and working classes, who commute to the city to work. Religious groups seek divine meaning though rural settlement. All these are groups on the move. All of them carry the potential for conflicts that the police will have to deal with.

Dynamic changes in ethnicity will confront Americans in the twenty-first century. Diversity is already remarkable in some areas. In Los Angeles, for example, more than 80 distinct languages are spoken (Kaplan 1998). These changes may profoundly affect police services. Consider Asians. In Minnesota, a state seemingly distant from the impact of migration, Asians tripled in number from 1980 to 1990, and then almost doubled again by 2000, to a total of almost 145,000 residents (U.S. Census Bureau 2003). Their in-migration creates unique police problems. The prone-out position many officers use to effect an arrest, for example, is the same position Vietnamese police use when they execute citizens. Vietnamese are sometimes terrified when "proned-out" and thus are more likely to run from the police (Taft 1991). How can police deal with public-order problems if they do not even share a common history, culture, and language with the citizens they serve?

As the United States becomes a truly international society, there is great demand for police to help people work together, to mediate ethnic frictions, and to find common ground. History books sometimes portray U.S. society as a *melting pot,* where different kinds of people blend together in harmony. Yet there is little evidence that Americans "melt together" or that we ever have, for that matter. On the contrary, some scholars warn that increased contact among different kinds of peoples contributes to increased group identity, particularly group religious identity (Huntington 1996).

Religious differences are an aspect of cultural differences. Demographic changes consequently are closely tied to religion. Religion has the capacity to become the basis of cultural friction across the United States, as was discovered in the aftermath of September 11, 2001, when some Americans turned their anger toward followers of Islam, as well as toward people of Middle Eastern descent. In the world of tomorrow, police will increasingly take on the responsibility of managing conflicts among religious groups, seeking to find common ground among them, and facilitating their coexistence.

Economics

Economic conditions affect crime, disorder, and the demand for police services. Economics change over time, and it is risky to predict them, as stock market investors know quite well. As this edition of the text goes to press, the U.S. economy is still struggling to recover from the 2009 meltdown in the financial system. Unemployment rates are up, home sales have not yet rebounded, government debt is rising, and police agency budgets are being cut. Hopefully these short-term trends will all be improving by the time you are reading this book.

One long-term trend in the nature of employment has been from hunting and gathering to farming to manufacturing jobs to service jobs and on toward the information-based economy. In 2009, about 79 percent of American workers were in management, professional, service, sales, or related jobs, whereas only about 21 percent were in construction, transportation, manufacturing, farming, and related jobs (Bureau of Labor Statistics 2010a). Employment today is more likely to be white collar, indoors, and in an office than in the past.

Employment markets are much more global today than in the past, as textile workers, steel workers, and others have learned the hard way. The promotion of free trade over the past 2 decades, as exemplified by the North American Free Trade Agreement, has created more opportunities for companies to move part, or all, of their operations to countries with lower labor costs, weaker environmental protections, and less concern for workplace safety. Until recently, this trend has mostly affected blue-collar employment and has helped account for the decline in manufacturing jobs in the United States. Currently, however, the same forces are also starting to affect white-collar and creative employment (Florida 2004). If these types of jobs, the very ones expected to take up the slack from declining manufacturing, also go "offshore," then the United States may face some serious unemployment challenges in the future.

Another big economic change has been in the participation of women in employment. In 2000, 58 percent of women aged 16 years and older were in the labor force (U.S. Census Bureau 2003). By comparison, in 1900 less than 20 percent of adult women were in the labor force (Infoplease 2003). This has changed the characteristics of the workforce that the police encounter, helped empower women economically, and affected whether parents are present or absent from the home with their children after school and at other times.

> Seven and a half million children in the United States between the ages of 5 and 14 are latch-key kids, according to the National Institute on Out-of-School-Time. Research confirms that kids are less likely to get into trouble when a responsible adult is watching them. In a study published by the American Academy of Pediatrics, researchers found that eighth graders who are unsupervised more than 10 hours a week are about 10 percent more likely to try marijuana and twice as likely to smoke cigarettes or drink alcohol as eighth graders who are unsupervised 0 hours per week. (*National Youth Anti-Drug Media Campaign 2003*)

The *unemployment rate*, which is measured as the percentage of adults seeking work who are not successful in gaining employment, is one of the most important measures of economic well-being. Since 1948, the monthly unemployment rate in the United States has varied between 2.5 percent (in May and June 1953) and 10.8 percent (in November and December 1982).During the past decade, the U.S. unemployment rate generally ranged between 4 and 6 percent, which is considered a low rate of unemployment, since some degree of joblessness is inevitable in a dynamic economy. However, unemployment rose to 10.1 percent in October 2009 and was still at 9.7 percent in May 2010 (Bureau of Labor Statistics, 2010b).

The unemployment rate can be deceiving, however. In August 2007, for example, the official unemployment rate was 4.6 percent. If marginally attached workers were included (those who are not working and are not actively looking for a job, but say they want one and have had one within the past year), however, the rate would have gone up to 5.5 percent. Then, if workers who had only part-time employment but wanted full-time jobs were included, the "real" unemployment rate would have been 8.4 percent as of August 2007 (U.S. Bureau of Labor Statistics 2007), almost twice the official unemployment rate. In other words, even in the strong economy of 2007, 1 of every 12 adult Americans was either unemployed or employed for fewer hours than they preferred.

Another important economic measure is the *poverty rate*. This statistic is even less precise than the unemployment rate, since defining how much income puts one above poverty is subjective, but nevertheless it is a closely watched economic indicator. In 2008, 10.3 percent of families in the United States had incomes below the poverty level, up from 8.7 percent in 2000, although still much better than the rate of 18.5 percent in 1959. Similarly, 13.2 percent of individuals fell below the poverty level in 2008, up from 11.3 percent in 2000, but down from 22.4 percent in 1959. So the long-term trends have clearly been positive, with ups and downs and a worrisome recent increase in poverty since 2000 (U.S. Census Bureau 2007a, 2010b).

Yet another key economic measure is *income inequality*, which indicates how much range there is between low-income and high-income individuals or families. In the United States, income inequality decreased from 1947 to 1968, but it has been increasing since 1968 (Weinberg 1996). In other words, since 1968 the rich have been getting richer. How much of a problem this represents is a matter of opinion, of course. Democrats and liberals tend to see income inequality as a serious social and economic problem and generally push for income redistribution remedies, such as progressive income, estate, and inheritance taxes and higher unemployment and welfare payments. Republicans and conservatives, on the other hand, do not necessarily regard income inequality as a problem, seeing it instead as a natural consequence of capitalism (market forces) and differences in peoples' abilities and willingness to work hard.

In sum, the U.S. economy thrived for several decades, and Americans are better off economically than most other people in the world. However, the current situation is difficult, and trends in income inequality, unemployment, and the poverty rate are worrisome. Also, globalization, the changing nature of jobs, and the much greater participation of women in the workforce all have ripple effects for social relations, families, and other aspects of modern society. Collectively, these are likely to affect the nature of crime, disorder, and the demand for police services in the future, albeit in unpredictable ways.

Immigration and Migration

Americans are becoming older and more diverse, and they face a challenging economic situation. One additional factor to consider is population immigration and *migration*, which result in large demographic variations among different states and regions. For example, Figure 15.2 shows the concentration of elderly residents in different states. The high level of over-65 residents in Florida (17.6 percent of all citizens, compared with the national average of 12.4 percent) is not much of a surprise, given that state's reputation as a retirement haven. Also not surprising is the state with the lowest proportion of over-65 residents—Alaska, with only 5.7 percent. But one might expect other warm-weather states such as Texas (9.9 percent) and California (10.6 percent) to have high levels of elderly, yet they do not. This is probably because of levels of in-migration (from other states) and immigration (from other countries) of younger as well as older persons into Texas and California.

Migration patterns within the United States lead to differences in the proportion of the population living in a state that was born in that state. The states with the highest levels of "native-born" residents (born within the state) are Louisiana, Pennsylvania, and Michigan (U.S. Census Bureau 2002b). The states with the lowest levels of residents born in the state are Nevada, Florida, and Arizona. These latter states are among the most transient in the country, and perhaps not coincidentally, all have higher-than-average reported crime rates.

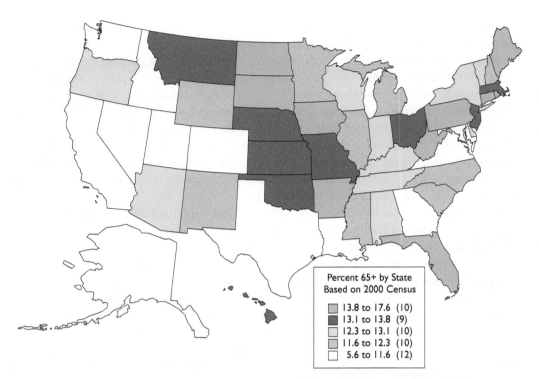

FIGURE 15.2 Persons 65+ as a Percentage of the Total Population—2000.

Source: Based on Census 2000 Data from the U.S. Bureau of the Census as presented in *A Profile of Older Americans: 2002* (Administration on Aging, U.S. Department of Health and Human Service).

States also vary dramatically in the proportion of their population that is foreign-born (the national average is 12.5 percent). According to 2008 estimates, California has the highest proportion of immigrants in its population (27 percent) followed by New York, New Jersey, Nevada, and Florida. The state with the lowest proportion of foreign-born residents is West Virginia (1.3 percent), followed by South Dakota, Mississippi, Wyoming, and Montana (Migration Policy Institute 2010).

One of the more dramatic demographic changes has been in the rural areas of America. In the nineteenth and twentieth centuries, population became heavily concentrated in metropolitan regions, as farm people moved to the cities to find work. This trend has changed in the past 25 years, as in-migration into cities has balanced and sometimes been overshadowed by out-migration. Growth has dispersed from the cities to outlying regions. Decentralization has given rise to edge cities, strip cities, exurbs, and rural sprawl. This centrifugal trend is characteristic of growth at the beginning of the twenty-first century. The states recording the fastest growth in rural areas are Nevada, Alaska, and Idaho. As new people arrive, the rural areas tend to lose many of their traditional elements.

The idea of rural communities conjures two related ideas for most people. First, we imagine small towns with a main street, a town square, and farmland or woodland on the outskirts. Second, we think of old-fashioned farm folk, sharing common customs and a common identity, rooted in American traditions. Today, both of these images are rapidly disappearing from America's rural landscapes, as they are transformed into exurbs inhabited by working commuters, retired people, and others seeking to escape big-city pressures.

Weisheit and Kernes (2003) identified several changes in rural areas. One is substantial growth in service industries. Another is that modern telecommunications have opened rural areas to many occupations that in the past were only practical in the cities. A third is that companies are drawn to rural areas by lower crime, lower taxes, lower wages, and a more peaceful lifestyle. There are also "modern cowboys," who include industrial engineers, shopping-center planners, software designers, and others. They can live and work any place and are linked by fiber-optic cables and wireless networks (Margolis 1993).

INSIDE POLICING 15.1 **SWAT in Small-Town America**

Rainbow City is a small community of less than 20,000 people, policed by a force of 19 officers. Only two or three cars are fielded per shift. Unlike many small towns, the department had a small tactical team, but the team was equipped only with handguns and shotguns. A Rainbow City detective, Gary Endrekin, was working an overtime patrol shift when Chris McCurley, the head of the Etowah County Drug Task Force, asked Endrekin to be part of a warrants service the following day. McCurley had personally worked up the case on Ezra George Peterson, the suspect and a 50-year-old probationer, and did not expect any problems.

Officers went to Peterson's house; Detective Endrekin and another officer approached the back while McCurley and others knocked on the front door. They were initially met with silence. When they tried to force entry, they encountered every officer's worst nightmare—a well-armed suspect opening up with an AK-47 assault rifle.

"I was around back with another officer and I heard the door crash in," Endrekin said. "I heard the sound of a high-powered rifle and it sounded like it was fully auto. I ran around to the front and was hit in the legs. Endrekin crawled behind a van on the property, but the suspect seemed specifically to target the wounded detective. He just kept shooting, ricocheting the shots off the ground," said Endrekin.

Without warning, the suspect came out of the house, moving directly toward Endrekin. "He was yelling, 'I'm going to finish you, you son-of-a-bitch.'" The experienced detective thought his life was over until his partner, Sergeant Tommy Watts, shot the suspect several times with a shotgun. The suspect went down, but he was not seriously injured because he was wearing body armor.

When the smoke cleared, the suspect had fired more than 200 rounds. Chris McCurley was dead. Gary Entrekin's legs were so badly torn up by the AK-47 rounds that he spent more than 2 months in the hospital and ultimately had to have one leg amputated. After this tragic incident, Rainbow City purchased H&K MP-5s and Colt AR-15s. The department also provided training with the weapons and upgraded the capabilities of its tactical team.

Should small towns have SWAT teams? Or is a SWAT team an unnecessary move toward militarization, as some critics claim? In Handcock County, Mississippi, Major Matt Karl is the commander of the Special Operations division, a joint-department, special-weapons team. About 3 years ago, he became concerned that the law enforcement departments in his area did not have the ability to respond properly to a tactical incident. Karl took the initiative to contact managers in two small, adjacent departments, Waveland and Bay St. Louis, and developed a plan for a multi-department tactical team. Three years later, the team consisted of 26 officers who handled any situation beyond the capabilities of patrol officers. The unit even assisted an adjacent county that did not have a tactical team after a barricaded suspect held the local police at bay for hours.

SOURCE: Adapted from D. Stockton, "SWAT's Small-Town Question: How Prepared Are You?" *The Law Enforcement Magazine* (1998) 22 (4), 20–24.

These changes herald new directions in the way rural police do their work. Increasingly, they are developing ways to deal with their new, not-so-rural residents. Drug couriers are using rural areas as principal routes (Weisheit, Falcone, and Wells 1996). Rural police increasingly use citizen surveys to assess the opinions of their constituencies (McGarrell, Benitez, and Gutierrez 2003). Departments are confronting increasing problems with extremist groups (Corcoran 1990). Order-maintenance problems are expanding, requiring a new breed of rural officer, one trained in problem-solving techniques and skilled in modern technologies. Weisheit and Kernes (2003) envision several changes in rural policing to cope with these changes:

- The most remote areas will see the rise of live interactive "video justice."
- Technology will play an important role in rural crime prevention.
- Improvements in automobiles and highways will be particularly important for rural police.
- There will be dramatic improvements in police communications.
- Technology will play an important role in training rural police.

Inside Policing 15.1 discusses one new phenomenon in rural policing—the need for SWAT teams. It seems increasingly likely that the Mayberry RFD model of rural policing, in which Andy and Barney handle whatever comes their way with old-fashioned common sense and, at most, one or two bullets in their pockets, is destined to give way to a more high-tech, legalistic, and professionalized style of small-town and rural policing, with fewer characteristics that distinguish it from urban and suburban policing.

Modern Problems

Besides the kinds of social and demographic changes described above, it is likely that the specific problems facing the police will change over time. These are quite difficult to forecast, so in this section we simply discuss five problems that exist today but are not likely to disappear any time soon. Two of these are chronic problems rooted in police work itself—racial profiling and eyewitness identification. One represents an area of overlapping responsibility with the federal government—immigration enforcement. The other two are specific problems in the community that police must deal with, one longstanding and the other fairly new—persons with mental illness and cyber crime.

Racial Profiling

Racial profiling, or "driving while black," emerged in the 1990s as perhaps the most serious and sensitive issue facing police departments in the United States (Buerger and Farrell 2002). It was the subject of lawsuits, civil rights investigations, and consent decrees. It was discussed and debated in the U.S. Congress and in the 2000 presidential election. Many states mandated new police policies and data collection systems, and even more local communities did so. Only the events of September 11, 2001, deflected attention away from racial profiling, and when the issue reemerged, it was focused more on the profiling of potential terrorists and the effects this might have on the rights of Middle Eastern and Moslem persons. Then Cambridge, Massachusetts, police sergeant James Crowley arrested Harvard University professor Henry Louis Gates, Jr., in 2009 for disorderly conduct on the steps of his own home, and racial profiling was back in the headlines, leading to a beer summit at the White House, with President Obama serving as host and arbitrator (Sherwell 2009).

The racial profiling phenomenon underscores the continued salience of race for policing. Given the emphasis on community policing throughout the 1980s and 1990s, with its focus on community engagement and the improvement of police–community relations, it might have been expected that police–minority relations would have been greatly improved. During the same period, however, the Rodney King incident occurred in Los Angeles, the Amadou Diallo and Abner Louima incidents occurred in New York, and many other instances of questioned police use of force against people of color occurred in other cities and states. Understandably, uneasiness and suspicion continued to characterize race and policing, creating the conditions for the dramatic rise of the racial profiling issue.

This issue clearly strikes a strong chord in minority communities and among those most concerned about civil rights and civil liberties in America (American Civil Liberties Union Foundation of California 2002). While most police have ardently denied that they use, or support the use of, any such profiles, 40 percent of African Americans believe they have been profiled by police, and a majority of whites believe the problem is widespread (The Gallup Organization 1999). It seems likely that the term "racial profiling" has gradually expanded in the public mind and come to signify larger issues of racial bias and discrimination by police. For this reason, the Police Executive Research Forum has encouraged police departments to address "racially biased policing," not just the narrower problem of racial profiling (Fridell et al. 2001).

As racial profiling–inspired data collection has continued around the country, it has frequently been discovered that minority drivers are overrepresented, in comparison to the population, in vehicle stops by the police. They are also typically more likely to have their persons and vehicles searched subsequent to vehicle stops (Durose, Smith, and Langan 2007). Studies have also found that black and Hispanic pedestrians are more likely to be stopped and questioned than white pedestrians (Baker 2010; also see MacDonald 2010). Whether this overrepresentation of minorities in vehicle stops and searches is the result of police profiling (discrimination) or, alternatively, a reflection of police deployment in lower-income neighborhoods, police efforts to address crime- and gang-related problems, or even differential driving habits, is currently not empirically known (Engel, Calnon, and Bernard 2002). It is the subject of much discussion and debate, however. In the most promising scenario, police and citizens will work together to collect and analyze these data, interpret the results, discuss their implications, and fashion appropriate responses (Farrell, McDevitt, and Buerger 2002). This approach employs the themes of community engagement and collaboration within the framework of community policing to encourage open conversation about a very thorny and complex issue, something that has not happened often enough with respect to race and policing in America.

Immigration Enforcement

Immigration was discussed earlier as an important feature of American society. It is not a new feature, of course. As a nation, the United States was established by immigrants and has long been known as a beacon and destination for people from around the world looking for freedom and economic opportunity. There are Native Americans, but they represent a very small proportion of the entire population.

Immigration has become a tremendously controversial political issue in recent years, particularly in regard to the porous U.S.–Mexican border and the large number of illegal and undocumented immigrants who cross that border in search of work. In difficult economic times like the present, it is not unusual for public opinion to turn against immigrants, especially illegal immigrants, since they compete with U.S. citizens for scarce jobs. Also, it is commonly believed that immigrants cause crime to increase, although the evidence on this is just the opposite (Wadsworth 2010).

Traditionally, the federal government has shouldered the entire responsibility for enforcing immigration laws. Over the past decade, however, pressure has grown to use local police to enhance immigration enforcement (Prince William County Police Department 2009). Often this has been in response to local concerns about immigration and frustration that the national government seems unable to deal with the problem. For the most part, local police have argued against this trend, mainly because it creates a significant barrier between the police and the immigrant community, making it less likely that crime victims and witnesses will freely cooperate with police (Dickey 2010). Most local police would rather focus directly on crime and disorder, leaving the enforcement of federal immigration laws to the federal government, but in today's political climate the pressure is sometimes so great that they have to compromise on this issue, against their better judgment.

Eyewitness Identification

Two relatively recent developments have brought the practice of **eyewitness identification** to the forefront. One is the spate of death penalty cases in the United States in which after-the-fact DNA analysis has led to convicted persons being exonerated. According to one account, mistaken identification by a victim or witness was a factor in 75 percent of the first 200 such DNA exonerations, the most common factor by far (Innocence Project 2007).

Of course, police and the courts have long known that eyewitness identifications can be mistaken. As safeguards, police have developed systematic methods for conducting photographic and in-person line-ups to make sure that eyewitness identifications are valid. In particular, police are careful to show witnesses several (typically six) similar-looking photos simultaneously in one display or several similar-looking live suspects simultaneously in a line and to refrain from any suggestive remarks that might point the witness toward any one suspect. However, recent research has revealed that this simultaneous method inadvertently leads to some number of false identifications because witnesses often believe that the perpetrator *must* be among the suspects displayed (why else would the police be showing me these pictures?). Thus, witnesses have a tendency, conscious or not, to select the suspect who seems closest to their recollection, instead of limiting themselves to a certain or positive identification, as instructed (Wells and Seelau 1995).

As a result of this research, sequential rather than simultaneous line-ups became the new recommended practice (National Institute of Justice 1999). Using this technique, witnesses are shown one photo or person at a time, with strict instructions to decide whether that person is or is not the person they saw committing the offense. As often happens, however, subsequent research has been less clear than the initial study about which technique is most effective (Mecklenburg 2006; Schacter et al. 2007).

One might be tempted to discount the importance of this eyewitness identification issue, now that forensic science and "CSI" have become so sophisticated. This would be a mistake for two reasons. One is that most cases are still actually solved the old-fashioned way, relying more on information from victims and witnesses than on scientific investigation (Cordner and Scarborough 2006). The other is that recent reviews of such standard forensic science techniques as fingerprint identification, ballistics, bite marks, and others have raised serious questions about their scientific validity (National Research Council 2009). In other words, it is not just eyewitness evidence that might be mistaken.

This situation is emblematic of an important challenge to the full professionalization of policing. A genuine profession takes its knowledge base seriously, including new knowledge, and especially new information that directly affects the lives of innocent people. Equally important, new knowledge is treated cautiously until it has been verified through replication—this is a standard principle of the scientific method. Unfortunately, much of what we currently think we know about any specific aspect of policing is typically based on one study conducted in one police department. As research into police practices becomes more common and more authoritative, it will be incumbent on police executives to develop better mechanisms to incorporate new knowledge into police practice, while not succumbing to the temptation to overreact to any one new study until its findings have been adequately tested.

Persons With Mental Illness

Police problems related to persons with mental illness are not new. American society adopted **deinstitutionalization** of the mentally ill during the second half of the twentieth century, mental hospitals were closed or downsized, and thousands of people with mental illness were brought back into the community. Deinstitutionalization was supposed to be paired with a major increase in community-based services for people with mental illness, but these services have always been underfunded. As a consequence, society has come to rely on the police more and more for dealing with people who have severe mental health emergencies and for handling people whose mental health problems lead to substance abuse, homelessness, and similar public order problems (Cordner 2006).

What makes this particular long-standing problem current and likely to remain vexing for the police is that (1) American society shows no signs of improving the provision of social services or health care for people with mental illness, (2) mental health problems are increasingly entangled with substance-abuse problems (so-called dual-diagnosis issues), and (3) police encounters with people suffering severe mental health crises continue to have tragic consequences. All too often, police use standard techniques, such as "command voice," when trying to calm people experiencing psychotic episodes, the techniques fail, the person makes what is interpreted as a threatening move with a knife or other weapon, the police shoot, and the person dies (Fyfe 2000).

Some police departments have developed alternative tactics for handling persons exhibiting serious mental health problems that are demonstrably more effective than the standard approach of dispatching a regular patrol officer to handle the call (Borum 2000; Reuland, Draper, and Norton 2010). The most common approach is to prepare some patrol officers to be specialists and to give them on-scene authority whenever they can respond to such calls (Dupont and Cochran 2000). This crisis intervention team approach has great promise, although it works best in metropolitan areas with nearby mental health professionals and is a much bigger challenge in a small town or rural area miles away from the nearest hospital. Perhaps the bigger problem, however, is figuring out how to police the chronic alcoholics, drug addicts, and homeless people who live on the streets in many of our cities, a large proportion of whom also have serious mental health problems. American society has largely abandoned these people—abandoned them to the police, who are clearly ill equipped to really help them. This is an example of a present-day chronic problem that will continue to exasperate the police unless they can find a way to convince the public to support the kinds of social services and health services that can actually address the real needs of people with mental illness.

Cyber Crime

One obvious new form of criminal activity is **cyber crime**, or computer crime. Three categories of cyber crime involve (1) the computer as a target, (2) the computer as a tool for the commission of a crime, and (3) the computer as incidental to the crime itself or, simply put, as evidence. Crimes in which the computer is the target involve individuals breaking into or attacking a victim's system and may include activities such as hacking, cracking, sabotage, or so-called denial of service (overwhelming a website). Crimes in which the computer is used as a tool are typically traditional crimes, such as fraud, theft, forgery, embezzlement, and even stalking committed in new ways. Finally, crimes in which the computer is incidental to the criminal activity could include using a computer to keep financial records of illegal business activities or sending a threatening e-mail message to someone (Brenner 2001).

Although numerous efforts have been undertaken to provide a better description of the incidence and prevalence of cyber crime, what we know is still limited. The National Crime Victimization Survey has added questions to examine fraud, identity theft, and stalking among its respondents, and the FBI has included a question in the National Incident-Based Reporting System to indicate whether an offender used a computer in the commission of a crime. A recent audit by the Office of Inspector General (2010) in the U.S. Department of Justice found that there were 10 million victims of identity theft in 2008 and that numerous initiatives are underway at the federal level to deal with this growing problem, but that there is a lack of coordination and an absence of a comprehensive strategy.

Today, most large police agencies have established computer crime units, while smaller agencies typically rely on assistance from federal agencies, state agencies, or multijurisdictional task forces (for links to a large number of units and task forces, visit the Electronic Evidence Information Center at http://www.e-evidence.info/index.html). Federal law enforcement agencies took a lead role in providing computer crime investigation assistance to local and state agencies during the 1990s; however, their focus has shifted more toward counterterrorism since September 11, 2001. As a result, local and state agencies have an even greater need to develop their own capabilities in this area.

Cyber crime is an interesting "future issue" for several reasons. One is the growing ubiquity of computers—in cell phones, cars, trucks, appliances, home security systems, and so on. Another is the severe lag time for police in developing sufficient technical expertise to compete successfully with high-tech offenders. It seems likely that the police will always be at least a few technology steps behind serious high-tech offenders, guaranteeing that police will continue to need a lot of assistance from outside experts. This reliance on civilian experts generally makes police uncomfortable, but it is probably a long-term necessity in such technical areas as cyber crime.

Also, cyber crime and white-collar crime are more and more closely related. Major fraud is often committed with a computer today, or at the least, the evidence of these financial transactions is stored on computers. Recent scandals and exposés concerning the Enron Corporation, Bernard Madoff's pyramid scheme, and questionable practices in the accounting, mutual fund, mortgage, and banking industries are reminders that the biggest thefts are committed by men and women in suits, not by armed robbers or shoplifters. Most police agencies have never really accepted the prevention and investigation of white-collar crime as an important part of their mission, in part because there is little public clamor for them to do so—community groups tend to complain about speeders and rowdy kids, not pension fund fraud. However, as state and federal law enforcement agencies refocus their missions more toward counterterrorism, it may become necessary for local police agencies to give white-collar crime more serious attention.

Modern Technology

Technology has clearly changed policing in the past. Patrol cars, two-way radios, 9-1-1 telephone systems, and in-car computers have changed the way police do their work and interact with the public. Similarly, automobiles, televisions, air conditioning, computers, and a host of other technologies have changed American society, patterns of social behavior, and consequently the police–community relationship. As technological change speeds up in the twenty-first century, these changes in society and policing are likely to occur even faster. One entity that tries to help police agencies adapt new technologies successfully is the National Law Enforcement and Corrections Technology Center system (see Inside Policing 15.2).

New technologies are not always as beneficial as expected and sometimes have unanticipated consequences. Putting police in cars, for example, improved their response time to calls from the public and allowed them to patrol wider areas, but it also made patrolling less

---

INSIDE POLICING 15.2 The National Law Enforcement and Corrections Technology Center System

Originally created in 1994 as a component of the National Institute of Justice's (NIJ's) Office of Science and Technology, the National Law Enforcement and Corrections Technology Center (NLECTC) system is now comprised of three centers serving different demographic regions of the public safety community. The States, Major Cities, and Counties Regional Center offers a resource and outreach mechanism for state, major city, and county criminal justice system partners, with a mission of ensuring that larger criminal justice agencies (those having 50 or more sworn personnel) have unbiased access to a full range of relevant scientific and technology-related information. The Small, Rural, Tribal, and Border Regional Center publicizes its programs and services to small, rural, tribal, and border agencies across the country. The Alaska Regional Center serves as conduit for agencies in Alaska.

The efforts of these centers complement those of NLECTC-National, which coordinates NIJ's Compliance Testing program and standards development efforts for a variety of equipment used in the public safety arena, and the Centers of Excellence (CoEs), which support NIJ's research, development, testing and evaluation (RDT&E) efforts in specific portfolio areas. The CoEs focus on the following topic areas: communications technologies, electronic crime technology, forensic science, sensors, surveillance and biometric technologies, and weapons and protective systems. The National Institute of Standards and Technology's Office of Law Enforcement Standards provides scientific and research support to these efforts.

As a whole, the NLECTC System provides the following:

- Scientific and technical support to NIJ's RDT&E projects.
- Support for the transfer and adoption of technology into practice by law enforcement and corrections agencies, courts, and crime laboratories.
- Assistance in developing and disseminating equipment performance standards and technology guides.
- Assistance in the demonstration, testing, and evaluation of criminal justice tools and technologies.
- Technology information and general and specialized technology assistance.
- Assistance in setting NIJ's research agenda by convening practitioner-based advisory groups to help identify criminal justice technology needs and gaps.

SOURCE: For further information about the NLECTC System, see http://www.justnet.org/Pages/About.aspx.

personal and interactive. Putting computers in police cars has given officers much quicker access to critical information, but it also tends to focus their attention on the computer instead of on the community outside of the car. Table 15.2 presents a recent perspective on high-impact and promising technologies affecting the police field.

TABLE 15.2 High-Impact and Promising Technologies Affecting the Police Field

CURRENT HIGH-IMPACT TECHNOLOGIES

- DNA testing equipment
- Integrated databases
- Geographic information system (GIS) software
- Computer-aided dispatch with global positioning system (GPS) tracking of patrol cars
- Video surveillance networks
- Wireless access in patrol cars
- Inter-agency radios
- Use of force computer simulators
- Fingerprint readers
- Conducted energy devices (such as Tasers)
- Investigative software (such as data mining software)
- Body armor

PROMISING TECHNOLOGIES FOR THE NEXT 3–5 YEARS AND BEYOND

- DNA testing equipment
- Integrated databases
- Computer-aided dispatch with GPS tracking of patrol cars
- Predictive modeling
- Real-time crime monitoring centers
- Inter-agency radios
- Video surveillance networks
- GIS software
- Investigative software (such as data mining software)
- Patrol car cameras
- Personal audio/video equipment (worn by officers)
- Aerial surveillance equipment (such as drones)
- Computer-based training and simulators
- Software for victimization risk factor analysis
- Next-generation 9-1-1 systems (with advanced text and voice capabilities)

Source: Police Executive Research Forum, *Law Enforcement Technology Needs Assessment: Future Technologies to Address the Operational Needs of Law Enforcement* (Washington, DC: author, 2009), pp. 7–8. Available online at http://www.policeforum.org/upload/Lockheed%20Martin%20Report%20Final%203–16-2009_483310947_612009144154.pdf.

Suspect Control and Officer Safety

Since the use of force is at the heart of police work, technology that helps officers control violent suspects and combatants more effectively is of utmost importance. Closely related is technology that better protects officers from offenders who might try to harm them. In the suspect-control category, police today have less than lethal weapons and equipment, such as OC (pepper) spray, Conductive Energy Devices (CEDs, or Tasers), and rubber bullets, that often help them disarm or capture offenders without having to resort to the use of deadly force. Experience so far with the Taser has been mixed. It has clearly helped subdue many violent and resisting subjects, resulting in fewer instances of police using their firearms and reduced injuries to police (Police Executive Research Forum 2009). However, approximately 400 people have died in the U.S. since 2001 after being shot with a Taser, including more than 50 cases in which coroners found that the Taser played a role in the death (Amnesty International 2010, 6). This demonstrates that the Taser is not always a non-lethal option; also there have been many instances of police using the Taser when they undoubtedly should have employed even less forceful options.

The other suspect-control situation that may eventually be solved by technology is the high-speed pursuit. The need in this regard is for technology that can stop a car as opposed to stopping a person. A few technologies are already available, including portable spike strips, but police are hopeful that some kind of electronic solution will be developed that can be activated from the pursuing police car. One need only consider the dangerousness of pursuits for police officers and the public to understand how beneficial a technological solution to this problem could be.

The most important technological contribution to officer safety has been soft body armor, which has saved the lives of over 3,000 officers who have been shot or involved in automobile crashes (DuPont 2007). Modern body armor (often called a bulletproof vest) is much lighter and more comfortable than in years past, contributing to the willingness of officers to wear it regularly, even in hot weather.

Crime Detection and Crime Solving

Another category of technological change pertains to crime detection and crime solving. Crime detection technology includes devices to detect weapons and drugs, cameras that can record illegal behavior (including traffic violations), listening devices that can intercept illicit conversations, and biometric techniques (such as retinal scanning) that can identify wanted persons. Needless to say, each of these types of technology raises concerns about privacy and civil liberties, since what they do is increase the level of surveillance in society. Most people would support additional surveillance that helps prevent serious crime, but they do not want their own lives subjected to more government prying. It is not clear that we can have one without the other, however, making these modern crime detection technologies quite controversial.

Crime-solving technologies create fewer privacy issue problems since they tend to focus on crimes that have already occurred. Improved techniques for finding latent fingerprints at crime scenes and linking them to suspects have helped solve many crimes in recent years. Similar improvements in finding other types of evidence (hairs, fibers, fluids, etc.) have been made, as well as in linking that evidence to suspects (most notably through DNA identification). The use of technology and science to solve crimes in the real world is not nearly as systematic or effective as portrayed in the popular *CSI* television series, mainly because most police departments cannot afford the latest equipment, and most crime labs do not have sufficient staff to analyze all the evidence submitted to them. Nevertheless, science and technology have improved police crime-solving effectiveness and are likely to improve it even more in the future (Cordner and Scarborough 2006).

Crime solving does raise privacy and civil liberty issues, however. Fingerprints and DNA evidence are most productive when they can be compared against large databases—however, most Americans do not favor the creation of universal fingerprint or DNA registries, so available databases tend to be limited to previously convicted offenders and military personnel. Similarly, although current polygraph (lie detector) techniques are not considered completely reliable, there is little doubt that more effective techniques will be developed in the future. When that time comes, how comfortable will we be with a device that allows the police (or anyone else) to tell for certain whether we are telling the truth or lying?

Information Technology

It is widely accepted that police work is all about gathering and using information. In previous eras this meant that good police officers had to be persuasive interviewers and needed to develop informants and other human sources of information about crime and criminals. These skills are still crucial, of course, but modern technology has added an entirely new component to the quest for information. Today, a tremendous amount of information is stored in computer databases (criminal records, arrest records, tax records, business license records, telephone records, etc.), and tools exist that allow police and others to access such information quickly and with ease.

Information technology (IT) refers to the whole system of information collection, storage, retrieval, and analysis that allows officers to check driving records from the side of the road, review previous calls for service at a particular address to which they are responding, positively identify arrestees during booking, and base their patrol tactics on up-to-date crime analysis information. This system is mostly composed of electronic (computer) hardware and software, along with analytical techniques that usually still require a degree of human judgment and expertise. The hardware elements of IT keep getting smaller and faster, so that personal digital assistants will soon be standard equipment for police officers in the field.

One of the most popular IT developments of recent years has been crime mapping (Vann and Garson 2003) and **geographic information systems (GIS)**. Mapping relevant police data (crimes, calls for service, traffic crashes) in a timely manner makes the data more user-friendly for most police officers, as well as for the public (see Inside Policing 15.3 for an example of crime mapping available to the public). When a patrol officer is specifically responsible for a particular geographic area, maps can help identify crime hot spots, stolen car drop-off locations, repeat call locations, residences of parolees, locations covered by domestic violence emergency protective orders, and lots of other useful pieces of information that might otherwise go unrecognized or be forgotten.

The important role that IT might play in solving serious crimes was illustrated in the Washington, DC–area sniper case in the fall of 2002 (Sink 2002). This case represents a situation in which information about several crimes and one or more unidentified offenders was tucked away in different databases, maintained by different agencies, some of which were not even aware that they were part of a larger pattern. IT could have efficiently searched different databases and pulled together disparate pieces of information that might have helped the investigators identify their suspects more quickly, possibly saving additional lives. Unfortunately, in this case, as in so many others, many pieces of the puzzle did not fall into place until well after the suspects were identified and captured through more

INSIDE POLICING 15.3   San Diego Robberies and Aggravated Assaults

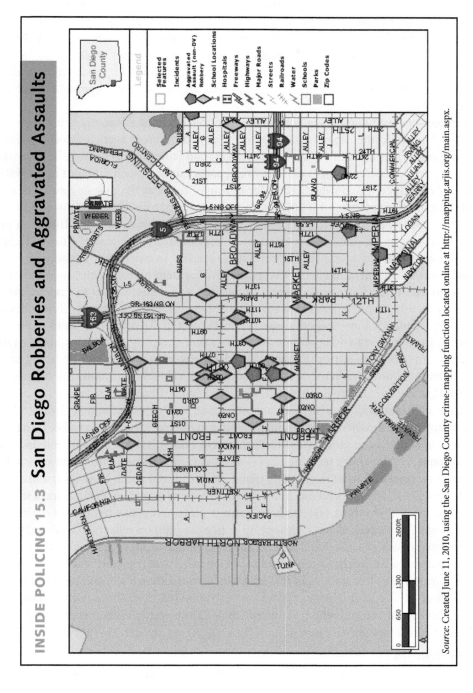

Source: Created June 11, 2010, using the San Diego County crime-mapping function located online at http://mapping.arjis.org/main.aspx.

traditional means. It will be very interesting to see whether modern IT can fulfill the high expectations that law enforcement currently has for it.

Communications and Interoperability

Since the introduction of two-way radios in police cars many years ago, police communications equipment has gotten smaller, more powerful, and more reliable. Nevertheless, police in many rural and remote areas still sometimes lack reliable communications between cars and with the communications center, and police in metropolitan areas sometimes have dead spots caused by massive buildings or access problems caused by heavy radio traffic on too few channels. These problems can be solved, of course, but at an expense that not every community can easily afford.

A bigger contemporary issue with respect to police communications is **interoperability**, which refers to the capacity of different units and different agencies to communicate between each other and also share digital information (computerized data). In many communities, the police department and the fire department have such different radio systems that they cannot communicate directly, for example. This was the case in New York and at the Pentagon on September 11, 2001. Also, it is frequently the case that town police and sheriff's deputies, or local and state police, cannot communicate directly. It is even more likely that local and federal authorities cannot communicate "car to car." This widespread lack of interoperability is sometimes just a nuisance, but in emergency situations it can be a significant impediment to effective response and incident management, as in the case of Hurricane Katrina. Efforts are currently underway at the federal level to find technology solutions to this problem, such as a so-called software radio that would allow officers to "dial" any frequency they needed to use (Vanu Inc. 2009). This solution faces opposition, however, from military and commercial interests that currently own the rights to most of the communications spectrum. In fact, the federal government is currently facing important decisions about whether to set aside more of the valuable communications spectrum for public safety use (Police Executive Research Forum 2010).

Police communications also play an important role in command and control—the police department's ability to deploy, manage, and maneuver its units in the field. The modern development of the **global positioning system (GPS)** has made it possible for police departments to keep closer track of officers and patrol cars. When automated vehicle locator systems based on earlier technology were first introduced about 25 years ago, they were resisted by police officers who did not want their bosses keeping such close track of them, but in the current era these systems have become more acceptable because of their role in promoting officer safety, as have cameras in police cars and on officers that record police–citizen interactions (Farrell 2009). In the future, command and control potential could be greatly enhanced by wearable miniature video cameras that transmit real-time video and audio back to the police station. In this scenario, commanders really will be able to control their officers in the field. This could reduce individual officer discretion and make operational decisions more consistent and predictable. Time will tell whether it would lead to policing that is more fair and just.

Social Media

Facebook, Twitter, texting, and other aspects of social networking and social media have burst on the scene in recent years, and some police agencies have been quick to adopt these new technologies (Barnes and Sipes 2010). One kind of application is for enhanced communication with the public—police departments can quickly and widely disseminate press releases, publicize their programs, and send out emergency notices. Perhaps more significantly, they can solicit information from the public in the form of tips, complaints, and suggestions. Used properly, these social media and social networking technologies can help the police engage the public and create a sense of community and togetherness.

Police are also using social media technologies in criminal investigations. Police have discovered that people will send texts and tweets to their friends and associates and post things on their Facebook pages that can be used as evidence (Hewlett 2010). Checking these kinds of "places" for evidence has become a standard step in the investigative process. Police investigators may also utilize social media more proactively to search out offenders and set up sting operations. As more and more human interaction occurs on the Internet and in virtual digital worlds, some of that interaction is related to real crime and disorder, making overt police presence and covert police surveillance an inevitable feature of virtual reality, just like in the real world.

Long-Term Trends

An important part of forecasting is to identify significant trends that are likely to have future consequences. Some demographic and economic trends were identified earlier in the chapter, such as aging and diversification of the population, increased participation of women in the labor force, and the changing nature of jobs. Also noted above was the trend toward more high-tech crime and police adoption of various modern technologies. In this section, we briefly discuss five other trends directly connected to modern policing—collaboration, privatization, federalization, militarization, and globalization.

Collaboration

Police have learned the value of collaboration over the past 2 decades, whether in the form of partnerships with the community or joint activities with schools, social service agencies, and other types of service providers. At one point in time, police had a tendency to think that they could deal with crime and disorder by themselves, keeping other stakeholders at arm's length. That is much less true today.

Two other forms of collaboration seem to be on the increase. One is with researchers and higher education. Traditionally, researchers and police had a hard time satisfying each other's interests because of differing basic assumptions, value systems, timeframes, and terminology (Buerger 2010; Stephens 2010). Increasingly, however, the problem-solving and "action research" frameworks have provided a bridge between the police and research worlds (Boba 2010; Scott 2010). Researchers are finding more opportunities to conduct interesting studies in and for police departments, and police are finding that research can be helpful to them in figuring out how to be more effective. Researchers can sometimes be "embedded" within police agencies, making real collaboration even more likely (Engel and Whalen 2010). To be sure, conflicts can still arise, but cooperation and collaboration have become more common.

The other increasing form of collaboration is within the law enforcement and public safety communities. Since 9/11, information sharing among police agencies and intelligence agencies at all levels has increased (Cordner and Scarborough 2010), along with increases in joint training, shared equipment, and shared or consolidated services. In the homeland security and emergency management context, police are now more closely connected to fire departments, emergency medical services, public health departments, and other significant elements of the safety sector than ever before. There is also a much closer working relationship between public police and private police/private security than in the past (International Association of Chiefs of Police 2004). Private security has not only grown in size over the past few decades, but also become more sophisticated and more professional, making them more legitimate and meaningful partners. Of course, there are still plenty of obstacles that interfere with the creation of true public/private partnerships, just as there are jealousies and turf battles that impede cooperation among public law enforcement agencies themselves (Emery 2009). However, the trend seems clearly in the direction of more and more collaboration, not less.

Privatization

Private policing is not new—in fact, private police preceded the formation of public police in London in 1829, and private detectives like the Pinkertons conducted most criminal investigations in the United States throughout much of the 1800s. Nevertheless, Americans are accustomed to thinking about the police as a public agency. Their public responsibilities, to represent the government and enforce the law, are central to the way most citizens believe the police should behave in a democratic setting. The public role played by the police today, however, may be shrinking in the face of **privatization**. Over the past 30 years, the traditional monopoly of the government over police services has diminished. Today in the United States there are three times more private security agents than public police officers (Bayley and Shearing 1998).

The trend toward private security is likely to continue, for several reasons. First, the police, by themselves, can only do so much about crime. Their behavior is constrained by due process in a democracy, as well as by social and economic variables outside their control. Yet, the public's fear of crime is not likely to decline and may increase. Private security has already begun to fill the gap for those who can afford to pay the price for extra protection.

Second, there is a change in the way we use physical space. The latter half of the twentieth century witnessed what Bayley and Shearing (1998) call the rise of *mass private property*—facilities that are privately owned but used by the public. These include shopping malls, college and school campuses, residential communities, high-rise condominiums, banks, commercial facilities, and recreational complexes. To that list could be added the increasing popularity of gated communities separated from their surrounding areas by tall walls and gates staffed by security guards. Private security specialists are the most likely form of policing for these kinds of facilities. Market-based private security will follow a market-based private economy. The outcome will be policing stratified by class and race.

Western democratic societies are moving inexorably, we fear, into a "Clockwork Orange" world where both the market and the government protect the affluent from the poor—the one by barricading and excluding, the other by repressing and imprisoning—and where civil society for the poor disappears in the face of criminal victimization and governmental repression (Bayley and Shearing 1998). This vision of the future raises important questions. Can we avoid a system where public crime control is carried out primarily against the poor?

Bayley and Shearing (1998) contend that we can, but only if we make two conscious policy choices. First, poor people need to participate in the market for security. Society should provide poorer communities with the ability to fund their own security. Such funding can only happen with the financial assistance of the federal government, interceding to prevent the continued split of American society into two camps—one well off and mostly Anglo, the other poor and mostly everyone else.

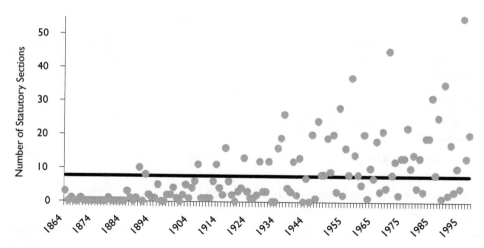

FIGURE 15.3 **Number of Federal Criminal Statute Section Enacted by Year (average number per year, 7.7, indicated by horizontal line).**

Source: Task Force on the Federalization of Criminal Law, *The Federalization of Criminal Law* (Washington, DC: American Bar Association, 1998), p. 8.

Second, community policing has to become the organizing principle of public policing. Since safety is fundamental to the quality of life, coproduction between the police and the public legitimates government, lessening the corrosive alienation that disorganizes communities and triggers collective violence. Community policing is the only police strategy that incorporates the problems encountered by the poor into decision making by the police. If society does not make a conscious effort to implement community policing and reinforce federal investment in local communities, it is possible that the character of policing could shift to private enterprise for the rich and public social control for the poor.

Federalization

A strong trend since the second half of the twentieth century has been the **federalization** of crime control and law enforcement (see Figure 15.3). In recent years, the U.S. Congress has passed more and more federal criminal laws, giving wider jurisdiction to federal prosecutors and federal police. Many crimes today, especially those involving guns or drugs, can be investigated and prosecuted federally as well as by state and local law enforcement. One might think that this would be an unmitigated positive trend, but an American Bar Association study (Task Force on the Federalization of Criminal Law 1998, 50) concluded differently:

- It generally undermines the state–federal fabric and disrupts the important constitutional balance of federal and state systems.
- It can have a detrimental impact on the state courts, state prosecutors, attorneys, and state investigating agents who bear the overwhelming share of responsibility for criminal law enforcement.
- It has the potential to relegate the less glamorous prosecutions to the state system, undermine citizen perception, dissipate citizen power, and diminish citizen confidence in both state and local law enforcement mechanisms.
- It creates an unhealthy concentration of policing power at the federal level.

- It can cause an adverse impact on the federal judicial system.

- It creates inappropriately disparate results for similarly situated defendants, depending on whether their essentially similar conduct is selected for federal or state prosecution.

- It increases unreviewable federal prosecutorial discretion.

- It contributes, to some degree, to costly and unneeded consequences for the federal prison system.

- It accumulates a large body of law that requires continually increasing and unprofitable congressional attention in monitoring federal criminal statutes and agencies.

- It diverts congressional attention from a needed focus on that criminal activity that, in practice, only federal prosecutions can address.

- Overall, it represents an unwise allocation of scarce resources needed to meet the genuine issues of crime.

It is particularly significant that the ABA Task Force reached these conclusions well before September 11, 2001. Since then, the nation's heightened concern about international terrorism and weapons of mass destruction has led to an even greater tendency to rely on federal laws and federal law enforcement. The ABA has continued to lobby against the over-federalization trend and Congress has recently held hearings on it (American Bar Association 2009), but there is little reason to think it will abate.

The biggest problem with this trend toward federalization is that it undercuts the very police officers and police agencies who are in the best position to deal with most crime—local and state police. It undercuts them in part because law enforcement resources are limited; more resources for federal law enforcement inevitably means fewer resources for state and local police. It also undercuts state and local police by sending a subtle message that they must not be effective or professional enough to deal with serious crime, thus the need for a bigger federal role. And finally, federalization undercuts effective policing because it "puts more distance between law enforcers and local community residents—in direct conflict with community-policing objectives" (Police Executive Research Forum 1997).

Militarization

The **militarization** trend is similar to the federalization trend. Traditionally, the regular military has been very restricted in its role in crime control and policing within the U.S. borders (the National Guard and Coast Guard are somewhat less restricted). Military police have had jurisdiction on military bases and with respect to military personnel, of course, but otherwise, the military has generally only been used for law enforcement or order-maintenance duties in serious emergencies, such as natural disasters or mass civil disorder, when martial law is declared. These limitations on the domestic police role of the military were enacted in The Posse Comitatus Act of 1878, which generally "prohibits U.S. military personnel from interdicting vehicles, vessels and aircraft; conducting surveillance, searches, pursuit and seizures; or making arrests on behalf of civilian law enforcement authorities" (U.S. Northern Command 2004).

While Americans have historically viewed the separation of the police and the military as an essential characteristic of their democratic heritage, this view may be changing. Kraska (1994) has observed a heightened level of activity linking the military to the police in the United States. He argues that the traditional separation of the police and the military is eroding today:

Changes in the post-cold war world and in the influence of contemporary militarism—the reliance on military-style force to solve problems—are eroding the separation between police and military activity, resulting in a military involved in law enforcement, and the police at times operating "militarily," all under the guise of ameliorating "social problems." *(Kraska 1994, 1)*

Kraska cited several examples of military involvement in domestic affairs:

- The Washington, DC, National Guard has used soldiers to assist federal and local police in air and ground transportation, lending military equipment, demolishing crack houses, and flying aerial surveillance missions.

- Portland, Oregon, in 1991 became the first municipality to deploy armed National Guard soldiers to assist local police in drug-related operations.

- Under the auspices of training, the U.S. military in southern Florida and Louisiana has conducted Andean-type exercises using military helicopters. Once the military locates a suspected operation and secures the area, the local police actually search and arrest suspects.

Military involvement in domestic law enforcement had been most common in conjunction with the so-called war on drugs until the terrorist attacks of September 11, 2001. Immediately after 9/11, it became common to see military personnel guarding airports and other critical facilities, and there have been calls for military participation in other types of counterterrorism efforts, such as controlling the U.S.–Mexican border. Similarly, after Hurricane Katrina hit New Orleans and other parts of the Gulf Coast in 2005, military assistance was instrumental in restoring order as well as providing humanitarian relief. In some citizens' minds, it is a fairly easy and comforting segue from U.S. Army Special Forces chasing terrorists in Afghanistan to U.S. Army units chasing terrorists in New York or California. For other citizens, however, the specter of U.S. soldiers patrolling the streets or knocking on doors in the middle of the night is frightening and antithetical to the American way of life.

Globalization

Another trend in modern policing is **globalization**. Developments in business, finance, trade, travel, communications, and computers really have "shrunk the world" in the past decade or two. It is far more likely now than 20 years ago that a local criminal investigation might involve international transactions and foreign individuals. These foreign individuals might have traveled to the local jurisdiction or they might have played their roles (as witnesses, victims, or suspects) from afar.

Many traditional crimes can have international features today, such as drug distribution and theft. Much has also been made in recent years of international organized crime, especially that involving Russians. Crimes committed with computers, including frauds, thefts, vandalism, and hacking, really know no boundaries. Then there are newer crimes (or perhaps crimes that are simply getting more attention today), such as human trafficking of women and children and illegal smuggling of immigrants, weapons, and even nuclear material. The term "transnational crime" has been coined to describe the increasingly international nature of crime.

Of course, international terrorism has become a huge concern for local, state, and federal law enforcement since September 11, 2001. Americans, and people all around the world, saw the death and destruction caused by a relatively small group of terrorists from the Middle East who had trained in Afghanistan. These were far from the first acts of international terrorism committed against the United States, of course, and in fact, other countries had been more seriously plagued by these kinds of attacks than the United States. The attacks of September 11 galvanized national and world attention, however, and drove home the new reality that crime and terrorism emanating from halfway around the globe could threaten American communities and American citizens.

Another aspect of globalization that has affected American policing has been the participation of local and state police in international policing missions in places like Haiti, Bosnia, and Kosovo (Perito 2002) and most recently in Iraq and Afghanistan. As the United States, the United Nations, the European Union, and other bodies have accepted peacekeeping roles in war-torn countries around the world, it has become evident that a key element in the restoration of order and civil society is effective policing. Typically, police and military forces in these countries were previously aligned with repressive regimes. Once the initial military phase of peacekeeping has been accomplished, the country needs reliable, professional policing to maintain order and reassure the citizenry of their safety. While a policing system is being rebuilt along democratic lines, police officers are brought in from around the world to provide police service and help train the country's new police.

Many American police officers have now had the experience of serving in such international missions, and many American police departments now see that part of their responsibility is to support the development of more professional and democratic policing in other countries. This is a relatively new awareness for American police and contributes to their sense of being part of a global police community. It is also a fairly new realization for those in the U.S. government responsible for foreign relations that "security is important to the development of democracy and police are important to the character of that security. Assisting in the democratic reform of foreign police systems has become a front-burner issue in American foreign policy" (Bayley 2001, 5).

It is difficult to predict all the future ramifications for policing of this trend toward globalization. Clearly, however, international issues and considerations once thought irrelevant for local American policing have become relevant and even significant. This trend can only continue.

Competing Police Strategies

In Chapters 2 and 4 we outlined the evolution of police strategies from the political era into the reform/professional era and then on to the community policing era. Community policing was widely accepted as the most effective and sensible policing strategy through the 1990s, but since then the events of September 11, 2001, serious economic difficulties and further developments within policing itself have complicated the situation. Today, two or three different approaches to the "big picture" of policing strategy are currently competing for the hearts and minds of police leaders, public officials, and the general public.

Terrorism and Homeland Security

Several years ago, Ed Flynn, then Massachusetts Public Safety Secretary and now police chief in Milwaukee, called terrorism "the monster that ate criminal justice" (Rosen 2003, 1). Since the events of September 11, 2001, terrorism and homeland security have dominated nearly every discussion about public safety in America, led to new legislation and a significant reorganization of the federal government, and dramatically changed national funding priorities. It is important to give these new priorities their due, and yet, at the same time, to remember that policing has many other responsibilities and concerns. Just to illustrate, every month in the United States there are about 1,400 murders, 8,000 rapes, and 37,000 robberies (Federal Bureau of Investigation 2007). Also, every month about 3,500 people die in fatal traffic crashes (National Highway Traffic Safety Administration 2007). To say the least, there are many very serious crimes and incidents demanding police attention besides those associated with terrorism.

The attack of September 11 demonstrated that a weapon of mass destruction could be delivered in the United States with catastrophic results. It also demonstrated that a small group of individuals from halfway around the world could have both the hatred and the determination to plan and carry out such an attack on American soil. As so many commentators have said, nothing will ever be the same again. For police, the fact that these individuals lived in American cities and towns for an extended period before the attack, taking flying lessons and making other preparations, raises the possibility that they might have been identified in advance if neighbors, patrol officers, and intelligence analysts had only been a bit more observant. Whether local police could possibly have anticipated the intentions of these terrorists has not been established, but certainly police are now trying very hard to identify any individuals or groups who might have similar intentions, as recent successful investigations and interdictions in New York and elsewhere have shown (Hays 2010).

One of the clearest lessons from the September 11 attack is the need for local, state, and federal authorities to improve intelligence analysis and sharing (Hoover 2002). At the local level, few police departments had sophisticated intelligence operations of any type, much less ones focused on international terrorism. At the national level, in the aftermath of the attack, it became evident that the FBI, in particular, had a very weak intelligence analysis capacity (Marshall 2003). For many reasons, but mainly its historic focus on criminal investigation, the FBI never developed a strong intelligence capacity in the counterterrorism arena, especially after the end of the Cold War. This shortcoming might not have been as serious if there was a strong tradition of information sharing among the federal agencies with intelligence responsibilities, such as the FBI, the Central Intelligence Agency, and the National Security Agency, but unfortunately, these agencies have historically behaved more like competitors than partners.

The federal government reorganization that created the new Department of Homeland Security was designed to improve information sharing and coordination among the various federal agencies with counterterrorism and law enforcement responsibilities. Time will tell whether the reorganization will accomplish these objectives. None of the major intelligence-gathering agencies, including the FBI, the Central Intelligence Agency, and the National Security Agency, was moved to the Department of Homeland Security, clearly indicating that interagency relations will still be key, even at the federal level.

New federal legislation addressing terrorism and homeland security is primarily to be found in the **USA Patriot Act** of 2001, enacted less than 2 months after the September 11 attacks. This act contains numerous provisions that can be summarized as follows (Doyle 2002):

- The act gives federal officials greater authority to track and intercept communications.
- It vests the Secretary of the Treasury with regulatory powers to combat corruption of U.S. financial institutions for foreign money-laundering purposes.
- It seeks to further close our borders to foreign terrorists and to detain and remove those within our borders.
- It creates new crimes, new penalties, and new procedural efficiencies for use against domestic and international terrorists.

The Patriot Act has been very controversial since its enactment. Critics have been concerned about invasions of privacy, including the much-celebrated authority to examine library records, the authorization of "sneak-and-peek" search warrants, and the expansion of government access to confidential information. By the same token, much of the investigative and intelligence-gathering authority in the act had previously been authorized for drug and organized crime investigations and was merely extended to counterterrorism (Olson 2003). Additional controversies have since developed over electronic surveillance of telephone calls and e-mails by the National Security Agency and over the detention and processing of terrorism suspects classified as enemy combatants. Despite criticism of the Patriot Act and the Bush administration's approach to the "War on Terror," the Obama administration has made few if any major changes since entering the White House in 2009 (Friedman and Hansen 2009).

The American people want to be safe and free. Over time, and especially in response to crime waves, drug epidemics, and, most recently, terrorism, the immediate concern for safety often gets stronger, leading to new laws like the Patriot Act and more funding for police and public safety. Usually, however, the countervailing desire for freedom helps check increases in government power and authority. Also, new laws and practices are subject to constitutionality questions, and sometimes the courts tell the executive or legislative branches that they have gone too far. Whether the Patriot Act went too far is a political and legal question that has been debated hotly since it was enacted, and that debate will no doubt continue. In the meantime, it will be up to law enforcement officials to implement the act with professionalism and restraint to maximize both safety and freedom. Balancing the public's twin desires for safety and freedom is something that local and state police have a great deal of experience with, and we must hope that they draw on that experience in this new era of terrorism and homeland security.

All five long-term trends discussed earlier in this chapter—collaboration, privatization, federalization, militarization, and globalization—have large impacts on counterterrorism and homeland security. Information sharing and joint initiatives among law enforcement and intelligence agencies are essential, as are partnerships with the community, including the Muslim community. Private corporations have some of the information that law enforcement might like to include in intelligence analysis, and private security has a major interest in protecting commercial assets from terrorist attack. Despite some rhetoric about "hometown" security, America's initial approach to homeland security has been further federalization of law enforcement. Counterterrorism and protection against weapons of mass destruction seem inevitably to give the military a larger domestic role and to further militarize local, state, and federal policing. And despite our longer experience with domestic terrorism, the more recent emergence of international terrorism dramatically demonstrates the global nature of the problem and the necessity for a global response.

Compstat and Performance Management

Compstat, the command accountability system developed in New York in the 1990s and later adopted in many other police agencies, was described and discussed earlier in the text. Clearly, Compstat has been a kind of two-edge sword. On the positive side, it has helped police executives focus their agencies' attention squarely on reducing crime by targeting current crime and disorder hot spots. It has elevated the role of crime analysis and crime mapping, making day-to-day policing more data driven (Shane 2007). In agencies where police tactics were traditionally rather passive, it has shifted them toward a more proactive and relentless approach (Henry 2002).

The downside of Compstat has been that it can lead to an excessively short-term and shortsighted approach to policing. The relentless focus on reacting to yesterday's crime patterns can deflect attention from longer-term trends and patterns. The hot spots orientation tends to lead to a "cops on dots" mentality that emphasizes deploying officers to precise locations, but only to create police visibility and engage in enforcement. Also, Compstat tends to put a lot of pressure on police commanders and police officers to show positive results—this has been found to lead to creative bookkeeping and manipulation of statistics (Eterno and Silverman 2010; Rayman 2010). One common adage in the management world is "you get what you measure." Sometimes, however, what happens is that you get what you measure, whether it really happened or not.

Compstat is part of a more general trend toward emphasizing performance management and "managerialism" as the key means of improving police organizational effectiveness (Loveday 2008). Traditionally, this has been difficult to accomplish in police administration, partly because data systems were inadequate and partly because it is so hard to specifically define and measure the most important dimensions of the police function. Modern data systems have made it *seem* more feasible to use performance measurement to manage police behavior and steer the police organization, but some critics think this is mostly a myth (Manning 2008). It may be that Compstat and managerialism are little more than high-tech versions of traditional bureaucratic management, based as they are on the assumption that managers need to closely direct and control the activities of police officers to get them to do their work effectively (Willis, Mastrofski, and Weisburd 2007). As Chief Richard Myers argues in his Voices From the Field, a dramatically different approach to police leadership and management may be needed as we move further into the twenty-first century.

COP, POP, and ILP

Compstat is not the only major innovation to have surfaced in the past decade or two, and terrorism and homeland security are not the only important issues facing police agencies today. Terrorism is such a serious threat, however, that some have contemplated whether existing police strategies are still up to the job. Because terrorists are so violent and so determined to commit dreadful acts on behalf of their causes, it has been suggested that policing strategies based on openness, consent, and cooperation must be reconsidered (de Guzman 2002).

While understandable, this point of view seems shortsighted and ultimately a concession to those who use terror to achieve their ends. Many others in the police field are more inclined to argue that community policing (COP) and problem-oriented policing (POP) represent the most promising approaches to homeland (and hometown) security (Burack 2003; Newman and Clarke 2008). Neither of these approaches, of course, precludes the use of supplementary and specialized responses to terrorism. But COP and POP still seem to be the most effective police strategies for controlling crime and disorder and reducing fear, while protecting the legitimacy of the police institution in a free and open society. Inside Policing 15.4 presents a resolution adopted by the International Association of Chiefs of Police in 2002 in support of a community policing approach to homeland security. A similar view was echoed by Charles Ramsey, Police Commissioner in Philadelphia and former Chief of Police in Washington, DC (2002, 6–7):

> While many U.S. law enforcement agencies have adopted community-policing strategies in recent years, traumatic events like the 9/11 attacks can cause organizations to fall back

VOICES FROM THE FIELD

Chief Richard W. Myers
Colorado Springs Police Department

Question: Besides technology, how will policing change in the next 25 years?

Answer: While technology and innovation have stimulated ideas and programs to nudge policing to a more progressive future, the remaining icon of policing that desperately needs to be moving toward the future is **leadership**. Leading police organizations in the future is likely to be significantly different than traditional police leadership, and it's not too soon to develop future models.

Some elements of leadership are NOT likely to change: strong interpersonal skills, the ability to communicate effectively, and the importance of inspiring employees will always be necessary components of a great leader. Leadership styles are quite varied, with some leaders practicing hands-on direction at the ground level, while others focus more on the big picture view. Regardless of present leadership styles, future models will surely draw some from the present, mixed with previously untested methods.

The classic leadership model that has always dominated in policing is the pyramidal hierarchy. Many progressive organizations have already begun the shift to more net-centric structures. In a networked model, the leader's job is to define the boundaries within which empowered employees can work with greater autonomy, persistently clarify the organizational mission, and provide the networked employees the resources they need to do their work. Providing the context of the mission and keeping the network intensely focused on its achievement will dominate the future leader's role.

Leadership will also have to change to reflect the profile of future employees: techno-savvy, diverse in thought and backgrounds, less responsive to autocratic direction, more mission focused than task driven. Applying traditional leadership with such a future workforce will likely lead to a dysfunctional outcome.

Just as leadership in the future will be different, the selection of police officers also will be different. Selecting candidates with high character indicators and effective communication skills will continue, but there will be far less importance on knowledge of law, police procedures, and even physical prowess. A team of blended skill sets, many previously undervalued in policing, is most likely to yield a creative and outcome focused work unit that can work equally well within the high-tech environment and the high-touch human community. Relying on the old "tried and true" selection tests will not identify the blend of skills needed for the officer of the future.

There's an old saying that the best day to plant a tree was 50 years ago; the second best day is today. The same could be said for planning and developing future police leadership models.

Richard Myers is a Commissioner with CALEA and a member of the Board of Directors of PERF. Prior to becoming police chief in Colorado Springs, he was police chief in Appleton, Wisconsin.

on more traditional methods of doing business. Some police departments may abandon community policing for seemingly more immediate security concerns. Community policing, however, should play a central role in addressing these issues.

In conjunction with COP and POP, some police leaders today are calling for the adoption of **intelligence-led policing (ILP)**. Like Compstat, this policing strategy emphasizes the use of real-time crime analysis, but it also incorporates intelligence analysis in the deployment of both specialized units and regular patrol officers (Carter 2004). In principle, a police department's resources could be targeted *each day* on the most serious immediate *and* long-term threats and problems facing the jurisdiction, based on careful analysis of calls for service, crime data, intelligence, and information from a variety of other sources. This is a far cry from the traditional police strategy of simply deploying one patrol unit to each beat on each shift with no more tactical direction than "be careful out there." ILP might be described as Compstat on steroids.

This model of policing has been in use in the United Kingdom and Australia since the 1990s (Ratcliffe 2008). It tends to demand more centralization of information and decision making than is common in American policing, as well as more analytical capacity than most U.S. police departments can muster. So far, ILP has appealed most to large departments such as the NYPD, LAPD, and New Jersey State Police (Fuentes 2006). However, many other police agencies are in the process of upgrading their analysis capabilities, plus the states have developed Fusion Centers, with encouragement and some funding from the Department of Homeland Security, to provide analysis services and products to local agencies (Rollins and Connors 2007). It seems likely that ILP will become more popular and more widespread in the decade to come as police departments improve the efficiency and effectiveness of their systems for collecting, analyzing, and disseminating information and intelligence to field officers and commanders. If it does develop and mature, a key issue will be whether it helps to support and complement COP and POP, or, alternatively, whether it seeks to replace today's dominant police strategies.

The most recent developments associated with ILP are predictive policing and "real-time crime centers." The aim of predictive policing is anticipation—using data not only to react to incidents and patterns more quickly, but also to predict them in the hope of taking preventive or preemptive action. Prediction has been the ultimate objective of crime analysis for many years, but the current argument is that modern technology and data systems make it more than just a dream. Predictive policing is still a rather general concept at this point, one of those phrases that sounds modern and appealing but does not come with many details. It also raises philosophical and legal concerns, since our criminal justice system is designed to hold people accountable for things they have done, not things they might do in the future. Police strategists and civil libertarians alike will be watching carefully as this predictive policing concept develops over the next few years.

Real-time crime centers operate more in the realm of reacting to crime, but reacting *really fast*. These centers incorporate some of the types of analytical capability mentioned in conjunction with Compstat and ILP, but their focus is specifically on incidents occurring at the moment. They try to use real-time call-for-service information, real-time intelligence, video feeds from public and private surveillance cameras, and all kinds of other real-time data to provide immediate input to patrol officers, detectives, and commanders in the field. These real-time crime centers are a cross between an analysis unit or Fusion Center and an emergency communications center. Their development probably owes as much to modern technology as to police strategizing—they take advantage of things we can now do, technically, without a completely clear rationale for why we should do them. In particular, the proliferation of surveillance cameras has created an avalanche of new data in the form of pictures. Real-time crime centers are one police response to the challenge of trying to keep up with that avalanche and actually make tactical use of it.

In policing, as in many other fields, practitioners and observers strive to anticipate "the next big thing." In the modern era, we have a tendency to expect technology to provide the

INSIDE POLICING 15.4   **Homeland Security: Community Policing—A Valuable Tool in the Fight Against Terrorism**

WHEREAS, the IACP recognizes that in the aftermath of the September 11th atrocities, there is a clear danger to the public of additional terrorist attacks; and

WHEREAS, the IACP recognizes that while technology plays an important role in countering terrorism, there is a recognition that human intelligence is a key factor in both the prevention of and response to these acts; and

WHEREAS, the IACP maintains that it is imperative that law enforcement maintains the trust and support of the citizens as partners in the co-production of public safety; and

WHEREAS, the IACP maintains that this partnership has been established through the successful implementation of community policing initiatives; and

WHEREAS, the IACP maintains that community policing efforts have fostered those partnerships that are aimed at supporting and facilitating the prevention of terrorist acts and the response to handling these acts when they do occur; and

WHEREAS, the IACP maintains that community policing should be an integral part of the measured response to the threats to homeland security; and

WHEREAS, the IACP recognizes that the principles of community policing are even more important post-September 11th than ever before. The philosophy it represents, the principles for which it stands, and the strategies it offers, should further enhance the capabilities of law enforcement agencies, public safety agencies, social service agencies, and the corporate community to improve public safety in connection with potential terrorist attacks as well as non-terrorist criminal activity; now, therefore, be it

RESOLVED, that the IACP will strongly support and employ community policing as a valuable tool to provide the best possible readiness, response and handling of terrorist incidents; and that the IACP encourages governments of the free world to actively promote, support and fund community-policing philosophies and initiatives in an effort to prevent terrorist activity and ensure the safety and security of their citizens.

SOURCE: Submitted by Community Policing Committee of the IACP and adopted by the general membership in 2002. Available online at http://www.iacp.org/resolution/2002Resolutions.pdf.

next big thing. It might be hoped, however, that the next big thing in policing will have just as strong a component of collaboration and democratic values so that when new technical capabilities are adopted, as they certainly will be, the end result will be better policing across all the different dimensions of the police bottom line.

Summary

American society has always been very dynamic, and the current situation is no different. Consideration of police *and society*, then, must take into account the changing nature of that society. A few important facets of ongoing societal change include the aging of the population, the increasing diversity of the American people, shifts in jobs and other economic conditions, immigration, and migration of the population from cities to rural areas and between regions and states. Among the most obvious factors affecting policing are the different cultures and languages they now encounter, increasing income inequality, and a vast increase in the number of families with both parents working outside the home, leaving more children unsupervised after school and at other times.

Changing times create new challenges and issues. Among the contemporary issues facing policing that seem likely to remain salient are racial profiling, immigration enforcement, eyewitness identification, persons with mental illness, and cyber crime. Police practices need continuous refinement to ensure that policing is done in an efficient, effective, and equitable manner. Crime and disorder problems in the community need careful analysis and attention, whether they are of a long-standing nature, such as dealing with mental health emergencies, or newer problems, such as computer crime.

There is probably no surer forecast than that technology will continue to change, and change ever faster, affecting society and policing. Improvements in less-than-lethal weapons, soft body armor, crime scene investigation and forensic science, IT, and communications are likely to make tremendous contributions toward more effective and efficient policing. It is harder to predict the unintended consequences that will follow from these new technologies, except to say that there will be some.

Significant long-term trends that seem likely to affect policing in the future include collaboration, privatization, federalization, militarization, and globalization. Together, these trends have the potential to radically change the distinctive nature of American policing—public, local, fragmented, and civilian. Whether the momentum behind these trends is inexorable or more temporary is open to debate. The increasingly complex and transnational nature of crime and the sudden emergence of international terrorism suggest that these trends can only increase in momentum. However, everyday crime and disorder are still much more common than sophisticated international crime and more of a threat to the average American, suggesting that our local police may not become an endangered species anytime soon.

Terrorism and homeland security have dominated the police agenda since September 11, 2001. As a result, the authority of the police has been expanded, federal law enforcement has been reorganized, and state and local police have accepted new high-priority missions. Exactly what these new missions are, at least at the local level, is still being worked out. In the meantime, Compstat, COP, POP, and ILP are all currently vying for the attention and allegiance of police leaders and other public officials.

Critical Thinking Questions

1. The American population is becoming, on average, older. How will this make your life different from what your parents experienced? What impact will this have on policing in the future?

2. The U.S. economy was once based heavily on farming and later on manufacturing. Now, most jobs are in the service, information, or creativity sectors. What are the implications of these fundamental economic changes for social relations, crime, and policing?

3. Cyber crime and other types of electronic and white-collar crime are very complicated and technical. Do you think the average small police department will ever have any personnel competent to investigate them? If not, and if state and federal police become more and more focused on counterterrorism, who will investigate these types of crime in the future?

4. Which of the five significant trends discussed in the chapter (collaboration, privatization, federalization, militarization, and globalization) do you think will have

the biggest impact on future policing? Why? Which of the trends concerns you the most and why?

5. Police commanders will soon have the technical capability to sit in the police station and monitor what all of their officers are doing in the field, thanks to miniature video cameras that can be worn by officers. What effect do you think this will have on police work? As a police officer, would you welcome this new technology? Would you welcome it as a member of the public?

6. The USA Patriot Act is a controversial law. What liberties and freedoms do you think Americans should be willing to give up to prevent major terrorist acts? What additional powers do you think police need to be successful at counterterrorism?

References

Administration on Aging. 2009. Projected Future Growth of the Older Population. Available online at http://www.aoa.gov/AoARoot/Aging_Statistics/future_growth/future_growth.aspx#age.

American Bar Association. 2009. Testimony of Stephen A. Saltzburg on Over Criminalization of Conduct and Over-Federalization of Criminal Law. Available online at http://www.abanet.org/poladv/letters/crimlaw/2009jul22_mandatoryminimumh_t.pdf.

American Civil Liberties Union Foundation of California. 2002. *Driving While Black or Brown: The California DWB Report.* San Francisco: Author.

Amnesty International. 2010. Submission to the United Nations Human Rights Council. Available online at http://www.amnesty.org/en/library/asset/AMR51/027/2010/en/2ca99987-f73b-4707-9ad5-7758434a75ce/amr510272010en.pdf.

Baker, A. 2010. "New York Minorities More Likely to be Frisked," *New York Times* May 12. Available online at http://www.nytimes.com/2010/05/13/nyregion/13frisk.html?ref=nyregion.

Barnes, T., and Sipes, L. 2010. "Three Years of Social Media—Lessons Learned," *Community Policing Dispatch* 3 (January). Available online at http://www.cops.usdoj.gov/html/dispatch/January_2010/social_media.htm.

Bayley, D. 2001. *Democratizing the Police Abroad: What to Do and How to Do It.* Washington, DC: National Institute of Justice.

Bayley, D., and Shearing, C. 1998. "The Future of Policing." In G. Cole and M. Gertz (eds.), *The Criminal Justice System: Politics and Policies,* 7th ed., pp. 150–167. Belmont, CA: West/Wadsworth Publishing.

Boba, R. 2010. "A Practice-Based Evidence Approach in Florida," *Police Practice & Research: An International Journal* 11: 122–128.

Borum, R. 2000. "Improving High Risk Encounters Between People With Mental Illness and the Police." *The Journal of the American Academy of Psychiatry and the Law* 28(3): 332–337.

Brenner, S. W. 2001. "Defining Cybercrime: A Review of State and Federal Law." In R. D. Clifford (ed.), *Cybercrime: The Investigation, Prosecution and Defense of a Computer-Related Crime,* pp. 11–69. Durham, NC: Carolina Academic Press.

Buerger, M. 2010. "Policing and Research: Two Cultures Separated by an Almost Common Language," *Police Practice & Research: An International Journal* 11: 135–143.

Buerger, M., and Farrell, A. 2002. "The Evidence of Racial Profiling: Interpreting Documented and Unofficial Sources," *Police Quarterly.* 5(3): 272–305.

Burack, J. 2003. "Community Policing in a Security-Conscious World: Working to Prevent Terrorism in Rural America." *Subject to Debate* 17(8): 1, 3, 7. Washington, DC: Police Executive Research Forum.

Bureau of Labor Statistics. 2010a. Employed Persons by Occupation, Sex, and Age. Washington, DC: U.S. Department of Labor. Available online at http://www.bls.gov/cps/cpsaat9.pdf.

———. 2010b. Labor Force Statistics from the Current Population Survey. Washington, DC: U.S. Department of Labor. Available online at http://data.bls.gov/PDQ/servlet/SurveyOutputServlet?data_tool=latest_numbers&series_id=LNS14000000.

Carter, D. L. 2004. *Law Enforcement Intelligence: A Guide for State, Local, and Tribal Law Enforcement Agencies.* Washington, DC: Office of Community Oriented Policing Services.

Centers for Disease Control. 2009a. "Births: Preliminary Data for 2007," *National Vital Statistics Reports* 57 (March 18). Washington, DC: U.S. Department of Health & Human Services. Available online at http://www.cdc.gov/nchs/data/nvsr/nvsr57/nvsr57_12.pdf.

———. 2009b. "Deaths: Final Data for 2006," *National Vital Statistics Reports* 57, April 17. Washington, DC: U.S. Department of Health & Human Services. Available online at http://www.cdc.gov/nchs/data/nvsr/nvsr57/nvsr57_14.pdf.

Corcoran, J. 1990. *Bitter Harvest: Gordon Kahl and the Posse Comitatus.* New York: Penguin Books.

Cordner, G. 2006. *People With Mental Illness: Problem-Specific Guide No. 40.* Washington, DC: Office of Community Oriented Policing Services. Available online at http://www.popcenter.org/Problems/problem-mentalillness.htm.

Cordner, G., and Scarborough, K. E. 2006. "Science Solves Crime: Myth or Reality." In R. M. Bohm and J. T. Walker (eds.), *Demystifying Crime and Criminal Justice,* pp. 104–110. Los Angeles, CA: Roxbury Publishing Company.

———. 2010. "Information Sharing: Exploring the Intersection of Policing With National and Military Intelligence," *Homeland Security Affairs Journal* 6. Available online at http://www.hsaj.org/?article=6.1.5.

de Guzman, M. C. 2002. The Changing Roles and Strategies of the Police in Time of Terror." *ACJS Today* 22(3): 8–13.

Dickey, C. 2010. "Reading, Ranting, and Arithmetic," *Newsweek* May 27. Available online at http://www.newsweek.com/2010/05/27/reading-ranting-and-arithmetic.html.

Doyle, C. 2002. "The USA Patriot Act: A Sketch." Library of Congress, Congressional Research Service. Available online at http://www.fas.org/irp/crs/RS21203.pdf.

DuPont. 2007. "Survivors' Club Salutes 3,000th Law Enforcement Officer Saved by a Protective Vest." Available online at http://www2.dupont.com/Media_Center/en_US/news_releases/2006/article20060307b.html.

Dupont, R., and Cochran, S. 2000. "Police Response to Mental Health Emergencies—Barriers to Change." *The Journal of the American Academy of Psychiatry and the Law* 28(3): 338–344.

Durose, M. R., Smith, E. L., and Langan, P. A. 2007. *Contacts Between Police and the Public, 2005.* Washington, DC: Bureau of Justice Statistics.

Emery, T. 2009. "It's Official: The ATF and the FBI Don't Get Along," *Time* October 24. Available online at http://www.time.com/time/nation/article/0,8599,1932091,00.html.

Engel, R. S., Calnon, J. M., and Bernard, T. J. 2002. "Theory and Racial Profiling: Shortcomings and Future Directions in Research." *Justice Quarterly* 19(2): 249–273.

Engel, R. S., and Whalen, J. L. 2010. "Police–Academic Partnerships: Ending the Dialog of the Deaf, the Cincinnati Experience," *Police Practice & Research: An International Journal* 11: 105–116.

Eterno, J. A., and Silverman, E. B. 2010. "The NYPD's Compstat: Compare Statistics or Compose Statistics?" *International Journal of Police Science and Management.* Available online at http://www.atypon-link.com/VAT/doi/abs/10.1350/ijps.2010.00.0.195.

Farrell, M. B. 2009. "San Jose Police Get Ear-Mounted Video Cameras in Battle for Image," *Christian Science Monitor* December 22. Available online at http://www.csmonitor.com/USA/2009/1222/San-Jose-police-get-ear-mounted-video-cameras-in-battle-for-image.

Farrell, A., McDevitt, J., and Buerger, M. 2002. "Moving Police and Community Dialogues Forward Through Data Collection Task Forces." *Police Quarterly* 5(3): 359–379.

Federal Bureau of Investigation. 2007. *Uniform Crime Reports, 2006.* Washington, DC: author.

Florida, R. 2004. "Creative Class War." *The Washington Monthly* 36(2): 31–37.

Friedman, L., and Hansen, V. 2009. "Obama's Terrorism Policy: Change if Necessary, But Not Necessarily Change," *Jurist* September 25. Available online at http://jurist.law.pitt.edu/forumy/2009/09/obamas-terrorism-policy-change-if.php.

Fridell, L., Lunney, R., Diamond, D., and Kubu, B. 2001. *Racially Biased Policing: A Principled Response.* Washington, DC: Police Executive Research Forum.

Fuentes, J. R. 2006. *Practical Guide to Intelligence-Led Policing.* New York: Manhattan Institute, Center for Policing Terrorism. Available online at http://www.manhattan-institute.org/pdf/NJPoliceGuide.pdf.

Fyfe, J. J. 2000. "Policing the Emotionally Disturbed." *The Journal of the American Academy of Psychiatry and the Law* 28(3): 345–347.

The Gallup Organization. 1999. *Racial Profiling Is Seen as Widespread, Particularly Among Young Black Men.* Princeton, NJ: Author.

Hays, T. 2010. "NYPD Undercover Unit Key in NJ Terror Arrests," *Washington Post* June 8. Available online at - http://www.huffingtonpost.com/2010/06/08/undercover-cop-unraveled_n_604094.html.

Henry, V. E. 2002. *The Compstat Paradigm: Management Accountability in Policing, Business and the Public Sector.* Flushing, NY: Looseleaf Law Publications.

Hewlett, J. 2010. "Lexington Woman Indicted on Manslaughter Charge for Fiery Crash," *Lexington Herald-Leader* May 27. Available online at http://www.kentucky.com/2010/05/26/1281229/lexington-woman-faces-manslaughter.html.

Hoover, L. T. 2002. "The Challenges to Local Police Participation in the Homeland Security Effort." *Subject to Debate* 16(10): 1, 3–4, 8–10. Washington, DC: Police Executive Research Forum.

Huntington, S. 1996. *The Clash of Civilizations and the Remaking of World Order.* New York: Simon & Schuster.

Infoplease. 2003. *Women in the Labor Force, 1900–2002.* Available online at http://www.infoplease.com/ipa/A0104673.html.

Innocence Project. 2007. *Eyewitness Identification Reform.* Available online at http://www.innocenceproject.org/Content/165.php.

International Association of Chiefs of Police. 2004. *National Policy Summit: Building Private Security/Public Policing Partnerships to Prevent and Respond to Terrorism and Public Disorder.* Alexandria, VA: Author.

Kaplan, R. 1998. "Travels Into America's Future." *Atlantic Monthly* August: 37–72.

Kraska, P. 1994. "The Police and the Military in the Cold-War Era: Streamlining the State's Use of Force Entities in the Drug War." *Police Forum* 4(1): 1–7.

Loveday, B. 2008. "Performance Management and the Decline of Leadership Within Public Services in the United Kingdom. *Policing: A Journal of Policy and Practice* 2: 120–130.

MacDonald, H. 2010. "Distorting the Truth About Crime and Race," *City Journal* 20 May 14. Available online at http://www.city-journal.org/2010/eon0514hm.html.

Manning, P. K. 2008. "Performance Rituals." *Policing: A Journal of Policy and Practice* 2: 284–293.

Margolis, J. 1993. "The Computer Cowboys." *Chicago Tribune* November 18: Sec. 2, 1.

Marshall, J. M. 2003. "The FBI: The Nineties and 9/11." *Understanding Government.* Washington, DC: American University.

McGarrell, E., Benitez, S., and Gutierrez, R. 2003. "Getting to Know Your Community Through Citizen Surveys and Focus Group Interviews." In Q. C. Thurman and E. F. McGarrell (eds.), *Community Policing in a Rural Setting,* 2nd ed., pp. 113–120. Cincinnati, OH: Anderson Publishing Co.

Mecklenburg, S. H. 2006. *Report to the Legislature of the State of Illinois: The Illinois Pilot Program on Sequential Double-Blind Identification Procedures.* Available online at http://www.chicagopolice.org/IL%20Pilot%20on%20Eyewitness%20ID.pdf.

Migration Policy Institute. 2010. *2008 American Community Survey and Census Data on the Foreign Born by State.* Available online at http://www.migrationinformation.org/datahub/acscensus.cfm.

National Highway Traffic Safety Administration. 2007. *2006 Traffic Safety Annual Assessment: A Preview.* Washington, DC: author. Available online at http://www.nhtsa.dot.gov/portal/site/nhtsa/menuitem. 6a6eaf83cf719ad24ec86e10dba046a0/.

National Institute of Justice. 1999. *Eyewitness Evidence: A Guide for Law Enforcement.* Washington, DC: Author.

National Research Council. 2009. *Strengthening Forensic Science in the United States: A Path Forward.* Washington, DC: National Academies Press.

National Youth Anti-Drug Media Campaign. 2003. *Keeping Latch-Key Kids Off of Drugs.* Available online at http://www.theantidrug.com/news/news_latchkey.asp.

Newman, G., and Clarke, R. V. 2008. *Policing Terrorism: An Executive's Guide.* Washington, DC: Office of Community Oriented Policing Services.

Office of the Inspector General. 2010. *The Department of Justice's Efforts to Combat Identity Theft.* Washington, DC: U.S. Department of Justice. Available online at http://www.justice.gov/oig/reports/plus/a1021.pdf.

Olson, R. 2003. "Responding to the USA Patriot Act." *Subject to Debate* 17(8): 2. Washington, DC: Police Executive Research Forum.

Perito, R. 2002. *The American Experience with Police in Peacekeeping Operations.* Clementsport, Nova Scotia: Canadian Peacekeeping Press.

Police Executive Research Forum. 1997. Position on Federalism. Washington, DC: Author. Cited in Task Force on the Federalization of Criminal Law. 1998. *The Federalization of Criminal Law.* Washington, DC: American Bar Association, p. 41.

———. 2001. *Racially Biased Policing: A Principled Response.* Washington, DC: Author.

———. 2009. *Comparing Safety Outcomes in Police Use-of-Force Cases for Law Enforcement Agencies That Have Deployed Conducted Energy Devices and a Matched Comparison Group That Have Not: A Quasi-Experimental Evaluation.* Washington, DC: Author. Available online at http://www.policeforum.org/upload/CED%20outcomes_193971463_10232009143958.pdf.

———. 2010. "FCC Officials Spar with Public Safety Leaders on Future Wireless Communications Needs," *Subject to Debate* 24 (March). Washington, DC: Author.

Prince William County Police Department. 2009. *Evaluation Study of Prince William County Police Illegal Immigration Enforcement Policy.* Prince William County, VA: Author. Available online at http://www.co.prince-william.va.us/docLibrary/PDF/10636.pdf.

Ramsey, C. 2002. "Community Policing: Now More Than Ever." *On the Beat* 19: 6–7. Washington, DC: Office of Community Oriented Policing Services.

Ratcliffe, J. H. 2008. *Intelligence-Led Policing.* Devon, UK: Willan Publishing.

Rayman, G. 2010. "The NYPD Tapes: Inside Bed-Stuy's 81st Precinct," *Village Voice* May 4. Available online at http://www.villagevoice.com/2010-05-04/news/the-nypd-tapes-inside-bed-stuy-s-81st-precinct/.

Reuland, M., Draper, L., and Norton, B. 2010. *Improving Responses to People With Mental Illnesses: Tailoring Law Enforcement Initiatives to Individual Jurisdictions.* Lexington, KY: Council of State Governments. Available online at http://consensusproject.org/jc_publications/tailoring_le_responses.

Roberts, S. 1994. *Who We Are: A Portrait of America Based on the Latest U.S. Census.* New York: Random House/Times Books.

Rollins, J., and Connors, T. 2007. "State Fusion Center Processes and Procedures: Best Practices and Recommendations." New York: Manhattan Institute, Center for Policing Terrorism. Available online at http://www.manhattan-institute.org/html/ptr_02.htm.

Rosen, M. R. 2003. "2003: A Year in Retrospect." *Law Enforcement News* December: 1, 4.

Schacter, D. L., Dawes, R., Jacoby, L. L., Kahneman, D., Lempert, R., Roediger, H. L., and Risenthal, R. 2007. "Policy Forum: Studying Eyewitness Investigations in the Field." *Law & Human Behavior.* Available online at http://www.jjay.cuny.edu/extra/policyforum.pdf.

Scott, M. S. 2010. "Policing and Police Research: Learning to Listen, With a Wisconsin Case Study," *Police Practice & Research: An International Journal* 11: 95–104.

Shane, J. M. 2007. *What Every Chief Executive Should Know: Using Data to Measure Police Performance.* Flushing, NY: Looseleaf Law Publications.

Sherwell, P. 2009. "White House Beer Summit: Race Row Policeman and Professor Make Peace," *Daily Telegraph* July 31. Available online at http://www.telegraph.co.uk/news/worldnews/northamerica/usa/5943630/White-House-beer-summit-race-row-professor-and-policeman-make-peace.html.

Sink, M. 2002. "An Electronic Cop That Plays Hunches." *New York Times* November 2: A1, A19.

Stephens, D. W. 2010. "Enhancing the Impact of Research on Police Practice," *Police Practice & Research: An International Journal* 11: 150–154.

Stockton, D. 1998. "SWAT's Small-Town Question: How Prepared Are You?" *The Law Enforcement Magazine* 22 (4), 20–24.

Taft, P. 1991. "Policing the New Immigrant Ghettos." In C. Klockars and S. Mastrofski (eds.), *Thinking About Police: Contemporary Readings,* pp. 307–315. New York: McGraw–Hill.

Task Force on the Federalization of Criminal Law. 1998. *The Federalization of Criminal Law.* Washington, DC: American Bar Association.

U.S. Bureau of Labor Statistics. 2007. Employment Situation Summary: August 2007. Available online at http://www.bls.gov/news.release/empsit.nr0.htm.

———. 2004. Labor Force Statistics From the Current Population Survey. Available online at http://data.bls.gov/servlet/SurveyOutputServlet.

U.S. Census Bureau. 2002a. *Demographic Trends in the 20th Century.* Washington, DC: author. Available at http://www.census.gov/prod/2002pubs/censr-4.pdf.

———. 2002b. *Geographic Mobility: 1995 to 2000.* Washington, DC: Author. Available online at http://www.census.gov/prod/2003pubs/c2kbr-28.pdf.

———. 2003. *Quick Facts.* Available online at http://quickfacts.census.gov/qfd/states/27000.html.

———. 2007a. *Historical Poverty Tables.* Available online at http://www.census.gov/hhes/www/censpov.html.

———. 2007b. *The 2007 Statistical Abstract: The National Data Book.* Washington, DC: Author. Available online at http://www.census.gov/prod/2006pubs/07statab/pop.pdf.

———. 2010a. *State and County QuickFacts.* Available online at http://quickfacts.census.gov/qfd/states/00000.html.

———. 2010b. *People and Families in Poverty by Selected Characteristics: 2007 and 2008.* Available online at http://www.infoplease.com/finance/economy/people-poverty-characteristics.html#axzz0yV2Nz48c.

U.S. Northern Command. 2004. *Posse Comitatus Act.* Available online at http://www.northcom.mil/About/history_education/posse.html.

Vann, I. B., and Garson, G. D. 2003. *Crime Mapping: New Tools for Law Enforcement.* New York: Peter Lang Publishing.

Vanu, Inc. 2009. *Software Defined Radio (SDR).* Available online at http://www.vanu.com/technology/.

Wadsworth, T. 2010. "Is Immigration Responsible for the Crime Drop? An Assessment of the Influence of Immigration on Changes in Violent Crime Between 1990 and 2000," *Social Science Quarterly* 91: 531–553.

Weinberg, D. H. 1996. "A Brief Look at Postwar U.S. Income Inequality." Washington, DC: U.S. Census Bureau. Available online at http://www.census.gov/prod/1/pop/p60-191.pdf.

Weisheit, R., Falcone, D., and Wells, L. E. 1996. *Crime and Policing in Small-Town and Rural America.* Prospect Heights, IL: Waveland Press.

Weisheit, R., and Kernes, S. 2003. "Future Challenges: The Urbanization of Rural America." In Q. Thurman and E. McGarrell (eds.), *Community Policing in a Rural Setting,* 2nd ed., pp. 137–147. Cincinnati, OH: Anderson Publishing Co.

Wells, G., and Seelau, E. P. 1995. "Eyewitness Identification: Psychological Research and Legal Policy on Line-Ups." *Psychology, Public Policy & Law* 1: 765–791.

Willis, J. J., Mastrofski, S. D., and Weisburd, D. 2007. "Making Sense of Compstat: A Theory-Based Analysis of Organizational Change in Three Police Departments." *Law & Society Review* 41:147–188.

GLOSSARY

abuse of authority Misuse of power by police that tends to injure a member of the police constituency. It can take the form of excessive physical force, psychological abuse, or violation of civil rights.

accreditation A process by which police departments are assessed in terms of standards of competency and professionalism. Accreditation typically involves a rigorous process of self-study followed by external review by an accreditation team made up of an official body of organizations. See also **Commission on Accreditation of Law Enforcement Agencies**.

actual danger Strong likelihood of harm in a situation based on the actual number and rates of deaths and injuries that resulted from similar situations.

acute stress A form of high-level distress caused by sudden emergencies such as shootings or high-speed chases.

advisory committee A committee composed of community leaders and upper-level and district police staff. Such committees are intended to create partnerships between the police and the community they serve.

affidavit A written oath establishing probable cause to obtain a search warrant; an officer describes exactly what is to be seized and exactly what is to be searched.

affirmative action plan An attempt to remedy past discriminatory employment and promotional practices.

andragogy An instructional method promoting the involvement of students and instructors in the learning process, stressing analytical and conceptual skills. See also **pedagogy**.

Arnold v. Ballard Court case (1975) that upheld the notion that educational requirements are legitimate and quantitatively verifiable conditions for employment as a police officer.

arrest The act of depriving a person of his or her liberty by legal authority for the purposes of interrogation or criminal prosecution.

balance of power The autonomy, authority, power, or status of groups or units compared with each other within an organization or a community.

beat meetings Regular meetings that bring together small groups of residents and beat officers, held to strengthen police–community ties.

bias crime A crime that is racially or sexually motivated, a hate crime.

bona fide occupational qualification A job-related standard that is permissible (Title VII of the Civil Rights Act) if a particular characteristic can be shown to be necessary for successful job performance even though it may discriminate against minorities.

bright-line rule A clear, easily understood, and easily applied standard in a specific situation.

broad police function Idea that the mission of the police is not confined to enforcing laws and apprehending lawbreakers, but also encompasses conflict resolution, victim assistance, accident prevention, problem solving, reducing fear, and social work. Broad police function is one of the central ideas underlying community policing.

broken-windows theory A theory proposed by Wilson and Kelling (1982) that posits that officers should pay more attention to minor infractions, such as public drunkenness and vagrancy. Attention to these minor violations may ease citizen fears and deter more serious crime from occurring.

career growth Occurs after an individual is recruited, selected, trained, and has completed probation in a police department. Career growth can involve officers learning new skills and techniques in their current positions as well as training for specific positions within or outside a department, new assignments, and promotion.

Carroll doctrine Provides for warrantless searches of motor vehicles if the vehicle is, in fact, mobile and if there is probable cause.

case law Written rulings of state and federal appellate courts that define when and how a procedure is to be used.

Castro v. Beecher Court case (1972) that affirmed the legitimacy of the Boston Police Department's requirement that police officers have at least a high school education.

centralization Retention of authority and decision making by the top levels of a police department.

certification A document (license or certificate) that states that a department or individual has met professional standards. It is typically given by a state-level organization.

chain of command Levels in an organizational (departmental) hierarchy; the higher the level, the greater the power, authority, and influence.

The Challenge of Crime in a Free Society Comprehensive report issued in 1967 by the President's Commission on Law Enforcement and Administration of Justice. The report documented the serious impact of crime on U.S. society and issued over 200 specific proposals for action. Particular areas of focus included police–community relationships and the low quality and education level of many police personnel.

change strategies Management methods used by a department to facilitate change.

Chicago Alternative Policing Strategy (CAPS) A big-city example of a continuing department-wide community policing effort, with measurable effects on crime, public opinion, citizen involvement, and problem-solving efforts.

Chief's Scholar Program A graduate program at the University of Cincinnati's Policing Institute in which highly qualified members of the Cincinnati Police Department are selected to become full-time (on-duty status) master's degree students in the university's Criminal Justice department.

chronic stress A form of low-level, cumulative distress that includes the day-to-day routine of the job.

citizen input Community policing belief that citizens should have open access to police organizations and input to police policies and decisions. Individual neighborhoods and communities should have the opportunity to influence how they are policed, legitimate interest groups in the community should be able to discuss their views and concerns directly with police officials, and police departments should be responsive and accountable.

civil laws Laws concerned with relationships between individuals (contracts, business transactions, family relations) as distinct from **criminal laws**.

civil liability The fact that a police officer, his or her supervisor, the chief, and the governmental unit of which the department is a part can be sued for monetary damages for negligent behavior; one of the most common legal methods to control police behavior.

civil service, or merit, system A selection method for filling government jobs determined by rank order based on the highest combined score on a written exam; oral interview; and physical, medical, and personal requirements; these requirements have often not been job related and therefore discriminatory.

civilian review board Group of citizens charged with investigating allegations of police misconduct.

class-control theory One of four theories to explain the development of police departments: to dominate the working class for the benefit of the industrial elite.

classical principles Rules governing a bureaucracy including specialization of work, assigning of authority and responsibility, discipline, unity of command, scalar chain of authority, centralization of decision making, and small spans of control.

coercion Occurs any time the police require citizens to act in a particular way.

cognitive learning Training that goes beyond learning a specific skill or task and instead focuses on the process that establishes logical and valid thinking patterns.

color of law The misuse of power possessed by an individual who is a "state actor" and derives power from the government.

command voice Firmly spoken order.

Commission on Accreditation for Law Enforcement Agencies (CALEA) National commission that accredits police agencies, public safety training academies, and public safety communication centers based on established standards and a process of self-study and on-site review.

community crime prevention An approach to crime reduction that emphasizes prevention through community-based activities such as organized blocks, safe houses, and citizen patrols.

community policing (COP) A mode of policing that is highly responsive to the identities and needs of the communities that a department serves. Among other things, community policing is characterized by philosophies and programs that promote ongoing police–community interaction, strong community partnerships, and a broad view of police responsibilities.

Compstat From "compare stats" it is a process that utilized timely crime data to analyze crime patterns on which to base appropriate responses, also known as an anti-crime program.

computer-aided dispatch A system that includes call taking, dispatching, and call disposition. The system also includes resource management, allowing departments to map crimes and alert officers of past problems in that jurisdiction.

computerized crime mapping A computer-generated map of crime information matched to a geographic area to help officers know where to concentrate their patrol activities.

conducted energy devices (CED) Weapons designed to disrupt a subject's central nervous system through the use of electrical energy (for example, the Taser).

consolidated agencies A type of police agency created through the integration of two or more police departments. This may involve two or more departments becoming one, or it may include two or more departments sharing functions, such as communications or training.

constable Official in medieval England appointed to assist the **sheriff**; later a British police officer.

constable–nightwatch System A system of law enforcement that began in England and prevailed in cities in the northeastern United States from the 1600s to the early 1800s; the constable provided limited daytime police services while the nightwatch patrolled after dark.

constitutional, or federally protected, rights Title 42 USC §1983 established that these rights need to be violated for plaintiffs to seek redress against police officers or departments; these rights are outlined in the Bill of Rights or the equal protection clause of the Fourteenth Amendment.

contingency theory Management based on the recognition that many internal and external factors influence police behavior and there is no one best way to run a department.

continuum of force A range of possible responses police officers use, from mere presence to deadly force, according to the intensity of resistance of suspects. The continuum provides officers with a standard for training in the use of force.

contract law enforcement A kind of policing that involves an agreement (contract) between two units of government in which one provides law enforcement services for the other.

controlling The process by which managers determine how the quality or quantity of departmental systems and services can be improved if goals and objectives are to be accomplished.

cop crunch Concern during the 1990s and early twenty-first century that police departments would not be able to attract and hire sufficient numbers of qualified applicants to replace personnel who were leaving.

counterterrorism Policing that aims to protect citizens from terrorist attacks. Counterterrorism activities must take into account the particular motivations and tools of terrorists and require new forms of cooperation between local police and federal agencies. Many current counterterrorism policies are controversial because of their effects on individual freedom.

crackdown An intensive, short-term increase in officer presence and arrests for the specific types of offenses or for all offenses in specific areas.

Crime Control Act Comprehensive federal crime legislation that led to the development of the COPS program and the hiring of an additional 100,000 police officers.

crime-control theory One of four theories to explain the development of police departments: to prevent or suppress criminal activity.

crime prevention through environmental design (CPTED) A strategy by which police and the community work together to control neighborhoods and buildings to reduce opportunities for crime. It includes target hardening and territorial reinforcement.

crime suppression Control and prevention of crime through the actual or implied presence of police.

criminal justice system Includes the police, judicial system, and correctional institutions. The police function as the "gatekeepers" of the criminal justice system because they make initial contact with law breakers and determine who will be cited or arrested.

criminal laws Laws concerned with the relationship between the individual and the government, especially in the areas of public safety and order (driving licenses, theft, rape, and murder), as distinct from **civil laws**.

criminal procedure The process by which a person accused of a crime is processed through the criminal justice system.

crisis intervention team Specially trained police officers given the responsibility to handle situations involving mental health crises. The team may work in partnership with other mental health agencies to bring understanding and compassion to the situation. A goal is to de-escalate the situation and perhaps resolve the situation without making an arrest.

critical-incident debriefing Counseling services provided to officers after an extremely stressful event.

cultural diversity A wide variation in racial, ethnic, and gender makeup of a police department; also of a community or society.

custody Situation where a person is deprived of his or her freedom in a significant way, such as during an arrest.

cyber crime Computer crime, involving the computer as a target, the computer as a tool for the commission of a crime, or the computer as incidental to the crime itself.

Davis v. City of Dallas The Supreme Court upheld the Dallas Police Department's requirement of 45 hours of college credit, even though it discriminated against minorities, because of the professional and complex nature of police work.

deadly force Level of force capable of killing a person; used to incapacitate a suspect who presents an immediate and potentially deadly threat to an officer or other person.

decentralization Delegation of authority and decision making to lower organizational levels.

decertification Process of suspending or revoking an officer's police authority. Typically exercised by a state board or council that oversees police training and officer certification.

de-escalation of force Behavior of the officer that may help to reduce the incidence of violence between the police and citizens. This may include nonaggressive behavior or effective communication skills.

defeminization The process whereby women who do not conform to sex-role stereotypes and are "tough" enough to gain respect as officers may be labeled as "bitches" or "lesbians" in an attempt to neutralize their threat to male dominance.

defense-of-life policy Policies that restrict the use of deadly force to those situations in which the officer's life or another person's is in jeopardy or to prevent the escape of a person who is extremely dangerous.

deinstitutionalization The closing or downsizing of mental hospitals during the second half of the twentieth century, bringing thousands of people with mental illness back into the community.

depolicing Phenomenon where, in the wake of a lawsuit, officers may feel the need to engage in fewer interactions with the public, particularly officer-initiated encounters. Officers rationalize this as a normal response to what they feel is an unjust situation and rationalize that their own likelihood of being named as a defendant in a lawsuit decreases if they interact with fewer citizens.

differential police response Differential response programs classify incoming calls according to their degree of seriousness and base the type of action police take on that classification. Such programs can decrease costs and increase efficiency.

directed patrol A proactive patrol method that uses uncommitted time for a specified activity and is based on crime and problem analysis. It utilizes computerized crime analysis and mapping to identify crime patterns and direct patrols to primary crime areas at primary crime times.

discretion The decision-making latitude of the police on whether to invoke legal sanctions. It may include the decision to investigate or not, to arrest or not, to pursue or not.

disorder-control theory One of four theories to explain the development of police departments: to prevent or suppress mob violence.

disorder index A UCR-like index used to standardize police calls for service (loud music, noisy juveniles, public nuisances). Over time, this index would provide police with an understanding of community concerns and priorities and be able to draw comparisons with other communities.

disparate impact A selection method can be considered to have a legally disparate impact when the selection rate of a group is less than 80 percent of the most successful group, also known as the four fifths rule.

distress Negative stress.

double marginality The situation in which minority police officers are not fully accepted by either the police or members of their own racial or ethnic group.

dual arrest In cases of domestic violence, the police arrest both parties involved.

early warning/early identification system A modern approach to police officer accountability that combines the bureaucratic and internal investigation methods; these systems track specific types of officer behaviors and then alert management when individual officers exceed the threshold for such behavior.

economic corruption The breaking of the law by officers to seek personal financial gain, for example, keeping drug money confiscated from dealers.

education Instruction in a general body of knowledge on which decisions can be based as to *why* something should be done on the job; concerned with theories, concepts, issues, and alternatives. See also **training**.

empirical evidence Proof based on systematic study of data.

enticement A police activity that purposely encourages someone to commit a crime.

entrapment Police activity that purposely provides a person with the opportunity and intent to commit a crime.

ethical formalism Idea of the absolute importance of doing one's duty. An officer who believes that police should "go by book" is an ethical formalist.

ethical relativism Idea that what is considered good varies with the particular values of groups and individuals.

ethical utilitarianism Idea that it is good results of one's actions that determines whether the action itself is good. For example, telling a lie (generally an unethical act) might save a life (a good result).

eustress Positive stress.

event analysis Refers to the police being aware of important dates, celebrations, anniversaries of events, and how these important dates may relate to upcoming situations. For example, the police need to be aware of the anniversary date of an act of terrorism and be alert to activity occurring on that date.

excessive force More violence that is needed to carry out a legitimate police task.

exclusionary rule A method for enforcing the reasonableness standard of the Fourth Amendment. It holds that evidence obtained by the government in violation of the Fourth Amendment's guarantee against unreasonable searches and seizures is not admissible in criminal prosecution to demonstrate guilt.

exoneration Clearing an officer of blame when an investigation finds a complaint is essentially true, but the officer's behavior is considered justified, legal, and within departmental policy.

experimental police district (EPD) A small, decentralized district within the Madison, Wisconsin, police department, serving as a test facility for new modes of leadership and community involvement.

external change Changes in policing practices or management that primarily affect a department's relationship to outside entities, people, or institutions, for example, the strengthening of police–community ties through beat teams and advisory committees.

extra-legal police aggression Acts committed by a police officer that are intended to injure someone physically or psychologically with no legitimate police function.

eyewitness identification Practice where an eyewitness identifying a suspect, often from a line-up, is considered convincing evidence in court.

false complaints Unfounded allegations of misconduct.

federalism A form of government in which some powers are exercised by the national government while many others are decentralized to state and local units of government.

federalization A strong trend throughout the second half of the twentieth century, the federalization of crime control and law enforcement means that the U.S. Congress has passed more and more federal criminal laws, giving wider jurisdiction to federal prosecutors and police. Many crimes today, especially those involving guns or drugs, can be investigated and prosecuted federally as well as by state and local law enforcement.

field operations Consists primarily of patrol and investigations but may also include units to handle traffic, crime prevention, victim assistance, and so on.

field-training officer (FTO) An experienced, well-qualified officer selected and taught to act as a mentor to a new recruit by providing on-the-job training.

fleeing-felon rule Guideline for use of deadly force in pursuit of someone hastening from the scene of a suspected grave crime.

follow-up investigation An official inquiry generally conducted by a detective to develop a case; includes identifying and locating a suspect, possibly obtaining a confession, and disposing of the case.

four-fifths rule See **disparate impact**.

frankpledge system A system for keeping order in medieval England based on tithings (10 families) and hundreds (10 tithings).

fruit of the poisonous tree doctrine An extension of the exclusionary rule that indicates that not only must evidence seized improperly be excluded from criminal court, but also must any additional evidence seized after that police action.

Garrity interview Compelled testimony for internal investigations; routine practice but not protected by the fifth amendment and cannot normally be used in a criminal proceeding.

general deterrence Patrol deterrence strategy focused on maximizing police interventions (e.g., attempting to reduce firearm violence by increasing motor vehicle stops for the purpose of seizing illegal weapons).

generalist A police officer who performs a variety of activities, some of which could be assigned to a specialist.

geographic focus A community policing strategy emphasizing the geographic basis of assignment and responsibility by shifting the fundamental unit of patrol accountability from time of day to place. Seeks to establish 24-hour responsibility for smaller areas, rather than responsibility for wide areas for 8- to 10-hour shifts; also seeks permanency of assignment for officers so they will know their community better.

geographic information systems (GIS) Computerized systems that enable spatial analysis of data, such as crime mapping.

global positioning system (GPS) A system or device that uses satellites to pinpoint locations on Earth, such as the longitude and latitude coordinates of a crime scene, traffic crash, or police vehicle.

globalization Developments in business, finance, trade, travel, communications, and computers have "shrunk the world," so now it is far more likely that a local criminal investigation might involve international transactions and foreign individuals. Many traditional crimes have international facets today, such as drug distribution and theft. International organized crime, cyber crime, and terrorism are also concerns.

goals General statements of long-term purpose. Goals are often used to identify the role of the police and in mission statements.

grass eaters Police officers who accept graft when it comes their way but do not actively solicit opportunities for graft, as distinct from **meat eaters**.

gratuity Something of value, such as free or reduced-cost beverages or meals, discount buying privileges, free admission to athletic events or movies, gifts, and small rewards. Most commonly it is beverages or meals. Some officers accept such gratuities from the public.

grievance arbitration In unionized agencies, this is an option for officers appealing recommended disciplinary action they believe is inappropriate.

Griggs v. Duke Power Co. Supreme Court case (1971) that held that even if an employment practice has discriminatory overtones, it may be allowed if the practice is job related (a "business necessity").

group norms Expected behavior from group members, which can be a powerful factor in resistance to organizational change.

highway patrol A state police force whose duties are generally limited to enforcing traffic laws and dealing with accidents on state roads and highways. See also **state police**.

homeland security The mission of protecting the nation as well as local communities from all kinds of serious threats, including terrorism and natural disaster.

hostile work-environment harassment A situation in which unwelcome conduct by other workers is so severe or pervasive that it interferes with a person's work performance.

hot pursuit exception A common exception to warrant requirements. Police may follow a felon or otherwise dangerous criminal into a place typically protected by the Fourth Amendment, such as a home, or may cross jurisdictional boundaries. Hot pursuits must be based on probable cause and the gravity of the offense must be taken into consideration. Once in a constitutionally protected area, the officer may search for the suspect and for weapons or evidence, but once the suspect is found, the search must cease.

hot spots Locations that have a greater amount of crime or disorder than other areas.

inertia A condition of doing things as they have always been done before; it is a strong influence in resisting change in police departments.

information technology (IT) The whole system of information collection, storage, retrieval, and analysis that assists officers in having ready access to information (such as driving and criminal records) and basing their patrol tactics on up-to-date crime analysis information. This system is mostly composed of electronic (computer) hardware and software, along with analytical techniques that require a degree of human judgment and expertise.

in-group solidarity A closeness and loyalty among officers brought about by the perceived danger of police work, the close-knit working relations among officers, concerns that outsiders cannot be trusted, and a common basis of patrol activity.

innovation The development and use of new ideas and methods.

in-service training A program to update all department members regularly on a wide variety of subjects.

intelligence-led policing (ILP) Policing model that emphasizes the use of real-time crime and intelligence analysis as the basis for deploying both specialized units and regular patrol officers.

intentional tort A tort (wrong) that an officer plans to cause some physical or mental harm.

internal affairs Section in a police department to respond to complaints.

internal change Changes in policing practices or management that occur within a department, for example, allowing for greater employee participation in the development and implementation of new policies.

interoperability The capacity of different units and different agencies to communicate between each other and also share digital information (computerized data).

interrogations Circumstances when the police ask questions that tend to incriminate the citizen.

job task analysis Validating selection and testing methods by identifying the behaviors that are necessary for adequate job performance.

job redesign An effort to enrich police work by broadening the role so the job will be its own reward.

jurisdiction The geographic area or type of crime for which a police force is responsible.

kin policing In early or nonindustrial societies, enforcement of customary rules of conduct by family, clan, or tribe.

lateral entry The ability of a police officer, at the patrol or supervisory level, to transfer from one unit to another, usually without losing seniority.

law enforcement Activities in which police make arrests, issue citations, conduct investigations, and attempt to prevent or deter criminal activity. A primary function of patrol officers.

Law Enforcement Assistance Administration (LEAA) An agency through which the federal government spent billions of dollars on the criminal justice system—focusing on the police—in an attempt to improve effectiveness and reduce crime.

Law Enforcement Education Program (LEEP) Established under the **Law Enforcement Assistance Administration** to provide financial assistance to police personnel, as well as to others who wished to enter police service, to pursue a college education; it significantly increased police programs in higher education in the mid-1970s.

leading Motivating others to perform various tasks that will contribute to the accomplishment of goals and objectives.

learning organization An organization that benefits from, and adapts to, its own and others' experiences.

legalistic style Policing that insists on enforcing the law in maintaining order.

less lethal weapons Weapons that are intended to knock down or incapacitate a dangerous suspect who has not responded to other techniques. They include bean bags and pepper sprays.

management Directing individuals to achieve departmental goals efficiently and effectively.

marshal A federally appointed official to keep order in federal territories (U.S. marshal); also a federally appointed local police officer (deputy marshal) and a locally appointed official (town marshal).

MBWA Abbreviation for "managing by walking around." Technique that police department managers use to better understand the challenges and issues that their employees face. Leadership that involves being seen, getting out on the "street," observing, and asking or answering questions.

meat eaters Police officers who actively solicit opportunities for financial gain and are involved in more widespread and serious corruption than **grass eaters**.

mere presence An officer's being in view in a situation, the mildest level of force.

militarization Involvement of the military with law enforcement. Traditionally kept separate, these two bodies now frequently work together in the so-called war on drugs and in anti-terrorism efforts.

Miranda rights Based on Fifth Amendment privilege from self-incrimination, police must take appropriate safeguards to ensure that a defendant's rights are not violated during arrest. Specifically, police must advise defendants that (1) they have the right to remain silent, (2) any statement made may be used against the defendant in court, (3) the defendant has the right to have an attorney present during questioning, and (4) if a defendant cannot afford an attorney, then the state will appoint one prior to questioning. The defendant must intelligently and voluntarily waive these rights prior to questioning.

National Advisory Commission on Criminal Justice Standards and Goals Commission that authored the highly influential 1973 *Report on Police*, a document that further advanced the higher-education recommendations made by previous commissions. The report included a graduated timetable for requiring additional higher education of all police officers at the time of initial employment.

National Advisory Commission on Higher Education for Police Officers A commission to study the problems of college and graduate education for police in the 1970s; a report in 1978 called for

significant changes in virtually all phases of police higher education, including institution, curriculum, and faculty.

National Incident-Based Reporting System (NIBRS) The FBI's redesign of the UCR program, which helps improve the quantity, quality, and accuracy of the crime offense statistics. NIBRS includes 52 data elements on 22 offense categories in the Part A classification and 11 offenses in the Group B category, for which only arrestee data are to be reported. It distinguishes between attempted and completed crimes, provides additional information on victim/offender relationships and characteristics, and includes the location of crimes.

negligent tort A tort (wrong) resulting from a breach of lawful duty to act reasonably toward an individual whom a police officer might harm.

nightwatch In olden times, group of citizens who patrolled at night looking for fires and other problems.

noble-cause corruption The abandonment of ethical and legal means to achieve good ends. Police may use both violence and subjugation of rights if they are more concerned about the noble-cause—getting bad guys off the streets, protecting victims and children—than about the morality of technically legal behavior.

occupational deviance Illegal behavior by an officer in the course of work or under the clock of police authority.

officer survival Major risks faced by police officers—officer stress, suicide, and threats—are countered through officer survival training.

Omnibus Crime Control and Safe Streets Act (1968) A major piece of legislation to deal with the national concern over crime; it created the Law Enforcement Assistance Administration.

open fields doctrine A search doctrine indicating that items in open fields are not protected by the Fourth Amendment's guarantee against unreasonable searches and seizures, so they can properly be taken by an officer without a warrant or probable cause.

order maintenance Patrol goal that may or may not involve a violation of the law (usually minor), during which officers tend to use alternatives other than arrest.

organization design The formal patterns of arrangements and relationships developed by police management to accomplish departmental goals.

organizational change A department's adoption of new ideas or behavior; a term often associated with community policing.

organizing The process of arranging personnel and physical resources to carry out plans and accomplish goals and objectives.

paramilitary model Formal pattern where the police are organized along military lines, with emphasis on a legalistic approach.

particularist perspectives Views of the police that emphasize differences among police officers, as distinct from **universalists perspectives**.

partnerships Programs, organizations, or police–community relationships that facilitate the community's participation in its own protection.

patronage system Unofficial practice in which public jobs are given as rewards for supporting the political party in power.

Peace Officers Standards and Training (POST) Organization that, in many states, sets standards for the evaluation of police personnel.

pedagogy An instructional method involving a one-way transfer of knowledge, usually facts and procedures, from the instructor to the student, distinguished from **andragogy**.

peer-counseling program A program in which police officers who are specially trained to recognize problems associated with stress from critical incidents provide support to colleagues and make referrals as deemed necessary.

perceived danger Harm that an officer of the public believes to be potential in a situation.

personalized service Stresses the personal, long-term relationship between a police official and the individuals they encounter. Police attention to personalized service can help create trust and confidence in the communities in which they work.

person-initiated danger An attack against a police officer by another person.

physical force Use of physical means to control or apprehend citizen suspects.

physiological stress A state resulting from physical, chemical, or emotional factors that can cause biological disease such as high blood pressure and ulcers.

plain view doctrine The principle that what police discover during the performance of their normal duties can be seized. For example, if a police officer stops a person who committed a traffic violation and the officer sees illegal items in the back seat of the car, then that contraband is in plain view and can be legally taken.

planning The process of preparing for the future by setting goals and objectives and developing courses of action for accomplishing them.

police brutality Excessive force, including violence, that does not support a legitimate police function.

police corruption Any forbidden act that involves misuse of an officer's position for gain.

police culture The informal, but important relations among police officers and the values they share. Police work is characterized by its own occupational beliefs and values, which traditionally include a perception of the police as sexist and macho.

police deviance Activities of officers that inconsistent with their legal authority, the department's authority, and standards of ethical conduct.

Police Executive Research Forum (PERF) An association made up of college-educated police chief executives; it passed a resolution calling for all police applicants to possess 30 semester units of college, increasing to a minimum requirement of a bachelor's degree for employment in policing.

police legitimacy Public confidence in the police as fair and equitable; the legitimacy of the police may be associated with the community's willingness to accept and obey the law.

police misconduct Actions that violate departmental guidelines (policies, procedures, rules, and regulations) that define both appropriate and inappropriate conduct for officers.

police paramilitary unit (PPU) A group of police that functions as a military special-operations team, primarily to threaten or use collective force.

police stressors Sources of stress for police, including departmental practices (e.g. authoritarian structure) and the inherent nature of police work (e.g., shift work, boredom, exposure to human misery).

police training officer (PTO) A new type of field training program developed for the purpose of initiating and training recruits in the two main components of community policing: community partnerships and problem solving. Differs significantly from traditional models and emphasizes adult learning (androgogical) principles and problem-based learning.

police violence Use of force to obtain confessions.

police auditor systems Developed more recently than civilian review boards, these systems do not usually investigate or monitor individual citizen complaints—that is left to the internal affairs. Instead, the auditor model focuses on the police organization and its policies and practices, ensuring that legal requirements are being met and that the most efficient and effective practices are being followed.

police–community relations Philosophy emphasizing the importance of communication and mutual understanding between a police agency and its community.

policewoman Female officer who attempts to maintain a "feminine manner" while performing police duties.

policewoman Female officer who tends to emphasize the traditional police culture, especially its law enforcement aspects.

political era A period, stretching from the middle of the eighteenth century to the 1920s, in which police derived their authority from powerful local politicians who utilized the police to maintain the status quo and retain political power.

positive interaction Positive interaction occurs when police talk with, assist, or form relationships with community members in their day-to-day activities. Positive interaction can help offset the negative (yet inevitable) effects of the more punitive and confrontational aspects of policing.

posse comitatus Group in medieval England called out to pursue fleeing felons.

posttraumatic stress disorder (PTSD) A psychological state caused by frequent or prolonged exposure to crises or trauma.

potential danger Harm that could exist in a situation.

predispositional theory The idea that the behavior of a police officer is primarily explained by the characteristics, values, and attitudes of that person before he or she was employed.

preliminary investigation An initial inquiry conducted by patrol officers of the purpose of establishing that a crime has been committed and to protect the scene of the crime from those not involved in the inquiry.

President's Commission on Law Enforcement and Administration of Justice Commission that issued **The Challenge of Crime in a Free Society** in 1967.

pretextual stops Officers stopping a suspect for a minor violation with the goal of eliciting another, more serious violation.

prevention emphasis Community policing strategy that emphasizes a more proactive and preventive orientation, encouraging better use of police officers' time by devoting the substantial resource of free patrol time to directed enforcement activities, specific crime prevention efforts, problem solving, community engagement, citizen interaction, or similar kinds of activities. Officers are encouraged to look beyond individual-incident calls for service and reported crimes to discover underlying problems and conditions.

primary aggressor laws Laws that encourage police officers to determine which of the parties in an intimate partner violence situation is truly the offender or primary aggressor.

private police Police employed and paid by an individual or nongovernmental organization.

privatization Trend in which public police are increasingly replaced or augmented by privately employed security forces. Privatization raises questions about racial and economic inequality.

proactive Proactive police work emphasizes police-initiated activities by individual officers and departments.

proactive arrests Arrests that occur as a result of a police initiative to focus on a narrow set of high-risk targets.

probable cause According to the Supreme Court, probable cause exists where the facts and circumstances within the officers' knowledge, and of which they have reasonably trustworthy information, are sufficient in themselves to warrant a belief by a man of reasonable caution that a crime is being committed. Hence, the officer has reason to believe that a particular individual has "more likely than not" committed a certain crime. Probable cause is the minimum legal standard necessary to make a custodial arrest of a person and it is a more rigorous standard than reasonable suspicion.

problem analysis triangle The problem analysis triangle (sometimes referred to as the crime triangle) provides a way of thinking about recurring problems of crime and disorder. This idea assumes that crime or disorder results when (1) likely offenders and (2) suitable targets come together in (3) time and space in the absence of capable guardians for that target.

problem solving Techniques to gain deeper insight into the issues that police are called on to address and to develop tailored solutions that have a longer-lasting impact on the problem.

problem-based learning Teaching method in which police trainees are presented with real-life problems that they must attempt to solve. Often part of PTO training programs.

problem-oriented policing (POP) An approach to police work that is concerned primarily with identifying and solving community problems, with or without input from the community.

procedural justice Refers to being treated fairly by police officers who are acting under the authority of criminal law, that is, being treated in an even-handed manner by police performing their law enforcement duties.

procedural laws Criminal laws that govern how the police enforce **substantive laws**.

professionalization Movement to help the police be more objective and effective in their decisions by forming a code of ethics, developing a scientifically derived body of knowledge and skill, and providing extensive education and training. These are all means to turn police work from an occupation into a profession.

protective sweep A limited examination of a home to determine whether there are others who could pose a safety risk for officers.

psychological force The use of nonphysical methods of coercion, particularly to obtain an admission or confession from a suspect.

psychological stress Anxiety. May challenge the individual's ability to handle or cope with the situation.

public information officer (PIO) An official who is responsible for managing the police department's public image, disseminating information, and interacting with the media.

public police Police who are employed, trained, and paid by a government agency.

public safety agencies Involves the integration of police and firefighting services (or other services like disaster preparedness, hazardous waste disposal, and emergency medical services). This integration can be limited to administrative matters or the cross-training of personnel to handle both functions. If cross-trained, it is usually the police trained in firefighting more often than the firefighters trained in policing.

quality leadership A department-wide management philosophy that includes principles of teamwork for planning and goal setting, data-based problem solving, a customer orientation, employee input in decisions, policies to support productive employees, encouragement for risk taking and tolerance for mistakes, and the manager as facilitator rather than commander.

quality-of-life policing Police strategy that targets the reduction of physical and social disorder so that community members will work together to promote neighborhood safety and concomitantly reduce crime.

quid pro quo harassment A situation requiring the employee to choose between the job and meeting a supervisor's sexual demands.

racial profiling The use of an individual's race or ethnicity by law enforcement personnel in deciding whether to engage in enforcement.

random patrol Police officers patrolling their beats at random (by chance) when not otherwise on assignment.

reactive Reactive police work is characterized by police responses to incidents when assistance is specifically requested by citizens.

reasonable suspicion Suspicion based on objective facts and logical conclusions that a crime has been or is about to be committed based on the circumstances at hand.

reform era A period, stretching from the 1920s to the 1960s, in which police derived their authority from the law and professionalism, which was critical to wrestle influence away from local politicians. The reform era de-emphasized the provision of social services by the police in favor of crime control.

regional police Regional police organizations are jointly operated by two or more local governments across their respective jurisdictions. Often overseen by a board or commission with representation from all participating jurisdictions, with funding provided by each on a proportional basis.

reliability The consistency of a measure in yielding results over time. If other observers conducted the same research in the same setting, they would probably come to similar conclusions.

reoriented operations An aspect of community policing that recommends less reliance on the patrol car and more emphasis on face-to-face interactions, replacing ineffective or isolating operational practices with more effective and more interactive practices, and finding ways of performing necessary traditional functions more efficiently to save time and resources that can then be devoted to more community-oriented activities.

research and development (R&D) A unit to help police departments to become learning organizations by going beyond mere statistical descriptions of departmental inputs and outputs and trying to develop new ideas, often based on research in the field

reverse discrimination The charge made by a group—usually white men—who feel that an affirmative-action plan in the selection and promotion process shows bias in favor of minorities and women.

rotten-apple theory of corruption The idea that corruption is limited to a small number of officers who were probably dishonest prior to their employment. The term stems from the metaphor that a few rotten apples will spoil the barrel; in other words, a few bad officers can spoil a department.

rule of law A principle of constitutional democracy whereby the exercise of power is based on laws, not on an individual or organization.

SARA model Acronym for "scanning, analysis, response, and assessment," a four-stage problem-solving process.

screening in Process of identifying police applicants who are the best-qualified candidates for the applicant pool.

screening out Process identifying police applicants who are unqualified and removing them from consideration, while leaving all those who minimally qualify in the applicant pool.

sensitization training Instructing an officer to be aware of the problems of victims as well as their own victimization; it should be conducted early in their careers.

separation of powers Principle of government by which power is divided between separate branches of a government. In the United States, power is divided among the executive, judicial, and legislative branches.

sexual harassment Unwelcome sexual advances that unreasonably interfere with a person's work or create a hostile working environment.

sheriff Originally an English official appointed to levy fines and keep order in a county; later in the United States an official, usually elected, who enforces the law in rural areas. In addition to patrol and investigations, a sheriff's duties often include managing a jail and providing services for courts.

situational crime prevention Crime prevention approach emphasizing the necessity of tailoring crime prevention responses to the specific characteristics of the crime problem being addressed, rejecting any one-size-fits-all thinking. It also focuses primarily on reducing opportunities for crime by, for example, increasing the effort required to commit offenses, increasing the risk of being detected, and reducing the reward should the offense be consummated.

situational danger A particular problem on the job, for example, a high-speed chase, that threatens an officer's safety.

slippery slope theory The idea that corruption at a lower level can easily lead to corruption at a higher level.

social services Police responsibilities that involve taking reports and providing information and assistance to the public, everything from helping a stranded motorist to checking grandma's house to make sure she is all right.

socialization theory Theory that police behavior—both positive and negative—is determined more by work experiences and peers than by pre-employment values and attitudes.

social-supports model An approach to police stress based on the premise that individuals are insulated against stressors when they have a support network of friends, family, and coworkers.

special jurisdiction police Police agencies that have limited functional jurisdiction (e.g., fish and wildlife enforcement) or limited geographic jurisdiction (e.g., campus police or transit police).

specialist A police officer who performs a particular kind of activity such as investigation, as distinguished from a **generalist**.

specialization The division of labor of personnel; the fewer kinds of tasks a person performs, the greater the level of specialization.

specialized training Instruction to prepare officers for particular categories of tasks or jobs.

specific deterrence Patrol deterrence strategy focused on targeted police interventions (e.g., attempting to reduce firearm violence by targeting/stopping suspicious-looking motorists for the purpose of seizing illegal weapons).

state police A state force that has bored law enforcement power, conducts criminal investigations, patrols roads and highways, and frequently has forensic science laboratories.

stop and frisk Practice where an officer may stop a person, temporarily depriving him or her of freedom of movement, if the officer has reasonable suspicion that the person is involved in a crime. Furthermore, the officer may frisk the person if there is reasonable suspicion to believe the citizen is armed and poses a threat to the officer for the duration of the stop.

stressor-outcome model An approach to police stress based on the premise that circumstances of strain or tension lead to psychological or physiological stress.

structural characteristics The features that police departments emphasize or do not emphasize, which may be discriminatory, especially against women.

subjugation of defendant's rights Overriding a citizen's civil rights to obtain a confession.

substantive laws Criminal laws that identify behavior and punishment, distinct from **procedural laws**.

suicide prevention training Instruction aimed at reducing police suicides by recognizing depression, developing communication skills, resolving conflicts, and maintaining close relationships.

sustained complaints Allegations of misdeeds by police that an investigation finds to be justified.

symbolic assailant Type of person the police officer thinks is potentially dangerous or troublesome, usually because of the way the person walks, talks, and dresses.

systems theory The idea that all parts of a system (organization) are interrelated and interdependent.

target hardening Crime prevention strategy that seeks improvements in doors, windows, locks, alarms, lighting, and landscaping to make illegal entry into homes and businesses more difficult and time-consuming.

target oriented A concept used by police officers to assess likely targets in their districts. A target-oriented approach monitors not only obvious places and persons who might be of danger, but also "safe areas" that may be vulnerable to disruption.

task forces A team of officers from two or more police agencies that works to solve a particular problem that transcends jurisdictional limits (e.g., a drug task force).

team policing A group of officers, working as a unit, who are stationed in a neighborhood and are responsible for all police services there.

testimonial evidence Proof based on the opinions of others.

thief catcher In olden times, a person hired to secure return of stolen property.

third degree Historical term for coercive police methods used to obtain confessions.

total quality management (TQM) A customer-oriented approach that emphasizes human resources and quantitative methods in an attempt at continuous improvement.

training Instruction of an individual in how to do a job; concerned with specific facts and procedures. See also **education**.

tribal police Law enforcement bodies on Native American (Indian) reservations.

unfounded complaints Allegations of police misdeeds that an investigation finds did not occur as stated.

universalistic perspectives Views of police behavior that look for the ways in which officers are similar, as distinct from **particularistic perspectives**.

unsubstantiated complaints Allegations that in the opinion of those making the decision cannot be sustained as either true or false.

urban-dispersion theory One of four theories that explain the development of the police department: to provide an important part of government.

U.S.A. Patriot Act Highly controversial law enacted in 2001 in response to the terrorist attacks of September 11. The Patriot Act gives federal officials greater authority to track and intercept communications, vests the Secretary of the Treasury with regulatory powers to combat corruption of U.S. financial institutions for foreign money-laundering purposes, seeks to further close U.S. borders, and creates new crimes, new penalties, and new procedural efficiencies for use against domestic and international terrorists.

use corruption Illegal use of drugs by officers.

use of force The legal authority to maintain order, demand compliance, detain individuals, use weapons, and, if necessary, inflict violence. Police are granted this authority to shield victims from dangerous felons; to control unruly, hostile, or physically abusive citizens; and to protect immediate threats to human life. Use of force is the most controversial aspect of the legal authority of the police.

validity Justifiability of a measure as an accurate assessment of the attribute it is designed to assess. Other people are likely to see the same thing the observer sees.

verbal force Persuasive use of words to control a situation.

vigilante Member of a voluntary band (usually men) who organize to respond to real or imagined threats to their safety; to protect their lives, property, or power; or seek revenge. Characteristic of the old West, they are also active today.

watchman style Policing that allows great latitude in maintaining order.

WHAM Acronym for "winning hearts and minds." A process to secure the cooperation of rank-and-file members of a department in implementing organizational change.

zero-tolerance policing A strategy of proactive arrests, based on the broken-windows theory of crime causation. In practice, this theory suggests that if police aggressively pursue minor quality-of-life crimes, the improvement in the quality of life in an area will indirectly lead to a lower rate of serious crime.

NAME INDEX

Bold page numbers indicate material in figures and tables.

Aamodt, M. G., 436, 466–467
Abadinsky, H., **36**
Ackerman, J. M., 249
Adams, R. E., 160, 172
Adams, T., 281
Alarid, L. F., 240
Alex, N., 390
Alexander, D. A., 436
Alpert, G. P., 204, 208, 251–252, 281, 284, 286, 292, 301–302, 325–326, 352, 360, 370, **376**
Anderson, D., 394, 406
Anderson, D. C., 322
Anderson, G. S., 426
Anderson, P., 326
Applebaum, P. S., 210
Araujo, W. J., 252
Archbold, C. A., 405–406, 425
Arcury, T. A., 160, 172
Armstrong, D. A., 467
Aron, F., 421–422, **422**, 424
Atherton, S., 210
Auten, J., 133, 281

Baehr, M. E., **229**
Bain, L. J., 429
Baker, A., 325, 495
Banas, D. W., 232
Banton, M., 303
Barker, J. C., **82**, 435
Barker, T., 292, 296, 331, 353, 378
Barnes, T., 100, 504
Barnum, C., 286
Baro, A. L., 456, 470
Barrineau, H. E., 75
Barrows, H., 204
Baumer, E., 136, 243, 246
Bayley, D. H., 174, 204, 235, 253, 259, 280, 283, **313**, 313–314, 371, **378**, 506, 510
Bazley, T. D., 361, 396
Beaver, K. M., 258
Beers, D., 324
Begin, B., 4
Benitez, S., 494
Bennett, S. F., 173, 467
Bennett, T., 92, 115
Benson, M., 114
Bercal, T. E., 128

Berenson, A., 327
Berg, B. L., 31, 37, 202, 372, 391, 407
Berk, R., 323–324
Berk, R. A., 249
Berkeley, G. E., 5, 393, 456
Berkowitz, L., 329
Bernard, T. J., 329, 495
Bernstein, M., 193
Bibeau, L., 445
Biebel, E. P., 114, **114**
Birzer, M. L., 203
Bittner, E., 18, 129, 204, 280, 311, 354
Black, D., 272, 284, 286–288
Blake, L., 240
Bloch, P., 394, 406
Bloch, P. B., 261
Blumberg, M., 342
Boba, R., 505
Bobb, M., 366
Bohrer, S., 252
Boland, B., 136
Bond, B. J., 247
Bonn, S., 471, 480
Bopp, W., **43**
Borkenstein, R., 48
Borum, R., 497
Bouza, A. V., 149
Bowdwn, L., 188
Bower, D. L., 445
Bowman, T., 463
Boydstun, J. E., 91, 139, 234
Bradford, D., 203
Bradley, D., 180
Braga, A. A., 23, **23**, 116, 243, 245, 247
Brandl, S. G., 171, 253, 257, 444
Bratton, W. J., 117, 136–137, 176, 245
Breda, D. R., 357
Brenner, S. W., 498
Brent, E. E., 313
Brewer, N., 234
Brodsky, S. L., 367
Bromley, M. L., 173, 280
Brooks, L. W., 281–282, 288–289
Brown, D. K., 103, 239, 340
Brown, J. M., 339–340, 343, **343**
Brown, L. P., 113
Brown, M., 406
Brown, M. F., 326
Brown, M. K., 303

Brown, R. A., 286, 289, 390
Brown, R. M., 37
Brunson, R. K., 139
Brzeczek, R. J., 434
Bucqueroux, B., 100
Budnick, K., 407
Buerger, M. E., 241, 494–495, 505
Bumphus, V. W., 362
Burack, J., 513
Burbeck, E., 196, 199
Burlingame, D., 456, 470
Burns, D. E., 389
Burrows, B. A., 172
Bynum, T. S., 239

Cahn, M. F., 240
Caiden, G. E., **43, 52,** 238–239, 297–298, **299,** 362–363, 365, 456
Caldero, M. A., 272, 275–276, 288, 302, 378, 423
Calnon, J. M., 495
Campbelis, C., 199
Campbell, A, 323–324
Caplan, G., 359
Carlan, P. E., 469
Carmichael, J. T., 341
Carte, G. E., 456
Carter, D., 292, 353, 356, 378
Carter, D. L., 328, 331, 400, 462, 467, 471, **471,** 473–474, **475–476,** 515
Cascio, W. F., 466
Cawley, D. F., 252
Celona, L., 176
Chaiken, J. M., 194, 466–467, 470
Chambliss, W., 284
Chapman, R., 255
Chappell, A. T., 212
Charles, L. E., 428
Charles, M. T., 251, 406–407
Cherkauskas, J. C., 286
Chermak, S., 150–151, 242
Chermak, S. M., 281
Cheurprakobkit, S., 466
Clark, J. R., 201, 243
Clarke, R. V., 94, 513
Clarren, S. N., 94–95
Clawson, M., 443
Cloud, J., 83
Cochran, J. K., 173, 280
Cochran, S., 497

Cohen, B., 194, 466–467, 470
Cohen, J., 136, 242
Cohen, M., 240
Cohen, M. I., 101, 240
Cohn, E. G., 342
Cole, G. F., **43**, 48
Cole, S. A., 258
Collins, M. L., 467
Collins, S. C., 411
Compton, M. R., 445
Conley, J. A., 412
Connors, E. F., 101, 240
Connors, T., 515
Coomes, L. F., 76, **77**
Cooper, L., 35
Cooper, T. W., 71, 73, 79
Corcoran, J., 494
Cordner, G. W., 14, 19, 21, 98, 101, 114,
    114, 116, 172, 239, 281, 287,
    354, 373, 444–445, 496–497,
    502, 505
Corell, J., 342
Cosgrove, C. A., 172
Costello, P., 197
Coupe, R. T., 240
Couper, D. C., 130, **131,** 161–162,
    164, 175
Cowper, T. J., 134
Cox, T. C., 199
Crabtree, A., 197
Crank, J. P., 19, 180, 231, 272, 276, 279,
    288, 292, **293,** 302, 323, 327, 378,
    423
Cronin, T. J., 434
Crosby, A., 197
Cubellis, L. J., 134–135
Cullen, F. T., 431
Cullen, J. B., 369, **370**
Cumming, E., 128
Cumming, I., 128
Cushing, M. A., 428–429

D'Arcy, S., 355
Dalley, A. F., 464
Dantzker, M. L., 470
Daum, J., 408
Davey, J. D., 432
Davidson, M. J., 436
Davies, J., 75
Davis, E. F., 252
Davis, K. C., 281
Day, F. D., 32
Decker, L. K., 191, 474
Decker, S. H., 172
Dees, T. M., 294
deGuzman, M. C., 230–231, 254, 470, 513
DeJong, C., 290, 393
del Carmen, R. V., 58, 62–65, 67, **67,** 69,
    71, 73–75, 78–79
Delattre, E. J., 302, 378
Delbeq, A. L., 157
DeLeon-Granados, W., 294
DeLong, R., 199
DeLuca, S. T., 132
Denton, N. A., 341
Deutsch, A., 458
Dickey, C., 496

Dishlacoff, L., 432
Dixon, T. L., 209
Doerner, W. G., 199
Donahue, M., 340
Dorschner, J., 298
Dowler, K., 437
Doyle, C., 511
Doyle, M. A., 147
Draper, L., 445, 497
Dugan, J. R., 357
Dunbar, R.L.M., 470
Dunford, F. W., 250
Dunham, R. G., 251, 252, **376**
Dunn, J. M., 428
Dupont, R., 497
Durose, M. R., 23, 228, 285, 315, **316,** 495
Dwyer, J., 325

Earle, H. H., 202
Eck, J. E., 102–103, 116, 145, 255–256,
    257
Edell, L., 128
Eisenberg, T., 193, 393, 425
Ekstrand, L. E., 116
Elgion, J., 325
Elliot, D. S., 250
Emery, T., 505
Engel, R. S., 140–141, 180, 280, 284,
    286–288, 444, 472, 495, 505
Epstein, A., 259
Eterno, J. A., 513

Falcone, D. N., 18, **18, 49,** 251, 494
Falkenberg, S., 193, 197, 199
Famega, C. N., 141, 272
Fanelli, J., 176
Farmer, D. J., 256
Farmer, R. E., 419–420, 437
Farrell, A., 284, 494–495
Farrell, M. B., 504
Farrington, D. P., 92
Faulkner, S., 321
Feagin, J. R., 284
Feder, L., 395
Feinberg, S. E., 239
Feldman, K. A., 468
Felkenes, G. T., 332, 391
Fell, R., 433
Felson, R. B., 249–250
Fenster, A., 464
Fielding, H., 32
Filer, R. J., 219
Finkle, E., 437
Finn, P., 424, 429, 444–445
Fitzgerald, L., 410
Fleissner, D., **92**
Fleming, J., 102
Fogelson, R., 370
Fornango, R., 136, 243, 246
Forst, B., 252
Fox, J. A., 339, **339**
Frank, J., 83, 113, 141, 172, 272, 286,
    289, 390
Frankel, B., 303
Franklin, C. A., 407
Franz, V., 134
Freels, S., 136

Friday, P. C., 161, 321
Fridell, L. A., 91, 111, 251, 286, 342, 495
Friederich, R. J., 332
Friedman, L., 512
Friedman, W., 209
Friedrich, R. J., 287
Froemel, E. C., **229**
Fry, L., 465
Frydl, K., 116, 139, 281, 287, 290, 372,
    394, 468
Fuentes, J. R., 515
Furcon, J. E., **229**
Furnham, A., 196, 199
Fuss, T, 194
Fyfe, J. J., 317–318, 323–324, 330, 338,
    339–342, 344, 497

Gaines, L., 433
Gaines, L. K., 193, 197, 199
Gallagher, C. A., 249
Gallati, R. R., 32
Gambino, J. A., 193
Garcia, V., 393
Garmire, B. L., 393–394
Garner, R., **479**
Garofalo, J., 260, 315
Garrity, T. J., 252
Garson, G. D., 502
Gartin, P. R., 241
Gaska, C. W., 434
Gau, J. M., 139
Geison, G. L., 369, **370**
Geistman, J., 210
Geller, W. A., 178, 180, 338, 340–342,
    344, 352
George-Abeyie, D., 391
Germann, A. C., 32
Gerth, H. H., 128
Gertz, M., 391
Giacomazzi, A., 180
Giacopassi, D., 343
Gibson, C. L., 432
Giles, H., 209
Goldberg, A. L., **233,** 400, **401,** 403
Golden, J. W., 323
Goldman, J., 367
Goldstein, H., 4, 98, 100, 105–106,
    128–129, 144, 292, 470
Goldstein, J., 281, 371, 376
Gore, B., 433
Gosnell, H. F., 389–390
Grabosky, P., 102
Graham, N., 359
Gray, D. O., **427**
Greene Mazerolle, L., 246, **248**
Greene, J. A., 79
Greene, J. R., 83, 104, 137, 144, 172–173,
    232, 239, 246, 272, 395, 409
Greenfeld, L., 315
Greenspan, R., 176, **177**
Greenstone, J. L., 428
Greenwood, P., 252, 255
Greenwood, P. W., 103
Griffin, S. P., 329, 470
Gruenewald, J., 151
Gu, J., 443
Guller, I. B., 464

Guralnick, L., 433
Gurman, S., 4
Gutierrez, R., 494
Guyot, D., 288

Haarr, R. N., 115, 211, 398–399, 411, 425
Hainsworth, B. E., 408
Hajek, C., 209
Hall, R., 369, **370**
Hansen, V., 512
Harcourt, B., 136, 246
Harmon, M. M., 378
Harris, M., 4
Harrison, M., 428
Hart, P. M., 420
Hartnett, S. M., 144, 158, 165–166,
      167, 172
Hassell, K. D., 278, 405–406
Hayeslip, P. W., 172
Hayhurst, D. L., 421
Hays, T., 511
He, N., 172, 397, 425
Headey, B., 420
Heinzlemann, F., **92**
Henry, V. E., 512
Henson, B., 197
Herbert, S., 136, **137**, 246, 272, 279, 284
Hewlett, J., 505
Hickey, E. R., 396
Hickman, J. H., **200**, 237
Hickman, M. J., 83, 192–194, 199, 205,
      217, 217–218, 227, 251, 258–259,
      316, 332, 390, 400, **401–402, 461,**
      461–462
Hill, K. Q., 443
Hinds, L., 210
Hinduja, S., 115, 173
Hirschel, D., 249–250
Hochstedler, E., 412
Hodes, C. R., 194
Hodge, J. P., 393
Hoffman, P. B., 396
Holloway, K., 92
Holmes, M. D., 337, 342, 353,
      361, 368
Hoover, J., 214, 216
Hoover, L. T., **257**, 511
Hopkins, E. J., 329, **330**
Hornick, J. P., 172
Horvath, F., 340
Hough, R. M., 80
Huberts, L. W., 141
Huckabee, R. G., 191, 474
Hughes, T, 75, 79, 81, 198
Huizinga, D., 250
Humphrey, K. R., 433
Hunt, A., 4
Hunt, J., 323–324
Hunt, R. L., 194
Huntington, S., 489
Hurrell, J. L., Jr., 422–424, **423,**
      431–432 436
Hurst, Y. G., 287

Iris, M., 360
Irons, N., 437
Ivanoff, A., 434–435

Jacobs, D., 341
Jefferis, E., 443
Jenkins, P., 248
Jesilow, P., 393, 396
Johns, C., 408
Johnson, C. S., 389
Johnson, D. R., **34**, 34–35, **36,** 39–42,
      47–48, 50, **51–52,** 52
Johnson, H. A., **34**
Johnson, K., **195**
Johnston, W., 466
Jolly, R., **402**
Jones, D. M., 134
Jordan, W. T., 186–187, 189–190
Jurik, N. C., 407

Kadleck, C., 148
Kahn, C., 3
Kakar, S., 467, 470
Kaminski, R. J., 442–443, 446–447
Kane, R. J., 291, 293, **293,** 296–298
Kania, R.R.E, 327, 341
Kaplan, R., 489
Kappeler, S. F., 73
Kappeler, V. E., 71, 73–76, 78, 134–135,
      199, 284, 286, 292, 294,
      300–302, 436
Kappeler, V. W., 433
Kaptein, M., 141
Karales, K. J., 340
Karmen, A. A., 37
Katz, C. M., 30, 246, 260
Katz, J., **195**
Kavanagh, J., 442
Kelley, T., 434
Kelley, T. V., 95, 159
Kelling, G. L., 37, 39, 40–41, 44, 96, 100,
      103, 117, 135–136, 138, 238, 245,
      283, 371
Kellogg, T., 428
Kennedy, D., 243, 368, **369**
Kent, D. A., 393
Kephart, W. M., 390
Kerley, K., 114
Kernes, S., 493–494
Kessler, D. A., 234
Kim, B., 173
King, W. R., 438
Kinley, L., 239
Kionka, E., 75
Kirkham, G. L., 33
Kleinmuntz, B., 194
Kleismet, R. B., 149
Klinger, D., 283–284
Klockars, C. B., 104, 272, 302, 327, 377
Klotter, J. C., 61
Knowles, J. J., 292
Knowles, M. S., 203
Konstantin, D. N., 441–442
Korbetz, R. W., 458
Kposowa, A. J., 466
Kraska, P., 508–509
Kraska, P. B., 134–135, 286, 301, 433
Kreisel, B. W., 364, **364**
Krimmel, J. T., 467
Kroes, W. H., 422–424, **423,** 431–432, 436
Kruger, K. J., 409–410

Kunzman, L. L., 466
Kureczka, A. W., **427,** 427–428
Kuykendall, J., 19, 171, **200,** 253–254, 340,
      370, 447
Kuykendall, J. L., 389
Kwak, D-H., 425

Lachlan, B., 150
LaGrange, T. C., 444, 466
Lamb, R., 321
Lambuth, L., 436
Landrum, L. W., 390
Lane, R., 34–35
Langan, P., 315
Langan, P. A., 23, 228, 285, 315, **316,**
      339–340, 343, **343,** 495
Langworthy, R. H., 272, 278,
      339, 341
Laramy, J. E., 219, 467
Larose, A. P., 275
Larson, J. A., 329, **330**
Larson, R. C., 239
Lasthuizen, K., 141
Lauritsen, J., 283
Lawton, B. A., 242
Lee, B. K., 80
Lee, C. B., 196
Leinen, S., 390
Lersch, K., 299, 302, 361
Lersch, K. M., 284, 396, 466
Levenson, R. W., 436
Levine, L., 75
Leviton, S. C., 428
Levy, R. J., 470
Lichtenberg, I. D., 442
Liederbach, J., 113, 278
Lilley, D., 115, 173
Lind, E. A., 139
Linden, R., 406
Linn, E., 19
Litzenberger, R., 426
Lobitz, S. H., 130, **131,** 161–162,
      164, 175
Locke, B., 463–464
Loftin, C., 248
Lonsway, K. A., 192, 409
Loo, R., 421, 427, 434–435
Lord, V. B., 161, 424, **427**
Loveday, B., 513
Lovrich, N. P., 397
Ludwig, J., 242
Luongo, A. J., 242
Lurigio, A. J., 158

MacDonald, H., 495
MacDonald, J. M., 446–447
Mackey, W. C., 327, 341
Madden, T. J., 251
Maguire, E. R., 133, 278
Maher, T. M., 299–301
Manning, P. K., 104, 272, 369, 378, 513
Margolis, B. L., 422–424, **423,** 436
Margolis, J., 493
Marion, N., 321
Marshall, J. M., 511
Marshall, J. R., 433
Martin, C., 289, 292

Martin, C. A., 426, 427
Martin, S. E., 259–260, 272, 286, 289, 394,
    400, 403–404, 406–409
Marvel, T. B., 235
Marzulli, J., 325
Massey, D. S., 341
Mastrofski, S. D., 22, 104, 113, 139, 172,
    176–177, **177**, 282, 287, 290, 373,
    466, 513
Matulia, K. R., 339
Maurer, M., 284
Maynard, N. W., 436
Maynard, P. E., 436
Mayne, R., 32–33
Mazerolle, L., 141, 230
McAllister, B., 373
McCampbell, M. S., 212
McCluskey, J. D., 139, 400
McCoy, S. P., 436
McCrary, J., 397
McDevitt, J., 245, 284, 495
McDonald, T. D., 18
McDowall, D., 248
McDowell, J., 407
McElroy, J. E., 172–173
McElvain, J. P., 466
McEwen, J. T., 240
McEwen, T., 101, 322–323
McGarrell, E., 151, 242, 245, 494
McGill, M. E., 470
McGurrin, D., 300
McKean, H. E., 426
McLaren, R. C., 128, 228–229, 394
McLaughlin, S., 83
McLeod, R. G., 443
McMullan, J., 351
McNulty, E., 323
Mecklenburg, S. H., 496
Megerian, C., 3
Melchionne, T. M., 393–394
Mendoza, M., 4, **210**
Messing, P., 176
Metchik, E., 196
Mieczkowski, T., 299, 361, 396
Miller, C. E., 252
Miller, H. A., 173
Miller, I., 427
Miller, J., 465
Miller, L., 436
Miller, M., 275
Miller, M. R., 318
Miller, S. L., 393
Miller, W., 34
Mills, C. W., 128
Milton, C., 393–394
Milton, C. H., 95
Milton, C. W., 159
Mire, S., 173
Miron, H. J., 252
Moelter, N. P., 234
Monkkonen, E., 35
Moody, C. E., 235
Moore, M. H., 23, **23**, 37, 39–41,
    44, 100, 102, 117, 138, 145,
    208, 368, **369**
Moran, R., 242
Moran, T. K., 398

Morash, M., 395, 409–411, 425
Morrison, G. B., 321
Moskos, P., 478
Mottaz, C., 470
Muhlhausen, D. B., 116
Murphy, P. V., 46, 359
Myrdal, G., 390

Navarro, M., 326
Nees, H., 462
Newcomb, T. M., 468
Newman, G., 513
Niederhoffer, A., 470
Nixon, C., 180
Norton, B., 445, 497
Novak, K. J., 19, 83, 171, **200**, 240, 246,
    272, 282, 286–288, 444, 447
Nurre, S., 366, **366**

O'Neill, J. L., 428–429
Obst, P. L., 432
Oettmeier, T. N., 373
Olson, B., 4
Olson, R., 512
Oppenlander, N., 249
Owings, C., 393

Padavic, I., 407
Paoline, E. A., 19, 280, 289, 396,
    466–467
Parks, R. B., 113, 139, 288
Parnas, R., 128
Parsons, D., 393, 396
Pascarella, E. T., 468
Pate, T., 239
Patterson, G. T., 431
Paulsen, D. J., 135
Payne, B. K., 289
Payne, D. M., 232
Peak, K., 321
Peel, R., 32–33
Pelfrey, W. V., Jr., 113
Pendleton, M., 420
Perez McCluskey, C., 400
Perez, D., 356, 365
Perfetti, R. L., 286
Perito, R., 510
Petersilia, J., 103, 252, 255
Petterson, W. E., 357, 363
Pettit, W. G., 445
Pflug, M. A., 18
Phillips, A., 325
Phillips, D. M., 172
Piehl, A. M., 243
Pierce, G. L., 245
Pierce, J. L., 157
Pinals, D. A., 210
Pinizzoto, A. J., 252
Piquero, A. R., 83, 285
Piquero, N. L., 425, 432
Pisani, S. L., **160**
Pitts, S., 214, 216
Plecas, D., 426
Polk, E., 467
Pollock, J. M., **376**
Pollock-Byrne, J. M., **375**, 376
Pond, S. B., **427**

Ponte, D., 214, 216
Pope, C. E., 456–457, 459
Potter, G. W., 436
Pratt, T. C., 258–259
Prendergast, J., 83
Price, B. R., 380
Prokos, A., 407
Puro, S., 367
Pursley, R. D., **36**
Pynes, J. E., 203

Rabe-Hemp, C. E., 290, 395–396, 408
Rafky, J., 194
Ramirez, D., 284
Ramsey, C., 513
Raskin, D. C., 194
Ratcliffe, J. H., 515
Raudenbush, S. W., 246
Rayman, G., 176, 513
Ready, J., 80, 327
Reaves, B. A., 11, **12–14**, 13–14, **17**,
    35, **36**, 192–193, 199, **200**, 202,
    204–205, **205–208**, 207, 212, **217**,
    217–218, 227, **233**, 237, 251, 400,
    401–402, 403, **461**, 461–462
Redlinger, L., 378
Regoli, R. M., 465, 370
Reibstein, L., **137**
Reichel, P. L., 46
Reisig, M. D., 283
Reiss, A. J., Jr., 18, 97, 239, 312
Reith, C., 7
Reitzel, J., 285
Ren, L., 425
Reuland, M., 445, 497
Reuss-Ianni, E., 146, **147**, 280, 370
Reynolds, M. K., 248
Rhoades, P. W., 373
Rice, S. K., 277, 286
Rich, T. F., 237, **238**
Richard, W., 433
Richmond, R. L., 432
Riksheim, E. C., 281
Roberg, R. R., 19, 130, 171, **200**, 203–204,
    219, 228, 370, 420–421, 447,
    464–465, 467, 471, 480
Roberts, N. A., 436
Roberts, S., 486, 488–489
Robinson, A. L., 395
Robinson, H. M., 426
Roche, W. M., 160, 172
Roehl, J., 246, **248**
Rogan, D. P., 242
Rokeach, M., 275
Rollins, J., 515
Rosen, M. R., 510
Rosenbaum, D. P., 92, 158, 173
Rosenfeld, R., 136, 243, 246
Rosenfield, M., 197
Ross, D. L., 73
Roth, J. A., 116
Rowan, C., 32–33
Rubin, P. N., 201, 409–411
Rubinstein, J., 278, 303
Rudwick, E, 389–390
Ryan, J. F., 116
Rydberg, J., 467

Sadd, S., 173
Sampson, R., 111, 283
Sampson, R. J., 136, 246
Sapp, A. D., 286, 300, 400, 462, 467, 471,
    471, 473–474, **475–476**
Saunders, C. B., 457
Scannell, J., **97**
Scarborough, K. E., 115, 496, 502, 505
Schacter, D. L., 496
Schaefer, D. R., 246
Schapiro, A., 255
Scheider, M. C., 116, 255
Schein, E. H., 368
Schroeder, D. A., 258–259
Schuck, A. M., 290
Schultz, D. M., 405
Schwartz, A. T., 94–95
Scogin, F., 367
Scolforo, M., 3
Scott, E. L., 193
Scott, M., 105, 111, 114, 338,
    341–342, 344
Scott, M. S., 505
Scrivner, E., 189
Seelau, E. P., 496
Seigel, L., 63
Selye, H., 419–420
Seydlitz, R., 248
Shane, J. M., 512
Sharp, D., 210
Shaw, J. W., 242
Shearing, C., 506
Sheehan, M. C., 432
Sherman, L., 339, 341, 372
Sherman, L. J., 394, 406
Sherman, L. W., 75, 95, 139, 159, 230, 232,
    239, 241–242, 249, 259–260, 281,
    284, 288, 292, 342, 445, 460, 469
Sherry, M. E., 91, 234
Sherwell, P., 494
Sherwood, C. W., 470
Sichel, J. L., 388, 395
Sigler, R. T., 294
Sigman, M. R., 426
Silver, E., 287, 444
Silver, I., 71
Silverman, E. B., 513
Simonetti Rosen, M., **209**
Simpson, A. E., 393
Sink, M., 502
Sipes, L., 100, 504
Skeem, J., 445
Sklansky, D. A., 400, 405
Skogan, W. G., 111, 114, 116, 131, 139,
    144, 158, 162, **164**, 164–166, **167**,
    168, 171–172, 281, 287, 290, 372,
    394, 468
Skolnick, J. H., 174, 283, 303, 317–318,
    330, 351, 371, **378**
Sluder, R. D., 284, 286, 292, 301–302
Smalley, S., 3
Smith, A., 442
Smith, A. B., 463
Smith, B., 83, 353
Smith, B. W., 128, 210, 272, 329, 337,
    340–341, 342, 361, 368

Smith, D., 283–284
Smith, E. L., 23, 228, 315, **316**, 495
Smith, M. R., 74, 446–447
Smith, S., 315
Smith, S. M., 466–467
Smith, W., 204, 281, 352, 370
Snipes, J. B., 287, 290
Snortum, J., 255
Snowden, L., 194
Snyder, J., 275
Sobol, J., 284
Somvadee, C., 410
Sorenson, D.W.M., 442
Sparger, J., 343
Sparrow, M., 368, **369**
Spelman, W., 103, 145, 239
Sproule, C. F, 197
Stack, S, 434
Steiner, L., 111
Stephens, C., 427
Stephens, D. W., 230, 400, 471, **471**,
    473–474, 505
Stewart, D. M., 476, **476–477**
Stockton, D., **493**
Stoddard, K. B., 470
Stone, A., 303
Stone, A. R., 132
Stratton, J. G., 436
Strom, K. J., 258–259
Stroshine, M. S., 444
Sulc, L. B., 336
Sullivan, M., 444–445
Sullivan, P. S., 390–391, 404–405, 408, 412
Sulton, C., 394
Sun, I. K., 289
Sunshine, J., 24, 139
Sussman, F., 194
Swando, M. J., 173
Swanson, C., 433
Swatt, M. L., 432
Sykes, G., 288, 292, 313
Sykes, G. W., 373
Szucko, J. J., 194

Taft, P., 489
Tannehill, R., 203
Tatum, K. M., 80
Taylor, B., 186, 192–193, 462
Taylor, R. B., 242
Teplin, L. A., 287, 444
Terezini, P. T., 468
Terrill, W., 283, 289, 315, 317–318, 327,
    362–363, 396, 466–467
Territo, L., 420
Terry, W. C., 420
Thorton, R. F., 197
Thurman, Q., 116, 172
Tien, J., 240
Tillyer, R., 286
Timmins, W. M., 408
Tita, G. E., 245
Tomz, J. E., 424, 429
Townsey, R. A., 394
Travis, L. F., 278
Trimmer, R., 321
Trojanowicz, R., 96, 100–102, 232

True, E., 391
Truxillo, D. M., 467
Tucker, W, 336
Tuohy, J., 3
Tuomey, L. M., **402**
Turner, K. B., 405
Tyler, T. R., 24, 139

Uchida, C. D., 438

Van Maanen, J., 274, 284, 303
Van Raalte, R., 340
Vann, I. B., 502
Varela, J. G., 196
Vaughn, J., 428
Vaughn, M., 330
Vaughn, M. S., 71, 73, 76, **77**, 79
Veltkamp, L. J., 426
Vena, J. E., 433–434
Veno, A., 436
Vermette, H. S., 210
Vetter, H. J., 420
Vickers, B., 445
Violanti, J. M., 419, 421–422, **422**, 424,
    427, 433–434
Visher, C. A., 286
Vollmer, A., 42, 371, 456, 480

Wadsworth, T., 496
Waegel, W. B., 252
Wagner, M., 434
Walker, J. T., 323
Walker, L. G., 436
Walker, S., 9, 30, 41–42, **43**, 148–149, 260,
    297, 337, 352, 357, 359, 360–364,
    361, **364**, 366, 368, 393, 396,
    400, 405
Walker, W. F., 463
Wall, C. R., 393
Wallace, B., 357
Wallace, P. A., 420
Wasserman, R., 281
Waters, J., 437
Watkins, R. C., 172
Watson, E. M., 132
Wearing, A. J., 420
Weatherit, M., 104
Webb, V. J., 246
Weidman, D. R., 261
Weinberg, D. H., 491
Weiner, N. L., 465
Weirman, C. L., 470
Weisburd, D. A., 116, 173, 176–177, **177**,
    241, 245, 513
Weisheit, R. A., 18, **18**, 493–494
Weiss, A., 136, 150, 242
Weitzer, R., 391
Welch, M., 325
Wellborn, J., 445
Wells, E., 251
Wells, G., 496
Wells, L. E., 18, **18**, 494
Wells, W., 294
Welsh, B., 92
Werth, E. P., 204
West, P., 362, 365

Westley, W. A., 276, 303
Whalen, J. L., 180, 472, 505
Whetstone, T. S., 405, 467
Whitaker, G. P., 21, 141
White, M. D., 80, 197–198, 258–259, 286, 291, 293, **293**, 296, 327, 340, 468
Wiersema, B., 248
Wilkins, V. M., 391
Wilkinson, D. L., 173
Wilkinson, O. W., 228
William, M., 255
Williams, B. N., 391
Williams, G. L., 373
Williams, H., 46

Willis, J. J., 176–177, **177**, 513
Wilson, C., 234
Wilson, D. G., 173
Wilson, H., 466
Wilson, J. Q., 16, 24, 96, 128, 135–136, 138, 277, 280, 282, 303, 317, 327, 371
Wilson, J. R., 426
Wilson, O. W., 128, 133, 228–229, 232, 371, 394
Withrow, B. L., 286
Witkin, G., 246
Wollan, L. A., 33
Won-Jae, L., 240

Wood, R. A., 18
Worden, R., 271, 273
Worden, R. E., 240, 284, 287, 290, 466, 468
Worrall, J. L., 57, 76, 79, 246
Wycoff, M. A., 111, 131, 159, 162, 164, **164,** 172, 252

Yeh, S., 173

Zalman, M., 63
Zawitz, M., 339, **339**
Zhao, J. S., 116, 130, 172, 278, 397, 425

SUBJECT INDEX

Bold page numbers indicate material in figures and tables.

Abner Louima incident, 425, 495
Accountability and ethics, 351–380
  early intervention alternatives, **361**
  early warning/identification systems,
    360–361
  ethical relativism and the law, **377–378**
  ethical standards, 374–378
    limits of, 378, 380
  external mechanisms, 362–368
    auditor systems, 365–366, **366**
    civil/criminal liability, 367
    civil rights criminal violations,
      367–368
    civilian review, 362–365, **364**
    decertification, 367
    exclusionary rule, 367
    legal control, 366–367
    pattern/practice litigation, 368
  internal mechanisms
    complaint outcomes, 356–358
    grievance arbitration, 360
    internal investigations, 354–356,
      358–360, 362
    organization, management, 352
    steps of process, 355–356
    written directives, 179, 352–354
  Law Enforcement Code of Ethics,
    374–375
  oversight mechanism limits, 368–369
  Police Officer's Bill of Rights, **355**
  professional standards, 369–374
    limits of, 378, 380
    professionalization movement,
      369–374
  rule of law and, 6–7, 57
  schools of ethics, **376**
Acute/chronic stress, 420
ADA. See Americans with Disabilities Act
Ada (Idaho) County Sheriff's Office
    (ACSO), 180
Advisory committees (Chicago), 167
Affidavits, 64
Affirmative action, 396–397
AFL-CIO (American Federation of
    Labor, Congress of Industrial
    Organizations), 148
African American citizens
  harsher treatment vs., 283–284
  Indianapolis brutality case, 151
  lynchings of, 37

  police discrimination vs., 45, 46
  racial slurs by police, 151
  youth being stopped, 209, 495
African American police
  black citizens relation to, 391
  CAPS program trends, 168
  Chicago juvenile data, 209
  community policing and,
    90–91, 111
  in Dallas, **392**
  double marginality dilemma, 391
  education requirements, 475
  employee organizations, 148
  employment data, 400, **401, 403**
  exam score comparisons, 197
  female officers, 397
  force/coercion issues, 325, 340–343
  gang programs, 245
  historical background, 389
  litigation issues, 399
  officer data, 289
  performance of, 390–392
  police-community relations, 90–91
  promotion data, 390, 404–405
  during Reform Era, 41
  S.F. officers association, 148
  underrepresentation of, 412
  unequal treatment issues, 389–392
  views of neighborhood
    problems, 111
Age factor (police selection factor), 191
Alabama Department of Public
    Safety, 399
Alabama v. White (1960), 58
Albemarle Paper Company v. Moody
    (1975), 190
Albuquerque Police Department, 401
Alcohol abuse, 431–432, 447
Amadou Diallo shooting incident,
    425, 495
Amen investigation, 297
American Bar Association, 458
American Civil Liberties Union (ACLU),
    71, 72
American Federation of Labor
    and Congress of Industrial
    Organizations (AFL-CIO), 148
American Medical Association (AMA), 6
American society. *See* Changes in
    American society

Americans with Disabilities Act
    (ADA), 201
Amnesty International (AI), 80, 446, 501
Ancient Greece kin policing methods, 31
Ancient Rome kin policing
    methods, 31
Andragogy (defined), 203
Anti-Defamation League (U.S.), 10
Arizona v. Gant (2009), 68
Arizona v. Hicks (1987), 64
Arizona v. Johnson (2008), 62
Arlington (Texas) Police Department,
    462–463, **463**
Arlington (Virginia) Police
    Department, **464**
Army's Rangers, 134
Arrests
  agencies with authorization, **12**
  BJS juvenile data, 248
  criminal procedures and, 63–64
  curfew crime arrests, 248–249
  defined, 61
  dual arrests, 250
  false arrest, 61–62, 63, 74, 78
  illegal arrests, 38
  mandatory arrest, 249–250
  proactive strategies, 241, 242
  probable cause, 58, 63
  rate calculation (NCVS), 144
  reactive arrests, 249–250
  Supreme Court cases
    Chimel v. California (1969), 63–64
    Maryland v. Buie (1990), 64
    Payton v. New York (1981), 63
    U.S. v. Watson (1976), 63
Asian Americans
  Dallas Police officers, **392**
  police-community relations, 90–91
  recruitment of, 187
    height discrimination, 192
    test performance, 197
Asian Police Officers Association, 148
Associates degrees, 456
Associations (labor movements),
    148–150
Atlanta (Georgia) Police Department,
    234, 405
Attorney General's Report to Congress
    (2000), 116
Atwater v. Lago Vista (2001), **60**

Auditor systems (external accountability), 365–366
Austin (Texas) Police Department, 132
Automated fingerprint identification system (AFIS), 257

Baby boomers, 488
Baby bust phenomenon, 488
Background investigation (police selection factor), 193–194
Baldwin, Lola, 393
Baltimore (Maryland) Police Department, 4, 141, 230, 425, 478
Battery, 74, 249
Bay Area Rapid Transit police (California), 16
Beat Health Program (Oakland, California), 246–247, 248
Beat meetings (Chicago), 167
Bedford-Stuyvesant (NYC) 81st Precinct, 176
Behavior (of police). *See also* Corruption; Deviance and misconduct
  classical studies
    behavioral varieties, 277–278
    city police, 278
    justice without trial, 277
    police discretion, 278–280
    violence, 276–277
  defined, 4
  deviance, 290–303
    corruption, 295–299
    drug wars, 301–303
    gratuities, 294
    prevalence of, 292–294
    sexual misconduct, 299–301
    types of, 291–292
  group behavior management, 145–148, 148–150
  individual variables
    career orientation, 290
    education, age, experience, 289
    gender, 289–290
    race, 289
  legalistic style, 278
  management, 128–129
  organization variables
    bureaucratic nature, 281
    neighborhoods, 282–283
    work periods, areas, assignments, 281–282
  perspectives of, 271–276
    organizational, 272
    particularistic, 273
    predispositional theory, 275–276
    psychological, 272
    socialization vs. predisposition, 273–275
    sociological, 271–272
    universalistic, 271
  service style, 278
  situational variables
    age, 286–287
    citizen's mental state, 287–288
    demeanor/attitude, 284
    gender, 286
    location/presence of others, 288

mobilization, 284
race, 284–286
seriousness of offense, 287
suspect-complainant relationship, 287
varieties of, 277–278
Bell, Sean, 325
Berghuis v. Thompkins (2010), 61
Berkeley Police Department, 456, 480
Berks-Lehigh Regional Police Department (Pennsylvania), 15
BFOQ. See bona fide occupational qualification
Bias crime investigative programs, 260
Bill of Rights (U.S. Constitution), 7, 57
Black and Blue (Alex), 391
Blacks. *See* African American citizens; African American police
"Blue wall" code of silence, 277, 296
Board of Evaluators (BOE) feature (PTO program), 216
Bona fide occupational qualification (BFOQ), 191, 473
Bootlegging, 38, 49
Boston Gun Project, 243
Boston Police Department, 35, **146**
Boston riots, 35
Bow Street Runners (Thief Takers), 32
Bowman, Theron, **464**
Bratton, William, 3, **138**
Brendlin v. California (2007), **60**
Brewer v. Williams (1977), 70
Bright-line rule *(N.Y. v. Belton),* 68
Brinegar v. U.S. (1949), 58
Broken-windows theory. *See also* Zero-tolerance policing
  community policing and, 98, **137**
  criticism of, 136
  defined/described, 96, 135–136, 138
  implementation issues, 138
  quality-of-life policing and, 246
  research on strategies of, 247
Brooklyn Grand Jury corruption investigation, 297
Brown, John R., **285**
Brown, Lee P., 405
Brutality/excessive force, 327–329
  Abner Louima incident, 425, 495
  frequency of, 331–332
  as a non-problem (viewpoint), 336–338
  PTSD as cause of, 428
  Rodney King incident, 212, 332, **333–335**, 368, 407, 425, 495
  treatment of prisoners
    by early city police, 35
    by kin policing, 30–31
    for securing confessions, 42
    by Texas Rangers, 46–47
    in the 21st century, 332–333
Buddy Boy corruption scandal, 297
Buffalo (NY) Police Department, 428–429
Bureau of Alcohol, Tobacco, and Firearms, 78, 192
Bureau of Internal Revenue, 52
Bureau of Justice Statistics (BJS) survey
  academy training programs, 202, 205, 212
  coercion surveys, 312

college requirement for officers, 461–462
community policing training, 205
computerized crime mapping, 237
departmental cultural changes, 400
drug use/testing, 194
in-service trainings, 217
job task analysis, 204
juvenile arrests, 248
new applicant screening, 199
physical agility testing, 192
pursuit driving, 251
recruit training hours, 204
Burlington Vermont Police Department, 188

California Commission on Peace Officers Standards and Training (POST), 49
California Personality Inventory (CPI), 195–196
California v. Greenwood (1988), 65
Canines
  NYPD deployment of, 319–320
  usage guidelines, 72, 323
  usage study, 324
CAPS. *See* Chicago Alternate Police Strategy (CAPS) experience
Career criminal investigative training, 259–260
Career fairs, 187
Career growth (human resource component), 216–217
Carroll v. U.S. (1925), 67–68
Castor, Jane E., **388**
Castro v. Beecher (1972), 473
Central Intelligence Agency (CIA), 8
Centralized/decentralized management, 132
Chain of command (in management), 126
The Challenge of Crime in a Free Society report (President's Commission on Law Enforcement and Administration of Justice), 457
Changes in American society. *See also* Cultural diversity
  ageing/growing population, 486–488
  baby boomers, 488
  demographic changes, **487, 492**
  elderly issues, 18, 100, 110, 486–487, 486–488, **488,** 491
  competing strategies
    Compstat/performance management, 512–513
    COP, POP, ILP, 513–516
    terrorism/homeland security, 510–512
  economics
    income equality, 491
    poverty rates, 491
    unemployment rates, 489–491
  long-term trends
    collaboration, 505–506
    federalization, 507–508
    globalization, 509–510
    militarization, 508–509
    privatization, 506–507

Changes in American society. *See also*
        Cultural diversity—(*Continued*)
    modern problems, 494–498
        cyber crime, 53, 494, 498, 517
        eyewitness identification, 331, 494,
            496–497, 517
        immigration enforcement, 494,
            495–496, 517
        mentally ill citizens, 497
        racial profiling, 71–72, 83, 91, 151,
            284–286, 494–495
    modern technology, 499–505
        communications/interoperability, 504
        crime detection/crime solving,
            501–502
        geographic information systems, 502
        global positioning systems, 504
        high-impact/promising, **500**
        information technology, 502, 504
        social media, 504–505
        suspect control/officer safety, 501
Charlotte-Mecklenburg (North Carolina)
        Police Department, 98, 424
Checkpoint Advisory Committee, 67
"Checks and balances" (U.S. government), 5
Chicago Alternate Police Strategy (CAPS)
        experience, 111, 165–171
    assessment trends (1993–2003), **169**
    beat meetings, 144, 167
    foundational work, 165
    key elements, 165–167
        city services component, 167
        community role, 167
        comprehensive involvement, 165
        crime analysis emphasis, 167
        permanent beat assignments, 165
        training commitment, 166
        WHAM component, 166–167
    lessons learned, 170–171
    Office of Management Accountability,
        168–169
    problem-solving struggles, 169–170
    rapid-response units, 165–166
    results, 168–170
    surviving leadership change, 171
    WHAM component, 166–167
Chicago Community Policing Evaluation
        Consortium, 111, 168–169
Chicago Crime Commission (1919), 41
Chicago Police Department, 10. *See also*
        Chicago Alternate Police Strategy
        (CAPS) experience
    changes strategies, 165
    commendation award, 169
    community policing policy, 237
    demonstration (riot) management, **43**
    resource determination, 234
Chief's Scholar Program, 472–473
Chimel v. California (1969), 59, 63–64
Christopher Commission (King
        investigation), 335, 360, 407
Cincinnati Criminal Justice Masters
        Program, **245**
Cincinnati Initiative to Reduce Violence
        (CIRV), 243
Cincinnati Police Department (CPD),
        180, 197–198, **244**, 472

Citizen input (in community policing),
        98, 100
Citizen police, 9
Citizen Review Process, 364
City police forces
    in the American West, 51
    behavior study (1973), 278
    1830s-1850s, U.S.
        class-control theory, 35
        crime-control theory, 35
        disorder-control theory, 34–35
        prevention/apprehension
            methods, 35
        urban-dispersion theory, 35
    failures of (Massachusetts), 47
    non-injury shooting data, 340
    Philadelphia study, 278
Civil/criminal liability (external
        accountability), 367
Civil laws/lawsuit experience, 7,
        81–82
Civil liability
    avenues of, 73–74
    color of law, 76
    community policing, 79
    costs in policing, 71–73
    in federal courts, 75–76
    impact on officers, 81–84
    intentional torts, 74–75
        battery, 74
        wrongful deaths, 74
    negligent torts, 75
        actual damage/injury, 75
        breach of duty, 75
    rights violations, 76–77
    in state courts, 74
    Title 42 USC Section 1983 defense, 74,
        75–76, 78
    21st century issues, 79
    use of force, 80–81
    zero-tolerance policing, 79
Civil Rights Act (1964), 190, 191, 394,
        397–399, 406, 409–410, 474
Civil Rights Division (U.S. Department of
        Justice), 335–336
Civilian Complaint Review Board (New
        York), 137
Civilian review (external accountability),
        362–365
Class-control theory, 35
Classical police management, 128
Clemmons, Maurice, **441**
Cocaine, in evidence skimming, 4
Coercion. *See* Force and coercion
Cognitive learning training, 203
College degrees. *See* Higher education
Color of law, 76, **77**
Colorado State Police, 47
Combined DNA Index System
        (CODIS), 258
Command voice (in continuum of
        force), 318
Commission on Accreditation for Law
        Enforcement Agencies
        (CALEA), 373
Committee on the Future (1984, Madison,
        WI), 162

Communication (human resource
        component), 208–209
Community-oriented policing and
        problem solving (COPPS), 214
Community policing (COP), 79. *See also*
        Chicago Alternate Police Strategy
        (CAPS) experience; Madison
        (Wisconsin) Police Department
    by Chicago Police Department, 237
    COMSEC study (Ohio), 95
    CPTED strategies, trends, **92–93**
    defined, 96–98
    dismissal of, 158
    early forms
        crime prevention, 91–94
        foot patrol/broken windows, 95–96
        police-community relations, 90–91
        team policing, 94–95
    elements of
        broad police function, 100
        citizen input, 98, 100
        geographic focus, 102–103
        partnerships, 105–106
        personal service, 100–101
        philosophical dimension, 98
        positive interaction, 104–105
        prevention emphasis, 103–104
        problem analysis triangle, 108–109
        problem-oriented policing, 109, 114
        problem solving, 106–109
        reoriented operations, 101–102
        SARA model, 107
        strategic dimension, 101
        tactical dimension, 104
    evaluation of, 115–116
    evolving strategies, 89–90
    implementation, 109–115
        individual community policy,
            112–113
        positive indications, 111–113
        questions/doubts, 113–115
    implementation restructuring, 132–133
    job redesign and, 171–173
    modern day (present era), 116–118
    national survey results, 111–112
    problem-identification interview, **97**
    socialization vs. predisposition theory,
        273–275
    stress and, 424
    surviving leadership change, 171
    training programs, 205, **206**, 207
    transition issues
        balance of power, 159
        factors, 157–158
        management style, 160–161
        misunderstandings, 158
        North Carolina study, 161
Complaints and outcomes, 356–358
    about use of force (2002), **358**
    studies of, 357–358
    types of (complaints), 356
    types of punishment, 356–357
Compstat (Compare Statistics) procedure
        (NYPD), **99**, 136–139, 169,
        176–178, **177**. *See also* Zero-
        tolerance policing
Computer-aided dispatch, 237

Computerized crime mapping (CCM), 237–238

COMSEC (Community Sector Team Policing Experiment), 95

Concord (North Carolina) Police Department, 161

Conductive Energy Devices (CEDs). *See also* Tasers
  Amnesty International concerns, 80, 446, 501
  civil liability issues, 80–81
  training guidelines, 321, 322

Confessions. *See* Interrogations and confessions

Consensual encounters (voluntary interactions), 61

Consolidated agencies, 15

Constable-nightwatch policing system (England), 31–32

Constitution (U.S.)
  Bill of Rights, 7, 57
  Eighth Amendment, **8**
  Fifth Amendment, **8**
  Fourth Amendment, **8**, 58, 61, 356
  functions of, 6
  police officers and, 19
  Sixth Amendment, **8**

Contemporary police management, 129–131

Contingency theory (of management), 130

Continuum of force, 317–318

Contract law enforcement, 16

COP. See community policing

Cop crunch, 189–190

COPPS (community-oriented policing and problem solving), **214**

Corruption (police/departments), 295–299
  causes of, 274, 374
  and code of silence, 277, 296
  defined, 292
  departmental characteristics of, **299**
  drug corruption, 301, 378
  economic corruption, 37–38, 301, 302
  grass eaters/meat eaters, 295–296
  and gratuities, 294
  investigative committees, 297
  Knapp Commission investigations, **295–296**, 297, 302–303
  liabilities for, 367
  management of, 126, 141.145, 230
  noble-cause corruption, 302, 378
  persistence of, 297–299
  political corruption, 37–38
  theories of, 298–299
  types of, 37–38, 299–302

Corwin, James, **179**

Counterterrorism, 8–9, 53, 117, 498, 509, 512

County of Sacramento v. Lewis (1998), **60**

County police departments, 12

Couper, David C., 44, **45**, 130

Couple Communications Program (Minnesota), 436

CPTED (crime prevention through environmental design), 91–93

Crime Commission (1965), 44

Crime Control Act (Violent Crime Control and Law Enforcement Act of 1994), 458

Crime-control theory, 35

Crime fighting vs. social service role, 20–21

Crime prevention methods
  community methods, 92
  CPTED, **92–93**
  situational prevention, 94
  target hardening, 91

Crime prevention through environmental design (CPTED), **92–93**

Crime suppression role, 229

Crime triangle (problem analysis triangle), 108–109

Criminal Investigation Division (IRS), 11, **12**

Criminal Justice Standards and Training Commission (Florida), 367, 411

Criminal justice system (defined), 11

Criminal procedures
  arrests, 63–64
  defined, 57
  inevitable discovery, 70–71
  interrogations, confessions, 68–70
  public safety exception, 70
  search and seizure
    of persons, 58–59, 61
    of property, 64–65
  stop and frisk, 62–63
  Supreme Court rulings, 57–58
  vehicle searches, 65–68

Crisis situations. *See* Line-of-duty/crisis situations

Critical-incident debriefing (counseling), 426

CSTAR (Comprehensive Strategic Team Accountability Review) program (Kansas City), **179**

Cultural diversity, 4. *See also* Diversity in police departments
  ancestry groupings, 488–489
  community policing and, 146
  contingency theory application, 130
  educational instruction on, 205, **206**, 479
  historical minority perspective, 46
  immigration patterns, 488–489
  POST training on, 372
  recruit training needs in, 185, 203
  resource allocation and, 234
  use of force issues, 283

Culture of police. *See* Police culture

Curran investigations, 297

Curriculum development, content (human resource component), 204–205
  updates, 207–208

Cyber crime, 53, 494, 498, 517

Cynical police behavior, 272

Dallas (Texas) Police Association (DPA), **392**

Dallas (Texas) Police Department, 191, 194, **392**

Dalton brothers (outlaws), **51**

Dangers to officers, 440–444
  felonious officer killings, **438, 439**, 441
  handling mentally ill people, 444–445
  killed in the line of duty, 26, 340, **438**, 446
  perceived dangers, 440–441
  person-initiated dangers, 441
  potential/actual dangers, 441
  self-protection strategies, 446
  situational dangers, 441

Daughtry, Sylvester, Jr., **379**, 380

Davis, Edward, **146**

Davis v. City of Dallas (1985), 194, 473–474

Deadly force, 318, 338–344
  defined, 338
  determination categories
    death, 338–339
    injury, 339
    non-injury, 340
  environmental/departmental variations, 341–342
  individual/situational factors, 340–341
  justifiable homicide data, **339, 343**
  legal and policy changes
    defense-of-life policy, 344
    fleeing-felon rule, 343–344
    racial considerations, 342–343

Decertification (external accountability), 367

Decision making/police discretion, 280–290
  officer variables
    career orientation, 290
    education, age, experience, 289
    gender, 289–290
    race, 289
  organizational variables
    age, 286–287
    bureaucratic nature, 281
    citizen's mental state, 287–288
    demeanor/attitude, 284
    gender, 286
    location, 288
    mobilization, 284
    neighborhoods, 282–283
    presence of others, 288
    race, 284–286
    seriousness of offense, 287
    situational, 283
    suspect-complainant relationship, 287
    work periods, areas, assignments, 281–282

Deescalation of force (human resource component), 208

Defense-of-life shooting policy, 344

Delattre, Edwin, **209**

Deming, W. Edwards, 162

Department of Homeland Security (DHS), 11, 53, 511, 515

Depolicing, 83

Depression
  female officers, 425
  post-critical incidents, 427
  recognition-training for, 435

Depression—(*Continued*)
   social support benefits, 437
   stress-related, 432
   suicide and, 434
Detectives/detective units
   Civil War era, 50
   community policing and, 91, 165, 171
   expanded duties of, 102
   follow-up work by, 227
   hierarchical position of, **127**
   investigative function, 252–259
   in Massachusetts, 47
   19th century England, 32
   patrol relationships with, 260–261
   promotions to, 220
   undercover, and sting operations, 261
Detroit Police Department, 4, 188, 363
Detroit Police Officers' Association v. Young
   (1978), 399
Development of resources. *See* Human
   resource development
Deviance and misconduct, 290–303. *See*
   also Corruption
   drug wars, 301–303
   gratuities, 294
   prevalence of, 292–294
   sexual misconduct, 299–301
   terminations, **293**
   types of, 291–292
Deviant officers
   code of silence and, 296
   grass eaters/meat eaters, 295–297
   Knapp Commission investigation,
     295–296
   rogues, 296
   straight-shooters, 296
   white nights, 296
DHS (Department of Homeland
   Security), 11
Diallo, Amadou (shooting incident),
   425, 495
Dickerson v. U.S. (2000), 69
Dillinger, John, **52**
"Dirty Harry" problem, 377
Discretion (defined), 7
Disorder-control theory, 34–35
Disorder focus (problem-oriented
   policing), 246–247
Disorder-index, 144
Diversity in police departments,
   387–413
   affirmative action, 396–397
   African American officers
     black citizens relation to, 391
     in Dallas, **392**
     double marginality dilemma, 391
     employment data, 400, **401, 403**
     female officers, 397
     historical background, 389
     litigation issues, 399
     performance of, 390–392
     promotion data, 390, 404–405
     underrepresentation of, 412
     unequal treatment issues, 389–390
   Alaska Natives, 400
   American Indians, 400
   Asian American officers, **392**, 400, **402**

Castor's view on, **388**
consistent growth data, 400–406
Equal Employment Opportunity Act,
   397–398
Hispanic officers
   in Dallas, **392**
   employment data, 400, **401, 403**
   female officers, 397
   Hispanic citizens relation to, 391
   promotion data, 404–405
integration of minorities
   defeminization process, 407
   police culture, 407–408
   police man/police woman
     identities, 408
   pregnancy/maternity, 409–410
   sexual harassment, 203, 286, 292,
     300, 401, 407, 410–411
   structural characteristics, 408–409
Pacific Islanders, 400
promotional opportunities, 390, 392,
   404–406
race/ethnicity chart, **402–403**
reverse discrimination, 398–399
stress/invisibility feelings, 425
women officers
   employment data, 400, **401, 403, 404**
   exclusion from opportunities, 398
   historical background, 389
   performance of, 394–396
   Police Foundation survey, 394
   pregnancy/maternity, 409–410
   promotion data, **392**, 404
   recruitment of, 402
   sexual harassment of, 203, 286, 292,
     300, 401, 407, 410–411
   unequal treatment issues, 393–394,
     398, 401
Divorce of police officers, 436
DNA testing, **45,** 257–259, **500**
DoD (Department of Defense), 11
Dog unit. *See* Canines
Domestic violence
   community disorder measures and, 142
   and dual arrest, 250
   primary aggressor laws, 250
   proactive arrests for, 241
   reactive arrests for, 249–250
   specialized trainings for, 205, 210
   suspect-complainant relationship, 287
Doolin, Bill, **51**
Double marginality dilemma, 391
Drug abuse, 431, 433, 447
Drug corruption, 301, 378
Drug Enforcement Administration, **12**
Dual arrests, 250
DUI (driving under the influence)
   by NJ state trooper, 3
Duke Power Company, Griggs v., 190

Early warning system (EWS), 360–361
Economic conditions, influence on crime
   income equality, 491
   poverty rates, 491
   unemployment rates, 489–491
Economics, influence on crime, 489–491
Education. *See* Higher education

Edwards v. Arizona (1981), 69–70
Eighth Amendment (Constitution), **8**
Elderly citizens
   community policing and, 100
   crimes against, 110
   dilemmas presented by, 486–487
   geographic distribution, 486, 491
   rural police work and, 18
Empirical evidence, 387, 394, 428, 469
Endrekin, Gary, 493
Engel, Robin, **244–245**
England. *See also* Fielding, Henry; Peel,
   Sir Robert
   Bow Street Runners, 32
   constable-nightwatch system, 31–32
   county sheriffs, 31, 36
   emigration to America, 34
   founders, 33–34
   frankpledge policing system, 31
   19th century policing, 32–34
   Peelian Principles, 32–33, 35
   posse comitatus groups, 9, 31
   thief catchers, 32
   12th/13th century policing, 31–32
Enticement, 261–262
Entrapment, 261–262
Entry (selection factor), 185–186
EPD. See experimental police district
Equal Employment Opportunity Act
   (1972), 190, 397–398
ERUs (emergency response units), 134
Ethical relativism and the law, **377–378**
Ethical standards
   code of ethics, 374–375
   ethical dilemmas, 377–378
   ethical formalism, 375
   ethical perspectives, 375
   ethical relativism, 376–378
   ethical utilitarianism, 375–376
   limits of, 378, 380
   schools of ethics, 376
Ethics and integrity (human resource
   component), 208, **209**
Ethnic diversity. *See* Cultural diversity;
   Racial considerations
Etowah County (Alabama) Drug Task
   Force, 493
Eustress/distress, 420
Evidence
   AFIS/DNA testing, 257–259, **500**
   Baltimore skimming problems, 4
   community policing and, 92, 99, 100
   confessions as, 69
   due process revolution and, 254
   empirical evidence, 94, 387, 394,
     428, 469
   exclusionary rule and, 58–61,
     63, 367
   filing complaints regarding, 149
   fruit of the poisonous tree doctrine
     and, 61
   inevitable discovery and, 70–71
   procedural law and, 7
   search allowances, 63–68
   terrorism/investigation and, 254–256
   testimonial evidence, 387
Evidence-based policing, **99**

Exclusionary rule, 58–61, 63, 367
Exoneration (from complaints), 356
Experimental police district (EPD),
    163–164, 170
External accountability mechanisms,
    362–368
  auditor systems, 365–366
  civil/criminal liability, 367
  civil rights criminal violations, 367–368
  civilian review, 362–365
  decertification, 367
  exlusionary rule, 58, 367
  legal control, 366–367
  pattern/practice litigation, 368
Eyewitness identification, 331, 494,
    496–497, 517

Facebook (social media), 100, 504
False arrest, 61–62, 63, 74, 78
Family and Medical Leave Act (FMLA,
    1993), 409–410
Family clan (kin) policing, 30–32
Federal Bureau of Investigation (FBI)
  fingerprint system establishment, 42
  founding/role of, 11–12, **53**
  historical background, 50–53
  Hoover's directorship of, 52
  National Incident-Based Reporting
    System, 142–143, **143**
  reactive investigation methods, 16
  recruit drug standards, 195
  role of, 11–12
  Uniform Crime Reports, 44, 52, 142, 144
Federal Bureau of Prisons, **12**
Federal Emergency Management Agency
    (FEMA), 207
Federal law enforcement (U.S.)
  Postal Inspectors, 50, 53
  Revenue Cutter Service, 50
  Secret Service, 50, 53
  U.S. Marshals Service, 50, 51, 53
Federalism (defined), 5
Felonious officer killings, **438, 439,** 441
FEMA. See Federal Emergency
    Management Agency
Females. See Women officers
Field operations
  focused interventions, 241–249
  intimate partner violence, 205, **206,**
    241, 249–250, 257
  investigative function, 252–255
    selected research, 255–262
  patrol function, 228–238
  patrol operations, selected research,
    238–240
  police pursuits, 250–252
  reactive arrests, 249–250
Field training (human resource
    component), 211
Field-training officer (FTO) program,
    211, 212–213
Fielding, Henry, 32
Fifth Amendment (Constitution), **8**
Firearms. See also Bureau of Alcohol,
    Tobacco, and Firearms
  carrying authority agencies, **12**
  training, **206,** 321

Firearms Training Systems simulators, 321
Flat organizational structures, 131, **132**
Fleeing-felon rule, 344
Florida Criminal Justice Standards and
    Training Commission, 367, 411
Florida v. Bostick (1991), **60**
Florida v. Powell (2010), **61**
Floyd, Pretty Boy, 51
Foot patrol
  abandonment of, 95–96
  advantages of, 98
  community policing method, 90, 96, 98
  England, nineteenth century, 32
  increasing use of, 101, 231–232
  in Newark, NJ, 232
  Problem-Identification Interview, 97
  resistance to, in NY, 160
  as tactical method, 24, 39
  vs. motorized patrol, 96
Foot pursuits, 252
Force and coercion. *See also* Abner
    Louima incident; Brutality/
    excessive force; Deadly force;
    Inappropriate force; Louima,
    Abner (incident); Rodney King
    incident
  defined, 311–312
  inappropriate force
    brutality/excessive force, 327–329,
      331–333
    historical background, 329–331
    NYPD escalation scale, **320**
  in police-citizen interactions
    citizen's complaint against, **358**
    context of force, 312–315
    Police-Public Contact Survey,
      315–316, **316**
    Survey of Inmates in Local Jails,
      316–317
    traffic stop actions, **314**
  Police-Pubic Contact Survey,
    315–316, **316**
  Survey of Inmates in Jail, 316–317
  training in use of, 317–323
    canines, 319–320, 323, **324**
    CED guidelines, **322**
    command voice, 318
    continuum of force, 317
    deadly force, 318
    firearms, 321
    flashlights, 322–323
    less lethal weapons, 318
    mere presence, 317
    OC spray, 318, 321
    officer survival, 322
    self-defense, 321
    Tasers, 321
    verbal force, 317
  usage controversies
    with the community, 324–325
    between norms, 326–327
    over policy, 325–326
Fourth Amendment (Constitution), **8,**
    58, 61, 356
Frankpledge policing system (England), 31
Fraternal Order of Police, 148
Free societies, role of police, 4–6

determination by government type, 5–6
  homeland security and terrorism, 8–9
  rule of law, 6–7
Frisk. *See* Stop and frisk
Fruit of the poisonous tree doctrine, 61
FTO program. See field-training officer
    (FTO) program
Fyfe, James J., **319–320**

Gallup Organization polls
  crime ranking (1968), 457
  racial profiling survey, 285, 495
Gang violence, 16, 91, 242–245
Garrity v. New Jersey (1967), 356
Generalist officers, 11, 132, 135, 227
Geographic information systems
    (GIS), 502
George v. Randolph (2006), 60
Gerard, Daniel, **245**
GIS (geographic information
    systems), 502
Global positioning systems (GPS), 504
Glover, Thomas, **392**
Goals of police
  agency level, 24
  dimensions of performance, **23**
  organizational expectations, 19
  priorities of the public, 24
Golden Gate Peace Officers
    Association, 148
Good faith actions, 78
Government and police, 5–6
GPS (global positioning systems), 504
Gratuities, problems with, 294
Great Britain. *See also* England
  police founders, 33–34
  Royal Commission Report, 7
Great Depression (U.S., 1930s), 42
Greece (Ancient) kin policing
    methods, 31
Greenville (Texas) Police Department, 476
Grievance arbitration, 360
Griggs v. Duke Power Company (1971),
    190, 398, 474
Griswold, Tina, **441**
Group behavior management
  of employee organizations, 148
  of police subcultures, 145–148
  of police unions, 148–150
Group norms
  defined, 158–159, 181
  development of, 283
  deviation from, 30–31
Guardian Angels vigilante movement
    (NYC), 37
Guns
  cognitive stereotyping and, 286
  departmental focus on, 4, 171, 243
  federal investigations of use, 507
  Firearm Suppression Patrol
    strategy, 242
  and gang violence, 242–245
  officers killed by (data), 446
  Project Exile strategy, 243
  restraint in use of, 320
  in search and seizure cases, 64
  SWAT team equipment, 134–135

Harassment. *See* Racial harassment (by police); Sexual harassment
Harrison Narcotic Act (1914), 52
Harvard, Beverly, 405
Hawaii Police Department, 13
HAZMAT (hazardous materials) training, 218
Height and weight (police selection factor), 191–192
Herring v. U.S. (2009), **60**
High Point (NC) Police Department, 3
Higher education, 455–480
  Arlington (Texas) PD requirements, **463**
  associates degrees, 456
  and attitudes, 463–465
  as bona fide occupational qualification, 191, 473–474
  Chief's Scholar Program, 472–473
  and discrimination, 474–475
  future research directions, 468–469
  impact on policing
    attitudes, 463–465
    community policing, 470–471
    force and liability, 466–467
    job satisfaction, 470
    leadership/promotion, 467
    performance, 465–466
    terrorism, 470–471
  incentive programs, 475–480
    education pay, **476**
    entry-level officer support, 479
    requirements/policy implications, 477–480
    for sworn officers, **476**
  and performance, 465–466
  police chiefs, promotion and, 462–463
  police executive's views on, **471**, 471–472
  program development, 456–463
    components, **475**
    Federal support, 457–458
    quality of programs, 458–461
    requirements for police, **461**, 461–462
Highway patrol, 47–48, 49
Hillsborough County (Florida) Sheriff's Office, 188–189, **189**
Hiring in the Spirit of Service (HSS) project, 188
Hispanic citizens
  force/coercion disparities, 342
  juvenile delinquency data, 209
  police-community relations, 90–91
  recruitment of, 187
    height discrimination, 192
    test performance, 197
    youth being stopped, 209, 495
Hispanic police
  in Dallas, **392**
  detachment/alienation from community, 391
  employment data, 400, **401, 403**
  female officers, 397
  Hispanic citizens relation to, 391
  promotion data, 404–405
Historical background (of policing), 29–54. *See also* United States, modern policing history

city police forces, U.S., 34–35
county sheriffs, 36
founders of British police, 33–34
Greek city-states/ancient Rome, 31
kin policing, 30–32
sheriffs/frankpledge system, 31
socioeconomic factors, 35
vigilance committees, 36–37
Holocaust (World War II), **10**
Homeland security, 8–9, 505, 510–512, 516, **516**. *See also* Department of Homeland Security
Homicide
  demographics of, 17
  NYPD Compstat strategy for, 136
  PPUs and, 135
Hoover, Herbert, 41
Hoover, J. Edgar, 44, **52**, 53
Hoover, Jerry, **214**
Hot pursuit exception (to search and seizure of property), 65
Houston (Texas) Police Department, 476
HSS project. See Hiring in the Spirit of Service (HSS) project
Hudson v. Michigan (2006), **60**
Human resource development, 201–220
  academy training topics, **206**
  career growth, 216–217
  communication, 208–209
  community policing training, 205, **206, 207**
  curriculum development, content, 204–205
    job task analysis, 204
    POST programs, 204–205
    updates, 207–208
  deescalation of force, 208
  duration of training/academy type, **205**
  ethics and integrity, 208
  field training, 211
  FTO program, 212–213
  in-service training, **217**, 217–218
  on juveniles, 209–210
  lateral entry, 219–220
  on the mentally ill, 210
  one-way/two-way knowledge transfer, 203
  philosophy/instructional methods, 202–203
  POST recruitment training standards, 201–202
  problem-based learning, 204
  program orientation, 202
  promotion/assessment centers, 218–219
  PTO program, 213–214, **215**, 216
  recruit training effectiveness, 210–211
  specialized trainings, 218
  terrorism-related training, 207, **208**
  topic breakdown (chart), **206**
Human Rights Watch, 333, 335–336

IACP/West Award for Excellence in Criminal Investigations, **244**
IAFIS. See Integrated Automated Fingerprint Identification System
ICAM crime mapping system, 237–238, **238**

Idaho POST academy, 204
Illinois v. Caballes (2005), **60**
Illinois v. Lidster (2004), 67
Illinois v. McArthur (2001), **60**
Illinois v. Wardlow (2000), 62
ILP. See intelligence-led policing
Immigration. *See also* Migration/ migration patterns
  demographic changes, 488–489, 492–494
  demonstrations related to, 3
  enforcement, 494, 495–496, 517
  illegal immigration, 325, 489
  legal immigration, 489
  modern patterns of, 488–489
Immigration and Naturalization Services (INS), 377
In-group solidarity, 276–277
In-migration, 489, 491, 492
In-service training (human resource component), 217–218
Inappropriate force, 327–338
  brutality/excessive force, 327–329
  by early city police, 35
  frequency of, 331–332
  by kin policing, 30–31
  Rodney King incident, 333–335
  for securing confessions, 42
  by Texas Rangers, 46–47
  in the 21st century, 332–333
  complaints about, 332
  physical/psychological, 329–331
Incentive programs (higher education), 475–480
  education pay, **476**
  entry-level officer support, 479
  requirements/policy implications, 477–480
  for sworn officers, **476**
Independent Commission on the Los Angeles Police Department, 212
Indiana University, 456
Indianapolis Police Department, 140, 394
Individual's expectations (of police), 19
Inertia, and resistance to change, 158, 181
Inevitable discovery, Supreme Court cases, 70–71
Information technology (IT), 502
Inner-city riots (U.S., 1960s), 363, 389–391, 457
Innovation processes. *See also* Compstat (Compare Statistics) procedure (NYPD)
  FTO program, 214
  intelligent-led policing, 255
  in organizational change, 4, 174–181
    areas for, 163
    civil liability and, 71
    in community policing, 95
    Compstat/Compstat-like process, 176–178
    defined, 174
    learning organizations, 178–179
    middle management utilization, 180–181
    organizational learning, 180
    police-researcher partnerships, 180
  in resource utilization, 237

Institutional theory, applications to policework, 272
Integrated Automated Fingerprint Identification System (IAFIS), 257
Intelligence-led policing (ILP), 24–25, **99**, 255, 514–515
Intentional torts, 74–75
Internal accountability mechanisms internal investigations, 354–356, 358–360, 362
    organization, management, 352
    steps of process, 355–356
    written directives, 352–354
Internal affairs investigations, 354–356, 358–360
    complaint outcomes, 356–358
    differences in, 356
    early intervention alternatives, 361
    effectiveness of, 362
    issues in, 358–360
        location/personnel, 359
        orientation of IA unit, 359–360
        sustained complaints, 360
    orientation of units, 359–360
    steps of process, 355–356
Internal Revenue Service, Criminal Investigation Division, 11, **12**
International Association of Chiefs of Police (IACP), **244**, 370, 373, 401
International Association of Directors of Law Enforcement Standards and Training, 367
International terrorism, 509, 511–512
International Union of Police Associations, 148
Internet
    for community-policing news, 111
    for crime reporting, 240
    data-collection capabilities, **479**
    increasing interactions on, 505
    police recruitment via, 186–187
    recruit via, 187
Interrogations and confessions
    arrests and, 63
    community policing and, 91
    criminal procedure and, 57
    custodial interrogation, 70
    defined, 69
    field interrogations, 241
    historical background, **330**
    inevitable discovery and, 70
    Miranda warnings, **59, 60, 61**, 68–69
    of police officers, **355**, 367
    proactive vs. reactive, 21
    right to attorney, 69–70
    San Diego study, 139
    Supreme Court cases, 68–70
Intimate partner violence. *See* Domestic violence
Investigative functions, 252–255
    historical development, 253–254
    intelligence-led policing, 255
    terrorism/investigation, 254–255
Investigative operations, selected research
    AFIS advances, 257–259
    bias crime programs, 260
    career criminal programs, 259–260
    detective-patrol relationships, 260–261

DNA testing advances, 257–259, **500**
on effectiveness, 255–256
enticement/entrapment, 261–262
principles for improvement of, 256
Inwald Personality Inventory (IPI), 195–196
IQ (intelligence quotient) markers (police selection factor), 198

Jackson, President Andrew, 37
James brothers (outlaws), **51**
Jersey City problem-oriented approach, 247
Job redesign (community policing), 173
Johnson, Lemon, 62
Johnson, Lyndon Baines, 44
Jordan, Robert, 198
Judgmental pursuit policy, 251
Justice Without Trial (Skolnick), 277
Justifiable homicides, **339**
Juveniles
    academy training about, 204, 209–210
    broad police function inclusion of, 100
    community policing and, 104–105
    curfew crime arrests, 248–249
    detective unit specialization, 252
    field operations and, 227
    foot patrol officers and, 96
    Vollmer's attitudes towards, 42

K-9s. *See* Canines
Kansas City Gun Experiment, 242
Kansas City Massacre, 50
Kansas City (Missouri) Police Department (KCPD), 38, **179**, 236
Kansas City Preventive Patrol Experiment, 238
Karl, Matt, **493**
Katz v. U.S. (1967), **59**
Kelley, Eric, **441**
Kelling, George, 138
Kentucky Criminal Justice Training Center, 204
Kentucky Law Enforcement Council, 372
Killed in the line of duty, 26, 340, **438,** 446
Kin (family clan) policing, 30–32
King, Martin Luther, Jr., **52**
King, Rodney, brutality incident, 212, 332, **333–335**, 368, 407, 425, 495
King County (Seattle) Sheriff's Office, 188
Knapp Commission investigations, **295–296**, 297, 302–303
Kylio v. U.S. (2001), **60**

Labor movements (unions), 148–150
Lakewood (Washington) Police Department, **441**
Lateral entry (human resource component), 219–220
Latino Police Officers Association, 148
Law enforcement (defined), 228
Law Enforcement and Administrative Statistics (LEMAS) survey, 133, 173, 332
"Law Enforcement and Society: Lessons from the Holocaust" training program (Anti-Defamation League), 10

Law Enforcement Assistance Administration (LEAA), 457–458, **479**
Law Enforcement Education Program (LEEP), 458–460, **479**
Law Enforcement Management and Administrative Statistics (LEMAS), 133
Law Enforcement Officer Advisory Council (Arizona), 372
Leadership management, 125
Legal control (external accountability), 366–367
Legal issues
    civil liability
        avenues of, 73–74
        color of law, 76
        community policing, 79
        costs in policing, 71–73
        in federal courts, 75–76
        impact on officers, 81–84
        intentional torts, 74–75
        negligent torts, 75
        rights violations, 76–77
        in state courts, 74
        Title 42 USC Section 1983 defense, 77–78
        21st century issues, 79
        use of force, 80–81
        zero-tolerance policing, 79
    criminal procedures
        arrests, 63–64
        defined, 57
        inevitable discovery, 70–71
        interrogations, confessions, 68–70
        public safety exception, 70
        search and seizure, 58–59, 61, 64–65
        stop and frisk, 62–63
        Supreme Court rulings, 57–58
        vehicle searches, 65–68
Legalistic style (of policing), 278
Legitimacy issues, 139–140
LEMAS. See Law Enforcement Management and Administrative Statistics
Lexow Committee investigation, 297
Lincoln (Nebraska) Police Department, 465
Lindbergh, Charles, 50–51
Line-of-duty/crisis situations, 425–431
    administrative vs. on the street, 423
    heart rate study, 426
    killed in the line of duty, 26, 340, **438,** 446
    PTSD, 426–428
    shift work, 419, 421, 424, 426, 428–430, 434
    social supports for, 429, 431
Los Angeles County Sheriff's Department, 366
    spouse training program, 436
    women officers, 393
Los Angeles Police Department (LAPD), 3, 12, 13
    complaint investigation, 360–361
    computerized tracking system, 237–238
    departmental diversity, 400
    foot vs. car patrol, 234

Los Angeles Police Department
  (LAPD)—(*Continued*)
  FTOs, selection and training, **213**
  Independent Commission, 212
  Rodney King incident, 212, 332,
    333–335, 368, 407, 425, 495
  team policing, 94
  use of canines, 323, 324
Louima, Abner (incident), 425, 495
Loveland (Colorado) Police
  Department, **195**
Lowell (Massachusetts) Police
  Department, **146**, 177–178, 247
Lynch, Colonel, 37
Lynching (term derivation), 37

Mace, 80
Madison (Wisconsin) Police Department,
  45, 130–131
  organizational change experience,
    161–164
    citizen involvement, 163
    Committee on the Future (1984), 162
    EPD development, 163–164,
      163–164, 170
    innovative processes, 174, **175**
    internal/external changes, 171
    lessons learned, 170–171
    MBWA, 175
    results, 164
    TQM leadership, 162–163
  quality management/problem solving,
    44, 130–131
Males
  being arrested comparisons, 286
  coercion (force) used by, 289–290
  exam score comparisons, 197
Management, 124–152. *See also*
    Accountability and ethics
  behavioral style, 128–129
  chain of command, 126
  classical style, 128
  contingency theory of, 130
  defined, 125
  goals/organizational performance,
    140–145
    behavior/supervisory style, 140–141
    changing measures, 144–145
    evaluations/measurements,
      141–-144
  of group behavior, 145–150
    employee organizations, 148
    police subcultures, 145–148
    police unions, 148–150
  hierarchical organization pyramid, **127**
  inertia and, 158
  LEMAS data, 133
  lower/middle managers, 127
  media relations, 150–151
  open/closed systems of, 129
  organizational design
    broken-windows theory, 135–136
    centralization/decentralization, 132
    Compstat process, 136–139
    defined, 131–132
    paramilitary design, 133–135
    police legitimacy issues, 139–140

sustained adaptation, 133
  tall/flat structures, **132**
  zero-tolerance policing, 136, 138
  processes of
    controlling, 125–126
    leadership, 125
    organization, 125
    planning, 125
  resistance to change by, 159
  top managers, 127
  total quality management (TQM),
    130–131
    principles, 131
Management by walking around
  (MBWA), 175
Mapp v. Ohio (1961), 58, **59**
Marital/family problems, 435–436
Martinsville (Indiana) Police
  Department, 3
Maryland v. Buie (1990), 64
Maryland v. Pringle (2003), **60**
Maryland v. Shatzer (2010), 70
Massachusetts Criminal Justice Training
  Council, 203
Massachusetts State Police, 46–47
Mayhle, Stephen, **441**
Mayne, Richard, 32, 33–34
Mazet Committee investigation, 297
MBWA (management by walking
  around), 175
McCarthy, Joseph (McCarthyism), **52**
McCurley, Chris, 493
Media relations management, 150–151
Medical condition (police selection
  factor), 196
Mentally ill citizens
  effects of deinstitutionalization of, 497
  strategies for dealing with, 319, 444–445
  Taser use, 327
  training in dealing with, 210, 466
Mere presence (in continuum of force), 317
Metro-Dade Police Department, **195**
Metropolitan Police Act (England, 19th
  century), 32
Metropolitan Police Department
  (London, England), **45**
Metropolitan Police Department
  (Washington, DC), **10**
Miami-Dade Police Department, 12,
  298–299
Michigan Dept. of State Police v. Sitz
  (1990), **60**, 67
Michigan State Police, 429
Michigan State University, 456
Migration/migration patterns, 488–489,
  491, 492
Minneapolis Domestic Violence
  Experiment, 249
Minnesota Multiphasic Personality
  Inventory (MMPI), 195–196
Minnesota v. Dickerson (1993), 63
Minorities in the police. *See* Diversity in
  police departments
Minority perspective on American
  police, 46
  Texas, brutal treatment of prisoners,
    46–47

Miranda v. Arizona (1966), **59**, 68–69
Mississippi State Highway Patrol, **49**
Missouri State Highway Patrol (MSHP), **49**
Missouri v. Seibert (2004), **60**
Mob suppression
  by disorder-control theory, 34–35
Mollen Commission, 297
Moore, Sir John, 33
Moran v. Burbine (1986), **59**
Mothers Against Drunk Driving
  (MADD), 273, 486
Motorized vs. foot patrol, 96
Motorola/Weber Seavey Award for
  Excellence in Law Enforcement,
  244. *See also* Engel, Robin
Municipal police forces, 9, 13
Myers, Richard W., **514**

National Advisory Commission on Civil
  Disorders, 44, 363
National Advisory Commission on
  Criminal Justice Standards and
  Goals, 186, 458
National Advisory Commission on
  Higher Education for Police
  Officers, 459–460
National Association for the
  Advancement of Colored People
  (NAACP), 6, 72, 187
National Center for Health Statistics, 248
National Center for Women and Policing,
  403, 404
National Commission on Law
  Observance (1929), 41
National Commission on the Causes and
  Prevention of Violence (1969), 363
National Crime Victimization Survey
  (NCVS), 144, 249–250, 498
National Incident-Based Reporting
  System (NIBRS), 142–143, **143**
National Incident Management System/
  Incident Command System, 207
National Institute of Justice (NIJ), 445,
  499, **499**
National Law Enforcement and
  Corrections Technology Center
  (NLECTC), **499**
National Law Enforcement Officers
  Memorial Fund, 438, 440
National Mortality Detail File (1985), 434
National Organization of Black Law
  Enforcement Executives, 373, 405
National Rifle Association (NRA), 6
National Security Agency (NSA), 8
National Sheriffs Association, 373
Native Americans
  immigration enforcement, 495
  police-community relations, 90–91
  tribal police, 15
Navy Seals, 134
Nazi Germany, **10**
Nebraska State Highway Patrol, **49**
Negligent torts, 75
Neighborhood Foot Patrol Program, 232
Neighborhood Watch program, 92, 96,
  111, 113, 116
Nevada State Police, 47

New Jersey state troopers, 3
New York City Police Foundation,
    176, 434
New York Police Department (NYPD),
    13, 35, 79
    Amadou Diallo shooting incident,
        425, 495
    Bedford-Stuyvesant 81st Precinct, 176
    canine officer training, **319–320**
    Compstat procedure, **99,** 136–139, 169,
        176–178, **177**
    corruption, 297
    dealing with mentally ill citizens, **319**
    fleeing-felon rule, 344
    foot vs. car patrol, 234
    Knapp Commission investigations of,
        295–296
    misconduct suspensions, 292
    resistance to organizational change,
        159–160
    Scale of Escalating Force, **320**
    training in use of force, 319–320
    zero-tolerance policing, **138**
New York v. Belton (1981), 68
New York v. Quarles (1984), 59, 70
Newark (NJ) Foot Patrol Experiment, 232
Newspaper ads (recruitment method), 187
Nightwatch (citizen groups) policing,
    31, 34
NIJ. See National Institute of Justice
911 calls, 90, 102, **110, 166,** 168, 170, 230,
    239, 282
Nix v. Williams (1984), **59,** 70–71
Noble-cause corruption, 302
North Carolina Justice Academy, 321
North Carolina Police Department, COP
    study (2002, 2005), 161
North Dakota Police Department, 13

OC (oleoresin) spray, 80, 318, 321, 396,
    446, 448
Occupational stress, 420–421
Office of Community Oriented Policing
    Services (COPS), 98, 116, **214**
Office of Management Accountability
    (Chicago), 168–169
Office of Science and Technology (of
    NIJ), 499
Officers' Advisory Council (OAC,
    Madison, WI), 162
Officers for Justice (African
    Americans), 148
Ohio State Highway Patrol, **49**
Oliver v. U.S. (1984), 65
Omnibus Crime Control and Safe Streets
    Act (1968), 458
Open/closed management systems, 129
Open fields doctrine, 65
Operation Safe Streets (Philadelphia), 242
Oral interview (police selection factor),
    199–201
Order maintenance (defined), 228
Oregon Fish and Game Commission, **48**
Oregon State Highway Commission, **48**
Oregon State Police, 47, **48–49**
Oregon State Traffic Department, **48**
Organization expectations (of police), 19

Organizational change, 156–181
    Chicago (CAPS) experience
        foundational work, 165
        key elements, 165–167
        lessons learned, 170
        results, 168–170
        WHAM component, 166–167
    description of process, 157–158
    innovation processes, 174–181
        areas for, 163
        Compstat process, 176–178
        defined, 174
        learning organizations, 178–179
        middle management utilization,
            180–181
        organizational learning, 180
        police-researcher partnerships, 180
    job redesign/community policing,
        171–173
    LEMA survey, 173
    Madison PD experience, 161–164
        foundational work, 162
        key elements, 162–164
        results, 164
    resistance, overcoming, 159–161
    resistance, reasons for
        balance of power, 159
        group norms, 158–159
        inertia, 158, 181
        misunderstandings, 158
        in New York, 159–160
    success factors, 157
Organizational design. *See also* Broken-
    windows theory
    centralization/decentralization, 132
    Compstat procedure, **99,** 136–139, 169,
        176–178, **177**
    defined, 131–132
    paramilitary design, 133–135
    police legitimacy issues, 139–140
    sustained adaptation, 133
    tall/flat structures, 131, **132**
    zero-tolerance policing, 136, 138
Organizational performance, goals of,
    140–145
    behavior/supervisory style, 140–141
    changing measures
        disorder index, 144
        evaluation of, 144–145
    evaluations/measurements, 141–-144
Organizational perspectives (of
    behavior), 272
Out-migration, 492
Oversight mechanism limits, 368–369
Owens, Ronald, **441**

Paramilitary units. *See* Police paramilitary
    units
Parker, William, **52**
Participatory management style, 160–161
Particularistic perspective (of
    behavior), 273
Passive reacting policing, 21
Patriot Act (USA), 8
Patrol function, 228–238
    in beats (sectors/districts), 236
    computer-aided dispatch, 237, **237**

crackdowns, 241
    crime suppression role, 229
    differentiation response to calls, 240
    directed patrols, 241
    historical development, 228–230
    ICAM crime mapping system,
        237–238, **238**
    job description, **229**
    Kansas City Preventive Patrol
        Experiment, 238
    methods, 231–232, 234
    Neighborhood Foot Patrol
        Program, 232
    Newark (NJ) Foot Patrol
        Experiment, 232
    Operation Safe Streets, 242
    proactive vs. reactive approach, 230, 241
    resource allocation, 236
    resource determination, 234–236
    response times, 239–240
    in shifts, 236
    staffing, 234
    targeted hot spots, 241
    and terrorism, 230–231
    use of resources, 234
Pattern/practice litigation (external
    accountability), 368
Payton v. New York (1981), 63
Peace Officer Standards and Training
    (POST) organizations, 49, 186,
    201–202, 372
Pedagogy (defined), 203
Peel, Sir Robert, 32, 33, 35, **45**
Peelian Principles (of London police),
    32–33, 35
Pendergast, Thomas "Boss Tom," 38
Pendleton Civil Service Act (1883), 185
Pennsylvania State Police, 47
Pennsylvania State Troopers, 3
Pepper spray, 80, 318, **320,** 321, 501
PERF. See Police Executive Research
    Forum
Performance dimensions, **23**
Personalized service (community
    policing), 101
Peterson, Ezra George, 493
Philadelphia Police Force, 34
Philosophy/instructional methods
    (human resource component),
    202–203
Phoenix Regional Police Basic Training
    Academy, 211
Physical agility, strength (police selection
    factor), 192–193
Pittsburg Police Department, 4, 242, **441**
Plain view doctrine, 64
Planning management, 125
Pleasanton (California) Police
    Department, **210**
Pleasanton Youth Commission, **210**
Police academies
    education requirements, 472
    ethics training, 208–209
    firearms training, 321
    performance study, 197–198, 468
    physical training component, 192
    post-training skills integration, 211

Police academies—(*Continued*)
recruit training phase, 201–205, 274–275
representation by women, 401–402, 408, 410
rural police and, 17
socialization component, 274
suicide prevention training, 435
Police Administration (Wilson and McLaren), 43, 229, 371, 394
Police agencies, 6, 8–11, **12**, 13–16, 23–25
Police-Citizen Advisory Committee, 72
Police-citizen interactions (use of force)
context of force, 312–315
Police-Public Contact Survey, 315–316
Survey of Inmates in Local Jails, 316–317
Police-community relations, 90–91
Police culture
building blocks of, **369**
characteristics of, 279
deviant behavior and, 300
education and, 462
informal/formal, 103
organizational expectations and, 19
of PPUs, 133–135, 151
research studies of, 276
secretive/self-protective elements, 354, 368
"single" culture, discussion, 280
studies of, 272
traditional, 113, 115
traffic enforcement viewpoint, 442
Understanding Police Culture, 279
and the use of force, 323–324
women and, 407–408
Police departments. *See also* Chicago Alternate Police Strategy (CAPS) experience; Management; individual police departments
accountability/ethics issues, 352–353, 357–365
behavior factors, 274, 277–278
city services delivery by, 167
Committee on the Future review of, 162
community policing and, 21, 91, 100, 103, 105, 109, 117
Compstat procedure, **99**, 136–139, 169, 176–178, **177**
constituency feedback for, 180
corruption within, 295, 297–299
county police departments, 12
discipline of officers, 326
field operations, 229, 235–236, 249, 257, 260–261
formal/informal aspects, 19
high-speed chase requirements, 326
hiring decisions, 235–236
historical development of, 36–39
internal/external oversight mechanisms, 352
management of, 125–151, 164
officers employment data, **200**
organizational variables, 281–282
production orientation of, 277
professionalization of, 229

role of, 160
selection decisions by, 185–186
training academy study, 197–198
use-of-force policy, 328
Police Executive Research Forum (PERF), 10, 186–187, 189, 321, 373, 462
Police Foundation survey, 394
Police Officer's Bill of Rights, 355
Police paramilitary units (PPUs), 151
criticisms of, 133–134
influence of, 134–135
Police-Pubic Contact Survey (PPCS), 315–316, **316**
Police Services Study, 21–22, 141
Police systems, United States, 11–18
agencies with arrest/firearm authorization, **12**
consolidated agencies, 15
contract law enforcement, 16
county police departments, 12
federal government agencies, 12
full-time sworn personnel data, **14**
jurisdictional differences, 11–12
local/state agencies by size, 12–13, **13**
municipal police forces, 13
public safety agencies, 15
regional police, 15
rural police work, 17–18
similarities-differences, 16–18
special-jurisdiction police, 16, **17**
task forces, 16
ten largest federal agencies, **12**
tribal police, 15
Police Systems in the United States (Smith), 128
Police training officer (PTO) program, 213–214, **215**, 216
Political model of policing (U.S.), 37
Polygraph examination (police selection factor), 194
POP. See problem-oriented policing
Posse comitatus (England, 13th century), 9, 31
POST. See Peace Officer Standards and Training organizations
Postal Inspectors, 50, 53
Posttraumatic stress disorder (PTSD), 426–428
causes of, 426
counseling for, 426, 428
financial impact of, 428
New Zealand study, 427
sensitization training study, 427–428
treatment for, 426, 428
PPUs (police paramilitary units), 134, 135, 151. *See also* ERUs (emergency response units); SWAT (special weapons and tactics) teams
Praefectus urbi (Roman public police), 31
Predictive policing, **99**, 515
Predispositional perspective (of behavior), 275–276
President's Commission on Law Enforcement and Administration of Justice, 44, 363, 457

President's Commission Task Force on Police, 219
Primary aggressor laws, 250
Prisoners, brutal treatment of
by early city police, 35
by kin policing, 30–31
for securing confessions, 42
by Texas Rangers, 46–47
Private world of policing, 9, 147–148
Proactive police work, 21, 230, 241, 242
Probable cause, 78
Alabama v. White, 58
in arrests, 61, 63, 74, 287
Carroll v. U.S., 67–68
in Fourth Amendment, **8,** 65
Illinois v. McArthur, **60**
Kyllo v. U.S., **60**
Maryland v. Pringle, **60**
search warrants and, 64, 78
Terry v. Ohio, 62
U.S. v. Leon, **59**
U.S. v. Ross, **59,** 68
in vehicle stops, **66–67**
Problem analysis triangle (crime triangle), **108–109**
Problem-based learning (human resource component), 204
Problem-Identification Interview (form), **97**
Problem-oriented policing (POP), 24, 109
advancement of, 99
CPTED overlap with, 92
disorder focus, 246–247
implementation of, 45, 109
key to, 90
problem solving vs., 107–108
SMART inspector unit, 246
street-level policing vs., 114
successes of, 111, 116
supervisory support for, 163
Problem-solving approach (community policing), 106–108, 162, 230, 471
Problem Specific Guide for Police, 109, **110–111**
Procedural justice, 139, 210
Procedural laws (defined), 7
Production orientation (of police departments), 277
Professional Range Instruction Simulators, 321
Professionalization movement
described, 369–370, **370**
professional criteria
autonomy, 370–371
certification/accreditation, 372–373
commitment to service, 373–374
education and training, 372
unique knowledge, 371–372
Reform Era, 40
Program development (higher education), 456–463
components, **475**
Federal support, 457–458
quality of programs, 458–461
Program orientation (human resource component), 202
Progressive Era (U.S.) policing, 40–42

Prohibition era (U.S.), 38, 49
Project on Policing Neighborhoods, 467
Promotion opportunities
    African American officers, 390,
        404–405
    assessment centers, 218–219
    higher education and, 467
    selection factors, 185–186
    women officers, **392**, 404–406
Property search and seizure, 64–65
Prostitution, 38, 39, **110**, 142, 143, 168,
    246, 378
Protective sweeps of homes, 64
Psychological condition (police selection
    factor), 195–196
Psychological perspective (of
    behavior), 272
Psychological stress, 419
PTO program. See police training officer
    (PTO) program
Public Information Officer (PIO), 150
Public safety
    accountability and, 379
    affirmative action and, 397
    agencies, 12, **14**, 15, 47, 196, 379, 399
    community policing and, 92–93, 99,
        114, 230
    exception, 70, 84
    police responsibility for, 57, 72, 379
    as possible threat, 326
    search/seizures and, 64
    Supreme Court cases, 59, 70
Pursuits by police, 250–252
    defined, 250–251
    foot pursuits, 252
    judgmental policy, 251
    national survey data, 251
    post-pursuit incident reports, 251–252
    restrictive policy, 251
    violent felony only policy, 251

Quality-of-life policing, 246
Quality Policing: The Madison Experience
    (Couper and Lobitz), 130
Quality/Productivity (QP). *See* TQM
    (total quality management)

Racial considerations. *See also* Racial
    profiling
    bias crimes, 260
    coercive actions issues, 289, 312,
        342–343
    deadly force use, 342–343
    harassment by police, **292–293**
    Justice Without Trial study, 277
    neighborhood diversity issues, 283
    use of slurs, 329
Racial harassment (by police), **292–293**
Racial profiling. *See also* Abner Louima
        incident; Amadou Diallo shooting
        incident; Rodney King incident
    ACLU challenges to, 71
    Brown's views on, **285**
    by Cincinnati Police, 83
    community policing and, 91
    defined, 284–285, 494
    examinations into, 286

by Indianapolis Police, 151
by Maryland State Police, 72
suggestions for stopping, 495
Rainbow City (Alabama) Police
    Department, 493
Ramsey, Charles H., **10**
Rapid-response units (Chicago), 165–166
Reactive arrests, 249–250
Reasonable suspicion, 58
Reassignment (selection factor), 185–186
Recruitment. *See also* Human resource
        development; Selection of police
        factors
    budgets for, 187–188
    camaraderie of recruits, 274
    cop crunch data, 189
    education requirements, 456
    HSS project, 188
    methods, 186–187
    PERF study on, 186–187
    POST standards, 201
    screening in/screening out, 186
    selection decision factors, 185–188
    targeting
        females/minorities, 187–188, **402**,
            408–409
        service oriented people, 188–189
    training effectiveness, 210–211
Reform Era (U.S.) policing, 40–44
    Great Depression reforms, 42
    local, state, national crime
        commissions, 41
    professionalization, 40
    reform themes, 43
    Spanish-speaking/black
        neighborhoods, 41
    Uniform Crime Reports (FBI), 44
    Vollmer's leadership, 41–44
Regional Community Policing
    Institutes, 115
Regional police, 15
Renninger, Mark, **441**
Reno (Nevada) Police Department, **214**,
    215, 216
Repeat offender project (ROP), 259–260
Report on Police (1973, National Advisory
        Commission on Criminal Justice
        Standards and Goals), 396,
        458, 478
Residency (police selection factor), 193
Restrictive pursuit policy, 251
Revenue Cutter Service (U.S.), 50
Reverse discrimination, 398–399
Richards, Greg, **441**
Riot Commission, 44
Riots
    in Cincinnati, 83, 150, **244**
    in England, 33
    force/coercion and, 325
    historical background, 33, 35, 41
    in Miami, 391
    problem-specific guides for, **111**
    U.S., 1960s urban riots, 44, 94, 231, 363,
        389–391, 457
Rodney King incident, 212, 332, **333–335**,
    368, 407, 425, 495
Role and purpose (of police), 18–25

activities and workload, 21–32
community expectations, 19
crime fighting vs. social service, 20–21
enforcement vs. politics, 20
goals and strategies, 23–25
individual expectations, 19
legal expectations, 19
organizational expectations, 19
Police Services Study, 21
proactive vs. reactive, 21
Rome (Ancient) kin policing methods, 31
Roosevelt, Franklin, 52
Roosevelt, Theodore, 37
ROP. See repeat offender project
Rotten-apple theory of corruption,
    298–299
Rowan, Colonel Charles, 32, 33
Royal Canadian Mounted Police, 48,
    204, 434
Royal Commission Report (on British
    police), 7
Rule of law
    community expectations vs., 20
    police accountability to, 6–7, 57
    terrorism and, 8
Rural police work, 17–18

Saarinen, Diane, **138**
Sacramento (California) Police
    Department, 341
Safety of officers, 438–447
    accidental deaths, **439**
    assaults on officers, **440**
    dangers, types of, 440–444
    felonious officer killings, **438**, **439**, **441**
    handling the mentally ill, 444–445
    reducing fatalities, 445–447
    self-protection strategies, 446
San Diego Police Department
    lessening of complaints against, 137
    problem-oriented projects, **114**
    Review Commission, 363
San Francisco Office of Citizen
    Complaints, 363
San Francisco Police Department, 4, 400
San Jose Police Department, 212, **214**, 366
San Jose State University Police
    Department, 16, 456, **459**
SARA (scanning, analysis, response,
    assessment) community policing
    model, **107**
Schneckloth v. Bustamonte (1973), 65
School shootings, 3
Schoolcraft, Adrian, 176
Sciullo, Paul, **441**
Screening in/screening out (of
    recruits), 186
Seabury Committee investigation, 297
Search and seizure
    of persons, 58–59, 61
        fruit of the poisonous tree
            doctrine, 61
        probable cause, 58
        reasonable suspicion, 58
        Supreme Court cases, 58, 61
    of property, 64–65
        affidavits, 64

Search and seizure—(*Continued*)
    hot pursuit exception, 65
    open fields doctrine, 65
    plain view doctrine, 64
    search warrants, 64
    Supreme Court cases, 64–65
Search warrants, **59, 60,** 63–64, 78, 84, 512
Seattle (Washington) Police
    Department, **195**
Secret Service (U.S.), 50, 53
Selection of police factors, 190–201
    ADA, 201
    age, 191
    background investigation, 193–194
    bona fide occupational
        qualification, 191
    education, 193
    general suitability, 193
    height and weight, 191–192
    IQ markers, 198
    medical condition, 196
    oral interview, 199–201
    past drug use, **195**
    physical agility, strength, 192–193
    polygraph examination, 194
    preemployment standards/testing, 191,
        196–197
    process summary, **200**
    psychological condition, 195–196
    residency, 193
    screening methods, **200**
    vision, 192
    written examination, 197
    written examination performance,
        197–198
Self-defense
    in patrol job description, 229
    training, 205, **206,** 321
Selye, Hans, 419–420
Sensitization training, 427
Separation of powers (U.S. government),
    5–6
September 11, 2001 attack, 8, **45, 99,**
    135, 498
Service style (of policing), 278
Sexual harassment, 203, 286, 292, 300,
    401, 407, 410–411
Sexual misconduct, 299–301
Sheriffs/frankpledge policing system
    (England), 31, 36
Shielded from Justice (Human Rights
    Watch), 333
Situational crime prevention, 94
Sixth Amendment (Constitution), **8**
Skimming of evidence, by police, 4
Small, Rural, Tribal and Border Regional
    Center, 499
SMART (Specialized Multi-Agency
    Response Team), 246
Sobriety checkpoints, 67
Social media, 100, 504–505
Social service role (of police), 20–21, 228
Social supports and police stress, 429, 431
Socialization theory (of behavior), 274
Socialization vs. predisposition
        perspective (of behavior), 273–275
    academy experience, 274

    patrol division work, 275
    preentry (to police career) choice, 274
    reality of police work, 275
Sociological perspective (of behavior),
    271–272
South Bay (CA) Association of Black Law
    Enforcement Officers, 148
Special-interest groups, 6
Special-jurisdiction police, 16, **17**
Special weapons and tactics teams. *See*
    SWAT (special weapons and
    tactics) teams
Special weapons and tactics (SWAT)
    teams, 134–135, 218
Specialist officers, 91, 102, 115, **127,**
    216, 227
Specialized trainings (human resource
    component), 218
SRTs (special response teams), 134
St. Louis County Police Department, 395
St. Petersburg (Florida) Police
    Department, 140, 466
Stakeouts, 21
*Standards Relating to the Urban Police
    Function* report (American Bar
    Association), 458
State Highway Commission (Oregon), 48
State police
    Colorado, 47
    highway patrol, 47–48, 49
    Massachusetts, 46–47
    Michigan, 429
    Nevada, 47
    New Jersey, 3
    Oregon, 48–49
    Pennsylvania, 47
    Texas, 46–47
    Texas/Massachusetts, 46–47
Step Up to Law Enforcement program, **402**
Stephens, Darrel, 98, **99**
Sting operations, 261
Stop and frisk
    distinctions, 63
    Supreme Court cases, 62–63
    unprovoked flight/suspicion, 62
Strategies of police
    defined/described, 24
    differentiation in, 24–25
    differentiation of, 24–25
    for reclaiming neighborhoods, 3
Street Cop's Code, **147**
Stress, 419–448. *See also* Posttraumatic
        stress disorder
    acute/chronic, 420
    common reactions (chart), **427**
    consequences of
        alcohol abuse, 431–432, 447
        drug abuse, 431, 433, 447
        marital/family problems, 435–436
        suicide, 433–435
    control strategies, 436–437
    eustress/distress, 420
    females, work-related, 425
    line-of-duty/crisis situations, 425–431
        heart rate study, 426
        killed in the line of duty, 26, 340,
            438, 446

    lack of sleep, 421, 427–430, **430**
    shift work, 419, 421, 424, 426,
        428–430, 434
    social-supports model, 429, 431
    stressor-outcome model, 429, 431
    occupational, 420–421
    officer safety, 438–447
        accidental deaths, **439**
        assaults on officers, **440**
        dangers, types of, 440–444
        felonious officer killings, **438,**
            439, 441
        handling the mentally ill, 444–445
        reducing fatalities, 445–447
        self-protection strategies, 446
    physiological/psychological, 419
    stressors
        administrative vs. on the street,
            423–424
        bothersome work aspects, **423**
        categories of, 421, **422**
        emerging sources, 424–425
        gender/minority variations, 425
        lack of sleep, 421, 427–430, **430**
        1974/1995 studies, 422–423
        rankings, 421–424, **422**
Stretcher, Thomas, **245**
Subcultural theory (of attitudes and
    behavior), 278
Substantive laws (defined), 7
Suicide
    murder-suicides, 253
    NYC Police Foundation study, 434
    by police, 210, 322, **427,** 431, 433–435
    police field observations, **229**
    prevention training, 435
    PTSD and, 426, 428
Supreme Court cases
    arrests
        Chimel v. California (1969), 63–64
        Maryland v. Buie (1990), 64
        Payton v. New York (1981), 63
        U.S. v. Watson (1976), 63
    discrimination in hiring
        *Detroit Police Officers' Association v.
            Young,* 190
        Griggs v. Duke Power Company, 190,
            398, 474
        U.S. v. Paradise, 399
    drug testing requirements
        Davis v. City of Dallas, 194
        Shield Club v. City of Cleveland, 194
    education requirements
        Castro v. Beecher, 473
        Davis v. City of Dallas, 473–474
        Griggs v. Duke Power Company,
            190, 474
    height/weight requirements
        Vanguard Justice Society v. Hughes, 192
    inevitable discovery
        Brewer v. Williams (1977), 70
        Nix v. Williams (1984), 70–71
    internal investigation
        Garrity v. New Jersey, 356
    interrogations/confessions
        Dickerson v. U.S. (2000), 69
        Edwards v. Arizona (1981), 69–70

A comprehensive and student-friendly introduction to policing in the U.S. with an emphasis on real-world issues

Now in its fifth edition, *Police & Society* offers a descriptive and analytical look at the process of policing, from police behavior and organization to operations and historical perspectives. Focusing on the relationship between the police and the community and how it has changed throughout the years, Roy Roberg, Kenneth Novak, Gary Cordner, and new coauthor Brad Smith explore the most important theoretical foundations and incisive research on contemporary policing practices.

Features of the Fifth Edition

- **Discussion of many new topics** including procedural justice, recruitment strategies for females and minorities, social media/social networking, and predictive policing
- **Enhanced coverage** of criminal procedure, officer stress and safety, intimate partner violence, brutality/extralegal police aggression, and more
- **Expanded glossary** of key terms
- **Engaging boxed features:** "Inside Policing" boxes that discuss real-world police issues and "Voices From the Field" interviews—six of which are new to this edition—with nationally recognized experts
- **Superior supplements:** A revised and expanded **Instructor's Manual** and an interactive **Student Study Guide** on CD (packaged with the text)

Well-organized, comprehensive, and concise, *Police & Society*, Fifth Edition, is an essential resource for understanding policing in the twenty-first century.

About the Authors

Roy Roberg is Professor of Justice Studies at San José State University.

Kenneth Novak is Associate Professor and Chair of Criminal Justice and Criminology at the University of Missouri-Kansas City.

Gary Cordner is Professor of Criminal Justice at Kutztown University of Pennsylvania.

Brad Smith is Associate Professor of Criminal Justice at Wayne State University.

Cover photo: © Serega/iStockphoto
Cover design: Oxygen Design/Sherry Williams

ISBN 978-0-19-977256-8

OXFORD
UNIVERSITY PRESS
www.oup.com/us/he

9 780199 772568
90000